Hometown Memories . . .

Rumble Seats
and
Lumber Camps

Tales from the Good Old Days
in Northern Michigan

A TREASURY OF 20TH CENTURY MEMORIES

Cow Chips in the Cook Stove—Tales from the Lower Panhandle of Texas
Moonshine and Mountaintops—Tales from Northeast Tennessee
When We Got Electric…—Tales from Northwest West Virginia
Outside Privies and Dinner Pails—Tales from Southwest Iowa
Milking the Kickers—Tales from Southwest Oklahoma
Rolling Stores and Country Cures—Tales from Northeast Alabama
Penny Candy and Grandma's Porch Swing—Tales from North Central Pennsylvania
Lye Soap and Sad Irons—Tales from Northwest Missouri
Almost Heaven—Tales from Western West Virginia
Hobos and Swimming Holes—Tales from Northern Wisconsin
Saturday Night Baths and Sunday Dinners—Tales from Northwest Iowa
Sod Houses and The Dirty Thirties—Tales from Northwest and North Central Kansas
Coal Oil Lamps and Cattle in the Crops— Tales from Northern and Mountain West Idaho
Morning Chores and Soda Fountains—Tales from The Texas Hill Country

Hometown Memories . . .

Rumble Seats
and
Lumber Camps
Tales from the Good Old Days
in Northern Michigan

A TREASURY OF 20TH CENTURY MEMORIES
Compiled and edited by Todd Blair and Karen Garvey

HOMETOWN MEMORIES, LLC
Hickory, North Carolina

Rumble Seats and Lumber Camps

Publisher: Todd Blair
Lead Editor: Karen Garvey
Design and Graphic Arts Editor: Karen Garvey and Laura Montgomery
Office Services Assistant: Laura Montgomery
Assistant Editors: Jodi Black, Greg Rutz, Monica Black, Heather Garvey, Lisa Hollar, Brianne Mai, Reashea Montgomery, Meghan Lawton, and Tiffany Canaday

ISBN 978-1-940376-02-8
Copyright © 2013

Published by

Hometown Memories, LLC
2359 Highway 70 SE, Suite 350
Hickory, N. C. 28602
(877) 491-8802

Printed in the United States of America

Acknowledgements

To those Northern Michigan folks (and to those few who "ain't from around here") who took the trouble to write down your memories and mail them in to us, we offer our heartfelt thanks. And we're sure you're grateful to each other, because together, you have created a wonderful book.

To encourage participation, the publisher offered cash awards to the contributors of the most appealing stories. These awards were not based upon writing ability or historical knowledge, but rather upon subject matter and interest. The winners were: Paul Mouland of Oscoda, MI; Theresa Donajkowski of Davison, MI; Jack Owen of Hillman, MI; and Jeanette Karsten of Millersburg, MI. We would also like to give honorable mention to the contributions from Wendell Orm of Onaway, MI and Walt Plavljanich of Gould City, MI. The cash prizewinner for the book's cover photo goes to Mariam Navachic of Traverse City, MI (you'll find their names and page numbers in the table of contents). Congratulations! It was extremely difficult to choose these winners because every story and picture in this book had its own special appeal.

Associate Editors

Priscilla Bennet
Sandy Berry
Kayla Koboski Briggs
Mary L. Dudo Bucklin
Newton Chapman
James Wyatt Cook
Margaret Crowl
Jeff B. Davis
Theresa "Terri" Dinajkowski
Tom Finger
Pattie Gordon
Annie L. Hooghart
Louise Kane
Jeanette Karsten
David Kent
Marie A. Ketz
Richard T. King
Evelyn "Penny" Kipley

Charlotte LaFeve
Joseph R. Lamie
Foster McCool
Hamilton D. McNichol
Darlene Graff Meske
Rebecca M. Norris
Marilyn Koski Olsen
Wendell L. Orm
James Orr
Martha Preston
Jerry M. Rehage
John J. Renauld
Clarice L. Sperry
Cindi Strong
Geraldine Sturdavant
Sharon Vadeboncoeur Switalski
Juanita Walt
Gloria Johnston Whipple
Leeland Wilson

INTRODUCTION

We know that most folks don't bother to read introductions. But we do hope you (at least eventually) get around to reading this one. Here's why:

First, the creation of these books is in its fourth generation after we took over the responsibilities of Hometown Memories Publishing from its founders, Bob Lasley and Sallie Holt. After forty-nine books, they said goodbye to enjoy retirement, and each other. Bob and Sallie had a passion for saving these wonderful old tales from the good old days that we can only hope to match. We would love to hear your thoughts on how we are doing.

Second—and far more important—is the who, what, where, when, why and how of this book. Until you're aware of these, you won't fully enjoy and appreciate it.

This is a very unusual kind of history book. It was actually written by 392 Michigan old-timers and not-so-old-timers who remember what life was really like back in the earlier years of the 20th century in Northern Michigan. These folks come from all walks of life, and by voluntarily sharing their memories (which often include their emotions, as well), they have captured the spirit and character of a time that will never be seen again.

Unlike most history books, this one was written from the viewpoint of people who actually experienced history. They're familiar with the tribulations of the Great Depression; the horrible taste of castor oil; "outdoor" plumbing; party line phones; and countless other experiences unknown to today's generation.

We advertised all over Northern Michigan to obtain these stories. We sought everyday folks, not experienced authors, and we asked them to simply jot down their memories. Our intention was by no means literary perfection. Most of these folks wrote the way they spoke, and that's exactly what we wanted. To preserve story authenticity, we tried to make only minimal changes to written contributions. We believe that an attempt at correction would damage the book's integrity.

We need to include a few disclaimers: first, many important names are missing in many stories. Several folks revealed the names of their teachers, neighbors, friends, even their pets and livestock, but the identities of parents or other important characters weren't given. Second, many contributors did not identify pictures or make corrections to their first draft copies. We're sure this resulted in many errors (and perhaps lost photographs) but we did the best we could. Third, each contributor accepts full responsibility for his or her submission and for our interpretation of requested changes. Fourth, because some of the submitted photographs were photocopied or "computer printed," their quality may be very poor. And finally, because there was never a charge, "fee," or any other obligation to contributors to have their material included in this book, we do not accept responsibility for any story or other material that was left out, either intentionally or accidentally.

We hope you enjoy this unique book as much as we enjoyed putting it together.

Todd Blair and Karen Garvey
August 2013

TABLE OF CONTENTS

The Table of Contents is listed in alphabetical order by the story contributor's last name.

To search for stories by the contributor's hometown or year of birth, see indexes beginning on page 473.

Barbara Kane	414	Dee Manning	87
Louise Kane	327	Betty J. Marks	214
Marguerite Karabin	430	Marian J. Martin	412
Jeanette Karsten	20	Robert R. Martin	186
Debbie Keene	443	Claribel Mason	280
Linda Kelley	386	Laurel. E. Mason	359
Morley Kellogg	212	Bonnie J. Matyanczyk	67
Teresa Louise Kenaga	30	Foster McCool	328
David Kent	375	Christine McDonald	373
Jim Kent	79	Jack McGee	374
Marie A. Ketz	65	Marcella M. McNabb	429
Donald Kidder	54	Hamilton D. McNichol	150
Phyllis Kilcherman	380	Viola McVey	404
James R. Kilgus	189	Kathy Mendoza	77
Richard T. King	183	Robert Merchant	211
Theodore King	146	Darlene Groff Meske	293
William R. Kiogima	151	Dilla J. Miller	393
Penny Kipley	70	Jan Miner-Heniser	303
Nelson Louis Kirby	365	Mark A. Mitchell	230
Richard S. Kler	341	Geri Moody	338
Joanne Kline	160	Ralph L. Moore	31
ConradKoltys	458	Agnes Moraitis	327
Joyce (Robarge) Konwinski	358	Justin Moreau	45
Elizabeth Ballou Koski	439	Cheryl Morgan	376
Frank Krajnik	223	Paul Mouland	17
Philip C. Kreft	428	Carolyn Mousseau	146
Leonard L. LaFave	181	Harold L. Mowat	190
Charlotte LaFeve	178	Ruth Moyer	213
Joseph Lamie	448	Valerie Murden	280
Frances Lamont	90	Diann Murphy	163
Grace Jean (Emerson) Langea	239	John J. Murphy	345
Jerry L. Lardie	25	Nina Burger Myers	85
Betty Wartella Last	145	Mariam Navachic	148
Allen L. Lawson	273	Philip Naylor	179
Alma Leist	243	Marion. V. (Fabera) Neely	256
Judith M. Lentz	441	Carole Newlon	398
Mary Jo LePage	432	Theresa Maher Nichols	424
Elvira LePard	211	Charles M. Noel	353
Joyce A. Leslie	292	Rebecca M. Norris	405
Marge Lipp	342	Ardath Norton	299
Judy Loy	147	Paul T. O'Dell	116
Mary Lyon	212	Robert P. Olds	23
Stuart MacDonald	57	Joyce Oliver	355
Bernice (Bee Houghton) Macy	294	Marilyn Olsen	173
Mike Madden	259	Peggy Schmidt Olsen	233

The Tales...

True stories intentionally left just as the contributor wrote them.

Nazi Germany Invades Oscoda
By Paul Mouland of Oscoda, Michigan
Born One day before Dirt

During the Great Depression, my father was a carpenter and worked for the government, building C.C.C. camps in northern Michigan putting men to work clearing the forest. He loved to hunt and fish so in what little spare time he had this gave him the opportunity to explore the great Michigan outdoors.

In the late twenties, my folks decided to move out of Detroit and relocate in a small place six miles west of Oscoda. At that time there was only one other inhabitant in a place called Foote Site Village and everybody called him "Dad Long." They built a two-bedroom home with a small general store on the front along with seven one-room cabins to rent. Later they added an icehouse, a manual Crown gas pump, and wood boats to rent on the AuxSable River. My father would take their guest on hunting and fishing trip without charging a guide fee; my mother would cook the wild game along with bake goods and share it with the guest. This had people coming back year after year.

Unfortunately, my folks lost my first brother three months after he was born and my dad bought a plot in the Oscoda Cemetery to bury him. They also lost my second brother when he was three.

When I came along, they decided to sell out and move back to Detroit where they had easy access to the medical profession.

Fast forward to 1948, my folks always kept a cabin in Foote Site and my father would bring my mother and I up as soon as school was out while he went back to Detroit to work. We would see him every weekend when he came up to fish. He was usually followed by relatives or close family friends who spent their vacation with us.

When I wasn't on the river fishing, I would be at the cove in front of the Foote Site dam swimming.

I had a rope that I tied to a tree and I could swing out to the middle of the cove and drop down in the center. I could also swim in front of the logs that had accumulated in the back and watch the turtles and fish underneath them.

There was a two-lane trail that went behind their original business to a road called The Dam Road. The logging bridge had washed out many years ago and the road stopped at Foote Site Dam. I would climb over the Consumers Powers fence to walk through the woods to the cove. One day in 1948 at the age of ten, I jumped the fence and started down the trail to the cove. All of a sudden, I heard a lot of gunfire. My first reaction was it's not hunting season so who's firing all the guns and I better hide behind a tree to protect myself. When I got the nerve to look around the tree all I could see were a bunch of men coming my way in Nazi uniforms. I wasn't sure how I was going to escape without being shot. Looking around just beyond the tree was a thick bush so I got on my belly and crawled underneath it. My heart was pounding and when they got close, I held my breath until they passed.

Once they were out of site, I got up and ran back to the fence, which I went over in a single bound, at least that's what I thought. I ran home to warn my mother to find cover because we were being invaded. Back then, there weren't many phones, and if you had one, it was a party line. My mother grabbed me and ran next do to the neighbors to call into town to find out what was happening.

Come to find out it was a motion picture company doing a film on WWII and using the air base and the woods as background. I later found out visiting the Wurthsmith Air Museum the movie was called "Fighter Squadron.

An Inconceivable Experience
By Theresa Donajkowski of Davison,
Michigan
Born 1929

A few years ago, my mother-in-law, who lives in a village located in northern Michigan, fell and broke her wrist and knee. Since she needed constant and extended care, each member of the family took a two-week turn staying with her. It was September when I left for my stay in Posen, and it was here that I had an inconceivable experience.

In order to escape the drudgery and monotony of the sickroom, it was customary for me to ride my bicycle every afternoon. It seemed to me that the countryside became more beautiful with each passing day, but on the eighth day, it had reached perfection and

17

was almost beyond description.

Although late September, the sun was warm but there was still a touch of crispness in the air. The autumn haze had gently muted the vibrant shades of red, orange, and yellow, and a hint of smoke from burning leaves mingled with the scent of second crop clover drying in a field. The only sound came from the soft rustle of falling leaves and an occasional call of a whippoorwill. It was as though I had ridden into a dream world. Spellbound by the beauty and peacefulness I barely noticed a bum rummaging in the ditch at the top of a steep hill but I do recall thinking, "He is so out of character here."

When I drew abreast of the bum, he gave one leap into the path of my bike. Astounded, I realized the bum was actually a huge black bear! Terrorized as I was, I was incapable of braking my bicycle and the downgrade of the hill only aided in accelerating my speed. The bear raced directly in my path, my front wheel prodding his obese backside. Blood-curdling screams pierced the stillness, echoing and re-echoing. This frightened me even more and it was only later that it occurred to me that I must have been the screamer. As we reached the bottom of the hill, my bike slammed into the bear because he had stopped and I fell headlong into the ditch, my face brushing against the smelly bear. Mercifully, I passed out!

I returned to awareness in slow motion. With my eyes shut tightly, I sensed that I was lying in the ditch on a bed of leaves. I could feel the cool metal of the bike's handlebars in the small of my back. Next, I heard heavy breathing and then I became aware of some sort of struggle going on. When the acrid odor of mangy, unkempt fur hit my nostrils, my eyes flew open, and I found myself staring directly up at the copious posterior of the stupid bear. He was wedged between the slats of a crude but sturdy wooden gate that was right beside me. Dumbfounded, I just lay there while the bear groaned and wriggled frantically. After what seemed an eternity to me, the gate creaked and then splintered. Free at last, the bear turned, glared at me, and giving a vehement shudder, fled into the forest.

Lying in the ditch, I knew that no one, not even my husband, would believe this story. I started to laugh as I visualized the bear stumbling into his den and gasping to his mate, "You won't believe this, but I just got run over by some stupid woman on a bike, and don't tell me I've been eating fermented berries again!"

Wolf Creek in the '40s
By Jack Owen of Hillman, Michigan
Born 1940

My grandpa's log cabin along Wolf Creek should have been a picture on a 1943 calendar. It was kind of a "Late" homesteader's home whereby logs were procured from the nearby woods. This unique place had an A-frame roof with dormers. That's the good news: the bad news was that the cabin was built before electricity reached this rural area and without a water well.

World War II had generated many jobs downstate, so my grandparents headed down below toward Detroit to find work. My parents decided to move into their vacant log cabin because it was close to Mack Lake where my dad worked for the U.S. Forest Service.

Dad was a C.C.C. member during the Great Depression, which brought him to the Luzerne Camp near Mio. Incidentally, this camp was designated for white men only. Mack Lake also had a C.C.C. Camp designated for black men. Segregation was the policy back then. Later, the Mack Lake camp was converted to the Huron National Forest headquarters.

Wolf Creek supplied our family with water during our stay at Grandpa's cabin. During winter, Dad chopped a hole through the ice to dip water for our needs. I stood on a rug in the kitchen (the warmest place in the house) for my bath.

Years before, Mio had provided "city water" from Wolf Creek by using a ram pump that pushed water uphill through wooden pipes to an open reservoir after which gravity ran water down to Mio buildings. Of course, it was an unwritten rule that if you had to take a leak, stay back from the creek or you would be shot. Of course, the deer couldn't read so many became meat for the table.

Grandpa had a pet doe before he moved, but it disappeared during hunting season. This was long before any doe licenses were issued. Venison was somewhat of a staple in the diet of many rural folks. We even had deer meat at school because "good" road kills were donated to our lunch program. Hot lunches cost $1.00 per week while some poor kids got free lunches. My mother was always nearby because she was a teacher. Mom had graduated from Mio High School and had the opportunity to attend County Normal School.

We had Montgomery Ward catalogs and magazines for entertainment before we got electricity. I remember pictures of the surviving Civil War veterans in a Life magazine: all five of them. All were over 100 years old. One of the vets had dark hair supposedly because he only washed it once per year! Later, there were pictures of Harry Truman following his re-election when he ran against Dewey. By that time, you could spread your butter thicker because government rationing had lifted: the war was over.

Northern Michigan had some mighty cold nights during the winters, so Mother always made up the beds with flannel sheets and many wool blankets. The wood stove was out by midnight because we burned slabs. So the cabin got cold, real cold. You talk about quiet. This was the place to experience absolute silence. There was no traffic, no appliances, and no nothing that made noise, except for an occasional crack from a freezing log. This was a night that you didn't want to go to the bathroom. It involved going down the stairs, across the creek on the bridge, and out to the privy in the dark. We were a little short on night-lights, especially if Mom forgot to buy matches.

When we finally got electricity, it made a tremendous difference in our lifestyle.

Jack's grandfather with his pet doe around 1944

Right away, Mom bought a refrigerator and a wringer washing machine. She only caught her arm in the wringer once! We also got a radio. How nice was that? Sometimes I'd listen to Jungle Jim; our whole family gathered around the radio and listened to the Joe Lewis championship fights. My parents always turned on the six o'clock news with Walter Winchell.

Dad used to drive an old Chevrolet from the late 1930s. It had suicide rear doors, so Mom always preached safety about keeping the back door closed during a trip. Otherwise it would blow off and you with it. Dad always drove 45 m.p.h. so a lot of cars passed us on the highway when we went south on M-33, the only paved road in the county. This always frustrated me because I wanted Dad to drive faster. Then one day he bought a 1940 Chrysler, which would go 105 m.p.h. It even had an electric starter: no more cranking. At my urging, Dad would pass every car on the highway, including Buicks, Studebakers, and futuristic Kaisers. Dad and I beamed while racing down the road; after all, there were no speed limits. Mom often napped during trips, but at high speeds, the engine rumble would wake her. She sounded like a mad duck until Dad slowed down.

Then one day, a nice big house in town had a bad basement fire. The owner was at a local tavern and was not aware that his floors were burning. When he finally went home that night, he fell into the basement. I guess the local fire department did not communicate to him that his house had a fire. He was taken to the doctor's house (we did not have clinics) and it was determined that he was not greatly injured. He decided to sell the house and we bought it.

Carpenters were hired to repair all the fire damage. When we moved in, I realized how nice it was to have modern conveniences. We had a flush toilet, a bathtub, and a coal-burning furnace that held the fire all night. I could go across the alley and buy a nickel bottle of Coke at a local gas station and play "far away" with my friends. (Coke bottles had the bottling plant town on the bottom of the bottle.)

Our new modern home in Mio signaled a move up in social status. I could walk to school and later joined the Boy Scouts. Ironically, Mother was my third grade teacher in 1949. Later, my dad was my Scoutmaster. As could be expected, my ratings were very high during these years.

Good times continued for another decade. By that time, I was old enough to go out into the world on my own. It was then that I "grew up" because I discovered that you had to get with it and produce: otherwise, your status would go down faster and further than the pristine waters of Wolf Creek.

Blame It on the Starlings
By Jeanette Karsten of Millersburg, Michigan
Born 1936

It was the summer of 1948, just two years after our family had moved up north. Our new community was dotted with tumbledown farmsteads, long abandoned by folks who had found the soil too rocky or the climate too severe for successful farming.

To us four kids and a family of our nearest neighbors these places seemed to hold great potential for high adventure. Who knew what wonderful treasures might be just lying there waiting to be found? And so it was that whenever we could escape from our chores we were off to explore. What we mostly found were horseshoes, square nails, and broken household trinkets. So by the end of

June boredom had set in.

Some of us older kids had spent many hours of our early wartime years staging hard fought battles with such ammunition as rotten tomato hand grenades. But WWII was over and done. There was peace in the world and no real foe to arouse our passions.

We needed an enemy to fight and eventually found one in the shape of a bird. The ubiquitous hated starling! Noisy disgusting bullies of the bird world. This foreign species had multiplied by the thousands all over the American countryside. They built their ugly messy nests in houses stolen from nobler birds such as swallows and purple martins. They also nested in barns, corncribs, and granaries. They feasted on farm crops, and were such a nuisance that for a time there was even a bounty on them. Imagine that! With hundreds of thousands of starlings in our world, a kid could get rich!   Why not?

Of course, there was one small hitch. Our only weapons were sticks, stones, and maybe a homemade slingshot. And these nasty birds weren't going to sit still waiting to be picked off. OK, so we would have to forget about the bounty, but maybe we could destroy this enemy in a different way. Maybe we could try to find their nests and get rid of their eggs and babies. This idea took our summer in whole new direction.

We set to work at this new gruesome business with a kind of religious zeal. It was our calling to rid the earth of this evil bird. We spent many hours raking nests of eggs and babies down from inside the peaks of ancient barns, and pulling them out of hollow trees or fishing them out of cracks in dangerously crumbling walls.

One time when we had finished exploring the out buildings of an empty house, we noticed we could hear nestling starlings squawking for food near the back of the place. The house stood on a high foundation with a steep downhill slope away from the back door. We had to drag an old piece of ladder up the embankment in order to climb up and try the door which (wonder of wonders!) proved to be unlocked.

We explored the first and second floors and even the attic. We determined that there was indeed a nest of starlings in the chimney. But our piece of ladder wouldn't reach high enough for us to get at the stovepipe hole in the kitchen wall, and anyway we had no tools to remove the circular metal cover nailed over it.

This house had a wrap-around porch along its east and south sides. We found that one of the upstairs windows opened easily so we climbed out onto the porch roof. From there we could crawl around the corner to the valley where two parts of the house fit together. The chimney rose above us at the towering top of that valley.

I was the first to go all the way up. Crawling flat on my stomach I clung to the hot brown shingles with all my fingers and toes. Angry birds flew at me fluttering and scolding. When I carefully stood up to peer into the sooty black flue, I nearly lost my grip as a bird rocketed out in my face. "Yes," I reported calling back down to my buddies, "There's a nest with a bunch of babies in there all right." But what in the world could we do about it?

This is what we decided. All eight of us, aged six to twelve, went down to a nearby rock pile, and carried armloads of rocks to the back door. Like ants with a good food supply, we built a huge pile just inside the door. Next, we lugged them up the stairs to a spot beside the open window. There we formed a relay team and passed them out the window from the youngest kids to the oldest ones. One stone at a time we passed them along to finally reach the big kid positioned astraddle the roof peak at the chimney. That person had to carefully stretch down to receive each rock and drop it down the chimney.

When our rocks were all gone, and the dastardly deed was done, we climbed back inside. We shut the window, went downstairs, and carefully closed the door behind us as we exited. We even returned the ladder to the old barn. When I looked back up at that steep roof, it made my knees feel wobbly! It had been a long day. I'm sure we were all late for supper. And somehow, we all knew without a word that we'd done something so unspeakably naughty... we must never ever say one word about it.

A few weeks later, the scene of our crime was purchased by a downstate couple who happened to be longtime friends of my parents. Soon they arrived with their truck full of furniture, and their hearts full of enthusiasm about bravely moving up to "God's Country."

My folks went to help them move in. BUT... Well... there was a very unusual problem. Their chimney wouldn't draw. The house filled with smoke and (of all things!) it was because the chimney contained several feet of large rocks!

We kids were questioned about it, but not very seriously. I mean, anyone with even half a brain would have known that a bunch of little kids could never have managed such a stunt. But because they were dear friends, my parents felt constrained to provide them with a roof over their heads while a new chimney was being built.

It was surely Divine Justice that, like it or not, for some very long weeks, my brother and sisters and I had to share with their family our own beds as well as our places at the dinner table.

Twenty Below and a Necessary Adventure
By Wendell L. Orm of Onaway, Michigan
Born 1940

Here in Northeastern lower Michigan we are having an old-fashioned winter, very cold and with lots of snow. It does remind me of winters in the mid-1940s and 1950s on the old family farm west of the Village of Hillman in Montmorency County.

During those winters, there was one event that was a very cool one when the temps hit 10 degrees above down to 20 below zero. That event was a necessary trip to the outhouse. Right from the first impulse, it was an adventure.

For one thing, that little palace was a good 70 yards from the farmhouse. That's great in the spring, summer, and fall, not so much in the winter. Putting on lots of clothes just meant more time spent in that icebox taking them off and putting them back on. Yet a body might near freeze to death during the process of getting there, being there, and then getting back, if not enough was worn. Speed in this event was a good thing.

Once at the destination the first order of business was to make sure the Sears or Montgomery Ward catalog was within reach. Then there was the glance down the chosen hole to see how high the inverted icicle of poo had gotten. It if looked as if it was too high hopefully someone else hadn't removed the shovel used to knock it down.

Then came the disrobing—or as little of it as could be gotten away with. Only the most absolutely necessary removal was done. And did you ever try to hurry that sometime slow and laid-back natural function? It's a good thing the seats were wooden and might actually be slightly warmed by a once-warm behind.

Once the job was done your task was to hurry to cover the uncovered parts and sprint to the house. Little thought was given to anything but covering that 70 yards to the farmhouse as quickly as possible. Once inside, the old wood heater was embraced as closely as one could without getting burned. Slowly but surely warmth would begin seeping back into a frigid body.

Ah, the joys of rustic living. Everyone under about age 50 should experience the thrill of a 20 below zero jaunt to the outhouse at least once in their lifetime. As it is, they just don't know how good they have it!

The Fraternity of First Class Bear Hunters
By Walt Plavljanich of Gould City, Michigan
Born 1940

"Good luck tonight Kip. Call me at McNeil's if you have a problem." "Thanks, will do buddy". With those parting words, Walt's workday ended at the Putnam Hunt Club. Driving his truck down the two and a half mile driveway to US-2, Walt wondered if today, September 19, 2011 would be the day Kip got his first bear. He had drawn a first season permit and had already been hunting bear for ten days. He had seen three bears on stands, but chose not to shoot because they seemed "too small." No hunter wants to harvest a small bear. He had seen enough bear over his eight years at the hunt club to know the difference between small and large.

Kip and Walt are caretakers at the 1,560-acre hunt club and part of their responsibility in the fall of each year is to bait for bear and serve as guides for guest hunters, the first of which was due to arrive in five days. Six bait stations had been prepared and were being baited since early August. The hungry bears had already consumed several hundred dollars' worth of granola, molasses, and assorted sweets. At about 5 o'clock, Kip began gathering his gear for the evening hunt, which included a small snack of tuna salad and crackers. Hunters have to eat too! He parked his pick-up on the edge of a field that bordered the woods where he was going to hunt. Quietly closing the truck door, he began the quarter-mile walk to the Northwest Blind. As the name implies, this hunt shack is located near the remote northwest corner of the hunt club boundary. The hunter in the shack faces a large cedar swamp and beaver pond to the southwest. As he neared the shack and bait station his slow walk in became even slower. Each step was preceded by an intent look at the bait station. It wasn't likely that a bear would be there this early, but nothing is for certain when hunting bear. He was inside the shack and settled at 5:30. Kip began the wait. The bait station was 45-yards away from the shack to the west. The breeze was out of the northwest and the sky was clear, ideal conditions. The shack had three small windows, one facing west to the bait, one facing north to the trail in, and the other facing south. The door to the shack is adjacent to the south window. After about an hour in the shack, he had seen partridge come and go, a skunk whose tail always seemed to point to the sky, and ravens, all visiting the bait station.

The sun was sinking low on the horizon. At about 7 o'clock he opened the tuna salad container and had his snack. After eating, Kip carefully put the tuna container into a baggie, sealed it up, and placed it on the shelf below the south window. "I have to keep that scent contained," he thought. Meanwhile, in the woods to the southwest a long distance away, a bear picked up the scent of the bait station and began to move slowly in its direction. This bear was not familiar to the area and was not one of the three he had seen previously. It was a much larger bear. There's a saying in hunting that is so true: "In 10 seconds you can go from nothing happening to the most exciting day you've ever had in the woods." Kip was about twenty minutes away from those 10 seconds.

As he sat quietly in his shack in the remaining hour of daylight, Walt sat at a table at McNeil's Bar along with 19 other patrons enjoying euchre night. With snacks set out on the pool table, drinks flowing, it was hard to hear the Detroit Tigers game on TV above the chatter and laughter of the crowd. Walt was sitting with his back to the door in the noisy bar when he thought he heard someone say, "Hi Kip". Walt turned around and sure enough - there he stood! Walt then looked outside and saw it was still daylight out there - immediately leaving his chair he went right to Kip asking, "What are you doing here? Why are you here? Why are you here?" It just didn't register with Walt why he was in McNeil's in daylight. He was supposed to phone the bar if he got a bear, not show up in person! Why did he leave his stand? At about 20 minutes after seven, he sat in the shack intently watching the bait station. From then until dark was prime time for a bear to appear.

As he stared straight ahead, a dark movement outside the south window to his left caught his attention. Turning his head to the window, he found himself looking face to face at a bear not more than four feet away! The bear was on all fours with his nose in the air following a scent coming from the shack. He grabbed his 30.06 and stood facing the window with the rifle's muzzle pointed at the bear. The bear then came right up to the shack, put his paw on the windowsill, and began to stand up when he pulled the trigger. The flash of fire from the gun combined with the explosion of noise in the closed shack more resembled a grenade going off than a rifle shot. The bear somersaulted backwards from the impact of the bullet, and then ran off into the woods. Kip stood there in disbelief and shaking from the close encounter. He opened the door and stood there for a few minutes listening for any sounds from the bear. After a while, he heard a deep, guttural groan coming from the direction of the bear's retreat. He had heard and read about the death moan, but to hear it in the woods was an eerie experience. He then found blood on the ground at the shack and followed it for about 10-yards into the swampy woods. He then decided to leave the woods and get help at McNeil's.

When Walt approached him at the bar, asking him why he was there Kip simply blurted out, "I got him, Walt, I got him!" Of course, everyone inside the bar quieted down and listened intently to him explain how the bear came in to the scent of the Bumble Bee Tuna Salad, how he shot through the closed window at point blank range, and how the bear tumbled backwards and ran off. His story shot a wave of excitement through the entire bar! Shortly after Kip's story was told a fella who didn't know him asked Walt, "Is he serious about that bear story?" That's how incredible it seemed to be - was he serious? Kip needed help finding and retrieving the bear, and most any and all of the able-bodied men in the bar would have volunteered. Shortly after finishing the Euchre games, Walt and Jim (a good friend and fellow bear hunter-guide) headed back with him to the Northwest stand. Death moan put aside, there is something more intense and exciting about going out into the dark woods to find a bear than looking for a deer. Flashlights sweeping the forest floor soon picked up the blood trail and after less than 60-yards, there the bear laid. High fives and "atta boys" were exchanged. A great moment of truth. Mission accomplished! The boys brought the bear back to McNeil's Bar (also a bear check station) later that night and were greeted with applause by the Euchre crowd who had patiently awaited their arrival. A great memorable evening it was. Congratulations Kip, you kept your cool and joined the fraternity of First Class Bear Hunters! So much for hundreds of dollars of granola – a $0.99 box of tuna salad and crackers did the trick!

The Water's Call
By Robert P. Olds of Wolverine, Michigan
Born 1935

I have been fishing the waters of Burt and Mullett Lakes, and the Indian and Sturgeon Rivers for sixty plus years and these waters do continue to call me back. I have a multitude of memories of days spent fishing, but I would like to share but one with you. It is of the morning my grandfather took me Muskie fishing at the tender age of eight years old. Our folks had taken us to Indian River to visit my father's parents. We were living in Plymouth, Michigan at that time. I suspect it was over Memorial weekend, as it was not uncommon for our parents to take advantage of those long weekends. Also, it was the time when the Muskie were spawning in the Indian River.

Our grandparents owned and operated the Olds Cottages on Prospect Street on the

23

Indian River. He, being a carpenter by trade, had built three cottages on the property they had purchased. It had a large home already on the land. Our grandmother took care of the cottage rentals, and our grandfather built cottages for a living. To the best of my knowledge, he never owned a car. He walked to and from work. His sawmill was located on the southeast corner of Club Road and Onaway Road. In later years, he built a new mill just west of I-75 and north of Onaway Road. At that time, I do not remember I-75 being built yet.

My grandfather and I were up early. We ate breakfast, and then walked down to his boathouse. There was no fishing gear to load into the boat as my grandfather simply left it in the boat. We backed out of the boathouse and headed down the river to Mullett Lake. When we reached the area where the Indian River emptied into Mullett, he turned the boat about and handed me a fishing rod. The wooden plug on the end of the leader had to be all of ten inches long and as big around as a shovel handle. I expect it was larger than any fish I had caught up to that time. He told me how much line to let out, and then he put his lure in the water. It

Robert's grandparents, Aden and Minnie Olds
1930s

was a buck tail spinner with blades the size of half dollars. All of this about blew me away. I did not get much sleep the night before, as I knew we were going Muskie fishing in the morning, and the picture of the Muskie my granddad had shown me the night before had not helped. The fish that my grandfather had been holding in the picture was longer than I was tall.

We began to troll back up the river, with me having a death grip on the rod, fearful that any minute a Muskie would hit the lure and I would most certainly be jerked over the side of the boat, never to be seen again. In those days, there was no drag to set on the level wind reel. The drag was your thumb on the spool. As we came by Bowersock's Camp (now The Landings), my lure bounced off a log or stump, and my heart leapt into my throat, for I was convinced a giant Muskie had hit my bait. I suspect my granddad was enjoying all of this even though he acted as if he was not watching.

Then we were in front of what Dad always called muskrat landing, and again my lure struck some underwater obstacle. I braced my feet so I would not be pulled from the boat. This scene repeated itself all the way back to the boathouse. Finally, my granddad said, "Reel in your bait." I remember actually being relieved, as my arms were tired and my thumb had lost a little skin where it had been pressed against the line on the reel.

No, we did not catch any Muskies that day, but it was still the most exciting fishing trip of my life. I learned a very valuable lesson that has stayed with me all these years. It's not only the catching of the fish that keeps you coming back to the waters, but the anticipation of catching the fish. I suspect when you lose that anticipation, you will lose your desire. I never put bait in the water without expecting that fish of a lifetime to grab hold of it.

Folks, these waters truly do call me back. I am so thankful my grandfather took the time to take his eight year old grandson Muskie fishing and in so doing instilled in him a desire that continues to burn within me yet to

24

this day. I am also thankful I had a dad who encouraged me to become involved in the things of the out of doors.

Friend, take a child fishing this summer. You could do worse.

✓ Eggs for a Stranger
By Betty Shirey-Thayer of St. Helen, Michigan
Born 1921

I lived in Youngstown, Pennsylvania at the time of this story. I was raised by my father and grandmother. I was five years old at the time.

My grandmother went next door to talk to the neighbor. There was a knock at the door and there stood a big, red-haired bum/hobo. He said he was hungry. I invited him in. I got a chair up to the stove and proceeded to fry him some eggs.

When my grandmother came in, she remained calm until he left.

When he finished his eggs (my first time cooking), he thanked me and, as he was leaving, he handed me a bright, new penny. I was so happy.

When he was gone, my grandmother's safety lessons began. I knew then she was not as happy about this event as I was.

✓ Did We Eat Too Much Watermelon?
By Gloria Whipple of Muskegon, Michigan
Born 1946

We lived on Clarion Avenue in Petoskey in the '50s and '60s, during our growing up years. The dangerous things we, my brothers and I, got into make me shutter now a days. The trains that came into Petoskey to the train depot just happened to be parked down the hill and across the river from our house. We loved the trains. The biggest thrill for us was grabbing a hold of the ladder on the train cars and climbing on top, standing up—right until the train got to rolling along and riding it into Petoskey til' it slowed down, climbing down the ladder and rolling off into the grass.

One day, someone left a refrigerator car open and curious as we were, we went inside and to our great delight, it was full of watermelon lying there in the straw. We each grabbed a watermelon, as did our friends and we took em' up into the hills and smashed em' open and handfuls of watermelon went into our mouths. The best tasting watermelon a child could eat. We always watched for the refrigerator cars after that. But to this day, my brothers cannot stand to even look or taste a watermelon. Hm, did we eat too much watermelon?

✓ Anything to Get Out of School!
By Nancy Root of Grayling, Michigan
Born 1944

The mischief I got into was when I was about 11 years old. My best friend and I liked to play hooky from school. We were always trying to think of how we could get out of going to school, especially on the warm days.

We knew where some poison ivy was in the woods near us, so we got the bright idea one day of rubbing the leaves on our arms and legs. Of course it worked, we got a red itchy rash all up our arms and legs. We were contagious! We were not allowed to go to school until the rash dried up in a few days. We lived two houses away from each other so we were allowed to play outside in our yards. I think we spent most of the time being miserable from itching and spent most of the time putting calamine lotion on. We never did that again. We decided it was not worth it.

✓ Leek Breath
By Jerry L. Lardie of Traverse City, Michigan
Born 1938

I am 74 years of age, and have lived all my life in Traverse City. I attended St. Francis School for 12 years. In the spring of 1952, I was in the seventh grade. The weather in late May was 75 to 85 degrees, and the last place I wanted to be was in a stuffy classroom. I really wanted to be in the woods or fishing or swimming. I had an idea! After school that day, my buddy and I went to the woods and got what we needed. We then took our fishing equipment to his garage. The next morning, with lunches packed, we met at his house. We got what we had picked the day before, leeks—large juicy leeks. On our way to school, we each ate two of them. When we got to school, the nun's wondered what that terrible smell was. They discovered it was us, and wanted to know what we had been eating. We told them we had eggs and onions for breakfast. They told us to go home and to not eat that again before school. Off we went to Boardman Lake for a day of fishing, swimming, and just playing. With our lunches packed and 80-degree plus weather, we had an all-day blast!

The following year, we did the same thing. All went well until we got home. The school called my mom because they thought something was fishy. We were busted, and had to make the day of school up on the next Saturday. What a bummer.

John G. Hanel

✓ Serving in Korea on Porkchop Hill
By John G. Hanel of Afton, Michigan
Born 1931

We lived in Walker Township on an acre off of my Grandpa's farm. They called it the Fingerboard Corners because people would stop and ask which was they needed to go to get to Cheboygan. They would always point to the left and say, "That way."

When we went to school, of course we walked. It was one-mile distance. When we saw a police care coming or going, all of us kids ran down into the ditch until the car was gone. When I said I was sick so that I could stay home from school, my mom would get the castor oil out.

When I grew up, I got married and had a son. When he was seven months old, I was working in Flint, Michigan and got called to the Army. I came back home and went from Cheboygan by bus for my physical. I passed with flying colors, so I went straight into the army on December 9, 1952. At that time, they weren't taking married men. I hadn't gone to the draft board to tell them that I had married, so they made me serve the 14 months in Korea on the frontline anyway. I received the Bronze Star for my acts of heroism.

I was in the last big battle on Porkchop Hill. We went up there with 337 men and only came back with 33. On the way up there, we got pretty close and the North Koreans had taken the hill from the Americans. We were there to take it back. As we were on our way up, the North Koreans threw this thing under my rifle. I asked the guy next to me what it was, and he got up and ran. I was currently lying on the ground, so I quickly flipped over with my head downhill. That was a good move because it was a concussion grenade. It hit me in the hip and my hip hurt me until the next day. If I hadn't have moved, I would probably be in the nut house today.

As we were walking in the dark to the hill, my squad leader side stepped and I was chosen to be the leader. I made it all the way to the top. I was the only one from Company K who was in the bunker. There were a couple of wounded China men and an older guy from World War II. He told me to take over. I think he was from Company L. There was also another young guy there from another Company. I went out and checked the area, and then I told this other young guy to check. I told him to keep his head down until he got out about 20 feet. I guess he thought that he knew better than I did, and got out of the bunker and raised his head. They got him in the neck. It looked bad but it was just touched. The blood had just spread and made it look like they had cut his head off! We tied a handkerchief around his neck and he was okay. It pays to listen!

John and the Chicken
By Roberta Delamarter of Ionia, Michigan
Born 1932

Living in a three-generation home had its advantages and its disadvantages. Neal, John, and Dick had to live up to all the adults' standards. From a young age, Neal and John, being only a year apart, were expected to learn to work like farmers. It was fun to learn how to milk a cow and drive horses. It wasn't too long before they could milk several cows and even drive the horses when plowing.

Grandma had chickens, which she called her egg money. That was used for fabric for clothing or wallpaper to cover the cardboard boxes that she nailed to make the closet walls. Grandma also bought a radio that they could listen to *The Lone Ranger* on. So, you could see how important Grandma's chickens were to her.

On his 9th birthday, John received a bow and arrow! What a wonderful gift, but how should he use it? Sitting on the fence in the backyard, it was just natural to aim at one of Grandma's chickens and let the arrow go. Oh my gosh, it went right through the chicken's breast! The chicken flinched a bit but continued to walk around. John just sat there and felt guilty and just awful. What if Grandma found out? After all, there was a chicken with an arrow through its breast.

After quite a period of deliberating what to do, John decided to pull the arrow out. The chicken seemed to recover from its trauma. So John decided it was best not to tell anyone. As far as John knew, no one ever knew what had happened, but one nine year old boy learned a good lesson without being taught.

I have to admit this is one of my favorite stories I heard John, my husband, tell. He always told it with such honesty and guilt!

The Crazy Horse Saloon
By Nan Shay of Kingsley, Michigan
Born 1943

Back in the day when I was ten years old, we lived on the corner of Santo Street and Baldwin Street in Traverse City, Michigan. Caddy corner from us was my good friend Karen Fisher. We had a whole neighborhood of friends that we hung out with. We used to raise chickens for Sunday dinners. When all the chickens were gone, the coop, which was pretty big, was empty. With my two sisters, Char and Bobbie, Karen and I would clean out the coop so that we could make a cowboy bar out of it. We got a big plank to use for the bar. We set some cement blocks on it. We made Kool Aid for our whiskey. We even had a corner which we put curtains around for our stage. We'd all take turns singing on the stage. When it was Karen's turn to sing, she sang *Singin' in the Rain.* She had my sister Char up on the roof pouring water through the cracks of the roof once to make "rain." Outside, we made a hitchin' post to tie our horses to. We made the horses out of wooden lath. We made cardboard saddles and nailed them onto our wooden horses. We saved the hair from the corn on the cob for the mane and tail. We pounded Pet milk cans on our heels with a rock. That was our horse hoofs.

Bobbie was really crazy about horses. She loved them all. She'd ride her horse back and forth like horses do when they get antsy. One day, we were playing cowboys in the saloon (we had made a big sign to put on the roof that said "The Crazy Horse Saloon"). We were drinking our Kool Aid as our whiskey and laughing. Someone came in and said; "The bank has just been robbed!" we all turned into a posse and ran out to get our horses off the hitchin' post. That was when Bobbie tripped over her horse and it broke in half. She cut her knee and it was bleeding. She was crying her head off, not because she got hurt, but because she broke her horse that she really loved. Our mother came out and saw that she was bleeding, so she went the emergency room. Ma brought a clean dress and was changing her on the way. Well, she had to get 18 stitches in her knee. When we got home, the first thing she did was start making a new horse. We still laugh about that to this day!

My Brave Dad and Grandparents
By Maryann Sheppard of Ludington,
Michigan
Born 1936

My dad was born in 1908 and shared a lot of family stories with us. However, this one was the scariest.

The year was around 1920. It was early evening, dark outside. And being farmers, the family was settling in for the night. Dad, his younger brother by five years, and Grandma and Grandpa were at the kitchen table while Dad read his lessons aloud by the light of the kerosene lamp. There was a disturbance in the yard. The dog yapping, horses stomping, and voices. When Grandpa looked out the window, he saw a neighbor's horse and wagon with five men dressed in KKK robes and hoods. He handed each boy a shotgun, blew out the lamp, raised the windows on each side of the door, and sent Grandma to the back of the house. He told the boys that if he told them to shoot, they weren't to ask questions, just pull the trigger. Then he stepped outside.

Grandma was foreign and Catholic. She was still considered an outsider by many, because she was Catholic. She was a hardworking housewife and mother, spending her days making bread, tending her bees, and doing the multitude of chores necessary in running a farm. She didn't "neighbor," and the nearest Catholic Church was over a day's ride away. She also kept a large flock of geese and made and sold goose down pillows when she had the time to spare. We always had goose for Christmas dinner.

Grandpa recognized a couple of the men and asked what they wanted. It soon became apparent they'd been drinking and were out for a "lark." The spokesman said they'd come for some of Grandma's goose feathers, as they were going to tar and feather Mrs. XXX, as she was living in sin with Mr. Y. Grandpa talked to them while they kept tipping the jug and passing it around. Finally, he talked them into heading home, explaining Mrs. XXX and Mr. Y had moved on. Some were concerned they wouldn't get back to their homes in time for morning milking and were losing interest in the tar and feathers project anyway. One wasn't feeling well at all and had made a mess in the wagon. After they left, the boys and Grandma went to bed. Grandpa kept watch for a while but finally went to bed.

Early the next morning, Grandma was frying up some side pork and pancakes for breakfast while the boys brought in the day's supply of fresh water and wood and got ready for school. Grandpa was pouring the morning's milk into the cream separator when a young boy galloped up, asking if anyone had seen his dad. Everyone had and told him what had happened the night before. The boy's name was Chris, and he said his dad had left the night before for a meeting in town and never returned home. He'd followed the wagon tracks as far as he could and wondered if Grandpa would help him look for his dad.

So Grandpa saddled up, and they headed out across the creek, picking up wagon tracks heading across the field towards the woods. It didn't take them long to find the horse and wagon. Seems everyone had fallen asleep, the horse had wandered his own way and, walking between two trees that weren't wide enough to accommodate the width of the wagon, was stuck until help arrived.

Several weeks after that incident, two couples drove up in a buggy to Grandma and Grandpa's for a visit. The ladies brought some of their canned and baked specialties and several quilt patterns, and they welcomed Grandma to the neighborhood. Nothing was ever mentioned about the tar and feather incident.

About 70 to 80 years after that incident, I bought one of those KKK robes at an auction. They'd been secreted away in a hidden room and were a surprise discovery for the heirs of that farm. It's a physical reminder to me of how brave my dad and grandparents were in protecting their home and Grandma. And of how forgiving they were.

A Cold Winter's Night

After World War II, my family (Mom, Dad, two brothers, a sister, and I) moved back to our home in the country on a chain of lakes. We'd lived in town during the war years because of my dad's job with the US Government and because of gas rationing. Our home on the lakes had been empty for all of those war years.

One very cold winter night, I was sent to fetch a pail of water from the pump, which was centrally located between our house, several cabins, and the caretaker's cabin, probably a couple hundred feet from the back door. I put on my coat and boots, grabbed the water pail, and headed out. It was a beautiful, moonlit night. So bright, I could see my shadow. The air was so crisp and cold, it froze my nose hairs, and the lakes were booming. If you've never heard lakes making ice, you've really missed one of Mother Nature's wonders. It sometimes sounds like thunder, and then it will roar like a lion, and sometimes it will sizzle and crack, like a rifle shot. So I stood very quiet and listened to this awesome mystery of sounds.

As I stood by the door, I heard yipping and howling and far down the hill past the pump came a deer, running all out, with a pack of wild dogs close on its heels. The deer ran for the lake and was on the ice when it was caught by the pack and killed. I went back in the house without getting the water and told my dad, who immediately loaded his shotgun. He took the pail to get the water.

We kids were driven to my grandma's house to catch the school bus for the next several days while a posse of neighborhood men were rounded up to get rid of the wild dogs. These dogs had started out as domestic dogs and had gone wild when abandoned by their owners, who were forced to leave their homes during this hard time. We found out the dogs were raiding hen houses and even a barn and creating other disturbances in the area, and getting less fearful of people. They had even killed a couple of farm dogs.

My Dad

My dad died at age 90 from a form of leukemia. He was born Catholic but didn't attend church. He said the woods were his church. He worked for the U.S. Forest Service and retired from there. Just before he died, he met a man of God who had been a POW during WWII on a Japanese held island in the Pacific. He developed a great admiration for this man and wanted him for his funeral service.

During the service, the minister was talking about Dad and telling how three days before he died, Dad had accepted Christ as his savior and asked for forgiveness for his sins. Behind me, one of Dad's buddies loudly exclaimed, "My God! That's cutting it close!"

Moonlit Serenade
By Dale W. Farrell of Alger, Michigan
Born 1946

It is a jewel, and has been named the sixth most beautiful lake in the world. It is a picture postcard painted by God's hand with its deep clear opal blue water and sandy bottom. The lake is encircled by tall red pines, white paper birch, oaks, and cedars. At the north end of the lake, long before a state park was developed, there was a rustic county campground that hugged its shore. It was here upon the cool waters of Higgins Lake that a sight not soon forgotten occurred. Notched among the cedars and pines were thirty or so campsites. Each site faced the lake offering its resident a breathtaking view of the new day's sun as its golden rays shimmered across the lake's surface. At the far end, the shadowed trees of Treasure Island called for the young at heart to explore its shore. Those who traveled from the city in search of tranquility found it here. These city folk, or flat-landers as we called them, pitched walled tents or parked their Airstreams in cutout cubbies, seeking to find nature's getaway from the hectic traffic, noise, and confusion of everyday life.

It was on a warm July night in the summer of 1961 that the lake came alive. In the peace of the evening after the sun had lost itself behind the fortress of trees that guarded the lake, campfires would be lit. The fire's glow was like a string of lampposts that spotted the shoreline. What a beautiful sight they were, flickering and dancing their golden yellow ribbons upon the slated surface of the lake as wisps of smoke shrouded the treetops. On occasion, a group of three or four of us cottage dwellers would take my grandfather's old wooden green rowboat out for an evening cruise along the shore. Other than a few boats that carried anglers hoping for a last catch of the day, the lake was serene. We would row to the diving platforms that the DNR had placed out in the lake for the amusement of the summer workers at the old CCC Camp. Then we would turn around and head back. It was so peaceful and beautiful. It was especially nice to glide along under the gleam of a summer silver moon. Sometimes there would be two guys and two girls, but on this particular evening, the trip consisted of me and three girls, Carol, Sharon, and Judy. It was during this excursion that the normally gentle and calm evening came alive.

As the four of us guided our craft past the campground, it was as if the lake and all that encompassed it from the heavens above to the crescent shoreline was ours alone. The silver glow of the moon lighting our course must have inspired us beyond self-consciousness and any embarrassment, as we broke into song. We bellowed out such old tunes as *Shine on Silver Moon, Down by the Old Mill Stream, Bicycle Built for Two,* and many more songs of yesteryear. Our voices, intertwined with melodic overtones, awakened the slumbering night with a newfound spirit. Oh, how glorious it must have been as our tribute in verse ran across the still water and echoed off the trees.

We turned around just past the cedar swamp and headed back to our place of departure. As we passed by the campground, we were taken by surprise. As though the lake was a stage and we were the main attraction, the shore came alive with spotlights, headlights, flashlights, lights of all kinds that cut through the darkness, pinpointing the subject of their amusement. There we were for all to see. A cacophony of hoots, whoops, whistles, and rounds of encore carried their way to our solitary craft. There was no place to go, no place to hide. The girls did the best they could to slouch down in the boat, giggling with embarrassment while I manned the oars.

As we passed out of sight, the tribute subsided and peace once again settled on the lake. Carol, Sharon, and Judy slowly emerged from their hiding place like three little gophers who stuck their heads up out of their burrow to see if all was safe. The rest of the way back to the dock we were silent. Unintentionally, we had become the summer's main attraction, a vaudevillian act on Michigan's largest stage. Before the summer season was over, there would be more serenades in the moonlit nights along the Higgins Lake shore.

Teresa's mother, Charlotte Chesler Brothers in 1964

√ Music, Rustic Cabins, and Trickery
By Teresa Louise Kenaga of Haslett, Michigan
Born 1946

I took in my first breath on a cold December day at Grayling Mercy Hospital. I was raised in the small town of Mio near the AuSable River with a population of about 2,000. Winters were long and cold, never seeing any bare ground until April. Now, living in southern, lower Michigan, I see thaw after thaw during the winter months. When I was old enough to understand, my mother told me she was grateful that I hadn't arrived any sooner than I did. An earlier arrival would have prevented my mother, nine months pregnant, from finishing her tasks for the season, the season being deer hunting season. I'm uncertain when I developed my dislike for the deer season, but I think it was at my first sight of deer strung from the trees.

My parents rented out five cabins from April to December. These cabins were called "rustic." Not having running water put them in that category. They rented for $3.00 for one bed and $5.00 for two beds. With this, renters had a clean, cozy cabin, which included an icebox, basin, plates, cups, silverware, pots, pans, hotplate for cooking, an oil burning stove for heat, electricity, table and chairs, a dresser, cute curtains, and a lock on the door. Oh, yes, out yonder were the old outhouses. I do believe my mother thought they should never offend, and so they never smelled of anything but bleach. I began helping at an early age. All the lessons in working well for the family have been a benefit for me through the years. My three siblings, the kids renting cabins, and kids from cottages surrounding our property that visited in the summer gave us many playmates. In the day or into the evening, we could be heard hollering, "Here I come, ready or not!" or "Pom pom, pull away." I remember many times gathered with my siblings around the woodstove in the kitchen. One year, to my delight, we hatched out baby chicks by the warmth of the stove. My mother cooked on this stove until I was 12 years old, when the new range took its place. She did her magic, serving delicious meals. I am amazed that she could successfully bake and cook in a wood stove. I wonder if Mother ever missed it. I never asked.

The fire from that stove died, but the music from the piano never did. I was born into a house of music. My dad operated a square dancing place for people to come to on Saturday nights. Roller skating was on Sunday. He played piano by ear (that still fills me with awe), played guitar, harmonica, sang, and did the dance calls. My mother loved music, playing the piano and violin. We often gathered around the piano in the living room and sang a variety of songs from *The Old Rugged Cross* to *Jambalaya*. One summer, to pay a vet bill for an injured stray dog, we put on a talent show for those in the cabins and anyone in the area we could get to come. We lured them in with popcorn and Kool-Aid. My sisters and I sang songs. We often sang as a trio at church, PTA, County talent shows with the stage name, "The Brothers Sisters," our last name being Brothers. Friends contributed their talents. After the last act, before they could disappear with their chairs into their cabins, we passed a hat around. It was a success, and all for a good cause! My parents had their ups and downs through the years with paying off medical bills. First, my dad had colon cancer and my brother had spinal problems. I learned how to be creative and thrifty in tough times.

I must admit that my sisters and I weren't always so good. You see, sometimes the city kids who came to Mio to stay at their cottages near my home were not so kind to the locals. Sometimes their words stung. Some of the

Letitia, Maxine, and Teresa

things they would say were, "Oh, you have a TV and a radio?" or "Really? You guys from the sticks have inside facilities?" We felt we were not given the respect we deserved from these city kids. Sometimes, we acted on it with a little northern prank. Hopefully, you will see our innocent humor. We did this by taking them for a walk in the wooded hills, not too far from our place, probably a mile, or two. We then told them there were mean hillbillies in these woods. We told them that they had long beards and torn clothes, and carried long guns. So, one of us would lag behind and toss a rock into the woods, making them jump. I may have seen a few tears shed. By the time we had them safely back, they thought we were very brave. It was very scary for them; it was very funny for us! We never told them otherwise. We felt we were paying tribute to our northern roots, which I loved and always will.

The Dutchman's Swimming Hole and Fishing Trip
By Ralph L. Moore of Onaway, Michigan
Born 1945

As active youngsters growing up in the small Northeast Michigan village of Millersburg my cousins and I spent a considerable amount of time wading the picturesque Ocqueoc River, fishing for brook and rainbow trout, as well as smallmouth bass.

We were fortunate that our Polish grandparents' wonderful old farmhouse, wasn't too far from the Ocqueoc and so therefore we were able to walk a mile or so down the narrow, dusty, dirt road and then take a short cut across our neighbor's back forty in order to get to one of our favorite fishing holes.

The old swimming hole, which we called Dutchman's, was a little further away—just east of town—and was also a popular hangout on the Ocqueoc. We were quite familiar with this particular spot because our uncle would often pack 3 or 4 of us into his old '56 Plymouth after a grueling day of haying under a scorching, summer sun and head for Dutchman's.

Not yet having the modern convenience of running water and a good hot shower in the old farmhouse, it was a fast and relatively easy way to get cleaned up. Most everyone else in the area did the same thing.

A couple of years later and still unable to drive a car on the highway, my buddy who was a year older than me at 14, suggested we take his dad's 1953 Ford tractor to the Dutchman's swimming hole and see if we could catch some bass.

The typical grey and red color on this 28 horsepower tractor was probably the only thing that was typical. The rear tires were oversized and the governors were adjusted to near the maximum. So, what we had here was a hot rod farm tractor capable of speeds up to around 35 MPH, which in the late 1950s was quite awesome for a small farm tractor.

We must have been quite an amazing sight as we went flying down the highway with me sitting on the left fender, hanging on to the rear light with one hand, and holding on to the fender with the other and occasionally passing a slow moving car, which we often did.

We had quite often seen fish around that deep hole while swimming, so we thought it would be a good idea to give it a try.

After about an hour or so we had each caught a couple of nice bass around 15"-16" and we were having quite a bit of fun trying to outsmart them.

The shoreline we were fishing had quite a bit of brushy material around it and every so often, we would snag on to it as we were casting. Consequently, my buddy did not think too much of it when on the start of his next cast he felt some resistance and jerked his pole to release it. There was only one thing wrong. It wasn't hooked up in the brush; it was in the bridge of my big old nose! .

Man, I let out a scream that scared him half to death. As he quickly turned around, he could easily see that I was doubled over in extreme pain, as the hook was embedded in my nose pretty good. Fortunately, it just missed my eyes. After cutting the line, we tried to pull it out with some pliers, but that last hard tug of his set the hook pretty good and it was just too painful to try and remove.

Realizing we couldn't waste any more time trying to do it ourselves, I said, "We have to get over to my aunt and uncle's house," which was about 2 miles away. After hastily loading everything up, we headed out across a small field to the winding dirt road that led to the highway near where they lived. What a

sight that must have been as we took off down the road and me sitting on the fender with a fishhook in my nose and a big night crawler dangling from it. I can still remember my aunt and uncle having an extended laugh as we came knocking on their door.

Anyhow, they drove me up to the Onaway Clinic, which was about 10 miles away, while my buddy headed back to the farmhouse to tell my grandma and grandpa what happened.

Upon reaching the clinic there was to be more red-faced embarrassment, as everyone in there had a good laugh at my humorous situation and Dr. Donald Finch, who was the physician at the time, probably had the best laugh of all. He thought it was a riot because the old dried-up worm was still hanging from the hook.

After freezing the tender area with an injection he was able to pull the long shank hook out without too much trouble. Other than that I do not remember much more about what happened after that except, whenever I had to go see Doc' Finch in the years following that hilarious episode, we would both be reminded of that day and have a good laugh about it.

✓ I Was a Peacetime Baby but Gave My Mother Little Peace
By Eleanore VanZyll of Wyoming, Michigan
Born 1918

Grandpa and Grandma came from Canada in 1882, and built a log cabin in Oliver Township, nine miles from the County Seat of Kalkaska, Co. It was at the time when all the virgin timber was logged off. I remember hearing Dad tell of easily being able to ride a horse through the big pine trees. The last sleighs of big timber west of our place were taken out when I started school.

I don't know how Grandpa made a living, but know that he had a sugar bush and made maple syrup. Five children were made to this union, my mother being the oldest. Grandpa's health was failing, but somehow mother went to Ferris Institute and others were boarded out at Kalkaska to complete high school and County Normal.

Before mother Anna was married, Grandpa and Uncle Chester ordered material for two houses from Sears & Roebuck. Our big 4-bedroom house was built about 300 feet from the log cabin where Mother was born. Mother married Amos McCool in 1915, and after Grandpa passed away, Grandma lived with us until she died at age 93.

I arrived on Nov. 1918, shortly after WWI. I was a peacetime baby, but gave my dear mother, little peace. Foster, my big brother arrived 2 years earlier. The two younger brothers came in 1921 and 1924. That made up our family along with Grandma and our faithful companion dog, Old Shag. Growing up, there were good times and other times that I got laughed at a lot. The only girl, I often had to try a stunt first; if I could do it, then the boys could. I had to chase the ball that big brother batted out, or it seemed that I always had to be "It," playing Hide 'n Seek.

Our big 4-bedroom house was a great place to play in. The attic, which held a feather bed, several trunks of old, clothes, and curtains that we could dress up in and the water tank, which held water, pumped from the basement. The second floor had the beds with high wooden headboards that we could jump from onto the bed until mother called for us to stop. First floor was the racetrack that we ran, or Foster could ride the wooden tricycle around from the kitchen through the hall into the front hall, into the living room to the dining room and back to the kitchen. There were many races, hide and seek, and sliding down the smooth, polished stairs. Mother tried to teach me to play the piano, but I was too lazy to practice the finger moves, so she gave up at that. I wasn't much for playing with dolls, and broke the china head of one, because it wouldn't sit up while I brushed her hair.

The basement was deep, dark, and cool. It held the big furnace, firewood, pump, along with all Mother's canned goods. Because it was cool, our cream, milk, and butter were also kept there, as we had no icebox. Remembering Mother's good butter, she won first place, a beautiful Hoosier cabinet at the Cadillac State Fair, one year.

Our house was one of the few with indoor plumbing. The water was pumped from the basement to the big tank in the attic. It was up to us kids to run up to the attic to see how full the tank was, so Mother could shut the pump off before it ran over and flooded everything below. I was afraid of that job, when I was small, I thought the tank was bottomless and I might fall in.

We had a Bell Telephone on the wall that we had to crank to make a call. It was a party line phone, and every time Dad wanted to call, he would become quite impatient, because the neighborhood gossips were on the line, and he had to wait until they finished, which he felt took too long.

Growing up, we were taught that there were certain jobs that we had to do. Turning the handle of the wash wringer, turn the crank on the milk separator and the one on a corn Sheller.

One year Dad worked up a half acre of land for us to raise pickles. It was up top us to keep the weeds out, pick the pickles, and take them to Spenser to put down in big tanks of brine. We also were required to pull weeds out of the garden and thin out the carrots and radishes so they could grow bigger. Every fall we had to pick up potatoes; a job I didn't like. At first, the potatoes were dug by hand and we would beg Dad and Uncle John not to dig any more. After Dad got the potato digger, the rows got much longer and more help was required. Some high school kids were let out so they could earn money picking up potatoes. Getting hay into our barn and thrashing, were big jobs, often with help from the neighbors.

Last, but by far the least, was gathering the cattle from the woods and cut over land west of our house. That task took a lot of walking in bare feet, watching where we stepped as we followed the cattle home with the help of Shag.

Mother's work was never done. There was three meals to prepare; make lots of bread and can everything she could, and then there was the laundry. Rainwater was pumped from the cistern and put on the wood stove to heat, then dumped into the washtub on the wringer stand. Everything was scrubbed on the washboard, wrung into, first one rinse, then into the bluing rinse. Finally, the basket of wet, heavy clothes were taken out to hang and in the winter, it had to be carried up to the attic to dry. Grandma helped a lot. She made the beds, dusted the floors, knitted caps, and mittens, and made almost everything we wore. I got my first store bought coat when I started 7th grade.

The village of Sigma was a small place about two miles from our house and established at the time of the big timber. There was a hotel, depot, along with a store and about 20 families. Kirby's store had groceries, hardware, dry goods, and medicine. I remember the boxes with clear front covers, so one could see all the different cookies. There were chocolate covered bonbons, pink and white bonbons with coconut on top, but my favorite was Mary Ann's, a crisp molasses one. We didn't get into Kalkaska very much, but I do remember going there to shop for Christmas. That meant the morning chores had to be done, the big sleigh filled with straw, and blankets or fur robe. We had to keep warm for the nine-mile ride to town. We were snuggled down in the straw, but not for long. We would jump out to slide in the smooth sled tracks. I remember one stretch where the evergreen trees covered with snow almost closed over the road making it like a tunnel.

In town, Dad stabled the horses and we went to Mother's cousin for lunch. Afterwards we took all our money, about a quarter, to shop. There were only two stores where we could find a gift for a dime. The hardware or variety store, but we got our shopping done, then, started home. We were all tired, so we snuggled down in the sleigh, not worrying about getting home, because the horse knew the way. It was dark before we got home; the sky filled with stars and the only sound was the muffled hoof beats of the horses and the squeaks of their harness.

I think I started school in 1924. School was a one-room, where we sat, a library, boy's and girl's cloak rooms with a chemical toilet and a wash room which held a basin and soap, and a pail of water with one dipper. Everyone drank out of that one dipper, but not many washed their hands. I don't know how many attended, but our ages ranged from 6 to 17 or 18. Most of the older boys would never graduate 8th grade because they had to do work a lot. There were Native Americans, black and very poor white children, but we all played together as one. There was a variety of teachers; one told us that he had a piece of rubber hose to use— so better behave. One woman tried to pound the lesson into one boys head with a yardstick. He didn't learn much, anyway.

One time the boys killed a snake and chased the girls with it. When they ran into the girl's cloakroom, I took the snake and followed them. Teacher reprimanded me for that stunt.

At Christmas time, a stage was erected at the front of the room, from which acts, songs, or poems were done in front of an audience. After that, Santa came in and gave out gifts, a really exciting time. We walked the half mile to and from school, but one winter there was a bad storm with lots of snow. Dad met us part way, carried the youngest and made a trail for the others.

Brother Foster trapped skunks and checked the traps before school. If he caught one, his clothes would smell and when he got to school the teacher didn't much like the odor he carried with him.

Growing up at the time, we had to entertain ourselves. We had the RCA Victrola with a wide selection of records. A Scotsman named Harry Lauder, Al Jolson and a coloratura soprano, Gally Churchi. We being country bumpkins didn't appreciate her singing. Later we got a radio. The adults had to listen to Lum 'n Abner, Amos and Andy and the news. For the kids, it was The Shadow Knows, we learned to yodel listening to WLS Barn Dance.

In our teen years, a theatre opened in town, so Saturday night we could go to movies. Other farm folks came in and the theatre often smelled like the barn. One movie we saw was Tarzan of the Apes, which brother, Foster tried to emulate, but all he got was rope burns as he tried to swing from our elm tree.

My high school days were not much for me, I had no goals, but Mother knew that we had to graduate. I had to board out of town. The first year I stayed with my first teacher and her family, other times with my uncle and aunt. The last year I worked for the local Dr. and family, but I was paid for my work, $3.00 a week with room and board.

Our home was a happy home even with hard work and hard times. We had lots of visitors, Grandma's brothers and sisters. Often, all the beds would be filled and much food to be prepared. The man that delivered gasoline always tried to get there in time for breakfast, because there was laughter and good food.

There are so many good times to remember, a train trip to Cadillac when I was about 6 or 7, my first plane ride in a biplane at the County Fair. The pilot did as many stunts as he dared and I was really thrilled, our cars, from the Model-T Ford, to the Essex. Learning to drive and bumping into the insurance agent's car, and sledding on the hill.

Too many memories for just 3 pages, and I cherish them all and try to save them for my children.

Thank You for Sharing Your Fish with Me
By Susan Erickson of Burton, Michigan
Born 1960

Everyone needs a 'big fish' story and this is mine. June of 1979 was the sixth year our family had vacationed in a cabin on Loud Drive on Lake Van Etten just outside of Oscoda. The cabin was small, but familiar to us and we always arrived prepared to supply our own entertainment with our aluminum outboard boat equipped with a whopping 10-horse power engine that, believe it or not, we skied behind, and a light aqua colored butterfly sailboat.

I am one of the youngest of six children and because we only stayed one week at the lake my parents were the perfect taskmasters at having us unpack, sort food and clothes, and make the beds. We would quickly rig up our small boats down by the dock so we could begin to enjoy vacation as soon as possible. As I wandered down to our redwood dock I noticed the next-door neighbor's dock looked like legs from an over turned picnic table, but in reality, the points sticking up were the four large fishing poles that he had permanently fixed to his dock and he was frequently seen checking them for fish.

The afternoon was pleasantly warm with a steady, often strong westerly wind. My dad, being encouraged by the good weather, decided to take the sailboat out for the first run of the season. He was making good time tacking and coming about, but sometimes a gust of wind can change a safe situation into a dangerous one. I was half way up to the cabin when I decided that I should stay near the motorboat just in case my father needed me. After a few minutes of sitting on our sunny dock, I became warm so I dangled my feet in the cool water and then quickly jumped in. I stood thigh deep in the water with my fingertips just below the surface. I swung my arms to and fro watching the drops of water separate as they sparkled in the sun. Suddenly, something moving just a few inches from me and slightly below the water's surface caught

Susan with her neighbor in 1979

my eye. What I thought was a pair of eyes was watching, coming toward me. I could instantly feel adrenaline shoot through my body. I covered my mouth with my wet hands to stifle a scream. In the back of my mind scenes from the movie "Jaws 2" briefly flashed. It had been a year since the release of that frightening movie and I was just getting comfortable getting back in the water. Needless to say, I didn't stay in the water to find out what it was driftwood or not. I ran to the edge of the water as fast as I could, lifting my legs high to gain all possible speed. I walked along the dock peering into the clear water, my hands still clenched over my mouth. Nothing. What was it? Or had it been? A reflection on the water's surface? A teenager's vivid imagination? Just moments later I saw exactly what it was and I

35

found myself screaming into my hands again. Calmly swimming toward me about four feet out from the dock was a very big fish. The biggest I had ever seen. It appeared to be stunned.

My sister's boyfriend Rob had just opened the back door of the cabin to say hello when I beckoned him to come as quickly as his legs could carry him. I jumped back into the water and Rob quickly grabbed a net from our boat that I used to pick up a 15-pound, 39-½ inch Northern Pike. He didn't put up much of a fight even when he was completely out of the water. The only visible injury was a clean, one-inch long cut on the top of this wildly beautiful fish near his fin. My dad supposed that the blade of a motorboat could have cut the fish. I knew well that we could barely fit half of a frozen chicken into the cabins small refrigerator freezer let alone such a large fish. After several pictures were taken, the elderly next-door neighbor named Marcus, who had a permanent residence on the lake, offered to keep the fish in his freezer until the newspaper could be called on Monday.

As it turned out Marcus ended up with his picture in the paper that week with the fish, captioned by the very believable story of how he caught it. His poor wife was mortified to have to be the one to tell my parents and me what he had done. I believe he felt it wasn't fair that some high-school senior who visited the lake for one week a year and didn't even own a fishing pole should be lucky enough to "catch" such a fish when he fished from his dock all season long. My parents felt anyone who wanted to pose with a fish for the newspaper promoted the popularity of fishing in Michigan and I agreed.

So how did I feel about how this story unfolded? For several reasons I was never upset and if I could meet Marcus today I would give him a big hug and kiss because I understood that that fish was his. I imagined that he had caught that fish a thousand times over in his dreams and because I never saw Marcus again he never heard the rest of this story. Just a few weeks later I started college at the University of Michigan. My first assignment in my first English class was to write a descriptive story. We handed the stories in on Friday and on Monday the professor came to class disheartened at the poor quality of the stories and the writing, except for one.

Then she began to read one story to the whole class, the story of the girl who caught a fish. When she was finished, she asked me to stand up, tell everyone my name, where I attended high school, and the name of my high school English teacher. "Now that's how you write a descriptive story," she said. I was beaming. So, thank you Marcus, thank you for sharing your fish with me.

Miracle Lights of Christmas, 1930
By Esther Dinger Gauthier of Traverse City, Michigan
Submitted by Claire Gauthier Boutain of Riverview, Michigan
Born 1903

Something mysterious and seemingly unsolvable happened to me on Christmas Eve, 1930. That was the time our country was suffering through an economic depression, which brought hard times to nearly everyone. Now, when the cycle of difficult times is returning for many, I want to share my heartening happening. Perhaps it will help others remember the mystery and joy that is sometimes found within insurmountable trials.

Our farm family had had more than our share of sickness, fires, and ill fortune, but we put a lot of effort into bettering out lot. My husband, Isadore, worked long hours farming all summer, so we always had enough to eat and wear. Our clothes were not fancy, but I remodeled hand-me-down clothes to fit each one's size and needs. We always had sufficient food canned in jars, dried, or salted which had been prepared when foods were season. And we thanked God at every meal for the good He provided.

Everyone in the country suffered for lack of cash. We could not pay our farm taxes or mortgage, nor buy farm equipment or even simple household items. It was certain that store-bought luxuries were out of the question for Christmas. However, we had exchanged someday work with an old neighbor who could fashion wooden skis for several of the children and with "new" made-over clothes for the rest of the children, everyone at our house would have something to wake up to on Christ's birthday.

A family with several small children and

a new baby had just moved from the city to a farm near ours. They had neither a good supply of food nor a paying job so their Christmas looked very bleak. We could easily count our blessings in comparison. So when a surprise package from my sister in a distant city came on Christmas Eve, our children agreed to share our unexpected treasures with our neighbors. We divided the cookies, candies, and oranges equally, and then added an item of clothing we thought might fit each of the neighbor's children. We felt like a corporate Santa making plans and I, Mom, was elected to deliver our birthday gifts for the King.

That night, as early as we could, we tucked the little ones in bed, and left our oldest daughter (nine years old) in charge while Isadore did the evening barn chores. I walked across the snow-filled fields. There were no snowplowed roads in the rural area of our Leelanau County, Michigan. In fact, all roads here were merely wagon tracks. That evening, even yesterday's horse and sleigh tracks that usually followed in those wagon paths were hidden beneath the gentle afternoon's snowfall. The skies were again bright and clear as I left the house, and the early evening moon made pretty pictures of the hills and trees around me. My feet left big footprints in the crispy and fluffy snow. I'd walked that way many times, and my joyful task made me feel like a child again, giddy and expectant. Like a kid, my mind filled with thoughts of Christmas, only a few hours away.

An easy snow began falling as I reached our neighbor's house. I found the husband babysitting while his wife attended a Christmas Eve doing at school. I stayed long enough to warm my limbs and give him our holiday surprise, and then I started home. Those big lazy flakes of snow that had started falling just as I arrived were no longer "lazy." A northern blizzard soon howled the moon from sight, so when I left the lamplight of our neighbor's windows there was no way to guess where the path should be. The hills and valleys could give no clue in that white blacked out no-man's land. I was sure I knew the way, but all too soon even cool instinct would fail. There was nothing to reassure me, and worrisome thoughts began to taunt me. Old settlers often told true tales of frontier persons who lost their way in snowstorms and who were found only when spring thaws gave up their secrets.

With a faith born from many past favors, I asked God for direction. "Help me get home! Please show me the way!" I was trying to be His hands, trying to bring His joy to the poor on his birthday! I didn't think He would fail me, but then why would He hold back His own natural forces of nature? He was wise and good. He had directed the simple shepherds. He would guide me as He had the Wisemen, wouldn't He? Our gifts weren't as rich as theirs, but they were as lovingly given. Time seemed an eternity, while doubt and trust exchanged places in my mind – like twin stars spinning around some great black hole of fear. My unbelieving side laughed at my faith-filled side. It echoed the truth of those who wandered in circles, freezing to death just outside their own lamplight and home. As firmly came back the stories of miracle rescues, too.

Suddenly, in that savage cold torment, a light appeared! No light seemed possible! The wind scrubbed snow streaked strands of my hair across my face. It was easy to see my hair in the light. I could see each strand was like a tiny electric filament, glowing just like a light bulb. But hair can't light up! So I hid the offending wisps under my cap. The light stayed with me. I thought it might be some sort of reflection, but there were no artificial light sources out in our rural area. Maybe it could be lights from some distant car shining. Common sense said there was no way car light could be showing in such a storm and there were no roads clear out in those fields. My thoughts would return to my hair and sure enough, when I let a strand of hair come from under my cap, it was aglow, and I'd push the scary sight away. I had to keep walking, unsure of the way or not. To stop in such a storm was the first step to freezing to death. Cold and frightened as I was, an ever so loving calmness came over me. It hinted the light was somehow guiding me and so guided, I should no longer be afraid.

"Go on! Keep going! Just keep going! Be unafraid!" I told myself. Finally, just a little distance away, I could see a flicker of lamplight in a window. I could see it was home, and this time when I pulled a hair strand to see, it was just hair, just my everyday brown hair. As I fumbled at the doorknob with frozen hands, my little daughter helped me inside.

Her relieved but startled face let me know I must look dazed and shocking. She helped me regain myself as she rubbed my hands and feet back to feeling. She trembled as she took my wraps and listened to the story.

Years went by and we often relived and tried to make sense of that Christmas Eve. Always it is as vivid now as then. We ask ourselves, "What if I had looked up?" Why didn't I? Do angels come in electric filament versions? Does God need physical signs of miracles when He performs them? Whatever this awesome experience God gave me, I should never have wanted to miss those Christmas lights.

Fun in the snow

Rocket Man
By Harry Elliott Colestock of Petoskey, Michigan
Born 1923

I was born in the Highland Park Hospital in Highland Park, Michigan, when we lived in Ferndale, Michigan. For the first few years of my life, I attended the Coolidge School in Ferndale, until I was ten years old. At that time, the Great Depression hit and my dad was laid off from his toolmaker's job, and we had to sell our house to put food on the table. With part of the proceeds, we bought a five-acre orchard about eleven miles west of Birmingham. That summer, we all lived in a big tent while Dad and we three boys rebuilt a house, which a company in Detroit had given us if we removed it from their property. Our goal was to get it rebuilt enough so we could move into it before cold weather came, which we did.

In 1933, we moved out to our five-acre farm and into our house when we got it finished that fall. Our heating system was by a big circulating heater that was wood-fired. Dad stoked it up before going to bed at night. For cooking, we had a wood cook stove in the kitchen, with an electric hotplate for added assistance when needed. It was my job to keep the two wood boxes filled from the woodshed out back. In the fall, we would have a weekend when we would buzz wood on a big three-foot tractor driven buzz saw. We would cut several cords of wood, enough to provide our heat for the whole winter until the fall when it was time to cut again.

After I helped my dad rebuild our house, he rewarded me by giving me tickets to Harry Blackstone Sr., the magician, who was performing at the local theater. Blackstone called me up on stage as a volunteer and made a big fuss over our first names being the same. This is what got me started in magic, where I started to develop a love for it.

Mother was a trained teacher, and she coached all of us with our schoolwork, which was extremely easy for me. I graduated as valedictorian of my class in 1941. When we moved to our new house on Maple Road, we attended the Walled Lake School System and were picked up by bus on Maple Road in front of our house. I had to milk a few cows down in Heliker's barn and run my thirty-five muskrat trap line before the bus came, so that forced me to get up at 3:30am to get everything done.

I skinned my rats the night before and stretched them on tapered shingles so I could take them on the bus to the Vreeland Fur House across from the school the next morning. I only got thirty-five cents a skin in those days.

Dad was only off work a couple of years from his toolmaker's job, and with everyone helping, we survived without having to depend on Welfare. We had a big garden and an apple orchard, and with everyone working, we survived nicely.

In high school, I went out for football and basketball, but football interfered the most with our harvesting and marketing the apple crop. As our trees became larger and more mature, our apple harvest increased.

Pop leased several other orchards, too, until we eventually had 46,000 bushels of apples, with 45 workers picking at our peak time. Since Dad was back at his toolmaker's job, I served as his foreman with both Bob and Bill helping me to collect the apples and get them into storage at the end of the day. Friday nights were our most difficult times, as we had our football games on that night, and also had very late collection times in the orchards. Each crate contained one bushel and weighed about fifty pounds. With all the loading and unloading of hundreds of bushels, my brother, Bob and I developed wonderful muscles for football.

In my senior year, I developed into the strongest kid on the team and could throw people around whenever I wanted. Coach Hursh would let me call the plays as I had them all memorized by this time, and I was elected Captain of the team. This year we also became the champions of our league.

School classes were very easy for me and I earned two scholarships to Michigan State, as well as my valedictorian ranking. I attended MSU for one and a half years before Uncle Sam came calling, and I was drafted into the service for World War II. I chose the Air Force and was assigned to the Air Transport Command. After some basic training, I was assigned to an air base in Newcastle,

Harry Elliott Colestock

Delaware. We flew up to Mitchell Field, Long Island to pick up our loads, and then out to the Azores in the Atlantic for a refuel stop, and then down to Casablanca, North Africa for another refuel stop, and then over to Cairo, Egypt for another refuel stop, and then on to Calcutta, India, where we dumped our loads. We were flying the four-engine C-54s and could not go over the "HUMP" so the smaller two-engine C-47s picked up our loads and flew the stuff into Chung King. Our return trips from Calcutta carried mostly hospital cases and GIs on furlough.

After the war, I found myself married to my high school sweetheart, Marian Thomas, and with one child, "Aichy" as we called him, as he was H.E. Colestock III. I needed a higher income than the GI Bill offered so I changed from MSU to the University of Michigan and found both a job and housing at Willow Run Village near the U of M campus. I worked as a Village maintenance worker and dovetailed my time with my classes. I graduated with a BS in electrical engineering in February 1949, with an immediate job offer with GE as a test engineer at Schenectady, NY. I also earned an MBA in 1973 from Northern Indiana University.

After several years, Marian became homesick for Michigan, so we moved back. I took a job as an electrical engineer with Pontiac Motors. After one year, an opportunity arose with the Weltronic Company on Eight Mile Road, which led to my being chief engineer in a short time. From this job, I went to chief engineer of the Burroughs Corporation in Plymouth, Michigan. It was here that we won the contract to design and build the guidance computer for the Atlas missile, the one used to put John Glenn into orbit.

In looking back over my last fifty years, one of the most important accomplishments has been the design and development of the guidance computer for the Atlas missile. In the 1950s, there were three main computer manufacturers, IBM, Burroughs, and Remington Rand. These computers were designed for business use and used vacuum tubes and air conditioners. NASA came to each of us and asked us to build a computer that was fail-safe. They hammered their fists on my conference room table and demanded that we <u>must</u> have a computer that will <u>not</u> fail. As chief engineer of Burroughs, I didn't know how to do that. All engineers are trained that everything has a MTBF, a mean time before failure. That night, I went home and prayed that God would show me how to best answer their needs. The next day, God had given me the idea to give the computer a problem that I knew would exercise every circuit. If it got the right answer to the problem, then it could be used for launch; if it didn't get the right answer, then the launch would be cancelled. We proposed this system and won the contract. This guidance system has been updated twice since it was designed, to give it transistors and to eliminate the air conditioner. The logic was left essentially the same, so that in December of 2006, it was used to send an Atlas to Saturn. It was most satisfying to have John Glenn come back after his orbit of the earth in 1962 and thank us for our contribution to his flight.

I was working as chief engineer at Ingersoll-Rand in Plymouth, Michigan and became involved in some of the most intricate automation systems in the world. We tackled all types of high-speed assembly and high-speed testing that you could imagine, installing these all over the world. My last job before retirement was a complete assembly line and a complete test line for a six-cylinder car engine for the Holden car in Melbourne, Australia. Holden is a General Motors Division and is like the Chevrolet Division in America. These two lines ran about five million dollars and used 125 robots to do the assembly. This work resulted in 42 patents.

After retirement in July of 1988, I spent two years developing two devices for the medical profession, getting patents for a new pump for heart patients and a new device for the melting of the knot at the end of a suture. Then, in the '90s, I started the development of my computer-controlled automaton. This was a ½-size replica of magician-ventriloquist Jay Marshall from Chicago from the waist up. I finished this early in 1997 and decided to present it at the annual show of the Magician's Collector's Convention in Shalmberg, Illinois on May 31, 1997. On stage as the closing act for a Saturday night show, I got a standing ovation, with everyone wanting to see the apparatus after the applause died down. The Michigan Technology Council awarded me $5,000.00 to take my automaton around to 67 high schools to demonstrate it and try to teach students to build one of their own.

During my early years, both my dad and mom made sure that all of us children understood our need to have a strong faith in God. They made sure we went to Sunday school every week, even when we lived in the tent. They helped us with our prayers every night. My dad especially made us look to God for guidance with our problems and with our decisions, we make as we go through life. He always had an active faith and felt that God had a plan for us, because of His love for us. This taught me to put my hand in God's hand when I need His guidance and His leadership. This I do even yet today. God has blessed my life with not only two wonderful wives, but two wonderful boys, four wonderful grandchildren, and at this point in history, six wonderful great-grandchildren, and I love them all dearly.

A note from Harry's wife:

Harry's oldest son was an Air Force Colonel in charge of intelligence for the Gulf War. He is now retired. Harry's other son has a Doctorate in plasma physics and is head scientist at the Los Alamos lab. He has experiments in outer space.

In Harry's "spare time," he met Albert Einstein, was deacon and elder in church, donated 125 pints of blood, and traveled around the world eleven times on business. He was president of the Kiwanis in Ann Arbor and on the boards of various clubs. Harry tutored, volunteered, gardened, published a book, Industrial Robotics (McGraw-Hill), and wrote beautiful poetry. He was an ingenious inventor, an accomplished artist, and a professional magician. Harry passed away on December 28, 2012 at age eighty-nine.

A Rookie Deckhand's Deciding Moment
By Donn K. Syrett of Gaylord, Michigan
Born 1943

Looking back at some of the things, I did as a young man often produces in me a shiver that has absolutely nothing to do with temperature or weather conditions. That shiver is almost always produced by a memory associated with a stressful situation, and/or a matter of life and death circumstance that was staring me in the face. There have actually only been however, a couple of times in my life when death was smiling at me.

One took place in 1962 while climbing a cliff on Sugarloaf Mountain near Marquette, Michigan. I was attending Northern Michigan University (it progressed from a college to a university while I was there) which was the second of five that I would go to before I gave up on trying to become a college grad. The effort was there, but not the passion required to succeed. And make no mistake about it; passion is a huge part in claiming success in whatever we attempt. However, believe me when I say it was fear that saved my life on that cliff, not passion. Well, fear and my friend Lou, who had already reached the top and was talking me through the last 10 feet.

That experience made a sizable impression on me to say the least, and probably was instrumental in keeping me from that kind of incident happening again. No more cliff climbing! To this day, I have no idea what it was that made me do such a dumb thing as that. Obviously, I was trying to quell some inner exaggerated desire to be something that I wasn't. However, the chance of falling 40 or 50 feet off a cliff hardly seems to me now to be worth it all. The fact that I have a bit of difficulty just climbing the basement stairs at this time in my life may have something to do with changing my point of view on that subject. Regardless, I am still alive now to tell you about the other event that could have robbed my wife of 45 years of connubial bliss.

That experience took place in 1965, one year before we were married. After working at the Calcite Plant in Rogers City for a couple of years, I decided to go sailing on the lake boats of the Bradley Transportation Fleet. I had not formed a plan of what I wanted to do with the rest of my life back then, and sailing the Great Lakes was the next opportunity to experience another possibility. It became very obvious to me, after the following event, that not even in the farthest reaches of my mind would I consider life as a sailor.

My first trip was on the *Cedarville*. It was early spring in 1965, and I was scheduled for only one trip as a replacement for a fellow who had become ill. The boat was on the way to the port of Cedarville, and had to pass Rogers City on the way. One of the Calcite tugs would be taking me out to meet her.

Climbing up a rope ladder to get on board was just the beginning of what was to come. I figured at that time if I survived the boarding,

everything should be downhill from there. I was right, downhill was the correct word to use to describe what was to threaten my life next. Actually, the best and most accurate way to describe it would be simply... down.

The port of Fort William lies on the northern edge of Lake Superior. After exiting the Soo Locks, a gentle turn to the port side after entering the Big Lake, and you're on your way there. The thought of crossing Superior had caused me a bit of anxiety due to the stories I had heard and read concerning the huge storms that spring up so quickly there, even though the worst of them occur in October and November. Thankfully, the lake that day was as calm as spring rain on a flat rock, and stayed that way until we made our way back to the locks and Lake Huron. In reality though, what was to take place before we reached the safe confines of Sault Ste. Marie is what this story is really about.

Being a deckhand on a huge lake boat at that time would appear to be a great way to experience the majesty of the Great Lakes. The blue sky and water; the sun reflecting off the rolling swells; a cool breeze; and the green of the land in the distance, all formed a scene any young man born and raised on the shores of Lake Huron would not only appreciate, but he should be chomping at the bit to immerse himself in such an adventure.

Well, I wasn't! I was then and still am a landlubber. As a kid, I enjoyed swimming, like most kids do, but immediately upon passing into the "no longer a kid" stage of my life, water became a necessity for drinking, for bathing, and for showering only. The reason I decided, after much thought, to sail was because I needed the money to continue my college education. I personally was not that excited about doing that, however, my mother was, and she was still at that time the dominant force in my life. Back to sailing!

And who needs to think of "immerse" while experiencing 6 or 8-foot waves and 40 mile an hour winds? Believe me when I say, not me! Yet here I was climbing up a rope ladder 20 feet off the surface of the lake, not knowing at all what was to follow, but depending on my youthful strength and stubbornness to see me through whatever dangers were lurking before me.

There are many dangers connected with sailing on lake boats. The most obvious

41

would be falling overboard. However, the one danger that turned into a life-threatening situation for me, I knew nothing about until I became aware of it at a safety meeting prior to arriving at Fort William. To describe it as life threatening, however, especially to those sailors who contend with it on a regular basis, would present it as an exaggeration. It even seemed that way to me until I had time to evaluate it, think it through, and finally arrive at the conclusion that my life was in mortal danger!

At the afore-mentioned safety meeting, I became aware of three things very quickly. Number one: some ports do not have dockhands to tie up a boat when it arrives. Number two: one of the deckhands from an incoming boat has to be put over the side to complete that task. And number three: I was the deckhand who was to be put over the side! I remember thinking at the time that although it sounded exciting, it was something I would not have considered doing on my own. In this case, I had no say in the matter. I was told that I would be the one. The captain explained to me the seriousness and the danger involved in the operation, and also told me to listen very carefully to the following instructions. Believe me when I say, I listened very closely.

The device and process that was used to put me over the side and onto the dock is as follows: a metal pole about 6 feet high with another shorter pole attached to the top of it forming a 90° angle that was made to swing out over the side of the boat. A very long rope ran through the ring that was attached to the end of the pole. The end of the rope was tied through the middle of a piece of wood that was about 3 feet long and 8 to 10 inches wide. The other end of the rope would be in the hands of two other deckhands.

The procedure was as follows: I was to stand on that piece of wood with a foot on each side of the rope. The two other deckhands would then pull on the rope, I would push off, and they would lift me off the deck, swing me over the side, and lower me down to the dock. After successfully doing that, I would then take the tie up cable that was dropped over the side of the boat, and attach it to the bollards on the dock. Upon completing that, the winches on board ship would then pull the boat up to the dock and hold it there. This was repeated at the aft-end, and once the boat was securely

attached, my job was done. I then could go back on board via a ladder that had been put over the side.

In retrospect, the process is really quite simple, but to a 21-year-old first timer, believe me when I say that simple was not what preoccupied my mind as I stood waiting to be swung out into space! The word, or more precisely stated, the feeling, was once again fear. And as I reflect back on that moment in time, it was the kind of fear that can only cause one to listen only to what is being shouted out in one's mind. Not, however, to the two deckhands controlling the rope that would soon have your life in their hands.

Those two guys had told me, with much fervor I might add, that whatever you do, don't push off until you hear from us. Are they crazy? I might never push off. In fact, they may have to throw me off! Well, with all the noise surrounding me: guys shouting, winches hissing, the clanking of metal on metal, voices over the loudspeakers, and a few unrecognizable sounds, I thought I heard someone holler GO! And being a first-time rookie, instead of checking to see if for sure they hollered go, I went!

I immediately knew I was in trouble when I very quickly found myself "down" between the dock and the incoming boat, about 6 to 8 feet from the water, and the same distance to the top of the dock. This was not the way this was supposed to go. It was almost a miracle that the two guys manning the rope were able to keep me out of the water. Well, with the boat coming in and the distance between it and the dock getting smaller, I decided that it was time for me to get out of there, and begin pulling myself up hand-over-hand. By this time the deckhands had recovered and began pulling me up. With our combined efforts, I was soon standing on the dock shaking like a leaf in the summer breeze. That shaking was on the outside of me; the inside was convulsing like an earthquake in California!

Through it all, I was able to handle the cables, put them on the dock bollards, and safely return back aboard only to be confronted by two angry, to say the very least, deckhands. Thankfully, I can't remember what was said, but I do recall that they did all the talking. That was just a preamble of what I was to hear from the Captain and one of the Mates.

So there you have it. I am sure that

somewhere and sometime in the 200 or so years of Great Lakes shipping, my experience surely must've been one of many such adventures. I would hope with a vengeance that I was not the only one to have been subjected to such a harsh learning situation. On the other hand, I am truly thankful to be alive to share this with those of you who have learned lessons the easy way. I can only hope that sometime in the near future I will run across someone's story that is exactly like the one I just told you!

✓ Charlevoix the Beautiful
By Kaye Balch of Charlevoix, Michigan
Born 1941

My brother, Brad, and I were born in southern Michigan in the early 1940s. When World War II ended and our father returned to civilian life, he became a toolmaker at the Kaiser-Frasier Corporation at Willow Run. Both sets of our grandparents lived in Charlevoix, Michigan. Our paternal grandmother was an excellent seamstress. She loved making dresses for me on her old treadle sewing machine. Her fabric was recycled from the feed sacks grandpa purchased, full of grain, from their local co-op. A couple of times a year she would send a new dress or two for me by parcel post. One time two dresses arrived that had been identical to each other. They were red with white polka dots and white collars. The dresses had full skirts and were similar to the one worn by Walt Disney's Minnie Mouse, except the dots on Minnie's dresses were bigger than the ones on mine. During the time I wore those dresses, the neighborhood kids thought I rarely changed my clothes.

When we were in the 2nd and 3rd grades, our parents decided to return to northern Michigan to live nearer to their families. Mom was a Charlevoix girl and dad had grown up on a farm in Ironton, which was seven miles down the road. Charlevoix is an extraordinary resort community nestled on the shore of Lake Michigan. For many decades, it has been known as "Charlevoix the Beautiful," a logo so undeniably true. The main thoroughfare, U.S. 31 Highway, also known as Bridge Street, lies between two small hills. The business district is just four, rather short blocks, in the valley between the hills. Round Lake is situated at the center of town with an exceptional yacht basin and adjacent public parks. In the 1950s Charlevoix was a quaint little fishing village and come springtime Round Lake would be peppered with a few hundred rowboats and perch fishermen. The fish were abundant. The southern edge of the lake was home to several fish tugs. Fishnets would be stretched over large wooden reels drying in the sun in preparation for mending. Three city parks faced the lake and shuffleboard courts were present in the larger, more centralized park. In addition, another popular attraction in East Park and the nearby park directly to the south, were three fishponds. Small "islands" were established within the ponds with decorative foliage as well as an ornamental lighthouse on one. These structures had been created to provide a shady habitat for the large trout that were stocked in the ponds each summer. Fishing from these ponds was prohibited.

At the north end of town there is a drawbridge over the Pine River, a deep-water channel, which flows to and from Lake Michigan into Round Lake Harbor and beyond into Lake Charlevoix. One can stand near the bridge and capture the beauty of the three connecting lakes. One of the five Great Lakes, magnificent Lake Michigan to the west, offers the pleasure of some of the most spectacular sunsets and is the site of our well-known lighthouse at the end of the south pier.

Round Lake and its harbor is the sparkling jewel in the town center and connects to Lake Charlevoix. This point was once the site of

Kaye at age 14 in 1955

43

Local fish tug going through the Pine River Channel

a railroad bridge, Swing Bridge that was in operation during that period. Twice a day the bridge tender would operate the levers to mechanically swing the bridge into place to allow passage of the trains. During the remaining time, the bridge was drawn aside to allow watercraft access between the lakes. Fishing off this bridge was a popular activity. Sadly, this familiar landmark was totally removed in the 1980s. During the 1950s, my friends and I would ride our bikes to the train depot and purchase tickets at 30-cents each to take the train 20 miles north to Petoskey. It was just a short walk from the train depot to the business district and a public park there. We would spend some time in town and then board the train for our return trip.

Lake Charlevoix is a fairly large lake and has four other small communities on its shores. In addition to Charlevoix, there are Boyne City; the village of Horton Bay, which is best known for the old-time general store and for the author Ernest Hemingway's many summers spent there; Ironton, known for the ferry that carries bicyclists, hikers, and as many as four cars at a time, 600 feet across the Ironton narrows; and the city of East Jordan, which is located down the South Arm of Lake Charlevoix. This overall area is truly a water wonderland. Through the years, my brother and I thanked our parents numerous times for raising us in their hometown and allowing it to become our town, too.

Dad became the owner of the local recreation center, Arcade Enterprises, offering billiards and card games as well as hunting and fishing licenses, rifles, ammunition, fishing tackle, and bait. The building that housed his store was located next to the drawbridge and the channel; we lived upstairs. The windows across the front overlooked Round Lake, the loading dock for the Beaver Island ferry, and U.S. Coast Guard vessels, as well

as the Railroad Bridge and Lake Charlevoix in the distance. From the windows facing north, the view was that of the channel and boat traffic, which included yachts, sailboats, speedboats, fish tugs, and smaller watercraft. From our kitchen, the view was that of the pier, lighthouse, and sunsets. We had rooms with a view; there was no doubt about it! And, on a clear day, you could see Beaver Island. You still can for that matter, but not to mislead you; one could not see the island from our apartment. However, it lies 32 miles out into Lake Michigan and is, at times, visible from our shores and from along U.S. 31 Highway going north to Petoskey.

Shortly after the opening of Dad's business, he added taxicab and rent-a-car services. Mom obtained a chauffeur's license and was the principal taxi driver for 17 years. I guess you could now call Dad's enterprise a "Mom and Pop" business. She was the first member in our family to cross the new Mackinac Bridge when she took passengers into the Upper Peninsula. One day, after bringing a passenger in from the airport, she mentioned he was a very distinguished gentleman who told her he had traveled all over the world and had never seen a more beautiful town than Charlevoix. Even then, I realized how very lucky we were to live in such an enchanting and awesome community.

We had a dog we all loved dearly. She was part beagle, blue tick, and red bone, her name was Boots. My bike was equipped with a large wire basket and sometimes I would place a pillow in the basket and Boots on top. We would venture off on rides, an occasional picnic, or to the beach. We were fortunate to have three public beaches watched over by lifeguards to keep us safe. I'd paint Boots' toenails with nail polish and dress her in shorts and tee shirts we had outgrown. One time I cut the legs shorter from a pair of my brother's long johns and dressed Boots in them with her tail exiting the rear slit. She could stand on her hind legs and turn the knob on the door into Dad's store with her manicured front paws. Then she would push the door open with her nose and in she would go. When the door slammed shut, all the card players would turn to see who was coming to join in their cribbage or pinochle games. They would chuckle upon seeing Boots in her get-up.

44

When one of my best girlfriends and I were about the age of 12, we were into reading Nancy Drew Mysteries and soon fancied ourselves amateur sleuths like Nancy. In addition to reading of Nancy's numerous adventures, every Sunday afternoon we could, we would listen to the radio programs *The Shadow* and *True Detective Mysteries*. At the end of each True Detective program a description of one of the ten most wanted criminals in the United States would be given. My friend and I would carefully keep notes of their distinguishing features - height, hair, eye color, scars, etc. One fantastic spring morning, with little to do, we took our notebooks with our descriptions and sauntered down Charlevoix's four main blocks in search of one of the "Most Wanted." In the 1950s, Charlevoix's population was approximately 2,000 in the winter months, which would swell to around 10,000 in the summer due to the resort season. Before the deluge of visitors, we knew just about everyone in town. As we engaged in our "sleuthing" that day, there weren't any people on the street we didn't know. Then an unfamiliar man of approximately 40-45 years of age (soon to be labeled "suspicious individual") parked his automobile and went into the telegraph office. We entered his description into our notebooks along with that of his car and license plate numbers. To be less conspicuous, we crossed the street and waited an appreciable distance for him to exit the building. Once he did, we lagged behind somewhat and leisurely tailed him down the opposite side of the street. We lingered through his next few stops and then followed him back to his car. As he drove away, I can still remember how annoyed and disappointed we were. We had lost our one "suspect" and we had to admit that in no way could he be deemed as someone who had behaved in a suspicious manner.

Later, when we had moved on to the other end of town, we spotted what we thought to be his car parked on a nearby side street. We checked our notes and sure enough, the numbers on the license plate matched the ones in our notebooks. We both realized he must have been "on to us" and had decided to ditch two pesky young girls and complete his errands in peace. Life was good and prosperity flourished in our picturesque little village. Those were carefree, idyllic times. It wouldn't be too many years before we would be forced to find summer jobs so that our parents would know where we were and as we all know, a busy child with a job doesn't have much time for mischief.

✓ Growing Up on Lake Avalon
By Justin Moreau of Hillman, Michigan
Born 1947

My parents purchased a hunting lodge on the East side of Lake Avalon in 1942. They already had seven children and my mom needed a place to rest for the summers and keep her children happy and safely engaged in all the fun a Northern Michigan Lake could provide. It was paradise for them, a three-story log lodge that sat just 20 feet off the beach of one of the clearest and most beautiful lakes in Michigan. By the time I came along in 1947, my five brothers, who were anywhere from 8 to 20 years older than me, already had their games and the rules for them clearly defined. They already had a reputation as a wild and mischievous bunch among the family campfires along the beach. The older ones and many of their friends were known as Moreau's Marauders and signed my baby book, as such.

We spent every summer there and, I'm sure their memories are as vivid as mine. I grew up fast and learned the rules of their games quickly, more often than not, the hard way. There was "King of the Castle" and "Capture the Flag." There was the family way to learn how to swim which, simply stated, was being thrown off the raft, and forced to dog paddle your way back from the drop-off, or the "blues" as we called it, that's where your feet would finally hit the bottom and you could walk. Thank God, I made it!

Then there was the number of forts built on top of the old hill. They were all top secret and I was allowed into them only by invitation and with a blindfold on to assure their secrecy. Memory has one of them as a zoological laboratory with shelves filled with jars of biology experiments soaking in formaldehyde from the County Normal School in town. These had been pitched at the local dump and given new meaning and life by my brothers. I was told, of course, that they were the body parts of aliens that had crashed their Flying Saucers into the sand pit half way down the hill. I, naturally, believed everything my brothers told me.

One summer, there was a contest as to who was going to the moon in a "rocket" they had built—myself or the nephew, Donnie, my oldest sister's oldest son, who was actually a year older than me. I don't remember if the winner was chosen by a draw of straws or a game of "Rock, Paper, Scissors," but all I remember was the huge disappointment of not being able to go on the adventure of a lifetime.

I do remember the paper plates flying off the roof of the barn as real flying saucers and the sawdust they threw at us as real cosmic dust. They had built a cardboard wall dividing the inside of the barn in half, and cut two small holes into it about shoulder height and stuck my dad's binoculars backwards into them, so when you looked through them, all you could see was a distant cardboard "rocket" on a fruit box launch pad. I believed every bit of it.

To this day it amazes me that flying saucers and cosmic dust were a part of my brothers' game playing imagination back in the mid '50s, but a suppressed memory, which returned to me about 25 years later made it all real to me again. Circa the summer of 1954, I was seated at the Sunday afternoon dinner table when I suddenly got up and left this room. Something you never did in my family without permission and a very good reason. No one called me back. I went outside. It was extremely windy, so windy that the sand stung my legs. The waves were three and four footers, which was unusual for Lake Avalon. I looked out over the lake and there I saw them. Seven or eight white objects that I can only describe as Uncle Ben's Converted Rice—in size and in shape. They were circling each other in a tight formation when suddenly they took off rapidly in completely different directions. In an instant, they were gone. Gone from sight, and gone from memory.

The wind died down. I went back into the dining room, sat down, and continued eating my Sunday dinner. No one asked why I left the table. It was though I never left the room. It was as though what I had just experienced had never happened.

And for 25 years, it didn't. When the memory returned, probably after watching the movie, "Close Encounters of the Third Kind," it all became quite real. The memory was as vivid as though it had happened just yesterday. I pondered the memory for some time and ended up chalking it up as yet another mystical and amazing example of the magic of Lake Avalon. But--enough said about that.

Donnie, his sister, Cindy, and I fished almost every day, mostly at the crack of dawn and until we caught about a hundred pan fish, some of which were so small you could practically see through them, sunfish, rock bass, perch and an occasional black bass. There were circles of "fish beds" all around the lake planted and weighted with cinder blocks by the Conservation folks, and we would drop anchor right in the middle of them.

We would dig for worms in the swamp in back of the lodge before the sun came up, pack a lunch of peanut butter and mayonnaise sandwiches and head out in the aluminum boat which was really too wide for just one of us to row. But, we'd get to one of our usual agreed upon spots and fish for hours. "Got one!" and "Back Lash!" were the words spoken most. None of us were very good at casting.

It was always the tradition to walk around the lake at least once during the summer. Deer trails meandered up and down the hillsides on the lake, affording beautiful views of the lake from many vantage points.

Until the '70s, my last attempt was around 1972 when I had to crawl under decks and around garages to find the old trails. "Beware of the dog" and "No Trespassing" signs were everywhere. They were signs of the times, but the beauty of the lake did not seem compromised to me and I knew more and more people wanted to own and have memories of their piece of it.

My five brothers and my two sisters pursued their lives as teenagers and adults, as the case may be. Campfire romances abounded. I dare say most of the east side of the lake is happily intermarried to this day, including one of my nephews and his wife from three cabins down. The kids my age, nieces, nephews, and cousins pursued their own interests. We all learned to water ski by the time we were six or seven.

Until the Bolen's got the first fiberglass speedboat on the lake, our aluminum boat with its 25 horsepower Mercury was the fastest boat on the lake. We usually started off on two skis and kicked one off after a short circuit around the raft. We always had a spotter, but in the '50s, not everyone knew the physics of pulling a skier. Once, one of my brothers turned the wrong way into whoever he was pulling and when the towline slack straightened out, it flipped the lightweight aluminum boat right over, with everyone and everything in it. What an event! Every boat from every dock on the lake was at the rescue in a matter of minutes, no one drowned; no one was hurt. Each boat though, brought a piece of the "tragedy" back to the beach in front of the lodge. Floorboards, gas tanks, life belts, slalom skis, you name it; everyone came with a piece of the flotsam. They talked for hours about what they saw from their point of view, why and how it happened, and what's probably wrong with the motor and why it won't start. Turned out, the "block is cracked." First time I ever heard that expression. It was the end of the summer's water skiing season. What else can we do?

Riding into town in the back of the pickup to see a movie at the Hillman Theatre was always a thrill. Spotting deer on the way back, kinda freaked me out, because the truck was always broadside to the road, but actually spotting one was also thrilling, as were our drives to Turtle Lake to see literally hundreds of them in the fields on an early evening in the summer.

Riding on the hood or the front fender of my Aunt Myrtle's Hudson Hornet was another thrill. She was the proverbial best aunt. She was a very funny and wonderful woman. She let us drive the back roads (and smoke) in our early teens and told the best campfire horror stories of all time, God Bless her. I loved her. I still own the cottage she had in Jackson Subdivision, overlooking the lake. I dearly remember the tales of the imaginary "Gerflats," who lived in the walls of the cottage.

She introduced sailing to us all with her rare, Wineglass Class sailboat from England called the "Cold Duck." I'll never forget her shouts of, "Hike! Get out there, Hike!" It was the sailboat to beat on the lake for many years.

Who could forget the fun times at the "Potholes," the "Hogback," or the "Snakepits?" These are places of special memories for my whole family. The berry picking patches and secret morel mushroom haunts must remain family secrets, however.

The winters on the lake were no less memorable. Games like "Scavenger Hunt" and "Fox and the Geese" were huge. Hockey games and figure skating on the ice were essential for a great weekend "Up North." But, when my dad tied the toboggan, the sleds, and the saucers behind the truck and pulled us all over the county. That was a thrill you never forget. No one does that now, because it's illegal and totally unsafe but back then, it was the best.

I will never forget growing up on Lake Avalon. No matter what big city I ended up in, no matter what coast I lived on, Hillman and Lake Avalon were always the hardest places to leave. It would take me days and, in some cases, weeks to adjust to the reality of returning "home" when home was always the lodge on Lake Avalon. That's why I came back, to rekindle my millions of memories here.

Today, January 26, 2013, marks the 17th anniversary of my return to Northern Michigan, to Hillman, to Lake Avalon. I'm home and never leaving again! Thanks for the memories. I create more of them every day.

Teenage Boys and Slingshots
By Joel V. Smith of Oscoda, Michigan
Born 1945

When I was 12 years old, the attitudes expressed by my friend, Fred, and me were pretty normal. We were a bit smart-alecky at times, and we fell for the clothing styles that came and went away rapidly. During any given three-month period, we might have sported Ivy League hats, or our shoes may have had the cleats on the heels, which made us sound tough when walking in the school's hallways. It's what every junior high student was doing.

We were reasonable and down-to-earth right up to the moment when we changed. I think it was around the spring of 1958, when I was 13 and Fred was 14, that we totally lost our minds. In that year, we became morally irresponsible, lacking in empathy for anyone's well-being or property. Frankly, we both became dumb as a box of rocks.

In a case like this, you normally look back from age 68 (my age now) and you try to think of someone to blame for failures. But I really can't think of anyone who did something to make me stupid. The utter lunacy just arrived by itself—along with chest hair, I suppose.

What happened was, we were inside a sporting goods store one day, and we spotted slingshots hanging from a board display. The wood of each handle was pretty, and we liked the fact that the elastic rubber was made of surgical tubing. It was sewed with strong white thread to a clean postage stamp of tanned leather. The best part of all was that the price for the whole weapon was only two dollars.

Fred and I eagerly laid down our two bucks, and we walked out with our new kid-weapons. We'd also purchased a small bag of steel ball bearings.

In the days that followed, we both marveled when we discovered just how incredibly far the tiny steel ball would travel when we aimed at the horizon at an approximately 40 degree angle. If a skilled golfer could drive a ball up to 300 yards, we found that the slingshot ball would go about twice that distance. Perhaps my memory is failing me now, but it surely seemed in those days that the little metal ball would travel up to 1/3 mile. At least half the time, we'd lose sight of it when it departed the weapon. Once lost from sight, there was never a hope of picking it up. You couldn't guess with any accuracy where it set down. But not knowing was a big portion of the thrill. We could dream up all kinds of romantic solutions to explain where the projectile might have crashed to earth.

From there, we progressed to a mental state, which required a deliberate firing above the roofing of nearby homes. We loved hearing a crash from an unknown target three streets over. We laughed hard, falling to the grass and holding our bellies and imagining a homeowner telling police that something just seemed to come out of the sky. We knew that the cops could never locate us from so many houses away. We were, no pun intended, home safe.

Since we got away with it so many times, we naturally presumed we were invincible. The patient reader who follows this tale to the end will learn that we really were uncatchable. We never got hurt in any way, and we were never even questioned by police. But let's not get ahead of ourselves. I'm sure there were many dozens of adults who wanted to get their hands on our necks, if they could only identify us. But they never got the chance.

During a warm summer evening in '58, we were riding in Fred's family's 1957 Dodge Sierra station wagon. In those days, the back window rolled down into the gate. We sat comfortably on the back deck, our arms resting on the clean metal. We passed another Chrysler vehicle parked on a quiet city street. Fred pulled back as far as the surgical tubing would stretch, and the ball was released. Fred's mother may not have heard the steel-against-glass contact. Or perhaps she did hear it and thought the sound came from something else.

A dent the size of a golf ball was in the center of the massive glass windshield. Little spider legs of the damage spread in all directions. We kept our laughing under control, lest Fred's mother should guess what was happening. In all the years since, I've wondered how frustrated the local police might have been. I think they'd have paid a huge reward if they could only locate us. I do dread, even now, what could have happened. I'm sure it would have involved juvenile court, and a judge putting the fear of God into our souls. Now I am 68, Fred is 69, and I don't want to think about it, even today. Where in God's name were our brains?

We performed an even greater level of idiocy during a hot night in the following August: The owner of the new Chrysler almost got his revenge. In fact, it could have turned out even worse than we deserved.

We were lying on our backs on our boat dock at my family's northern Michigan home. I'm not sure if it was Fred who got the idea to fire a heavy glass marble straight up toward the stars. Perhaps it was me. Anyway, he pulled back and ball was out of sight in darkness. We counted off the seconds... one thousand one... one thousand two... one thousand three. At about five-point-five seconds—give or take—the marble hit about an arm's length from our foreheads. That ball made a sound like SPLOOMP in the quiet water.

"I can get closer to us than that," I said. I pulled back all the way. The glass ball went straight up. We couldn't see it, of course. The gods in their heavens wept. Perhaps they protected us and we did not know it. In five seconds, the heavy ball went Whack!

on the crosstie of the dock, inches from my eyes. I think I might have said something of substance; something like Oh Wow, that one was really close.

The next morning, in the perfect and warm daylight, we found a dent in the wood of the dock. It was not far from the point where I presumed my head had been resting.

By autumn, we returned to school. Fred went to a Roman Catholic junior high; I attended a local public school. I was in the eighth grade. The 1959 model cars were coming out. I recall thinking that everyone in Detroit's studios must be on some kind of drugs. The designs of the 1959 Cadillac, the Chevrolet Impala, the Dodge, and the Mercury were just absurd. Perhaps obscene would be a better word. But we loved their strange shapes; especially the back ends, the tail lamps, and the trunk lids. It was a joyous time to be alive.

When the cold autumn rains came, we thrilled at standing in the grassy field behind Fred's house and sending a steel ball sailing toward a distant garage roof. We were better marksmen by then. We lost sight of the ball in the darkness and the cold October rain. In a moment, the ball would strike a glancing blow on the roof shingles. The sound was a kind of SO-WOOO! A small spark jumped from the roof with every strike.

It was some kind of goofy fun. I'm glad we did not get hurt. I hope the owners of damaged property eventually forgave us. I suppose they did not. If it had been my new car, I certainly wouldn't have thought about such a thing as forgiveness.

Grandmother's Washday
By Gail Schrader of Lewiston, Michigan
Born 1939

Grandmother's day began at the crack of dawn with Max the rooster announcing its arrival.

Mondays were always washday! After breakfast grandpa would go downstairs and put water from the cistern into the cooper boiler, and set it on the two-burner kerosene stove to boil. Meanwhile in the kitchen grandmother would put the finishing touches on an apple pie, and put the makings of a soup on the back burner of the cook stove. Grandpa gave her a kiss on the cheek and went down stairs and poured the hot water into the washer.

Next down the steps, she would go to her washing. The hot water would be in the Maytag washer, us girls would call it the green monster with its giant rollers just waiting to grab our pigtails. Into the washer, she would add shaved Ivory soap, its clean scent rising into the steam; next, she picked up the brown jug of Roman bleach, its eye biting fumes penetrating the air. Now she added cold water to the cement laundry tubs, one clear and the other tub with Agro starch, when I asked her, "Why the starch?" she replied, "Why Missy when you get peanut butter and jelly on your school dress it will come out next week and I won't need to use the scrub board." Now she would put the whites into the steaming water to wash.

Up the stairs and out to the clothesline she went, with a wet rag to clean the lines, you see that's where the songbirds perched.

Back in the kitchen, she set to making bread and putting it on the shelf over the cook stove to rise.

She next went downstairs and picked up an old broom handle now white from repeated dunks in the hot water. Out of the hot water and thru the wringers to the rinse water, and wrung into the laundry basket. Grandmother would now put in the colors, shirts, dresses; grandpa's going to meeting pants.

Gail in the scrub tub

49

Outside after she hung the whites, I saw her smiling into the warm sun, at the dazzling whites billowing in the soft breeze. Back in the kitchen, she formed the bread and rolls into pans, and up on the shelf to rise again. Now the apple pie went into the oven to bake.

Down again, out came the colors, and this time they got rinsed in the starch. The darks were put in, coveralls, barn jackets, and red long johns. Back outside after hanging the colors, she put grandpa's pants into wire frame to form a tight crease.

In the kitchen, the pie came out and she put it in the open window to cool, the lace curtain kissing the top of the pie sending its aroma of warm apples, cinnamon, and sugar rising to engulf the kitchen. Next, the bread and rolls went into the oven.

Outside down came the colors and taken into the kitchen to be sprinkled and wrapped in flour sack towel and put in the icebox to be ironed tomorrow. Tuesdays were ironing day!

Hearing her humming and descending the steps she took out the next load of darks rinsed them and in went the rugs, the water now as cold and muddy as a spring creek.

Outside you could hear the rumbling of thunder, and the wind kicking up. Up went the darks while she looked over her shoulder hoping to finish before the storm broke. She ran back downstairs and grabbed the rugs out and pulled the plug on the tubs to drain. The rugs got hung in a hurry. Meanwhile she could hear the men folks coming in from the fields for the noon meal.

Into the kitchen, grandma pulled the bread and rolls out of the oven, the warm bread set in the window to cool, its earthly yeast scent filling the room and the rolls on the warming shelf to keep warm.

Grandmother rushed outside and took down the darks and took them downstairs and hung them next to the furnace to finish drying.

Up in the kitchen, she filled a kettle with hot water from the cook stove reservoir, and carried it out to the porch, set it next to the rain barrel, washbasin, and Boraso soap for the men to wash up. Inside she set the table with fresh churned sweet butter, warm rolls, tall glasses of cold spring water, and large steaming bowls of ham and bean soup. The men came in, sat, and talked about their morning.

Grandmother wandered out to the screen porch, with sweat running down her back, and goose bumps on her arms, she wiped her red hands on her apron, and sighed, "Well, I guess the rugs will get another rinse."

And that was grandmother's washday.

Grandmother after her washing was done

Visit to meet our Grandfather in Iron Mountain, Michigan Thanksgiving weekend, 1957
By James Orr of Posen, Michigan
Born 1944

It was cold as heck that Thanksgiving Day morning... 6:30am and my brother and I are dressed, packed and waiting for our father to pick us up.

We are going to meet our 92 year old grandfather for the very first time... and the trip is an "all-day-er." Iron Mountain, Michigan is 350 miles from our home in northside Detroit... thus the 6:30am departure time.

A plus for the journey was the fact that the "Big Mac" bridge had just recently opened for traffic. We would be amongst the "cool-cats"... having crossed it so soon after it opened. (*Dad said*)

Soon after our father arrived, we were loaded and on our way... Van Dyke Ave. for the most part... and then M-25. When we stopped for lunch at a truck-stop type restaurant, (grilled cheese and soup) we tried to envision the bridge spanning the waters that were once crossed only by ferry... (*Well, still are)*

Another plus... we arrived at the bridge while it was still light out... mid-afternoon.

The magnificence of it was breath-taking... and being able to see the water down below as we crossed was a pure adrenalin rush. We went slowly across... as Dad wanted to saturate himself with the splendor of modern technology. At the time, it was the longest Cable-supported bridge in the world; *(might be still)* boasting 5 miles between shores.

Once across, Dad stopped at a grocery store to buy some canned goods for his dad... My brother and I got to pick out a treat to hold us for the remainder of the trip. *(Dad was planning to prepare dinner at grampa's)*

Dad drove right through to Iron Mountain... and finally, turned off the main highway, and started down, what seemed like only a hiking path... sitting up straight and hands tightly around the steering wheel, Dad asked us to be quiet for a while. Those last couple of miles were better suited for a four-wheel drive vehicle than they were for Dad's Oldsmobile.

After about 20 minutes and several "scouting" stops along the way, we finally arrived at our destination... Dad relaxed and said, "This is it." Darkness had set in so we really couldn't get a good look at the outside, but enough to make out that we were at a log-cabin. Everyone took their packs and in we went...

Inside, the dimly lit one-room cabin was Gramps... whittling something in a rocker.

Dad put the bags of groceries on the kitchen table, turned to his father and said "Dad, I've brought your grandchildren with me." Grandpa acknowledged that we were there... then went back to his task at hand.

Being 92 years old allows a person to pretty much conduct themselves in any fashion they so choose. Being of Scotch-Irish descent just amplifies that ditty.

Dad went around and turned up the sap-lights *(that's right, not gas lights)* illuminating the one room cabin well enough that we *(brother and I)* could see the only bed was a single-bed, situated in a corner with a full-length curtain behind the head-board. We wondered just where we would be sleeping... and would it be warm enough... the cabin was rather chilly and dank.

Dad motioned for us to come over to where he was standing *(by his Dad)* and then he introduced us formally to our grandfather. "Dad, this is Kenneth Robert, 15 years old... this is James Edward, 13 years old." Ken and I both held out our hands, anticipating a shake. We didn't get one, but instead, we got a sincere look-over from our new family member, and then he spoke. "Good looking youngsters" is all he said. I tried to read his eyes, steely, yet with compassion, wondering if he would like us or not.

Dad told his father that he had brought him some groceries... and that he'd put them away for him. Murmuring softly, Grampa said, "Why bother? It's all crap."

In any event, Dad started to put the groceries away, and while doing so, was explaining how the cupboards came to be... his dad had made them... by hand. Grampa made every single piece of furniture in the cabin; the bed frame; kitchen table and chairs; the rocker; made the cold-storage lockers for his veggies too. We were amazed at how everything fit so perfectly and sealed tightly.

There wasn't any city water, electricity or any other city-type utility... just a hand-pump in the middle of the kitchen sink. The small 6 foot high building outside was where one did his "duty"... had a sap-light, matches and real toilet paper though.

At nearly the same time, Ken and I both asked Dad about dinner. He said for us to check the wood-stove... and to add some wood if needed. Ken lifted a burner cover and said it seemed to be O.K. with wood... Dad said "Great" and brought a large skillet over to the stove. Ken and I looked around; apparently, that wood stove was the only "heat" supplier for the cabin.

While Dad was busy preparing dinner... and gramps was whittling... Ken and I started nosing around... we asked Grampa if we could open the storage lockers to see what was inside. He said, "Be sure to close them tight."

We were opening them slowly (didn't want any surprises) and could feel the suction from the lid as it separated from the locker-box. There were potatoes in one, onions in another, beets, corn, squash, (acorn, I think) and one had eggs, berries, and apples in it. Two others were loaded with wood, one had small wood chips and the other had "discs" that were seemingly made that way. All were perfectly round and about the size of a hefty pancake… maybe ¾" thick.

All together, we counted 8 storage lockers, about 2 foot high, 2 foot deep and not quite 3 foot wide. They were neatly tucked together in a single row along the wall.

Ken and I checked out the "Sap-lamps"… apparently carved out from tree branches. They had a hollowed-out bowl and what looked like a cottontail reed (or tree moss) saturated in a sap-like substance in the bowl. We counted 10 of them.

After about a half an hour, Dad had dinner on the table. Ken and I were already sitting there… running our fingers over the perfectly smooth top… searching for flaws… we couldn't find any.

Grampa was last to sit… on his way, grabbing some sort of jerky from a box in the cupboard. Dad asked him why was he not eating the stew… Gramps said that he might try it a little later.

As if someone turned his "time to talk" switch on… Grampa began asking Ken and me all sorts of questions. How were we doing in school? Did we have love in our lives? What sports were we into? How was Dad treating us? It went on all through dinner… and then, just like that, it stopped. Ken and I cleaned up the table and put the dishes by the sink… not knowing from where we were going to get hot water. *(Dad had the pot of water on stove, heating while we were eating)*

Dad told us to get the wash-basin out from under the sink… put the hot water in it and then scrape off some "soap" from the block of soap. *(About the size of a house brick)*

By the time we had everything cleaned and put away, still marveling at the craftsmanship of the cupboards, it was nearly bedtime. So we asked… "Where are we sleeping?" At that, Dad walked over behind the bed in the corner, pulled the curtains aside… and there was another huge room with 4 beds in it. It was a little "cool" but we slept like babies.

Waking to the smell of eggs and sausage and "grilled" toast… Ken and I went to the outhouse, me first, then Ken. *(Best brother anyone could have)* When we came back inside, Dad and Grampa were both sitting at the table… 2 plates were set opposite them with eggs, sausage and toast… it was a perfect breakfast.

We spent most of the day listening to stories of how Grampa and Gramma met, got married and raised 4 boys in that cabin. Gramma had died at the early age of 38, some kind of miner's disease. Grampa had to raise the boys without benefit of a "woman's touch," until they went off on their own, in their late teens. Grampa then spent the next 50 years growing, harvesting, fishing, hunting, and trapping his own food… all by himself. He even had about a ¼ acre of tobacco hidden in with his crops. *(Believe that? tobacco growing in Iron Mountain, Michigan)* The "other" outhouse wasn't an outhouse at all; it was his "curing" house. *(Grampa's lips and fingers were stained yellow from smoking his own tobacco.)* There were about 2 dozen of Grampa's Sap-lamps in the curing house as well… sap bowls carved perfectly in all.

He showed us how he made fuel, from sap, for his lights; how he used animal dung for mixing with sawdust and wood chips for a "super-hot" fire. And told us how he used to walk the path up to the highway to wait for his ride to town for cheese and dry-goods.

He told us how he knows when his chickens can no longer bear eggs… how he used to walk several miles a day, through the woods, checking his traps… how he fished with his own hand-made lures… and how he nearly died from eating mushrooms that he thought were safe… and there wasn't anyone around to help him. He weathered through it with his "home-remedies." *(Probably, he was still alive, because his body had a tremendous immunity system.)*

We listened with eager ears… awe-struck at his ingenuity, his daring, his fearlessness. He said he once met up with a black bear, while checking his traps. Armed with only his "prodding stick" *(a walking stick with about a 4" sharpened spike on the bottom end)* he simply froze and said he didn't even breathe. The bear came within a few feet of him, head bobbing up and down, sniffed a little, then hobbled away.

All-in-all it was a great trip… Gramps was about as "cool" a person as you could find… mentally and physically sound… at the age of 92. He was a "Master"… at self-preservation and "how to live off the land. The reality of his existence, alone, in the woods… in his cabin… with no one to rely on for help… ever… was beginning to sink in.

He shook our hands the day we left… and

gave each of us a token of his handy-work… bone knives, made from a deer's antlers. I could not ever replace this "Treasure."

That was the only time we saw our Grandfather alive… but I think he liked us.

Amos and Andy—Summer, 1952

There really isn't an abundance of entertainment available to 8 and 10 year-old boys… living on the farm in 1952. There was no TV, no Video games, and no "electronic" fun things by any nature.

But… there was Amos and Andy, a radio show that came on at 7:00pm every night. They were the 1950's era Smothers Brothers… only they weren't being broadcast on live TV… they were being listened to on the radio.

All day long… from first light until dinner time… doing chores; helping Gramma with meals, by collecting eggs from the chicken coop; picking tomatoes, (sneaking a taste or two of those red-ripe ones) and helping (as best as an 8 and 10 year old boy can) with the livestock feeding and care. Sweeping the stalls in the barn, changing the straw beneath the chicken's roost.

On certain days, we'd get a bucket full of "rain-water" from the barrel outside… and knew it was time for Gramma to shampoo her hair.

But… after dinner… and the dishes were all dried and put away… we'd gather up the chairs and put them in a half-circle around the radio… and wait for it to "come alive" with the announcement that "it's the Amos and Andy Show".

We'd all look at each other with smiles on our faces, Gramma, Uncle Merlyn, my brother, and me… because it was time to be "entertained."

We'd listen and laugh with attentive ear all through the ½ hour show… we could "see" in our minds what pranks the two of them were up to… and we'd laugh even harder when they'd inevitably get caught.

Then… the infamous sign-off… "What you talk'n 'bout Andy" would be heard, and it was off to bed. Tomorrow we'd get to do it all over again… and, as we did every day, anxiously await our time to, once again, be entertained.

Thanks, in part, to Amos and Andy... life on the farm wasn't a chore at all.

Things Mom and Dad Didn't Know
By Esther Vargo of Dearborn Heights, Michigan

I am now almost 78 years young. I am fourth oldest of ten children, brought up during the depression.

I can remember my father raising our house and digging a basement. We had a wood stove in the living room and many mornings standing close to feel the heat. After the basement was in place, a huge coal furnace was installed. We had to stoke it often. There was a room in the corner where we had tons of coal delivered.

My mother had a ringer washing machine and we girls hung the clothes outside on a long double clothesline. Every Saturday was bed stripping and house cleaning day. Dad washed the car so it was clean for church on Sunday. Back then, there were no seat belts. We all sat on someone's lap with four in front.

We always had a large garden and oh, how we all hated to hoe it and pull a plow while dad pushed it. Mom canned all the vegetables. Dad made barrels and crocks of pickles and sauerkraut. Our friends liked to get a huge pickle and eat walking down the street.

When we were older as teens, we would crawl out the bathroom window after mom and dad were asleep. We would go to "Margie's Dairy Bar" for a milkshake or sundae, and then sneak back in the house.

Another thing mom and dad didn't know was we had to cross a railroad track to get to school. Sometimes they would be switching cars and was moving slow. We could hear the first bell ringing. We were late after the second bell, so we would crawl under the train

1939 Ford

and run the last two blocks. They never knew this.

My father at one time was a barber and oh, how we hated it when he cut our hair. My mom bought feed sacks real cheap. They were all different prints she made all our clothes with a singer pedal sewing machine.

We had to take turns getting new shoes. If your shoes had holes in the sole, we had to put cardboard inside them, until it was your turn for new shoes.

We had one old bike that had been given to us. We took turns to ride it.

At Christmas, we all got new sox and underwear, we slept three to a bed with homemade feather blankets. They called them "feather ticks."

I remember we had to get government stamps to buy gasoline and other stuff as there was a ration on.

My grandfather had cherry trees, which all we kids had to pick around July 4th. He grew grapes and made his own wine. He even made dandelion wine.

All 10 kids in 1970

√ My Memory of Benzonia
By Donald Kidder, Frankfort, Michigan
Born 1928

This is my memory of Benzonia, Michigan starting about 1930 by Donald Kidder.

The main street of Benzonia at that time consisted, on the west side of the street, starting from the River road, the Spellman grocery, Case's Garage, Maddock's grocery, a small office building, the Masonic hall, and then into residential. Starting at the same corner, on the east side, was a gas station named the

In-between, Post office, Huntinguin millinery shop, the Bennett funeral home, which was also used in the summer as a collection point for green beans.

Heading north from the River road on the east side of the road, was the Benzonia Academy, which consisted of the school, library, gym and study hall combined, the superintendent home, and a campus. The school burned down several years later, and was never rebuilt.

About one quarter mile further north, the Benzonia High School was built. It was the only high school in the area, and pupils from the surrounding area, who had finished the eighth grade, were brought to Benzonia to finish high school, or, as many did, drop out.

During the WPA days the school was added to, and included a gymnasium, so now, instead of using the old academy, we had one at the school. The new addition to the school was made with concrete, and was hand mixed using wheelbarrows to transport and pour.

I mentioned the In-between house; it was used by the greyhound bus line for a lunch stop. It was half way between Traverse City and Manistee, thus the name. After the bus no longer needed a stop, it was hand sawn into, one-half was moved about three quarters of a mile down River road, and became a home, and the other half was moved back across a small valley and became a home.

The congregational church was located on River road; it is now the historical museum.

The water supply for the village in 1930-1935 was a hand pump. Anyone without their own well had to carry water for drinking. Most people had cisterns, which furnished water for baths and washing clothes. Washing clothes consisted of a ringer washing machine and two metal tubs.

√ The Burning Cigar
By G. Tom Whetter of Kalamazoo, Michigan
Born 1936

Back in the Forties, it seemed as though almost everyone smoked. All my relatives did at least the men. My dad worked as a purchasing agent for an aircraft company in Detroit, Michigan. Salesmen brought him small gifts and samples because of his position with the company. My dad did not smoke cigars, but many of the gifts he received were just those cigars!

One salesman gave him a very expensive five-dollar cigar that was encased in a beautiful expensive looking glass tube with a cork on the end to keep the cigar fresh and moist. Somehow, this cigar ended up in the glove box of my dad's new 1946 Fleetline Chevrolet. I was ten years old and this ten-year-old boy wanted to sample that sweet looking, expensive cigar. But how could I do this without my dad noticing that it was missing in the event that he came looking for it sometime in the future? How could I cover my tracks and take the cigar but still have it in the glove box? I thought that I was smart enough to pull this off

This is what I did. Like most people, dad kept many of his gift cigars in his smoking stand, next to his overstuffed chair and his floor lamp, along with his tin canister of Kentucky Club pipe tobacco. He kept an apple core in the can to keep the pipe tobacco moist. I took one of the many cheap cellophane covered cigars and removed the cellophane. I knew he wouldn't miss one of those. I removed the cork, poured out the soft expensive cigar, replaced it with the old cheap cigar, and then resealed the tube so that he would never know. I went in our tiny two-car garage, closed the door, and lit the beautiful cigar with one of my mom's wooden kitchen matches. I took two long puffs like I had seen people do in the movies.

I wish I could say that I enjoyed that puff, but to tell you the truth I immediately got sick. It was all I could do to keep from throwing up my lunch. It didn't taste as good as it had looked. It took me a while to get rid of the evidence as sick as I was.

One Friday evening my dad's friend Henry and his wife Gertie dropped over for a visit and to listen to the Friday night fights on the radio. Not to disturb the women in the living room, the two men and I retired to the backyard to dad's Chevy and the car radio. It was a beautiful spring evening. We sat in the car with the doors open.

My dad knew that Henry was a professional cigar smoker. Henry reached in his vest pocket to pluck out one of his cigars. Dad, remembering that he had stored that fancy rich cigar in the glove box, offered it to Henry. "How would you like an expensive cigar, Henry?" Dad asked as he leaned in the car door and opened the glove box.

I was sitting in the back seat listening to all this. I couldn't believe my ears and wondered what was about to happen. Would he notice? Would they know? My heart was pounding, fast! I felt like running away. I never expected THIS to happen! So I just watched in frozen silence, scared to death.

I watched Henry from the back seat. His eyes lighted when he was offered the cigar. He recognized that it was probably the best and the most expensive cigar that he had ever smoked! But it was a cheap cigar! It was old and dried out. The first layer of tobacco was hanging down. It looked terrible, not like an expensive cigar. But being the fact that Henry had never had an expensive cigar like this before and being a gentleman, he didn't say anything.

Henry took out the cigar, licked it, bit off the end, and spit as they do. He then took out a large cigar lighter and lighted the end of the cigar. When he did, it burst into flame! I was afraid that he was going to catch on fire! The first layer of tobacco flamed up and started to fall on his shirt, and I was afraid that he would burn his suit coat. He grabbed the cigar out of his mouth and swiftly flung it out on the driveway pavement.

I was horrified! I was in panic mode! My dad was sitting in the driver's seat and completely taken by surprise. He jumped out and ran around the car to stomp on the burning cigar and help Henry out of the car.

I heard them talking. I stayed in the back seat, for the look on my face would have given me away. "Well, so much for a five-dollar cigar" My dad said as he was helping Henry out of the car.

My smart father never questioned me about that evening. I would like to know now if he ever thought that I had anything to do with that cigar. By not being questioned, I didn't have to lie. What would I have done? Would I have lied and said I didn't know anything about it, or would I have told the truth? Then again, perhaps he was smart enough to know not to ask me about it. He may not have really wanted to know. After all, I was my father's son.

I've told this story many times, but it wasn't until after Henry and my dad passed away that I told this story to Henry's widow,

Gertie. She thought it was funny and laughed long and hard.

✓ Charley You Can Come Out
By Marian Story of Houghton Lake,
Michigan
Born 1928

We lived in a small town called Galesburg, between Kalamazoo and Battle Creek. Gram was 7 years old when she "came across the pond" as she called the ocean. She was born the last of November and her twin the first of December 1854.

Every afternoon my great grandma took off her morning cap, took out her curlers, and combed her, snow-white hair. She put on her black dress, gold pin with her name, sat in her velvet red armchair, and greeted whoever came to see her. She was Gram to everyone, when she and her husband came to town, there were only eleven people. Her husband was a blacksmith. He made the town's flagpole. Their shop was on Mill Street, on this day, the chief, and deputy called on Gram. They said, "We know you have a chicken hawk, and you're not allowed to, will you let us have it?" Gram said, "I can't do what I don't have boys, but you're welcome to look." They searched the house, the woodsheds, the outhouses, but no chicken hawk. They sat and talked awhile, got her a shuttle of coal, and bid her good-bye, and left. She waited a while, she sang to me, I lay on the couch; I was five at the time. Then she lifted her apron and said "Charley you can come out, and out came the chicken hawk, he'd been lying beneath her apron on her lap all the time!

We had all kinds of pets; we had a skunk, coon, dogs, cats, and a parrot. Our house was the third from center of town. We had pumps for water right up to 1949. We cooked, and baked on a range. We had one in the kitchen, and one in the first woodshed. My granddad, her son, went to bury our skunk who'd passed away, he asked her again did you de-smell him, "oh yes" as gramps always did, the pet skunk slept with gramps, on this day he found Gram's hadn't oh was he mad.

Grandpa's wife would come out on Sundays she worked in town and our coon would get up on her lap walk in circles lay down, and after a while she'd look at all of us and say "he hasn't done it" the moment she said it he put out his paws, pat her and pee on her every time.

Grams was at the sewing machine sewing and I sat on the stair steps, Polly was on Gram's shoulder. Gram called her the flycatcher, she saw a mole on Gram's neck and swack, bit it off. All that Gram said was "Polly what you do?" Polly return bad Polly put up her feathers and hid her face. I fell downstairs.

✓ The Ghost of Pearl Street
By Jennifer Folkerts Cupples of Onaway,
Michigan

How did this ghost get its acclaim? I'll explain as I go to give you an idea based on my childhood journeys.

Gladys West, who was my neighbor and so-called stepmother or adoptive mother, remains in my memory the "maternal love" as a little girl. I loved her so much as a second mother who trained me and so guided me through the age of 12 into the daring.

Before the numerous television shows that abound on ghosts, paranormal and monsters, Gladys was my guiding light in my life at the early stages in the 50s and 60s. Spiritually minded she was so supportive of my growing interests in odd things of the unexplained phenomena. Fire, for example, was to behold for Marvin, her son and I. The force of fire utterly amazed me, even now, that such a force of nature could do so much good and so much harm representing the duality of all. Marvin and I were somewhat close as I was the "tomboy" and shared similar interests.

Firecrackers, cherry bombs, and 3-foot sparklers were the greatest inventions in our terms of consciousness. So we tried them all, when at the time all were legal. At the time in Hazel Park, Michigan, many were still using coal to heat their homes. That black stuff, that coal substance, could really provide the nation with a warm sense on their interiors. Another interesting factor.

Small mini laboratories were the craze especially with the boys in middle class society on the border of Detroit. As a tomboy, I fit right in to the land of labs with the experimentation of chemicals, fire, and others. How astonishing and fascinating things of science could be. Sir Isaac Newton and Leonardo DaVinci would have of enjoyed too our explorations.

So what was that white, gray, black smoke coming out from the liters? Sometimes these chemical reactions looked like mists, spirits, or a ghost as an aftermath. Where was Vincent Price and his explanations in his movies? These experiences lead to vivid discussions of the earth and the natural sciences.

I was, as you can imagine, one of the kids who ran home from school to watch "Dark Shadows" either at my house or at Gladys. I so much enjoyed Glady's discussion of the U.K. and especially England where her lineage ran. Of course, ghosts and spirits came up as a possibility in our world of the strange. Presbyterian was she, Marvin, and me a strong, staunch follower of Martin Luther in the Missouri Synod. Thus began our quest of checking up on those dark shadows in the abandoned and condemned house on Pearl Street.

Smack on the corner of Pearl Street and Ford Road was the pink-bricked house where I saw my first ghost. He, I believe, was a male entity of tall proportions. Gladys West was who I ran home to or rode my bike to further explain or discuss the happenings. Childhood imaginations as some could say, yet, I saw what I saw. This happened before such as the word as skeptic became popular.

My bike riding paths past the pink-bricked house remains ingrained in my memory of "The Ghost of Pearl Street." As life grew on, my parents separated me with Gladys as we moved to the east side of Hazel Park and the great divide of I-75, which ran the north and south. It began to be more challenging to visit Gladys, Marvin, and her family. By the age of 12, my interests changed, yet not forgotten my paranormal experiences. Boys, concert band, dances, and work became the new order.

Here I am, my credit due to Gladys West, author and investigator and researcher leading various grassroots movements in Michigan and around the world. Thank you Gladys West for the visions of the other side and the experiences of a lifetime. Join me on Facebook under Jennifer Folkerts Cupples and also look up the Michigan Wilderness Paranormal Club and press "Like"

Thank you Gladys West for "The Ghost on Pearl Street" experience. Rest in peace.

✓ A City Boys Adventure
By Stuart MacDonald of Yarmouthport, Massachusetts
Born 1938

My momentous trip in Michigan began in the green yards of East Detroit cutting lawns for 50 cents each. I was born and raised 2 miles from the Detroit City Airport. This gave me the ability to rent a 5 horse Johnson outboard motor but I'm getting ahead of myself. Every summer for 13 years upon awaking at 3am on a Saturday morning in mid-July, we would drive from East Detroit to the Upper Peninsula. My mother would make a beef stew, wrapping it in tin foil. My father would place it on the hot engine block. We drove up one and occasionally two lane-winding roads to the ferry at Mackinaw City. I remember many of the trips starting when I was four years old. First trip was in a 1938 Buick, 4 door sedan, and boxy car with a giant trunk. The trip for this story occurred in 1952, I was 14, a fairly sturdy lad, track star and freshman football player at Birmingham High School. The car we had for this trip was a 1948 Pontiac, also a four door sedan but with an automatic transmission, black, beautiful, with lots of chrome. We left very early in the morning. Sometime just before noon we would be in line for the ferry at Mackinaw City. The ferry would take us to St Ignace in the UP. The ferry held many cars as well as train freight cars, busses, bicycles and walking passengers. Loading from the stern, it would sail straight across to St Ignace and the vehicles would then depart from the bow. I remember some of the names of the boats. Vacationland, City of Petoskey and the City of Cheboygan come to mind. We took the Vacationland that year as pictured on the last page. We lined up, busses in one line, cars in another. When the lanes were full, chains went across. I don't remember how long it took but it had to be too fast for me. Rumbling off the big boat, we went east for a short trip and ended our trip at Ehele's log cabins, just across the road from the water. After unpacking the car, we removed the beef stew from the engine. It was our Saturday dinner. We fished, swam, and got reconnected with the area Sunday. Early in the afternoon, we took my dad to a local airport and he flew back to Detroit to work for a week leaving the car with us.

Pete, my older brother and I would look up all our friends who were also up at the same time every year, Pete would find a girlfriend for the two weeks, usually a local Indian girl. My little sister, Susan, would wander down to visit with her grandmother. My grandfolks had one of the two cabins right on the water. Monday morning, I could hardly wait as my mother would take us to Cedarville and I would rent the motor for my boat. That afternoon I would mount the motor on a 14 foot, wooden boat and explore the local islands in the Le Cheneau islands. On Friday, at the end of the first week we would return to the airport and pick up my dad. He would be with us for the week and then we would all return home together.

I say my boat because I was allowed to rent a 5 horsepower motor from a marina in Cedarville, 10 minutes down the road by car. The motor and gas money came from the lawn cutting I had done earlier that year, plus, some birthday and Christmas money I had hoarded away.

One morning in the second week after tiring of the many visits to the same haunts, I thought why don't I gas up and take a trip to Mackinaw Island? I could barely see it in the distance but having been there once before by ferry I remembered how much fun it had been to visit. I had been to Mackinaw Island when I was much younger and I remember eating outside on a really long porch. I didn't know it was about 15 miles away across open water, at the age of 14 I didn't have the ability to factor that into my trip. I filled numerous small cans and bottles with gas, carefully mixing in the additional oil the 2-cycle motor required. Then I left without telling anyone where I was going, just me, a life preserver, two oars and no food or water. I motored basically SW passing the end of Brûlée Point road on the last point of land east of Search Bay. This last bit of information coming from Maps on my iPad, I hadn't a clue back then as to my route, only my destination. Thank God, there never was any fog. At this point, I have to inject some thoughts that have been building up to this point. And they are how incredibly naive I was! Stupid meaning total lack of knowledge. Between the ages of 18 to now, I have spent 4 years in the Navy on 'boats' over a thousand feet long weighing 60,000 tons.

Have taken seven sailing courses, 2 Coast Guard courses and captained 12 different boats from 8' to 40' long. Chartered a 40' catamaran and was responsible for five people in the BVI, a 160 square mile area for 8 days. Have had my own sailboat sailing in Michigan, Massachusetts, Vermont, and Florida for 15 years. I have read and heard of so many lives lost and accidents it would make your hair stand on end. I can only explain my return because there is a God. He had to have had a very busy day with me somewhere around July 15 1952.

OK, back to the boat. I'm guessing, but it appears the distance might be 15 to 17 miles across the open water. As I recall I tied up at a very high dock right next to where the ferries landed with less than a pint of gas left of my meager supply. I climbed up the dock and refueled. I don't remember if I went into the gas pump area with an assortment of cans and bottles or not, I must have been a sight, a little kid with a motley collection of gas holding containers! I do remember that I had about 75 cents left over. I contemplated sending my folks a post card from the island or buying some fudge, I did the latter. But I remember thinking what a shock it might have been for my mother to open a card from her son who had made a trip like that. I devoured the fudge with a large gulp of water.

The trip back was long and tiring, stopping at one point on the tip of Brûlée Point to just sit on dry land for a while. After a short rest, I could NOT get the motor started and panic set in. I did not know what to do. After a period of thinking and rethinking, it dawned on me that I had turned the gas shut off. After turning it back on, it started on the first pull, phew!

I was less than a few hours to go and home was getting closer. I was invigorated, but still held cruising speed so as not to consume fuel at a high rate. As I entered the area just south of Hessel, I noticed the waves had substantially picked up, the wind was onshore. The boat was now pitching up and down quite radically. I had to steer in corkscrew fashion to avoid burying the bow or stern to avoid taking on water. Then I saw a rather unexpected situation, all the boats had been taken out of the water! I picked a slot onshore unoccupied and drove the boat onto land lifting, the motor up just as the bow beached.

Thank God, I was home, very tired, mentally and physically.

I came into the cabin and my folks looked like they were seeing a ghost. They didn't ask and I didn't tell them for years later what I had done. I don't think they wanted to know. I do remember not being spanked, then or ever again, as was what I usually expected and got for my errant actions.

Many of us have 10 minutes of fame in life, thank heaven most of us don't have 12 hours of scariness. I think if I ever wanted to repeat the trip I would take a 25' or more, fully gassed up twin-engine boat and check the weather first. Better yet, I'd get onto one of the Star Line Ferries and let them take me over and back.

✓ Good Old Days
By Flo Anderson, Kaleva, Michigan
Born 1922

Good old days in a two-story school, kindergarten to half of fourth grade was on the first floor, and the other half of fourth grade to eighth grade on the second floor. There were five kids in the eighth grade. My team lost the

Flo's parents, Sadie and Michael Czarnecki

spelling bee so we had to put on a play for the school. I loved it because we got out of class to practice. If we missed a class of our own, we were exposed to previous lower class, as well as higher class. We marched up to the front of the room. One man teacher pulled the hair back of students when they were noisy or for some other reason. I loved it when the downstairs teacher married the upstairs teacher.

Mom went to "keeno" and brother and Dad went to pick up food and dish prizes. She was so lucky. A Maytag washer was delivered and she didn't like it. They didn't pick it up so she had Dad and my brother put it in the alleyway. I loved the Easy washer, she used bluing, and she boiled sheets for whitening in a boiler on the kitchen stove.

Mom and Dad were of Swedish decent, and moved to Kewanee, Illinois. Dad came from Sweden and Mom worked in Chicago. He worked in boiler works and the doctor said if he didn't quit he'd be dead in a year. Mom blind folded him and sat him near a USA map with a pencil. Kaleva was the area they came to and found out later the land wasn't as good as the seller said.

He got a job in auto production and came home on weekends. He had to leave the car at the bottom of the hill, as all roads didn't get plowed in the winter. He farmed in the summer. I remember Saturday baths in a wash tub in the garage. Mom was cooking on a kerosene stove and almost lost the barn to a fire.

We went to a movie with ten bread wrappers. We ate lots of white bread so I'd have a few wrappers for whoever needed just a few more. I remember going into Manistee on Saturday for church wearing this brown dress with a lace collar that I loved. There was a downpour, as we had to walk from church to Kosciusko to catch the bus, and it started shrinking. Both my friends, boy and girl, were pulling my dress down (crinkle crepe).

Winter weather, yes, one year my brother skated all around Filer City because it was frozen. My dad hosed water for a skating rink in the front yard, and I had bob skates. I plowed through snow to get to school. We had a two story house. Mom hung wash up in a bare room, and we had feather ticks and had two quart jars of hot water to go to bed upstairs in the winter. As we lived on a farm

George, Sadie, Michael, and Flo in 1931

we had peaches, which usually froze out, cherries, apples, sometimes corn and cukes. City people would drop off their cats. We had thirteen cats at times.

Yes, we had a milkman, also the baker truck. I loved to get those baked goods. Dad put up a closure by the front door, and if you didn't pick up the quarts of milk frozen cream would lift the cap.

The front room always had window shades down before Christmas, for opening on Christmas morning. I remember seeing a blue dress that I got for Christmas, in an upstairs room, no more real Santa Claus.

We had sleds, toboggans, and slip jacks. There were hills nearby so we'd have fun–I hit a tree and got knocked out. Friends pulled me home and I had to stay at home for a while. The teacher brought homework for me to do.

I had mastoid so I had to go to the doctor every day at 11:00 am. At Easter, the doctor gave me a paper basket with jelly eggs. I loved it. I learned to drive and so I had a car to put on a play at the Masonic Temple in Manastee. One stormy night the windshield wipers stopped, so I had to stick my hand out to clear snow. We had many quilts and kids packed in the car, as I had to take them home. Mom and Dad were so happy when I got home. There was too much snow to get into the garage so I left the car in the alley.

My brother built lattice work for the chicken yard. I was holding up the lattice when he went to get more nails. A rooster came at me, and no more rooster. Later I just couldn't clean a chicken and eat it the same day.

We had a two seat outhouse and a night time potty. I remember a date with another couple and two wanted to use our bathroom, which didn't flush, I was so embarrassed.

Castor oil always seemed to be a cure-all. When I was growing up Sunday afternoon, we'd go for a car ride usually to Ludington where they had a playground with more than just swings. My brother was pushing me and I let go, went flying, but landed in the sand.

When my husband and I moved into his Mom and Dad's house, we saw where the door had been moved three times. Grandma had a green thumb and had an English green fern from ceiling to floor.

Life Was Better Then, Than Now
By Marlene Rood of Dimondale, Michigan
Born 1950

I grew up in Lewiston, a small town that was really a village. One of the first things I remember is going to school. Our kindergarten class was held in the same room as the first and second grade class, with the same teacher. Third and fourth grade was in another room, fifth, sixth, seventh, and eighth in another. Each grade had approximately 10-12 kids. At that time, the elementary schools were K-8. At recess time, we sometimes just sat in the back of the room and danced or played games. When it was time for lunch, the cooks brought the lunches to each room, they would serve up our trays, and we would sit at our desks and eat. At lunchtime, we would be able to move our desks together.

There were a couple of times when I would have to use either the outhouse or a chamber pot (or thunder bucker as it was sometimes called). Of course, back then, outhouses were made of wood and the odor was something you never forget. When we would visit my grandparents, there was no bathroom upstairs, so under the bed was a chamber pot and thankfully, there was a lid.

My parents both worked and there were seven people in a small house for the first twelve years of my life, grandma lived with us until her passing. The kitchen was about 6X12 with the table up against one wall. To this day, I'm not sure how we did it but we all sat around that table and we all ate together.

Castor oil was a wonderful thing. Mom would line my brothers and myself up and with tablespoon and bottle in hand, we each received our dose of castor oil.

Phones back then were the wonderful rotary phones but I was never a girl that liked to talk much on the phone but when you wanted to make a call or if you were on the phone, it was frustrating. The one good thing was, if you were calling someone in the same town, you only had to dial the last four digits. It was kind of fun when you wanted to make a call and there was someone already on the line, you could listen and hear what they were talking about. When you wanted to make a call and they would not get off the line, you sometimes had to let them know that they were on the phone long enough.

Our wringer washer was in the cellar. There was always the washer and two rinse tubs. On laundry day when one load was done we used the curved end of a cane to get the clothes out of the washer, then put in another load of clothes-in the same wash water, back then you didn't have the luxury of having clean water after each load. Then put the washed clothes in the first rinse tub, then the second. After they were rinsed the second time I would have to wring them out by hand, put them in a basket, and take them outside where they would be hung on the clothesline to dry.

Since we didn't live that far from the elementary school, about a half mile, we walked to school. The bus didn't pick kids up that close. No matter what the weather you walked to school. Girls would put wool pants on under their skirts then once at school we would have to take them off. There were times in the winter when walking home during a blizzard was exhausting and bitterly cold. But, I have to say that every once in a great while, if mom wasn't working at the store, she would come and pick us up, if it was pouring rain.

Sadie Hawkins Day was a fun day at school. It was the one day you wore your old clothes with patches all over them to school. It was a L'il Abner type day. At night, there was a dance and the gym would be decorated in hay bales, you'd dance and there might even be games to play.

During the summer, we spent most of our days either at the lake or in the woods playing. Back then, there was never the fear of someone grabbing a child. So after breakfast my little brother and I would usually end up in the wood climbing trees, hiding in the tall grass or picking berries of some kind. Then we would change into our bathing suits and walk to the lake, about a mile away, and spend the afternoon. Mom always knew where we were. If it was lunchtime, and she was home from work, if we were in the woods close enough to hear her, all she had to do was yell out the door for us to come home. In the evening, it wasn't uncommon to find us playing outside until bedtime. We did have one of the first televisions in town, which was exciting to us, and, of course, we could only get three channels, and they weren't very good. Every once in a while, someone would have to jump up and move the rabbit ears, or go outside, and turn the antenna to bring the picture in better. There was no remote, you had to actually get up and change the channel, or turn the volume up or down.

Lewiston, in the 1950s, had approximately 700-800 people, just down home people, so when it came time to go to Gaylord, a larger town 30 miles away, to do some shopping we got dressed up for the trip. These shopping sprees were a treat.

Being the only girl of four kids, I did get some new clothes, especially for school, but for the day to day clothes I did get some of my older brothers clothes to wear when they outgrew them, and I also got some hand me downs from the older girls next door. I remember after my father's mother had passed, she lived with us until I was about 12, I needed a winter coat, and there just wasn't the money to spare, so mom took grandma's winter coat and cut it down for me. That coat was blue and it looked like and older person's coat, but it was warm and that was all I cared about. I remember that mom did make some of my clothes.

There was no bullying, oh sure just some little nit picking, but it didn't really bother anyone, and we had some dirt-poor kids in our school. It seemed like no one really cared about your clothes, as long as you were clean and didn't smell, but those who did, didn't really bother anyone.

At Christmas time, we would all get in the car, dad with saw in hand, and drive until we found the right tree. Cut it down and drag it to the car. That is part of what Christmas is all about for me, the smell of a fresh cut tree in the house, with all the lights and decorations on it.

Life in the '50s and '60s was great now that I am an adult and remember all these things and much more, even the music was better than it is now. Country music was country music not this rock country type stuff they sing. Oh, yes, life was much better then, than now.

√ The Farm
By Nancy Jane Starlin Sanders of Copemish, Michigan
Born 1941

My earliest recollections in childhood are happy and wrapped up in family—mother, father, and sister.

My first memories are of living in Mason, MI and coming up to the farm near Mesick, MI on weekends. (I later learned my father had purchased the 160 acre farm almost on a whimsy—this little side story I have to share because it wouldn't happen to just anyone). My mother and father were living in Manistee at the time and had seen the farm with the small creek running through it. Dad liked the land and the buildings and stopped by to see if it were for sale. The owner, Claud Curtis, a ginseng farmer said it wasn't. So, Dad gave Claud his address and said if he ever decided to sell to let him know. (Several acres of trees had already been cleared when Cummer and Diggins owned the property.) I don't know how much time passed, but one day along come Claud and told dad that he was ready to sell for the sum of $1,900—mind you that was quite a bit back in 1938. Dad wanted that farm and he jumped at the chance.

As the new owner, Dad tried farming for a while but couldn't make a go of it and make the payments too. When the war broke out in the early '40s, (Dad was 4-F due to a health problem) Dad was lucky enough to land the job in a drop forge where he worked until the end of the war. This served two purposes, it helped the war effort, and he was able to put aside the money to pay for the entire farm he had purchased.

My mother lived in the home up north for

Nancy's father, Paul Starlin with his first team of horses in 1939

that first winter. In the spring when Dad was able to find a home for us to rent, we joined him and went to live in Mason for the next two years. Occasionally we come north to stay weekends at the farm. I remember the family's treks included a stop at the gas station for a fill-up at the sign of the "Flying Red Horse," a purchase of a box of Fig Newton cookies, which we all enjoyed, and searching for the Burma Shave signs to read as we journeyed northward. Cars in the 40s took a lot longer to travel a distance than they do today and it seemed like it took forever to get to the farm. We had a great time once we arrived though.

We moved back to the farm after the war. Interestingly enough the farmhouse was the one of few in the neighborhood to have indoor plumbing and lights. While the rest of the neighbors still struggled without the necessities of life, we lived in the lap of luxury, or so I thought. I was unaware of the fact that we were indeed near penniless most of the time. Living on the farm, we never had need for food or other basic things in life. Basic needs were always plentiful. We grew our own vegetable garden—canning in abundance each year. One transparent apple tree provides plenty of applesauce— Lee's horses and gotten out of the fence and trampled down the rest of the row of fruit trees that Dad had planted. Wild raspberries and blueberries were bountiful. We enjoyed picking and canning them. Meat was never a problem, as we raised chickens, pigs, and cows, and on occasion a rabbit or two.

Since our family canned many fruits and vegetables each year, that meant that first we gathered the fruit. About the week of July 4 each year when we seen Dad heading out the door with his milk pail over his arm in mid-morning, we knew it was time to pick wild blueberries (huckleberries) in the pinery— the pinery was state owned land in back of our farm. Both my sister and I were expected to go and do our part. We each had a two-quart bucket that we were counted upon to fill before we come home at day's end. Mom packed a lunch and off we went. Some days picking was easy, some days it was scarce. I remember one day when my pail was nearly full and I sat down on a mounded-up hill of pine needles to pick the leaves and twigs out of the huckleberries. It wasn't long before I jumped off that pile of pine needles and ran as fast as my legs would carry me, with Shirley doubled over in laughter. The mound I had

Nancy and Shirley in 1949

made my rest upon was a huge fire ant hill. My full pail of berries toppled over as I made my exit. That was the only time my parents let me off the hook and go home with an empty pail.

On the farm, there weren't many hazy, lazy dazs. Farm work was hard. If we weren't helping dad hoe the cornfields, we were weeding the garden, hauling wood, helping mom with the housework, and canning… all this to support dad's dream of having a successful farm. However, in terms of the world's success it never was. In terms of offering a secure childhood to a family, it was a huge success. I have appreciated this more than I can say as the years go by. What I didn't realize at the time was that our individual family unit was being built—brick-by-brick--family members relying on each other to do their part in both work and play.

Many a day would go by that we only saw one another, or perhaps a nearby neighbor. So, as a family we were pretty tightly bonded. Saturdays were reserved for going to town to sell the cow's cream to the local creamery and perhaps purchase a few groceries. Sometimes during those visits, we stopped at the drugstore where, if we were lucky, dad would buy us an ice cream cone. Another treat for us was to visit the "Dalquist" store. You could always find lots of things to buy there. Blue Waltz perfume was one of my favorites and I would save my allowance for weeks just to get a bottle. Blue Waltz perfume and little tin cookware was what I spent my ten cents allowance on back then.

Saturday nights in the summer were usually spent going to the "free" show in Mesick. That, too, offered us the opportunity to buy groceries and visit with other neighbors. One lingering remembrance I have is of the Salvation Army Band that always played in front of Clark and Olson's store. Girls and guys would pair off and make their way up and down the main street of Mesick as strains of "Onward Christian Soldiers" filled the air. If the milking had been done in time and we arrived early enough, we tried to get a parking place to watch the show from the car, if not; we had to set on the benches out underneath the stars--not a good situation on rainy nights. The shows were sponsored by local storeowners, in hopes of bringing farm families into town for buying and trading. These shows lasted well into my teen years. I'm not real sure when they were discontinued, but a movie theater opened up in Manton and soon after the free shows became a thing of the past. After all, why go to a free show when you could pay to see one?

Good Neighbors

This story would not be complete however unless I mention some of the many adventures the neighbor children and I experienced throughout the years. I recall the summer when the back pond was dug on the farm. It wasn't very wide and deep only at the end near the dam but we thought it was the best. Because there was no boat to be found, we children decided to take an old copper clothes boiler and float across the pond. I was selected to get inside the boiler and my friend Sylvia pushed me out as far as she could into the water. Needless to say, that old copper boiler was no boat. It sunk to the bottom in short order with me in it. I tell you I had some tall explaining to do to my irritated mother as to why my clothes were dripping wet and full of mud.

The copper boiler may not have been much fun as a boat that summer, however, later that winter we resurrected it when the pond froze over and had a blast skimming across the pond seated inside. That frozen pond brought many friends out to ice skate with.

Summer was equally as much fun. During the hay season, we worked hard bringing in the bales. Before hay balers came to our area, haying was done with loaders. The loose hay would be loaded onto the wagons with the loader and hauled to the barns to be stored in the mows. My family had its own little enterprise worked out when it came to getting the hay from the wagon into the haymow. Dad stood atop the loaded hay wagon where he would put big hayforks attached to a rope and pulley around a load of hay and yell to one of us girls, who were stationed out in front of the barn to "let it go." We in turn would wave at mother where she was on the tractor waiting to pull the other end of the rope, taking the load up into the barn where dad would "trip" it at the appropriate moment, causing it to drop in the right mow. I remember the day when he backed up to trip the rope and fell completely off the hay wagon. Boy was he mad! Surprisingly enough he wasn't hurt, other than his pride. Once the mows were filled with hay, the neighborhood kids would have a sleep over in each other's barns. The only thing is, we didn't get much sleep.

There wasn't much excitement at our house unless the relatives come, except the night my Dad caught an invader in the chicken coop. Mother always raised chickens and would get a little extra spending money from the eggs we didn't use during the week. So it was important to her if she wanted a few nice things that she had her egg money. However, disappointment ran high when something started killing her chickens during the night. It being a warm summer we slept with the windows open and mom kept an ear to the ground to hear the hens if they started clucking. Several times, she sent Dad to the chicken coop after noises of clucking in the night. This went on far too long and finally one night Dad was fast enough to reach the coop before a badger emerged with his nightly meal. A couple of shots from Dad's rifle put an end to the raids on mom's chickens. Mom went back to raising chickens and selling eggs. That was the first and only time we ever seen a badger on the farm.

With the food in great supply on the farm when my sister, Shirley, and I were younger, we were rather chubby children. However, we reached a point, she was in the eighth grade, and I was in the sixth, when we decided being plump was not appealing. So, Shirley found this diet in one of her magazines that promised if followed precisely we would take off ten pounds in two weeks. At that time, my mom was working in a sewing factory and not around to help us much, but we decided we could do it by ourselves. So we followed the diet to the letter and did lose weight throughout the first week. When Saturday lunchtime came, we once again set the pot of water on the stove to boil, as usual, for our boiled hamburger, dropping the ball in at the appropriate time. Being it was Saturday; Mother was home watching her with a perplexed look. After a bit she could no longer contain herself and inquired as to what we were doing. "Boiling our hamburgers," we replied. "Could I see the recipe," she asked. After examining the diet magazine she said, "Broiled hamburgers, not boiled," and burst into laughter.

That was the last rubber ball hamburger I ever ate.

One Day When Gypsies Were Approaching
By Marie A. Ketz, Manistee, Michigan
Born 1928

My story begins in Germany where my grossmutter, (grandmother) Anna Kroepke from Berlin met and fell in love with a young Prussian soldier, my Grossvater, (grandfather) Julius Sievert. Anna's family forbid her marriage to Julius so she left her dowry behind and married. They had two little girls and decided to come to North America.

In 1883, Anna and her sister, who was married to Julius' brother, came first with all their children to America. Julius and his brother followed shortly but their ship ended up in South America. They gained passage to get to North America by working their way doing carpentry jobs and playing music on their violins. Grossvater also brought his prize possessions-grape vine cuttings, which he carefully tended on his long trip and planted after arriving in Michigan. He had the most beautiful grape arbors that extended into the lot adjacent to where they made their home. He made wonderful wine. Manistee, Michigan, had had a fire that destroyed many homes and there was a need for workers to rebuild. Grossvater, being a carpenter and mason had plenty of work. The same year they arrived, 1883, my father, Ernest Sievert, was born, as were other children later.

Grossmutter never spoke English, but Grossvater, because of his business, had to learn to speak it. My father, Ernest, was born with a heart defect, but worked with his father as a teenager and learned the trade. He also could play the violin. As he got older, he saved his money and bought land at Canfield Lake three miles south from the town of Manistee.

About this time, my other maternal grandparents Ephrom and Lavina Alspach and family, came from North Dakota with a horse and covered wagon. Their daughter Dessie was my mom. Ephrom worked along with my fraternal grandfather, he was also a mason and plasterer. My father had horses and one special horse, a Kentucky trotter. My mother loved horses, and took a fancy to that trotter. My dad had an eye for my mother but she was only fourteen or fifteen at the time, and he decided to wait for her.

She became engaged to him at eighteen

Marie's grandparents, Lavina and Ephrom

and he was thirteen years older than her. They married a year later, on December 22, 1915, and moved to a small cottage at Canfield Lake. They had seven children, some cattle and chickens, but needed more land and a larger house. It was depression time and my father made a deal with a kind banker to buy an eighty-acre farm just two miles further south, and the deal was to fix up the old buildings and farmland. There was a windmill but no electricity.

Dad built a two-story house and fixed the other buildings. The family moved, and three more children were born. I was the eighth child, a daughter named Marie, two boys came later. My mother now had ten children within sixteen years. Our mother worked very hard washing clothes by hand with a washboard and canned hundreds of jars of fruit and vegetables, made butter, homemade bread, and pies, and would hitch up the horse and buggy and deliver the eggs, butter, and buttermilk into town. She also had a loom, and made rugs to sell. Our mother was a midwife for many of the neighbor women. She also had a beautiful flower garden that she enjoyed when she had a little time to be by herself.

Our father was a beekeeper and we had lots of honey. With his heart problem, my father's work was limited. He still did carpenter work and made our sleds, hope chests for his daughters, and toolboxes for his sons. He fixed a wind charger on the house

65

Ernest and Dessie Sievert and 8 of their 10 children around 1930

for lights besides the gas lanterns. Our father also thought ahead for our future, and had ten parcels of property divided equally at Canfield Lake in our names.

All of us had our chores to do, milking cows and feeding fifty pigs. We younger ones had to ride the horses that pulled cultivators down the rows of corn and potatoes for weeding. Some of us usually the younger ones, took the herd of cows along North on Maple Road to Canfield Lake to graze and drink, and back home to be milked later. In summer, we would all pile up in a truck and go to Canfield Lake in the evening for our baths and swimming. Our baths at home were in the old washtubs- girls' first then boys. We were on a party line with the old windup telephone. We would giggle and laugh when our dad spoke in German to Grossvater. None of us ever learned to speak German. Every day, dad would read to us a few verses out of the Bible to start our day right.

The highlight in our lives was when the neighbor's threshing machine came down the road to our house to separate the grain. Neighbors came to help and mom cooked the big meal. It was the same thrill when we had to help filling the silo with cut corn. We younger ones were barefoot, and packed it, as it was blown into the silo.

Our horses were a main source of help in our farming and our mother had two favorites, Trixie and Midnight, which she trained to nuzzle a kiss on her cheek in exchange for a lump of sugar.

We attended a one-room country school for all eight grades. It was a half mile from our farm. In the winter we would skate there on our and the neighbors' frozen fields. Our teachers sometimes boarded with a neighbor if they were from another city or town. There were monthly PTA meetings and we had wonderful Christmas programs with plays, and music recitations. When I was very small, I remember how terrified we were one day when gypsies were approaching and the teacher made us keep very quiet. She pulled the shades down until they passed. There was a neighbor, Mr. Pruess, who was working in a field close by and the gypsies made him undress to his underwear, and they stole everything he had including his clothes. There were two outhouses- boys and girls. The school had a bell tower with a large bell that we took turns pulling the rope to ring at morning and recess time. While growing up our family liked music and some of us learned to play guitar, violin, accordion, and mouth organ. We sang duets and in trios at our school and other schools' functions at various times.

There were lots of mishaps during our childhood. My brother, Don, was riding in the truck with our dad, and bees were in the cab. My dad lost control, the truck tipped over in a ditch, and cut my brother's ear almost off, no damage to his hearing. My sister, Mara Lee, had a serious appendix attack and landed in the hospital at age fifteen.

Once, when the milk had to be delivered to Ross Dairy, it snowed so bad the plows couldn't make it out so, my three brothers used two by fours put together and loaded the 10 gallon cans on, and pushed and pulled for three miles to get them delivered. It took half a day to go a half mile.

Lysol was a constant help for our accidents. My sister, Betty, got butted in her butt by a cow's horn. We were always barefoot and stepped on nails, wire, etc. Mom cut up an old sheet and used Lysol. When I was about ten years old, our father tore down our old

10 of the Sievert children

granary. The roof was so much fun to play on and I fell, and was unconscious for several hours. I woke up sore and throwing up. Mom kept me in close watch until I was better.

One time while I was cleaning the barn I took a wheelbarrow load of manure up a board ramp. A wagon was nearby, and so was our big bull. I jumped on the wagon and was screaming as loud as I could. The bull was trying to tip over the wagon with his horns. My brother ran to my rescue in time.

Almost always, as we milked the cows, they would swish us in the face with their tails. I got the bright idea to tie a brick on the end to hold it down. The darn cow lifted it and swung it towards me; another lesson learned.

My brother Les, when he was a teenager, had come home from hunting and the gun accidentally went off and hit him in the leg. My older brother was getting grain for the animals and a mouse ran up his pant leg. He ran and dove into the horse tank. We had an old rickety house in a pasture next to us and we thought there were ghosts in there. My brother had so much fun teasing our cousins from out of town.

We sisters had to help bale hay. One sat and pushed the wires, and the other one tied. One day my brother checked the oil and I, like a good sister, said I would take care of it. I put the oil in the wrong place. I took the cap off the air cleaner and poured in a quart of oil. I never heard the end of that.

Halloween was fun for my brothers and the neighbor boys. They took the wheels off a wagon, put the wagon on the roof of the school, and put the wheels back on. They tipped over and moved some out houses. They also took the wheels off of cars and trucks belonging to our neighbors.

During watermelon season, we went at night and did some watermelon snitching. Some of us got scared sick to our stomachs. I'm sure if some of my siblings were still around there would be some pretty tall tales left untold.

Our father died of heart failure at the age of fifty-seven, leaving our mom, who was forty-four, to care and raise ten children, from ages six to twenty-two years old, and run the farm. When we all left and got married our brother-in-law, who was a carpenter, built a new house for our mom at Canfield Lake where she spent her last sixteen years, still gardening

and making rugs with a loom. She lived to be 94 years old. My brother and his family still live on the farm home. Our days on the farm were quite the adventure I'll always treasure.

Lemonade, Lemonade Show Us Something If You're Not Afraid
By Bonnie J. Matyanczyk of Lake City, Michigan

When our family moved to Michigan, there were eleven children. When we were up north, there were three more boys born, that made seven girls and seven boys.

There were enough children for sides when we played games. Some of the games we played were "Crack the Whip" the last one at the end always yelling. "Inny Eye Over" where each team was on their side of the house. One team threw the ball over the house, the other tried to catch it and run around the house and tap a player of the other team, and if he did, they had to join them. We always had our own teams for baseball, volleyball, and a baseball game called "work up."

We had a game we played called "Lemonade." Two people picked the players for sides. You measured about twelve feet from each side, you said, "Lemonade, lemonade, show us something if you're not afraid." If the other side guessed what you were acting out, you had to run to their side before they tapped

Bonnie's dad at Andorfer's in 1947

your arm, you had to join them if they did. Today it's called charades!

Our family all had talents. Our dad played a harmonica and accordion. Mom played piano, mandolin, and organ. My mom once played the piano with the Toledo Symphony Orchestra. I have a pamphlet dated June 9, 1924.

I, Bonnie, played piano, sang in operettas in high school, sang in contests with a boy named Stormy, also wrote two songs. The hymn was called "Tell Your Troubles to Jesus" it won first prize at a fair. The other was called "Do You Remember" I had copyrights. I had a song sheet made of "Do You Remember?" and sold quite a few of them. Mr. Larry Collins helped me on the music. I also wrote "Christmastime" and the choir sang it at the high school Christmas program. I was so proud.

My sisters and brothers talents were; playing piano, organ, harmonica, guitar, accordion, singing, and yodeling. Many of them have passed on but I remember them and their talents fondly.

Remembering childhood is fun. Some of our treats would be a tablespoon of brown sugar on tin children's play dishes. Mom would put a bag of candy on top of the green wooden cupboard. You dare not touch it. Once a month we each got one piece of candy. We would be good.

Once a month, mom would line us up, we each had to take a tablespoon of castor oil, and we'd all run and vomit. Mom said it would clean our bodies of germs. Now children wouldn't understand our way of living. I think we appreciated things more.

My brothers would make scooters with wood, and use old skates for wheels. Our uncles would save the caps from pop and beer for the decorations.

When we would ice skate on our pond, we all used one skate. We also did the same on roller skates. It was no surprise when we would leave our shoes on so we would fit the skates.

Our cowboy and Indians was Roy Rogers and Gene Autry. The brothers made the guns out of wood, and we would use dad's big toolbox for our fortress. The ones who were Indians put feathers from the chickens in their cap.

Dad built a closet at the top of the stairs

Bonnie with her parents in 1982

for girl's clothes. Judy and I came out of the bedroom, and what did we see, but a man's shoes sticking out of the curtains. We were stunned! First, came a whimper from both, then a small scream, and down the stairs we ran. Of course, you know Harold got it from mom, so he stood in the closet for a while for punishment.

Another trick was played on us when Harold was very sick with a fever. Mom, Judy, and I would take turns checking on him. It was my turn, so when I walked into the bedroom, he wasn't breathing, his mouth was open, and he had his eyes rolled up! I yelled for mom and Judy, of course we were all crying. He had to give in and breathe. Mom was so scared and so were we.

Another event happened when our brother Terry was with us. Harold had it all planned that he would put ketchup all over Terry's body, and he would roll down the stairs and yell like he was hurt. It worked at first, and of course, we were scared. But mom tasted the supposed blood. She said "its ketchup" both got a spanking!

At times when we call Harold on the phone, we'll say, "What's new?" He'll answer laughing, "New York, New Jersey," funny, weird Harold.

Remember the song "Here we go to Grandma's House," well I loved to go to grandma Voll's any chance I had.

It felt like an honor to do anything for her. She lived in Toledo, Ohio in an apartment. And when you lived up north in Michigan, it was as if you lived in the wilderness. No electric, an outhouse with Sears and Roebuck paper to use, cook stove, pump outside. Well, grandma had all the conveniences. The milkman brought her milk in a glass quart jar, and she would let you have the cream from the lid. The bread man came with fresh wonder bread, and rolls. My favorite was a fresh glazed donut, um, um, good!

A man came around called "The Sheeney Man," he was spooky. There were two horses that pulled his wagon. On it was all kinds of utensils, almost everything but the kitchen sink, and we could put anything out in a bag for him to take. Our aunt had us so scared of him that we'd hide under the table, or under the buffet. His horn he blew sounded so scary. You could hear him coming, boy would we hide.

On Friday nights, she listened to "Inner Sanctum," "Lights Out," and the "Hit Parade," I loved music and you learned songs that way. When the first two programs were on, she turned out all her lights. I was cuddled on her lap and never moved, also I covered my eyes. You'd hear the sound of a squeaky door opening at the beginning of the show.

Jed's Bar was across from grandma's apartment on Bush Street. Grandma and I would sit on our chairs and watch people come out of the bar drunk and fighting. The police would come and take them to jail. I could hear the music playing loud. I thought it was fun to watch then, but I wouldn't now.

When you wound her victrola for her, went half a block to the store, dug up dandelion

Bonnie's mom and dad's 50th anniversary

greens, hung out her clothes, got to shine her silverware, admire her jewelry, take a fine tooth comb to scratch her head, empty the pan under her ice-box, these were the precious memories of grandma Voll's.

Grandma Voll stood upright and tall, a beautiful, wonderful, person.

My first love was so real. He was in the sixth grade and I was in the seventh. There was no one as handsome as Ralph Webster. No other girl could look at him or get near him in 1947.

For Valentine's Day, he bought me a card and signed, "I love you, Ralph." He also gave me a heart shaped bottle of perfume called "Blue Waltz." That was a treasure to me. Now they're bringing it back in magazines, and I bought some. When we would play "post office" we never called anyone but each other.

Mom had a Halloween party for me; she invited around twenty-four kids. Ralph and I never got away from each other, when we played the game "Wink Em" he held my shoulders so no one could get me to be it, when they winked at me.

In 1946, my parents moved from Holland, Ohio to Moorestown, Michigan. Ralph and I felt like our hearts were broken. I went back to Toledo, Ohio to work at Willy's Overland. A friend took me to Holland, Ohio to see a show, a drive-in. Ralph was there, in his army uniform. I thought I'd faint. He followed us to my grandma's house. The friend left, and Ralph walked me to the door and kissed me goodnight. What a thrill. We wrote when he got back to his station, then, he met a girl, and I got a Dear John letter.

Through the years, our mates both passed on and we got in touch with each other. The story doesn't end sadly. Ralph and I talked on the phone, e-mailed each other, sent letters, and had picnics. Then, he had a stroke, but we still talked on the phone. His last words to me were "I love you, girl." Never will I forget Ralph. "Girl" was my nickname. He was my "first love."

Christmas, was a special time, especially the precious times with my mother. She passed away March 1, 1987. Some Christmases ago dad made one of us girls a double-decker bed out of wood for our dolls, and wouldn't you know it, mom made a pretty dolly quilt for the bed; she even did crocheting around the edge.

I'll never forget my last Christmas with

my precious mother. Mama only had two months to live, but her courage was something to see. She was worried the gifts wouldn't be wrapped. I just knew those precious, soft and aging hands would help me do all the wrapping, even though her hands were tired and shaky. You see there were forty-eight grandchildren and thirty-four great grandchildren. There were also six sons and their wives, six daughters and their husbands that is twenty-four more, and also dad. We had to wrap one hundred and seven gifts!

Mama's attitude was remarkable. She wouldn't go to bed until midnight two nights in a row to make sure all the presents were wrapped, and every gift she picked would be what they wanted. I assured her they would love everything. I was amazed how she had enough strength to do this to please everyone. I knew my mama was a strong woman. She would tackle any task.

Three brothers arrived from Montana with their families, one night when she was very ill, at Christmas time. She had all us girls, daughters, and daughter-in-laws, stand at the foot of her bed and sing Christmas carols. She joined us singing the carols. What a mama!

This last Christmas wasn't a sad one with mama. I have so many beautiful memories stored away in my heart forever, of my times with mama.

My friend through grade school was Irene Twigg. In high school, it was Lois Coon and Alice Wright. We were nicknamed "The Three Musketeers."

Now my daughter Lisa is a secretary in the new high school. I still love to hear the hustling and bustling of the children in the hallways, their laughter, the smell of crayons, see the puppy love, smell of blackboards and erasers.

Up north as we grew older, a man who had a house in Stittsville, Michigan, would bring us boxes and bags of clothes. It was like Christmas in June or July. We were so happy to try on these clothes, new coats, shoes, and dresses.

As we all got married, us girls would get together with bags of clothes, shoes, and purses. It got to be a habit, so we added wigs, straw hats, then we started to bring masks, funny glasses and whatever we could think of.

Now that we're older, we five girls have a bingo party once a year at one of our places.

Sometimes we all wear pajamas. Sometimes it lasts one day, sometimes two. We have a blast, and we all take home a lot of gifts!

Little Pins Got in My Pocket
By Penny Kipley of Traverse City, Michigan
Born 1928

My parents moved our family to Wallin, Michigan when my sister was six months old, and I was two and a half years old, in the spring of 1930. We lived for a couple of years in an apartment above a grocery store in Wallin. I started kindergarten in the little one room schoolhouse on the banks of the Betsie River. I was the only one in kindergarten, and my teacher was Carl Lindy, son of Berga Lindy, who owned the grocery store in nearby Thompsonville, and later became the probate judge in Beulah.

We had a Christmas program, and since I was the only one in kindergarten, I had a short poem to recite. "I'm not very big, I'm really quite small, but I wish a Merry Christmas to one and all." Well, I looked out at the sea of faces, and completely lost it. Carl Lindy was behind the curtain holding up a Hershey bar, and when I saw the chocolate I suddenly remembered my lines, thus a chocoholic was born.

It was the next spring when we moved to a house on Webber road. Chris and Theresa Webber lived about a block down the road from us. They had three children, and one on the way. When he was born, they named him Wayne. My mom, sister, and I went down the road to meet Wayne Webber. Theresa was showing us all the neat things they had received for the new baby, including a package of gold safety pins. Somehow, those little pins got in my pocket, and when we got home, my mother discovered I had them. Well, she proceeded to let me know that what I did was stealing, and marched me right back down the road to return them. I never took anything again!

When Wayne was five years old, the family moved to the Detroit area. Chris worked in the auto plants. They would come back every summer and always came to visit my mom. I never saw Wayne, and never heard what became of him, until it was in the news that Wayne and Joan Webber had donated eight million dollars to Munson Hospital. Wow, I stole his baby pins!

A few years later, we moved to the next road over, highway 669, about three miles north of Thompsonville. I went to school in town, until I was in the fifth grade. When we moved again, further north on 669, I had to change schools. Now I went to a little one-room schoolhouse, called Rust School, named after Charley and Emily Rust, who lived on the road of the same name.

Rust school ran out of money when I finished eighth grade, and we were bused to Thompsonville until I finished the tenth grade. When they ran out of money, we were bused seventeen miles to Benzonia School. In the winter, we got on the bus in the dark, and got home in the dark. I graduated in 1946 from Benzonia, with a class of twenty-one girls and five boys. When boys were old enough, they went into the services.

When we walked to Rust school in the winter, the snow banks were so high we had to walk on the top, and could touch the telephone wires. Of course, we were told not to touch the wires. I guess none of us ever did because we all survived.

When we went to Thompsonville, the bus picked us up, and one very cold day the bus didn't come. There was something special at school that day, maybe it was dress rehearsal for the Christmas program. We decided to walk, and stopped at each house along the way to get warm. When we got to school, we were told the buses were frozen. When they got them started, they would take us home, because the pipes were frozen in the school, and it was closed. We later learned that it was 40 degrees below zero…brrr.

My best friend Margie and I were so upset when we were sent to Benzonia. We did not want to go to a larger school. In Thompsonville, ninth through twelfth grades were in two rooms in the basement. At Benzonia, we had to change rooms for every class, so when it came time to order class rings, we decided to order our rings from the Montgomery Ward catalog, for $5.96 with T.H.S. instead of B.H.S. They still let us graduate.

There was nothing doing in Northern Michigan in 1946. My grandparents took me to Detroit, and I worked at Henry Ford Hospital, and then for a couple of doctors, and finally, found my niche as a telephone operator, until I married, and had my first daughter in 1950.

No one in those days had any money, and there was no way I could go to nursing school, thus the hospital and doctors filled a need, but I only made $20 a week, and gave my grandma $6 a week for room and board.

In Thompsonville in the summer, we picked fruit, cherries, strawberries, even cucumbers and beans because there was a pickle factory in town. One summer, my friend Margie, my sister, and I rode in the rumble seat of our teacher's model A or T, and drove to Dayton Willard's orchard on the north shore of Crystal Lake to pick cherries. It was cold in the morning going, but coming home it would be very hot. So, because we were sticky from cherries and spray, we often stopped and took a dip in Crystal Lake before we headed home. One day my mom asked us to bring home a lug (25-30 lbs.) of cherries so she could can them for winter. At that time, salt and sugar came in brown paper bags that looked alike. Somehow, the bags got mixed up, and mom canned the whole lug of cherries with salt. Later, when she opened up the first jar and tasted them, she cried.

In the fall, anyone who wanted to pick

Evelyn Marie age 15 months

apples or pick up potatoes could be excused from school. In the summer, there were free movies in town, and everyone would take chairs or blankets and sit on the ground to see the movie. My favorites were Lassie or Roy Rogers and Dale Evans. Gas was rationed and we didn't have a car, but Margie's parents had a car, and no gas. My stepfather was a farmer, and had gas delivered to a 50-gallon drum. If we were good, he would fill a can with two gallons, and we would take it to Margie's, and go to the movie. One day, Margie and I got into an argument, and she knocked my glasses off, I said, "Just see if we bring gas down tonight to go to the movie!" time came to go, and Joanie and I trotted down the road as if nothing happened.

When I was a teenager, I babysat all night for a neighbors two children, while he and his wife went to Yuma to play his clarinet in a band. He would pick up the piano player, Alma Rensherger, who was the postmistress, and play until 12:00 pm. I stayed all night for thirty-five cents, and an orange. When I was older I went to the dances with them, and his wife had to stay home with the kids. I loved the dancing because when we lived in Wallin the dance hall was directly across the street. Mom would take blankets and pillows for Joanie and me, and put us up on the stage, and we were supposed to go to sleep. Sometimes we did, but I watched the dancing, and that's where I first saw square dancing. So, in 1975 my husband and I took lessons, and have danced all across the country from Maryland to California.

In 1938 my brother Ed was born. I was nine years old, and the oldest, so I had to go to the closest neighbor to have them call the doctor. Ed was born at 11:30 pm, the night before my 9th birthday. I was terrified because, I had to go through the swamp and I'm sure I ran all the way, knowing there were wild animals in the swamp. The doctor was called and he stopped at the neighbors took me home.

When Ed was a toddler, he followed Margie, Joanie and me all over. We would do everything to get away from him, we'd run out in the hayfield and hide in the tall grass and not make a sound, little Ed would always find us and grin from ear to ear.

When I graduated in 1946, my dad gave me a watch because I wanted to be a nurse (I knew there was no way that would ever happen, but I got a watch). Margie's mom gave me a bottle of "Evening in Paris" cologne, and

The Kipley's in 2011

mom gave me my first lipstick. There was no money for gifts. There was very little money for food. We ate a lot of beans, applesauce, potatoes and anything we grew on the farm.

After I went to work, I always felt bad that I wasn't able to send money home. There wasn't much left of a twenty-dollar bill after I gave my grandma six dollars, bus fare, lunch money, and clothes. I was lucky my grandma sewed almost all my clothes.

During the war years, so many things were rationed and we had coupons for sugar, meat, coffee, gas, and shoes. My grandparents didn't use all their coupons for shoes, and we were a family of six so they would send us their coupons. I remember neighbors who used to hoard sugar in a brand new garbage can. We all hoped the ants would get in it! They loved lemon pie! Margie was their niece, and she made a great lemon pie, her uncle bragged about that. That's why we wished ants would get into the sugar, because he was such a braggart!

My mom cooked on a wood stove, and to this day every time I use the microwave, I think of her. She also did the laundry on a scrub board using Fels Naptha bar soap and hung laundry on the clothesline outside, summer and winter. She didn't have electricity until after I left home in 1946. She baked all our bread and on Fridays, we could smell the fresh bread and baked beans when we got off the bus, yum!

My mom passed away at 54 years old of cancer. She had a very hard life and never complained. Her name was Florence Swisher, God bless her!

My good friend Teeny Maginity's father was our mailman and when Crystal Lake was frozen, he had a fishing shanty on it. Sometimes after school, Teeny and I would walk down the hill to Beulah and out onto the ice and have a cold sandwich with her dad and get back to Beulah in time to catch the train (around 11:00 pm) to Thompsonville. The next day in school, needless to say, we nodded off more than once. We usually did this Friday nights.

I remember another super cold day when my mom said I would have to pump water for the cattle. I had no mittens, so when I put my hands on the pump handle, it took the skin right off. I went into the house crying and I said, "That God damn pump," and my mom said, "What did you say?" and I repeated it, and she said "Do you know what that means?" and I said, "It means I hate that GD pump!" She said, "Honey, it means –God, destroy this pump. Then what would we do without water?" I had learned another lesson from my dear mom.

We have now lived in Traverse City for thirty-four years.

✓ Frozen Cream in the Milk Bottle
By Laura Weighman of Bellaire, Michigan

The good old days started for me in Mid-Michigan, at least that's what I thought it was called. I was born in Saginaw, Michigan. My dad died when I was 4 years old. When I was about nine, I would come home from school and go upstairs and say my prayers for the people who had polio. I felt that must be such a terrible thing for anyone to have. I prayed that no one in my family would get it.

I always liked to get up early because we had a milkman who pulled his milk wagon by a horse. I liked to see the horse and I would beat everyone to the frozen cream that popped out of the top of the bottle.

After breakfast, I would sometimes curl my hair a little. We had a curling iron that you warmed up on the burner. Saturday we would heat up the bath water and dump it in the tub. Mom lined us up from the cleanest to the dirtiest.

Saturday was also movies, depending on which theatre we went to. Northside theatre was 9 cents and The Janes was 12 cents. The Temple, which was a little fancier with red velvet curtains, cost a little more. My parents usually picked The Janes because of transportation. Gas was expensive at 10 cents per gallon. I like The Northside because they 3 movies and The Jane's because they had the News Reels. The News Reels gave us all of the information on the wars.

I listened to the radio at nighttime for the radio show and sometimes I played records on our old time Victrola. I also liked listening to the ball games in the afternoon.

The most important thing back in those days is that the teachers were allowed to teach about God. The singing teacher taught us about God and taught us what some of the words in the Christmas songs meant.

In later years, we moved out into the country. We had a cow, a garden, and a player piano. We had a great time playing that piano and singing.

Well, I am running out of time. I hope you have as much fun reading this as I did writing it.

✓ Springtime Blizzard
By Judith Ann (Lewandowski) Smith of
Flint, Michigan
Born 1947

As long as I can remember whenever the subjects of giving birth or snowstorms came up, my mother always told this story.

The year was 1947. The small town of Posen, Michigan, located toward the tip of the eastside of the Lower Peninsula also known as the mitten of Michigan, located in Presque Isle County was hit with another major snowstorm. It was the end of March and our town of Posen was getting slammed for the second time in three months with a major blizzard. Posen had already experienced a terrific snowstorm in January 1947.

My mother was about to give birth to her first child. Her due date was March 27th. My parents, Dominic and Kay Lewandowski, lived in the small farming community of Posen, Michigan on North Grand Lake Highway, with my Grandma Rose. This is my dad's mom. Rogers City, located on the shores of Lake Huron, was the nearest town. Dr. Edward Arscott's office was located in Rogers City. Dr. Arscott was my mom's doctor. There was no hospital in Rogers City. Just a maternity home where women went to have their babies. Alpena was the nearest town with a hospital, but it is twenty-five miles away, so they decided to use the maternity home in Rogers City. That was the plan, until the snowstorm hit Posen.

Since my mom's due was near and the storm started, my parents decided to go stay at my Uncle Benny and Aunts Martha's house at 695 South Lake Street in Rogers City until it was time for my birth. My aunt and uncle talked my parents into having their baby that would be me at their house. Also, Dr. Edward Arscott was able to be at the house for my birth. Finally the big day arrived, Wednesday, April 2nd at 5:30 P.M., I was born, Judith Ann Lewandowski.

The blizzard was so bad that it took the Presque Isle County Road Commission weeks to clear all the roads. We stayed in Rogers City for two weeks. We could not get home by car yet, so I was brought home by sleigh and horses. At this time, the main road US 23 was cleared, but the other roads to my Grandma Rose's house were still impassable. After two weeks, my mom's dad—Grandpa John Pokorski met them at the junction of US 23 and M 65. He was safely able to get the new family back home to Grandma Rose's house.

Four siblings were soon to follow. Their births were not as exciting as mine was; they were born in the hospital in Alpena.

Berend and Grace Gernaat Story
By Ken Gernaat of Lake City, Michigan
Born 1936

They had six children: Minnie born September 12, 1894—died May 7. 1975, spouse Albert Vis—died December 18, 1972, Alice born 1896—died September 13, 1910, Kate born 1898—died December 6, 1918,

Albert born June 26, 1902—died September 15, 1980, Helena Hoekwater—died July 9, 1956, Herman born December 1, 1908—died April 28, 1990, Minnie Borgman—died May 28, 2003, and William born 1911—died 1911.

Berend was commonly known as Ben born 26 May 1871 was the son of Albert born 29 August 1839 and married Tjaakje Elderman in 1865. Ben was the fourth child of eight. There were three brothers and four sisters and they lived in a small house in Oostwald near Germany. They were fairly close to a Dutch Reformed Church, a school, and a cemetery where his mom and dad are buried. The house he was born and grew up in is still being used, has been refurbished, and looks great.

In 1893, Ben was 22 years old and the economy was bad in the Netherlands, I know nothing of his personal life except that he had a girlfriend. The story is that they wanted to get married but the culture was different so this was a problem.

Well the next fact of his life was Ben and Grace Gremmer his friend boarded a ship to New York U.S.A. they arrived in May of 1893. They traveled to Michigan, probably by train and wound up in Missaukee County. Think about this move at 22 years old, not married, going to a different country with a different language, leaving family and friends. He didn't know anyone in America that I heard of. What do you call people like this, crazy. Some say they were adventure some, others say they had guts, some say they were in love, or had a vision. Whatever it was, I for one am glad they did it.

I talked to Ben in 1960 to find out about his move but I didn't have a recorder and he was 90, I waited too late, but I will tell the story as best I can. Ben and Grace got married in September of 1893. As near as I can tell they lived on a 160 acre parcel of land where the big Gernaat farm is today on Stoney Corner Road. I went to the county office in Lake City and found the 160-acre parcel that was given to Jacob Laymen, a military person as bounty and in 1867. He then sold it to Delos A. Blodgett, a lumber baron and probably took the trees off the land. Possibly Ben bought 120 acres before he came to America from a post card that showed the land in a winter scene with snow. It looked flat but when Ben got here in the spring, it was all stumps. We could not find a record of when Ben bought it, but are quite sure he lived in a cabin on this property when they got married.

Ben worked in a logging camp somewhere for a number of years. It was a tough life and hard work. I'm guessing Ben worked for the lumber camp to build a house and a barn, where he raised a family. His first child was a girl named Minnie born 12 September 1894. The second was a girl named Alice born 1896 then came Kate born July 8, 1898. On June 26 came Albert the first boy, 1 December 1908 came Herman and then in 1911 came William who died 1911.

In 1912, Ben bought an 80-acre parcel from John Lutke that joined his land to the north for $750. From what I remember about Ben, he always walked with a limp supposedly one leg was shorter than the other but it didn't slow him down. Because of the primitive life style, a lot of disease was around and caused death. It affected the family of Ben and Grace as well, Alice died September 14, 1910 at age 14 from typhoid fever. Kate was a schoolteacher in a school close by the farm and she got the flu at 20 years old and died December 6 1918.

One story was that an Indian was hanging around the house, he and Ben got in a fight, and Ben killed the Indian.

Ben and family grew the farm with horses, cows, chickens, and pigs to where it was a successful farm. In 1938, he bought a new Chevy that is still in the Gernaat family. Ken's son, Kurt has it and it has 39,000 original miles on it. Ben's son Herman took over the farm. And then his son Gerry grew the farm into a large dairy with over 1800 cows. Now his son Chadwick is taking over, if only Ben could see it now. Ben helped his son Albert (my Dad) get started on a farm in Aetna Township in 1938.

Ben and Grace moved from the farm in 1946 to Vogel Center to retire, but continued to help Herman on the farm. Grace died March 7 1959. Ben died September 8, 1961 at 91years old and never drew any Social Security.

I can't wait to see him again on the other side. Grace was born on 17 May 1861 in the Netherlands to Stoffel Gremmer the first child of three. While Ben was working at the lumber camp, Grace was starting to grow the farm. They were both hard workers.

The SheeNee Man Summer 1955
Submitted by Carole Lynn Orr as told to by
James Orr of Posen, Michigan
Born 1944

Some things just don't change that much… and taking out the trash is one of them. For the past 50-odd years… we've all endured this dreaded word on a weekly basis… "trash"… and as kids, we knew it was time to head for curbside.

Today, a rather humongous truck rolls slowly down the street… grabbing trash containers with octopus-like arms and sweeping them into the back of the truck. One good shake… and the containers are right back where they were… empty.

But that wasn't how it was when I was a kid… we couldn't wait for trash day. It was, quite possibly, the best day of the week… because, after it was at curbside, we'd pick a house and wait patiently on the front porch… eager to hear the eventful sound of what soon would follow.

Finally… we would hear… clop, clop, clop… his one-horse wagon would be making its way down the middle of the street…eyes peering left, then right.

And then he would stop at a particular trash pile… The "SheeNee" man had cometh. And, while he was sifting through the pile of rubble, we'd all grab our carrots or apples and run to the wagon. With rhythmic anticipation, we waited our turn to feed his horse… petting him and wishing he was our very own. He wasn't a trash-wagon horse to us… with his coat always perfectly groomed, he was grandiose in stature … he was our "Black Beauty."

The SheeNee man would return to the wagon, broken toaster in hand, always smiling. Pointing to the toaster, we'd ask him… "What are you going to do with that"? He'd say, "I'm going to see if I can make it new again." *(He could fix anything)*

He'd put the toaster carefully in the back of his wagon, climb aboard, and grab the reins… "Move it Charlie"… and down the street they'd go.

We'd all go back to the porch… and tell of how "Charlie" liked "My apple best."

The SheeNee man would be back next week… most likely, the toaster would be by his side on the seat… all shiny and looking like new… price tag affixed.

And we'd get to do it all over again… life was good.

Coal Dust Dead of Winter, 1954

Today… most Americans can sit in the comfort of a warm and cozy home… enjoying whatever pleasure they choose… and not give a single thought about how that home got so "warm and cozy". We just dial a number on our Thermostat… and our home is warmed to that temperature… done deal.

To most Americans, heat, is just a routine "utility" payment… nothing more.

But it wasn't always as simple as that… not at our house… not in 1954 anyway.

We didn't have a Natural Gas line to bring gas to our furnace… mainly because we didn't have a gas-fired furnace… we had coal. And the coal wasn't delivered via an automated pipeline delivery system… it was brought to us by truck.

Coal delivery day was usually during the dead of winter… it was always early on Saturday morning (bath day) and always a 3-man job. My brother and I would handle the basement task… while the driver would unload the coal from his truck.

First… we would shovel away any snow from the coal bin's delivery chute window… then remove the window. Next… we would guide the coal delivery-chute through the window until it was about a third of the way into the bin. Then the driver would throw us the bottom end of the tarp *(used to cover the delivery-chute so the coal dust stayed pretty much contained.)* The bottom end of the tarp was weighted, so it didn't flop around during the delivery.

Finally… we'd get our scoop shovels and yell for the driver to "Bring it"… and in the coal came. As it hit the floor, we'd frantically shovel it under the chute and into the corner of the bin… this activity is where we'd turn ourselves into "coal dust magnets" and pretty much end up black as the coal itself before we were through.

As the coal-bin filled… we would have to bang on the chute with a shovel to let the driver know that the chute had to be brought up a few feet… this, depending on how much we were getting this time, would occur two or three times.

After our load was fully delivered, the driver would pull the chute out from the window and then put the window back in place. I was always the one that ran upstairs and outside to retrieve our free "furnace sack of coal"… simply a potato sack full of coal… it was heavy, but that was my job. The driver would leave and we'd fill the furnace from the "free sack" first… then my brother would set the air-intake cover-plate *(air damper)* to the proper notch… and we were done… almost.

We kept a whiskbroom in the coal bin and spent another 10 minutes "dusting each other off" before we were allowed to go back upstairs. And then it was straight to the bathtub… my brother first because he was older… I had to wait at the kitchen table, where Mom had put newspapers on a chair for me.

After our baths… and clean clothes… we'd all gather by the warmest register, the one in the parlor. *(right above the furnace)* Since the coal furnace didn't have a modern "forced-air" blower… the heat was gravity channeled through the ducts… and the parlor room was the closest room to the furnace… it was always the warmest room in the house.

In the morning, my brother would go back to the basement and "feed the furnace" more coal… and before bed, the furnace would get fed again. This routine would continue from the first sign of winter *(usually when the temps got down to the low fifties)* right on through until mid-Spring, when the temps got back up again.

Also, important to note… since the degree of heat wasn't thermostatically regulated, the air-intake damper was never to be moved once it was set. *(Mom did, however, have my brother open it up a little whenever she had company.)*

Full-Service Stations Circa… Early '60s

Suppose we were driving along… and noticed that we were low on gas. Wouldn't it be nice if we didn't have to give a thought to the torrential rain or blowing snow or freezing temp outside. If we could simply pull into our local gas station and out would come an attendant. "Yes Ma'am" he'd say. "What can I get for you today?"

And, while sitting in our warm car, the attendant would fill our gas tank, even check our oil; check our battery; check our tire pressures; and clean our windshield… all because we were a "customer."

Yep… that sure would be nice…

76

Well… that's exactly how it was back when I was a teen driver… even into my early '20s.

During my final year of high school, I worked evenings at J & D Standard station… a FULL service station that routinely did all of those things.

When a gas customer pulled up to the pumps, I would greet them respectfully and begin the ritual. While the gas was pumping, I'd check the customer's oil, check the Electrolyte level in the battery, check all tires for proper air pressure… and fill as required. I'd check the brake fluid and wipers too… just because.

Then… I'd make the windshield spotlessly clean.

It didn't matter if it was pouring rain, snowing like the dickens or cold as heck… I still did my job…with a smile.

If the customer was a little low on oil or battery fluid, even windshield-washer fluid, I'd top them off. Hoping, by doing so, the customer would return to this station… and maybe tell a friend or two.

When we started accepting credit cards, my job became a little harder… now I had to take a customer's credit card, fill out the credit slip, process the card through the credit card machine and return to the customer for signature. Took a little longer than simply "swiping" your credit card at today's modern gas pumps.

Our work ethic was simple… "Perform the attendant's tasks without making it look like you're ticked about having to do it." Pretty simple… yet sometimes difficult to do. Especially when a customer would roll down his window and say, "Hey… you missed a spot"… pointing to a miniscule bug spot on his windshield… or an iota piece of ice.

I remember some of the girls, in my high school classes, talking about getting gas after school at a particular station. They were going to where the "cutest guy ever" worked as an attendant. I guess that's only fair… I know some of my buddies had found a Clark station that had a "cutie" of a girl for an attendant… it all evens out I guess.

Then came along the front runner of today's gas station…"The Self-Serve" station. Back then, there weren't any convenience stores associated with the Self-Serve stations… those came a little later. But, it didn't take long for the Self-Serves to catch on… mainly because their gas prices were lower. They didn't have to pay an "attendant" to deliver it… so they could lower their gas prices and still maintain their profit level.

Not so very long after the Self-Serves emerged… so did the associative convenience store. After all, when a customer had to go inside to pay for his gas… he'd maybe pick up a soda while doing it. Made good sense… still does.

The main drawback to getting your gas at a self-serve was, of course, you then had to perform all of the tasks that an attendant would normally perform. But, to save some bucks at the pump, there wasn't a lot of complaining about that.

I quit working at J & D Standard (now Amoco) just before I graduated… but I could tell his business had already declined… kind of made me sad.

About a year after graduation, I went to visit Doug (the "D" of J & D.) I couldn't believe my eyes when I went into the station. There… a whole new checkout counter and several food shelves were in place. He had "modernized."

That "modernization" cost the day attendant his job… but Doug was still in business… and doing quite well as a "Self-Serve" station.

Today, we all pump our own gas; clean our own windshield; check our own oil and tire pressures… it's just a "normal" thing to do. Albeit not pleasant when the temps are at freezing… or it's coming down like Niagara Falls. Or you've pulled into a station that requires "pre-payment" before you can operate the pump. Inevitably, that results in a "double" walk inside… because the amount you've given the cashier will not be the same as the amount you've pumped… never is. I try to steer clear of the "pre-pay" stations.

√ **Big Families**
By Kathy Mendoza of Harbor Springs,
Michigan
Born 1937

In Cross Village, Michigan, in Northern Emmet County where I was born and raised, many of the families were so much larger than they are today. Being mostly farmers, as well as Catholics, our part of the state was well

Kathy's mother, Lois Keller making pies

their army cots in the living room at night for a place to sleep. For a while, we four youngest kids, all girls, slept together in a double bed, two on each end. I expect you can imagine the giggling that went on during those nights, and the cover pulling, especially on winter nights.

Sometimes when the summer heat was on, my older brothers were allowed to take a blanket and pillow and go sleep on the grass out in the yard. Ma wouldn't let us girls sleep out, though. Maybe that's why when I was grown and married I loved to go camping.

When it came to eating supper, though we did have a big farm table, we still ate in shifts whenever most of us were at home. Pa sat at the head of the table in "Pa's chair" and the youngest kids lined up on the homemade benches at the side of the table. After we were finished, Ma would sit down with the older kids after everyone was served.

When it came to clothing, all of us younger kids usually wore hand-me-downs, which the older kids had outgrown. Ma did a lot of mending, to be sure.

When we four little girls were big enough to join 4-H, Ma couldn't very well afford to buy the green and white outfits for us. Instead she bought some green dye and dyed each of us one of our skirts to wear with a while blouse, which was what the girls in our school were wearing for 4-H anyway. We loved learning the 4-H songs.

Several things were nice about coming from a large family. An important and fun thing in our big family was singing in harmony together, as Ma taught us to do. She was in the adult choir at church and as each

populated. Many of the families had eight or ten children, and yet those weren't the biggest families. One family in our parish had fifteen children and one had sixteen, so our family with seven daughters and six sons wasn't an exception. There were two other families who, like my parents, had thirteen children.

This is so different from today that one of the newcomers to this area asked me, "How on earth did your mother ever keep you clean with that many children and no running water or electricity?"

The answer wasn't that difficult. We hauled water in barrels from a neighbor's well. We also caught rainwater in barrels, which sat under the eaves trough. At times, we even melted snow for water when the snow was too deep to get to the neighbor's well. We heated our bath water on the kitchen wood stove and poured it into one of Ma's laundry tubs. In warm weather, we did plenty of swimming in the creek and in Lake Michigan, always taking soap along. We didn't feel we had it rough, as we had nothing with which to compare our style of living; all of our friends lived as we did. We all grew up with outhouses.

Sleeping arrangements did, at times, get crowded in a big family. I remember my mother portioning off different areas of the upstairs by hanging blankets over poles hung from the rafters to give us more privacy. When some of my older brothers came home to stay for a while from the Army, or from jobs downstate, sometimes they would set up

Lois and John Keller

of us girls got old enough, we got to join the children's choir. The boys all liked to sing, too and most of us learned to play instruments as our parents did. Another way having plenty of brother and sisters helped was when the older ones were studying at home; we got to learn right along with them, so we always had a good head start in school. Maybe the biggest thing, we always had someone to play games with.

And now, in our final years, though we have lost some siblings, we are not yet alone as those who had only one brother or sister, so I do believe the number thirteen has been lucky for me and mine.

√ Going North
By Jim Kent Atlanta, Michigan
Submitted by Maureen Kent

When I was seven years old, my folks decided to go north; so my dad bought an old horse, as I remember, that looked like Barney Google's horse, "Spark Plug," and an almost new wagon. He bent strips of wood for the roof, boiled paraffin wax, painted it on canvas, and stretched it over the roof he made. We now had a covered wagon to travel in. Our neighbors also got a horse and wagon and followed us up where we now live in Atlanta, Michigan.

We took all summer getting here, but we did a lot of camping out. We stopped at most lakes to fish and we picked a lot of blackberries along the road. I remember one-day close to West Branch, Michigan, when we camped by a small creek, my dad went to get a pail of water. He was gone almost an hour, but finally he came back with the water. He said he was trying to catch some trout out of in the pail but they kept flopping out, so he made a net of an old burlap sack and put a hoop around the top with a handle on it and went back to try his luck. As I remember, he caught some real nice trout for supper.

A few days later, we were driving along the road and met two men with a horse and wagon. We wanted a better horse so they traded right there on the road. Their horse was a nice looker but the wagon wasn't worth much. Our wagon still looked good but old "Spark Plug" was about worn out. That same night, (we didn't know what time) they came

to our camp and took the horse we got from them and left our old wagon. They were very thoughtful because they left our old horse tied to a tree!

We kept coming north until we got about twelve or fifteen miles from Atlanta. We found a log cabin on a lake not far off the road and moved in. My dad got a job in the woods cutting timber and my mother got a job in the cook camp, taking us three kids along. I can never forget the way those lumberjacks ate! They would take their potatoes, meat pie, bread, and desert, or whatever it might be, and pour Karo syrup over everything they had on their plate! I don't know what nationality they were, but they sure had a tougher stomach that I ever had.

One day my dad and his partner, who came up with us, took his horse and wagon and went duck hunting at some lake. They tied the horse to a tree and went off hunting. Well, they didn't come home that night nor the next day, so my mother told the boss of the camp about it, so he took his old Model T Ford and started looking for them. He found the horse standing in a hole that he had pawed out of the ground. My dad's hat and his partners were by the lake not far off road so he decided they were lost. He got on an old logging road and started looking for them. My dad's partner had a brother-in-law who had come up to see him and he had gone with them.

My dad told us later they had slept on the ground with some boughs under them to make it softer. During the night, they heard coyotes howling. Two of them can make enough noise to make anyone's hair stand up and if you never heard them before, you might flip your lid! They sounded like a dozen wolves. Well, I think this fellow flipped his lid as he got up about midnight and took off, running through the woods, leaving the other two where they were! It just happened he came out on the old log road where the fellow with the Model T was looking for them.

The boss saw him come out of the woods ahead of him and tried to catch up to him, but he started running for the woods so the camp boss stopped the car and ran him down and tried to find out where he might find the other two. He said he didn't remember anything, so the boss took him back to camp where we stayed. As soon as he got out of the car he yelled for his wife to start packing their suitcases, and that they were leaving for Flint right now!

They went to the little shed where the train would pick up anyone who flagged them down. We never saw them again. They didn't stay long enough to find out if my dad or his partner got out or not. The men finally came out over by Onaway on the fourth day. They said that they had got lost while hunting and for over four days they ate mostly wintergreen berries. Onaway is about twenty miles north of Atlanta.

✓ Chicken Foot Soup
By Christophe Chagnon of Onaway, Michigan

On a June afternoon in 1963, my siblings, and I had been playing outside all day and we were famished. Mom stood on the back porch and called us in for dinner. We took our seats at the table anxiously waiting the wonderfully smelling meal that she had prepared on the old wood-burning cook stove.

Mom was always trying to be creative but frugal with dinner. She was raised in the Corktown district of Detroit during the Great Depression when food and money were hard to come by. She made meals from the simplest fare, like chicken gizzard stew, goulash from the poorest of beef parts, and head cheese from even more unpleasant ingredients. That afternoon she had made a special concoction that she hoped would become a new entre on her weekly menu.

Mom lowered the heavy cast iron door of the stove and slid a heaping pan of golden skinned, baked chicken legs onto a thick towel, and set it on the dinner table. A swirled mound of mashed potatoes over flowed from the bowl's rim. Gleaming in a buttery wash, freshly baked bread sat unsliced on a wooden cutting board next to a tub of pale, yellow, homemade butter. Then, she returned to the stovetop, and retrieved a cast iron pot. Setting it squarely in the center of the table we waited and wondered in great anticipation what gourmand delight would frighten us this evening. We felt the ache of hunger within our empty stomachs but were made to wait. Mom's strict devotion to Catholic rules required us to pause until grace was said. Mom removed her checkered apron and hung it over a cupboard door.

We lowered our heads and recited, "Bless us O Lord, and these thy gifts which we are about to receive from thy bounty, through Christ, our Lord, Amen!" Finishing with a hasty sign of the cross, we filled our plates with succulent drumsticks covered in crusty corn flakes, fresh butter on bread, and mashed potatoes with a rich pool of volcanic, melting butter streaming over its peak. Then, as proudly as a kid displaying a completed model airplane, Mom lifted the lid of the cast iron pot and dug deep into the caldron with a wooden ladle. Out from the pot rose a claw, and then another that revealed a boney, scaly appendage that was held together with sinew and skin. It was chicken foot soup. She, watchfully, poured the pungent broth and feet into each of our bowls, and with a bright smile she said, "Wha da ya think, boys? Chicken foot soup! Umm." Without pause, she sat at the table, and carried on as though nothing was unusual.

Through our protesting turned up noses, and profound "ew's," the scary entre was never included on the weekly menu again.

✓ Fixing Mr. Doright
Mr. Hall, our high school principal, warned me and my friends, Larry, Jimmy, and Roy many times about cutting class and skipping school. But it was a warm October day in 1968, when Roy, and the boys pulled into my driveway with his orange 1960 Chevy panel wagon to pick me up for school. All of us were adventurous sixteen year olds always looking for a break from school. Roy screeched the 'three on the tree' shifter into first gear and we headed up M-33 Highway towards school.

Knowing the consequences that awaited us if we skipped again, Roy was tempted by the warm breeze and bright October sun, and defiantly offered a tantalizing suggestion.

"You guys wanna skip and go climb the fire tower by Atlanta?"

"You know what's gonna' happen if we do," I said uncomfortably from the backseat.

"Yeah, we'll get smacked with Mr. Doright!" Larry laughed referring to Mr. Hall's heavy oak paddle that was perforated with hundreds of holes allowing it to travel faster.

"Don't worry, guys, I've got a plan to fix

him," Roy promised.

"Oh yeah, what is it," I asked.

"We're gonna' stuff a stack of lined paper in ar' pants and we won't feel dang a thing," Roy revealed.

So we fell to the temptation of fun that we were going to have climbing the old fire tower, and trusted Roy's solution to 'fix' the wrath of Mr. Doright who we were certain to face the following day.

We sped past the school's entrance on M-33 laughing without remorse, and joked we about the other students that were stuck in school on the beautiful day.

The old, worn out panel wagon puffed clouds of grey smoke that made its way into the cab, and our eyes burned. We bounced and rocked on our way up the long potholed two-tracker that led to the fire tower.

The State of Michigan had condemned the decrepit, rusty tower years earlier and the first two flights of steps had been removed. We had to make a harrowing climb along the framework to get to the remaining steps that led to its top. The other boys were raised on farms, and I was a naïve 'city slicker' kid living in town. They had climbed the tower before and weren't afraid of heights, but I was scared to death traversing the rusted framework.

"Ay, I can see Onaway High School," Larry's voice echoed above the scraggly Jack Pine trees below, "Suckers!" he called out with his hands surrounding his mouth.

"There's Atlanta," Roy said pointing to the south.

I clung to the tower's frame like a scared kitten stuck in a tall tree. They stood high above me on the rotted wooden deck and teased me.

Sensing my fear, the farm boys held the feeble railing and shifted their weight back and forth causing the tower to creak and groan as though it was going collapse around me. The tower gyrating like a flagpole in a stiff wind. In spite of my begging pleas to stop, they continued until I made it back to the safety of terra firma and the security of the panel wagon.

"Hee hee. Chicken!" They shouted from atop their fragile perch, but I didn't care. I was safe again.

The next morning we made it to school on time. Larry and I shared first hour English class. A crackling voice came through the speaker hanging above the door announcing, "Would Chris, Larry, Jimmy and Roy, please come to Mr. Hall's office now." Larry looked at me with a dose of apprehension showing across his face. I wasn't worried; Roy promised that his plan would work. We lifted the lids to our desks, and grabbed thick stacks of line paper for defense against Mr. Doright. When Larry and I rose from our desks, an ominous hush came over the class. They, too, knew what awaited us.

The lined paper was in place and we walked down the hallway like rigid stick figures. Jimmy and Roy, also prepared with paper, were coming our way, and we entered Mr. Hall's office.

The tall, wiry principal leaned over his desk, and peered over his black rim glasses, "So, I guess you boys thought I was kidding?" Behind him, hanging on a nail, Mr. Doright waited within arm's reach to be brought in action. "Follow me," Mr. Hall said, and he removed the oak paddle from the nail.

He took us to the vacant typing class down the hall. "Okay, boys. Grab a desktop and lean over. We did. We were going to get one smack apiece for skipping.

We lined up like boys reversed faced to a firing squad of two, Mr. Hall and Mr. Doright. Mr. Hall practiced waving the paddle back and forth like a batter in an on deck circle. In a long sweeping swing, Mr. Doright whistled through the dour air like a jet plane and landed with a loud thud on Larry's behind. Not a 'smack', but a dull sounding thud. Larry feigned a flinch pretending he was in pain, and Mr. Hall shook his head in disbelief. Then he moved down the line to Jimmy.

If Jimmy wasn't such a jokester, we may have gotten away with our 8.5x11 defense. When Mr. Doright struck his rear end, Jimmy let out a contagious laugh that spread to each of us like the plague.

"What the ..." Mr. Hall mumbled. He knew that farms boys were tough but not tough enough to laugh at the end results of his mighty swing. He discovered the paper in our pants, and we were busted.

We removed the stacks of paper, and once again, we grabbed the desks. The punishment was increased to two whacks even though he complimented us on our creativity. Something he suggested we should apply in class.

On our slow and painful march back

to class, we looked over to Roy who was brushing tears from his eyes. Larry said, "So you know how to FIX IT, do ya? Wade a go, Roy!"

Something else was discovered that day, farm boys cry just as hard as a 'city slicker' kid from town.

✓ Tawas Community
By Dorothy Vassler Jennett Teplansky of San Diego, California
Born 1946

It's unfortunate that a dot on a map can't allow you to visualize the vibrant life of a city or town. You should be able to put your finger on it and be flooded with the rich history of its people and what made the community special. I think of the Tawas community as one of those special places.

I will try my best to categorize my memories:
People
Father "BOB" Morrison of the Episcopal Church on W. Westover who went to school with Edward (Ted) Kennedy
Teachers
1963 in the Tawas Area High School
Mr. Savanko who taught bookkeeping and math
Mr. Wiltse who taught American History
Dr. Sutton & Dr. Brinkman
Stores
Demick's Drug Store- had an old style soda fountain
Dorothy Hermans 5 & 10
Sis's Dress Shop- her best items were in the back of the store
Merschel's Hardware- always around for a nice chat (however, no pot belly stove)
Henniger's Clothing/Department Store
Freel's Market
Klenow's Market- great meat, always open
East Tawas Moccasins
O'Conner's Pendleton Shop
Hester's IGA
Dairy Queen
A&P on Main Street- living near the store, our dog "Sarge" would run to the A&P and step on the mat and the electric doors would open for him every time. Dad would have to retrieve him inside the store.
Mooney's Ben Franklin

Look's Pontiac & Buick
Mill End- things smelled burnt after they had a small fire.
Perry Drugs
Brennan's Jewelry Store- Mr. Brennan was nice to loan me $100 in the '60s for a typewriter when I went to college. I paid him every penny and I purchased many items through the years because of his trust and kindness.
Restaurants and Bars
Sid & Imees Restaurant
Miolo's Coffee Shop
Midway on US23
Gino's Pizza
Whispering Pines
Barnacle Bills
Bowling Alley- hand set pins
Blue Water Bar
Waubins
Buckhorn Bar
Lixey's
Ginii's (Name of first owners on a ceiling beam)
Marion's Dairy Bar & Greyhound Bus Station
Public Buildings
Water Department next to the bait shop on Newman at the beach
Community Center- when it was located on the beach
City camp ground where the Holiday Inn is now
One-room schoolhouse at the corner of Sand Lake Rd and M55
Library on W. Westover
Activities/Places
The POINT was city owned not STATE owned
Silver Valley toboggan slide
The town dock when it was only one section and you could drive up to it.
Lumberman's monument
Tawas Beach Road
Hobby Lot- hole in one for a "Free game"
Other
Falkner's Veterinarian Care on North US 23 with Dr. Falkner and Karlene
Wurtsmith Air Force Base in Oscoda
Log cabin on the corner of Shirmer Rd. & Tawas Lake Rd. - old cabin stood alone in the woods
Tawas High School
Paid the kids 1 cent per minute to work at the school
Real homemade food was served at the

cafeteria
American Legion on Newman Street
White's Motel
Moehring's Greenhouse- beautiful flower arrangements
Holland Hotel
Martin's Hotel
Verlac's Real Estate
Barber's Oil
Green Gables Resort
Tawas Drive-In
Family Theatre (one screen only and Disney characters on the walls)
Detroit Mackinac Railroad (Owned by the Duffy's)
When the lighthouse was at the point- not much land beyond

Ruben, Silva Jean, Mable, Gwen, Faye, and Lee Brooks

The Miracle of the Shoebox Baby
By Silva Jean Brooks-Freeman of Atlanta, Michigan
Born 1937

The spring of my birth was exceptionally wet and muddy making traveling the backcountry dirt roads of Montmorency County a nightmare for everyone. My parents, Ruben and Mabel Brooks lived on a farm in a small rural valley just south of Atlanta, Michigan. My father worked as both farmer and woodsman while my mother spent her days caring for her children and doing the endless work involved in keeping a house in the '30s.

At that time, our family consisted of two boys and two girls. Two other brothers had died after being born prematurely, one only eleven months before my arrival. I was to be baby number seven. When my mother again showed signs of an impending premature birth, the local doctor, Ray S. Young of Lewiston, Michigan urged her to find a place to stay in town so that he could be more readily available to attend what was sure to be a precarious birth. The bad roads would have definitely hampered his ability to arrive on time.

Arrangements were made for my mother to stay with her sister, Mary Mogg. Aunt Mary was a housekeeper for the Pettinger family in Atlanta and lived with them in their home. A room was found for me there. On April

29 just as Dr. Young feared, I arrived weeks too early at 3:45 P M weighing in at about 3 pounds. Knowing that my survival depended on my staying warm during those first hours following my birth I was wrapped in a blanket and placed in of all things—a shoebox! This was then put carefully on the open oven door in the kitchen. This became my incubator and surely helped save my life.

The next challenge was getting me to eat. My mother had never been able to nurse any of her children and I was so small and weak that this was even more difficult for me. So, I was given what was known as a "sugar tit." This was a cloth that held a bit of sugar and then was dipped in milk. Somehow, I managed to suck on this until eventually after much time and persistence from my mother and probably my Aunt Mary, I was strong enough to drink from a bottle. Incredibly, I survived and in time even thrived.

The local schoolteacher boarded with my family during this time and had brought my siblings to me shortly after my birth. They came to the house to find their new little sister lying in that shoebox and resting where it had been placed on the oven door. My sister, Gwen took one look at me and exclaimed that I looked like a little doll. My brothers being typical boys didn't give me much thought even though I was born on my brother Lee's birthday.

Now as I look back and consider this story of my birth I can't help but wonder why I lived when so many other babies did not survive in similar circumstances. How did I survive? I think of all my mother and others must have done to keep me alive. Did God have a special purpose for my life? I think this must be so. I am now 76 years of age with a large family of my own including many grandchildren and great grandchildren. They are carrying on the legacy of life that began for me in a simple cardboard shoebox.

Growing Up on the 80-Acre Dairy Farm
By Bernard H. Yantz of Traverse City,
Michigan
Born 1958

In 1965, I was 6 years old starting school in the one-room schoolhouse (up to grade eight) just short of a mile walk from our two-story Farmhouse built in 1900. Yes, one way was nearly a mile and I had to pass Steve Rau's place, our neighboring farm on M-30 on the way. He had a big MEAN Collie and it took great delight in biting the back of my legs each time I passed. Cow dogs were a great help in bring in the cows for daily milking. We kept ours under control and after several months of trying to sneak by that farm without being bit, the dog was hit by a car and my daily life became much less stressful.

Life on the Farm was strict with daily chores and the only way out was sickness or try to fake being sick. Black Sauve or iodine cured and cuts or scrapes, aspirin or a visit to the dreaded doctor was for all else. I was the king of stitches. Starting with my older brother throwing a sand bucket at me and me catching it with my face, seven stitches under my left eye. In 1963, when we moved into the Family farm business my Grand Parents beloved cow dog (Big collie) came with the territory. With me being so young and not knowing NOT TO KICK the new dog, that was good for around 40 stitches of cat gut in my nose and around my mouth. My Father was very upset to have to put the dog down (after 10 days of being tied up) and he let me know it. I can still see him yelling at me "I had to shoot a good dog because of you."

My older brother took some matches from Grandmother's cupboard, we went under the corncrib where there was no grass and lit the dead grass surrounding it. The dead grass burnt very quickly and we were in serious trouble. The fire just blackened the wooden corncrib and went out. Out back of the barn went older brother with Dad. I got Grandmother this time. She was a very very nice lady and a schoolteacher. I remember she said, "This hurts me more than you" and whacked the back of my hands with the back do a hairbrush. I never played with fire again.

Daily chores: The pigpen was between the house and the barn. There were about 20 pigs with super natural hearing living in the other barn just past the chicken coop. Brother and I would try to sneak to the milking barn to do chores without getting trampled. We sometimes had to jump into an apple tree on the way. There was one light bulb in the haymow, near the top of the barn and very dim at night. Older brother and I had to roll bales over to and down the chute to the lower level for feeding. We had to work together to roll one and it was a very long way up to the mow and down to the lower level. We fed them while they were in their stanchions. We did have one bull with a large ring in his nose for control while moving him. I used to tease him until one day he lifted his head real fast and got me with the ring on my forehead. Hurt. Dad had no sympathy.

Around 1965, Farming took a turn, you had to go big or get out. We were milking approximately 14 cows and not getting by. Dad sold the cows and the tractor for a chain saw and small saw mill. He and Lloyd Winters went into the sawmill business (Winter and Yantz Wood Products) built on our 80 acres. Now known as Knight's Mill.

My first job was nailing pallets. I was pretty quick at rolling nails and hammering out pallets. Purchased my first car for $110 (1968 Plymouth) 25 cents per pallet, when I was 17.

In 1884, my great Grand Father Anton Yantz, (was spelled Jantz in Canada, changed it when they came to Michigan) Great Grand Mother Catherine Yantz brought seven Sons from Kitchener Canada (was known as Little Berlin) in 1884 to the 80-acres on M-30, Three miles south of West Branch Michigan. They built and stayed in a log cabin from 1884 to 1900 until the present day home was built. My Grand Father, Francis Xavier Yantz was the youngest and together with Olive (Bishop) Yantz had my Father, Richard Benedict Yantz. We inherited the Family Farm in 1963 when Francis Xavier (Soff) Yantz passed away from Cancer. I remember the neighbors stopping in to pay their last respects to him before he passed. During that same time, I like to visit my Grand Parents house because they had a black and white TV set. We did not. I watched the John F Kennedy funeral and little John solute his Dad's coffin, while my Mother cried her eyes out.

✓ **Climbing the Family Tree**
By Nina Burger Myers of Merritt, Michigan
Born 1909

I can never recall a time when I was not interested in our family history. I have often heard my grandfather speak of different events that had occurred when he was young, but never had the privilege of hearing all of the history until last Friday evening.

I spent the evening with Grandpa Long. I asked him if he would give us the family history. He consented by telling us to draw our chairs up to the table to write as he sat down in his easy chair. He said our ancestry came from England.

Grandpa Long left home at the age of 20. He had read books about the United States and wanted to come and see it himself. Grandpa worked for a farmer (Mr. Porterfield) in Ohio for three years.

He returned to Ohio in 1868 from Canada and rented 40 acres of land for farming. He married Ruth J. Cummings on August 24, 1868 in Mercer County, Ohio. They had twelve children, three died in infancy. The children were named: Jacob, Lewis, George, Ivan, Amanda, Wilbur, William, Etta, Oliver, Margaret, Ethal, and John.
My grandparents also took in a little boy (Samuel Mead) when he was only one day old and raised him as their own as his mother died in childbirth. Grandpa and part of his family moved to Michigan in 1909. His boys came up on an excursion train.

My mother, Margaret, married James V. Burger on March 31, 1906 at Wapakoneta, Ohio. To this union were born Ruth on April 30, 1907 and Nina on February 10, 1909.

It is always a pleasure to hear Grandpa Long tell stories of real life. He was nine years old when he received his first pair of shoes. When the weather was very cold, he used to wrap his feet in old rags to keep them warm. Grandpa said the school he attended was built

of logs. It was 18' x 22' and contained one door and one window. Along the side of the door, there were six glasses 8" x 10". For their seats, they had split logs 10' x 12". These logs had holes bored into them and legs fitted into each one. Their desks were made the same way except they used larger logs. They had school in the summer time only because in winter the roads or paths were drifted too much for the children to travel. My grandfather went to school 61 days in his lifetime. He can read very well now. His mother taught him how to read and write before he went to school and he has always been studying and teaching himself. I would say he is a well-educated man.

Grandpa was a very strong and gritty man. He and a group of men were cradling a neighbor's field of wheat and as they were walking to the house for dinner, he picked up a large stone and tossed it over his shoulder. The men laughed and Grandpa said, "I bet you men cannot do that." Each of them tried, but no one could even lift it to his shoulders with both hands. Grandpa said he "bet" he could carry it 10 steps on one hand. They did not think he could, but he did. Instead of letting the stone roll off the side of his hand, he tipped his hand and let it roll off his fingers and he broke his first finger at the first joint.

He ate dinner and finished cradling working through the pain. In the morning, his hand was turning black. The doctor refused to take his finger off. His hand got worse. Finally, he had Grandma hold a chisel on his finger while he hit it with a mallet. He put a puffball over it, stopped the bleeding, and wrapped the finger.

When Grandpa Long was two weeks old, his parents moved into a log house that was 16' wide and 18' long. Just think of it! A family with seven children all living in such a small house. Their house was chinked with moss taken from trees and the roof was covered with bark. They had only a dirt floor. Grandpa lived in this same house until he was 12 years old.

In 1856, he and his father built a log house that was 20' x 30' and two stories high. They had no nails to use, so the rafters were pinned on by boring holes into them with an auger and using wooden pins to hold the rafters in place.

Grandpa says that carpentry seems natural

to him. He has built homes, schoolhouses, and barns. He built the house and barn where he now lives. His farm stands about 15 miles southeast of Lake City, a mile west, and a mile north of my home. He built our barn too. He not only built it, but he hewed out the timbers with an ax and planned the entire barn. Grandpa has hewed out and built three barns after age 80. One still stands in Butterfield.

He has hewed out timbers for his neighbors, made sled runners, neck yokes for oxen, and almost everything in the carpentry line. He farmed up until about five years ago. Since then he has let one of his sons (Oliver) take care of the farm. Grandpa always raised one of the best gardens in the community each year.

He has also been a lumberman. He used to cut timber for $3.00 per acre. Grandpa also did ditching for tiles, dug wells, and walled them up with brick or large round stones. He owned a threshing machine in Ohio and did all of the community threshing. If any livestock became ill, the neighbors almost always would get Grandpa to help doctor them. In short, I guess that I should say that Grandpa is a handy man no matter where he is.

✓ Fun in the Orchard
By Ann H. Gerke of Herron, Michigan

My family's large orchard was a source of lots of fun for my siblings and me during the 1960s. There must have been around thirty fruit trees. The majority of them were good eating apples that ripened from summer though fall. Whoever planted the trees was wise to include plums, pie cherries, sweet cherries, pears, and peaches.

Using farm lumber on hand, we were able to construct three tree houses in the big-limbed trees. This was way before cordless tools. We used a handsaw, hammer, and nails. This project kept us busy while building them, but then they became clubhouses for many days of fun.

A large garden was planted between the trees, so once the vegetables started to mature, we had convenient fresh snacks for eating out of hand. The peas would be the earliest food. The wonderful white sweet cherries on very tall trees ripened in July. The birds and the children ate their fill of the fresh delights. The salad tomatoes were also a good choice. If we could not wait for ripe apples, sometimes a sprinkle from the saltshaker would reduce the sourness. Over eating of the green apples often led to a tummy ache.

One extra-large Northern Spy apple tree had the perfect branches for four or five tire swings. We could swing towards each other without quite colliding! During the hot summer, this was a shady spot to play.

We did have to take a break from the outdoors to help preserve the tasty produce for winter eating. We learned to peel apples for lots of fresh pies and many more for the freezer. My mother would make the tender crusts from scratch and assemble the pies. The crab apples, cherries, plums, and pears were canned in glass jars. We did not have to worry about chemical added as preservatives in our food. We ate well!

Many bushels of fresh apples went in the basement for winter eating. But some of the later trees held onto apples on the top branches. We would watch out the window as the squirrels scrambled for a meal of frozen apple.

Some of the trees are gone now. A new cow barn and tractor shed are in the center of the original orchard. But I still think of all the summer fun in the orchard.

✓ The Three Speed English Racer
By Dennis G. Cline of Owosso, Michigan
Born 1952

I grew up in Lewiston, Michigan during the fifties, sixties and seventies, a great time and place if you like people few and far between. It did get crowded in the summer time when the tourists came to the area. My mother always called them flatlanders.
Well, to get to the point of this letter. When I was about thirteen or fourteen, before I was of legal age to drive (I may get to a story about that later) my folks bought me a Sear's three-speed English racer bicycle. The name made it sound fast, alas if that were only true. It had twenty-six inch wheels, a friend of mine had one of those little bikes with high rise handle bars, a banana seat, those little 20 inch wheels and FIVE speeds and was faster.

I did say I would get to the point of the

86

letter. OK, here goes. As I said earlier, people were few and far between. So if I wanted to visit with any of my friends, it meant that I either walked or rode the bike. Well, on one of my trips when I was at a friend's house, it rained and I mean rained (we thought about building an arc). By the time I headed for home it had stopped and the roads were mostly dry. I was wary of cars passing when I was near any puddles along the road. A block or so from home, I spotted a huge puddle.

I had her in third gear bent over the handlebars pedaling for all I was worth. I thought I would make the water fly. Things were going well right up to the point when I hit the deepest pot hole you'd ever saw. Well I flew that day, the flight was short and I would like to say sweet but it wasn't. Although in my defense it was my first water landing. The only thing that was really hurt (most of me was wet) was my pride. Oh I did puncture the front tube when the pot hole stopped my advance.

I walked her home and patched the tube and she was as good as new for a while. Then one day her transmission went. I thought I was back to walking everywhere, that was more exercise than I was into at the time. But I remembered my brother's old bike was still around. It was a standard rear wheel with a coaster brake instead of cable brakes and it rubbed the frame when I finally got it bolted on. One of the last missions the old girl and I went on was a ride up fire tower hill southwest of town. It was about three miles just to get to the road up the hill. The rubbing tire and deep sand slowed me down. My friends beat me to the top but we made it and they even let me rest before we headed back down. She lasted that summer then gave up the ghost.

A Charmed Life
By Dee Manning of Lincoln, Michigan
Born 1951

We 5 kids lived a charmed life. We grew up on a farm north of Hale, a small town in NE Michigan. Our grandparents lived nearby. Back of Grama Fruin's just up the road were lady slippers growing along the wooded ravine, looking for all the world to us kids like a pixie land. To a little kid, sparkly snow looks like diamonds. My granddaughter Sativa came out of church with me one night and I pointed them out to her. She said, "Those are little ones. Let's dig down to the BIG ones!" Diamonds in the snow. So pretty. Mark Twain once said, "If there were only one soap bubble in the world, what would it be valued at?" I'd lay on my belly watching ants going in and out of their homes, picturing their tiny furniture. Our parents always had a big garden. Mom told me I could have my own little one. She showed me how to shake the dirt out of the sod and plant radish and lettuce seeds, my choice. Soon as they were big enough to harvest, I'd gather some and make sliced radish, lettuce and mayo sandwiches. Funny how no one else wanted to join me, haha. I still like them.

Our country cousins would come up as often as possible. We'd jump from the hayloft onto the pile of loose hay on the barn floor. A treat to them, having no barn in the city. But they could show us tricks on our bikes... stuff we'd never tried. A cousin from a different part of the family once visited and the bad words and jokes that came out of her mouth... was shocking to a little kid like me. My kindergarten year of school... I was sitting with my older sister about half way back on the bus when some of the senior boys behind us started swearing. When I couldn't stand it any longer, I turned and asked them, "Don't you know Jesus is listening to you!" They chuckled but quit. Oh, the age of innocence, haha.

I remember a few times Dad had to save us. My sister Louise and I were playing upstairs at Gra'ma's and put our heads through the stair rails so we could look down the stairs and then couldn't get back out! He came up and had us scooch midway up and pulled back on the bars enough that we could get unstuck without pulling our ears off our heads! We didn't try that again. Another time while camping at Wagner Lake near Mio, I was riding my bike down the big hill and headed right for a big pine tree. He ran between me and the tree and grabbed the handle bars, taking all the speed into his strong arms. My hero! He was a good man.

We'd spend most of the summer barefoot. Once while walking back for the cows, I didn't see a garter snake crossing our path ahead and stepped right on it as it slithered on its way. Eew. Another time, one of us kids discovered a snake in the garage that had just swallowed a frog. Horrors! Our brave Mom had to kill the thing with a hoe to release the frog to make us happy. Not sure if the frog lived through the ordeal. So years later when I had the chance to touch a huge python at a zoo, I figured it would be wet and cold like our farm snakes so didn't want any part of that. The guy standing beside me said, "Chicken…" so I touched it and was surprised to discover it was dry and rock solid muscular.

Bees were part of country life, too. When we were downstate for a family reunion, I stepped on a bee barefoot and it did what bees do… ouch! Years later while washing the car in the driveway, I heard a roar and saw a black mass flying overhead… was a swarm of bees moving to a new location with their queen. My favorite insects are dragonflies, with their gossamer wings and darting ways and tickly feet as they land on my arm.

About Growing Up During the Great Depression
By Nancy L. Ferrar of Traverse City, Michigan
Born 1923

While our country was learning to survive the Great Depression our Latham family: 3 boys and 5 girls, including twin girls, were encountering hard times in another Great Lakes city, Duluth, Minnesota.

Soon after the twins were born, the Swedish maid inquired the names of the twins. Our mother answered, "Nancy and Jane." Hildur Erickson cried out, "Nancy! That is the name of a goat!" My three brothers teased me, "Nanny goat!"

The Depression brought out some ingenious ways of survival. Our father was a bookkeeper for several businesses. A dry cleaner owner recompensed with dry cleaning tickets to my father.

By newspaper advertisements, Dad swapped the tickets for goods and services. By the ads, the family received 8 quarts of milk, piano lessons, a rug, a pool table, grocery delivery, and a lousy picture. At holiday time, the grocer gave us a crate of apples.

The older sisters handed down clothes to their younger sisters, and sometimes we sewed our own clothes.

My mother had a sorority sister whose

Latham and neighbor kids on Halloween

daughters outgrew their clothes. The woman sent a box of clothes periodically to our family. The four younger sisters became excited when each box arrived. The sisters ranged in size, so the sister who fit an apparel became the owner.

My mother sewed snow pants for me using old striped pants Dad discarded. When I wore them the neighbor boy teased me, "You're wearing your Dad's pants!" I laughed to myself, as the boy was from a family of seven children. We were all in the same boat.

Somebody was often worse off than we were. At times, a beggar appeared begging for food. Mother supplied sandwiches and coffee. At other times, Mother asked him to cut the grass. Another pauper was selling rags from his open truck.

In the early years, washing was done by hand and a scrub board, using a hand wringer for squeezing out the water. Later Mother bought an electric machine with a wringer.

Bedding was a problem in the wintertime. The clothes were hung outside on a circular clothesline with wooden clothespins. When the sheets stiffened from the wind and cold, they'd be placed on the metal radiators in each room to dry.

Wrinkles in cotton sheets and pillowcases were pressed out with a mangle or ironer, a machine for pressing dry laundry by passing it between heated rollers. Ironing was an all-day affair.

Coal and ice were home delivered. During warm weather, a cardboard sign was placed on our front window with the number 25, 50, 70, or 100. The sign told the iceman how many pounds of ice to deliver.

Coal was delivered through the basement

window by shunting through to the storage room. Coal was needed to heat the furnace, which supplied warmth by water passing through a radiator in each room.

During rain, snow, or sun, we children walked to grade school, ½ mile to and from, including home for lunch. Those who lived on a farm in the country rode on a school bus, taking their lunch in a paper bag. On the walk to school, we avoided passing a decrepit house by taking a short cut through Mrs. Germain's field. We were picking wild flowers; we sisters gathered daisies, asters, and dandelions and presented them to our teachers. Later that day the principal informed us that Mrs. Germain had phoned to complain that we were trespassing. To rectify our mistakes, the principal suggested we gather up the flower gifts from each teacher and return them to Mrs. G.

During the fourth grade, the teacher assigned us to memorize Henry Wadsworth Longfellow's "The Children's Hour." At home, my twin Jane kept reciting "…laughing hyena…" I told her, "Jane, you are going to repeat hyena instead of Allegra in class." She responded by still practicing "hyena" and promising to say "Allegra" on day of recitation.

When the time came to recite in class, I anxiously awaited Jane's turn to recite. When she began the poem, she blurted out "laughing hyena."

The teacher made Jane stay after school. When the class dismissed I ran home, laughing all the way, to tell Mom, "She did it, she did it!"

School days remind me of the wooden desk with a hole near the right hand corner for an inkwell. A wood pen with metallic point was used to dip into the well containing ink for writing.

When I was 10 years old, a nearby neighbor tourist home operator contacted my mother who asked me to work for her. I cleaned the table, scraped off the left over food from the plates, and helped her making the beds for 10 cents an hour.

A loaf of bread was a dime's worth. Candy bars, such as Baby Ruth, Snickers and Mars Bar, or a cup of coffee were worth a nickel. A penny could buy one lollypop, a stick of gum, or a licorice stick.

During teen years, after school we rushed home to play the Victrola with some loud records of the latest Hit Parade: Bing Crosby, Frank Sinatra, and the Mills Brothers. Then we danced the jitterbug and foxtrot.

When Dad saw us sisters dressed for high school and wearing bright red lipstick, he blurted out, "Take the lipstick off!" Our response was, "But all the girls are wearing lipstick!"

For clothing in those days, girls usually wore skirts and blouses with brown and white saddle shoes. Long stockings were made of lisle, a fine smooth cotton.

The trouble with silk stockings is that they were expensive and easy to get runs or holes. During mild weather we went bare legged and drew a dark line on the back of our legs, pretending a seam.

Sometimes when only the youngest siblings were around, we got into mischief. One day my brother David caught many moths fluttering around the light of a bridge lamp. He was trying to help us with a nature project. When he returned home, we twins were sleeping, so Dave opened the bedroom door and let loose the moths, which went flying around the room.

Where was our Mother that day? She was teaching child training with the WPA, the Works Progress Administration.

Note: The WPA was the largest and most ambitious New Deal agency. It was a national program operating projects in cooperation with state and local governments. Between 1935 and 1943, the WPA provided almost eight million jobs. Through this and other New Deal programs, President Franklin D. Roosevelt's administration helped our country get back on its feet.

Nancy's parents with their children

As I Remember

By Frances Lamont of Bear Lake, Michigan
Born 1922

I am 90 years old and love to reminisce on the good old days.

I lived out in the country six miles from any town. Winters were rough as I walked 1 ½ miles to school. Winters were harsh as we had more snow then. It was as high as the fence posts. The mailman came on a cutter and horse at times. Roads weren't plowed often.

Our House

The house was built by my grandparents after their arrival in Michigan. We didn't have storm windows so we kids could write our names on the frost inside the windows. We had two wood stoves. One stove was in the kitchen to cook on and for heat. Another stove was in the living room. We had our Saturday night bath next to the living room stove in a washtub. It was so hard filling the tub and emptying it. We baked on one side near the stove and froze on the other side.

Outside Toilet

Our outside toilet was unusual as it was a portion of the milk house. One night my two sisters visited the toilet. My Dad thought he would play a trick on them by covering himself with a horsehide robe to look like a bear. They were so frightened that he said he never would do it again.

There is another story about that toilet. When I was a baby, my two sisters sat me on the lid of the toilet hole. It slipped and let me fall in. My mother and my foster sister took me to the well to clean me up.

This toilet was different as all the waste went in a big box and my Dad and horses took it out and dumped it.

We had a windmill to pump water. When the wind didn't blow, we pumped by hand. We had a large storage tank in the kitchen. It was my older sister's job to clean it as she had long arms to reach the bottom.

School

I went to Big Four School for 8 years. All the children were in the one room with one teacher. There wasn't any electricity, so on P.T.A. nights, gasoline lanterns hung from the ceiling. They were pumped up and had mantels, as I remember. The whole family went to P.T.A. meetings and often the students put on a program especially at Christmas. We wore black knitted leggings to school, made by my grandmother

Rogers Walk Through the Snow

At one time, my sister, Lenore, wasn't well so my Dad bought a little Shetland pony and a buggy for us to ride to school. Jack, the pony had a mind of his own and often balked. Once he threw my cousin and me off. The man who lived near the school often made him start for home. I remember riding to school once in the buggy with my hand outstretched. A big bird flew over and dropped his dirt on my hand. It is strange I would remember an incident like that.

Many times I walked 1 ½ miles to school and on my way home from school; I went down to Bear Creek to get the milk cows.

Farm Animals

I always helped milk cows at night, sometimes five cows. I didn't mind, but I hated to be switched by their tails, which had dried manure on them. It felt like "cat of nine tails" hitting me. When I brought them home from the pasture, one cow let me ride her part way to the barn.

Mother raised chickens, geese, and turkeys. She was upset when the turkeys nested in the woods and the little turkeys were in danger. The old gander was a threat to us, as he would pinch our legs and then twist. It sure did hurt.

The county Fair was in Onekama about 6-8 miles away. Dad and our cow dog, Prince, drove cattle to exhibit at the fair and got prizes. The family also took baked goods and hand crafted items and won prizes.

Crops

My Dad always raised lots of raspberries for his cash crop. Finnish women and children came from Kaleva, 6 miles away, to pick them. They talked in the Finnish language and we always thought they were talking about us. My mother said that people thought the Fins carried knives and were dangerous. But they were wrong, as the Finnish people were honest, hard-working people. My Mother told me that a Finnish woman bought a cow from them and walked the 6 miles every month to pay $5 for it.

Grain thrashing time in the fall was a busy time. A big heavy thrashing machine was all the horses could pull up our sandy driveway. My mother and Aunt Eva cooked huge meals for the neighborhood men who helped. My

Dad would go help them when it was their turn to have thrashers.

My Dad had huge bins of several kinds of grain in the granary. It was fun to jump and play in it. Dad took grain to the gristmill to get it made into flour.

Dad raised a lot of potatoes. When we got home from school, there was a note saying to come to the potato field and pick up potatoes. It was a hilly field and some of the potatoes rolled down hill. The potatoes were hand dug with a fork.

Some of the potatoes were put in a pit in the ground near the potato field and the pit was opened in the spring. Carrots, rutabagas, and other vegetables were put in too. Some of the potatoes were put in the basement of our house in bins. During the winter, we sorted them for sale. We ate the little ones.

During the springtime, Maple Syrup was made for the use of the family, as sugar was uncommon. They used horse and sleigh to gather the sap into a big storage container. It was later boiled down in a big long metal pan that had a wood fire under it. When the sap was just about to the syrup stage, it was brought to the house for the final boiling.

Big stones had to be removed from the fields in order to work the ground. Dad had two big piles of stones, one on the edge of the woods, and one by the barnyard. The one by the barnyard had stinging nettles growing over them. Boy, did they sting your bare legs and feet if you played on the stone pile. The way the big stones were gathered was on a sled called a stone bolt drawn by horses.

Household chores

I used to turn the crank on the big barrel churn to make butter. Sometimes I thought the butter would never come. I remember when oleomargarine first came out. Sellers didn't want it to be in competition with butter so a yellow-colored substance had to be worked into the white oleo.

My mother canned everything, as there was so refrigeration. She canned in a big copper wash boiler on the cook stove. I remember she fried pork and put it in a crock and then poured lard over it to preserve it. I never liked it, as it tasted rancid. Milk, etc. was kept in the basement, as it was cool.

Mom was always fighting bed bugs. Every time we had a new hired man, he brought us a new batch.

Our House:

My grandparent's first home in Michigan was more like a rustic log cabin. Later they built a beautiful house and big barn. Other outer buildings such as a hen house, milk house/wood shed/toilet combination and another wagon shed were added.

Our house had what you call a "parlor." This room was used for special occasions only. There were possibly four funerals and three weddings that took place there. My folks were the first couple to be married. The second was my foster sister's wedding and then my own wedding on Nov 18, 1942. My wedding was a simple affair with just open face sandwiches, cake, and ice cream. My dress was a white formal with lace, which cost only $13 dollars, but a lot of money back then. One of the nuns from Mercy Hospital where I graduated offered to make my veil. My sister had a good script so she hand wrote the invitations. It was World War II times, and everyone tried to economize, not like the lavish weddings now days.

Washday and electricity

Mom washed on a scrub board with tubs of water. There was a wringer, which I turned. Later she got a gasoline washer, which made a lot of noise and had an exhaust hose.

We didn't have electricity until 1943. Dad had a "Delco" plant in the basement, which produced electricity by batteries. It wasn't very successful and had a different voltage.

World War II

During WWII, many things were rationed like sugar, gas, tires, etc. We even saved toothpaste tubes for the aluminum. We were encouraged to make Victory Gardens although we always had a big garden in front of the house.

My Dad watched for enemy planes on top of O'Rourks Store in town.

✓ Dad's Father's Day Present
By Carlotta Myers Palozzilo of Merritt,
Michigan
Born 1941

Butterfield Creek runs through Butterfield Township located in Missaukee County, Michigan. It was the home of the Myers and Burger families before, during, and after the Depression.

Claude Myers built a log cabin along the creek prior to his marriage to Nina Burger. I was born here in the log cabin on Father's Day, June 15, 1941. After that, I was referred to as his Father's Day present.

We did not have electricity in the home, as the power company had not run the lines in yet. In the evenings and on dark days, the kerosene lantern burned brightly. I watched the shadows dance on the walls from my crib. Dad and Mom usually had supper after the milking and other barn chores were finished and by that time, it was usually dark.

My first pair of high-heeled shoes were bright red three-inch heels. The next morning, I began dressing for church and put on the new shoes, but my foot wouldn't go in because there was something hard in the toe. I turned the shoe upside down and a couple of smooth stones fell out. I could tell by the twinkle in her Dad's eyes that he knew all about it. Dad was a tease.

At the edge of the woods, Mom planted long rows of yellow daffodils, narcissus, and jonquils. When they finished blooming, the purple and yellow iris and yellow and orange lilies began blooming. She also grew plenty of asparagus, and when much of it went to seed, she used it as lovely greenery to put in with her floral arrangements.

The wood cook stove became the focal point in the home. We used it for cooking, heat, and hot water through coils connected to the wood stove. All meals were cooked on it, as well as homemade baked bread, pies, cookies, and cakes. It was important to have the fire just right. Should it become too hot, the food or baked goods would burn, if the temperature fell too much, so would the cake.

Mom had the garden while Dad worked growing crops for the horses and cattle. We had oats, wheat, buckwheat, field corn, and potatoes. He raised cattle for milk and cream, sheep for wool, and pigs, chickens, and rabbits for meat. There was always work to do on the farm and everyone had to pitch in and help.

One year, Dad grew contract pickles, which meant they would be sold rather than used by the family. This happened to be the year I was given a cap pistol for my birthday. It was nearly harvest time and the sun had set turning daylight into dusk when a car pulled off the road out by the garden. Three young men jumped out and headed for what they thought was a melon patch. At the same time, I stepped just outside the door and opened fire with my cap pistol. You should have seen them run for cover back to the car.

It might have been the Cornish rooster or hen, but one of these nasty chickens used to fly at me and peck my legs whenever I went into the chicken park to feed them. I hated that ugly old chicken! The Cornish were touted for their meat. They had large breasts, legs, and thighs, but small wings and backs.

Dad was working at a neighbor's field and since Mom wouldn't kill chickens, it was up to me. I told Mom that fried chicken would be great for supper and she agreed and suggested I kill one and clean it and she would cook it. It was music to my ears I was more than willing because I knew which chicken we were going to have for supper that night. It wasn't any trouble catching the chicken for it came running full speed to peck me. I reached down and grabbed it.

"Surprise, you get to be supper tonight!" I fairly crowed.

A pail of hot water had already been prepared to dip it in and pull off the feathers. A short trip to the chopping block with my trusty cleaver in hand was all it took to make that chicken history. It was the best fried chicken supper bar none!

I hated it whenever I felt I had disappointed or displeased my father for he was a very gentle man and never spanked me. He would raise his voice once in a while though. I was a mischievous kid to raise, but then I couldn't help it since I was a chip off the old block.

There were numerous times that I watched my Dad cut down a tree with his axe. He always explained to me what he was doing and why. So when he said you always notch a tree first in the same direction you want it to fall, I listened.

One day I put the theory to test. I took my little hatchet and went out to the chicken park and picked out a tree about five inches in diameter. I notched it on the side away from the fence and proceeded to chop at it from the opposite side. Pretty soon, there was a cracking sound followed by a mighty roar and "ka-boom" as it hit the ground right in the spot where I had planned.

I thought everybody would be happy that I knew how to chop down a tree, but not so. Dad was only happy to see I hadn't been hurt and that the tree didn't fall into the chicken park and find a new way to kill chickens. My hatchet days were numbered and were over almost before they had begun. From then on, the only contact I was to have with wood was to carry it into the house, stack it in the wood box, and keep the fires burning. Paula Bunyan I was never to be.

Growing up in Lupton, Michigan
By Kim (Rakestraw) Gildner of West Branch, Michigan
Born 1956

Growing up in Lupton was a wonderful experience. Kids aren't as lucky nowadays as we were. We didn't have electronics, cell phones, or computers, but our imaginations took us farther than any airplane could have.

We went to a two-room school house that I was lucky enough to go to through second grade until at that time the school closed and we had to start riding a bus to go to Rose City School. In Lupton School, I had a pretty big class with 5 or 6 of us. Some of the classes only had 2 or 3 people in them. We would walk the couple of blocks to school and brought sack lunches. There was only one teacher, which must have been quite a job for one teacher to teach all the grades. One particular memory was when I was in kindergarten and we sat at a round table. Teacher was busy with one of the other classes and I had learned the song Home on the Range. I wanted to teach the other kids how to sing it. Apparently, my singing was interrupting the other classes and the teacher told me to stop. I just couldn't stop because I had to teach them so teacher came back and made me go stand in the corner until

Rick and Kim Rakestraw in 1961

I understood that I could not sing in school. I was quite upset that she could not understand that it was necessary for them to learn to sing the song too. We had a nice little playground with swings, teeter-totters, slide, and a Merry-Go-Round. We would eat our lunch and run to play, getting plenty of exercise. After school, we would run down the hill and head for home. If you went behind the school and headed back through the woods and over the stepping stones on the creek, across the street and a little more woods, you would come to Green Lake. A couple of times my brother was nice enough to let me go with him to go fishing over there and that was the route we would take.

On the way home from school, there was a lovely elderly lady who lived in a very small house, named Daisy. She would wave and holler out the door as we went by and one of us would run over to her house to help her with anything she needed, or maybe run to the general store and get her something she needed and then when we would bring it back, she would give us a bright shiny quarter. That was exciting because then we could run back to the store and find quite a few "penny candies" or something great to buy for that quarter. The gentleman who ran the store was R.G. Reid, a very nice man. He had somebody working at the counter to wait on customers, but he would be back at the meat counter and had on his white apron. He would ask how we were doing today and maybe if we were really lucky he would take his black marker that he wrote on the meat packages with and draw a little picture on the back of our hand of an Indian or horse head.

We would all play until dinner if our homework was done and there were plenty of kids around town to play baseball or shoot hoops through a ring on a tree or hooked to the garage. We had plenty of games to play (none of them in a box or store-bought) like Eeney Einey Over, Mumbly Peg, making mud pies, climbing the big maple tree, or maybe playing in the lilac bush, where if you used your imagination, it was actually a big mansion. We would crawl inside and in the middle you could climb up and that would be the upstairs, underneath was the kitchen and living room, and under one of the other bushes that connected to it was the bedroom. We would get all sorts of old dishes and dolls and play in there for hours. Mumbly Peg was a game we played with jack knives (every kid had one). You would put the open knife on your elbow, shoulder, or knee and flip it over and try and get it to land in the dirt. I bet you can't find a parent who would let you do that today, but I don't remember anyone ever getting hurt from it.

My father worked at the mill, but also was the janitor at the Lupton School so after dinner, we would head up to the school and help him clean. We would sweep the floors after putting some reddish colored sawdust stuff on the floor that would help sweep the dirt off the wood floors. He would do most of it and would assign us some jobs to do too. I thought it was a lot of fun.

At the country school, we had a Christmas play each year and someone constructed a stage for us to sing and do our little plays. After Santa would come and we were all very excited to each get a bag of candy.

On weekends, and summers, practically every kid in town would get together and play baseball. There was no shortage of playmates and we were outside in the summer from the time we hopped out of bed to dinnertime when mothers would call for us to "Come Eat." We could ride our bikes to explore, swim, or camp, although when we were quite young the only camping we did was out under the stars or maybe with some blankets hooked to the clothesline in a makeshift tent. Before we went to sleep, we might try to catch some fireflies or play hide and seek in the dark. We had the run of the town, every kid was safe, and everybody knew everybody. We would build forts out of old slabs. There was a sawdust pile left from one of the old mills, and any kid that ever lived in Lupton played for

hours on the sawdust pile, climbing, jumping, and sliding. We could either walk or ride our bike to the creek which had a little swimming hole area right by the road. The road was about 10 feet or so up higher than the creek and we would stand at the opposite side of the road, run across, and jump into the air into that creek into the deep part. In the winter, we would all head up to Tucker Hill, which was near the cemetery north of town. It seemed like a huge hill to me and we had so much fun sliding the hill on toboggans or sleds. My father told me that when he was young, they slid on their sleds all the way from the top of the hill north of the cemetery, all the way into town, and then would hike back up that road and do it all over again. That would have been quite a sledding hill.

There were a couple of summers that my brother found a crow's nest and brought a baby crow home. They usually would stay for just a summer and then go. We named each one the same name, "George." To this day whenever I see a crow, I say "Hello George." Those crows would terrorize the neighborhood to our delight. They would steal the clothespins off the neighbor's clothesline and steal shiny objects. I have had many kids after they grew up mention, "Didn't your brother have a crow." I heard from a man not long ago that knew about our crow when he was a child and now years later he had to re-shingle the roof of the house I used to live in. He found all sorts of shiny objects under the old shingles that the crow had stolen and hidden up there.

When I was about 5, my mother was helping a friend with a wedding. My sisters were helping with the dinner, and my brother and I were to be the ring bearer and flower girl. I am not sure who was in charge of getting me to the rehearsal for the wedding, but we lived near the church and I knew I had to be at the church for rehearsal. I had some time before rehearsal so I went out to play, climbing the maple tree, then climbing in the pine tree (I picked up some pine tar on my hands so I wiped it off on my shirt). Then I dug some dirt up, added water, and made some mud pies. I walked to the church, walked in the door and people were laughing at me, but my mother's mouth was hanging open seeing mud, dirt, and sap. I couldn't understand what the big deal was.

Something our family did at deer season

Lupton Friends Church Bible School
1960

was open our home to hunters from the city. My whole family slept in my parent's room and we rented out the upstairs rooms to the hunters and the extra rooms in my grandparents' house next door. We would get up before sunrise, help mom cook breakfast, and then serve them breakfast at a big table. Dad would take them to hunting spot. We would make ground bologna or ground beef roast for sandwiches and pack each hunter a lunch and a thermos of coffee. They would come back at night for dinner, which we fixed. Hard work, but much fun, and wonderful people.

Another favorite memory was going with dad on Saturday nights when dances were held in Rose City. I was too young, but he would let me ride with him to pick up my older sisters. While waiting we would go to the "The Grill." Those burgers were the best burgers and time spent with my dad was even better. Coca Cola was really a special treat. On Sunday mornings at my house, my dad would sometimes bring home a six-pack of coca cola and a bag of potato chips. We would sit and watch Abbott and Costello, or the Three Stooges and eat our chips and drink pop and then usually chicken or a roast with the fixings and of course all sat at the dining room table together for Sunday dinner. My dad fixed us potato soup for dinner on most Sunday nights.

We did have a general store in Lupton but once a month on Saturday, we would head to the big city, West Branch, and get groceries at A&P store. As a child, it seemed like such a long drive, and such a big place. Always when I think of A&P, I remember the smell of the coffee when people would grind it to buy.

Nowadays, you cannot feel as comfortable about letting your young children sleep outside under the stars in the field, and instead of cell phones, we still got the message it was time to come home when you would hear the mother's hollering "time for dinner." We would never have dreamt that you could sit inside on computer or electronic device instead of out in the fresh air. If chores and homework were done, we were outside playing or inventing our next game. Imagination took us everywhere and we enjoyed every minute of it.

✓ **Heaven on Earth**
By Scott R. Jones of Clay, Michigan
Born 1950

Although I am in my '60s, my memories of life on Higgins Lake, in northern lower-peninsula Michigan will never completely fade. Each year, at the end of the school year in mid-June, our family would re-locate to the west shore of Higgins lake, Michigan. We had a cottage, built by an un-licensed builder named Samsul (I was told), who put together a house that was both a nightmare and a dream. The nightmare was that it was so poorly built that, if someone walked across the floor in the main room, the record would skip on the phonograph playing there. The main beam under the floor was held up by two tree trunks in the basement. The upstairs was comprised of "beaverboard" (an early form of particleboard) over studs set at least 24" apart. The dream was that, on any given night, 13 people could sleep there (though, some levels of privacy were somewhat violated at times). To us kids, it was heaven itself.

Morning started with a "morning dip" (instituted by my dad sometime just before my birth). All of us would be summoned from our warm beds with cries of "OK, you panty-waists, let's go!" To be clear, none of us ever knew exactly what a "panty-waist (or waste) was, but it sounded like a serious slacker of some kind. We would dutifully pull on a swimsuit and head for the beach. All except for my mom, which would become very important upon our return to the cottage later. Someone would be detailed to bring a bar of Ivory soap. Ivory soap was necessary because it floated, so it wouldn't get sand in it. The cottage had a bathroom, but the shower was woefully lacking. It was a box with a plastic curtain. The lake provided our means of personal grooming.

Higgins Lake was spring fed. That meant that, if you had three or more cloudy days, the water would be about 60 degrees. Morning dips were not always comfortable. We gutted it out, though. Cleanliness was next to Godliness, after all. The walk back up to the cottage was accompanied by chattering teeth, oftentimes. The treat was that my mother (staying behind to start breakfast) would have a hot water foot bucket on the side porch to welcome us back with. My sister (much smaller then) would half immerse herself to get warm.

Breakfast was taken at a custom built, 14-foot long picnic table in the main room. Waffles were made in a waffle iron that had come out of the 1930s. It was chrome, with a drip pan built in, and a fiber covered cord, with a spring at the base to keep it from kinking, and a "flipper" wood handle to allow opening it without burning yourself. The waffles themselves were not so lucky, however. The first few stuck, and were reduced to crumbles, which went on the plates of the most impatient diners. As the waffle iron "seasoned," however, the waffles became more "photogenic."

Cleanup, conducted at an old time kitchen sink, consisted of washing the dishes in a round aluminum dishpan, rinsing them in another pan, and immediately hand drying them, and putting them away as we went along. We didn't have room enough to set them up in a rack for drying. I'll never forget one day, when we were using paper plates, my sister jokingly tossed them into the dishwater. Not to be outdone, my mother washed and rinsed them, then took them out and hung them up on the clothesline to dry. The lady next door had such an expression on her face....

My mother had an amazing ability to find blueberries. We would grab a pile of mismatched pans, jump in the 1956 Buick Special (the one with the grille that looked like some mean guy baring his teeth), and set off up the "fire trails" through the woods west of the lake. Mom would park in some spot, which she somehow knew about, and we would all pile out of the car. She would lead us down a narrow two track or path through the woods for about 35 miles (actually, probably only a hundred yards, but we were little, remember), and we would emerge in a blueberry bog. The bushes were absolutely loaded with berries. Even using our "one for the pan, two for me" picking strategy, we still got lots of blueberries to take home. Mom would sort them (since we were a little casual in our selection criteria), and bake a killer blueberry pie. This still left lots for putting on cereal the next day, too.

The lake was, of course, still the main focus of most of our activities. Mom always said that she didn't worry about us if we were in the water, only when we were near the road. Boy, if she only knew! How any of us survived to adulthood, I'll never know. The great thing about Higgins Lake was that it had a nice sand bottom that stayed shallow enough to walk for (in our stretch) about 150 feet out. Once it was deep enough that you had to swim anyway, the bottom turned "squishy," but it didn't matter. We had all manner of floating craft, from paddleboards to sailboats, but no motor boat (until later on). We spent more time under the water than on top of it, I think. We all were proficient in the use of mask and snorkel, and became intimately familiar with the bottom of the lake (down to about 20 feet or so). Early on, we had a swimming raft, which was a wood platform, floated on some 55-gallon drums strapped on the underside. This was anchored in about 10 feet of water, chained to a big chunk of concrete. When a storm would hit, the chain had a habit of breaking, and we would have to retrieve the raft from wherever it drifted to. A wooden ladder bolted to the side allowed us to climb on to "catch some rays." The seagulls liked the raft as much as we did, which led us to leave an old broom on board, so we could sweep off their leavings. It was pretty rank some days.

Later on, my father designed and built a diving platform, which was constructed of pipes and a wood platform. The pipe structure would sit on the bottom. This made it stable enough that we installed a diving board. Close calls, and one collision by a passing boat, proved how very stable it was. Installing it at the beginning of summer, and removing it at the end took at least six of us (and by then we were big, strapping kids).

Very early in my memories we had a "boat," which was actually a cement-mixing trough. We called it "Gizmo." Simple pleasures for simple minds, right? My dad thought the design would translate into an actual boat, so he built "Gizmo II" one winter. This was a mixing trough shaped boat 3' wide, by about 6' long. It had seats, oarlocks, oars, and even foot grids, all built to scale. With a couple of really little kids, it was cute as a button, but didn't maneuver worth a darn. Dad even put a motor mounting board on the back, which was only tested once.

My older brother had rebuilt an antique "Sea King" motor that he got from somewhere. He clamped it on the back of Gizmo II, and he and I set out to do a test run. We were too big to really be in such a little boat, and there was only about three inches of freeboard between us and swamping the boat. He got the motor running, but just then a large motorboat came by out in the deeper water. Seeing the wake coming at us, he quickly unclamped the motor, and lifted it clear as the boat sunk beneath us. We were only in hip deep water, but now a serious problem came up. The motor was still running, and he couldn't let go with one hand to shut it off without dropping it. He held on, while it spun him around in a circle. He yelled at me to lean in on the next pass and shut off the lever, which I did. Video tape equipment was not available at that time, thankfully, or we would have "gone viral" for sure. "Hey, Martha, look at these two dopes!"

Although lunch was usually "catch as catch can," dinner was always a full family affair. We had a large bell on a post, which was rung to summon us home from wherever we were at the time- usually within earshot. When we were really little, we sat on books to prop us up to table height. Dinner conversation consisted of relating the high points of the day. (The low points were, of course, conveniently avoided.) After dinner, we would go over to one of the two motels that were next to us. The closest one was The Oaks Resort, which had six cabins. Many of our friends would return year after year to spend one or two weeks. They usually had a bonfire every night near the beach, and we would have sing-alongs. Interestingly, the songs were often from many decades in the past. "Shanty in Old Shanty-town", "Wait 'till the Sun Shines, Nellie", and one of my very favorites, "Moonlight Bay."

Eventually, the bell would ring, and we would run home to "hit the sack." On warm nights, I would sleep with the window open at the head of my bed, and fall asleep listening to the fading songs drift from next door. The gentle lap of the waves on the beach provided the heartbeat of the lake. Heaven on earth.

Elberta, Michigan a Peach of a Place to Live
By Shirley Groesser Balentine of Muskegon, Michigan
Born 1940

In 1940 in Frankfort, MI in an apartment above the A&P Store on Main Street on Saturday a birth took place. A baby girl was born to Jake and Dorothy Godfrey Groesser they named her Shirley Kay and that is who is writing this story.

I was raised in Elberta, MI, which is around the Betsie Bay from Frankfort. It was the time the Ann Arbor Railroad the Ann Arbor Carferrys were busy bringing all sorts of supplies and transporting people in and out of the area. I use to watch the yard engine going back and forth on the tracks in the yard and picking up railroad cars and making the long trains that the big engines would carry out to Owosso, MI and other towns on their way. Sometimes I would watch the train load the boxcars into the boats and they would also load the people's cars that wanted to take them across the lake.

When I started school, I was only 4 yrs. old and wouldn't be 5 yrs. old until February. I was not ready for school but I put up with half days. The next year they told me, I had to go all day. About the second week I had enough I went home for lunch and didn't go back to school. Then I thought where am I going to hide until school is out that day? Well why not the big play ground for all the kids in Elberta the big hill that overlooks Elberta. I set there waiting for school to get out. I watched all the kids leave then I was getting scared to go home. Then I saw my Mother looking for me and she went to my Grandparents, Clyde & Tillie Godfrey's house so I came down off the hill and stopped there. They ask me where I had been and I told them on the hill and I didn't want to go to school all day. My Grandpa who never said a lot but you listened when he spoke if you do that again the Truant Officers will be looking for you. Well I thought about that and never skipped a day again until my senior year I skipped a half a day and I didn't get caught. In the sixth grade, I had a very nice

97

Elberta 6th grade class

teacher her name was Mrs. Brown. She only stayed one year in our school I hope it wasn't because of what I done. Why I done this to my best teacher I will never know. I liked to joke around a lot and I sent for some things out of a comic book. One thing was a squirrel tail that would stick to the back of your clothes the kids thought it was cool. Then I had a big black spider and Mrs. Brown went out of the room and I put it under the book she was using and when she came back in the room she picked up the book and screamed out loud and Mrs. Edison came hurrying in from the next room and ask if she was ok. I was sorry I had done that and no one ever told on me.

In the summer time, we would ride bikes, scooters, roller skate and we would play all kinds of games outside hide and seek, hopscotch, jump rope, and a few others. Rainy days we played cards, colored, and other things. My Grandpa made rubber guns for me and my cousins Buck and Jim Acre they were made out of tires. He made all of us stilts that we walked around on. We use to play on the church hill we would climb up to the top where the big water tank was for the village water supply. We would sometimes take our kites with us and fly them over Elberta and we would go over to Lake Michigan with extra string and fly the kites off the bluffs so far they looked like a dot in the sky. Most of the kids in the hood use to spend a lot of time at the beach in the summer. One day my cousins were there and they took me over to the boat docks that they didn't use anymore. The pilings were high and they got me to jump off one I thought I was never coming up again. I decided that was not a safe place to play. One day my Step dad Herschel Holmes (Pud) took me and my brothers Ron and Deryl Holmes

to the beach to teach me to dive off the diving board that was on the pier. I showed him how deep it was by standing on the bottom and holding my hand up which was out of the water. He dived off the board and hit bottom and I saw his feet stop and he slowly came up and made a couple of lunges to the pier. He got to the ladder and went straight down under the water I screamed for help and went down to pull him up. I got him under the arm and held him until Dick VanBrocklyn came running out on the pier and helped me get him up. He was trying to walk up the pier. We got him on the pier and Bob Beughnot swam out and came up the ladder and turned him over on his stomach and pushed on his back and some water came out of his lungs. By that time, the Coast Guard that had heard me scream came up to the pier and took him to the hospital in Frankfort. All he had was a sore neck thank the Lord. I was only 15 and had to drive my brothers up the steep hill from the beach.

In the winter, we spent most of the day playing on the hill. We had sleds, jumpers, toboggans, and skies that we used. My jumper was made by my Grandpa. We would go off the main and make trails around trees and bumps with cardboard that we sat on. If the cardboard wore out, we used the seat of our snow pants. I can't member how many times over the years that I got in trouble for wearing out the seat of my pants. Around noon we would go home with our legs crossed looking

8th grade cheerleaders in 1953

98

funny trying to walk fast enough to get home to the bathroom. We would warm our fingers and toes and restored our energy and back to the hill. We would play until suppertime and head for home with our legs crossed again and starving. One summer there was a glass mining co. that mined sand on top the hill. They left a mound of sand at the bottom of the hill were we played. That winter when I was 9 yrs. old, I came down the hill on my jumper and hit that mound of sand and flew off it like a ski jump. I landed on my left shoulder and broke my collarbone it was Thanksgiving Day.

We had an oil burner in the living room and a wood burner in the kitchen. It would be so cold in the mornings that my brothers and I would run to the oil burner in the living room and back up just as close as we could to get warm. A little later, the wood stove in the kitchen would be going and that was warmer. We use to have to go to the outhouse in the day and at night, we used a chamber pot. Than one Halloween some boys tipped over the outhouse and the folks decided it was time to get an inside flush toilet.

When I was 5 years, old the sirens went off and I was scared. People were coming out of their houses with pot and pans and banging on them and shouting the war is over the war is over. World War II had just ended.

Some of us kids would go to the Post Office where the mail cart sat that was used to go to the passenger train and get the mail from the mail car. The cart had 2 big wheels on it, a flat bed, and a long handle Perry Richley who was an elderly man would pull on the handle and we would push on the back. They would throw a couple of mailbags on it and we would help him push the cart back to Post Office. You know what? He could really do it all by himself. When I was older, Pud worked on the railroad and he would clean the coaches and the mail car. I would help clean the coaches but I didn't help with the mail car after I seen him empty the spittoon where the mail sorter worked.

One day there was some excitement at the boat dock. When the boats turned around and backed into the dock so they could line up with the rails on the boat and the dock and it under the bank. The cars parked alongside of the boats fell into the sinkhole.

They got all the cars out but I don't know if they were still useable.

Our family would listen to the radio in the evenings. There was The Squeaking Door, The Shadow, and The Grand Old Opera. On Sat. am it was Buster Brown and Howdy Duddy Time. Sometimes we would all go to the Garden Theater to a movie in Frankfort?

In 1956, two of my classmates (Ella and Vivian) were in a car accident. I would have been with them but I had a date that night of the Honor dance. There were five girls from Elberta in the car Bonnie Anderson was driving Mary Church, Teddy Tanner, Ella Hammond, and Vivian Huhnke. Vivian had 6 skull fractures and lost some hearing on one side. Four of them lived but Teddy passed away 10 days later. The accident was the fault of the boys.

After I graduated, I went to college to become a nurse. That summer I worked in the canning factory. They canned and froze cherries and after they were done, they made apple juice. When we were younger, we would go to the factory when they were making apple juice and the back doors were open where the presses would squeeze juice. The guys would give us the nice fresh juice right off the press it tasted so good. The factory burned down about 1970.

After my Mother passed away, my husband Richard Balentine and myself bought the house that I was raised in at Lincoln and Sherman. Our three girls spent a lot of time there with us and visiting grandma. They

Richard and Shirley Balentine in 2010

99

have enjoyed a lot of the same things I did growing up. They have also brought their families here to play and enjoy this beautiful area. Two of my granddaughters and one great granddaughter and myself have come here every year for the past 5 years for our Girlie Days. We ride bikes on the trail, go to beaches, playgrounds, shopping, crafts, designing our t-shirts and many more things. This year we have the Sleeping Bear Dunes on our list.

Last year we had a reunion for the neighborhood kids that have moved way that grew up together. There was John and Wanda Acre, Priscilla Bramer, Sally and Kay Beughnot, Ron Holmes, and me. There were two that couldn't make it that day Deryl Holmes and Molly Luxford. What a wonderful time we had reminiscing. We are planning another one this year.

Elberta was named after the Elberta peach. Elberta is a Peach of a place to grow up.

✓ I Never Called Him Charlie
By Tom Finger of Mesa, Arizona
Born 1929

Mention the sleepy village of Lupton and "gangster activity" will not leap into your mind unless you lived nearby back in the 1920s. During the prohibition years, the Purple Gang out of Detroit owned a large stretch of land that run from Lupton east to Lake Huron, which was posted "no trespassing" and was enforced by armed men patrolling the area.

At some time a large bar, dance floor, and lodging clubhouse was constructed in Lupton and called Graceland, long before Elvis ever thought of it. The purpose was not only for a place to relax and party for gang members, but for the Lake Huron beachfront property. This was not for swimming or sunbathing, but only to receive boatloads of prohibited whiskey from Canada, which was hauled down to Detroit and sold to speakeasies.

Graceland was a large log structure with a well-appointed interior of mounted hunting trophies and comfortable seating. The bar and liquor display was a magnificent hardwood structure, and a long walkway surrounded the upper walls just under the windows I assume for observation of the area outside. It was a place for gang members to bring their girlfriends and party, and what happened at Graceland, evidently stayed in Graceland.

When gang members wanted to relax with their wife and children, they came up to Kenyon's resort on Sage Lake a few miles away where they appeared to be no different than friendly vacationing families.

The above information is true to the best of my memory as a 16 year old observant kid that lived and worked at the nearby resort of "Kenyon's on Sage Lake" as stoop labor delivering ice or anything required by the guests. Also, I hauled garbage, swamped boats, carried hotel luggage, trapped skunks, and ran errands.

This was in 1945 at the end of WWII when I was paid $10. per week and tips and observed things that made me curious. How did all these obviously wealthy people find this resort at the end of a gravel road way off the beaten path on a small lake in Ogemaw County? They all drove big cars, Cadillacs, Packards, etc.

There wasn't a Chevy to be seen, and luggage was not just cardboard suitcases, much of it was monogrammed leather, which I had never seen before.

My Job at Kenyon's

How I got that job was that my folks and I were visiting my uncle up in Rose City in the spring of 1945. I had found the add in their newspaper looking for an intelligent young man to do resort work. "Intelligent young man" seemed to fit me perfectly and I wanted a summer job. My folks had both been raised in Ogemaw County and knew Mr. Kenyon from years past, so we stopped at Kenyon's Resort going home.

Mr. Kenyon said he needed someone to haul ice from the ice house to the hotel and about 15 cottages as well as haul garbage from all them places to his sons pig farm up the hill behind the resort. This sounded like a lot of hauling to me and the job wasn't so appealing until he asked me, "Can you drive a pickup truck."

Now I really wanted that job because I loved to drive. My mother thought I was too young to live away from home all summer, but my dad said, "Well, you might as well start making your fortune while you're smarter than anyone you know."

Now I knew the old boy was being cynical, possibly with good reasons, but I wanted the job and I got it. But making a fortune escaped me somehow.

As an adult in later years and still curious and skeptical, I returned to that area and talked to older locals who reinforced my memory of possible gangsters in that area. With the advent of computers and internet, I searched the history of Lupton and the Purple Gang, which removed any doubts I had. In August 2012, I stayed at Kenyon's for 2 nights and learned of things I was never aware of back in 1945.

The hotel is well known to have tunnels and secret passageways when the new owner purchased and remodeled the hotel in 2006. The resort is now restored, modified, and offers all the creature comforts of lodging, and fine food demanded by today's travelers.

Graceland had burned down in 1978 but the intrigue remains. I remember the interior of Graceland from stopping once to nervously buy a bottle of coke and leave quickly in case there was still a hit man in there. Remember I was only 16 at that time and not very worldly.

Resort History

Charles Kenyon Sir started his resort in 1903 and this is not to say he was a Purple Gang member, but he seemed to have very good connections during the war with possible black market rationed products. This original building on the Kenyon complex was at one time a store, a post office, and now storage.

Charles Kenyon a former Ogemaw County Sherriff in his younger days who was perhaps in his late seventies in 1945. This was his store/office where he sold basic items and ran the resort with Charles Jr. and his daughter, Roxy. But the old guy was the boss of everything, and there was no question in my mind about that.

Through this store passed many truckloads of no doubt black market items, liquor, cigarettes, and many unattainable things during WWII. I remember unloading a truck in the middle of the night and questioned Mr. Kenyon, "Why don't we unload this truck in the morning when we can see what we are doing." His response was, "Just unload the truck and don't talk about this to anyone." This was another red flag to me that indicated unusual activities.

A New Experience

The day after these deliveries were made a tall well-dressed guy possibly in his mid-30s driving a flashy red car would appear and stay for several days. I suspected he was there collecting for them deliveries.

I don't remember the guys name but for some reason he seemed interested in me and asked many questions about me, my family, and other forgotten things.

When I told him I was from the Frankenmuth area down state but I do have an uncle that lives in Rose City nearby, he asked, "Have you visited him lately." I hadn't, but explained that I work 7 days a week and had no days off. The next day he approached me and said he had talked to Mr. Kenyon for me and I could have the day off the following Sunday to visit my uncle. I was surprised but explained that I would have to hitchhike, and there was 15 miles of gravel road between here and the road going north to Rose City, which would be a hard place to catch a ride. He seemed insistent that I visit my uncle.

Now this is unbelievable but a true story. He said, "You can take my car." I was a licensed driver since age 14 so on Sunday morning I was driving his late model V12 Lincoln Zephyr with a push button radio to Rose City. (I knew cars at age 16)

My Aunt Lulu was pleased to see me and fixed a great Sunday dinner and we enjoyed the day. However, my uncle Rube was nervous as a cat on a hot tin roof until I drove out of his driveway. I think in his mind, he was sure I had stolen that car and I was out joy riding around the state. No one in their right mind would loan this car to a 16 year old teenager. I know he wouldn't have loaned me his car.

After the fact, I think if I had wrecked that car, that guy would have just gone out and stole another car. Looking back I wonder, did that guy loan me his car as a favor, or did they just want an inquisitive kid out of the resort for that day?

Mr. Kenyon

Mr. Kenyon was a great influence on me as a young lad, and every teenager should have a mentor such as him. He was a tall well-built man who talked softly but no doubt could go bear hunting with a switch. When he told me what needed to be done, I somehow knew it was not a suggestion, and I did get it done. I seldom questioned his instructions as I would my father, and I did listen to him.

An example of how trusting he was, I was given the keys to the truck and a large amount of cash to drive to West Branch to pick up a dishwasher and all the plumbing and material to install it. I was to pay the hardware man a fair price but no more. The man that rode with me was an alcoholic about 50 or more years old who Mr. Kenyon didn't trust, but he would know what we needed and would select the material. And I was not to stop at any beer gardens along the way.

I don't recall the amount of cash, but it seemed like a lot of money to me, so I was nervous and determined to bring back the right dishwasher and material as well as the balance of the cash he gave me. The only challenge was when the old guy got cranky on the way back and insisted I stop at a bar because he needed a pack of cigarettes. I told him I would stop, but would not wait for him and he could get back however he could, and I would return to Kenyon's alone, which I did. All the way back, I worried that I would catch hell for leaving the old guy there. I was relieved and proud when Mr. Kenyon just said, "You did the right thing Tom, you did good." I still had my job but I never seen that old guy again.

My wakeup call in the morning before daylight was when Mr. Kenyon parked his truck with a rusted out muffler next to the store and raced the engine a couple times. I knew it was time for me to hit the floor with both feet running. We had breakfast at the hotel kitchen and I got my instructions for the day. By mid mornings I was always hungry and would buy candy bars at the store until Mr. Kenyon said, "You shouldn't eat so much candy, it will give you pimples" I explained that the cook, an older lady that didn't care for me, said I ate too much and all that food would rot in my stomach and I would die. His response was, "Whenever you're hungry, go to the kitchen" Next morning I did, and the old girl couldn't be nicer to me and fixed anything I wanted to eat. She evidently heard from Mr. Kenyon.

I loved that old man!

✓ Penny Candy and 10-cent Soda Pop
By Joyce Villeneuve of Alpena, Michigan
Born 1944

I was fortunate enough to grow up on a farm. There was work but, also, lots of fun swinging in the haymow, playing house with my sisters, lying in the sun on nice days and

Snow covered gas pump in the 1940s

playing outdoor games with my siblings. In the nice weather, all helped to weed in the large garden. The worst chore for me was picking the potato bugs off the plants and filling a pail, after which the older children burned them. "Haying" was fun but also hard work (our farm was not automated). The youngest children rode on the wagon and pressed down the hay by walking on it, while the older pitched it up from the field. When the wagon was full, the hay was pitched into the mow and the process was repeated. I still recall how the hay felt down my neck and everywhere else by the end of the day. The chickens were free range, although we did not call it that then. I often fed them by scattering the food on the ground. Our outhouse shared the back yard with the chickens. The catalogs we received often wound up there to be used as "necessary" paper. They were also handy if you wanted to sit awhile. We had electricity but not running water. It had to be pumped and carried into the house. Eventually the water was installed in the house. My uncle had a phone, which we did not. Each house

102

had a ring, but all on the "party" line could hear all calls. There were often spats with neighbors over time spent on the phone or those listening to other calls.

Every evening, we scoured the acreage for the cows. They were obstinate and did not come when called. We had to wait until we heard their bells and gather them one by one. They were milked in the evening and morning. The product was separated, milk kept and the cream sold, except for a little for home. I remember being very little and stirring the butter churn while sitting on the table. It took a long time. I often rode with my father to the creamery to drop off the cans. That building no longer exists. We also often went to the feed store. That building is still there today, but is a fruit grower's distribution center. The animal food came in patterned cloth bags and the material was used to make clothes, dish-towels, or bed linen.

I usually walked with my sisters to the gravel pit on summer afternoons. We had no idea whose property it was on and it was deep but I preferred it to the nearby river because there were no leeches. Another favorite activity was to walk down the tracks and buy penny candy and 10-cent soda pop. We had no television but some of our favorite radio programs were "The Shadow" and Gene Autry. Every Sunday, our mother would visit her sister and my sisters; cousin and I would walk to downtown and see a movie. That was my favorite day of the week. It was fun to see them and sometimes we picked up other children as we walked. The movie was always preceded by a cartoon and cost 10 cents for those under twelve. Even at 11, my sister was accused of being older and forced to pay 25 cents, the adult cost.

Our schoolhouse held about 35 children from kindergarten through eighth grades. Our long-suffering teacher managed all the classes with the help of a few eighth grade girls. My brothers were naughty and often threw crayons on the coal stove when the teacher was busy, causing a smell to permeate the room. We were allowed to go outside until it aired out. Another trick was plotting with a developmental disabled boy, who would stay in the woods after lunch hour was finished, and the teacher would send everyone back out to find him, extending lunch break. My Dad always said that, if the teacher had to

spank you at school, you would get twice as a much when you got home but I do not think the teacher ever told. I loved learning, books, and being read to from the beautiful IDEAL magazines, which our teacher read to us on special holidays. Laurie Ingalls was my favorite author back then and I read all the school owned. By the time I was in third grade, a new school had been built and the one-room schoolhouses were history. My father worked for a contractor and laid many of the blocks in the new school. When my sister graduated from eighth grade, the school sponsored a trip across the new Mackinaw Bridge, which my Dad had also worked on. Two years later, I was able to go. It was a rare treat. The new school had a wooded yard and the pine trees were a perfect shelter for play. I would use the branches to sweep the needles up, so I would have a clean "house." My favorite teacher's husband drove the milk wagon in town and I had occasionally seen him dropping off the bottles to homes.

It was a more innocent time: doors remained unlocked and children wandered in their neighborhoods without fear. I wish the innocence of the late '40s and '50s would return for our children and grandchildren. But advances in electronics and health care have improved mankind and extended life. And the important things have not changed–love, relationships, and God.

The Hill
By Dave Beck of Berkley, Michigan
Born 1948

My Mother-in-Law would always graciously allow my wife and I to take over the family cabin in Mio every 4th of July. This way we could have family, friends, and all the kids up north for a few days of nothing but fun. We would fit as many as we could in the cabin and the rest pitched tents throughout Ma's 5 acres. There would be anywhere from 20 to 25 people, adults and children, that converged on "The Hill." That's what we called this wonderful slice of heaven in the woods. "The Hill". It was like our mini Woodstock.

Our July 4th excursions lasted for several years but the best one was our last one. Besides going to the swimming hole, cookouts, horseshoes and snipe hunting, we had the "Kids Olympics." Featuring Water balloon toss, 3-legged race, sack race, and water-in-spoon relay. To open the games we had a moment of silence as my best friend, Tom came bursting out of the front door of the cabin with his Bic lighter ablaze - The "Kidlympics" flame. Let the games begin! A great fun day, and after all was said and done it was victory ribbons for all the kids. Not to mention ice cream and cake!

In years past we always had bon-fires and some form of fireworks but the unusually high temperatures and lack of rain put the fire danger at "very high." No bon-fires, no fireworks!

I always made my own cassette tape compilations and, always wanting to fill the entire 90 minutes of the tape, I had many sound effects albums that I would use for the endings. Learning that the fire danger was going to reach at least "High" in Mio the cassette I was compiling for our July 4th Fun Fest I decided to add fireworks sound effects to the end of the tape. I knew my buddy, Tom was bringing his boom box, and since mine was a dual cassette player AND I had blank tapes we decided since we couldn't have actual fireworks we'd simulate. We copied the sound effects onto a blank tape. Now we had two copies. So far, so good.

When darkness settled in around us, we had the kids and adults gather 'round the fire pit. We put a small flashlight in the pit that was our bon-fire. Then Tom and his son with their boom box stood on one side of the fire pit and my oldest son and me with our boom box on the other side. All four of us had bigger 6-volt flashlights and once everyone was settled in, we started the boom boxes. As soon as the fireworks began playing Tom and I and the boys pointed our flashlights toward the sky and began turning them on and off intermittently, our fireworks. The adults immediately started "oohing and ahhhing". All the kids immediately looked at us like we were completely insane! It didn't take long though and the kids began "oohing and ahhhing" right along with us! It wasn't the real thing but it certainly was quite a fun, memorable time.

Fannie Hoe

Between remembering what I could at age 6 or 7 and what my folks and sister told me, our vacation trips to the Upper Peninsula were incredible. Adventurous? Yes, you could say that.

My parents were never in a hurry to get to any of our destinations on time. Opting for roadside lunches and numerous side trips. Don't get me wrong, my sister and I never complained. It was so cool, always wondering what was next!

Since there were so many side excursions, we usually would arrive at our next stop pretty deep into the night. There wasn't much that would light your way back then as you traveled the U.P. so the dark of the night seemed even darker. This allowed my Dad to tell us stories, spooky stories that would scare us no matter how many times we heard them.

Copper Harbor was our main destination. Especially Lake Fannie Hoe. So many memories, swimming, fishing (with no luck), feeding the ducks, and skipping stones. At night, before bed, we'd have a bon-fire. We'd roast marshmallows while Dad would tell us more stories. Like the story about the Indian maiden who drowned in Lake Fannie Hoe. Dad told us the town folk had all searched and searched for her but she was never to be found. At night Dad said when the wind was just right you could hear her call out, "Fannie Hoe," Fannie Hoe." Only two times and then silence. It chilled our spines the way he told it. But not as much as when we were almost asleep in our cabin beds and from the outside hear the eerie cry of "FANNIE HOE, FANNIE HOE"! Covers over our heads. Scared the crap out of us. Thanks Dad.

Northwoods of Michigan

As a kid, my family and I used to go up north all the time. Didn't make any difference what time of the year it was. When Dad said, "Are you kids ready?" Our eyes would light up and smiles would quickly grow on our faces. Then as time moved on and family too, the trips to the Northwoods became less and less until they weren't any more.

Now fast forward and I'm in my twenties and I'm taking my first trip north. It's been too many years since. My girlfriend, Barb, who is now my wife of 40 years, and I were on a journey to visit friends who were attending Michigan Tech University in Houghton near the top of the Upper Peninsula. It was winter and with snow covered, slow going roads it was going to be a long trip, coming from down state. Barb and I decided it would be wise to make the trip in two days. So she arranged with her folks for us to spend the night at her family cabin in Mio. The bonus was that her Dad, Mom and brother were already there and waiting for us!

I pulled up their driveway and shut off the car. The first thing I noticed when I got out was my breath dancing in the night as I talked to Barb. AH! Breathing in that fresh northern air. We were surrounded by snow covered pine trees and bathed in Mother Nature's night light. Barb and I hugged and said nothing. And what did we hear? Nothing. So silent. So quiet. So serene. So peaceful. I looked up to see a beautiful full moon and that's when I gasped and slowly said, "Oh, Wow!" I was gazing at more stars than I had ever remembered seeing in my entire life! It was like so many twinkling diamonds in the sky. The Northwoods of Michigan just takes my breathe away!

Jacqueline, Joy, Jean, and Joanne Peterson in 1945

Northern Michigan is Still My Home
By Vivian Jacqueline Peterson Secrist of Flushing, Michigan
Born 1929

I was born in Flint, Michigan. There are six of us children, four girls, and two boys. When I was about two years old, my brother was hit by a car in Flint. My parents decided then they didn't want to raise six children in a city, so they moved to Atlanta. They knew people who lived in Atlanta on Kellyville Road by the name of Downings. We homesteaded 40 acres on Kellyville Road. My mother worked around Atlanta. One place she worked was Claude Mowery's restaurant. My father also worked around Atlanta. One job he had was a job working on M33 when they paved that road.

We children went to school in Atlanta. We rode the bus. The bus we took was always late or early. We had to walk ¼ mile to catch the bus. This one time when the school was having a program at Christmas, we missed the bus. We all wanted to go to the program very much, so we took off and walked down the old railroad track to the school. We were all pretty young but we went.

After we had lived on the farm for 10 years, we moved to Big Rock on Beltz Road. We still took the school bus and walked ½ mile to catch the bus. We lived about six or seven miles to Atlanta. We would walk to town quite often. There was little snack restaurant about one mile west of Atlanta called Mae and Wards. All the teens went there. We could eat or dance. It was a nice place. We had a lot of

Atlanta High School and Elementary School in 1940

fun.

After I graduated from Atlanta High School, I worked different places for a couple of years. Then I got married. I married Vernon Secrist. He lived with his Aunt Fanny and Uncle Floyd on Manier Road. He had quit school after 10th grade and joined the Navy in 1945. After he had been back a few years, we got married. Then we moved back to Flint. He worked in the Buick Plant there.

We were back up north quite often. My mother was still living there and a sister, Jean Smith and a brother, Fred Peterson. We go to the 4-H County Fair a lot and other things they have every year. We go to Clear Lake, and my family does some fishing. I feel Atlanta is still my home.

My classmates and I still go north and celebrate our class reunion every year. Last year, we celebrated our 65th Reunion. There are only eight of us left, but I still enjoy seeing the ones who can come. We graduated in 1947.

The Good Ole Days
By Helen Woodward of Pellston, Michigan
Born 1938

I grew up in Harbor Springs, Michigan in the Forties. Harbor Springs is a small town on Little Travers Bay. I lived on West 3rd Street, across from the Catholic School and Church. The school is gone now. It was an Indian boarding school. I was a day scholar.

Summers were spent at the beach with friends. The beach was two blocks from where I lived. Those days for fun the kids in the neighborhood would get together and play kick the can in the alley between 3rd and 4th Streets, collect and exchange comic books, and play baseball in the school playgrounds.

There was a movie theater in town, a dock by the bay where we could fish or see Navy boats or passenger ships when they came in to dock. When passenger ships would leave, the people would throw coins to the kids on the dock.

Those days, we listened to radio programs. My favorite was *Sargent Preston of the Yukon*. Others were *The Lone Ranger*, *Jack Benny*, *Burns and Allen*, *Fibber McGee and Molly*, and *The Shadow*.

As a Girl Scout in those days, we went door to door selling cookies. I think they were about 35 cents a box.

Our winters, with a lot of snow, were spent taking our sleds to the sand hills to slide or going to the ice rink up behind the high school. Or we spent time in the library.

Things I remember from when I was a child are iceboxes, an ice house where we would buy ice blocks, an iron we'd heat on the wood stove to iron clothes, heating bricks and then wrapping them to put at the foot of the bed, coal furnaces, and getting a dose of cod liver oil or castor oil if we needed it.

As they say, those were the good ole days.

A Muskrat in the Fishing Shack
By William Welk of Alpena, Michigan
Born 1931

I was fishing for pike on the Thunder Bay River one day. I was spear fishing for the pike in a shanty, and I could see anything that came in the hole I had cut in the ice. It was extremely cold that day, and the ice was thick. There was a lot of pressure on the river that day, which made a loud noise every now and then. This would scare me, which in turn would make me jump off my seat in the shanty.

Wouldn't you know, a muskrat came up in the hole for air and scared me half to death. It ran around inside the shanty until finally it went back down the hole.

When my fishing partner showed up, he said, "What happened to the roof of the shanty?" I told him what had happened. He laughed at me, because I had put the handle of the spear right through the roof of the shanty trying to get that darn muskrat back in the hole.

A Muskrat in the Fishing Shack
By William Welk of Alpena, Michigan
Born 1931

I was fishing for pike on the Thunder Bay River one day. I was spear fishing for the pike in a shanty, and I could see anything that came in the hole I had cut in the ice. It was extremely cold that day, and the ice was thick. There was a lot of pressure on the river that day, which made a loud noise every now and then. This would scare me, which in turn would make me jump off my seat in the shanty.

Wouldn't you know, a muskrat came up in the hole for air and scared me half to death. It ran around inside the shanty until finally it went back down the hole.

When my fishing partner showed up, he said, "What happened to the roof of the shanty?" I told him what had happened. He laughed at me, because I had put the handle of the spear right through the roof of the shanty trying to get that darn muskrat back in the hole.

✓ Hospitality in the Old Days
By Lorraine Hansen of Cheboygan,
Michigan
Born 1924

I was riding with my son and granddaughter one day as she was learning to drive. Five miles outside of town, in the country, we passed an old house where I had lived 65 years ago. It was on Old Mackinaw Road. I told her I wasn't as lucky as her today, for there were no school buses back then. Mine were usually the first tracks in the snow as I walked every day to Cheboygan High School on Sherigan-Divison Street. Sometimes I met two ladies who worked at the bank, or if I was lucky, I got a ride with the milkman.

Coming home, walking, I would get so cold I would stop to get warm in neighbors' homes. Hospitality was a very natural thing in those days, and I would be treated to a nice warm drink of hot cocoa. I would thank them and be on my way again. If I walked all the way, I would get home in time for supper.

My granddaughter didn't say anything, but I could imagine her thoughts.

✓ The House That Was Paid for by Trading Stamps
By Jeanne Crawford of Rogers City,
Michigan
Born 1953

Did you ever purchase S&H Green Stamps as a kid? Well, I hope you enjoy reading the true story about my wealthy and famous great-great cousin, I think named Shelly B. Hutchinson. My Great-Grandpa, Herbert C. Hutchinson, had an uncle named Shelly B. Hutchinson who built a Queen Anne style mansion in Ypsilanti, MI at the turn of the twentieth century. Did you ever hear the saying, "Save that coffee card from Café Luwak"? Well, that's exactly how Shelly Hutchinson made enough money to build the biggest house in town. He had the idea for trading stamps, and his partnership with Sperry made them a fortune.

The materials for the mansion, his thirty-three room, single family dwelling, came from all over the world. He included many unique features, such as an indoor pool, a two-story ballroom with an orchestra loft, one of the country's earliest elevators, and a dining room that is a replica of that found in Kaiser Wilhelm's mansion in Germany.

Young Shelly started out as a dancing master and seems to have enjoyed some success as such. He was well known for his ability and even made a tour of the west. Yet it was while working as a clerk in a store at Battle Creek, MI, that he first developed his idea for a trading stamp business. With that great business success, Hutchinson moved back to Ypsilanti, built his big house, and then lost it.

Once he lost his home business and money, Hutchinson moved to New York. Little is known of how he spent the next forty years, although something was said of him selling real estate. He visited Ypsilanti at the age of ninety-one. He is buried in the family plot in Highland Cemetery, just north of his house on the hill.

✓ To the Man Who Saved My Life
By William R. Frank of Roscommon,
Michigan
Born 1947

Roscommon, MI is where I grew up in the late '50s. We had activities all summer long, and they were all free! The local Rotary Club sponsored the Summer Recreation Program for all the kids to enjoy. Open gym all day long, baseball, and swimming at Higgins Lake every morning and afternoon. Not just any lake, the sixth most beautiful lake in the world per *National Geographic*.

One hot summer day, I was swimming at Gerrish Township Park. I, being ten going on eleven, had it all figured out. I thought I was a pretty good swimmer. This lake goes out very gradually to about six feet deep, and then there is a drop off. Black water is what they call it, easily one hundred feet deep. Someone had anchored a raft right at the drop off. Usually only the high school kids went out that deep. On my way out to the raft, I found out I wasn't as good a swimmer as I thought. I was in water over my head and in trouble. Suddenly, one of the "big boys" jumped in and saved my life. It all happened so fast, I don't know if I thanked him properly.

Fast forward to about 2009, and I am reading the *Houghton Lake Resorter*. I see a picture of a fifty-year Houghton Lake High School class reunion. In the listing of those attending, I see a name that instantly takes me back to that summer day at Higgins Lake. It was a man named Herb Smith, now a man of late sixty years of age. As I would find out later, he was a career military man and highly decorated. Reading his name made me appreciate the large gift he had given me. Without his unselfish effort that day, I would never have graduated from high school, gotten married, started a business, had four beautiful girls, or have a special granddaughter going on three. A few years after reading of that class reunion, I read his obituary. He had passed away in his early seventies.

It was then again that I wondered did I ever thank him properly?

✓ Moving Down on the Farm
By Jane Poirier of Fort Myers, Florida

We were living in the suburbs of Detroit in a seven bedroom, red brick home with a three-car garage, just three houses down from the beautiful Lake Saint Clair. All seven (at the time) of us children attended a parochial school, where we were instructed in the archaic teaching of the Catholic system, but from time to time, we did manage to have some fun with our large family.

I remember when Mom and Dad said we were moving to a farm in northern Michigan, and I began to panic. I had dreamy childhood plans on moving to Detroit and getting a job when I was 18! Perhaps I would be a secretary for a large firm and maybe marry a lawyer.

It was April and we had a huge snowfall throughout Michigan. When we finally made

The farmhouse

it to the farm, it was pitch dark, a darkness that I had never seen in the city. "Where is the house?" I asked Dad as he parked the truck. "Down there," he said as he pointed into the black night. We were at the end of a 400-yard long driveway that was lined with barren black walnut trees that seemed to have arms that would grab me as I walked through them.

When my eyes adjusted, I could see the outline of a dark shape on top of a small hill and other ominous objects spread throughout the landscape. The snow was three feet deep, and we had to grab only what we would need for the next day. So we bundled up what we could carry and made that long walk through the deep snow.

As I reached the end of the driveway, I saw this long-neglected house that was so dilapidated that I thought for sure Mom and Dad had made some sort of mistake. "This is not our house," I said to myself. I looked at Julie and said, "This looks like a haunted house." I was so scared and by the look on hers' and Kelly's faces, I was sure that they were, too.

We looked around as we made that trek into the darkness and saw a broken down garage. Slightly to the left and behind that was what looked like a huge shed. Later, I found out it was a bunkhouse used to house the migrants for what must have been a working farm at one time. Behind that there were apple trees frozen in the snow. To the right and behind the decaying garage was a smaller building that was used as a chicken coop. To the right of that was a path that led to the "back forty." To the right of the path was a barn that was in the best condition of all the other buildings on the compound, including the house itself. Further to the right was another barn in decent shape.

And to the right of that, as though it was from a horror novel, was a swamp! I had never felt such dread until that point in my young life.

The First Night

Kelly, Julie, and I were told that our bedroom was at the end of the hallway upstairs. Of course, it was right next to the attic! We walked into the room with our flashlight, as we had no electricity yet. We looked around at the walls that we would be spending the best years of our lives; talking of school and boys, and girls that we didn't like, etc., and saw holes the size of fists, peeling wallpaper, and our own breath billowing out of our gaping mouths. We were so cold as we laid out our sleeping bags on the unvarnished wooden floor and quickly climbed in them. "I don't like it here," seemed to come out of our mouths at the same time. As if on cue, what must have been a mouse ran through the walls and was joined by his friends. I think it was Julie who said, "Did you hear that?" We didn't sleep that night.

Being thrown into that situation was the closest that we three girls had ever been, along with many other scary nights to come.

Snakes in the Barrel and Snakes in the Hay
By Meta Johnson of Reed City, Michigan
Born 1925

We lived two and a half miles from town, so that was the distance we trekked to school. In 1936-1937, when the big snowstorm came, the roads were filled from shoulder to shoulder. We headed out, but there was nothing identifiable except the row of fence posts that peaked out of the snow for two to four inches. We walked on the fence each day until the snow softened, and there with each step we sank as far as we could go in the snow. The locals dug the snow out by shovelfuls and hauled it away on a sleigh. The road was plugged for six weeks while the main roads were slowly cleared.

Growing up, we never had a water well with a pump or a windmill. We carried water one eighth of a mile from a spring along the road. Occasionally, there would be a frog or snake in the barrel that was set in the spring. Rainwater was caught in washtubs for laundry, and a good spanking was imminent if we were caught messing with it. One day while hauling water in cream cans on a stone boat, the horse dropped dead and we ended up carrying the water that day and from then on. In the house, there was one pail of water and a dipper for everyone's use. Daily wash up was in a basin with a washcloth and sponge baths were the norm. Laundry was done in washtubs with a scrub board and was wrung out by hand. Whites were washed first, then colors, and overalls, etc. last. The same water was used for the entire wash. Later, there was a washing machine with a gasoline motor that packed a good kick. In the winter, the clothes froze to the clothesline and were later brought in to finish drying.

Haying was done by horse drawn mowing machine and a dump rake. It would be raked into a window and later stacked. At hauling time, we would dig into the stack and throw it onto the wagon where someone would distribute it so the load would be even. It was my job to place it on the wagon, and everyone thought it was hilarious when they would throw up a snake with the fork full of hay. That was a way to get me off and running away from the hay wagon. To this day, snakes and I are not friends.

Back Then
By Maxine Pettinger of Manistee, Michigan
Born 1936

Growing up three-quarters of a century ago, my parents, their friends, or even the doctors and nurses did not use terms such as "obsessive," compulsive," or "politically correct," just "it's a habit" or "she'll outgrow it."

We didn't live in a city or even a small town, just an area called Stickney Township, near a crossroad on the highway from there to somewhere. We could climb up and sit amongst the trees on the bluff and watch the cars whiz by. There was a railroad spur where the engine was left for a while. My friends and I could climb around in it during the long summer days and play all kinds of imaginary games and adventures. Eventually, they moved the engine and pulled up the tracks. During my last visit out "there," the bluff seemed pretty small to me. I stood and gazed at it and wondered was it ever there? Did it just seem like I was climbing a hill?

I remember back decades ago, helping Mother prepare Jell-O. How I loved that and the wondrous boxes that contained the wax paper packets that were folded to hold the flavored gelatin crystals. After mixing the colorful powder with the boiling water, my reward was to lick the waxed paper wrap. Nowadays the children don't have that luxury. How sad.

At the time, I lived in "my small wooden castle," even with what, I imagined, were the same drafty rooms during the winter as the large stone castles I had seen in the movies. I would think of it as the castles in Northern Ireland or Scotland, the castles of my ancestors. Instead of a giant fireplace that we had to chop wood for to provide heat for the castle, we had an oil stove to keep us warm. This oil stove, when filled with oil, glowed red with heat that would drive the cold drafts as a legion of knights chasing the enemy toward the shore and their boats.

There was nothing I wouldn't do to keep that legion riding, so when my mother assigned me the oil chore, I was the obedient serf. My job every other week was to keep oil in the stove. I filled a five-gallon can from the two hundred fifty gallon drum, which stood on the far side of the garage. I was proud to be the provider of the necessary fuel to feed "our fire-spewing dragon," which protected us from the cold.

At age twelve, I could not carry the full can all the way into the house. I would carry it a bit, stop, sit it down, rest, and then start out again. My father worked out of town, and my only brother was only a year old. So my older sister and I shared this job. But my reward was the knowledge that the next morning, I would be able to jump out of bed and warm my hands next to the stove. Each morning, it was my habit to run out of my room to the "wonderful warm dragon" and sit and stretch my arms toward the stove with hands opened wide to warm myself. No good deed went unrewarded.

Another old time appliance was our wringer washer, which was in our detached garage. So the best time of the year for the laundry chore was spring and summer when we could open the doors and let the sunshine in. I remember one sunny day, listening to the radio while doing laundry when it happened.

I was putting the clothes through the wringer, and as I had been warned not to do, I was pushing the clothes with my fingers too close to the roller. Sure enough, it happened; the roller grabbed onto my fingers. I got one out, but my index finger was wrapped into the sheet. I screamed like bloodied Mary, but with the radio on, I wasn't sure anyone could hear me. I was crying, screaming, and then I closed the rest of my fingers around my thumb and pulled back. I'm not sure how exactly it happened, but my dad was there, holding me around the shoulders, the wringers were sprung up, and my hand was freed from the flesh-eating monster. To this day, my right index finger is a quarter inch longer than my left index finger. Proof you should listen to mothers when they say don't put your fingers in the rollers.

That was then.

✓ Campers and White Sand
By Paula Vivyan of Central Lake, Michigan
Born 1952

I have lived in Michigan my whole life. Currently I live with my husband, Ray, in Central Lake and work in Bellaire. This is a story my dad told me when he was 79 years old and battling cancer. I had never heard him talk about it before. My husband and I were sitting with Dad, recalling old times.

Paula's brother, Paula, and her dad

Paula and her mom on a camping trip

Dad was a "Jack of all trades" in every sense. He religiously read *Mechanics Illustrated*, as well as many "how to" trade magazines.

So, when I was five years old, in 1957, Dad decided to build the family a travel trailer for camping. He spent every spare moment he had on the project, welding the frame out of a large truck chassis, and then he constructed the body and interior. He fashioned it a bit like the popular Airstream trailer. The trailer had all the amenities: a kitchen, a bathroom, a couch that folded out into a double bed, and a kitchen table with two benches that also folded into a double bed. It was amazing. He finished it in six months, got it licensed, and we were on our way. Everywhere we went, people came over to check out the camper.

This story begins at Grand Haven State Park. We were on a three-week adventure, heading north. It was our first two-night stay at Grand Haven. My older brother, who was fifteen at the time, was responsible for watching me while my folks went fishing. He was way more interested in the girls on the beach than he was in keeping an eye on me, so he left me to entertain myself in the sand.

We spent two glorious days at Grand Haven, and then we pulled up stakes and headed north. We were so excited. We were cruising up Highway 31 when Dad noticed something a little off. He thought the brakes were locking up on the trailer, because when we were trying to navigate up the hills, our '53 Chevy station wagon was groaning. So he pulled off at a small roadside park to take a look.

He began by crawling under the car and trailer to inspect everything. It left him scratching his head. While we were waiting, my mom made us sandwiches in our little kitchen. She happened to notice a little white sand on the floor. She looked a little closer and began trying to find the source of the sand. It seemed to be coming from under the table. When Dad came in to eat his sandwich, she mentioned the sand.

They spent the next hour talking about the problem, and then my dad got a look on his face. He made us all get up from the table and he opened the bench seat. He sat down on the floor and laughed until he cried, and then my mom and brother broke out laughing. While we were in Grand Haven, I had entertained myself by filling both storage compartments under the bench seats with sand, using my small yellow bucket and shovel.

We spent the next three hours getting all the sand out so we could head north again. When we returned home from our camping trip, my dad put a huge tractor tire in our backyard and filled it with white sand.

Bananas, White Boots, and the Lake
By Joan L. Cole of Taylor, Michigan
Born 1944

I remember going north to Mikado to my grandparents' farm with my mother and uncle. It was on US10, a dirt road, and one way was 238 miles and about eight hours. When we got to Oscoda, my uncle said to me if I wasn't good, he would throw me in the lake and how close he could get to the water.

Then when we get to Goddard's road past Goddard's farm be getting to Grandpa's farm. He was in a bed with a rope tied to the ceiling for his leg exercises. He had a stroke. He had white hair and a mustache. Grandma had gray hair in circle braids on top of her head.

The La Cure truck came and Grandma got bananas, pink candy, and other things. The fruit bowl sat on a dresser in the bedroom. She put the bananas in it. I was the first to go to bed, so the bananas went down me. The peels went over the headboard. Sick, oh boy! I thought I was going in the lake.

I'd go out when my other uncle would do the milking. I could get some warm milk then. One time I wore my new white boots to

111

the barn, and the cow raised its tail. Off to the house I ran, barefoot. I thought my boots were ruined. No more milk for me.

About a mile south were an Indian settlement, a church, and a cemetery. In between was a small cabin where Old Man Buster lived. We would go to check on him for Grandma.

My other grandparents lived in Glennie. They passed before I was born.

My mother worked at Oscoda Hotel. My mother's uncle had a dairy farm in Harrisville. He had to keep his cheese in the dairy house. I saw cottage cheese, butter, and cream made. My aunt worked midnights at the nursing home in Harrisville and still had a beautiful farmhouse.

There were outhouses on both farms and everywhere else. The joke was on my sister-in-law. She was about 5 feet and ninety pounds. I was about five four and one hundred sixty pounds. We went to the outhouse. My brother, six feet and two hundred thirty pounds, goes behind the outhouse, does like an Indian sound. My sister-in-law ran to Mom and Dad's house with her pants down. I peed right through the mini-scare. It was a good laugh then.

I only have a few cousins left. My grandparents have all passed. My uncle bought the farmhouse and everything changes. My dad and mom retired and built a place across from Goddard's farm. Then they passed. Now there are trailers, small houses, and empty lots. Mom and Dad's house went into foreclosure.

In 1998, my husband bought a seventy-five foot trailer on Pine River in Kill Master. He had a stroke and passed in 2010, so her I sit with health issues. I have three dogs, a pug, Lucy, and two small poodles, Dam It (Pop's name for her before he passed and Coca.

I had a lot of uncles. One took my boy to see one last Indian, Wal be Kat, in his cabin. How my son talked about that to everyone at school! Today, that son has the trailer and takes his grandchildren and his friends all around. His wife is from Alpena.

I have one cousin who owns Winslow Doors. A nephew owns a shop in Harrisville. One sister is in a nursing home in Harrisville. One cousin retired after working in a Harrisville drugstore from high school until age sixty-six. That is a lot of years. One of my brothers is in Alpena.

John's Story
By John P. Belasco of Margate, Florida
Born 1936

Glad to be out of the snowstorm and cold of 1940, five year old John Belasco climbed the stairs to the tenement apartment where he lived with his parents and a younger and older sister in Brighton, Massachusetts. Halfway up the stairs, he would hear his dad playing the piano and practicing his beautiful Italian tenor voice. Too young to know of a man's dreams of singing opera at Carnegie Hall, he sneaked into the room and sat on the floor to listen. What a handsome man, what a beautiful voice! He wondered why the other tenants complained about his dad's practice. To him, everything his dad did was perfect. He never questioned anything he said or never failed to act when his dad told him to do something. He slipped off his shoes and put his hands over his feet to warm them.

His dad finished his practice and stood up. He said, "John, I need these things from the store." He spoke the list slowly to him while John struggled into his wet shoes. Living with a father with a photographic memory, he listened carefully to the list so he would not disappoint him.

He shuffled down the steps, out into the snow, where it was deeper than just a short time ago. He pulled himself up on the fence that separated him from the store. He climbed to the top and jumped into the snow. Once inside the store, he quickly located the items for his dad and slugged his way through the snow to Bracket Street. At least he didn't have to worry about getting beat up by Irish kids on a night like tonight. They sometimes strayed from the next alley into Italian streets.

Home once more, John climbed the stairs, but there was no piano playing or singing this time. He could hear his parents screaming and swearing at each other, each blaming the other for having kids to care for. An object hit the wall, making a crashing sound. John huddled on the stairs, holding his breath. His father's voice broke the silence, "I told you to get rid of that boy before you brought another mouth to feed into the world. Other women do it, why couldn't you?

His mother's clear, Irish voice was shrill, "Come a step closer to me, and I'll put this knife into your guts."

The door opened and his dad fled past him down the stairs. John slumped, crying on the steps. He wiped the tears, climbed back up the steps, thinking his dad would be back soon. He went to the window, watching dirty pigeons digging through the filth the neighbors threw out. He looked down at his clothes. He was as dirty as the pigeons. He waited for a long time, but his dad never came back.

His mother was forced to take any work she could get just to feed the three kids she was solely responsible for. There was no time for niceties like bathing them and keeping their clothes clean and certainly no time for hugs and kisses. Spring came, and he slowly realized his dad was never coming back.

By age seven, he was home alone for most days and night. His mother worked two to three jobs to try to keep the family together. She did take time to check John's grades at the Catholic school he attended, and a failing one got him a spanking. Her spankings were nothing compared to his punishments at school. He was left handed, a trait the nuns were determined to correct by whacking him on the left hand when he was using it to write. He still has scars on his left hand from the ruler. He ended up not being able to write with either hand. One nun took a personal interest in him and provided the nurturing he so needed. He began to learn how to care for others. A young priest liked to work with kids and had a positive influence on John.

When he was eight years old, his mother announced they were moving in with her boyfriend. They packed with great anticipation of having a dad, a home, and becoming a family again. The new dad taught him how to read, and when he put stories in front of him to read, John was delighted that he knew the words on the pages. But it wasn't all school work. The new dad was an Indian and taught John how to hunt and trap. He put a cigar box with money in it on the counter and told John he could borrow from it, but he needed to put it back. When the money was gone, John asked for more. "John, if you borrow money, you need to put it back before you get more," his dad told him. Although his mother still worked, she was home to prepare meals and wash his clothes. He felt secure and safe at last. It was almost too good to be true.

After they had been there for about a year, John had settled into a routine. One night he was awakened from his peaceful sleep by his mother's screams. Her sobbing and moans frightened and confused him. He ran to his new dad for help. He recoiled in horrified unbelief as he saw his mother's bloodied face from his dad's fists. John ran across the room and started pounding him as hard as he could. His dad picked him up and threw him against the wall. His mother screamed for him to run. He went back to his room and piled into his bed that was no longer a safe haven. Anger swelled in him like a volcano. He wanted to go back to his dad and hurt him, but he was powerless.

His mother moved into a one bedroom apartment with John and his two sisters. John hung out with the neighborhood kids of the streets. In the summer, they played hide and seek on their bikes. In the winter, they skated down the streets behind a chair. They always gathered around to watch when there was a street fight. On one such occasions, one of the boys left because his dad was coming to visit. A couple of days later, a street fight brought the boys out to watch. As they got closer, they saw it was the visiting dad, beating his son.

At fourteen, he joined a street gang. The gang didn't lie or steal from each other, but above all, they didn't betray one of their own. That was what he was looking for. They strutted down the street, carrying brass knuckles, knives, and some of them had guns. They drank, swore, and lived by their golden rule, Do unto others before they have a chance to do unto you.

At sixteen, John gave up his struggle to read and write and quit school. He went to work in a tool shop. At seventeen, he once again grew weary of his failures and joined the Navy. He was assigned to the boiler room, where kids without high school diplomas went.

Out of the Navy at 21, John had no skills for a job and nowhere to go. He did get a job driving a truck. As he watched gang members plan attacks on others, it was crystal clear to him that he wanted a different life. He went to his mother's house and phoned his dad, who had called him from Colorado and offered him a job in his catering business and restaurant. John went to work with the pastry chef and learned a lot about baking. He later went to work in the bar of the restaurant and learned about wines and liquors.

He dated a lot of girls, but none of them seemed sincere. He talked to his co-worker about his frustration with the girls he was dating. "I know just the girl for you. Her name is Judy. She is beautiful, smart, and plays the violin. I'll introduce you tomorrow night," he said.

When John and Judy started to date, she invited him to go with her to Church of Christ. He not only fell in love with Judy, but he loved and respected her mother. She had major surgery and survival was not certain. She had tremendous faith in God. John told Judy, "Whatever that woman has, I want it."

At church, he learned of a God who could love and forgive. In March 1959, he married Judy and his life made a U-turn. In February 1959, he was baptized, called his mother and told her he wanted to be a minister in spite of unbelievable odds.

School was always a struggle; reading was slow and laborious because he was an auditory learner. He would have to work because he had a wife and a daughter. Nevertheless, he took the entrance test at a university in Colorado and began the first semester. At the end of the semester, he had all F's; at the end of the second semester, he had all F's. People began to tell him he should give up the idea of becoming a minister. He was prepared to pay the price of his call, which included 110 hours of work a week plus school. He had determination, grit, and a new-found faith to persevere. He wanted to tell people about this God who had mercy, this God who loved them no matter what they had done. By the third semester, he had raised two of the F's to D's. He felt encouraged and was just beginning to understand how to study. One of his instructors had told him to find a study group of good students and then observe the habits and methods of the A students and do what they did. John followed this advice all his life and developed the motto of, "if you do what they do, you'll be what they are." He was getting more successful at school, but the scars of his past life showed up in the form of anger and fights.

John became a talented fund raiser for missions and for the churches where he served. He studied Jesus' life and the early Christians so he could do what they did and become like them. He and Judy had five children and took in two abused foster children. He spent 29 years as a pastor of Royal Oak Church in Michigan. He worked tirelessly in the community as well as in the church. He served 1,700 people in the area. If people needed medicine, John bought it. If a family needed food, John took it to them. If they needed clothes, John gave them money. They often became members of the church. He taught and lived grace love, and forgiveness.

Pastoring a church is much more than delivering sermons, visiting, and eating church fellowship meals. It's butting heads and breaking hearts with the leaders in the church. Personalities clash over everything from theology to grounds keeping. Power struggles exist in almost all churches, but John says he has met some of the most spiritual, sincere men in church than anywhere else.

In 2012, John left the ministry. He and Judy moved to Florida where he became involved in missions, one of the loves of his life. He had a lot of experience raising funds. John became the director and fund raiser for the Royal Ok Church of Christ for the Mission Clinic International. Dr. Jason Moore, an emergency physician in Michigan, started and manages the Panama Mission. His plan is to heal both body and spirit. John is training a number of men in the art of raising funds for the mission.

"If I could say something to my reader," John said, "it would be to live each day as if it is your last, because it might be."

✓ Country Life
By Dorothy Wendt of Bear Lake, Michigan
Born 1926

I am an 86 year old widow. I've had quite a good life. I was born in a small town in 1926 by the name of Kaleva, a Finnish town. I was the youngest of twelve children, six boys, and six girls. My parents worked, and I was sent to school when I was four. We didn't have very much but never went hungry or without clothes. My mother made a lot of all our clothes, some out of feed sacks and flour sacks.

When I was five years old, my mother sent me down to the store to get P&G Soap to do the wash. Yes, we could go anywhere

Dorothy's parents, Georgia and John Gannon

and no worries. Well, while I was in the store, some men robbed the bank across from the store and shot Mr. Billman, who we all knew very well. They were caught and put in prison.

We moved to a town called Manistee, a bigger town than Kaleva. I went to my first dentist, and he pulled a tooth. I cried going home. He was a good friend of our family in the end.

We then moved to a farm of 640 acres of cherries and apples. My father and three or four brothers all worked there. As we younger ones got old enough, we picked apples and cherries. I got real good at it in later years.

I had some excellent teachers. I don't believe I was a teacher's pet though. We went to a small school through eighth grade, and then we had to go to a bigger school where some of us graduated. We had to walk about one and a half miles to New Land School. In winter, it was hard. We had a lot more snow back in those days. We wore long socks and long johns. The bus, when we went to Onekama School, didn't pick us up at our yard or drive. I walked out the mile to get to it.

We didn't any of us kids get too sick or break many bones, one brother, and one sister. My mother gave us kids castor oil once in a while but I couldn't give it to my kids. When I was four or five, I had an ear ache. My dad worked on the railroad, and he took me to a doctor in Copemish by handcar. It was one of those hand-pumped ones. I got an Easter bunny from him. I guess I must have been

good.

I guess we didn't take too many baths back in those days. I suppose once a week. We had outdoor toilets until we moved to Manistee, and then we had it all.

When I got 14 years old, my parents had a car, and I got to drive. It had a rumble seat and if I could afford it, I'd have one today.

I was 16 when we moved off the farm. We lived in Onekama, a small town but a nice lake, Portage Lake and Lake Michigan to the west. I had a few boyfriends while in high school.

Yes, I lived through the Depression years, but we did what needed to get along. As I said, we didn't go hungry and with nine to ten people to feed. My mother made a lot of stuff, good food. I'm sure some came from people who had more than we did. We had chicken every Sunday. We all played games outside or inside, plus a lot of neighbors.

We had no TV or telephone. I we had a message for someone we walked there to tell them. We did get a phone when we got to Onekama and finally a TV. There were not too many channels back then, seven, or nine up this way. I could live without it but not my radio. Our first phone was one where we had two or more rings to get someone, like one long and one short. I worked in a telephone office where we rang up people. We could listen in on a few conversations. The manager and I would play dominos where we weren't busy.

I finally married and had two children, one girl, and one boy. My husband lived until 1999 and we celebrated 53 years together. I have two grandchildren and 6 great-grandkids, two

The Gannon Boys

115

to fourteen years of age. My great-grandkids have all the electronic games to play with, and I just don't like them (the electronics). Kids don't know how to carry on a conversation with anyone – too busy texting, etc.

We had several dogs but our favorite was Ginger, a small dog we had for 13 years. She was three when we got her from friends. We don't have her anymore.

We live sort of in the country on two acres. There are not many snakes around here; a few blue racers years ago. I hate snakes anyway so I don't care if there are any around.

Now with spring coming on, we'll be busy out in the yard and garden. I don't do much anymore but I do like to raise a few things, fresh tomatoes, pickles, and berries. Yum.

✓ Oakridge Tom
By Paul T. O'Dell of Presque Isle, Michigan
Born 1936

During the latter part of April, in a Michigan forestland, a North American Legend, the symbol of Thanksgiving, Tom Turkey, set the stage for the greatest hunting experience of any sportsman's dream. This story was the culmination of six years of this sportsman's dream to hunt for, study, fantasize, yearn for, and literally pray for the chance to fill his Wild Turkey Hunting Permit in the wonderful man made wild turkey range in the northern lower peninsula of Michigan.

It was another year, another opportunity to obtain a wild turkey hunting permit in the Michigan Department of National Resources Lottery's method of choosing several thousand hunters, out of which only five percent will be successful. No matter how ridiculous this sounds, the challenge is magnified to the extent; it has created a hunting trophy second to none. Imagine if you can, the approximately 800,000 Michigan deer hunters heading into the opening day woods with only the chance of 500 being successful. These odds are what the aspiring wild turkey hunter faces. Do you know what this means in terms of incentive to an optimistic hunter? It is like a drug that confuses the senses. It tells him that on one hand, he will be lucky to be permitted to participate. On the other hand, he could become

the envy of all hunters when he bags the most mysterious of all game birds. It is the degree of difficulty that establishes top trophies and certainly, a transplanted Pennsylvania turkey in a Michigan environment qualifies.

In Scene I, the anxious turkey hunter is planning which season offered in the lottery he will choose this year. His decision is the 30th of April and the first three days of May. This decision has to be made before the end of March. Next, even before knowing if the permit is drawn, a seminar is offered to further tease and whet the appetite. Of course, the hunter and his companions charge ahead as if no obstacles exist. The imagination runs rampant. The hunting paraphernalia is considered: camouflage, grease paint, calls, both box type and mouth type, decoys, and location on opening morning.

Scouting is performed prior to the season to determine the wild turkey's whereabouts. Hours of blowing owl and crow calls in the evening after dark to get a Tom to respond. A labor of love for a chance to encounter the greatest game bird of all.

The object is to get an answer from a male bird on his roost. If an answer is received, it is certain the bird will remain at that location until daylight. It is then important, of course, to be in a position before daylight to encounter Mr. Tom when he comes down from his roost to have breakfast and some turkey love, whichever comes first.

The Hunt
The morning sky was overflowing with stars. As of yet, there was no hint of sunrise on the eastern horizon. I weaved my way along the edge of a huckleberry swamp, trying to avoid the fallen trees and low-hanging branches illuminated by the starlight. I had picked my spot for the opening day of this Michigan turkey season several weeks before, based on pre-season scouting. For some reason, I had this strong desire to find a place to settle down before I had even reached the first of three ridges I had planned to cross. I gave in to the urge and knelt down in a glacial pothole on a side hill of the first ridge I had come to. There, I would wait for the beautiful dawning of a spring morning in the northern lower peninsula of Michigan.

As the blackness of space between the millions of twinkling specks in the sky began fading to gray, the skyline to the east was taking on a fluorescent glow that increased in intensity in unison with the chorus created by awakening birds and wood sounds. The lovely stillness, the peacefulness of the morning, was worth all the effort expended, that I might be present to be a witness to it. The hunting of a Michigan gobbler was secondary at this moment. I had already been rewarded by a natural resource that did not require a license, just the senses of the mind, soul, and body.

The musty aroma of the dead oak stump I leaned against was strong like a spice, delicious to the nostrils. Two owls sent morning mating calls back and forth over a quarter mile of treetops as a jay swept along their communication route, adding caws like static to their conversation. Crows let their presence be known by unpleasant squawking. Occasionally, something sounding remotely like a turkey gobble would follow their lead. This familiar response reminded me of what I had set out to do this morning. I slowly removed the Pennsylvania box call from my camouflage parka. I had borrowed the call from a friend who was born in Redding, PA, and swore to its authenticity. I gently scraped out three series of "keouks" on the oak and mahogany instrument. Silence prevailed as the seemingly unnatural sound quieted the forest. Several minutes passed before the distant sound repeated. It was most assuredly a Tom, anxious for companionship before breakfast. I knew if he was really interested, he would be shortening the distance between us, excited to meet his next conquest. Silence was my best weapon. Fifteen or twenty minutes had passed before I reluctantly decided to break the silence with a forced "took, took, took…took, took, took" on my mouth call. The effort produced an absolute calm, not even the squirrels or frogs thought it worthy of an answer. I waited what seemed like an eternity (about five minutes). Then suddenly an explosion of sound shook the forest, raising the hair on the back of my neck! The double gobble bounced around the trees like a ricocheting bullet. I froze. My heart pounded in my ears, and my knees shook. My only salvation was the fact that I had stopped behind an oak tree large enough in diameter to conceal my form and elected to remain standing. The tree was directly between me and "old thunder tonsils."

A peak around the oak in the direction of the bird's answer was astounding. Through the winter torn brush was a black form resembling the inflated display posture of the only Michigan big game with wings! I immediately ducked back behind the natural blind and began to wonder what the Hot Tom would do next.

I slowly raised my single shot Stevens 12 gage hand over hand from its leaning position against the oak, until I had its stock in my hands with the barrel tip strait overhead and directly behind the tree trunk. I knew if I had any chance for the gobbler to come into range, I'd have to remain as still and quiet as I ever had in my life.

I barely peered around the tree again and observed a most beautiful sight. This magnificent game bird was steadily strutting up the ridge toward my stand. His bronze tipped feathers shone iridescent in the morning sun, topped off by his dominantly white head. His head was accented with blue and red fleshy formations, known as wattles, loosely hanging from his neck. With each jerky step, the male turkey's most discriminating identification, a coarse horsehair-like beard, swung pendulum style from the gobbler's chest.

I felt that the next few moments would determine the outcome of this encounter as the Tom drew within fifty feet. I was almost enjoying the experience too much to bring it to an end when the large bird stopped and lowered his head to the ground, pecking at the matted oak leaves left from the heavy winter snows. It was my cue to lower the barrel and set the hammer, which in doing so created a telltale click that fortunately went unnoticed by my prey. As he lifted his head and cautiously began progressing in my direction again, I could hear the rustle of his clawed feet on the forest floor. The aroused Tom was intently surveying the spot he had pinpointed from my earlier turkey talk.

The distance between us had narrowed to a mere ten yards, and just a few more steps would provide the clear shot I'd been waiting for so long! My arms were aching under the weight of the old 12 as I stared down the camouflage barrel to the shining brass head at the end. I sighted the shotgun at the big gobbler's head, and then raised it slightly to cover my target with the end of the barrel. I squeezed the trigger, holding the aim firm. The resounding blast was deafening, but it had the desired results. The majestic bird fully displayed at the shot's impact and fell backward into the opened fan of its tail feathers, then slow motion-like, rolled over onto his side. He was dead before he reached the ground. The number six load had patterned from the ground in front of his feet to his lower neck, shooting lower than anticipated.

The hefty twenty-pounder sported a ten-inch beard, one and a half inch spurs, and an impressive, mature spread of evenly matched tail feathers.

The thrill of the hunt was over, but its memory will last a lifetime. To insure it, this acorn-fed trophy hangs precariously from the wall of a Hale, Michigan hunting lodge owned my by hunting companion, Curly Bragen. Curly, a transplanted Pennsylvanian, not unlike the turkey, and avid hunter/sportsman in his own right, deserves some of the credit for this outstanding morning in the oaks. Due to his diligent pre-season scouting and masterful sundown bird imitations, so important for locating gobblers going to roost, the dream of bagging an Oakridge Tom came true!

From Rotary Phones to Computers
By Jeff B. Davis of Alpena, Michigan
Born 1955

PR6 (Prescott)-9720: I remember as a child that was our home phone number. I remember my dad calling my mom at home saying he would be home late, as he had a sales call or some sales calls at dinnertime or after. Just save some dinner for him in the oven on warm. My mother always told me, "If you ever get in trouble, you tell the policeman your phone number is Prescott 6-9720."

My dad, when he was older, got into professional insurance sales as an occupation, because the plants had passed management by after the war. We lived in an essentially working class community in Michigan, and for certain a lot of working people were first coming home at dinner time as a time to talk, whatever shift they were on, or after dinner if by chance they worked by day employment. My dad was very good at reading a policy and would explain the inclusions and exclusions

Jeff on his go cart that he and his dad assembled in 1960

in the coverage to the potential clients as his sales skill.

Dad made a lot of money in sales. He even wrote the comprehensive insurance for the city as one of his big premium payments. My mother had clerical skills, with typing and shorthand. She worked for the county, a state college, and a major insurance underwriter. Her real skills were better at deftly ironing shirts or clothing alterations. She sewed for herself and made napkins, placemats, tablecloths, and drapes. She should have sold them, as she could have made a lot of money. This would have defined the typical American family from working class to middle class in

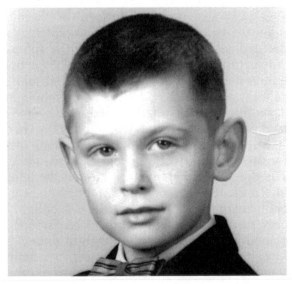

Jeff Davis in 1958

Denise, Jeff, and Janelle in 1956

the sentiment of the baby boom as the rise of prosperity in America. Dad had over thirty years as a laborer in car manufacture and had passed that tradition on to me.

When I was a child, there was still a lot of hope for me. There were first balsa wood airplanes, rubber powered, with the street as the runway. Later I had a balsa wood gas model Flying Wing I had attempted to build. There was a kit AM-FM radio I had attempted to build and an electronic signal key to learn Morse code for flight or nautical use. Later, there were model rockets. I followed the space program with intimate detail from television and the newspapers.

One time, I was beaten up by the neighborhood bully, and it took my beautiful red-haired cousin, Jeanelle, to beat the living hell out of him with some Sonny Liston imitation moves. The neighbor never recovered from her accost. She with ribbons and bow flying in a pretty Easter dress her mother had selected.

Then there was a time for sickness. Well, like a child of the times, there was a lot of disease about, either from the wars or from the United States still having just emerged from a primitive wilderness. I got sick as much as the other students, I suppose, though I wasn't at school when I got sick. I got hard measles, German measles, chicken pox, mumps on one side, and tetanus from playing with ice in the yard. I got hit in the head twice with toy pistols from another neighbor bully and almost ended up in the hospital with a concussion and stitches!

I never tried to cheat at school or gym class. I always liked gym class and learned basic calisthenics, as well as square dancing.

I never wanted to skip school, but if I did stay home, I could watch Rita Bells Prize Movie, which was during the school period. She was amazing with the history of Hollywood. I remember some of the movies quite well. I remember Charles Laughton was one of my favorite film heroes. Didn't he start out in silent films? I remember Lamont Cranston. Wasn't he the Invisible Man, maybe the original one? I will never forget one time when I was sick; my folks had to go out for the evening. As was the ritual, the teenage neighbor, Tommy, pretty much got to take care of me. The original television showing of *The Day the Earth Stood Still* was my privilege. After seeing that, I was sure that I, or maybe all of us, was going to die.

Tommy was this nice high school student who looked like Clint Eastwood, and wore a muscle shirt and dress trousers to school. I figured out, however, as he liked studying himself in my mother's vanity, that his trigonometry problems and Bruce Lee were about the same. Tommy liked gymnastics and jujitsu, and looking at him in the vanity looked a lot like the movie *Enter the Dragon*, where Bruce kills Han in the room full of mirrors. Much to my horror!

Well, now we are in the twenty-first century. I am sitting here at my computer today. My cell phone index is the same as the alphanumeric pad that is the reference to all those phone relationships. I kept a rotary phone connection for my later house out of love for the previous family and my computing interface. Whether the infrastructure is telephone city, your server reference, or your online commitment, only your future is out there in cyberspace. Is your smart firewall a smart barrier and is the boundary you perceive a smart encryption cloud? An ideal password is an asymmetric code that is the random inverse between two symmetric sequences in the global parlance. We all went safe computing and happy family love and activities for all of us! The rotary index and the digital index are much the same in the augmentation of modern weapons technology!

Applesauce, Ice Skating, and Walking in Circles
By Betty Plough of Traverse City, Michigan
Born 1943

Back in the early 1950s, we had a phone number of 590-M in our small town of Traverse City, MI. My friends and I went to one of the local movie theaters every Saturday, and when we would come out of the theater, we would give the cashier our phone number, and she would call our parents to come and get us. I did this one Saturday only to have the telephone operator say that the number had been changed. Well, I knew that could not have happened, but I ended up walking home, totally puzzled as to why she would tell me this. It even got me to thinking that maybe my family was trying to lose me! I was totally relieved when I got home and found out that the phone company had indeed changed our number to 886-J.

My father was a fireman in our town and because of this, we had a scanner that was on twenty-four hours a day. If he was on duty for a 24-hour shift, he would call home several times during that time just to check on things. There was no call waiting back then, and if he had tried to call and one of us was on the phone for an extended period of time, he would just keep getting a busy signal. After trying many times to reach us, we would hear on the scanner, "Windsor 6-6092 is still busy," and we knew we had better get off that phone so he could call!

I was a teenager before we got our first television, and I totally remember sitting around the radio in our parlor listening to Jack Benny, *Amos and Andy*, *Bobby Benson and the B-Bar-B Riders*, *Sky King*, and the very scary *The Shadow*. I can still hear the words, "Only the Shadow knows what lurks in the hearts and minds of men," and then that evil-sounding laugh.

We had a wringer washer in our kitchen, and I can still remember my mom letting me put the bluing in the rinse water. I was always amazed that adding that inky substance could actually made the clothes whiter. That never made sense to me. I always thought it would stain the clothes blue!

One of our elderly neighbors had an icebox in her kitchen, which was a big deal to me since we had an actual refrigerator. The ice truck would deliver big blocks of ice for her, and whenever we saw the truck stop, we would run over and have the ice man chip off a piece of ice for us to suck on. That was such a big deal to us back then.

Many people had milk delivered to their doorsteps, but we were lucky and had a little mom and pop grocery store at the end of our alley, so we bought our milk there. I can remember that whenever I was given a nickel as a reward or just because I asked for one on occasion, I would go to that grocery store and buy myself a small jar of baby applesauce. I thought that was just the best stuff in the world, even better than candy!

When I was a teenager, my friends and I hung out at the local ice skating rink just a few blocks from our homes. Every night, it was get the dishes and homework done, and then head to the rink until it closed. I had some of my best times at that rink. But I was scared to death to walk home alone in the dark, so after the last of my friends and I parted at the corner by her house, I would walk the rest of the way home, turning in circles so no one could come up behind me and scare me. If there was a stray dog or cat around, I would coax it to walk with me until I got home. To this day, I am afraid of being alone in the dark outside. I don't know where that came from, but it's been with me for a long time.

My Father's Leg
By Judith Shinn of Manistee, Michigan
Born 1947

This is a true story from my father's young life in rural Manistee, MI as he told it to me. His name was Lloyd Joseph Hughes, and he was born August 15, 1909 to John and Anna Hughes. My father died in March of 2009 at almost one hundred years of age.

"On the farm in those days, farmers would often buy wild horses that were shipped by train from out west. Ma and Pa brought three horses home one day in the Model T truck. The young horses were only about as tall as calves, but Pa had a heck of a time breaking them in. Their names were Nellie, Dolly, and Billie. Pa eventually sold Billie to a neighbor. The other two horses were used for plowing the fields and for riding. I often rode a horse when Pa wanted me to bring in the cattle or go search for a lost cow down by Cooper Creek. Nellie and Dolly were always a bit wild and knew how to throw the rider if they so desired.

Spearing season was almost over, and Ma was anxious for me to bring home some fish for supper. I was fourteen years old, and on this particular day, I tied my long spear to Nellie and headed for Guerney Creek. The long handle of the spear dragged along the path as we rode. All of a sudden, the horse decided to buck, and she threw me to the ground. The spear caught my left leg and cut deep into my thigh. I somehow managed to yank it out and started to limp home, blood pouring out of my overalls. Fortunately, carpenters were working on the roof that day and came running when they heard me hollering for help. The men carried me the rest of the way back, and Ma and Pa then took me to Doc McMellan. He bandaged me up and sent me home to bed. No one knew until much later that an artery had been severed deep inside my leg.

The accident happened around the end of April in 1923. By September, I was still in bed with a lot of bedsores and a leg swollen to three times its normal size. My leg was like a big red ball and very painful. I didn't want anyone to touch me. Ma had some Indians come over from time to time to try to draw out the infection with herb potions. I remember a time when Grandma Modjeski and Ma were sitting in the other room, and I heard one of them say, "It's a shame, a young man like that..." You see, they didn't expect me to make it.

One day a neighbor, Mrs. Wissner, came for a visit. As soon as she saw me lying on a cot, she insisted that I go to the hospital immediately. I was carried into her Dodge touring car, and I remember looking up at the beautiful clouds in the blue sky as she drove me to Mercy Hospital, about eight miles into town.

I was scheduled for an operation the next morning. Pa was allowed into the operating room because of the seriousness of my condition. I was so weak that the doctor said I would not make it through an amputation if one needed to be done. He first opened the wound. Dad told me later how the doctor took out handfuls of coagulated dark blood from my swollen thigh. He then tried to sew up the damaged artery that had been bleeding

internally for so long. Doc sewed and the artery would break; he sewed and it would break. Finally, he was able to stop the bleeding. If my leg turned black in the night, he would amputate. The doctor told my pa, "The boy is so weak he may not make it anyway."

The next morning, the doctor was amazed! The tips of my toes were black, but that was all. The nurses attended to my foot and the dead flesh eventually shriveled away and the toes healed. I was in the hospital for a month and on crutches for a year and a half. But I still hunted for rabbit and got so I could dance around real good on those crutches.

As my leg began to heal, it was quite bent, so they had me put weights on top of my knee to straighten the leg. My bad leg got so straight it could bend better than my good leg. To this day, it is like that, except I never could bend my ankle much because of all the stretching. I used to be able to count all the stitches in my leg from the top to the bottom, but that's all faded now. They said I'd never walk again, but look where I've gone and what I've done with this leg."

Lloyd Hughes, as told to his daughter, Judith, in 1998.

✓ On the Lake Up North
By Carol Sue McWain Goodenough of East Jordan, Michigan
Born 1948

In the 1890s, property was available on the beautiful, clear, blue waters of Lake Charlevoix, then known as Pine Lake, almost for the asking. The lumber era of Michigan that had been booming in the 1860s and 1870s was almost over. Businesses, homes, and cottages began springing up around Lake Charlevoix.

Frank and Amelia McWain, my paternal grandparents, explored most of Pine Lake in their launch, a boat having a one-cylinder gas engine, called the *Never-Row*. At the end of their search, they selected the forty acres that we now know as Chula Vista. Chula Vista is on the south shore of Lake Charlevoix, about seven miles west of Boyne City. The property was purchased from the Grand Rapids and Indiana Railroad, who had received it by grant from the State of Michigan.

It was the dream of Frank and Amelia that the Chula Vista Resort should become a community of relatives and friends. Frank's sister, Mary Jane (McWain) Lewis, named the resort Chula Vista after the town she had visited and liked in California. The site Frank and Amelia selected had 1,500 feet of beautiful sandy beach, and it was located on a natural harbor. The north 500 feet of lakefront was divided into 50-foot lots, each 120 feet deep. Thus, ten lots were lakefront and an additional 23 lots about the same size were plotted behind the lakefront lots. Most of the lots were either given to the original owners or sold to them for a nominal amount of $50.00 each.

The first cottage built in Chula Vista is our McWain family cottage, Wantocombak. Before Wantocombak was built, the family tented on Karlskin's Point. Frank's sister, Sadie Dale (McWain) Maurer, hated it because she always saw snakes there, and she was terrified of them. The family moved further down the lake and sacrificed the beautiful sunsets for the sandier beach. The original cottage was built by Fred Stahl and some other McWain friends. It was 28 feet by 16 feet, with a shed on the back for dining and a 12-foot porch on the front.

Judson McWain, born in Boyne City in 1906, son of Frank and Amelia, told many stories of his boyhood at Chula Vista. He remembered the early days in Chula Vista when the "resorters" arrived in boats. There were no roads from town at first. Ferryboats traveled the 40-mile trip two times a day around Lake Charlevoix, from Boyne City to East Jordan to Charlevoix. The boats were about 40 to 50 feet long and carried freight. They had steam engines and traveled about eight or nine miles per hour. Captain George Weaver ran the *City of Boyne* and the *Cummings* and was a familiar sight in Chula Vista.

There was usually a long dock extending into deep water and when someone wanted a boat to stop, a white flag was put on a pole and the *City of Boyne* would come over from Horton Bay, across the lake. Additional stops were in Advance, Ironton, and Eveline Orchards. The captain often let the children steer the boat, sometimes to their enjoyment. When Frank worked in town and Amelia and their children lived at the cottage, he sent groceries out by boat.

Around 1911, plans were made to have a boat dock built in Chula Vista, near Wantocombak. Frank bought an old sailing boat, known as the *Ebenezer*, as salvage to build the new dock. The boat was about sixty feet long, and it was built of very heavy beams and decking boards. It was believed that the boat had sunk in a storm near Charlevoix in Lake Charlevoix (Pine Lake). Apparently, the boat grounded before sinking and still had some buoyancy to it. The boat was towed to Chula Vista and plans were made to salvage the excellent timbers and decking boards to build the new permanent dock.

The boat sank, however, before any

Carol Sue McWain in 1952

McWain family in 1905

salvage was accomplished. It sank on the channel bank and protruded above the water line, making it a navigational hazard. Captain Weaver protested the danger caused by the sunken hull of the *Ebenezer* because when the wind was blowing there was danger of his boat running on it. The Coast Guard dynamited the *Ebenezer*, and though they were successful in blowing off most of the super structure the main hull remained intact and is still visible today below the surface of the water.

When the dynamiting occurred, many large fish were stunned by the explosion and floated on the water. Chula Vista resorters took advantage of the easy fishing, and many had fish dinners for the next few nights. For years after the explosion, timbers and other parts of the *Ebenezer* were washed up on shore. As children, we found pieces occasionally. The boat is now on the maps of the lake as a shipwrecked vessel, and Scuba divers come to dive on the boat and see what is left. They cannot take anything off of it anymore. Fishermen find it a good spot to fish, too.

I remember that, as children, we thought the boat was haunted, and we refused to go near it, except as a dare. Believing it too scary to go near it, we never swam over it or water-skied over it. Today we still tell the story of the "Green Hand" that will come up and grab any children found near the *Ebenezer*. As the lake levels go up and down, it becomes more visible and more of a hazard.

Lynne Chandler was my next-door childhood friend, and we spent many wonderful days playing in the sun and using our imaginations to come up with a lot of adventures. Many a warm, sunny day was spent swimming near the docks. We never left the water all day and our parents had to remind us to come in for lunch and dinner. Our imaginations made the docks a castle, or a movie set, or even a house where future families were planned. On the beach, elaborate

sand castles were built using the drip method. Several tiny towns were built throughout the summer before they were washed out. We made artistic animals and pots out of the gray clay found in the lake. We dipped Queen Ann's Lace flowers into multi-colored chalk to make lovely colored bouquets. We also gathered cattails to soak in kerosene to later light as torches along the beach. We were very dramatic and often wrote, directed, and acted in plays. We cast other children in the many parts, gave tickets out to the adults, and made it a festive evening. Costumes were as elaborate as we could make them and we borrowed many outfits and props from the cottage owners.

Rainy days did not bore the children of Chula Vista. We played with our Ginny dolls and read books like Nancy Drew and The Hardy Boys. Game marathons were held. *Monopoly* was a real favorite, often the same game went on for days. *Aggravation*, *Yahtzee*, Chinese checkers, and *Uno* were also favorite games.

Outdoors, we played badminton, volleyball, hide and seek, and other active games. One favorite game of the children was Draw a Circle on the Old Man's Back. We used all the acreage of Chula Vista as the playing area. Two were chosen to begin the game. The first shut their eyes and put their head against a tree trunk, the second person used their finger to "draw" a person on the back of that child, saying, "Draw a circle on the old man's back. Put two eyes, a nose, and who will draw the mouth?" the second child then pointed to someone to put the mouth on. After that was done, the first child turned around and guessed who they thought it was, giving that person a large task to do. It might be "run to the McWain's dock, touch the end, and then return to the tree." He then guessed who made the mouth. If the guesser was right, he told the mouth drawer to do the task, but if he was wrong, the child who drew the mouth tells him to do the task. Some tasks were very multi-tasked but always fun, and all ages loved to play the game.

As we grew up, we added swimming to the neighbor's raft, rowing, sailing, and water skiing to our days in the sun. We never forgot those early, lazier days at the cottage when we were younger, though. We now tell our children and grandchildren the stories.

Those memories are cherished forever. Chula Vista is still a special place in the hearts of the descendants of the McWain family, and family and friends continue to have fond memories of their days and nights "on the lake up north."

✓ The Japanese Flag Sortie

By W. Thomas Stege of Manistee, Michigan
Born 1925

The night of December 7, 1941, was something to remember. It was a quiet Sunday here in Manistee, and that evening a number of us went over to the Congregational Church, which hosted a little get-together every Sunday evening for the young people of the community, of any faith.

When arrived at about 7 P. M. I found the others all talking about an incident they had heard about a few hours earlier; an air attack on our navy at Pearl Harbor in Hawaii. There was a radio in the lounge and we all listened to it for a while as the news kept coming in. At about 8:30 P. M. the meeting broke up and we all went our separate ways.

Four of us wandered down toward town, and found that the newspaper was putting out an EXTRA EDITION, but practically no one was on the streets, they were all at home listening to the news. I suddenly had an idea for a prank that would have a shocking effect on the community, despite the serious nature of the event.

Why don't we put a Japanese flag up on the high school flagpole that night so that it would shake everyone up the next morning? The four fellows that were together at that time were Bill Catton, Clifford Christianson, Kurt Illig, and I, all of the Manistee High School class of 1942.

We went to the Masonic Temple, the front door of which was always open, and went down to the basement, to the room assigned to the DeMolay membership. We needed a large white cloth with which to make a flag, and we knew that they stored tablecloths in a safe next to the door of the DeMolay room. We looked at the door of the safe, and noticed that someone had written some numbers with a lead pencil on the surface of the black steel

door. We decided to try them as a combination for the safe, and it worked!

We found the tablecloths, took a large one out, and shut the door to the safe. Kurt Illig went home to get some red paint and a paintbrush. I stayed there and drew a design of a rising sun on what was to be the Jap flag.

Kurt came back with the paint. I had used pages of an Esquire magazine to cover the pool table, so it wouldn't be damaged by paint. I then painted the flag of the rising sun, using the lines I had drawn on the cloth while Kurt was gone.

When it was all done, I used a pencil and wrote in several of the white sections of the flag, "Down with Japan" and "the dirty yellow dogs." Then the flag was rolled up along with the newspapers and the four of them began their journey up to the high school.

First, we walked up Maple street to the front of the library, then crossed the street to the gas station on the northwest corner of First and Maple, then west on First street to Oak street, then south on Oak to Second street, and at the southeast corner of Second and Oak, we stuck the paint brush into a culvert under the sidewalk. As we went along, we were letting the papers loose, a few at a time until we got to Sixth Street, and then they were all gone. We had made sure that we left no fingerprints on the brush or any of the papers.

By that time, both Cliff Christianson and Bill Catton had second thoughts about the caper, and decided to opt out and head for home. That was their choice and it made no difference to Kurt and me.

We then went to the flagpole in the front of the building facing Maple Street, untied the halyard, attached the homemade flag, and raised it up to the top. We then stepped back and looked up in the dark, and saw that the flag was not quite up to the top. We untied the line and raised it up a little more. Unfortunately, we tugged a little too hard, and the line that had been attached to the bottom of the flag came loose and fell to the ground. The flag was up there, flying in the breeze, but there was no way to take it down.

Fortunately, it was a rare December, and there was no snow on the ground, therefore, no footprints along the way. Kurt and I then walked down the front lawn of the school to the southwest corner of Sixth and Maple, where I suddenly remembered that I had left a

Physics book, belonging to my girlfriend, Lea Thompson, at the base of the flagpole. I had to go back up and look all around the ground beneath the flagpole until I finally found the book. It had her name on it, and the whole event would have been given away the first thing in the morning.

I woke up the next morning, had breakfast, and started up to school. I went through our backyard, across the space between the Guardian Angels' church and school, then across the open field behind Jack Kann's house, to the corner of Sixth and Maple. I then started up the long walk to the north door of the school. Part way up the walk, I saw the large group of people by the base of the flagpole, and it wasn't until then that I remembered the event of the previous evening.

I continued up the walk and into the school, up the stairs to the third floor where my locker was located. Everyone was all in a buzz about the appearance of the Japanese flag. Mr. Bendle, the principal, was walking up and down the third floor hallway, his face as red as a beet, and he would once every so often go into a classroom and look out the window at the flag.

The flag was up too high to get down with any kind of ladder. They eventually called the fire department, and they sent a ladder truck to get it down. It was almost noon before that was accomplished.

In the meantime, the city police and the state police had arrived, and were part of the crowd viewing the spectacle. Up in the hallway, Cliff Christianson told Kurt Illig that we had better confess to our part in the act. Kurt replied, "If you say anything, I'll break your neck." On the way down the walk during the noon hour break, "Aggie" Batzer said to Kurt, "Come on Baron, we know you did it". Kurt's face turned pale, but he just kept on walking down the walk without answering. Kurt was in a tough spot, as his dad, on several occasions, already been accused of being a Nazi sympathizer. If his dad knew what he had done, he might have been horsewhipped.

When I got home for lunch at noon, my sister, Cynthia, was already there and giving our mom and dad the whole story about the flag. I listened but said nothing.

A few days later, a newspaper article appeared that indicated that the authorities had completed their investigation and had come to the conclusion that it had indeed been just a prank.

In the meantime, the war went on, and in time, each of the perpetrators of that now famous prank was in some branch of the service. Three of them were in the navy and one in the Army. All four served either at sea or overseas. Shrapnel from a bomb dropped on his aircraft carrier, the Ticonderoga, wounded Bill Carton; Kurt Illig was wounded and captured in the Battle of the Bulge in Belgium, on Christmas Eve of 1944. After the war ended in Europe, Kurt was released and came home.

Many years later, out at a men's stag at the Manistee Golf & Country Club, Mr. Bendle, who had retired as the principal of the high school, was enjoying an evening with some friends at that event. I went over to his table and decided that it was time to tell him the true story of the Japanese flag on his school building in 1941. In a sharp contrast to his reaction, that morning many years before, he now almost fell off his chair laughing. He now thought it was the funniest thing he had ever heard of. At several stags after that, he would call me over to his table and ask me to tell the story once again. He really enjoyed it every time.

I never did find out what happened to the flag. I always thought that it should have been displayed in a picture frame and hung in a hallway of the high school. On several anniversaries of the occasion, for many years afterward, I would make another Japanese flag and put it up on the high school flagpole on the night of December 7. By early morning, the janitors had removed it, and toward the end, they probably didn't get the significance of the reference to the original night.

✓ **War Recollections**
By June Crawford of Kackson, Michigan
Born 1928

There was a crowd forming outside the store. They seemed fairly congenial until the doors were opened. Then my eyes widened as I saw them running, pushing, rudely passing others who had been in front of them before the doors opened. I turned to another of the cashiers. She smiled and said, "This is the day we receive our cigarette delivery."

It was the summer of 1944, one year before the end of World War II. I was 16, and it was my first day as a cashier at the local supermarket. I had completed my training on arranging all the rationed items on the counter before entering the prices manually. Green stamps were for canned vegetables, red stamps for meats and butter, and another coupon was for sugar. But I wasn't prepared for the run on cigarettes, which weren't rationed. The store did limit one carton to a customer. After that hectic morning, I vowed never to smoke. Of course, the health issues were never acknowledged back then.

There were many lessons learned during that time period. Mostly people shared, bought War Bonds, wrote to servicemen, and didn't complain. Many young people had jobs vacated by women who had taken jobs done by men who were in the service. My 18 year old brother was in the Army in the South Pacific. My 19 year old sister worked in a war related company, wrote to over 20 servicemen, and volunteered at the USO. I was too young for the service or the USO, but I did write to several servicemen.

I was a senior in high school, and already most of the boys in my class had been drafted. They received their diplomas despite missing the last few months of school. They also missed the proms and graduation services. We girls missed the boys. Actually, I attended my senior prom with a junior.

I was 13 years old and just arrived home from church that Sunday morning, December 7, 1941, when the radio blurted out the news that Pearl Harbor had been bombed by the Japanese. I have to say, at first, people scoffed at little Japan attacking us and figured we would clean them up in short order. And to add to our indignity, two of their representatives were in Washington at that time, discussing peace. I don't know what happened to them. It didn't work out that way, of course.

As the War escalated and Hitler and Mussolini became involved, we saw most of our city's young men go to war. Many were drafted, however, many enlisted. The streets and neighborhoods of our small industrial area city, River Rouge, Michigan, were inhabited by women and children and either pre-eighteen or forty-plus year old men.

A 15 minute "Eyes of the World" newsreel at the local theater gave us a brief glimpse of the war. There were also the radio and newspapers. The newspapers didn't use many photos at that time. In fact, the general public didn't even know that President Roosevelt was confined to a wheelchair most of the time.

On a more personal level, there were sacrifices, though we really didn't think of them as such. We were very concerned about our men over there. We read the casualty lists once a week in the newspaper. We were thankful when no one we knew was on it.

We were allocated one pair of real shoes per year. There were shoes made of straw and other non-leather materials, which were available, and I think my feet are still feeling the results. Some clothing materials were also quite scarce. Girls all wore dresses or skirts and blouses. The thought that jeans would someday be fashionable never entered our minds. Nylon panty hose were also a casualty of the war. I don't know what the material was that replaced it, but it always wrinkled at the knees as well as other places. And our undies, panties, were held up by buttons. Elastic was another scarcity. That caused an almost embarrassing moment for me once. After that incident, I always reinforced with safety pins.

Gas was also rationed so we walked a lot. We walked to school twice a day, as we went home for lunch. There wasn't any school cafeteria or fast food places back then. The teen hang out was an ice cream parlor that had a jukebox with all the big band selections and cost a nickel a tune.

Well, that was quite a journey back through time, but an era I remember well. Sometimes I think despite those sacrificing years, we are healthier as a generation. We walked, we worked, we canned fresh fruit and vegetables, and we had victory gardens.

Both rich and poor men were drafted or enlisted, there were no protests, and eventually we all celebrated that August day in 1945 when it ended. Our city officials didn't waste any time remembering our city's servicemen. On March 30, 1948, 2 ½ years after the war ended, a free-standing monument with the engraved names of all those from our small city who had served in the military forces of WWII was dedicated.

Home, Finally
By Barbara Whitaker Palin of Gaylord,
Michigan
Born 1935

I was born in December of 1935 in Mt. Pleasant, Michigan, the first grandchild on the Whitaker side of the family. I was destined to be the only grandchild on the Fuller side. My dad, Dick Whitaker, worked for the refinery in Mt. Pleasant as a truck driver when I was about three, and we lived in a house that he had built out by the airport. Dad heard of a man in Farwell, my mom's hometown, who had a grocery store for sale and who also was looking for a house in Mt. Pleasant, so they decided to make a trade. We moved to Farwell and opened Whitaker's Grocery store. We lived in a small apartment behind the store while Dick drove back and forth to work at the refinery. Marion managed the store during the day. Everything seemed to be going well until Dick was called into the refinery office and was questioned about the arrangement. He admitted that he owned a grocery store in Farwell and, at that, he was told that he was done at the refinery at the end of the week. The reasoning was that if he owned a store, he didn't need another job; there were other people who needed the job more. This was a blow, as the store was not doing too well, and my folks had just started payments on a new car.

Barbara Whitaker Palin and Toby in 1938

So Dick took any kind of supplementary work he could find: cutting fence posts and other kinds of work in the woods. This was 1939 and business was poor all over. The stock was going down in the store and the future looked grim, when a man came into the store saying that Dow Chemical in Midland was looking for pipe fitters. Dick drove to Midland, where he learned that they wanted experienced men. He would have to serve an apprenticeship, and he would have to go through the Union. He was sent to Battle Creek to talk to the Business Agent and sign up with the Union, after which he was sent to Flint to work. This necessitated that Marion run the store during the week, and Dick would be in Farwell on weekends only, an arrangement that she did not like at all. Every week, I wondered if my daddy would come home again.

We were still living in the back of our store in Farwell when I started kindergarten in the fall of 1941. I attended my first day at school with my friend, Gail. We had played together since before either of us could remember. We were all asked to do a show and tell, so I told the story of "The Three Bears," with a lot of expression and hand gestures. Everyone applauded and from then on, storytelling was a part of me.

I had not been in school long when Dad got a chance to sell the store, and we moved to Flint where we could all be together. We lived in two different apartments and I attended two different schools, always feeling like the new kid. To me, all the homeliest little girls were named Barbara.

I had just had my sixth birthday when we were visiting at Grandma Fuller's house in Farwell for the weekend of December 7, 1941. Dinner was over, and we were gathered around the Philco Radio, listening to the symphony broadcast from New York, when the announcement came that the Japanese had bombed Pearl Harbor. None of us had heard of Pearl Harbor, but we knew that this must be serious.

All the men were enlisting in the military, but Dad had an exemption because of his work on refineries and government projects. Later that spring of 1942, we were moved to Lansing. We never seemed to stay in one place long enough to make friends. From there, we moved back to Mt. Pleasant, where we stayed part of the next year, living on High street near Fancher School. Our neighbors and landlords, Joanie and Floyd Eckleston were a young couple who were newly married, and we shared many good times with them. Later, they eventually had two kids and named them Dick and Marion Barbara.

I particularly remember my seventh birthday party that year when I was in first grade at Fancher School. My teacher, Miss Robertson, was a favorite, and she and all the little girls in my class were invited to my party. I had a wonderful cake with a music box inside that played "Happy Birthday," and everyone picked prizes out of a paper pie.

The summer of 1943 was our family's favorite. Dad worked in Ludington, and we rented a cottage on Hamlin Lake, right on the water. We socialized with three other families (the Bruces, Sears, and Linkmeirs) whose fathers also

Whitaker's Grocery in 1939
Barbara's parents, Dick and Marion Whitaker

worked in pipefitting, and we had a wonderful summer together, with picnics, fish fries, and hikes across the sand dunes. In the fall, we moved into Ludington as I entered second grade. But before long, we were on the move again, headed for Texas in the company with one of the families, the Bruces from Indiana.

Going to Texas was like going to another world. First, we lived in Freeport on the Gulf coast, in a government trailer court on a bed of oyster shells. The trailers were triple foldouts, and the bathrooms were across the court and shared by everyone. We shopped at an Army commissary. While we were there, Dad bought a small, chestnut cowpony named Brownie, but we called him Texie. He was fun to ride and had enough get-up-and-go to satisfy Mom. I'd come home from school every day and ride, herding the livestock, which ran free at that time, away from the

trailers, playing cowboy. One time, when two year old Curtis Bruce was playing by himself out between our two trailers, a great rumble arose as a whole herd of horses galloped right through the court, heading straight for Curtis. We were all horrified, but as they approached, those horses divided and thundered right around that little boy.

Christmas that year promised to be a bleak affair for all of our family. Uncle Ken Paullin, who had just started his own men's clothing store in Mt. Pleasant, received his draft notice and was in Mississippi in the Army with Aunt Wanda. And here we were in Texas, far away from home. Dad had to work every day we were in Texas, except Easter Sunday, and we had a terrible time finding a proper Christmas tree. We were heartened, however, when a big box of presents arrived from the Whitaker grandparents in Mt. Pleasant, along with "the Holy Family," an ancient set of small figurines depicting the Nativity.

Toward spring of 1944, we moved to Bay City, Texas and had a pleasant but tiny apartment. It was only two rooms and a bath, another government project. There I had a friend, Narkita, whom I enjoyed as a playmate. We started home to Michigan in late April, trailering Texie. On the way, we stopped in Houston, where my folks bought a real Mexican serape and a rag doll for me. I named her Narkita.

When we returned to Michigan, we lived with my mom's parents in Farwell while I finished out the school year. When asked by the teacher and other students how far away Texas was, I told them, "at least 100 miles." And I had come back north with such a thick Southern accent that hardly anyone could understand me.

That summer, 1944, we lived in Lansing again, where Dad was working. We lived with another family, (the Perrys) a widowed mother, Ruth, and her three sons, Carlyle, a teenager, Ronny, who was mentally handicapped, and Mac, who was my age. They were an odd, sad family. Ruth worked long hours and the boys were not allowed to have toys because "they'll only break them," was Ruth's excuse. Perhaps they simply couldn't afford them. While my mom, Marion, kept house, Ronny was a constant companion of Mac and me and, sad to say, we often teased Ronny. One time when we were down in the basement, we teased poor Ronny to the limits of his endurance. He grabbed a butcher knife, which had carelessly been left out, and he came after us, chasing us upstairs. Mom disarmed him, but after that incident, we moved to another place for the remainder of the summer.

In the fall of 1944, we moved back to Mt. Pleasant, this time to a three room garage apartment at 1205 East High, across the field from the hospital. Mom had known our new landlady, Ruth Russell from being in the Child Study Club when we had last lived in Mt. Pleasant. My folks were concerned about all the moving around we had done in the last few years: 15 moves and 9 separate schools. They had decided to make Mt. Pleasant our home base until I was out of school. Dad would work wherever in Michigan he could and only come home on weekends, a great sacrifice for them.

East High Street was a kid's paradise. At last, I had a whole neighborhood of friends to play with. There was a tree house, a swing, and fields to play in; kick the can, football, baseball, and many hours playing Army, pirates, and cowboys. In the winter, the neighborhood fathers flooded and groomed the tennis court that was beside our garage apartment for skating and hockey. We had finally come home.

Good Fun with Great Friends
By Judy Ann (Pettier) Dempsey of
Cheboygan, Michigan
Born 1948

I was born and raised in Cheboygan on Pinehill Ave. I attended Cheboygan Catholic High School from '62 to '66. There are many things I remember about the growing up years.

I still have many fond memories and newspaper clippings of being a Girl Scout in 1961. Girl scouting was very popular back in our grade school days. One event that was always memorable and always held in February was the Sweetheart Banquet, where each girl attending would pin a heart on her dad with their names. Prizes were always awarded to the father with the most daughters and also for the dad who was first to arrive and last to arrive. The evening was spent with a delicious dinner. Each girl was responsible for bringing her table service for herself and her father. The Kiwanis Club was a very big sponsor and usually provided the chicken for the meals. The girls' moms usually prepared the meal in the kitchen. We also had to bring a dish to pass. The evening was spent being entertained by each Girl Scout Troop putting on skits and plays. I do not see this kind of activity going on now with scouting. Selling Girl Scout cookies was also a big event in each girl's life, as was who could sell the most. Another thing we also enjoyed was camping at Wilderness State Park for a week in the month of June. Again, this event was also sponsored by the Kiwanis. Great memories also during this week of fun.

I remember well the rotary telephones and the party lines. When a long distance call came through, it was a major event, especially if an aunt or uncle or grandparent called long distance. It was a special time for everyone to get their hellos in.

Remembering back to my high school days during the fabulous '60s, I remember snake dances down Main Street prior to Homecoming. We also had huge bonfires behind CCHS, where the football team always collected most of the firewood, usually from outhouses. Football games were always held on Saturday nights, followed by a Homecoming Dance. I remember Sadie Hawkins Dances in the early fall, where each girl would have to ask a guy to the dance. The dress code was overalls or blue jeans and sneakers and straw hats. I fondly remember hayrides, especially through town, being pulled by a tractor and everyone singing.

Band Canyon was the hangout of the '60s for rock bands, local and distant. I especially remember one particular band called the Bed of Roses. My sister became friends with one of the band members, and since they had no place to sleep that night after playing, my sister invited them to spend the night in their van in our backyard. Well, when my parents got up on Sunday morning, they were appalled. Back then, the word spoken was, "What will the neighbors think? Get them out of this yard, or I will call the police."

Thinking back to the teachers we had back then, how very different from now. Teachers took no guff, especially the Mercy nuns, who often time smacked our hands with that large crucifix if we were talking or chewing gum in class. But we did learn. Of course, now it would be considered abuse.

As kids, we spent our summers riding our bikes to the city beach and the Dairy Queen. We often camped out in the late summers in our backyard, listening to our transistor radios, trying to get the radio station WLS in Chicago so we could listen to Wolfman Jack and all the latest hits.

We spent our winters on the ice rink located on Western Avenue. Of course, we were always looking for the boys, and the rink cop always kept us in line. He was there to make sure we kept curfew, which was nine o'clock on school nights and ten o'clock on weekends. We always obeyed, since he knew most of our parents and would not hesitate to call them if we sassed back. I also remember making our own skating rink with all the neighborhood kids. It was located in the Stempkey Field and ran through Pinehill Cemetery. Most often in the late fall it would flood from the heavy rain and then freeze. All of us kids would shovel off this rink and skate. The boys, of course, played hockey.

Getting back into our summers during the high school years, we would spend Sundays out at Aloha State Park with friends and sunbathe, and then go home and get ready to go to Proffitt's Platter Party, which was a drive-in that served wonderful hamburgers, fries, and Cokes. The disc jockey would sit up in the little house on the roof of the drive-in with a feed line next door to the radio station, broadcasting from there and taking requests from every car to hear favorite songs dedicated to some special person. Back then, we had no cell phone, iPods, iPads, or PCs, and we grew up to be responsible adults.

One particular memory that should have been considered dangerous was swimming at the dam and the spillway, jumping off the John F. Bridge, swimming in the river near the Riverside Sport Shop. We also learned to waterski down in the Mackinaw Turning Basin. Back then it was allowed to have waterskiing and swimming in the river. John McLelland was the waterski instructor. Smelt fishing in the early spring and sucker spearing and a case of beer was also a popular activity with the high school kids back then.

Another fall event that was always memorable was decorating the homecoming floats. It was also a time to pile in a car and go what we called back then "cooning" apples at Northern Orchards. But if we got caught it was a dollar fine for every apple in our possession, not to mention the wrath we would suffer from our parents and our teachers, especially at Catholic school.

It is hard to remember all the fun times back then, but we did have a lot of activities while growing up. There was always a neighborhood baseball game. We had roller-skating on the sidewalks across the street. Not to mention siting on a neighbor's porch, drinking Kool-Aid on a wooden swing. We spent our late summers picking raspberries, catching fireflies, and looking at stars. One rite of spring most of us grew up with was burning the grass in the backfields with Dad. Many of the neighborhood kids were all like little firebugs. I can still smell that familiar scent of burning grass. As children back then, we also went to a lot of Sunday matinees at the local movie theatres. Back then, they were twenty-five cents a person. Mom would give us fifty cents each, and we thought we were rich.

I have so many great memories. It's too bad the kids of today do not have these same opportunities. It seems the parents never had a lot of money, but we had good times, and we made our own fun with good friends.

✓ **Born in a Chicken Coop**
By Paul Edward Doane of Evart, Michigan
Born 1930

I was born in a chicken coop in Sylvan on February 28, 1930. Sylvan was nine miles from Evart, Michigan. It consisted of a church, a school, a hall, a store, a parsonage, and a

Uncle Lewis, Cousin Edward, and Paul's dad, Earl

couple of houses. There was a cemetery an eighth of a mile east. I have reasons to know the distance to town well. I walked it after football practice several times, after a game, and once with a full suitcase, plus a couple of miles more to the farm where we lived then. Well, actually, the place wasn't a chicken coop then, just a shack that was a quarter of a mile west. My uncle bought it later and built a long, low building for the chickens and then decided to live in that and use my birthplace for a chicken coop.

I remember one place where we lived when I was a little kid, I could go through the little door that was for the chickens. Maybe I felt at home there. My folks moved so much that my mom told a cousin that she never unpacked. We lived in over seven places in Sylvan alone. Where we lived, the longest was a 200-acre farm two miles north of Sylvan near the Grindstone Creek. My mother's folks lived across the road and on the north side of the creek, which ran through their property. They got all their water from a spring near the creek. They never had a pump. It was my mother's job to go get fresh water. A long walk. There was always a pail of cold water in the kitchen. I didn't care for it after seeing my grandpa take a drink and then pour the rest of the dipper into the pail. I remember as a little kid running up from the creek hollering, "Snakes, snakes." I probably saw one and panicked. They had an old car in the barn, but I never saw them drive it. Don't know if they did, but must have gotten groceries.

Most of my early schooling was at a one-room school in Sylvan. Dad went to the same one. Even had the same teacher for a while. My siblings all went to grade school there. I had a picture from 1911 of the kids by the school. My dad was wearing his brother's cut off pants, which he hated. Also, pictures with my sisters and I. We had a lot of games at recess; pom, pom, pull away; crack the whip;

ante eye over; pigtail; tag; and like that. My sister, Florence, was four years older than me, Ruth two. I was the baby of the family for twenty years, until Dick was born. Two years later, Bob was born. All with the same mother and father.

Most homes we had there had the outdoor privies. They were smelly in summer and cold in winter. We had our choices though. *Sears and Roebuck* or *Montgomery Ward* toilet tissues. I quickly learned that the shiny colored pages weren't the best. Too slippery. At Halloween, some of the little houses got tipped over or moved. Ours never did. I had moved out and was working before the folks had indoor plumbing. That place had a flowing well. Nice. What I hated about the Saturday night bath with the galvanized laundry tubs was the fact that I was the youngest and had to take a bath in the same water after my sisters. Yech.

Money was tight, so Dad went to Lansing to try to get a job. I think he had $2.00, and his brother-in-law lent him $2.00. Gas was a lot cheaper then. He got a job in a factory, but couldn't stand it long. He'd get sick.

I took kindergarten at Maplewood and my sisters went to Everitt. We lived close to school, so I walked. The first lesson I learned

Paul's mother, Ella Barthomew

131

was don't sass the teacher. I did and was kept after school. She wouldn't let me take a picture home I had made. I bawled as I left, and the crossing guard sympathized with me. (I think) It was a tough neighborhood. One big kid held me while another sharpened up a stick and stuck me in the face. I guess they wanted to see if I'd bleed. I did. Still have the scar.

Our little abode there had a chemical toilet in the cellar. Don't remember just how that worked but don't think I want to know. The mean kid had the mumps one day, and my mother told my sister to stay away from him. He saw she was scared so he was over there trying to kick her with his skates. Dad came out, and he took off. His skates shot out from under him and he went down. Dad laughed. We also lived near an airport for a while. The girls came home from school with some project. Trying to see it, I knocked over a bucket of hot water mom was scalding a chicken with. They didn't rush us to the doctor back then. Just had a bit of skin come off with my pants. No big deal.

Then back to Sylvan. We lived across from the cemetery. Dad had a few cows and two buckskin horses, Jim and Ginger. My job was watering them all. We had a pitcher pump in the kitchen with a pipe running out the window. No running water or electricity, of course. Kerosene lamps. We did have a mantle lamp, which was a lot brighter but tended to be fussy. The mantle would start to turn black, and we'd have to put salt on it. I don't remember Dad planting it, but he had a big field of watermelons. It must have been a tremendous job. Each hill was covered by a hot cap. I have a picture. People would come from miles around to swipe them. Also had a garden with a lot of tomatoes. I didn't care for them at that time. After they were getting overripe, us kids pelted each other with them. Good clean fun. Our mothers probably didn't think so. Dad used to peddle them at various places. Once at Cadillac, the police stopped him. Said he had to have a license. He went to the station with them. I was afraid he wouldn't come back. He did. I think they just made him buy a license. I heard afterward that some local went into the melon patch at night. One guy slipped on what is now known as dairy dew and fell with the melon on top of him. I started my education there, reading the funnies and some comic books someone gave me. Batman was round even then. And Jiggs and Maggie, the Katzenjammer Kids, Terry and the pirates, Brenda Starr, Blondie (she must be pretty old by now), Flash Gordon, and a lot of others. The one room school didn't have a lot of books, but I was reading about the Greek gods when I had barely started the first grade; Odin, Thor, and Lodin the Mischief Maker, and like that.

Our father never laid a hand on us, but he would make us sit in a chair if we didn't behave. Somehow, the chairs always ended up closer together. When we lived by the cemetery, I had a nickel or two and wanted to go to the store. Mom told me to wait for the girls or I'd get a licking. Candy was a penny. Pop a nickel. Gas was twenty-five cents. Too much temptation for this kid. I gave in and got my licking when I came back. Actually, it didn't amount to anything. Then we moved to the 200-acre farm where Dad worked on shares. Shares of the increase and in stock and crops.

Then as World War II started winding down, we moved back to Lansing. Dad got a job with Nash Kelvinator, making airplane propellers, and I got jobs digging for Victory Gardens and mowing lawns for fifty cents an hour. Good pay. It was 1943. The only place we could find to rent was an unused gas station. It still had the pumps and people kept stopping. Rationing was on. Dad missed sugar, which was scarce and was tempted to buy it on the black market. Seems like we lived mostly on tomato soup and Spam.

I always had trouble with my hearing and the teachers at the school wanted me to go to the deaf school in Flint. I didn't want to. An office girl encouraged me to enter a victory garden poster contest. I won. Two girls and I got our picture in the State Journal as the winners in our schools. We also got $100.00 prize money.

After that year was up, we went north again. We lived at an uncle's place in Clare. A few years later, that place burned as their daughter tried to start a fire in the kitchen range. She was pregnant. They managed to save the baby but she died. The same thing happened to my dad's oldest brother in Sylvan. He was a bachelor and never had a car. Don't think he ever took a girl out. When the stove exploded, he took time to shave.

132

Went to a nephew's who lived nearby. Said, "I don't think I'll have to go to the doctor, do you?" His nephew said, "Yes!" Took him to the doctor and he died the next day.

When it was time to start high school, we stayed with relatives until the folks moved back to the 200-acre farm. The Grindstone Creek started way back to the west, and I used to fish on a beaver pond. Then it ran over to a neighbor's and on to my grandpa's. It was two miles from our road to M66 and much longer as the creek winded. I never had too much luck with worms, but once I discovered spinners, I could get my limit every time. The big ones were in the middle. One pool had a dandy. He'd hit every time but I couldn't land him. A couple of times, I waded the creed twice from 66 to our road. In the middle was a big pool and this huge trout would hit the lure every time. Go flying through the air and toss it. I never did land him.

I got in pretty good shape on the farm, as I'd till a big field with a three-section drag and three horses. I'd clean the cow barns with a scoop and wheelbarrow. Run it up a plank and dump it on the manure pile. Helped with the buzz rigs and piling the grain in the granary while the threshers were there, too. Our horses were in one pasture and the cows in one a little farther off. I'd often go back and get one horse so I could ride him to get the cows. He didn't like going away from the barn. I'd get him to running. No saddle. Come to a mud puddle and he'd slam on the brakes. I'd go over his head but manage to keep the reins. As kids, we loved to go barefoot. Couldn't wait for spring. I like to sing. I used to sing Happy Birthday to my son and he'd motion me away and say, "That's enough." Funny the way the cows never seemed to mind. They did switch their tails but I thought it was because of the flies.

I didn't marry until I was 62. I tell my wife I waited until I found the right girl. One that would have me.

Commercial Fishing and a Restaurant Family
By David F. Juilleret of Charlevoix, Michigan
Born 1937

I feel I've been very lucky to have been born into a commercial fishing and restaurant family in a northern Michigan town. I was born in 1937 in Petoskey Hospital, located on Bear River by the mouth of the bay. We lived in Harbor Springs with Grandpa Juilleret. Memories of that time are not too vivid, but I can remember we were told not to play on the fishing reels, nets, and drying structures and we could not go into the icehouse. This was all part of the fishery business. We also had lumber piles of rough-sawn lumber for sale, random links, great springboards.

Grandpa at this time had the restaurant in Harbor Springs. Dad worked for him. It was called a café at this time. I remember The Blue Room, a room off the ally entrance. This room was for Indians, only they could not hang out in the café or bar, as the staple income was beer and wine.

We went to Charlevoix when I turned five as I started kindergarten there. We had a fishpond in the center of the room. I loved to fish already at this young age. Dad always said I was the first to catch all the goldfish out of the pond.

Dad had gone back to commercial fishing. He is listed as a commercial fisherman on my birth certificate. I was told the family at one time operated three tugs out of Harbor Springs. Harbor springs, Petoskey, and Charlevoix closed in 2010. Then a good friend called a few years back to give me platters with our name on them.

We lived in Charlevoix until '42. Dad had fished shares. Own your own nets to set, work on the tug as a hand, tug takes share of profit. Booth fishers was in Charlevoix at this time. I believe there was over twenty tugs running out of here then. I can remember knowing the sound of Dad's tug and running to the docks at Booth's to see the fish, fish boxes full of fish and the fish bigger than the boxes. This was the beginning of the end to the big fishery. The lamprey eel was in strong with the fish being over fished.

In Charlevoix, I made many friends. We were here three years and lived in four houses. One had the toilet in one of the bedrooms, but there was no tub. We had to go next door to the neighbor's on bath night. We were poor. I don't think we knew what poor was, as we didn't know anyone any better off. We were all equal, except of course for the resorters.

In 1944, Grandpa had a stroke. We went back to Harbor Springs where Dad did a partnership with his brother, Joe, and his dad. This is when and where I really grew up and had a lot of good memories. We bought our first home on the hill by the school, almost in the schoolyard. The ice rink and football field were right out the back door.

My granddad became my mentor. He was semi-retired after the stroke. He had five rowboats left from the gillnet fishing. I helped get them ready for perch fishing rental. I tended them; being sure, they were bailed out and tied properly. They were kept at the city dock where the Pier Restaurant is today. I learned to seine minnows, which we kept for sale at the restaurant. He had five fish shanties, which I helped Grandpa tend for rental in the winter.

I loved to go fishing with Grandpa. Perch, smelt, and cisco was all that was left in the lake. One spring, Grandpa and I speared up twenty suckers that had been killed by lamprey. We put them on a board, took a picture, circled the lamprey kill marks, and sent the picture to the Detroit Free Press. We were trying to get some attention to what was going on in the lakes.

Grandpa was probably one of the first fishing guides. We took two boats to Wilderness State Park, Waugoshance Point, to fish for small mouth bass. We would leave Harbor Springs around three in the morning, getting back home around six or seven in the evening. I learned a lot about watching the weather. We mainly rowed the boats in and out of the small bays. The old icehouse we had filled with leaves so we had our own night crawlers. Grandpa was a heck of a fisherman and got to be well known for his ability to catch fish.

I loved growing up in Harbor Springs. Mom did not like me out on the dock fishing with my hand line. I was always trying to get someone to go with me. A lot of times, I just said someone would meet me there and off I would go. Dad would buy any perch over 8 ½ inches, the commercial legal size, to sell at the restaurant. I fished before and after school. I loved to fish smelt with a cane pole and Coleman lantern at night in the fall. Seining for minnows one night at the Harbor Beach, we came up with a sturgeon. It had twelve lamprey eels on it and another ten holes. We hauled it over to the Conway Hatchery, where they had a sturgeon pond. It lived for a long time there.

I learned to work in Harbor Springs. I started sorting beer and pop bottles, ran a potato peeler, and washed dishes. I got 25 cents an hour; four hours equaled one dollar. That was good money for an eight year old. The summer I was eight, I caddied at Harbor Point, a nine-hole course at that time. I only took ladies with four or five clubs one round a day. I did that for two years and then moved on to Wequetonsing for eighteen holes twice a day. The summer I was twelve, I went to go to work. They said I had to be thirteen with a work permit. I lucked out and got a job on a berry farm. I loved it and learned a lot and made some money. I started peddling the *News Review* when they first established routes in Harbor. I had one fourth of the town. I had to collect on Fridays and was usually late for dinner those nights. It seems there was a lot of blizzards that winter. We moved back to Charlevoix after a year with the papers.

While in Harbor Springs, my mom wanted me to play the piano. She had me take lessons from a Catholic nun. I went to Holy Childhood School to do this. The school always smelled of boiled cabbage. I knew that it was full of Indian kids living there. I thought they were all orphans. I had no idea they were being forced to live like the white man. I really think that was a dark time in our society. It had to be terrible for those kids, while we were all having so much fun just being kids growing up in God's country.

My dad's family partnership went to heck in 1949. He looked at restaurants in East Jordan, Boyne City, and Charlevoix for sale. The East Jordan one near the foundry was the best year around gross. The Boyne City one was better in winter than in summer, as skiing was getting a good start at Boyne Mountain. The one in Charlevoix, The Coffee Cup, was made affordable, so back to Charlevoix we went. Mom and Dad ran it twenty-four hours a day, seven days a week for over a year. We could find no place to live at this time in Charlevoix, so we lived in the basement for a couple of months and then found a place nearby to rent. I lived in the rental until I left for the Navy the summer I graduated in 1955.

The summer before coming to Charlevoix, my dad called me late one night to ask if I would like to go half-and-half on a boat. Boy was I excited. We had to go out on the beach in the full moon to look at it, as he needed ten dollars right then. We got there just as there was an eclipse of the moon. So that was what we named the boat. I loved that boat. The first summer in Charlevoix, we kept it in the city slip. I'll bet I rowed that boat out on Round Lake perch fishing every day. I loved being on the water. I got my first outboard 5 hp. Johnson from Bellinger Marine in 1952. First one to have a neutral in for starting. So then, I was all over Lake Charlevoix.

We had a lot of fun as teenagers. We went dancing at the Grange Hall every Saturday night. I think every farm area had a Grange. We drank beer and danced all night; square dances and polkas. There was no rock yet, but it was on its way.

I worked in the food business from the time we came to Charlevoix until I went in the Navy. I went in the Navy to go to cook's school, which I did. I went back to work for Mom and Dad the same day I got out of the service.

A little about the food business. I was born into a family that the way I understand it was commercial fishing, and as that got harder they started to sell the fish through a restaurant started by my great-grandmother. The planked fish came from the fact that when lifting gill nets on the tug, the first fish was tied to a maple plank and set behind the warming stove. When I was young, I would go to the restaurant with Grandpa. His hound was always asleep on the big furnace register. Rats and roaches were very common, as there was nothing to kill them. There were traps for mice and rats. I remember D-Con killed a rat but where did he go. As for food, everything was homemade. We had ice cream and all the toppings. The food business had changed so much. I recall we had our own butcher, as beef came by the side. Imagine no frozen food, no prepared food of any kind.

A little about the sports fishery that I have been so lucky to enjoy. In the '50s, all fish were gone except some perch. I got out of the service in 1958. We fished perch and small mouth bass in Lake Charlevoix. In the early '60s, the DNR started to plant lake trout, steelhead, and brown trout I fished them long lining and started doing very well. We started fishing lake trout in the big lake in the late '60s; we used wire line. It was a lot of fun. We came up with homemade down riggers and releases

to fish deep with lighter tackle. Salmon were introduced, and they are a ball. I did great in the food business with all the fishermen. I did all my baking and prep work early 3:30am. So I opened for the sportsmen. We also have great ice fishing. I built a portable shack years ago. It has been a lot of fun to see all the new tackle come on the market.

Indian fishing rights almost wiped the fishery out again. I'm glad that gill netting is a lot of work. They should be lifted every day or the quality of the fish deteriorates fast. They did put some rules on themselves. We had quite a time trying to stop gill netting, a lot of bad stories. I just pray we have it all worked out.

✔ Sachem
By David Twining of Stone Mountain,
Georgia
Born 1954

Heroes are common. If you study history or read the paper, there are many to be found. Most achieved against great odds, believed in things they never saw, and cut a path through life with little more than the strength of their character. Many of us cherish the essence of these amazing people who inspire us to go on, especially when personal challenges seem impossible or provide motivation when there is none immediately at hand within. And lucky are those who actually meet their heroes, touch them, or spend time discussing the more ordinary topics of life. Beyond all the miracles and good fortune, I have known and enjoyed over the years, my hero was, and still to this day remains, the single greatest experience and influence on my life.

At the age of six, I began a quiet journey of life-changing experiences while developing an understanding of what my personal hero was really all about. Our relationship was not unique; he was my grandfather on my father's side. I remember at first, he often appeared to be serious and introspective. Over time, I would view him much differently. He was a rare type of man who spent fifty years shaping the values of young boys from every walk of life across America, and even from distant countries, through his life's passion, camping. It wouldn't be until I was in my thirties that I fully understood the magnitude and impact

135

his vision had in my own life, especially in my approach to spiritual matters and an appreciation of the outdoors.

Great-grandfather Fred operated a logging tug, the *Charles W. Liken*, mainly on Lake Huron, log driving large islands of trees from Au Gres down state to the sawmills in the Bay City area. I can only imagine how wild and sparsely populated the northern region of Michigan must have been in the early 1900s. As a young man growing up in the little town of Twining, Michigan, Grandfather was always very athletic and excelled in baseball, bowling, camping, and sailing. He loved being near or on the many lakes of northern Michigan. When he was in his teens, the family moved to Bay City, where his father started a brick business.

Herbert Harrison Twining, Sr. would not follow in his father's footsteps on the Great Lakes or in the brick business, but instead attended college at the University of Michigan and graduated with a degree in business administration. During summer jobs with the YMCA in Indiana, he discovered that he had a strong desire to work with young boys while at camp and also made a lifelong friend names George Jones, or Jonesy, as he was called. By the time Herbert graduated, he knew that building and directing a boy's camp was his dream.

After college, in the winter of 1925 and with financial help from his mother, he set off to find a suitable spot to establish a camp somewhere in the northern Michigan region. It wasn't long before he found a perfect location known as The Elms on Burt Lake. The mile long, lake front property was vacant except for the hotel, and he used snowshoes in -60 degree weather to walk the land that would

Founder and director of Camp Algonquian, Herbert H. Twining, Sr. in the 1940s

eventually become well known as Camp Algonquin. In 1935, when the Camp Director's Association was reorganized into what is now the American Camping association, he would lead and be their first president.

"Headquarters," as Grandfather called the hotel, was positioned at the center of the sprawling camp on the shores of Burt Lake, a four mile wide, and seven mile long, deep, fresh water expanse. With a huge stone porch and spacious two stories behind, the building was easily seen from nearly any point on the lake. In the grassy area immediately in front were two flag poles at either end. At center was a large ship's anchor painted white. This was the assembly area for daily flag raising and lowering at the beginning and end of each day, complete with trumpet player, adding just a touch of military flavor and discipline to the ceremony. Grandfather would always position himself in front of the ship's anchor as he addressed the assembled campers who were lined up dress right dress.

A massive dining hall was added to the headquarters building. The completely open room was filled with tables end to end, with wooden benches for seating. At the north end was the kitchen, with an eight foot stainless pass-through. At the opposite end was a mammoth stone fireplace. Just to the left, in the corner, was an old scroll-type piano. Windows and an ample covered porch wrapped around three sides of that wing of the building.

All of the structures that were built were of the same open rafter, shell-like framing and added to the sense that you were always "roughing it" out in the woods. Directly behind the headquarters and dining hall was a theater of sorts. About the same size as the dining hall, the theater had a stage with large black curtains; bench seating, another mammoth stone fireplace off to the left, and a small concession stand out on the large porch. The rest of the camp consisted of small cabins at the far ends of the property, arranged by age groups that could accommodate seven boys and one counselor. The ages ranged from 6 to 17 years. Each group was identified by different Indian tribe names of the Algonquin nation. The youngest were the Chippewa, and then the Cree, Ojibway, and the Mississauga were the oldest boys.

The back half of the property was terraced well above the lower lake level, much like a high plain. This was where the barn, corrals, and pasture were for the horses. There was also a rifle range, craft shop, and infirmary toward the forward section of the rim overlooking the lake.

Grandfather had a wonderful way of combining traditional Christian faith, his love and respect for nature as creations of God, and the spiritualism of the northern American Indian tribes into every aspect of camp life. What I thought at the time were fun activities to keep us busy were, in reality, his way to lay the foundations for male values, many of which were no longer commonly passed on in the quickening pace of contemporary living in 1960s America.

At the camp, we would learn to swim, to shoot a rifle or a bow and arrow, ride horses, sail, canoe, tie knots, navigate, hike and also to be self-reliant, trust worthy, confident in ourselves, and even explore creative skills. Most activities lasted an hour. A large bell would be rung from the headquarters building to signal the change to the next activity or meal. Each day started early and ended just about at dusk. There was little time that was not structured in some way.

There were a host of other activities, not unlike "rites of passage," held in secret ceremonies before great bonfires deep in the forest late at night. Perhaps the youngest boys were the most profoundly affected by these events, but as I got older, I also appreciated participating to make the experience as memorable for the younger boys who would follow as the years passed. I remember wearing something like a breach cloth, being wrapped in a blanket, and blindfolded. We were led in single file into the woods. Along the way, we would hear the distant screams of Indians and were startled by the noises of shaking leafy branches or animal sounds. After what seemed like a very long time, we could begin to hear a distant pounding of drums, which became louder and louder, until it seemed they were right ahead or behind us. The crackling heat of a fire could be felt as we stopped. After several incantations and feverish beating of the drums, our blindfolds were removed. Our vision was blurred and not ready to view the amazing, huge fire, perhaps twenty feet in height, just a short distance in front of us. The council ring, as it was called, was a circular clearing bordered by irregular stump seating. It was evident that the entire camp was in attendance, but the ocean of on-looking faces was silent, as the "Sachem" spoke of the responsibilities were now required to prepare for. The older campers applied paint markings to our faces, signifying our first step of many that would lead us on a quest of manhood. These initiations bonded us together, and many of the boys I looked forward to seeing year after year would return a little older or more experienced, but we all grew to love the outdoors, belonged together as brothers, and found common images of God and family despite the diversity of our backgrounds.

So much growing took place there during those summers and with an awareness of really being alive that I didn't find so readily once I went back again to my home in Ann Arbor. Finding out what you were capable of or not capable of was a daily event, but there were always ways for every boy to strive for excellence and demonstrate wholesome competition through games or learning new skills. It was the common experience of things like friendship and fellowship we were not getting the rest of the year away from the camp that made us return year after year.

Grandfather was careful not to single out my older brother, cousins, or myself with special privileges or undue attention. We were no more or less than every other camper. Yet I felt closer to him when I would find him reflecting or praying as he gazed out toward the lake, sitting on a pine log bench. And I liked it that he didn't stop to acknowledge me watching from a distance, because I knew it was something deep and moving to him. By his example I learned that men must be thinkers as much as doers and that it is important to be alone with God in your own way so you can nurture personal meditations in the outdoors. And although he never said it to me, I knew that's where his mind was during those moments. He would often remark with conviction to, "Put God first, the other fellow second, and yourself third."

There, under the trees on Sunday mornings, we would worship together as a camp. I had no trouble absorbing whatever grandfather or the other senior counselors would speak about. The sermons were always simple and tied to nature, and maybe that is why they always reached me. Herb, as he was sometimes called, was the personification of what it was to be a man of faith, but not a weakling at the same time. More than that, Grandfather would be one of the few men I knew personally who really lived his faith each and every day until his death in 1971. I think that understanding was also, what was in the hearts of all the men who attended the funeral, men who were once boys, discovering the same things I had found over those many, many summers at Camp Algonquin.

No compliments or words of gratitude will ever repay him for the secrets he shared and lessons he taught to me, but unlike so much of modern day to day life that comes and goes so quickly now, his personal wisdom, his reverence for God, and his appreciation for the abounding nature of northern Michigan is still etched clearly in the values I have kept as my own.

For my father, Herbert Harrison Twining, Jr. and in loving memory of my sister, Patrice Ann.

Good Memories of Traverse City
By Martha Preston of Traverse City, Michigan
Born 1944

In 1949, our family moved to Traverse City, Michigan. I was five years old and the eighth child in a family of nine kids. We moved into a house on 11th Street on the 600 block, and we lived just ½ block from the highway, or as we called it, Division Street. If we walked from our house west and crossed over Division Street to the other side, we would be on the grounds of the State Hospital. The State Hospital was a mental institution run by the State of Michigan. I don't know how much property they owned, but it was quite large, and we, as kids, used to play in that area. There was a creek called Kids Creek, and we used to play in and out of the creek all year long, winter, and summer.

The first year that we moved into the house on 11th Street, it was 1949 and getting close to Christmas. Now as you can guess by the size of our family, we didn't have a lot of money. Our family did not own a car until my older sister purchased one in 1956. Until that date, we walked everywhere. My mother not only didn't own a car, she never learned how to drive one. Anyway, the incident I wanted to tell you about took place that first winter we were in Traverse City.

Two of my brothers, Tony, ten years old, and Leo, eleven years old, wanted Mom to purchase a Christmas tree for the house, but Mom explained to them that the trees were too expensive. We had just moved everything we owned from down state to Traverse City, and there just wasn't enough money for extras like Christmas trees this year. They would just have to wait until next year. So imagine our surprise when we saw my two brothers coming home, dragging a very nice Christmas tree behind them. Because I was only five years old, I thought it was the greatest thing they could possibly have done. My mother, on the other hand, had other ideas. After questioning them about this tree, they told her that there were a lot of Christmas trees just ½ block away, and all they had to do was cut them down and bring them home. My mom looked out of our front door, and she saw the drag marks the boys had made bringing the tree home. She followed the marks down our front porch, down our front walk, down the city street, across Division Street, and straight into the State Hospital grounds where a stand of pine trees were growing. She saw the drag marks go right to a stump of a tree and realized what the boys had done. As I have said, she was in no position to pay any fine or any penalties, having no money. So she did the only thing she could do. She turned around and walked back home and spent some sleepless nights waiting for the knock on the door, which thankfully never came.

Even though we didn't have much money,

138

Traverse City was a wonderful town to grow up in. We lived only about one dozen blocks from Clinch Park, which is a public beach located on Lake Michigan. We spent our summers in the water. We grew up with neighbor kids, and I still see some of them and keep in touch with them, even after we moved over 60 years ago. We lived on the 600 block of W. Eleventh Street and there were kids all around us for playmates. We had many baseball games in the alley between 11th and 12th Streets. We would sometimes be able to go to the movies on Saturday afternoons. In those days, it cost 25 cents to go to the movies. We would see a newsreel, a cartoon, and the main show, and if we were allowed to stay longer, we could stay and see the whole thing again for free. They never kicked us out of a theater like they do today.

There were three theaters in town when I was growing up, the State Theater, which is still in business, the Michigan Theater, which is no longer in business, and the Tra-Bay Theater. I'm not sure how to spell the Tra-Bay Theater, because I can't find any information about it. I only remember the building being on the south side of Front Street, and I can't place where it was, exactly. If my memory is correct, I understand why it didn't stay in business for long. The theater only cost five cents to get into and watch a show. But the shows were all the cowboy movies like Hop-a-long Cassidy, and they all seemed to be "cliff hangers." I can't remember ever seeing a movie there that ended. We had to go back the next week to see the conclusion. Again, I have to admit that my memory could be faulty.

I attended only on Saturday afternoons, and only if my mother made our older brothers take me and my sister, who was one year older than I am. They agreed to take us to the moves on Saturday so that they could go themselves. Sometimes we would see a move at the State or Michigan Theater. Again, my brothers, Leo and Tony, were forced to take us. They did not want to be seen with little sisters. But they knew that Mom would insist we go with them, so they said okay. There were two boys my brothers' ages that lived across the street from us, Loren and Roy, who always came with us to the movies. I can remember how it was in those days. Loren and Roy would bring a huge brown paper bag like you get in the grocery stores, full of fresh-popped popcorn, and

they would take it into the theater. I've often wondered what would happen today if anyone tried this. But in those days, it was standard for people to bring whatever food they wished into the movie. I remember sitting and eating popcorn until I was full.

As I said before, my two brothers did not want their two little sisters dragging along with them, but they were afraid to tell Mom that they didn't want to take us to the movie. So their solution was simple, they thought. When my sister and I, being around seven and eight years old, walked with them, they made us walk a half a block behind them. Then when it was time to cross the street to go into the movie theater, they would hold our hands until we were all in the middle of Front Street. Then they would let go of our hands and run across the street, leaving us in the middle of the road. In those days, Front Street ran both ways instead of the one-way road it is today. We would stand in the middle of the road and beg them to come and get us, and they would say they would if we promised to tell Mom that we did not want to go to the movies with them the next week. We always said we would promise to tell her that, but of course, we never did. We also never told her about them leaving us in the middle of the street. But you must remember this would have been in the late '40s and early '50s, and there were probably 10 cars on Front Street at any one time.

I can remember the neighbors in the fall, after most of the leaves had fallen, raking the leaves into the street along the curbs. I don't really remember if it was planned or not, but it seemed as if it was spontaneous. Someone would start to burn the leaves. We, as kids, were just delighted. That signaled the marshmallows would be coming out soon. Before we knew it, all of the neighbors were in the street burning leaves, visiting with each other, and giving the kids marshmallows to roast. I realize that burning of leaves can be hazardous to our health, but it is too bad that we no longer get to know our neighbors like we used to in days gone by. I now live about 10 miles south of Traverse City and I pass subdivisions and city streets almost daily. I am sad to see how empty the yards are. I miss seeing and hearing the kids playing with each other, unless it is organized sports or something along those lines. I am sure that my grandkids and great-grandkids will have wonderful lives also, and I hope they will forge bonds and good memories like I have.

Last Days of Innocence
By Ardis Streeter of Lupton, Michigan
Born 1948

Lupton School sets on Cherry Street in Lupton, Michigan, where it was built by an early settler, Alex Reid in 1903 and 1904. The land was donated by George Stanley, who was also an early settler. The first year, the school had 98 students and classes were held at the school until 1964. In the '50s, when the story begins, the kindergarten through seventh grade was taught in two rooms that was called the little room and the big room because of the ages of the students. The little room had students, kindergarten through grade three, while the big room was fourth through seventh. In the very early days, a flowing well was in the yard and a stack of wood piled in the basement to provide for the water and heat. Later, a well was drilled for the school to have running water, and also a gas furnace was installed in the '60s.

School started with students standing and every voice heard from the smallest to the largest saying the Pledge to the flag followed by a prayer. Students studied math, reading and writing, and some history and geography. Art was taught by making art projects for school programs and decorating for holidays. Music was taught by singing in school and for

Ardis's teacher getting ready for school to start the board reads Monday March 1, 1960

programs such as the Christmas play and the Spring Festival.

When Ardie was in kindergarten, she met her favorite teacher, Miss Koin. She was not only beautiful, but she loved her students and loved teaching them even more. She wore full skirts with large, colorful flowers. During small groups, she sat in the center of the group and spread her skirt so that each child had a piece of it touching him or her. The students sat spellbound, with her skirt spread to all of them. The sun streamed through the windows and helped to create a magical place as she read to them.

The magic was broken for the little room students when it was time to get ready for the long walk home for lunch. A few of the students brought their lunch because they came on the bus or wanted to eat with their friends. Joyce looked forward to her sandwich made with thick slices of her mother's homemade bread. While she ate, she thought of her mother making the bread in the large crock bowl. Everyone said it was the largest one they had ever seen. She stirred the bread together and set it in a warm place to rise. The smell of the yeast bread soon filled the whole house. Joyce took small bites and wondered if she could still smell the yeast or did she taste it. She shrugged her shoulders, put her lunch bag away, and ran outside to play.

The students who had gone home wolfed down their lunches so they could hurry back to school to play. They gathered under the big oak tree in the schoolyard. There was no division in their group. Some seemed rich and others poor, but it didn't matter. None formed a click, no one was an outsider. Everyone was accepted and the same in all their eyes. The big room students looked out for the little room ones.

With their jackknives in their pockets, they decided it was time to start their fort in the woods behind the school. It couldn't be too far from the creek, so they could get washed up before going back to school. It would be big enough for several to get inside. They began to cut out the brush to form the floor. The little kids were sent to bring branches that they could gather from the ground. Soon they were joined by the kids from the big room, who cut branches and cedar boughs, pulled fallen trees along the ground, and gathered load after load of branches. The hour flew by and before they knew it, the air was filled with the sound of the big bell on the school. Time to go to the classroom. One of the big room students would grab the heavy rope that rang the bell, and swing through the air with his feet a flying up and down with the rope while the bell clanged to be heard all over Lupton.

The next day, they could hardly contain their excitement, because they were starting to put the walls of the fort up. First, they put some small branches down to define where the walls would be. The roots and limbs were filled in with cedar boughs, branches, and leaves. By the time the bell rang, they had a base for the fort. They could even use it if they wanted, but tomorrow they would start the roof.

The next day, some of the kids went for long branches. They needed to be long enough to reach across the top to form the roof. They also had to find two stumps to place on the sides of the fort for the tallest kids to stand on. Two kids from the little room found a nice round stump and together they rolled it to the fort. One of the larger boys was behind them with another stump. The two tallest boys set the stumps and jumped on them. The first boy was handed a long, bushy branch. No matter how hard he pushed, he couldn't get it to the other side. They decided to take it down and trim it so it could be passed to the other side. Trimming took a long time with their jackknives. The girl who lived closest to the school agreed to bring a hand saw the next day. When they got back in the classroom, she could hardly do her math because she was trying to decide if she should ask her dad for the saw or just sneak it out. When she explained that night what they were doing, of course, Dad agreed that the saw would be needed at school. The next day, there were several kids who brought saws and hammer and nails. Now they could finish the job.

School started the next day as usual, with the Pledge and a prayer, and then the teacher announced, "The woods will be off limits from now on, since a bear was spotted by someone in the community."

Our hearts sank! We would never be able to see our fort finished. Some weeks later, a fence was put up around the playground so we wouldn't be tempted to wander off into the woods again. Many times, we would look longingly across the fence at our unaccomplished project and dream and talk about what it could have been.

We never had a lack of things to do at recess. Some played jacks on the cement square by the well; some had a baseball or kickball game going, while some played red rover. One of the favorite games was mumbly peg. We sat in a circle and took turns using our open jackknives to stick in the ground by flipping it off different points on our bodies. First, we started with the knifepoint on our wrist, then onto the elbow, shoulder, chin, forehead, and so on. As soon as the knife fell to the ground without sticking, it went on to the next person's turn. A peg was driven into the ground and hit each time the knife missed its mark. At the end of the game, the loser had to pull the peg up out of the ground with his teeth. By that time, the peg was pretty far into the ground!

Class went on as usual, with each class meeting with the teacher while the others were working on their assignments. We always had plenty to do. When our assignments were finished, we could always practice our penmanship, or read, or help the younger ones, or work on putting up bulletin boards.

Every fall, we had the Harvest Festival to raise money to keep our school repaired, new windows, furnace, or whatever was needed at the time. Every family would bring all kinds of garden produce, apples, pears, breads, pies, cookies, handcrafted items, and even some live bunnies in cages. One year, we were all surprised when one family brought a big cage with a huge white turkey to sell for some lucky family's Thanksgiving dinner. Everything was displayed on several big tables for all to see. Once the auctioneer, who was one of the parents, got going, a group of us kids would sneak out the door and head for a well-known good garden to get a few more watermelons and pumpkins to help out at our fundraiser. No one seemed to notice that we were gone and never asked where the extra produce came from.

The Christmas program took all priority. We began practicing lines for plays, pieces, and songs every day long before Thanksgiving. As it got closer, some dads came and brought the stage up from the basement. We opened the big doors between the big room and the little room and pushed all the desks along the south wall in the big room. The men started assembling the stage. We continued our schoolwork in spite of the sound of hammers and nails. We worked hard, knowing that we didn't have much time left before the big night. We used evergreen boughs to fill in around the bottom of the stage since it was about three feet off the floor.

One family brought a big spruce tree and stood it to the side of the stage. Now we could decorate. We popped popcorn and strung it on long pieces of thread, and every fourth or fifth piece of popcorn we would put a cranberry or raisin. We made handmade decorations and long paper chains made out of construction paper to hang on the tree and from corner to corner of the rooms. Every space in the school looked like Christmas. Now we were ready for the big night!

There was great excitement when the night of the performance finally arrived. Everyone wore their best, and there was standing room only. It seemed like everyone in the whole community came. The little kids sat in chairs in front of the stage and waited their turn to perform. The bigger kids helped get the smaller ones on and off the stage, and the little ones sat quietly and patiently while their bigger brothers and sisters performed. At the very end of the evening, all the kids, both big and little, would all go onto the stage and begin the final song, which was "We Wish You a Merry Christmas." We would sing it over and over, with all eyes on the door with great anticipation! Finally, the big moment would come. A sound of jingle bells would be heard in the foyer. The door would open and a real Santa enter, shouting, "Ho, Ho, Ho!" He would have a huge sack on his back with enough bags of candy for all of us. We would all clap and shout, "Merry Christmas!" After all the treats were passed out, it was time for all to go home. We would all work together to clean up the school the next day and the men would come and take down the stage and carry it to the basement for the next year.

In the spring, we had a Spring Festival with folk dancing. Before school was over, we always took a trip of some sort. The whole school would go.

On the last day of school, we cleaned the school from top to bottom. We said our good-byes, knowing that we would see most of the kids at church every Sunday until the next school year.

As seen through the eyes of Joyce Oyster Gould and Ardis Rakestraw Streeter.

No Better Place than Home
By Alphonse Bruski of Houghton Lake, Michigan
Born 1930

I went to St. Casimir's Catholic School in Posen, Michigan, where all of my thirteen brothers and sisters attended school. I remember Sister Mary Valentine as the first nun I ever had for a teacher. She was a tiny nun and very gentle with the children. I also had her in first grade.

In grades second and third, Sister Mary Alfred was my teacher. My younger sister, Regina, joined me when I was in the second grade. Although she was in kindergarten when I was in first grade, the school board decided it would be easier on my parents if Regina skipped first grade and was in the same class I was. Therefore, we could share the same books and walk together to and from school. Regina was able to skip a class, because she was one of the smarter kids in class. At that time, we had double desks, and we would sit together, sharing the same books and everything. There we were, Alphonse and Regina, the only boy and girl in class sitting together. At first, I felt uneasy about it; because I thought, the kids would be laughing at us or something. They did tease us about it during noon hour, but after a while, they stopped teasing and everything was alright.

Alphonse's parents, Frank and Cecelia Bruski

I guess having a brother or sister in the same class can either be good or bad, depending on how you look at it. It can be good because you tend to study better. However, it can be bad, because if you do something bad in school, your parents are liable to find out sooner.

Three times each day during school hours, we went outside to play. When we were small kids, we would play on the merry-go-round, the swings, the slide, etc. During noon hour, we would play tag or just stand around in a bunch and talk. In the wintertime, we would play in the snow or on the snow banks. Or we would have snowball fights. Sometimes, if we got hit in the face with a snowball, it would really hurt.

I had younger and older brothers and sisters going to school, and it seems like we always walked together. Sometimes we left the house at different times, so we did not walk together. However, if we saw somebody lagging behind when coming from school, we stopped and waited for them to catch up, and we would walk together. There sometimes was a reason for one of us to stop and wait for the other one. The one that usually waited did not have any money to buy candy at Frank Jesionowski's candy store. That was our favorite place in town.

Mother used to fix our lunches to take to school, but as we grew older, we fixed our own. Because we came from such a poor family, our lunches were not the best. Sometimes, a sandwich consisted of lard instead of butter, and cream with sugar and pepper on it. Later, my parents could afford to put meat between the sandwiches. With that, we got homemade cookies, pie, or cake and occasionally an orange or banana.

There was a special passenger train that went by, and we called it "The Street Car," because it resembled one. It used to drop off and pick up passengers at the depot. Just about every summer, my aunt, Helen, boarded the streetcar in Alpena. Helen arrived on this train from Chicago. Before she left Chicago, she wrote Mom a letter and told us when she would be coming. We either picked her up at the station or she just walked to our house. When we saw her coming down the road, we got so excited, because we always enjoyed it when she came to visit us. She often brought her son, Eugene, and daughter, Betty. My sister, Helen, was always glad to see Betty,

Alphonse's grandparents, Grandpa and Grandma Buza

because they were the same age, and they would have a lot of fun together. My brother, Archie, and I were glad to see Eugene come, because he was our age. We played "cops and robbers" together. Cousin Eugene always liked to play this game. Now I can see why; he grew up to be a detective. Mom was also glad when Aunt Helen visited her. Although she had a lot of brothers, Aunt Helen was her only sister.

When I was a kid, I always wanted to be a cowboy or a baseball player. I was a big fan of the Detroit Tigers. I knew all of their names and the names of the players from the other teams in the American League. I had a scrapbook of pictures and articles of baseball players. My favorite player was Ted Williams of the American League and Stan Musial of the National League.

I always wanted to see a Tiger game in Detroit. I remember the first time I got to go to Detroit when I was about twelve years old. It was during the time when my oldest brother, Aloysuis, was driving trucks for Pete Purol. He would haul cattle, sheep, or potatoes. One time, he had to take a load of cattle to Detroit, and he asked my brother, Art, and me if we would like to go with him. We couldn't believe it. Imagine, leaving the farm for a few days and going to the big city of Detroit in a truck with our big brother. We couldn't wait. Of course, we had to ask Mom and Dad if we could go.

The thing I remember the most about the ride is when we were past Alpena, and the truck had to climb the Harrisville Hills. Behind the semi-trailer, it had a heavy load

Alphonse Bruski with his dog

of cattle, and it seemed like the truck would not make it to the top of those hills. But my brother went through those hills many times, so he knew just what to do.

When we arrived in Detroit, my brother first took us to Uncle Joe's house, and then he went to have the cattle unloaded. One time when Aloysuis was in Detroit with a load of cattle, his truck and semi-trailer overturned right in the city on an intersection. The cattle got out, and they ran all over the place. Police on horses finally rounded them up. It must have been quite an experience for him.

Anyway, we were glad to see our uncle and aunt. They used to come to the farm to see Mom and Dad just about every summer. It seemed so different in the city. The houses were so close together. While we were waiting for Al to get back, we were outside Uncle's house and just looking around. When Aloysuis finally came back, we climbed into Uncle Joe's car, and he took us to a place where they had some animals. It was like a park. As we were walking from the car, I saw all these monkeys in the distance. I had never seen live monkeys before, so I started running off by myself toward them. Al had to holler to me to get back. He said that I could get lost among all those people by myself. To me,

the monkeys were such fascinating animals to watch. We walked around in the park and looked at all the other animals. I really enjoyed that.

Afterwards, Uncle Joe drove and showed us the factory where he worked. On the way back, he bought Art and me each an ice cream cone. By this time, I was getting carsick from riding around the city. I really didn't care for the ice cream cone at that time. But how could I say that I didn't want it after he bought it? I ate some of it, but when we got back to the house, I pretended I had to go to the bathroom and flushed the rest of it in the toilet. I felt so guilty flushing down that ice cream cone, but at least I didn't offend Uncle's feelings. Later, I realized that Uncle would understand if I only told him I was carsick.

After spending a day in Detroit, we said goodbye to Uncle and Aunty and headed back north to Posen. When we got home, we told Mom and Dad about our trip and our stay in the big city.

I'd like to tell you of an incident that happened in the house next door that Mom and Dad owned and rented out to a couple. They were Louis and Martha Bronikowski. The kitchen in this house had an opening in the floor where we could spill potatoes through to the basement. One day when Martha went grocery shopping, Dad and I went into the house to replace the linoleum in the kitchen. We were ready to cut out the piece of linoleum where the hole was. Dad went downstairs and was sitting on the steps looking up and marking the outline of the hole with a pencil. Just as he was doing this, Martha came rushing into the kitchen with grocery bags in her arms, not knowing what was going on. As she went toward the cupboard, she stepped right on the middle of the linoleum where Dad was marking the hole. She went right through the linoleum, bags, and all, and landed right on top of Dad. Luckily, nothing happened to them, but we had a good laugh. I still have to laugh when I think about it.

Next to our garden was the apple orchard. I have fond memories of that orchard, because as a kid I used to play and climb the trees. Robins and other fine birds would build their nests in those trees. I would climb the trees and look into the nests to see if there were any eggs yet. The robins would have three or four nice, pale blue eggs in their nests. But

I did not touch them, because we were told that if we did, the birds would abandon the nest. Occasionally, I came back to see if the eggs were hatched. I could usually tell when the eggs hatched, because the robins would get nervous and do a lot of squawking when I came close to the tree.

One day when I was helping my dad and brother with the fence, I had an accident. Dad and my brother were stretching the barbed wire, which is nailed right above the fence. Where I was standing, I noticed that the barbed wire was hooked on to the fence below and did not let go. So I got up on an old tree stump to loosen it. As I grabbed the wire, it broke just behind me, knocking me to the ground. I fell on my right arm. But the force was so great that it broke my arm. Mom and Dad took me to the hospital in Alpena, where I had it straightened out and put in a cast. It really hurt when two doctors were trying to straighten out my arm, because it was bent where it was broken. It hurt so bad, but I didn't complain, because I wanted them to do a good job.

I would have to say that I have very fond memories of my boyhood days on the farm. There was the feeling of nature around me, which I enjoyed. There was hard work, but it did not seem to hurt me. But there was enough time to play and to do things that I enjoyed to do. There were sad times and good times. I was fortunate to have good parents who stood by me as well as all my brothers and sisters. I've heard of kids running away from home. That was never a consideration for me, because there wasn't a better place to run to.

Sun-Warmed Canvas Bathtub
By Carol Paul of Rogers City, Michigan
Born 1937

When she was seven my older sister got worms. My other sister and I hoped we would get them too so we could take worm medicine instead of Castor oil or Cod Liver oil, as it was really bad.

I stayed at my uncle's farm in the summer. They had a big canvas bathtub that sat in the sun all day. In the evening, my aunt would take a bath, then us girls, then my uncle. The boys came last, oldest to youngest. The water was pretty dirty by the time they were done!

My mother was working so my oldest sister decided to do the wash for her. After she was in the basement for a while, she started hollering, "Help, girls, help me!"

We ran down stairs and there she was with her hair, right up to her head in the wringer. One of us, I don't know who was smart enough, hit the release bar.

My sister wore her hair parted on the side the rest of the year so no one would see her baldhead.

A Commitment to Education
By Betty Wartella Last of Cheboygan,
Michigan
Born 1924

I was born in Moran, Michigan, in August 1924, 88 years ago, 14 miles north of St. Ignace, MI, which is on the straits of Mackinaw between the upper and lower peninsula.

We had a two-seater outhouse with a Sears Roebuck and Montgomery Ward catalog for toilet paper. We had a well house with a pump and had to carry water in pails.

I moved to Cheboygan, MI, for my Junior and Senior year of high school, because the Moran School only went to the 10th grade. Three years before, my sister Ruth went to Sault Ste. Marie, MI, to graduate. We are the only two in our family to graduate.

I graduated and married during World War 2 and stayed in Cheboygan all these years. I cooked on a big black cook stove that burned wood. We had an indoor toilet but no bathtub until we remodeled.

I am the 12th of 13 children of 8 girls and 5 boys. My sister Ruth is 90 years old. We are the last of our family. My sister Gertrude passed away in 2012 at the age of 95; she outlived all my brothers and sisters.

Cranky Model T
By Charles Huntington of Petoskey,
Michigan
Born 1927

In the middle 1930s my parents would often visit my Uncle Collins at his farm outside Mason, Michigan. My brother and I were always able to amuse ourselves while they visited. My uncle owned a Model T Ford

145

truck for use on the farm.

One Sunday afternoon on one such occasion my brother, age 12, asked Uncle Collins if we could start the truck and drive it around the barnyard. Dad had taught my brother to drive a couple of years earlier, he being more mature than his age would indicate. My uncle said fine and told my brother about the ignition. Having no starter it had to be cranked. So we set the crank at its topmost position, Bud got behind the wheel while I, age 10, climbed up on the bumper with one foot on the crank. Bud set the ignition and said "Okay." Holding the radiator cap, I put both feet on the crank and rode it down. The spark caught but as sometimes happens, it backfired and lifted me in the air three or four feet and I landed, completely unhurt, in front of the truck.

Both of us had a good laugh about that, then proceeded to try again with better results and had a great time driving around the yard that afternoon.

The Bus Tipped Over
By Lucile Sandeen of Mancelona, Michigan
Born 1926

I checked with my friend Dorothy Hunter and we think we were eight to ten years old when this incident happened. I am now 86. Our bus driver was Alvah Crothers. In the winter, he had fixed a bus with a double sled out of pressed material of some kind. He had a small potbellied stove for warmth. A team of horses drew it. North of Alden was a long steep hill called Nemo Hill. It was very steep at that time, but since then the hill has been cut down on the top of the hill. We were going down the hill and the snow was very deep. The bus tipped over on its side. Mr. Crothers had to stay with the horses. We all piled out and pushed the bus back up. The only causality was the bus driver's son, Percy. A small lid on the top of the stove caught him on the back of the hand. It was quite a small burn. My lunch pail top came off and my lunch spilled out. I loved boiled eggs and my mom frequently had one in my lunch. The boys had a great time passing it around before giving it back to me. We arrived at school all safe and sound and full of our story to tell.

World War II
By Theodore King of Alpena, Michigan
Born 1922

I was born October 1, 1922. Outhouses and chamber pots, I remember them well, I hated to use the chamber pot, because it was a cold seat especially when the fire in our potbelly stove went out and the outhouse was even colder on a stormy night or any night. The chamber pot could be smelly, if it wasn't emptied regularly. We used lime in our outside toilet to keep the smell down; ours was just a two seater, one small and one large.

I enlisted January 10, 1941. I served six years in the U.S. Navy. My first ship, the U.S.S. Destroyer Sturtevant – 240, I served this ship for 13 months to the day it was sunk in the gulf of Mexico on April 27, 1942. Made four or five trips to Iceland before the water supplying the British with food and arms. When we reached Iceland, the British would take over the convoy to England, for us back to the U.S. for another convoy. It was the quiet war as I referred it to my pay was $7.50 every two weeks or $15.00 a month. We paid $6.00 per month for our life insurance. In 90 years of age, October 1, 1922 I first spent time in the North Atlantic, then patrol in the Caribbean. Ship was sunk in the Gulf April 26, 1942. I was serving in the North Atlantic when the Reuben James was sunk. She lost 101 men including my hometown friend; we enlisted together. Six months later, we got sunk in the Gulf. We lost 17 men. I went on to serve on two more ships, completing six years of my enlistment.

Flowers for Mom
By Carolyn Mousseau of Cheboygan,
Michigan
Born 1935

One great story comes to mind when me and my twin sisters were kids. We lived in Livonia, Michigan, which at that time was a township with gravel roads (actually cinder), a lot of fields, woods, and space.

I am now 77 years old and retired in Cheboygan, Michigan, "God's Country," with my hubby of 55 years. My one living sister, Cindy, lives in Gladwin, Michigan. She is a widow. And Claudia, the other twin, lives in "God's Country," literally.

When we were kids 7-9 years old we would hide behind the old church by the little cemetery and wait for a funeral. After everyone left the service, we would go and pick my mom a pretty bouquet. Needless to say, these little surprises to Mom did not last long. Moms are wise. About the third time, we had to take the flowers back, put them on the grave, say a prayer for the departed, and say we were sorry.

Carolyn's twin sisters Cindy and Claudia

Whittemore School, Sledding, and MYF
By Judy Loy of Tawas City, Michigan
Born 1944

My name is Judy (Dickey) Loy. I was raised at Whittemore, Michigan a loving town where everyone cared and helped each other no matter what. First, my family lived on a farm outside of town but when I was about 12 years old, we moved into town because of my dad's illness. We had the second house down from United Methodist Church.

Back then, we had lots of snow. First, when school was called off kids shoveled snow. When that was done, we got our sleds and slid down a side road by our home. Kids came from all over town, bundled tightly. We'd sled for hours. So much fun!

I attended Whittemore School. The best teachers were in elementary school: Mrs. Biglow in 2nd grade and Mrs. Jenny Valley in 3rd grade. Back then, teachers would take time to help children and they could hug a child when needed.

I attended United Methodist Church in Whittemore. We had a MYF for young kids. We used to have taffy pulls and go out at Christmas time and sing for those who could not get out or were ill. We had Bible school in the summer. The same kids went to school, sledded together, and attended church. It was like having a huge loving family. At Christmas time, the Chamber of Commerce held a drawing and one year I won $25. That was my Christmas shopping money. Back then, a person could buy nice gifts for family and friends. We used to have a milkman come. He'd bring milk and cottage cheese. We never had to lock our homes like we do today. I always felt safe and secure at home in Whittemore, Michigan.

Of course, in summer the racetrack was always a huge hit, as it is today. My dad would take me to the first and last races. In between, I'd climb out on the flat roof of the house and watch and hear the announcer at the track.

I had a Toy Terrier dog named Peanuts. I would take him for walks in 1965—that's when I met my husband. We dated one year and married in 1966. We have two children, Julie and John Loy. We've been married 46 years. Recently my husband had to be put in the nursing home. He has Alzheimer's and lots of other illnesses. But living over to Whittemore is my best and wonderful life, as people there are so caring and loving. Of course, the biggest share of them are gone now, and the kids I grew up with live elsewhere.

Mother "Won" an Electric Sewing Machine
By Martha West of Marion, Michigan
Born 1948

My grandfather, Peter Flum, was born in August 1876. He said he was the third white child registered in Missaukee County here in Northern Michigan. In those days, the area was populated with wildlife. Grandpa told

147

many stories about the wildlife.

He said his dad brought bear cubs home on one occasion. The boys treated them as pets, playing with them until they got too large and too rough. Then their dad took them back into the woods and released them. On another occasion, my grandpa was taking meat to a lumber camp to sell to the ones who were running the camp. A pack of wolves must have smelled the meat, and came up to him. One of them put his paws on Peter's shoulders, howling in his ear. Peter dropped the meat quickly. The wolves started fighting over the meat, which gave him a chance to get away. As he ran, he heard a noise behind him and thought the wolves were following him. Instead, it was leaves, which he was kicking up as he ran through the woods. He was certainly relieved when he realized that it was leaves and not wolves following him.

After Peter had married and had children, he had a car that he made look like a pickup. When he would stop the car/pickup for the day, he would take the coil out, wipe it off, and bring it in the house for the night. He would put it into the warming oven of the Home Comfort cook stove, and it would dry overnight so that it would be ready to start his vehicle in the morning.

At one point, Peter worked on the lake. In the winter, he would cut ice into chunks so that it could be stored in sawdust to be kept for summer. The ice was used in the iceboxes that people had in their houses.

My mother was a seamstress and made clothes for her siblings after her mother died when my mother was 10 years old. She would develop a pattern, cut, and sew the clothes. Of course, she was using a treadle sewing machine to sew the clothes. After my mother married my dad in 1946, she continued to use the treadle sewing machine. She made her maternity clothes as well as her other garments. She ended up with five daughters and sewed our clothes as well. I may have been in high school before I wore many store-bought dresses. My mother finally received an electric sewing machine in a rather unusual way. My aunt was living in a nearby town, and did her grocery shopping locally. The store had a drawing on a sewing machine. My aunt entered her name in the drawing and thought, "If I win, I will give the machine to Lota." She won! Then she requested that the electric sewing machine be delivered to my mother's address instead of to her own address. My mother even got a demonstration on how the machine operated. Her sewing time suddenly improved.

Incidentally, I started to learn how to sew on the treadle sewing machine before we had the electric machine.

The Popcorn Business
By Mariam Navachic of Traverse City, Michigan
Born 1918

John Ramsay of Kalamazoo County married Sarah Henderson of Oswego, New York and moved to Michigan in 1875. They operated the county poor farm in Niles, Michigan with their five children: Mary, Willis, Nellie, Alpheus, and Adalbert. When Willis was 18 years old, the family moved to Northern Michigan. They cleared the property and built a home, which is now known as Ramsay Road in Grant Township, Grand Traverse County. The home still stands today. Later, they bought the property across the road and built a large barn.

John was the first man in Grant Twp to own a team of horses named Collie and Cyp. They did quite a bit of logging in the area. They made money by helping other settlers clear their property to build their homestead. While eating popcorn one evening, Willis talked to his mother and suggested making fresh popcorn in the morning and selling some to the passengers when the train stopped at the Wexford Depot. Sarah made fresh doughnuts and coffee to send along. The passengers were mostly employees at the Hannah Lay coal docks. They were more than happy to purchase the offerings. They even asked if he could bring sandwiches and perhaps a slice of cake too. Over time, Willis made a great deal of money. When the railroad realized what a lucrative business Willis had they made a dining cart for the train. Some passengers took their time to convert but as the business slowed and the railroad didn't want their depot used as a stand to complete with their own dining car. Willis gave up and purchased property across the road for his future farm of 180 acres. This property had a very good gravel pit and Willis managed to sell several

Fun times at the lake in 1927

loads of gravel. He built a barn to shelter several horses and cows. Also, he built a large chicken coop with bars for the chickens to hop to different levels, to nest in at a higher level away from drafts and predators.

Meanwhile, Emma Lawrence of Syracuse, New York moved into Wexford County and met Willis. They were married at Monroe Center. They eventually become the parents of eight children: Fern, John, Clare, Nellie, Isabell, Alfreda, Perry Hannah, and Carrie. Carrie was the only child born in Willis' new home in 1900. This home is in good condition and standing today.

Willis donated 40-acres to build the new neighborhood school. This school still stands however the property was sold along with the building and concerted to a home with a stairway to a loft. The owners say it's haunted and sometimes they hear laughter of a kid giggling or tools being moved. Willis was a firm believer in education so when each of his children finished the 8th grade they went to Traverse City for two years to study any project that interested them. John studied bees and went into that business. He also had a small fox and mink farm. Clare studied business and farming. Isabell went to Grand Rapids and became a registered nurse. Alfreda received her teacher's certificate. Perry Hannah took up gardening and worked a while for Henry Ford and then returned to his father's farm to raise cattle. His home still stands and it was the first to have a full basement and a furnace within enclosed coal bins allowing him to have heat registers in every room. It also had a washroom with an indoor pump and water, a pantry accessible to the dining room and kitchen.

I Am Still Here
By Sharon Switalski of Manistee, Michigan
Born 1943

I was born in 1943, in the beautiful port city of Manistee, Michigan, near the shores of Lake Michigan and one block from the Manistee River channel. It was a great place to experience childhood; though we were poor, we had many riches. We had two rooms downstairs, a toilet in a closet, and we bathed in a galvanized washtub. The bedrooms were upstairs and mine faced the wooded sand hills, as well as the lake where I could see the lighthouse! Though I had younger siblings, my Brother Don who was a year older than me and I were buddies. Across the street was the path through the woods to the sand hills where we spent much of our summers playing. The sand was scattered with clamshells, snail shells, pretty stones that sparkled with fool's gold, or iron pyrite, and there were dead poplar trees, which had tall main trunks; we used them as a frame for our "teepees."

We took the small bushy growth and laid the fragrant branches intertwined across the frames. Inside was cool and we would enjoy with our friends our bagged lunches and jugs of water. There was a huge cement circle about four or five feet high. When my father was a boy and also lived near, he recalled that a huge engine would end there as a turn around. All the gears and tracks are long gone. It served as a pet cemetery for birds, rabbits, or whatever we found that had met its end. We tied twig crosses and placed pretty stones for markers.

Not too far away was the country club for golfing! My younger brother, a young entrepreneur, gathered stray golf balls found in the woods and would sell them back. There were bittersweet vines in the area of woods as well. He would cut bouquets to sell to the ladies on the Hill in Manistee, a more affluent area. They loved to see him come and admired him for his efforts, so they hired him to shovel snow in the winter. The hill, Cedar and Second Street, was closed off for the winter and became our town's favorite and best sledding hill. One block to the right of all this was the River Channel and our neighbor's fish shanty. Their daughter Gail and I would spend hours there playing with cats and new litters of kittens, watching her father Stanley and my grandfather, and dad, mending nets that were wound on large wooden framed reels. Oh, how I wish we had a picture of that. Sometimes we were allowed to go out with the men on the tug Atomic and watch them set the nets. We watched them with their catch setting them on racks in the smokehouse.

I loved where I lived. I loved the experiences I had. Not many toys, not much for a house, but it was my home, my wonderful memories. As I fall asleep some nights, the glow of the lighthouse would come into my room and the sound, the low and deep sound of it calling home the ships. I hear them still in time calling out to me. "I am still here," even though the landscape I speak of has changed. I call back in my heart and memory, "I am still here too!" with a very enriched life because of it.

✓ The Fort
By Ines Brocht of Marion, Michigan
Born 1930

In April of 1991, I bought Mark and Matthew, our twin grandsons, two sheets of plywood for their birthday. It was to be the floor for our fort the kids and I planned on building in the woods south of my house. We hauled old pallets and whatever we could find to the site. With a lot of luck, we built the fort. Our neighbor Betty gave us two big skylights, which we used for the roof. It was quite a thrill to sleep down there and watch the stars.

The first year a porcupine chewed a hole through our wall and got inside and chewed the legs off a little table we had in there. That summer we scrounged up enough tin to tin up our fort.

I and one to four grandkids have spent many nights down there, usually eating breakfast in the woods. Now eighteen years later the fort still stands and the grandkids and their kids always visit it yet.

My dad was a farmer with a very small income. I started school when I was five years old. We had to walk a mile and a half to school. I had two older sisters to walk with. We all, girls and boys both, wore long underwear. Us girls also wore tan colored long cotton socks. It was really hard to fold those long underwear to look neat in your socks. We also all wore four-buckle Artics over our shoes.

The first through fourth grades got out at 2:30, the fourth through eighth grades got out at 4 pm. Most of the time I walked home with a little neighbor boy who lived one half mile from school. One day our river hill road was so slippery with ice I couldn't get up it so Donald Dean, my friend, took our dinner pails to the top, then came back down and helped me up. I stayed at their house that night.

We had lots of fun playing games of tag, red light green light, and Mother, May I. No swing sets and no phones to call school off.

At Christmas time, we and about twenty kids aged 5 through 14 would put on a Christmas program for our parents. Everyone had a piece to say and usually two or three plays. Also, someone had to pull the makeshift curtains across a plank stage. After the program, we usually got one gift, as we drew names, and also pencils or something from the teacher. And everyone got a box of candy and peanuts, which was a big treat.

I can remember trading my jar of fruit to a friend for white crackers, as we never had crackers at home. But my mom always canned many cans of blueberries, blackberries, and applesauce.

One sad day of my life was when I was in eighth grade. I hit our teacher's little four year old boy in the mouth with the swing and knocked two of his teeth out. There was blood everywhere and no phone to call for help.

When I started high school, the bus didn't come out to our place so I had to stay with an elderly couple and work for my board. One night he came in and asked me if I could help him get his cows back in as they had gotten out of the pasture. Of course, I was used to cows so I just ran fast around and soon we had them in. For weeks when anyone came, he would say, "Boy, you should see that girl run." I thought how silly he was but now I'm his age and understand. The school bus started picking us up when I was in the eleventh grade. I graduated second in my class.

✓ Reclining on the Beach, Watching Aerial Combat
By Hamilton D. McNichol of Oscoda, Michigan
Born 1942

Imagine yourself very young, swimming suit clad and chestnut brown tanned by the summer sun.

You're loafing on the warm sands of a beach and watching, with great fascination, aerial combat taking place above white capped waters. No, it's not 1944 and you're not on the beaches of Normandy. Instead, it's sometime between 1950 and perhaps 1957 and you're safe and comfortable on the shores of Lake Huron and the beaches are those of the Oscoda Township Park.

Though it wasn't actually aerial combat in the strict sense of the word, it still qualified as high drama for myself and my school chums, free from curricular obligations during those glorious summer days. The first indication that the show is about to begin comes with the deep, rumbling cadence of twin diesel engines. Those engines, powering a pair of WWII converted PT boats under the command of USAF officer Grady Greathouse, could be heard for miles along the Lake Huron shoreline. Painted a conspicuous orange and white, they were moored at the mouth of the Au Sable River, a port from which they were launched to monitor forthcoming operations and provide a safety net for the pilots above. Soon after the audio alert, the boats would be spotted exiting the mouth of the river and with a soul-searching rumble turn north and speed out into the lake.

Sprawled upon our beach towels, all eyes would begin to search the skies above the lake for the first glimpse of the P-51 Mustang prop driven fighter aircraft. However, the first aircraft to come into view was usually the DC-3 tow plane that dragged a long, rectangular shaped target for the fighter aircraft to attack.

Quite possibly, a full quarter mile of cable attached the target to the tow plane.

Soon following the appearance of the crash boats and the DC-3 tow plane, the high pitched whine of fighter aircraft engines could be heard. Perhaps five or six of the fighters would sweep out over the lake in formation from their Wurtsmith AFB home, (formerly Skeel Field), and approach the target from the northwest. Then, as the squad closed in, each plane would break off in turn and dive on the target. The fighters would bank and pull well away before the ratta-tat-tat of their machine guns became audible to kids and adults watching from the beach. During the summer months, this impromptu air show was often witnessed by locals and visitors alike.

Since the DC-3, on its return trip to the airfield, could not land with the target in tow, the pilot would descend over an uninhabited forested area west of the landing strip and release the cable. Perhaps, he once released at too great an altitude, or maybe a high wind carried the target off. At any rate, the military personnel assigned to recover the wayward quarry were unable to locate it. However, my father and I, who frequently found reason enough to be in the brush with berry pail, fishing pole, or shotgun, came upon one such cable with its deteriorated target and returned it to the Air Force. That's how I know that the target was always towed by a very long and very heavy cable.

On your next visit to the Alpena, Alcona Area Credit Union, if you look on the wall behind the tellers' cages you will see a painting of two brightly painted PT boats resting at their Au Sable River moorings. I often wonder if the pretty young teller processing my transaction knows the origin and significant of that painting. She may wonder why I always have that silly, nostalgic smile on my face as I stand there gazing upon it. I hope that she knows, but if she doesn't I hope that she buys your book.

A Profitable Swim
By William R. Kiogima of Harbor Springs, Michigan
Born 1930

My name is William Raymond Kiogima. I was born in Harbor Springs, Michigan. My parents were Augustine and Katherine. They were both members of the Little Traverse Bay Bands of Odawa Indians. The Odawa Indians settled here in Northern Michigan in the late 1600s. They called this land "Wah-guh-nuhk-sing" which means Land of the Crooked Tree. Both of my parents spoke the Odawa language fluently and so it was easy for me to speak the language.

When the area became Harbor Springs, there was a community on the western city limits. There were about 25 families living there. These people were all Odawa and so that meant there were a lot of kids there. I was one of those kids along with my five brothers and one sister. We didn't have much to do so all we did was play. In the summer, we would go swimming either out on the bay or the swimming beach in Harbor. When the boys got big enough they would go caddy at the Harbor Point Golf Club or the Wequetonsing Golf Club. The girls would go to the resorts and see if they could wash dishes or walk the dog. We were happy to be making a few pennies but we were happy too, just to be playing. We didn't have TVs or ipads or cell phones and we were glad if we had a radio to listen to.

One of the events that happened in Harbor Springs in the summer was the arrival of the cruise ships. There would be sometimes as many as six or seven cruises that came to Harbor Springs in the summer at different times. Two of the ships that I remember were named the "Vacationland" and a side-wheeler called the "Western States." These cruises were formed in the larger cities of southern Michigan or Wisconsin. There were a couple of the cruises from Chicago. There was a cruise from Detroit that came up Lake Huron. These cruises visited the towns "up north." When they came to Little Traverse Bay, they would visit all the towns along the bay.

When they came around Harbor Point, they would give a blast of the ship's horn. This would let the people of Harbor Springs know that a cruise ship was arriving. The mayor and all the dignitaries of Harbor Springs would go down to the city dock to welcome all the people of the cruise as they got off the boat. The people of the cruise would walk all over town and visit all the shops in town. Some of the people would walk and see the resorts of the area. When the farmers who lived close enough to town to hear the boat horn heard it, they hooked up a carriage and came to town to take the tourists on a horse and buggy ride to tour the area. This was profitable for them as well as all of the shop owners in town. They must have had a set time that they could visit because when the ship's horn blew, it meant that all of the tourists had to get back to the city dock and prepare to board the vessel.

This is when all the fun began. As the tourists boarded they all lined the railings facing towards the dock. Then they began throwing money down on the dock. It was mostly change that they threw, so when it hit the dock it bounced and rolled around. If no one caught the coins as they rolled around, the coins would fall down in the space between the dock planks and drop down into the water. They would go down and settle on the sand, where you could see them by looking through the cracks in the dock. After the ship pulled away from the dock, all of us kids, Indian and white, would jump from the dock and dive down to start picking up the coins. If you could hold your breath and had a keen eye, you could have a very nice swim.

Model T-Powered Hog Butchering
By Roberta Hanna of Lewiston, Michigan
Born 1919

I was born in October 1919, and have witnessed more changes in living, inventions, commerce, travel, and technology than any other generation. I have written my childhood story for my children; this is one segment.

Butchering day was an important day on the farm. Even though we kids had to work, it was an exciting day.

It was a winter chore and we butchered three or four hogs to provide pork for the year. It was a neighborhood affair because the help of a couple of neighbors was needed.

We got up long before dawn and Dad started a fire under the butchering kettle. We carried water to fill it and then did the barn chores. Dad kept the firewood burning under the kettle, we ate breakfast, and by that time, the water was near boiling. The first hog was shot with a "22" rifle and hung by block and tackle over an open-ended fifty gallon drum firmly set at an angle and partially filled with the boiling water. The hog was dipped into the water until the bristles could be scraped off with a sharp knife. That hog was hung and quartered while someone else started on the second hog.

The heart and liver were removed and fresh liver was fried for lunch. The entrails (intestines) were emptied and a couple women cleaned, turned, and scraped them. They were dropped into salt water and saved to be later used for stuffing sausage.

We did not have a smoke house. Sides were sliced for "side meat" and the hams and shoulders were prepared for "sugar curing." A mix of sugar, salt, and pepper was placed in the small center area of several layers of

Hog butchering time with Roberta's family in 1920

newspapers. The ham was placed on the mix and remainder patted to cover the entire ham. The newspaper was wrapped neatly around the ham, and then dropped into a clean muslin bag. It was tied with binder twine and hung with bone end down in a cool place. When spring came, it was ready to use. By this time, the ham was covered with green mold. It was sliced; the mold trimmed off, and then fried. Sugar cured ham had a distinct flavor that could not be matched.

The side meat was sliced, fried, then packed into jars or crocks and covered and sealed with hot lard. Sausage was also fried and sealed in lard.

The scraps of meat and perhaps a shoulder were cut for sausage and it was ground by my dad's ingenious method. He jacked up a rear wheel of the model "T," cleaned it good, and tied the grinder handle to the wheel with a long piece of binder twine. The grinder was mounted on a plank, which someone sat on and fed the meat into the grinder.

To complete the sausage, the ground meat was put into the sausage stuffer, the entrails were strung onto the spout, and when the geared lid was turned down, presto! We had sausage coming out of the spout.

All the fat was cubed and along with fat trimmings was put into the same butcher kettle cooker in which the water had been heated that early morning. When it was fully cooked, it was dipped into the sausage stuffer. As the geared lid was turned downward, the hot lard came from the spout into a lard can and the remaining pressed scraps were "cracklins." We kids stood by waiting anxiously for the cracklins to chew.

Much of the meat was canned in quart glass jars, which were processed for three hours in boiling water.

Butchering a beef was much less complicated. Today's Health Department would condemn and ban every phase of such meat preservation. No one was ever ill from eating the meat.

No Child Escaped Swimmer's Itch
By Carole Underwood of Maple City,
Michigan
Born 1943

The cabin court, which was about one mile east of Mackinaw City, stood on the shore of Lake Huron. When I was young in the 1950s, we stayed there on trips up north. Inside the cabin was a metal double bed, a scarred wooden dresser, and a rollaway bed brought in for me. A closet-like structure had been attached to the back wall and contained a sink and toilet. In the evening, we sat in lawn chairs on the beach and watched for lake freighters.

Mackinaw City, which was literally land's end in those days, reminded me of old western towns I had seen on the new medium called television. The main street was lined with souvenir shops, fudge stores, and a few restaurants. I still have a small plaque, which we bought, in one of the shops – the plaque has a scene of a mountain cabin and a waterfall. I remember running around the dilapidated old Fort Michilimackinac before it was renovated for tourism at a later date.

After an early breakfast, we drove to the dock to catch a boat to Mackinac Island. We took a carriage ride, passed Arch Rock, and ended up at the fort where I skipped ahead and peeked into all the buildings. The Grand Hotel was very impressive to my child's eye, along with the beautiful mansions lining the streets.

Another day we arrived at the ferry dock to ride the Chief Wawatum across the Straits to St. Ignace. I recall being seasick on that ride and was happy to get to the U.P. We drove to Soo Junction and took the Toonerville Trolley through the woods to the banks of the Tahquamenon River where we boarded a boat that disembarked us above the falls. Waking along the riverside pathway was pleasant and the falls thundered into the lower river. I met a girl from Detroit on the trolley that day and she and I have exchanged Christmas

153

cards for the last 60 years. We also traveled to Sault Sainte Marie to see the Soo Locks on that trip. The Big Mac Bridge has made crossing the Straits easy today, but many of us have memories of waiting for the ferries in the old days. The trusty Chrysler sometimes took us through Traverse City on the way back to our cottage on a lake, but on other occasions, we chose Rt. 27 directly south. It was a two-lane highway then and we spent hours getting home.

I am sure that my experiences growing up in summer at a lake cottage are the same as those of other seasonal children all over the state. We swam every day and put up with the swimmer's itch, which no child escaped, learned to water ski, and when we were very young, caught turtles upon whose shells we painted our initials with fingernail polish and then tried to catch them again later. On rainy days, we played Monopoly and Park and Shop and read books. By the time we girls reached our teens, we were more interested in flirting with boys than catching turtles. My best friend and I used her powerboat to cruise to the middle of the lake, shut off the motor, and pretended that we were having engine trouble. Since the lake was small, rescuers arrived shortly, the engine mysteriously repaired itself, and we met a lot of boys that way.

In those days, we watched movies with titles like *Beach Blanket Bingo* and *Bikini Beach Party*. We listened to 45 RPM records; "Lazy Summer Night", "Moonlight Swim", "Love Letters in the Sand", and "See You in September". We danced to Glenn Miller's "Moonlight Serenade," an atypical summer night found us on someone's pontoon boat with a portable radio, a grill, and food. We cruised around the lake innumerable times before coming to shore and lighting a bonfire. The lovely Michigan moonlight and warm breezes enhanced our summer romances. We sang songs and sat on sandy beach towels and never thought about an ending to those halcyon days and nights.

Summer cottages were Spartan then compared to luxurious lakeside homes today. Our cottage had two small bedrooms, a living room with a brick fireplace, kitchen, front porch, and half bath. The fireplace was the only heat source because the bathroom lacked a tub or shower; we bathed and washed our hair at the end of the lakeside dock. Any laundry was done with a scrub board in a bucket of water. But we had much fun and did not feel deprived. Now I consider myself fortunate to live on a different lake amid the beauty of northern Michigan. I have come full circle from those magical summers long ago to the unforeseen charm of these later years in Leelanau County, truly the Land of Delight.

I Would Go to Bed and Cry
By Margaret Crowl of Hubbard Lake,
Michigan
Born 1934

I was born in 1934. I grew up over two miles from school, church, store, or other place of business. Our closest neighbor was over one mile. Our play was making sand villages, we used old car seats and crates, or other things we could get to make playhouses in the woods near the house. We had a few cut out dolls, but our biggest pleasure came from a catalog given to us by a friend or relative. We cut out people, furniture, clothes, or whatever else we needed. Sometimes a person would resemble someone we knew. We had families, store, and other neighborhood places.

The King's from New York sent our family several things. One day they sent a bicycle. My sister Betty and I pushed it up and down hills all the way home. She never learned to ride it, but I soon was able to ride it and it was much more fun riding than pushing. The King's had also sent a sled and we took turns sliding down the hill or sometimes we would pull each other. We also made snowmen and angels in the snow.

From time to time, my dad would hook up a battery to a windmill to charge it. Then he would hook the battery to a radio and we would stay up until 3:00 a.m. listening to music. We had a Victrola and would crank it up and enjoyed listening to some old 78 records. I still remember some words to songs we enjoyed such as "100 Years From Now," "Folks Like Us are Dumb Where I Come From," and "Giggling Gertie."

We had an outside toilet and covered slop pail in the house that needed to be emptied daily as I had two older sisters and several younger. We lived on a farm and had cows, pigs, chickens, a horse, a goat, geese, and ducks.

Margaret Crowl's family

We also raised rabbits for meat to sell. We had a dog and a cat. We never butchered the cattle and it didn't bother me when they butchered chickens or a neighbor came to help butcher a pig, but when my dad butchered the rabbits I would go to my bed and cry. Sometimes I took the cows to my grandparents land, a mile away, on the way to school and got them on my way home. Sometimes it would be raining with thunder and lightning. I didn't mind if I had located the cows. In winter, I would go chop a hole in water at the bog and take the cattle there to get a drink. I carried water to the other animals. In summer, there was a well with a hand pump and a big tank way back. We pumped the tank daily and used the Fordson tractor and trailer to haul big cream cans of water to the house, as we did not have water or electric. We got water in the winter from relatives or neighbors. Our washing machine was a washboard and a crank wringer or by hand. We used kerosene lanterns to take to the barn and kerosene lamps to read. We had a gas lamp that hung in the center of one big room downstairs.

Because of the long walk, I started kindergarten when I was seven. Our school was quite similar to other one-room schools in the 1940s. We however, were able to have our Christmas programs at the church through my 6th grade, until a ban was put against it, so the boys built a stage at school. Every student took part in songs and plays. The parents came and we exchanged gifts and Santa passed them out and a bag of candy.

There were not many cars used on our road back then and if we saw a car, we did not recognize we would run out in the woods and hide until it went by. A few years later, I walked to church several times a week. When I was in my early teens, Mr. King came to our place. My oldest sister was married and lived near Alpena. I rode with Mr. King to my sisters where we both spent the night. Back then, it was not illegal to pick trailing Arbutis, so we picked some and mom would pack them in Moss from the bog and mail them to the King's. We also cut Spruce Trees and sold them by a big truckload to a man who hauled them to Detroit to sell. Sometimes we picked cranberries from the bog and wild flowers.

Crocks in the Creek
By Marylin Riley of Alpena, Michigan
Born 1940

The beginning of my story is that I was born in July 1940 in Rust Township, Montmorency County, in a log home my father built out of logs and mortar. The doctor came to the house to deliver me.

We had two rooms downstairs and two upstairs. In the kitchen, we had a small hand pump for water, a Home Comfort wood stove, and a trap door that lifted to reveal a stairway that went to the basement, which had a dirt floor and bins for potatoes, apples, carrots, etc. And lots of shelves for home canned goods. There was an outside cellar door.

We had a Delco battery radio run by Delco batteries. On Saturday night, we took a bath in a washtub in the kitchen; the water out of the reservoir on the side of the stove gave us hot water. Then we listened to the radio. One story I remember was the Squeaking Door. It was very scary. The old radio would crack and fade out at times. My folks always listened to the news and everyone had to be quiet so they could hear.

The barn, outhouse, corncrib, garage, and chicken coop were all away from the house a ways. We had a team of workhorses and my dad would let me ride one, with him leading it, down to the creek that ran through our property to drink.

Mom kept crocks in the creek to keep our butter, cream, milk, and salt pork so it would keep cold, as we had no electricity. We lived on Mom's canned goods and our own meat:

pork, venison, rabbits, and squirrel. Mom baked our own bread and baked goods.

Dad had an old Chevy flatbed truck and every week or so he would take the grain to town to the mill to get ground into flour. Mom would send me with Dad, as they put the flour in cloth sacks that came in pretty colors and Mom would send me to pick out the material as she made her long aprons out of the sacks and also other items. The mill where we had our grain turned into flour is now Brush Creek Mill, a tourist attraction. It still has the water wheel. Then we took our cream to the cream factory to sell, called the Creamery.

We had a wringer washer and we hung clothes outside which in the summer was nice because they smelled so fresh. But in the winter, you froze your hands hanging them outside. You would go to the line and get what you needed and hang them around the stoves to thaw out. I had to wear long cotton stockings; tan colored and held up by a garter belt. I wore heavy high top shoes with a little fur on top so could you tell boys shoes and girls shoes apart. I had to walk a mile to school across fields with very deep snow with a hard crust on top. As you walked, you would drop through the crust and it would cut your ankles.

We had a one-room school and it was always so cold until the teacher or an older kid would get there to build a fire in the wood furnace. The furnace sat in the back of the room.

We had to use an outhouse to go to the bathroom. We also had to use hot water to thaw the outside pump for water. The teacher would melt snow on top of the furnace for this.

Storms then were terrible, lots of snow and cold, but they had school anyway. And yes, my dad had a car with a rumble seat. My cousin and I rode from my uncle's place in Spruce back to Hillman. It was fun. As for toys, my dad whittled out whistles.

We also butchered our own pork and Dad saved up the bladders and blew them up with a straw and they were so tough you could not break them so we always had a ball for football, basketball, or whatever.

I was born and raised on a farm, so I was taught to help with chores early in life. We were so busy that there was no time to get in trouble. One time my friend that lived across the road from us got us in trouble. We lived one half mile off the main road, so we played in the woods a lot. One day we were about 7 or 8 and we thought we found four little black and white kittens so we took them home. As soon as my dad saw them, he marched us two girls with our kittens back to where we found them. They were baby skunks.

In 1948, my dad bought a John Deere tractor and we also got electricity. Things started getting a lot better.

✓ Delivering Without a Doctor
By Edna Demorest of Flat Rock, North Carolina
Born 1928

My grandmother, Mable's life was cut short by a house fire. My great grandfather, Orvile Bailey, was bedridden in an upstairs bedroom and Mable was trying to get him out the window when the floor gave way under her and both perished. They had been able to get all the children to safety. I would have loved to know my Grandmother Bailey. From things my mother had told, she must have been a strong and loving lady, with much courage. Mom has told of a time her mother wanted to go to Boyne City to see her folks and grandpa would not go so she hitched her horse to the buggy and with Alice, about 11 years old took off for Boyne City. The trip took them two days to get there. At that time, the roads were no more than dirt trails through the woods, no motels, or restaurants along the way. Grandpa Bailey was a woods man and life must have been very hard on him after losing his wife and father both at the same time in such a tragedy. He was left with a 14 year old and a 2 year old, girl to care for. Alice lived with her dad and took care of the house and little sister, Winnie, until she married Alfred at the age of 18. After that, Winnie lived with brothers and sisters for several years. As she got a little older she came back to live with her dad in his little cabin in the woods. Later Aunt Winnie married Harley Stow. She has always been a very special part of our family.

My earliest memories of Grandpa Bailey were his little house in the woods, by a small creek, and his big yellow cat named Spike.

Grandpa was a quiet man who liked to just commune with nature. Back then, many neighborhoods had dances in someone's home on Saturday nights. One night Uncle Clifford took Alice to a dance 10 miles away to the Tennant Settlement. There she met Alfred Tennant, which was the beginning of over 48 years together for them. Alfred and Alice were both making plans for their wedding day. Alice was busy hand stitching a blue dress for her wedding. Alfred was busy building a little house deep in the woods for their home. Alfred and Alice Bailey were married November 28, 1925 at Onaway, Michigan. They celebrated their wedding by going to the movie "Hunch Back of Notre Dame." Then they spent the night with Alfred's sister, Nina and Steve Thomas. The next day they moved into their home. They were set for the winter with a cedar saw, an ax, and a side of beef hanging on the outside wall. Now they were ready to set up housekeeping. According to a picture, it must have been a rather small and rustic house. From a note on a picture, they lived there until January.

October 20, their first child was born. Clyde Orvile was born in a house across the road from dad's sister, Aunt Francis Hilliker; naturally, Aunt Frank took care of Bud's birth. I think they had a doctor for that birth. If anyone was sick or having a baby in the neighborhood, Aunt Frank was always the first to be called.

I don't know when they moved to Loon Lake where the Powers family lived, but they lived beside of them. There Edna Alfreda Tennant was born on November 26, 1928. No doctor came but I was in good hands. Aunt Frank and Granny Powers was there to welcome me. Sometime later mom and dad moved again. This time to a house on what is known as Kinney Island. Grandpa Tennant built a home site there. While living there at Kinney Island on February 17, 1931 Norman Harvey Tennant was born. My first memories are of our home at Kinney Island. I had never been back there after we moved, until many years later, Bud walked back there to Chuck and I. the old trail with the big rock along the way which we always ran ahead to climb up on was still there, but not near as big anymore like I remembered it. The old home site was a still very clean, picture in my mind after 60 years later.

Dad built a little house on Uncle Herb's property across the road from Aunt Frank, when I was four years old. This is where Edith Mable was born on January 22, 1934.

One year later history repeated itself for mom. Our house burned in the middle of the nigh January 31, 1935. Fortunately, they were able to get us all out, but lost everything they had. Norman was the only injury as a bedroom drape fell on his arm. He carried the scars the rest of his life. We were all taken to Aunt Frank's where we stayed a short time until another house was ready for us. We all had bad coughs from the smoke, but Aunt Frank doctored us with bear grease. Uncle Dell and Aunt Amy had a small house where they had lived sometime earlier, so everyone got together and fixed it for us to live in.

The summer of 1935, they were able to buy 40-acres of land surrounding the Hackett Lake School. While dad was building our house beside the school, we lived in a tent on the far end of the property for most of the summer. It must have been hard on mom to take care of four kids and do the cooking on an old cook stove outdoors. I remember one day it was pouring rain and she was trying to keep the fire going enough to cook the food. Bud and I slept in the car and Norman and Edith were in the tent with mom and dad. We were able to move into the house before the weather got bad. That fall I started school, Bud and I walked up the old road about a mile each day for school. Hackett Lake School was a one-room school with all eight grades. There was about 19 or 20 kids in school, all except five or six were Tennant cousins. In the eight years of school, I had only three different teachers. Harold Ross was born in the new house December 2, 1936. Again, Aunt Frank was there for the delivery of another new nephew. As I was growing up life was rather hard with very little money and much work to do. We had five or six cows, a team of horses, and a flock of chickens to be taken care of. Besides the farming dad made what money he could by working in the woods, cutting fence posts for sale, plus cedar boughs and Christmas trees. All through December, we cut and sold trees for $0.10 each. Everyone with trees to sell stacked them near the road and truckers came around looking for them to buy. They took the trees to the cities to sell. I have pulled many trees out of the thick woods with snow half way to my heck. All the kids who were big enough to walk through the snow helped by pulling out the trees as dad cut them.

I didn't do many outside chores as Bud and Norm were in line for that. My job was to fill in for mom when she was out in the field or somewhere helping dad. I learned at an early age to cook meals, keep the old cook stove going, bake bread, take care of the younger kids, and many other things.

Growing up Uncle Herb's daughter, Rosabell, and I were very close. They lived a half mile from us and we were the only two girls our age in the neighborhood. Her brother, Sam was the same age as Bud and they did many things together also. One year Uncle Herb made them each a set of skis. We took hers up a long hill to learn to ski. It was a long wait at the top of the hill for the other one to come back. We solved that by each taking one ski and sat on it to go down the hill. We had fun but neither one learned to ski. Hackett Lake was a small lake on Uncle Herb's land and by the time we were 11 years old, Bud and Sam started to skate. They would shovel off an area on the lake and we all had fun. Rosabell had a pair of clamp on skates and I had a pair of higher shoes so we put her skates on my shoes and took turns with them. Many Sunday afternoons were spent on the ice. The next year we each had new skates, but soon the boys tired of skating. We tried to interest Norm into the joy of skating so he could help shovel the snow. That was not Norm's thing. He much preferred to curl up by the stove and read a book. We had to either do it ourselves or talk her dad into helping us.

Dad always loved to fish so many hot nights they would do milking early and mom got the fry pans and potatoes ready to go to the lake. The lakes had cooking grills so mom would find wood and get a good fire going and start the potatoes frying. Bud, Norm, dad, and I would start to fish. As fast as one was caught the younger kids were busy taking them to mom to clean and cook. They always tasted good to us. Then we went in the lake with a bar of soap and cleaned up and cooled off.

I learned to sew at a very young age, when I was 10. Our teacher, Kate Wilson, brought her sewing machine to school and started a 4-H sewing class. My first year I had to hem two towels, one by hand and one by machine, and make a darn and a dress. My dress was yellow chambray with fine green rickrack trim with small green buttons. That year I was the only one to get a gold seal on my project. Rosabell and I took 4-H sewing three years. Several years earlier mom taught me to crochet. We had one small kerosene lamp in the middle of the table. Any reading or needlework was done there and the light was not very bright. Mom would only crochet with very fine thread so that is how I learned. Since then I have used many miles of thread. I graduated from the 8th grade May 5, 1943. All country kids were required to write a special county exam in order to pass from the 8th grade. The exam was given at a school seven miles away. Two months before my exam I came down with the measles. By that time, mom was not feeling very good. After several days, all the other kids came down with them also. Even though I was not feeling well yet, I had to help take care of things. I missed three weeks of school, just a month before my exam. The exam day came. At 2:00 that morning I was up as it was time to call Aunt Frank again. That time mom had the doctor present also. By 6:00 a.m. Myrtle May and Myron Morse was born. Dad was the janitor at school, so I opened the school and got the fire going, then walked a mile up the road to get a neighbor to stay with mom and got the kids off to school. Someone took us 8th graders to our exams. After writing our exams, we walked the seven miles back home. Later my 8th grade diploma came in the mail and I could not believe I had passed the exam.

Blackberry Brandy
By Dennis Huggler of Alpena, Michigan
Born 1928

When I was a youngster where Abitibi (now DPI) was built, there used to be fines from the washed stone quarry Wyandotte Chemical owned. They would run pipelines with sluice, which were the fines they built the base for the present company. We used to play golf on this property. I was lucky enough to have a two iron we would sink coffee cans into the fines for cups. There also was a field there that would burn all summer long as there was peat under the grass. My home was two

158

Denny's brother, Melton and Denny

blocks from there on the corner of Oldfield and Merchant Street on the north side of town. We had two lots where our house was, with two fish ponds stocked with catfish and rock bass.

I watched the construction of the Second Avenue Bridge and received a flash from a welder and my mother put wet tea leaves on my eyes to ease the pain. We used to play down by the Thunder Bay River as we lived only two blocks away. One time I fell in, that was before I could swim, there was a dredge in the river working, and one of the guys saw me fall in. He pulled a string of boats from one to the other finally getting to where I was hanging onto the bow of one of the other boats. He gave me a severe scolding and told me he never wanted to see me down there again. I learned how to dog paddle, after that I swam every day and became good at it.

I remember the tugs in the river one was called tramp owned by Piepkorn. Piepkorn also owned other tugs in the river. There was coal on the dock that also belonged to Piepkorn and was distributed by tuck. The fellow that handled the truck went by the name of Ellar, he was a good worker, and he whistled all the time. The Second Avenue Street was paved with brick and was smooth as glass. We owned an icebox where the milk and perishables were kept. The ice was delivered via horse and wagon house to house. We used to chase behind the wagon and chip ice off the blocks to suck on. We also played in the freight shed where the train would deliver goods for pickup by the local business, things like fencing, shotgun and 22-shells, and many other products.

I also remember the winter snow when we had to walk to school in a couple feet of snow. We didn't think anything of the snow. One year on the corner of Truckey and French Roads, there were 20-foot high snowdrifts that I stood on top of and watched trucks try to move it. They couldn't move it with the plows so they had to get a snow blower to do the job. I owned a 1934 Chevrolet that had snow tires and chains on the back wheels and it would go through a lot of snow. We had to take it to work, as my dad's car would not make it through that much snow.

I remember when the Memorial Hall was the only place that would hold enough people for a big party. It would hold at least 600 people. I used to roller-skate at the German Hall, which was located at the end of Second Avenue and Hubert Street. I met many pretty girls at the roller rink. My first girlfriend was a girl by the name of Lenore Jones; her parents lived about three blocks down Merchant Street from my house. We would sit on her front porch and smooch for a while then I would go home before her dad got there. I met her when she broke her arm trying to get away from me and my homemade scooter, which was made from an orange crate, 2x4's, and an old pair of roller skates. The roller skates clamped on your shoes with a special wrench.

I remember my 12th birthday. We were eating dinner and my dad said there was a cop outside looking for my brother and I. When we went out, there were two brand new bicycles on kick stands for us. I got the blue one and my brother got the other one. I remember bowling at the Trianon Lanes, located above the furniture store just north of the Second

Avenue Bridge, when we were in high school. I had about a 165 average that was high for the year. I also set pins there when I was 13, you were supposed to be 16, but I was a big kid, so I lied about my age and got the job. We were paid $0.03 per line, but we went on strike and got $0.05 per line. I did that for three years.

I remember skip day in our senior year of high school. We drank a bottle of blackberry brandy with the end result of getting sick. I have not been able to drink that kind of stuff since. As a teen, I worked at Swallow's Hardware on the corner of Fletcher Street and Second Avenue. They paid $0.20 per hour. Then I worked at Cohen's Hardware, which was also in the first block north of the Second Avenue Bridge. During the summer while I was still going to school, my buddy and I built fences for the Habitat Company. There we were paid $65.00 every two weeks. We filled special orders for different kinds of fences. They were made with cedar pickets that were sawed in two and pointed. We finished all of the orders and they laid us off, which was okay as it was about time to go back to school. After I graduated, I went to work at the Huron Portland Cement Plant. We worked on a cement mixer. It took six shovels of gravel, six shovels of sand, and three shovels of cement. There were three of us feeding that machine. They were making concrete to pour the bases for the new kilns, which were numbered 10 through 13. The contractor was a company called Gilliland Construction, which was owned locally by a man named Bill Gilliland, he was a nice person. I stayed at the cement plan until retirement in December 1986, which was then owned by National Gypsum.

There used to be a place called the Marine Market, it was a butcher shop and would supply the boats with groceries and meat when they came in to port for cement or stone. The store was located where the Post Office is now and next to it was a hamburger joint. Then on the corner of Fletcher and Second Avenue was a gas station called Renors where the men could buy gas or play cards in the back room. My father used to run the poker game; they would rake the pot according to the size of it. He did this after working all day at the cement plant, needless to say we didn't see very much of him.

✓ The Unexpected Vacation
By Joanne Kline of Traverse City, Michigan
Born 1929

The year was 1953. I had graduated from college in 1951 with a bachelor's degree and a secondary teaching certificate and had married a man who was determined to become a physician. He had depleted his V.A. benefits in undergraduate school, having previously served two years in the Air Force. This meant that upon acceptance to medical school, Kirksville College of Osteopathic Medicine, we were totally dependent on my income in a small community with an abundance of married students with wives seeking employment, several of whom were qualified teachers.

We settled into a college–owned two-room apartment, under pressure as (my husband's classes began and I learned that my chance of obtaining a teaching position was slim to none. With great trepidation, I applied for a job as a nurse's aide in a nearby hospital. I did not have experience; I had no desire, nor real knowledge of what my duties would be. Besides, I would need to buy uniforms and shoes. Furthermore, my husband had made it clear that he would never marry a nurse. In the midst of my great anxiety, thankfully, a knock came on our door and it was the superintendent of an outlying small school district with an offer of a position in a one room rural school, where the previously hired teacher failed to show up. School had already begun and in the meantime, mothers, though unqualified, were attempting to hold some kind of order.

Although this offer of employment was even more frightening in many respects than the position in the hospital, the pay was better, the hours on the surface were shorter, and it seemed at the time to be my destiny, and even perhaps, God's intervention! And so the adventure began. Getting to this school, Ringo Point School meant driving 14 miles to the small town of Novinger where the consolidated high school was, then taking a school bus that went into the county to pick up high school students. That was a route of about 11 miles or so, but it didn't go as far as Ringo Point. That meant that I got off the bus and hiked a half mile or so, over a couple of barbed wire fences, through a snake infested cow pasture, to the school yard, which

160

included a rickety outhouse that appeared to be barely clinging onto a small hill, and an outdoor hand pump for water.

Needless to say, I had some serious reservations about my decision to accept this "opportunity," but really, I had no choice at this point. The schoolhouse door was unlocked and as it opened, I could see 15 or 20 mice scurry from the tops of the desks to wherever they hid out when the room was occupied. I made a mental note to bring some poison the next day. Before long, I heard the sound of a bus unloading my students, 18 of them ranging from 1st to 8th grade. I don't know who of us were more frightened. There they stood, barely inside the only door, huddled together and looking at me as though I were from outer space. I might as well have been, I shared with them that I was from Michigan, I might as well have said, "Mars." Most of them were barefoot. Needless to say, I found preparing lesson plans for eight grades, plus a kindergartner five days a week, overwhelming. But it soon became clear that I would have no discipline problems. These children knew that if they caused any trouble in school, and if their parents learned of it, they would be in big trouble at home.

One ongoing problem involved a little 2nd grade girl who either couldn't hold it or chose not to leave her desk to go out to the outhouse. I can't say that I blamed her. So frequently, the noise of liquid splashing onto the wood floor was heard, along with some quiet giggles. This was not her only problem, but she was clearly loved by the other students. Her name was Judy. Then one spring day as I was teaching the older students and using the blackboard, I heard what sounded like a light knocking in the area of the chimney behind me. It persisted so I sent one of the older boys outside to see if anything was amiss. He quickly returned and said he couldn't see anything unusual, but then a rather rhythmic sound persisted even as I continued with the lesson. So I reluctantly decided to take a break and go outside myself to check the source of the noise. To my chagrin, the chimney was on fire! Did I mention that a coal furnace in the basement heated the building, which was also under my supervision and part of my janitorial duties? Needless to say, my mind and my body went into overdrive and I knew that first and foremost, I must get the children

out of the building, not at all difficult. Perhaps it was the most exciting thing they had ever witnessed.

Well, in the midst of my disaster, the neighbor nearest the school, where one of the older boys ran for help, came roaring out of his driveway, in his truck and leaning on his horn without a break. He sped past the school and up and down every local two-track. Miraculously, within minutes, the schoolyard was filled with trucks, tractors, and other odd farming implements, loaded with ladders and buckets. The ladders were quickly placed against the wall nearest the chimney. I frantically pumped water from the well, the children carried the water to the men on the ladders, all like a well-organized machine and time having been suspended, before long the flames and the smoke were defeated! And as a bonus, I got to meet some of the parents of my students as well as others who obviously cared about them, as well as the schoolhouse.

So school was suspended for a few days while repairs were made and I along with the children had an unexpected vacation. I spent many hours trying to get the black stains out of my clothing, rather unsuccessfully. That Christmas I decided to knit mittens for every student. I had observed that some of them came to school mittenless. Somewhere I have a picture of myself with the 18 pairs of mittens spread out on my bed. I don't know how they felt about it, but I felt content. That was the last year that Ringo Point School was open. The following years those students would be bussed to Novinger, the location of the newly consolidated school district. Every once in a while I think of those days and those students. I never had a single discipline problem. The 8th graders would be 60 now. I wonder where they are, what they're doing, and if they remember the day the schoolhouse caught fire.

My Montmorency County Adventure
By Sandy Berry of Brooklyn, Michigan
Born 1935

When I was sixteen years old, my cousin Norm took me deer hunting with him.

Living in a pup tent for a week with snow coming every day or so, it was quite an exhilarating and joyful experience for a

Sandy and the dog Star in 1992

young fellow. I remember a quarter inch of ice on the inside of the pup tent from our body heat. If you rolled at night, you wouldn't raise your arms—they'd get wet in a hurry. In the morning, we would crawl out the small door pushing snow as we went. Boots and clothes were the first things on the agenda. Next, the wood fire for breakfast and coffee. We'd set the coffee pot on the fire's edge and the iron skillet inward somewhat. Of course, all this was done by flashlight. That year, 1951, was my first year, so I was assigned to shoot the camp deer for meat. There were two camps that shared the wealth.

Did we get our license limit? You bet we did. There were not any doe permits back then. I learned how to read the land: scrapes, rubs, trails, areas where the elusive buck roamed, how to hunt in cedar swamps. Our spot was most likely one of the best areas a hunter could want, good hardwood, and hills to the North and a two-mile long cedar swamp to the South. It was and still is amazing how many deer you can see that way as they travel to and fro.

It took a while to identify the smaller bucks. Those ears sure do cover up a pair of spikes nicely. All in all, it was an experience I will never forget.

It didn't stop there, though. We went every year afterward. In 1954, the DNR came out with doe permits. I remember those first years of doe season. Hunters (I should say that loosely) would shoot at most anything that

moved. It also added a lot more people to our area. Someone hit the tree where I was sitting about six inches above my head that first year.

Another year I lost my cushion to one, when I went back to camp for lunch. I trailed him when I got back to my stand because we had snow. When I caught up with him, he was polite enough and gave it back.

In 1952 or 1953, my cousin Norm and Uncle Ellis bought a small camper trailer. It slept five of us warmly: Uncle Ellis and Aunt Celia, Norm and Marie, and myself (Sandy).

Down from where we camped yearly there was and still is a "40" in the middle of all that state land. For many years after that time, I took my wife and children as they were born. It was a joy living in a tent: straw on the ground under our sleeping bags, and an oil heater that you had to keep the wick trimmed or you'd have black soot and smoke. One time and you learned to trim your wick daily. The joyful years were back then. It's a lot different nowadays. If you set at a tree now all day you'd have four-wheelers and snowmobiles out looking for deer and for their pleasure.

How about that 40? Years later, it came up for sale and we bought it, my wife and I. The cabin was half level and half tilted to the ground. "Porkies" did quite a job on it. I cut long poles from the swamp, used 20-ton bottle jacks, and leveled her up. We did a lot of work on it as we got vacations from work. It was our cabin in the woods in the middle of hundreds of acres of state land. A very peaceful haven.

We would lay out feed corn, beets, and hay, and bread and donuts from the local bakery (day old stuff they didn't sell). We had rabbits, raccoons, bobcats, deer, bear, and a lot of birds. This was about 50 feet from our front door. It was a beautiful sight on a daily basis. I used to sit on the front porch and watch them and talk to the bear. All they would do, after they got used to me, would grunt a little at me as if they were answering me. We took some home movies back then. It's nice to watch them now. Nowadays you cannot feed them due to a bait/feed ban because of T.B. We eventually sold the 40.

I'm 77 years old now and sure wish I hadn't done that. I would fully enjoy my last years living there and cutting cedar to build log cabins for others. Cutting cedar trees and managing the land for further growth was a memorable time in my life. We built a few homes in the area. We enjoyed doing things for people who wanted their homes built right and with heart. We also built some rental properties up and still have them today. It would be nice to sell them though. I'm getting on in age now and my wife doesn't want them after I'm gone. She'll move downstate with her family I presume. They have strong family beliefs to care for one another. I still love the Northern part of Michigan today, and wouldn't change a thing.

√ Growing Up on Breakfast Point
By Diann Murphy of Grayling, Michigan
Born 1946

When I was young, my mother and father frequently took my siblings and I on camping trips and outdoor adventures. Although we lived in Chelsea, where my dad worked in one of North American Rockwell's plants, we spent many summer weekends, as well as our vacations, in the Grayling area. My parents bought a 10-acre parcel on Timber Trail southeast of town in the early 1960s. I-75 had not yet reached Grayling, so the trip ''up north'' was always on the two-lane highways such as US-27. Four-Mile road was still, basically, just a sand trail, and we had to hike the last 200 yards or so to get to the camper trailer that was permanently parked on the property. There were seven of us kids, so it was always a challenge to get one's fair share of space in such cramped quarters.

But my dad always wanted to be "on the water," and my folks spent many days looking for such a location. They eventually purchased a piece of property east of Grayling on the Au Sable River. Access to the river could only be had by way of the long-since abandoned bed of a railroad spur that had been used during the lumbering days. Typical of such spurs, the "ties" were nothing more than appropriately sized trees that they cut as they cleared the intended route. When they'd finished clear-cutting the area, they just pulled up the rails on the last trip out, and left the "ties" to nature. So, that rail bed had to become the driveway to get to the river. The problem was, it ran most of its distance through the swamp, and the ''ties'' had long since rotted away in the muck. My folks couldn't afford to pay to have a driveway built, so, for at least five or six years, we'd go to the Timber Trail property almost every weekend, and while we kids were having a camping trip, my dad was hauling sand in his pickup truck to build a driveway almost half-a-mile long. He shoveled it on, and shoveled it off. The owner of a local sandpit gave him permission to take it for free (something else that doesn't happen anymore).

As he shoveled, he collected all the stones he encountered in a 5-gallon pail, and once the river frontage was solid enough to become a yard, he started building a stonewall along the water's edge, so their property would have a pleasing appearance from the river. Anyone who regularly canoed the Au Sable River will remember the property on the south side with the stonewall and the big pile of driftwood, both of which are still there today, and "OLD GRAYBEARD" who faithfully entertained the river traffic with his Scottish music recordings.

Also, the river at this location still bears the hallmark of the railroad spur's bridge that crossed here, in the form of the pilings that even yet, in 2013, jut up from the riverbed, often causing unsuspecting canoeists to tip over in the 3-foot deep water. My dad was told by a few of the locals that the Peters Salt & Lumber Company owned the spur. I spent many years of my youth splashing and playing in the river there with my brothers and sisters. We all brought our own kids to Grayling through the years to do the same thing, and they brought their kids, and now they are bringing their kids. My mom and dad, who both worked in the Willow Run factory building B-24 Liberators during WWII, would be happy to know that their "homestead" is still in the family, and that their descendants are still enjoying it.

My mom passed away in 1982, so my dad was left to carry on alone. But he was a vigorous individual: Although he and my mom both worked at Willow Run, his term there only lasted until he was able to get into the Navy. He served on the USS Atlas during the war and was at Normandy for the invasion of Europe. When he passed away in 2002, his ashes joined mom's on the property at the river, which is known locally as Breakfast Point.

Speaking of Breakfast Point, Dad chose this name for his road because the locals always referred to his place as "oh, you live on breakfast point", so one day he had a local tell him the story and they told him that the old trappers and guides always stopped at the site of Dad and Mom's homestead on the river to have breakfast. So, when 911 came to our area and we had to name our driveways and roads for the telephone company, there was no question in my dad's mind what to name his road, hence "Breakfast Point" and the old locals all agreed with him.

A further bit of historical information is connected to the site of my parent's homestead. As recounted in the book, <u>The Old Au Sable</u> by Hazen L. Miller, copyright 1963, page 70, according to Chief David Shoppenagons related to H. C. McKinley in the book <u>The Au Sable River</u>. There was a pitched battle that took place literally in the front yard of the property between a party of Chippewa and Huron Indians, many years before even the very first white man arrived in this part of Michigan. They had encountered each other while traversing the river in opposite directions.

A few other memories from the early days of their homestead:

The telephone was a party line until 1985.

The 14 x 70 mobile home they put on the river was eventually "logged in" by my dad, with cedar trees he cut from the swamp himself *in his 70s*, so that, from the outside, it had the perfect appearance of a log cabin.

My dad loved to tell stories of his youth, including the memories of listening to his great-uncle, who was a Civil War veteran, tell his own war stories.

We May Not Have Had Money, but We Always Had Each Other
By Mary Lou Williams of Traverse City, Michigan
Born 1948

I was raised in Muskegon, Michigan, the youngest of five children, three boys, and two girls. Due to the fact that my dad died when I was only five, there were a lot of struggles. It should be noted that although we were dirt poor, we were a happy and healthy bunch. Mom was a stay at home mother and refused to take help from welfare or other agencies, feeling as a family, we were responsible for ourselves.

We were outside most of the time after school playing either touch football (girls included) climbing trees, swimming near the local Muskegon River or some other outdoor activity, coming in just in time to help with dinner, eat, clean up, and out until bedtime. At night, we would often play cards including Poker and Rummy being favorites. We used toothpicks for Poker stakes. We would also gather around the radio to listen to the *Red Ryder*, *The Green Hornet*, or my personal favorite, *The Lone Ranger*. Finally, one family got a television set and we would gather around on Saturday morning to watch *Casper the Friendly Ghost* or *Hopalong Cassidy*. *The Lone Ranger* finally came to life on that television.

One of my sister Nancy's and my favorite thing to do in the summer was to climb on top of an old outhouse that was right under a green apple tree. We would steal the saltshaker form the house and pick apples above our heads we were stuffed! Mom used to say we would get the "bloody flucks" (whatever that was), but we never did. We lived in the country and there were wild fields everywhere. All five of us kids were outside playing on good days most of the day, coming in only to wash up and help get dinner or at bedtime after we cleaned up the kitchen. We used to climb the trees in the area and in one location, there were many trees and several grew by small mounds. One day as we went to play on our favorite trees, an excavation crew was there and had blocked it off not letting us play there anymore. They declared it a major discovery of an Indian Burial Ground. That was awesome!

Another favorite activity was to tie a rope to a tree and swing down over the sand dune by the field. It never occurred to us we might hit a rock or another tree on the way down. The ropes were often frayed with many knots in them because they kept breaking. We would compete to see who could go the farthest. In the winter, we would slide down the hills on a broken toboggan or use sleds. We did this with our mother as well.

Often either after dinner, on weekends, or during the day in the summer, the neighborhood kids would gather to play marbles, or softball, touch football or Kick the Bucket. We would collect fireflies in jars and often lay down to look at the clouds and imagine shapes in them. There was lots of time to be kids. There was no money for dance classes or other expensive past times.

When we were very little, my sister, Nancy and I would entertain ourselves by playing house outside. Milk pods were eggs and whatever else we could fill in to be food for our imaginary table, like acorns, leaves, etc. we used to find old broom or mop sticks and make horses to ride on. We would put a sock filled with sawdust over one end and draw a face on it, used some old baling twine or rope for a bridle. Boy did we ever have fun with those. Never did we have expensive toys, but always a great imagination.

Since money was tight, my mother Pearl had a big Maxwell House coffee can on the kitchen counter to collect all income that might come our way. My three older brothers, Billy, Jerry, and Raymond, would bring money in by collecting night crawlers to sell, working at a seasonal fruit stand in the summer and in the winter, shoveling snow for $0.50 on the high end. My sister Nancy and I would either help mom with the laundry she took in from the neighbors or would babysit if available. There was no such thing as allowances and no expectations that there should be. We pulled together as a family to survive with all monies going into the can. No one ever took a penny from the can without permission. Even though we did not have a father and over the years, the country neighborhood deteriorated to basic poverty, not one of us kids got into trouble of any kind because we had too much respect for our mother.

My mother would wash all of our clothes every Monday's on a cranky wringer washing machine, but often it did not work and she would use a plain old washboard in a big metal tub. After mom would wash the clothes, my sister and I would help hang them out to dry on the clotheslines, even in the wintertime. All extra clothes would be strung up some place in the house. I remember my mother's hands being cracked, red, and sore most of the winter. She never complained.

Mary Lou and her sister Nancy

Since we lived in a two-bedroom home with five kids, we had to share a bedroom and my sister and I would sleep together and of course my brothers. There were two at one end of the bed and two at the other end. We only had one small stove that sat in the living room to heat the house and often in the winter, we would throw our winter coats over the top to warm them up before jumping in bed. This helped add heat to the two blankets we had.

Although we washed up every night, we only took a bath once a week on Saturday nights. We did not have running hot water so mom would heat up some in pots on the stove and use a big round metal tub that she sat in the middle of the kitchen floor. After stringing up a curtain to block the kitchen from the living room, mom would fill up the tub halfway with cold water and add hot water as needed. My sister and I used to go first and then my brothers. They always seemed to be dirtier. My mother would check each of us behind the ears, our necks, and knees to be sure we didn't miss anything. Since we could not afford pajamas, we slept in whatever we had. We got clothes twice a year for each of us. Back to school and Easter. This included underwear, socks, shoes, and a new dress or in the boys cases, shirts and pants. Other than that our clothes got sewed up and mended or were hand me downs.

Christmas was always full of love. Each one of us got one gift. Our stockings were one of our own socks, hung up on the doorframe. Of course the bigger the kid, the bigger the sock. We got oranges, cookies, or apples in the sock. My brothers and sister and I would sing Christmas carols with our mother and play games or listen to the radio. We were a very close family. One Christmas the family next to us had nothing and my mother had us each give one of the kids something of whatever we had. We wrapped it up in newspaper and gave it with an open heart. That was a very special Christmas and taught us the importance of giving.

Easter was special. Mom would always hide colored eggs and it was fun to guess where she hid them. No toys were given. Twice while growing up, my mother was able to make an Easter basket for each of us. That was very special.

My mother was from the south and we grew up on fried foods. Every night we had fried potatoes, bread, and meat when we could afford it. On Sunday, we had a special dinner of fried chicken, mashed potatoes, gravy, and a vegetable. There were times when there was no food, but my mom somehow made into a game. My sister and I once shared a half piece of bread with mustard on it and a glass of water for dinner. My mother made it seem we were having a tea party. Every school day my mother would get up very early and make homemade biscuits for our breakfast and lunches, insisting that we all had to eat breakfast before the long walk to school. She watched us to be sure we ate and always made our lunches if there was enough food. As a family, the older kids always helped the younger to get dressed or what the need was. My mother instilled pride of self and accomplishment in each of us as well as integrity.

School was long ways away and in good weather took about an hour to get home. My mother did not know how to drive and since we didn't have a car, we walked. For elementary, the nearest school was about two miles or more and we walked through a big field to get there. There was trestle that went over the Muskegon River and we had to cross it to get to school and then up a big hill to finally get to a sidewalk. The trestle was icy and dangerous in winter. Two of our neighbor boys Billy and Bobby died when they slipped off of the trestle. My mother taught us to put our ear to the railroad tracks to listen for a rumble, which meant a train was in the distance. If there was no rumble then we went as quickly as possible to the other side. The trestle is still there. My mother would meet us kids at the trestle to walk us across and keep us safe. Billy and Bobby got killed; they did not come home with us after school. My mother would listen to our day as we walked home.

We look back often and realized that as kids, yes, there were times we had no food, money, or enough staples, but we always had each other and are still very close. There were no credit cards and life was simple. We grew up giving back because we did not always have, and it taught us compassion, we worked hard because that is what we always did as a family to survive and knew we could have whatever we wanted if we were willing to work for it. That gave us a strong work ethic. Most of all, we grew up with integrity and a tremendous sense of humor, learning to laugh at ourselves when life dealt us another blow. Each one of us has been successful in our own way; we took pride in ourselves.

A Little Bit of Heaven
By Helen Braun of Midland, Michigan
Born 1925

I am the second child, but the first daughter born to Jennie Annie Pyle and Roy Charles Arthur Pyle, in Shepherd, Michigan on April 19, 1925. I grew up on a small farm near Coe, Michigan. I attended a school at a little country school called Cohoon, which was approximately ¼ mile from our home. We walked a couple miles to attend Christian Church with my sister Anna at Coe. Our grandparents Pyle picked us up to attend Methodist Church in Shepherd with them, where Anna and I were later baptized by Revered Henry Hulme. We spent lots of weekends with my widowed Grandma Palmer who lived alone a couple miles the opposite direction, near Forest Hill. I slept in her feather bed. We made mud pies on her front porch stoop. We learned how to sew from mother, the Cohoon Sewing club, and 4-H Club at an early age. Mother was a beautiful seamstress and also taught cooking, cleaning, and childcare.

I have three brothers and two sisters living and two deceased sisters. I graduated 8th grade from Cohoon School with ceremonies at what is now Central Michigan University in 1939. I attended classes at Shepherd High and after completing freshman year, I was asked to stay with Revered Henry Hulme's family and help Mrs. Hulme in care for Methodist Parsonage and daughter Janet. I resided there through my sophomore and junior year; room and board was $0.50 a week. Summer of my senior year my parents bought a farm in the Alma School District. Having been asked by Mr. Huber, Superintendent of Shepherd High School, to help Mrs. Huber with their house and family, since she also taught, I accepted and received room, board, and $2.00 a week. Good memories of Shepherd and the families I resided with.

World War II was declared December 7, 1941, so there was no senior trip. Students worked on farms when not attending classes because of manpower shortage. My Brother Basil entered the army during my 10th year; there were lots of tears and prayers. I graduated high school in Shepherd, Michigan in 1943. After graduation, my cousin Irene Stowers transported me to Midland, Michigan where I applied for work at Michigan Bell Telephone Company and was hired. After a three-month training session, I became a full-fledged telephone operator. I shared an apartment with my high school chum, Berneda Converse, and three other girls.

I met Ulmont Bardwell in the fall of 1943. It was love at first sight! We were married April 8, 1944 in Hope, Michigan at the Methodist Parsonage where Ulmont was from. He was inducted into the first Marine Air Wing Headquarters Command in May of 1944. Our son Richard Leroy was born January 1945. There was a lot of loneliness, tears, and prayers. I spent the summer of 1945 in San Diego, California with Ulmont while he attended the Marine Fleet Air West Coast, Construction and Maintenance School; completing it with a 3.8 grade point. He was in route for the invasion of Japan when VJ Day was declared and was then sent to China where he spent the next year. With an aching heart, I returned to Michigan and our baby. I went to work for the Union Telephone Company awaiting his return. The summer of 1947 Ulmont was discharged and we resumed our life together. He returned to his employment at Dow Chemical Company. There was no shelter for veterans in those days, so Ulmont's grandfather Samuel Havens, allowed us to use four rooms in the Aaron Haven's homestead that now belonged to him. We lived there a year and then purchased and remodeled a house in Beaverton, Michigan, where I worked part-time at the telephone office. We lived there three years and Ulmont had a chance to go to school at Dow Chemical and continue his employment; he continued taking courses throughout his year and retired in 1982 as a multi-craftsman.

We moved back to Midland, Michigan and purchased a two-bedroom home on Glencoe Street. Our Valentine, Cheryl Ann was born in 1951. I returned to work at Michigan Bell Telephone and worked until they cut over to dial. Ulmont remodeled the Glencoe Street house, but we needed an additional bedroom, so he decided to build a new house on Belmont Street. In 1955, we purchased a lot on Sturgeon Creek where in 1956 Ulmont drew plans and built a three-bedroom, full basement, two fireplaces, brick home where we resided until his death in May of 1983.

After the Michigan Bell layoff, I stayed home being a mom for a year and then returned to work for the city of Midland in the Water Department for five years then transferred to the Finance Department for 20 years; retiring with 25 years of service in 1980. I worked for the city when cut over to computer. I volunteered at First Methodist Church when we cut over to computer.

Our Midland years were spent skating on Sturgeon Creek that was behind our house. Tobogganing down the hill on our family built run of snow under the stars in winter. What fun! Cross-country skiing, a raft trip down the Colorado River, mule trip down the Grand Canyon, camping trips to Alaska, Ostego Lake, Burt and Higgins Lakes and many others. We did a lot of fishing, boating, hiking, mushrooming, and campfires in Leland, where we rented and then purchased property. We called it "A little bit of heaven" with our Leland purchase in 1966. We had a mobile home for 18 years. We made many trips, wonderful friends, and wonderful memories.

Our son Richard married Barbara Brown. They were blessed with two wonderful sons, Richard Eric and Chad Leland. Cheryl Ann married Stanley Kerr. They had a beautiful first granddaughter, Heather Suzanna and then a baby boy, Anthony Craig. High school graduations, college graduations, and baptisms were the order of the day. Ulmont Bardwell passed away May 11, 1983 of colon cancer. I built the house in 1983 following my husband's death. Our plans were to build that house in Leland – so I did. I still own my little bit of heaven today.

I met and married a retired chemical engineer, Theodore Braun, who was a widower, in July of 1991. He has four children and two grandchildren. Ted and I both loved polkas and had many wonderful times. We took a square dancing course through Delta College for senior citizens and did lots of square dancing. We went on many wonderful trips to New Jersey, Wyoming, Florida, California, and Ann Arbor, Michigan visiting the family; also many trips to Leland.

We celebrated the marriage of grandson Eric to Becky Gullion in 1994, the marriage of our grandson Chad Leland to Jennifer Ann Deming in 1996, and the birth of a great-granddaughter, Micaela Margaret, in 1997. Chad Leland couldn't deal with the bi-polar disorder that Jennifer was diagnosed with and after marrying her two times had to divorce her. Chad was given complete custody of the children. Chad met and married Nikki Turner while serving in Afghanistan and they are expecting their first child in March 2013. Marilyn Svochak passed away in December 2006. My son Richard Bardwell passed away March 21, 2008. Theodore Braun passed away on July 30, 2011. The sustaining thread of my life journey has been my faith in God and his everlasting arms to hold me when the going gets rough. I feel I was truly blessed in meeting and marrying two wonderful men and enjoying life's best. Who can ask for more!

The Duckling Named Tonie
By Denise Dewald of Au Gres, Michigan
Born 1954

Every fall my gramma got a ton of coal dumped in the yard. She carried it in buckets to the basement. Since my Sister Gail and I lived in a small trailer with mom and dad just across the driveway, we helped her when we were big enough. One year, when all of the coal was in the basement, I saw a piece of metal sticking up out of the ground where the coal had been. I tried to pull on it but it wouldn't budge. I called mom and gramma to come out and look at it. They were baffled too. They called dad out to look at it. He got a shovel from the garage and began digging. I thought it was probably a buried treasure chest filled with all kinds of gold and diamonds! Finally, when the hole was about two feet deep, we saw that the metal was an entire sheet of galvanized metal, bent into a circle. After more digging, what looked like a piece of leather came into view. Dad grabbed it and pulled. Out came a black lace-up shoe from the 1800s. Right next to the shoe was an old Sears's catalog, the pages rotted away. But the date on the cover was legible "1898." Dad pulled it out and I took it from him and began flipping through what was left of the pages. I found shoes in it that matched the one we found perfectly. I wanted to keep looking through everything in the hole, but dad covered it back up. He told us it was just somebody's dump from a long time ago. I still wonder what other things were in that hole.

In the cold winter months, when several feet of snow were on the ground, I used to love to stay at gramma's house and sleep on her couch. I'd lie under her handmade quilts and listen to the wind howl around the eves. I watched the flames from her stove through the little openings in the door as they cast dancing shadows on the ceiling. The darkness was pushed to the far corners of the small living room. I could see the big overstuffed chair where gramma rocked my sister and I. if the night was extra cold, she put more coal on left the damper open so the air could feed the flames. Sometimes if the fire was bright enough, I could even make out the paisley curls of frost on the windows, which I miss today. Modern windows may be more efficient, but they lost their charm along the

Denise Dewald age 20 months

way.

One bright cold day close to Christmas, Gail and I got home from school and were treated to a beautiful sight. Sleet had fallen while we were in school and now coated the big trees in the backyard. They were bright silver and sparkling in the sunshine. We ran into the house to tell gramma about it. As soon as I was in the door I exclaimed, "Gramma! Gramma!" I ran to the window and pointed and said, "Look at the trees! They're all silver!" She smiled at our delighted faces. "I decorated them with tinsel while you girls were at school," she said. I thought she was just wonderful for doing that. I tried to picture plump gramma climbing the trees and wrapping tinsel around every branch. I just couldn't do it.

Like most kids, Christmas was what we lived for. All year long, we thought about what we wanted. I still remember a lot of the toys I received: Chatty Kathy, Barbie, Casper the Friendly Ghost, which talked when you pulled the string in his back, Thumbelina, toy kitchen sets with plastic food, and coloring books and crayons. To this day, I still love to color.

Gramma had running water in her kitchen sink and a cistern in the basement. In the winter the water froze, as well as the hand pump outside. We took milk cans from the barn and hauled water from a neighbor who lived four miles away. Two of us got on either side of the cans and carried them to the car when they were full. Then we brought them in the house when we got back home. My sister's feet and mine got numb from being out in the cold so long without good boots. Gramma used to take our feet in her hands and blow on them till they were warm again.

Gramma had what was called a Michigan basement. She stored potatoes, canned goods, and coal for her stove down there. Old oil lamps that once belonged to my great-grandmother hung from nails in the overhead beams. Among the other items scattered around the basement were farm implements, a butter churn, and the scrub board she washed her clothes on. Big crocks of sauerkraut and dill pickles lined the cement floors. Her water cistern was to the right as you entered the basement.

Whenever there was a bad storm, mom, Gail, and I went with gramma down to the basement. We watched from the little westerly window as the summer storms whipped the trees into frenzy. If we stayed in the small

Denise and her sister, Gail

169

trailer we lived in just across the driveway during a storm, the wind rocked it until it felt like it was going to tip over. I used to have nightmares where the wind did blow it over. The dizzying sensation of flying through the air was terrifying; I woke up to the abrupt impact of hitting the bed beneath me, waking my sister up with my jerk.

I liked the small room my sister and I shared at the back of our little trailer home. The walls and ceiling were all wood with curved seams at the top. I thought the rounded edges made the room feel cozy. Rain pelted the metal roof so loudly that we used to have to shout to be heard. But when a light drizzle fell, it lulled us to sleep at night. In cold weather, I would lie in bed and watch frost form in the seams of the walls. But Gail and I were kept warm with one of gramma's big feather ticks. One winter morning after a snowstorm hit during the night, mom tried to open the door to go outside, but it wouldn't budge. She kept pushing till she finally got it open a little ways. She saw that she was pushing against a wall of snow! The entire northeast side of the trailer was covered with an enormous drift that continued right over the roof. I wanted to go outside and climb to the top of the trailer, but mom didn't think it was such a good idea.

There was a little country store not far from where we lived. Every Friday I bought used comic books with the covers torn off for nine cents apiece. Mom always bought Neapolitan ice cream and Paramount Potato Chips ("I'm Slim Chipley, the guy you see on the Paramount potato chips bright red pack.") Even though most campers today are larger than the trailer I grew up in, I cherished Friday nights when we all sat around on the daybed, eating ice cream and chips and reading comic books.

My 3rd grade teacher was my favorite. She was one of those special teachers who had a way with kids. She gave everything she had and never seemed to get riled over anything. All of us kids liked to gather around her on the playground. One bitter day at recess time, we were all crowded around her as usual. She was smiling at us. "Does anyone know why I like mittens better than gloves?" she asked us, looking from one face to another. We all shook our heads. "Because," she said with a twinkle in her eyes, "all my fingers can snuggle up together and keep each other warm." I pictured all my fingers as little people snuggling together, staying warm and cozy. I imagined them talking to each other and being happy under their wool mitten blanket. After that, I always wore mittens if I had them.

One of my favorite places to go to when I was a child was the barnyard, where the ducks, geese, and chickens were. The geese would surround me as I sat on a cement block. They would honk softly and nibble on the buttons on my shirt. They even tried chewing on my long hair. I ruffled their feathers and talked to them. Whenever a plane or jet flew by overhead, all the geese tilted their heads sideways with one eye to the sky. I laughed at their comical little faces. When I did, they looked at me as one, as if to say, "What?"

We had a mother duck sitting on eggs. One morning when I went to check on her, there were about a dozen little babies running along beside her. They were adorable! They were no more than three inches high and made soft little peeping sounds. I walked to the barn to get the feed. On my way, I saw one lone egg still on the nest. I tried to get the mother to sit on it, but she kept kicking it off the nest. I knew the little guy was okay inside his shell home because I could hear him scratching around and peeping. I decided to help him hatch out; I couldn't bear to leave him to die. I brought the egg inside and placed it in a pan with a soft cloth in it. I turned the oven to warm and placed the pan on the rack. My Sister Gail and I checked the egg all day to make sure it wasn't getting too warm. Toward evening, we saw that the poor thing was no closer to hatching out. We agreed we should help it out a little. We could hear where it was trying to break the shell, so we began gently peeling away the cracked shell. Soon we saw a tiny beak! We were so excited. With the opening started, the duckling had an easier time of breaking free. Before long, I was holding the tiniest little duck I ever saw. It was all wet and wiggly, peeping away. We kept it wrapped in the cloth till it was dry. Then we fed it some warm milk with bits of bread in it. Our plan was to keep it in the house for a few days till we were sure it was ready to join its brothers and sisters. Gail named the duck Tonie because she said it could be a girl's or a boy's name. It was soon clear that Tonie saw me as his mother. I had a box next to the bed for him to sleep in, but he cried loudly until I picked him up and put him on my chest. Only then would he go to sleep. I loved how sweet that was, but I wasn't getting much sleep with a duck on my chest.

Well, the day finally came when Tonie was ready to go to the barnyard and join his family. I was afraid the mother duck would reject him again. I brought little Tonie out and set him on the ground next to the rest of the family. He immediately waddled to the group and he never looked back. He fit right in; it was like he was never apart from them. I was a little heartbroken that he didn't seem to miss me in the least, but I thought he seemed happy. And besides, I knew I could visit him every day.

✓ Cod Liver Oil Treatments
By Betty White of Kalkaska, Michigan
Born 1924

I was born in McBain, Michigan in 1924. My first home was on Bois Blanc Island, Michigan. While living there, my parents introduced me to a sister in 1926. My maternal grandmother passed away and my father was requested by my grandfather to return to Kalkaska County, to run the farm while he continued to work for Henry Ford. He was helping support the family on the farm as my father had four brothers still living at home. This is where I grew up. My mother was thrust into a large household of mostly men that needed a cook and washerwoman, at a tender age of 20.

A farm is a great place to raise children, as there is so many things to keep you busy, doing chores, and playing games with the other children in the neighborhood and at school. In the morning, our breakfast consisted of fried pork, eggs, oatmeal, and sometimes pancakes or toast all made on our kitchen wood stove. The bread went into a wire rack and placed on the stovetop. At noon there was a large dinner consisting of the usual farmers fare, as the men worked hard in the fields and we had a large bell on a post to call them into meals. Supper consisted of soups, bread, and milk or Jonnie cake with warm milk from the evening milking.

The cows were milked by hand and the men brought in pails of milk, which was put through a separator, which sent the milk into one container and another for the cream. The milk went to the calves and pigs and the cream was sold after we took out enough for our butter. We had a large crock with a paddle and a long handle that went through the cover, so we didn't get splashed. If we were in a hurry for the butter, it could be shaken in a glass fruit jar. If we girls got up early as our father was about to do the milking, he would scrape the thick foam from the cream, and put it on bread with sugar on top, a good treat! The rest of the cream went into a five-gallon can, to be picked up by the cream man. My mother baked several loaves of bread at a time, which hardly lasted all week then she made the best biscuits for some of our meals, also good cinnamon rolls, along with the bread.

With the men busy with the farm chores, my mother was busy, cleaning house, cooking, and washing on a board. The men carried the water, pumped from a well, quite a distance from the house, with two five-gallon cream cans, one in each hand. It was emptied into a copper boiler to heat on the stove with a bar of Fels Naptha soap shaved into the water along with some bluing to soak the clothes with stains. A plunger was used to help get the clothes clean. More soap was used while scrubbing on the scrub board. There was a rack that held the tubs, one for wash water, and one for rinse water with a hand wringer in the center. One of the uncles cranked the wringer for the heavy clothes as some of the work clothes were brought home from the winter work in the lumbering time. In winter, the clothes were washed in the kitchen and hung on lines in the upstairs and a few heavy things were dried outside and brought in frozen to finish drying by our wood heater in the living room where all of the boots, gloves, and mittens were also dried. In the summertime, my mother washed out by the clothesline. The ironing was done in the living room in summer, as the kitchen stove had to be kept burning to heat the sad irons.

One of my uncles had worked with machines in the lumbering time that were fueled with steam from water and he had several steam engines in the yard. They were used for threshing the grain, filling the silo with the corn that was made into silage for the cattle in winter. Also, they were used to buzz up the logs that were brought into the yard

171

for our winter wood. Later, my father along with his brother's bought all of the necessary farm implements to do a better job of farming. So there was a lot of activity going on most of the time. Men came to help with some of the threshing and filling of the silo and they had to be fed, some of the neighbor women came and helped. They made a real large meal for all of these men, including luscious pies. They also got together at butchering time or building a barn or a house.

After the uncles moved to homes of their own, we acquired another sister in 1928. We were now three and five with our parents. In the summer, we had picnics by the Manistee River where we learned to swim. We traveled there with our team of horses and wagon. People gathered to play baseball and danced at the local Grange Hall on Saturday nights.

One time, my sister and I ran away with the horses. We were very young. My mother always maintained that we were three and five. We visited some children in the little town of Sharon, three miles away. We coaxed the two friends to ride with us, but they were afraid. We decided to let our horses drink from the river. We got the idea of riding the horses into the big Manistee River that still had logs lying on the bottom of the river, from the lumbering days. My sister's horse stumbled and that worried us, so we got out and rode home. My father wasn't concerned, but my mother was, he told her we would probably be bringing the cows with us. There was one that was on her way home to feed her calf, so we brought her home. We did not tell where we had been but a little later, a neighbor told on us. My sister gave out with the information about her horse stumbling on a log. We got a good talking to; we had already suffered sore bottoms from our ride. Now we were given permission to ride, as my mother had been fearful of our getting hurt.

When I was a little older, my nightly chore was to take the farm horse and ride after the cows. They went to graze on some open land near the river. They wore bells and I had to listen for them, to know which direction to take, as they sometimes were two or three miles away. Our dog was always with me. She helped to round them up and drive them home.

Early on, my father had an old 1924 Chevrolet Touring car with a top that came down. It had side curtains and isinglass in them to see out. There was only heat from the engine to keep warm and a windshield blade that was turned by hand. I only remember riding to town one time with my father in that car. My uncles used it to stretch barbed wire fence and pulled the transmission out from under it. We did not have a car for some time after this.

One time I received a scratch on my leg when the horse got too close to some barbed wire fence. Infection developed. It was fall and few neighbors had cars. My uncle had drained his for winter. It just so happened that my father's sister from Bois Blanc Island came to visit. She grabbed me up and took me to a doctor. Without anything to help the pain, he pierced a hole in my leg and pushed some gauze into the hole with some medicated ointment on it. I was screaming all the while. I have always been thankful though, as he saved my leg. Along with recovering from that, my sisters and I developed the Red Measles, which we received from contact with an uncle that was staying with us. I did not go to school for several weeks.

I lost weight and my mother being concerned, requested my father to notify the doctor when he was in town for supplies. The doctor came to see me and left a bottle of Mandrake Bitters. I refused to take it and my grandfather tried to entice me by saying he would bring me the funnies from the paper. Finally, my father offered to take them along with me. Eventually I got better and was now able to go back to school. I don't remember taking Castor Oil, but we took Cod Liver Oil to help keep from getting serious colds. In the spring, my aunt that had taken me to visit the doctor sent me a pair of ducks. They were fun to watch. They could not get the corn as quickly as the chickens. My father put the corn in their drinking water and the water spurted out both sides of their bills as they ate the corn.

We had serious storms in the summer with much lightning and thunder. Our tree near the house was hit several times, also the granary. The grain was tossed around and the bolt went outside and knocked a spoke out of a car wheel. We didn't have a party line, but we had a line between our house and a neighbor's, so my mother could call if she had a question about our health, as the neighbor was a former nurse. When we had a bad storm, fireballs would fly out of the phone. Of course, we stayed away from that. In the spring, we picked Trilliums. Dog Tooth Violets and the Tiny Blue Violets we found in the damp areas of our woods. Our mother was presented with many large bouquets.

We played a lot of games at school, which was across the road from our house. We played Anti-I-Over the schoolhouse, with the one catching the ball running to the other side to tag someone. We played Pom-Pom-Pull-Away between the schoolhouse and the fence. The one with the ball called out Pom-Pom-Pull-Away and everyone ran to the other side while he tried to tag someone. We played Work UP with a soft ball and as one was called out, everyone moved up from the field to 3rd base and on up until they were at bat.

I always missed living on the farm and when there was a recession and no work, my husband, and I took our sons to the farm and they had two years in which to enjoy the area. They had to carry in the wood and haul the water on their toboggan in winter, but they also enjoyed the big hill behind the barn with their toboggan and Christmas skis. They also were able to attend a country school too. They were healthy and grew with all the good bread that I baked in my mother's old kitchen range, which had been returned. They ate meat, vegetables, fruit and we also made lots of cookies. We picked blackberries and made jam for school lunches. We went to Traverse City and found a farmer that let us pick some cherries for jam too. The neighbor had a rhubarb patch; we picked it for fruit to can for winter. We were given food commodities and $12.00 to live on, but no gas to get to town. A neighboring storekeeper helped us out with gas for the car as we shopped at his store.

✓ The Barrel Ride of a Lifetime
By Marilyn Olsen of Benzonia, Michigan
Born 1938

My brother and I were both born in lower Michigan, Springdale Twp. near Bear Lake. Millard was born in a tarpaper shack that mother rented from Lillian Hammond. There were no lights, running water, or inside plumbing. The roof leaked and the drips in pans scared me. The doctor came to the house and delivered Millard breech. Mother named him after the doctor. I was born across the road in the Haskins home in a slop jar. We moved up north to Fullers Spur, a few miles from Watersmeet, Michigan. Mother rented a 10x12 shack, no lights, running water, and our heat was with wood. I contacted whooping cough at three months old. Mother did get me to the doctor, but I wasn't expected to live. She cut up pieces of men's old wool underwear, cooked onions, and plastered them on my back and chest and held me to keep me warm. She said she had to pound me to keep me breathing and I bled from every hole in my body.

When my brother was five and I was three years old, mother would take us through the deep snow to check her snares. She would set several to catch rabbits for us to eat. We never saw her clean the animals. She taught my brother how to make snares. We had a neighbor named Lewie Demers. We called him grampa. He would give us a cookie. His house is still standing and used as a hunting cabin. I was three and I thought his house was a mansion. I went back 72 years later, the house still stands, and the rooms are as I remember them. Mother was alone with us in the 1940s. There was a total eclipse of the sun. She was scared so she set us in the middle of the floor and sang to us. The songs were some she learned as a youngster. The Titanic, Marim Parker, and the Fate of Floyd Collins.

The tarpaper shack was moved into Watersmeet in the winter, pulled by a truck down the snow-covered road. When they got the house into town, it had to be turned around. Spencer Clark hooked chains and skids under it and his team of horses, which belonged to Harry Gilbertson, pulled it around to face the road. My father Lewis Koski who owned and flew his own airplane would come to Watersmeet. He would fly over and buzz Herman Manifields home. That was his signal to go to the small airport and pick him up. It is said that my dad kept his plane together with tape and wire. Mother never let him take us kids in it.

Mother and father were divorced in 1941. We moved back down to lower Michigan. Mother remarried and after WWII, our stepfather bought 40 acres on Grace Road, outside of Elberta, Michigan. There had been a house on the property that burnt down. A part of a barn was standing. We lived in the barn until the house was built. They covered the barn walls with cardboard and put a door on. We stayed in it all summer. It was like camping, us kids thought it was fun. There were no lights, running water, or bathrooms. We were lucky to have the two-seater outhouse. Our refrigerator was a square box set in the upper spring with water running through it. It kept everything ice cold. The Watkins man came once a month selling household goods and cooking supplies. Mother bought a root beer pop mix. Mother made it and it was kept cold in our spring refrigerator. Our summers were really hot in the valley where we lived. The spring ran below the house and we would dam it up with rocks. It would get deep enough for us to float our wooden boats my brother made. There is still a huge rock we played on by the spring. It doesn't seem as big now. We spent many hours playing there. Mother cooked on a two-burner kerosene stove. A bottle glass jar of kerosene had to be tipped upside down and placed at the end of the stove. The stove had four legs and a metal over, which would sit on top of a burner. Farmer matches were used to light it.

My brother was very creative and whatever we didn't have he could make. He made an airplane big enough to hold me. We both pulled it to the top of the long hill. He put me inside and gave me a good push. I took several rides before it crashed. He never got a ride since he couldn't fit inside. My uncle gave me my first and only barrel ride, down the same hill. He pulled the empty barrel up the hill. I got inside and had the ride of my life. It made me so sick, one ride lasted me a lifetime. He had a good laugh. Mother wasn't too happy with him. We played in our woods, building tree houses, climbing small tress that would bend and swing us around as we kicked. My brother and I climbed a big Maple tree along Grace Road by our house; we each had a cowbell. As the cars came down the hill and about to where we were hiding in the tree, we would ring the bells as hard as we could. The people would stop their car and look under and around it. We thought it was so funny. It was until mother caught us. My brother found roots in the bank of the spring. They were about as big around as a cigar. The inside had small holes so when sucked on you drew air through. We called it smoke root.

Millard and Marilyn Koski

Brother took some matched from the house and we smoked. It tasted awful and it didn't burn good. We had a large Catalpa tree by the house. It had long bean-like capsules that hung down. They were filled with flat seeds. We planted the seeds in the sand hill to grow bananas. The tree had beautiful flowers that we picked and sucked the sweet nectar out of. We even had our cousins eat the flowers. We played store with cardboard boxes, empty cans, jars, and boxes. Our money was stones. We used weeds for coffee and vegetables. Our stepfather junked an old car in the yard and we played in that a lot. Pretend driving to many states.

I was real naughty and had my cousin bite into a jack-in-the-pulpit bulb. It burnt his mouth for two hours. He carried a wet washcloth on his tongue. In the winter, we would slide downhill on a wringer washer lid or piece of cardboard. If we were lucky, we would get a box that had wax on the inside. The store would get fruit and vegetables in them. Later my brother had a jumper; he always made a jump at the bottom of the hill by packing snow. He would make it high enough that you would fly up and come down and hurt your backend. He also made igloos large enough to stand up in and hold four kids. We seemed to have more snow then and it was deep enough to make tunnels.

My second cousin is nine years older than me. In the summer, I would spend a couple of weeks with her. She was like a big sister. She entertained me by riding me on her bike handlebars, she made fudge, she colored with me, we milked cows, and we smoked corn silk wrapped in toilet paper or catalogs in the outside toilet. We picked strawberries and pickles. She also took me to the free show in Copemish. We picked cherries with our mother in the summer. Our money was spent on school clothes, which was usually two flannel shirts, jeans, and one pair of shoes a year. My last year of picking I was able to order a record player and two records out of the Alden's catalog. The case was metal and a crank up or electric could run it. It was fun to order from the Alden's catalog. You never knew what you would get. One time I got shoes, both shoes were for the same foot. We all got a good laugh over that. The waiting for the package to come was like forever. Another time I got a coat I didn't order.

On Tuesday nights in Elberta in the summer, there was a free show. We picked cherries all day, then pulled weeds in the garden, so we might be able to go. Usually mother was too tired. The show didn't start until dark, which was around 10:00 p.m. we were given a dime for candy. You could get lots of candy for a penny. We would sit on a blanket with mother and sometimes us kids would fall asleep. There was always a big crowd with the streets full of summer workers. The shows were usually in black and white. In later years, we got a drive in theater in Honor, Michigan. It is still in operation to this day, two dollars a carload, but higher now.

I was about 11 years old and during the month of December the story of the Cinnamon Bear (Christmas Story) was on the radio. We would get off the school bus and run into the house to listen to the 15-minute program. It would run until the day before Christmas. My daughter got me the CD story set when I was 70 years old. I still like the story. The sad thing about Christmas was before we could get a Christmas tree I had to clean the whole house. My brother and half-sister didn't help me. We never got bikes, sleds, and stuff like that. We usually got an orange, coloring book, plastic bubbles, and nuts. Mother always made candy, popcorn balls, and cookies. My brother got to listen to stories on the radio such as, *Tom Mix*, *Superman*, and *Captain Midnight*. Sometimes he would get a box top and $0.10 to send for a whistle or ring.

In 1946, a candy all day sucker lasted all-day and longer. A sucker cost a nickel and was about three inches in diameter. It was a light pastel color and as hard as a rock. I would sneak five pennies from mother's red tobacco can for a sucker. I had to hide the sucker or brother would tell on me. If I were caught, I would get a whippen. Mother would make me go outside and get a stick; it had to be the right size too, for a good whippen. I usually got my share too. I was in mother's purse and found a package of sin-sins. They were small black pieces that tasted like licorice. I ate them all. They were for your breath. I never got caught at that!

When I was 11 years old, mother and our stepfather left us kids at home alone. My brother and I decided to make candy. We used mother's old candy cookbook. The recipe called for corn syrup, which I couldn't find in the cupboard, but I found cornstarch, so I used that. The candy was awful. We had to eat it all so mother didn't find out. Lesson learned! My brother made most of our toys through the years; he even made me my first bra. I can't remember wearing it but it sure looked funny. It was made of scrap material; I wish I had kept it. I did keep a picture my brother drew on a bleached feed sack, of a plane and parachutes, which mother embroidered. When brother and I saved a few cents we would buy mother a gift. Which was a pretty glass dish with candy for $0.29 at the Frankfor Dime Store.

Life's Journey
By JoAnn Croff of Punta Gorda, Florida
Born 1938

I was born and raised in a little town called Oden Mech, with a population 300 in the winter and triple in the summer, that's when all the summer people arrived. My grandparents owned the town's only grocery store, it sat on one side of the railroad tracks and the depot sat on the other side. Above the store were bedrooms where we always watched the trains stop and the summer people arrive. I always wondered what it would be like to have nice shiny shoes and pretty dresses and nice cars to ride in and people who love each other, a family, of course little did I know most of the time the nanny's raised the children and the chauffeurs drove the nice cars.

My gramps was a shoe cobbler and made some of the finest shoes around, people would order them at the end of summer, and the next year when they came there would be a nice new pair of custom made shoes. Besides the store gramps had some property on Pleasant View, we called the "Sugar Bush" where every spring we would go there until the sap was done running.

I learned how to drive on an old Diamond Rio truck. There the boys gathered the sap and my job was to drive the truck, I could barely see over the wheel but gramps always said, "Put it in creeper gear and watch the trees fall off the path and I did." He, my uncle, and my brother cut a lot of the trees off from nubs nob what they call scare face and we haul them down the road to the sugar bush and in time, the boys would go there, cut it smaller, and haul it home. Then they would have a weekend of cutting it up with a machine called a buzz saw, he always had a lot of help. Neighbors were a lot different then; if you were outside working, they would come and help. Of course, grandma always made fried chicken and biscuits, and homemade blackberry Cobler.

Grandpa also made a big ole' sleigh, which took all of the town, kids to pull up the hill and then we would all pile on and ride down. About five times, we were ready to call it a day. We would go home, wash up for dinner and after dinner we would help with the dishes and hurry to the radio to listen to "The Lone Ranger", "Inner Sanctum", or "The Shadow", just to name a few and by then it was time for bed and we were glad to go. We made our fun and we never had to go to the gym to workout. If you had any energy, left grandma and grandpa could find something for you to do. But times were not too bad, but this was all to change shortly.

We lived with grandma and grandpa because our father said to our mom one day, "I need to go south to find work and when I

JoAnn Croff

find something I'll send for you." Well that never happened. He met someone in Saginaw and divorced our mom, he didn't even know she was pregnant with my sister and mom never told him. It almost killed her, but she loved him so much. I don't even know what he looked like except for a few pictures I have seen, but life goes on and on it did.

Mom got a job in Petosley and went to work for Coling Packing Company; it was cold work, but we moved on. One day grandpa said to mom, "The house behind the store is for sale. I am gonna buy it for you and the kids." What a great grandpa and grandma they were, but grandpa said your gonna have to help with electric and pay the taxes, otherwise it is yours. We moved in our own rooms, life was looking good.

I remember mom saying close to Christmas, "There isn't gonna be money for presents but I will do my best to make a nice dinner for us all." We were sad as all young kids looked forward to presents. On Christmas Eve, we were all sitting around feeling sorry for ourselves when there was a knock on the door and a man in uniform was there and he had a big basket of turkey, potatoes, pumpkin pie, etc., all the trimming for a great Christmas dinner and in the basket was a gift for each of us. My brother got a truck and my sister and I got dolls. I still have mine, she sits on my bed, and every day I am reminded of these people. They were from the Salvation Army. What a great Christmas we had because of them.

Just as we thought things were getting better, they were gonna get worse. One day mom came home with this man his name was Lee (the devil in disguise). Mom was in love, but oh my god we hated him from that day forward, he was a mean man. One day he said to mom, "Come live with me." She couldn't pack us up fast enough, why I don't know. From that day forward for the next few years life was hell on earth. At 10 years old my brother said, "Sis, I am running away." He liked my brother least of all, so one day he came up missing and nobody ever went to find him. I knew where he was, but I was never going to tell.

Then came the big surprise, he said, "Take that baby to your mother and leave her, I can't stand her." Oh no, what about me, leave me too. We wound up in a little town in Texas and for the first time he got a job to hauling gas and mom was waiting tables, yes all day long to myself – locked up in the trailer, but it was better. I asked mom if I could have a tablet to write on and she sneaked one in to me. So during the day I would write songs, I filled up the whole notebook at one time. I had four notebooks full of songs until one day he found them and burned them. I had nothing else to do, I could not go outside, and to this day, I am very Closterphobic. I was placed in foster care to heal and slowly I began to remember. When I could remember I had a grandma, the people helped me call her and she said, "Your mother was here trying to get your sister." No grams you can't let that happen. I need money to come home, so a bus ticket was sent and I went home. As soon as I got off the bus we went to the courthouse and asked for a special meeting with Judge Murphy, it was granted. I had the police report and the hospital report. It was a done deal. Custody was granted.

When my mom came to get Jane, she saw me and it was all it took, she left and I never saw her again for 40 years. I wound up taking care of her in the end. My brother and sister wanted nothing to do with her, but I believe she was almost as sick as him and love does crazy things to people. When I sleep at night I have no regrets, she has since had to answer to a higher judge than me. My brother had gone into the service and my sister was safe and going to school and me, I am free at last.

As time goes on grandma was having heart problems. We were all worried. One day I said to grandma, "I am going to quit school so I can help you more. I can get a job at least help out with money." So I moved into Petoskey, got a job, and sent my grandpa and grams all I could and it helped. I was able to get a room in a boarding house for $5.00 a week. Can you believe that? It was all I needed.

I was working for Ma Wilson Cafe, just down the street from where I lived. She was another great person, she treated me like a daughter, and I loved her like the mother I always wanted. It was a very busy little place; the cops always got free coffee, so they were all there at one time during the day.

Well one day I looked up and in he walked, a new policeman on the beat, and I was in love. I didn't even know if he was married or not, but I'd adore him from afar if he was. He was tall and handsome and I found out he was single. Wow, but what chance did I have to find a man like him. Well one day as I was closing up he looked in and said, "Any coffee left?" I said, "You bet, but if not I will make one." He put a nickel in the jukebox and I locked the door. He looked at me and said, "Dance." Oh my God, yes, and dance we did. Afterwards he said, "Are you all closed up now?" I said yes and he then said, "Go for a bike ride." I said yes, it's how it all started. How I met my prince charming. But I found out he was also seeing another girl, it broke my heart and I had heard different things like he was a ladies man, but low and behold we were married and had three children together. Something was always missing in our relationship though - it was love. Did he love me? Yes, I think he did, but only one time did he ever say it and I needed it desperately. It was all I ever wanted, a simple, "I love you," or I am so glad you're here. We were divorced after 15 years and I cried for weeks, I lost my prince.

I decided to move to Traverse City, make a new life for my children and myself and so we did. I buried myself in work. I need to stop and regress a bit here. After Ma Wilson got burned (the fryer blew up on her) the restaurant was closed and I lost a great friend. I found a job working for the Palace Cigar Store on Lake Street. It was a deli up front and a pool house in the back. Bob McMasters was the owner and he turned out to be the greater person in my life, he changed me into a princess. He was my rock to rely on like the father I never knew. We had a great relationship. I worked very hard for him and I knew he over paid me, but he always said, "I would need two people to do what you do." One day he came to work and said, "There is a contest going on for Petaskey Winter Queen, why don't you enter it?" Hey, I don't have clothes or talent to do something like that. He said, "Not to worry"

177

and left, I couldn't even begin to dream. A short time later, he came back with the big bag of clothes and pair of ice skates. There were nice slacks, a beautiful formal, shoes, a white fur coat, which I still have, everything but I didn't even know how to skate, and so off we went to the skating park. Sometimes he would come and watch and sometimes not, but I worked really hard at it every chance I had. I would be at the park and practice. The day the contest was held Dan Reuther came up to me and said, "Good luck." Well I can hardly believe it to this day. I won! I was Miss Petaskey of 1957.

Favorite Pet
By Faye Plume of Rogers City, Michigan
Born 1952

Our favorite pet was called Foxy, the Fox. My father brought him home one winter's day. It was all red and curled up in a ball. My older sister, Jane, and I loved Foxy very much. He would run around the house. His real home was in the crawl space of the house. When Foxy died, we were very sad and heartbroken.

The LaFeve Farm
By Charlotte LaFeve of Fife Lake, Michigan
Born 1937

People of Fife Lake remember the "LaFeve, Wife and Daughter Cochon Farm" from 1973-1984. It was a 100-sow operation complete from breeding to the market and also sales out of a small store in the garage of their home. Thus became LaFeve's famous pork burgers.

Sometimes the aroma from the farm would sneak into the village of Fife Lake—not good! However, when Jim LaFeve would hook up his five roasters on the lake on the 4th of July and roast five hogs, the village loved the aroma!

The "LaFeve, wife, and daughter Cochon Farm" was well-known to people in the area and to people downstate where Jim would get orders for pork and deliver it to them.

To this day people will still remark about Jim's good pork burgers, such good pork, and the family that worked together.

Our Wild Horse
By Randy Buyze of Mancelona, Michigan
Born 1951

One memory that stands out in my childhood is when my mother told us (my two older brothers and I, ages eight, nine, and ten) that if we could catch a loose horse running around our farm we could have it!

We had goats, pigs, chickens, dogs, and cats, but what we really wanted was a horse to ride. We spent all day trying to catch that horse and finally corralled it in a neighbor's corral about five miles away. About that time, our dad was coming home from work and asked us what we were up to. He burst our bubble when he told us we couldn't keep the horse. It belonged to someone else.

Finally realizing how much we wanted a horse, dad brought home a donkey and buggy. It wasn't exactly what we wanted, but all three of us could ride him at once through the woods and fields. He could also pull the buckboard buggy and we would pick up the neighbor kids and cousins and go on many adventures. One rule we had to do in the summer was pick a basket of berries for our mom before we could come home. It was easy to do, and then we could spend the rest of the day playing in the woods.

Tip Up Fishing
By Beverly J. Prell of Atlanta, Michigan
Born 1937

Many years ago, my friend and I used to play innocent jokes on one another. Bill always said he could beat me with a better practical joke. Well, I decided I'm going to get you good this time Bill.

Back then, we were big on Tip Up fishing on the ice. This one night, Bill and Dee went away. It was bitter cold. I had seen him put out a Tip Up. Now, here's my chance. I suited up and found a large plastic bottle and filled it with water. Went out on the ice and spudded out his Tip Up. Hooked the bottle on and lower it in and set the flag.

In the a.m., to his delight, he seen the flag up. The hole was froze shut and he worked hard to get it opened. Then he started to pull up the line and pulled and pulled. He thought he had a dandy Northern Pike. I was watching with my binoculars and when he pulled up the bottle and seen what it was, he turned in my direction and was shaking his fists at me. I was laughing so hard I was on my knees.

Well, my dear friend Bill is gone now, but the memories, the laughter, the fun we had is priceless and cannot be forgotten.

✓ Bingham to Lincoln
By Pat Gamage of Lachine, Michigan
Born 1936

In the 1940s, when I began elementary school, I attended the Bingham School, which is now the Arts Academy. From our house on the corner of Seventh and River Streets, it was a pleasant walk. There were houses all along the way and other Bingham students lived in many of them. However, as I reached the upper elementary grades, it was decided that there were too many children at Bingham and not enough at Lincoln School. Therefore, those of us closest to Lincoln were told we must attend there. The problem was that Lincoln was across the river from where we lived. Instead of a pleasant walk through a familiar neighborhood, we had to walk up to Ninth Street, to cross the river on the Ninth Street bridge, then walk down Oldfield Street where there were very few buildings on the riverside. The wind off the lake got a nice sweep down both the river and Oldfield Street and made for a very cold walk in the winter. Once the river froze over, of course, the walk could be shortened considerably by walking across on the ice. Unfortunately, our mother instructed us NEVER to step on the ice. It was known to be unstable and we might break through and drown or develop hypothermia. Being the good little girl that I was, of course I walked by way of the bridge all year long. My brother, Ken, who was a grade ahead of me, and our neighbor, Bob, decided it was quite safe and often took the shortcut across the ice. I was too chicken to go with them, but also too chicken to tell mother what they were doing. So they took the easy way and I took the hard way. I'm sure that in today's world, if children had to travel that far to school, a bus would pick them up in their neighborhood. But this is how it was in the "olden days."

✓ Growing Up In Northern Michigan
By Philip Naylor of Lincoln, Michigan
Born 1953

I have a memory of my favorite pet, a dog named Peanuts. He would follow the mailman from our house to all his route and, we found out later, all the way back to the post office. And at the end of the day drop the dog off at our place by car on his way home from work at the post office.

I had an old, rusted out car I used to drive. It was so rusted that when a bunch of us guys would go out driving down old, country roads, someone would ask the driver (me) to slow down. "I have to pee," because the floorboards were so rusted, you could pee right through the floorboards onto the ground.

I had a teacher that would catch us chewing gum and make us put the gum on our nose and wear it 'til the end of class.

Getting in trouble from dad for throwing darts in the garage at all the cans on the shelf and putting holes in them so they would leak their contents all over.

Getting in trouble from mother for filling an old, burlap sack full of garter snakes and taking them home and showing them to her. She would say take them right back where I found them.

Camping with my parents when next to us was a pop-up camper. In mid-afternoon we were all sitting around when all of a sudden the back end of the pop-up camper broke (where the bed is) and out rolled a man and woman stark naked. They scrambled to the door of the camper, but they had locked it from the inside so they had to scramble back to the now open end of the camper and scramble back in.

As a small child, for amusement would catch grasshoppers and throw them into spider webs and watch the spiders come out and spin their web around them.

My dad told me he never told my mother this. He kept this secret 'til his death at age 85. My mother, who is still alive at age 87, still doesn't know this and I will never tell. My dad told me when I was about three years old, and I am now 60 years old, him and me was walking on the ice on a river when I started to fall in. (On any river or lake it is knowledge that when you leave your ice fishing hole to always mark it so no one would fall in, because even though it is iced over again, it is not as thick.)

My dad says he caught me by the collar just in time. Otherwise, I would have drowned and, because of the current in the river, I wouldn't have been found 'til spring. He never told my mother because he says she would never have let me go ice fishing with him again.

Son of a Great Lakes' Lighthouse Keeper
By Richard A. Campbell of Mackinaw City, Michigan
Born 1930

My life began in a small northern Michigan town on the shores of Lake Michigan. Most of the population was of Native American descent, as was my father.

Times were very hard. Father took a job as a lighthouse keeper on an island in the Detroit River. Our life was very interesting. Father took us kids across the river in a skiff each

Dick and John Campbell in 1943

day to Wyandothe so we could go to school.

A few years later, dad transferred to Huron Island in Lake Superior, located just off the Huron Mountains. The island was an outcropping of stone, one-quarter mile wide and one mile long, and a high elevation. During the summer, our family lived on the island with my father. My sisters and I spent the summer swimming, fishing, and exploring. We had none of the usual conveniences. There was no refrigeration or running water. Once a week, weather permitting, we went ashore for supplies.

When school was in session, our family lived on the Chippewa Indian Reservation at Baraga, Michigan.

My father later transferred to Old Mackinaw Point in Mackinaw City, Michigan. Civilization at last! This was a whole new life for me—cars, stores, neighbors, and friends— and I was about to enter high school.

Lighthouse living was very interesting and because at times we were so isolated my father taught me how to exist, physically and mentally. I also learned seamanship, fish net making, machinery, and diving.

As I look back, I realize how important these early experiences were as they formed my future ways.

Jane, Dick, and Helen in the 1930s

The Toy Train
By Leonard L. LaFave of Onaway, Michigan
Born 1940

I was born on a small farm in northern Michigan in January of 1940. I now live on that farm and I sleep approximately 100 feet from the bedroom of our old two-story farmhouse where I was born.

I can well remember that old two-story farmhouse had four rooms in the upstairs, which was three bedrooms, and one room was used as a catchall or the junk room or storage room, so we called it.

When I was four or five years old, I entered that room and discovered a homemade toy train. We never had a surplus of money and Christmas was due real soon. Other such homemade toys for my sister were also being created but not done yet. My mother had skills for this kind of project and a loving heart so we could have a real happy Christmas even though no Christmas money existed. She had painted a round oatmeal box and caused it to become a train engine with wheels made from spools that thread for sewing machines came on. A toilet paper cardboard center was the smokestack. She sure had talent and as I said, she loved her family.

I did not touch anything as I retreated back out of that room and allowed the toy train to be a surprise Christmas morning. I did not tell my mother about my discovery until after I was married and had a family of my own. Mother would have had a broken heart if I had told her that I had discovered my toy train. Instead, she would always remember how happy the surprise toy made me Christmas morning.

I never could appreciate any boughten toy like I appreciated that one.

Grandfathers' Outdoor Adventures
By Rick Fowler of Harbor Springs, Michigan
Born 1952

I really never knew that much about my dad's dad. He was just grandpa to me and passed away when I was eight years old. I knew from what my dad said that he was an avid fisherman and hunter, yet my one and only memory of fishing with him was one spring smelt excursion when I begged to go along with he and my dad to the Carp River. They finally relented and stowed me like baggage in the back seat of our station wagon. I must have slept the whole way because my next memory is of waking up to a roaring bonfire and watching him and my dad scooping up netfulls of the silvery wonders and then begin the process of cleaning them. As the night turned into the early morning, they poured ice onto the hundreds of filets, packed up the gear, and headed back home. I never did have another outing with my grandpa, but my dad would relate many stories of their excursions onto the waters of northern Michigan.

One such story was about the "stringers of walleye" that they would catch on Burt Lake, especially in the late 40s and early 50s. As a kid who was just beginning to explore the bounties of the outdoors, I was captivated by these tales of lunker walleye and nasty pike. It was hard to envision the excitement they both must have felt until I happened upon a picture taken by my dad of grandpa coming up to the launch, beaming broadly as he held up what was indeed a "stringer of walleye." This one solitary picture of a man so proud of his catch could have been the catalyst to a myriad of memories but now will never be retold.

My mother's dad loved to fish too. In fact, one of his passions was ice fishing on Mullet and Burt Lakes in particular for sturgeon. I was six years old when my dad and grandfather included me in their plans, which involved spearing sturgeon from their shack on Mullet Lake. My grandparents lived in Indian River, Michigan and, since the lake was only a couple of miles away, we had ample time, a place to get quickly if we needed to warm up (meaning me), and we could get home and get something to eat without all of us having to leave the shack.

Both my dad and my grandfather had speared a sturgeon before and loved to talk about their experiences to anyone who would listen. This morning had been slow and we had seen nothing swimming by in the clear cut hole of the shanty. Dad and grandpa decided to visit another shack nearby, to talk to them no doubt about how they had speared their sturgeons and it had taken at least 20 minutes to land the monsters (every year the pounds, length, and battle times seemed to get longer.

While they were gone, they instructed me

to keep an eye out for any fish that swam by and to holler if it was really big. Now, I had never seen a sturgeon before and therefore could not envision how massive they were. Within minutes of their departure, I got down on my hands and knees to get a clearer picture of the world below me. At that same moment, the dinosaur of a fish decided to make his presence known and swam by the hole without a care in the world. Little did that fish know that up above a six-year-old kid screamed at the top of his lungs, busted down the thin-skinned door in his attempt to get away from the monster, and went running to his father.

They never, ever let me forget that moment!

Now, I don't want to rush my venture in grand parenting, believe me. However, when (and if) the blessing of grandchildren is bestowed on me I hope my tales of the outdoors will be shared with them. Indeed, anglers and hungers need to pass on many of the legacies of fishing excursions, shore lunch, hunting camps, and opening days. We cannot omit any opportunity to instill a sense of what this great state of ours has to offer present and future generations as a result of past generations. Maybe one day my grandchild will write an article about ice fishing, using a picture of his grandfather as the spark for the theme, instilling yet another generation of outdoor heritage.

Suttons Bay
By Cleo M. Boone of Traverse, Michigan
Born 1937

I grew up in Suttons Bay and was born on September 24, 1937. I attended the old stone schoolhouse for the kindergarten year and the first grade where I took my brother, as he is few years younger, very shy. My mother would come meet us and we would walk home which was a few blocks from home. My mother didn't learn to drive when she was young, grew up on a farm, large family, had to help with the younger children, and her father was very sick with Typhoid Fever and almost died and had a little brother who died as an infant. My mother also had the Fever as a young girl, lost all her hair, so she never was real strong and it affected her heart and they found out in later years. She used to take in laundry for

Cleo's parents, Earl and Helen Priest with their children

resorters to make extra money. Used a wringer washer, heated water for the laundry on an oil stove, made her own soap for the laundry. She hung out all the laundry, ironed everything, starched some of the things, did a great job. I can still see her beautiful, white laundry in my thoughts. My dad was a share worker, took his job serious. He worked for the Leelanau County road driving truck, trimming trees in summer. We had a rotary phone and it would ring so many times for each family and you could listen in if you were real quiet. I went to a Catholic school nearby and they had outhouses, which were pretty common. We went to church every day as they had a chapel right in the schoolroom. We had nuns for our teachers and they were pretty strict. We had a fire escape right in one of the rooms so we would have to use that ever so often for a drill and we liked that. My sister and I used to have to help after school being we lived close by. Sweep floors, etc. My mother used to make clothes for my sister and I out of other things or we were given clothes from other families. Really loved getting them. She made pants for brother Jack and gave him haircuts with those pinchy clippers, which he hated. We had a record player, the wind-up kind with large records that we played. My brother has it now. We used to visit our grandparents pretty often and they had farm animals, which we loved, good food like pickles, homemade bread, smoked ham, cake pies from scratch made on wood stoves. I have had a great life and have four grown children, six grandchildren, and a husband for 57 year February 11. What more could a person ask for?

Barn Living
By Richard T. King of Manton, Michigan
Born 1925

I was born in 1925; the last of eight children, and my father was a police officer in the city of Chicago at that time. The history of Chicago has long indicated the existence of many corrupt officials in high offices. My father died when I was about 15 years old and I can never remember of him speaking about those days as a police officer. Perhaps it was because of those activities that my father decided to leave the police department after 17 years and move North to what I've always referred to as the wilderness area in Manistee County, Michigan. Our destination was a 40-acre wooded tract near what is now called Timmerman Lake in Norman Township. When we first arrived there in 1932, it was referred to as Mud Lake. If you got close to the lake, the earth would sink beneath your feet. It was said that a farmer in the area had lost some farm animals there that got too near the lake and were unable to get free. There was only one small area where a boat could be launched for fishing and it is my belief it is still the same today.

Even though this was the era of the Great Depression, my parents believed we could live off the land. We would use a crosscut saw and cut all our own firewood. Though my father had never farmed, we would have a big garden. We could shoot wild game for food and be self-sufficient. However, our first task was to get some type of housing constructed before the next winter set in. Frank and Ida Timmerman were my aunt and uncle and they lived within walking distance. They lived in a small log cabin, had some cows, a team of

horses, and a small barn. Upon our arrival, our family stayed with them and my brothers and I slept in the barn on the hay. Because of lack of time and money, it was decided by my parents we would build a small barn to live in and then sometime later we could build a house. Although these plans were probably well intended, everything we accomplished that summer seemed to go awry. The barn house was completed with two small bedrooms on one end and the remainder was open living area. There was no insulation in the walls or ceiling and the outside was covered with heavy tarpaper. The garden, which was planted on new ground, produced hardly anything.

As the summer days began to cool down, there was talk of school. My brother and I would go to a two-room elementary school, which was located in the small village of Wellston some five miles away. About the first two miles of road from our house was what we called a "two track," which wandered like a snake around the trees, stumps, swamps, and over hills. It then entered on a seasonal dirt road near the Pine Lake area. The only other house along this road was much closer to the village of Wellston. Still, even living in this remote wilderness, we were provided with transportation to school and our bus turned out to be a Model T Ford driven by a Mr. Claud Halstead. He chewed tobacco, stuttered a lot, but was a fine old gentleman with a lot of character. This then was our position as we faced our first winter in our barn house.

In the open area of our house, we had a large wood-burning cook stove with an oven. Near this stove was a sink with a small hand pump for our water supply. A rather large round table with chairs and a couch completed our meager furnishings. In another area stood a heating stove and the stovepipe went straight up and thru the roof. As time went on and it got colder, we all huddled around the heating stove that never appeared to produce enough heat. At this time, we had an old car and gas was only ten cents a gallon. But if you didn't have the ten cents, your car didn't move. Or perhaps it needed a tire or some repair that you just couldn't afford.

As the coldest part of the winter came, we wore our warmest clothing all day and were still cold. Our heating stove was not working well because the wood we cut was green and did not burn well. Our food source was meager and we were often hungry. As the snow got deeper, the old Model T added tire chains, which helped a lot. But then one day after a rather severe blizzard, the old T never showed up and it was weeks before we could get to school again. It was now about the middle of March and the sun, when it did shine, had a little warmth in it. We longed for spring and the sight of bare ground and what a new season would bring. As the snow began to melt, there were little trickles of water running everywhere. What we didn't know at that time was that this area between Pine Lake and Timmerman Lake often flooded in the spring snowmelt. Some years before we moved to this area a ditch had been dug by the W.P.A., which was intended to help drain some of this vast area. Our little barn house was built on a knoll and, when the snow had melted, our roadway went into this flooded area and it was several weeks before it dissipated. On one side of our knoll, there was some higher ground and by walking about three-fourths of a mile, we could get to the Udell Hills road. So Old Claud, our faithful bus driver, started picking us up on that road, but it was a lot further that way.

Sometime that summer something good finally happened. My father was accepted into the Civilian Conservation Corps and was stationed near Brethren about ten miles away. He was much older than most of the other men but I believe he was accepted because of his background and the hardships his family was enduring. He would be able to get home about once or twice a month and we would now have an income of $25 a month. For those of you who long for the solitude of the wilderness, be careful what you wish for. As a family, we were held captive by poverty, terrible roads, flooding, and blizzards. But probably the worst was the terrible loneliness we endured in this area. We stayed in that area for some two-and-a-half years and then moved into Wellston. And what a happy event that was. It was a happy time and area to grow up. Every day the old steam train would come into town to drop off mail, freight, and tourists that stayed at the local hotel. I could walk to school and have some friends. And in the summer, we had a nice lake for swimming or fishing. And here I spent the next nine years attending school and growing up before Uncle Sam made me an offer I just couldn't refuse.

I have never been back to that barn house in the wilderness but I often wonder if much has changed in that area. It seems like such a long time ago.

New Guinea Hens
By Clarice L. Sperry of West Branch,
Michigan
Born 1933

In the first chapter of my life, I was born at home in Lansing, Michigan in the late Depression years, in 1933, the youngest girl, and the seventh child in a family of eight children. My parents were quite poor. My mother never worked outside the home and never learned to drive a car. My father was a self-made carpenter and worked hard to make a living for his large family. My mother took pride in keeping a clean house, and although we had hand-me-down clothes, they were clean, and darned when necessary. She had a regular household routine. Monday was always laundry day when she spent much of the day in our old Michigan basement washing clothes in a wringer-type Maytag washer. She hung them outside in good weather and in the basement when the weather was bad. Tuesday was ironing day, using a heavy electric iron. Wednesday and Thursday left time to bake and clean, and Friday was always an extra cleaning day to get ready for the weekend. She baked her own bread and pies, and we never went hungry. We were expected to be home promptly at suppertime, which wasn't always meat and potatoes, but sometimes bean soup. Although we lived in the city, we owned an extra lot where my parents grew vegetables to supplement our needs and my mom canned a lot of these for winter. My mom always reserved a small area in the garden for flowers and had a lilac tree that bloomed just in time for decorating the graves of relatives for Memorial Day, a yearly routine.

One of my dad's regular routines included a Saturday morning, every week, for sharpening his saws for his work the next week. I can still hear the sound of the rasping of the file against each of the saw teeth.

At the age of four, I became ill and the doctor diagnosed it as infantile paralysis (polio). I was paralyzed in my neck and my right leg. What caused polio, at that time, was generally unknown. In my case, it was decided that it must have come from my drinking water from a community cup at Sunday School. The doctor, not being sure how to treat it, brought over an ultraviolet lamp to be used on my paralyzed neck and leg. He visited me at home, coming late at night after his office hours were over. He also instructed my parents to give me anything I wanted to eat. My parents told me they soon grew tired of the roast beef I always requested.

I started school a few months before I was five years old and, the school being a mile away, I was allowed to bring my lunch and stay during the lunch hour to avoid the extra trips a day, having to drag my paralyzed leg. Gradually, I overcame the paralysis and was able to walk normally.

One day my father carried me over to a neighbor's home where new puppies had been born and let me choose one. We brought home a cute, little, red part-Chow puppy, and we had "Teddy" until he was well over ten years old.

Our entertainment was occasional radio programs such as Jack Benny, Perry Mason, and Amos 'n Andy, for my folks, and the Grand Ole Opry for my dad, soaps in the afternoon for my mom, when she had time, and on the weekend, for the kids, there was The Green Hornet, The Hermit's Cave, and Suspense. TV was not available until I was in my teens.

Some of my earliest memories were seeing the ice truck drive in, delivering 25 pounds of ice for our icebox. The ice blocks in the truck were covered with burlap and the neighborhood kids gathered when he drove in, begging for the ice chips he chipped

Geraldine and Clarice

off for us as a treat. We also welcomed the milkman who delivered milk to our home from a wagon-cart pulled by a horse named Peg. The glass milk bottles had to be shaken to distribute the cream at the top of the bottles.

My cousins, all girls, lived next door and, fortunately, the three girls in my family each had a cousin close in age as friends. We were never allowed to summon our friend by knocking at their door, but by calling their name from outside so that we would not bother their parents. My cousin-friend was Geraldine and I would stand outside her house and call, "Geraldine," and wait for her to come out. Unlike the teens today, who spend their playtime with electronic toys, we spent most of our time outside playing Kick the Can, Hide & Seek, and Tag. A nearby vacant field served as a place for softball. Sometimes, after dinner, we would play outside until it was too dark to see, but always close to home.

I remember the coupons that we had to use for sugar, butter, and soap, and other items that were rationed during the war years, and many times, when these supplies became available, we stood in line at the grocery store, hoping they did not run out before we got to the head of the line. One of the items I remember was a plastic bag of oleo, containing an orange capsule in the bag that we needed to pop and then squeeze through the bag contents until we changed the oleo to the color of butter.

Two of my brothers went away to war, one in the Army who ended up in New Guinea, and the other in the Navy, stationed on an LST. Neither of them would talk about the war when they came home, except that my

Navy brother told me that the LST in front and behind theirs was bombed, narrowly missing them. My brothers sent letters home and I remember I felt privileged when my Army brother sent me a little letter. It was in a government-provided letterform called V-Mail, which was microfilmed, screened for security, and reduced in size to about six inches. I remember my brother told me that one of the soldiers wanted to tell his parents where he was stationed and in his letter, he asked their parents how their New Guinea hens were doing and, of course, they had no Guinea hens.

As I grew older, I found my father did not believe in girls dating until they reached the age of 18, but with my mother's help I managed to get a gown for my Senior Prom and a date. My dad was on a hunting trip so I was able to get to the prom.

Those were my earliest memories and even though we were poor, I never felt underprivileged or poor, even though we didn't have a lot. I earned 50 cents an hour babysitting and working after school and Saturdays in a small grocery store nearby, which allowed me to buy the extras I wanted and taught me good work ethics.

I graduated from high school and was able to start the next chapter of my life, working and, later, marrying a wonderful husband who became an attorney and later a judge, who is now deceased. We had seven children of our own and I feel truly blessed and thankful for the memories and teachings of my past.

The Smelt Run
By Robert R. Martin of Traverse City, Michigan
Born 1937

My name is Robert R. Martin. I am 76 years old. I was born and raised in northern Michigan.

In 1946, my parents and my dad's niece and her husband bought a resort on Lake Huron, just halfway between Cheboygan and Mackinaw City, right next to a roadside park.

Right beside the house was a creek, about six feet from the house. It was fed by a large beaver dam about a mile up in the woods. As far as I know, the creek had no name. Every spring the smelt would run up that creek. After the smelt run, the Red Horse Suckers would run, and then the Lamprey eels would come.

The water was only about six inches deep. The creek was about five to eight feet wide. Every year my folks would let people come in and get all the smelt they wanted, but they had to catch them with their hands, which was no problem, as smelt are small and very rough.

One evening we had a large crowd of people there and my dad told me to partner up with this tall, lanky man with glasses. The man told me to call him Jim. I was supposed to show him how to catch smelt. We had a great time that evening. Later on, I found out the man was Jim Gains, the owner of Gains Dog Food.

I was told he wrote my folks a nice letter thanking them. We always got a Christmas card from him.

There used to be a bar and dance hall about four miles north toward Mackinaw City, owned by an Art Lesperance. Dad got to be good friends with Art. Dad used to call square dances there on weekends once in a while. (It is now the Comador Inn.)

So in the spring when the smelt quit running, the suckers would come upstream. Art would smoke about 500 of them every year and dad would pass them out during parties on the beach in the summer. He always had a lot of beer on hand, but the people would have to wade out into the lake to get a cold beer.

About 1948 or '49, the DNR put a trap (they called it a wier) in our creek to catch Lamprey eels. It was my job every morning before I went to school to check the wier. I had to measure the depth and temp of the water and keep a tally of all the eels we caught. I was supposed to release any trout that came in, which I did, right to mother's kitchen!

My family has always been avid deer hunters, from my parents, grandparents, aunts, uncles, etc. They always camped on public land in Roscommon County, more on that later.

One morning (14th of November) I am not sure of the year, '46, '47, '48, my mother was getting us kids breakfast of oatmeal in the kitchen, dad was still in bed. It was still dark out, but right outside the kitchen window, we had a large yard light. The kitchen window was made up of individual 9" x 9" panes of glass. We looked up and there was a big, eight-point buck standing under the light, watching us through the window.

My mother ran in to get my dad. He came out in his white long johns with the button-back flap, bare feet. All of the deer rifles were packed in dad's 1932 Model A Ford pickup outside. The only gun we had in the house was dad's single-shot, 16-gauge shotgun. He got the gun out of the closet, put a #6 shot shell in, and shot through the window, taking out two or three panes of glass. The deer was only about 25 feet from the house, down it went. My sister and I had to get on the bus shortly so mother kept saying over and over, "Don't say anything to anybody about this," which we did not.

When we got home that evening from school, my father was gone to deer camp. The deer was in the freezer.

One thing I forgot to mention about the smelt, at times they would be so thick in the creek that they literally pushed themselves out of the water onto the edge of the bank.

One time my dad and a bunch of his friends caught enough to fill the back end of his Model A pickup. He then put them on our garden and plowed them under!

My parents, aunt, and uncle (Wilbur and Waunetta Brown from Petoskey) used to tell a story about my aunt who, by the way, married my Uncle Bill, as I called him, when she was 17 years old.

Aunt Waunetta came into camp one day at noon to have lunch. She said she had just missed a very large buck, but she said it came out and stood broadside less than 50 feet away. She said she shot five times, emptied her rifle at it, and it just stood there. While she was trying to reload, it just walked away.

So after lunch they all went to the spot where she said she had shot at the deer. She walked over to where she was standing and said, "Look, there are my empty cartridges." Well, they looked all right, she had just levered the shells out of the rifle. She had forgot to pull the trigger!

My family always camped in the same spot every year. My uncle even made a wooden platform for his large tent.

For an outhouse, they would place a new pole between two stumps and place a tarp around it.

One year my Uncle Bill cut a new, fresh Spruce pole for the outhouse. My Uncle Percy was the first to use it the next morning. It was cold back then. Uncle Percy was a very hairy person. When he got up off the pole, they said you could have heard him holler all the way to town (six miles). The heat from his body melted the pitch in the wood and the hair from his bottom stuck to the pole. My uncle said afterward they had the only fur-covered outhouse log in Roscommon County!

In 1950 my dad and my Uncle Wilbur bought 40 acres (which we still own) about one-and-a-half miles from where they used to camp for almost 20 years.

During the next three years, we built three cabins. They set in a triangle about 100 feet apart.

At that time, we all had old, potbelly wood stoves (we now have propane space heaters). One evening the most of us were in my aunt and Uncle Bill's cabin visiting.

Aunt Waunetta was sweeping up debris and leaves from around the stove. She would then throw it in the wood stove. On this evening somehow a full clip (five shells) of my uncle's 300-Savage ended up in the debris that went into the stove. You never saw so many people move so fast as they did when those shells started going off!

To back up a bit, when my parents purchased the resort on Lake Huron we had no phone. Our first phone was a wood, crank phone, on a party line, 19 families on that one line. Every time the phone would ring, you had eight or ten people on the line.

One thing I forgot to mention was our resort consisted of nine housekeeping cabins. They were named after Snow White and the Seven Dwarfs, plus Willie. People would ask dad where Willie came from. Dad would tell them, "That's how Snow White had the seven dwarfs!"

Is there a Santy Claus
By Richard Slater of Roscommon, Michigan
Born 1930

Santa won't come if you're not asleep Christmas Eve. In 1935, we lived on the farm and I slept with my brother to keep warm, and my mother said, "Now you two boys get into bed and go to sleep, or Santa won't come."

I couldn't sleep—I laid awake, thinking: how could he fit down our chimney; it's too small, and my brother said, "I told you a hunnert times there ain't no Santy Claus, it's ma and dad—they put out the presents now go to sleep."

He thought he knew everything just because he was nine and I was only five.

I still couldn't sleep. I laid awake, listening.

I heard the wind rustle our corn shocks stacked around the house. It made the leaves squeak and scratch at the window. It sounded like somebody or something trying to get in. There was a light under the bedroom door. Somebody was out there in the living room.

The door opened and my mother stood there. "Richard," she said, "Are you asleep?" And I said, "Yup," And my brother said, "You dummy."

Dorothy W. French

✓ Beautiful Teal Blue Long Dress
By Dorothy Wilhelm French of Traverse City, Michigan
Born 1925

My grandfather, Anthony J Wilhelm, age 6 arrived in Traverse City, Michigan from Prague, Bohemia when Traverse City was 8 years old. Traverse City held a Centennial celebration in 1947, the year I graduated from The University of Michigan. The men grew beards and women wore 100-year-old dresses if they could find them or have one made. I was thin and was able to wear the most beautiful teal blue long dress with a 21" waist. I have a picture taken of me and have made it into a greeting card.

As an adult, my grandfather built a brick store on the corner of 8th and Union in Traverse City and opened A.J Wilhelm Department Store in 1886. His first wife died. Kate Smith who was born on South Manitou Island came to Traverse City after high school and he hired her as a clerk. They were married a few years later and had 3 sons—one my father. My grandfather was 50 when my father was born and 90 when he died.

When my Uncle Ralph and my father George graduated from college, they ran the business and he retired. My mother met my father at Olivet College. She came out to Michigan from Wilton, Conn. Because of the store, my family had things many people didn't. When most people still had an icebox with ice delivered by the iceman, we had a G.E. monitor Top Refrigerator in 1927.

Wheelock's had a farm near Long Lake. They made butter and it was put into crocks and brought in to the store on Saturdays and picked up the washed empty crocks. Ours was not salted at my mother's request.

We also had a cold cellar off the basement and the door was kept closed except to get food. There were bushels of potatoes, squash, apples, and a few canned items.

We heated our home with coal. There was a coal bin with a window in the basement and the coal trucks emptied coal through this window. The coal had to be shoveled into the furnace door and banked at night. My father bought a stoker, which automatically put the coal into the furnace, and it needed to be filled just once a day. My brothers could do this when they were older.

The laundry was done in the basement with a tub and a wringer and a rinse tub. My mother had the first Bendix washing machine in 1936. It was installed in the kitchen near the door to the basement and side yard. There were no detergents back then -just soap. Mother put some soap in and turned it on. Shortly after the kitchen floor was covered by an inch of suds! I can still see this in my mind when I think about it! It was a job to clean it up but my brothers and I helped. She

188

soon learned how very little to use. She still had to hang the clothes outside on nice days and in the basement on lines when it rained or snowed.

Good friends of my parents had a cottage on Crescent Shores on the west side of Long Lake. My parents bought the lot next to them in 1930. I was five years old. There were only about 8 cottages out there and no electricity or water or telephone. We pumped our water and had kerosene lamps and stove and an icebox. At the end of school year, we moved out to the cottage and our fathers drove in to Traverse City to work. If our mother wanted something my brother's and I walked 2 miles to a small country store and called my Dad. The main road out to North Long Lake is now called Rt. 610. It was just a gravel road in the '30s. You never knew how long it would take you to drive out because Gallegher's Farm (which is still there) had cattle and the herd crossed the road at different times each the day.

Gerald Ford became the 38th president in 1974. During this time President Ford attended the Cherry Festival held in July. (Cherry crops are big business in this area.) He was invited out to Senator Robert Griffin's cottage on North Long Lake. Security was very tight during the festival. Windows in buildings along the route were not allowed to be open. Wilhelm's store second floor front windows were all closed. Secret Service and a large entourage headed out for dinner on North Long Lake Road. Unexpected to the FBI and Secret service-the group came to a standstill while the cattle walked across the road. President Ford was a "sitting duck"! After all the plans!

Locals knew about the cattle but no one bothered to check. My brother was manager of the store at that time. He knew. Today there is an underpass for the cattle and they do not cross the road!

√ Freckles is Home for Lunch
By James R. Kilgus of Beulah, Michigan
Born 1944

I grew up in the great 1950s. Those were the days when everyone had an old, warped wooden storm door on the side door with that long spring that would close it with a slam when us kids would run out to play.

No modern aluminum doors with hydraulic closers then. Everyone had a pet, then, too. We had a big tiger cat named Freckles. No one ever considered having a cat "declawed" back then since they were always out at night and needed their claws for self-defense. They may have come home missing a part of an ear or part of their tail, but they always came home for meals and to sleep.

I recall one day when my mother had some ladies over for lunch. Midway through the meal, there was a knock at the side door. Not thinking that my mother had heard it, one of the ladies said, "There's someone knocking at the door." My mother, unconcerned, said, "It's just the cat, wants to come in for lunch." The lady, unbelieving, said, "How can a cat knock at the door?" "Well," my mom said, "You can let him in if you want". Sure enough, when she opened the door, there sat Freckles waiting to come in! And in he came. Cats are ingenious, Freckles had learned that he could hook his claws on the bottom of the wood storm door that warped outward and shake it so it sounded just like someone knocking on the door! We always knew when the cat wanted to come in! Just one of many fond memories of the 1950s!

√ Saving for a War Bond
By Mary L. Duda Bucklin of Zephyrhills,
Florida
Born 1937

The red two-story sandstone school sat high on a hill overlooking Lake Superior's Keweenaw Bay. In 1943, when I was in first grade the L'Anse, Michigan Elementary School housed grades kindergarten through fourth grade.

The rug under me became wrinkled and the wood floor and I felt hard on my back. The classroom was quiet but I could hear the soft murmur of Miss Theirit's voice and the regular breathing of near-by classmates. It was first grade and we still had to take a nap. Actually, I think Miss Theirit needed us to take a nap. Ours was a classroom of 27 six year olds. Admittedly, some of my classmates did doze off.

"Mary Lou." I heard Miss Theirit softly call my name. The room was darkened by the long pull shades that covered each of the five windows that extended from wall to wall. They were tall windows and double hung, beginning three feet off the floor and nearly reaching the high ceiling. A first grader standing next to one of the windows could see the playground.

I quietly stood up and tip toed around my near-by resting classmates. I knew what the teacher wanted. It was my turn to buy a war bond stamp. Fumbling in my dress pocket, I found the white cotton hanky that mom had given me. Tied in one corner was a dime. By the time I reached the teacher's desk I had loosened the knot mom had tied to secure the dime and handed the coin to Miss Theirit. She handed me a stamp and placed my stamp album at the corner of her desk. I licked the stamp and placed it in the empty square next to the row of pink stamps. Miss Theirit took my stamp album. She placed it in the drawer of her desk until next week and my next dime.

In 1940, President Franklin Roosevelt's advisors were searching for a way to finance a war. The war bond was seen as a voluntary loan system. It was implemented in the fall of 1940. Sold for $18.75 the bond had a maturity date of ten years and a redemption value of twenty-five dollars. For those who found it difficult to purchase an entire bond, ten cent saving stamps could be purchased and collected in treasury approved stamp albums until enough stamps were accumulated for a bond purchase.

As I found my way back to my rug, I heard Miss Theirit call the name of the next purchaser of a war stamp.

When my stamp album was filled, Miss Theirit gave it to me to bring home. Mom took the album to The Commercial Bank of L'Anse and exchanged it for a U. S. War Bond.

Back to the Farm
By Harold L. Mowat of Evart, Michigan
Born 1937

The trips back to visit the farm near Evart were a couple of times a year, but I did get to stay the summer when I was about fourteen. This was really neat for a teenager—that is, after the first night when the folks had left for home. Man, was I lonesome (thought the world had ended and they really hated me). I'll be good, if you'll come back!

By morning, all of that was forgotten. I got to drive the tractor (this was Uncle Earl's tractor, as Grandpa never had one). I believe it was a Farmall 300 or 400. Grandpa was going to cut hay this particular Wednesday. Now, Wednesday was prayer meeting night at Ogilvie Wesleyan Methodist Church at the corner of Sylvan and Avondale Roads. (This property came from my great-grandfather Daniel Ogilvie, hence the name). So I brought the tractor up by the house like he asked me to do, to lower the sickle bar on the mower. He said, "Unlatch the bar and kick it out," so I did as I was told (always did what I was told), only to see Grandpa with his fingers in between the guards, pulling something out. There went the bar and there went his index finger! It cut the end clean off, except for a small piece of skin holding it on. He grabbed his finger and into the house he went. Grandma took immediate action. First, she put his hand into the big water pail at the pump—the same pail we drank out of all the time. Then she put the finger back on, wrapped it up in some home remedy made out of cow s%#t or some other poultice material and back to work we went. We were cutting hay on Uncle Fred's 70 acres on 11 Mile. He would cut the hay, load it with the slat hay loader on to the wagon, and I would take it down to the barn. I don't know if I unloaded it or whether Uncle Earl was there. But it was cool, because I was driving by myself. I pulled out of the drive and headed up Avondale Road. I put it in road gear and jammed the gas full and away we went, the wagon bouncing all over the road. I made it to 11 Mile, turned on 11 Mile, hit a few bumps, and the pin flew out of the tongue. The wagon tongue dug into the road and overturned the wagon and really bent up the reach under the wagon. I went and got Grandpa. We came back, turned the wagon over, and headed for the field. The wagon kind of looked like a dog trying to hump something. Needless to say, Grandpa was not too pleased at this time. We hooked the bent wagon to the hay loader and away we went.

Grandpa was on the tractor and I was stowing away the hay as it came off the loader. It was late in the day and Grandpa said we would go one or two more times around and then head for the barn. It was time for supper, to milk the cows, and then head to church. Well, we picked up some tree branches in the loader and before he got stopped we had hardly any slats left in the hay loader. After a few choice words and a little work, it couldn't be saved. By the time we got back and took care of the cows, it was too late for prayer meeting. Grandpa never missed church, but with a little help from his favorite grandson, he missed this one.

Friends from Charlevoix the Beautiful
By Kayla Koboski Briggs of Durham, North Carolina
Born 1947

I was born in Petoskey, Michigan in July 1947. My mother's family lived in Charlevoix. When I was little, I would sometimes take the Greyhound bus in the summer from Petoskey to Charlevoix to spend time with my Great Grandma Aggie and Grandma Lill. The Greyhound bus station stopped at Wags Coffee Shop in Charlevoix and it is where my Grandma Lill waited on table. I would walk up the hill two blocks away and stay several days. I would walk to the beaches (mainly Michigan Beach by the lighthouse, Depot Beach, which was warmer, and once in a while Ferry Beach).

In the summer of 1962, I stayed at my Grandma Lill's for the entire summer to help my Aunt Edna take care of my Great Grandma Aggie for she could not see any longer. Also, I would help my Aunt Edna with the housework and my Uncle Bob with the yard work. I met MM that summer and she introduced me to several of her friends (SS, PP, and BD). We called ourselves the Four-squared + BD for four of us had double initials (KK, MM, SS, and PP). We went to the beaches and stayed at a church camp cottage one night telling stories and scared ourselves so we did not get sleep that night. We enjoyed going to Schroeder's soda fountain and having Lime Rickey and Chocolate Phosphate drinks. Also, going to the movies and having the delicious buttered popcorn, which they made fresh. Once in a while, we would stop at the A&W root beer stand and get some take away root beer, which they sold it in white, wax-coated megaphones. We would pull off the bottom to yell through the container/megaphone. Loved downtown Charlevoix and walking around to see the boats docked plus going through the channel out into Lake Michigan and seeing the bridge go up and down and the "mushroom houses" (Earl Young homes) were my favorite. My family left for Anaheim, California at the beginning of August. I left at the end of August with my cousin Vicki, her husband, and daughter, via Route 66. I wrote letters to my Charlevoix friends over the years.

In the summer of 1965, I flew from Los Angeles, California to Chicago, Illinois as a high school graduation gift. I stayed with my Aunt Marg in Chicago for 10 days then took a Greyhound bus from Chicago to Charlevoix. I met up with MM, SS and BD but not PP for she was busy with her horses. The talk was about the Camp Charlevoix counselors and where we would be going to college in the fall. One of the Camp Charlevoix counselors had black hearse car, which we all climbed into and drove around in. The Camp Charlevoix counselors only got off one or two nights a week so several of us (girls) sneaked into Camp Charlevoix one night to see our friends. It was a very daring escapade! One very hot day in the early evening we (girls) met at the Michigan beach (to the right of the channel and lighthouse when you are looking out towards Lake Michigan) for it was more private area. We decided to take off our bathing suits and tie them to the inner tube we had with us. After swimming around for a while we decided to go in and found that the top of one of our swimsuits was missing. We looked and looked and could not find the top so the rest of us went to shore and got a towel and shirt to cover up with so we could go home. Several days later one of our families was out walking on the beach and found the swimsuit top washed up on shore and wanted to know what it was doing there! There definitely was a discussion about this but we survived it. At the end of summer we had a party and said farewell to each other.

Over the years we have seen each other and it is now 2013 and each Christmas we (KK, MM, SS, and BD) still exchange Christmas cards and letters.

Grandpa's Gone Fishing
By Edith Thompson of Three Rivers, Michigan
Born 1926

Back in the 1930s, my grandfather, Willis Bailey, was a widower living alone in a little log cabin out in the woods about a mile south, of the Black river where it crosses Black River Rd. There was a little creek, crossing his place where he went fishing every morning. One year on the day before trout season the only fish that bit on his hook was a nice brook trout, even though he knew it was not trout season yet he decided to keep it and eat it. On the way to his cabin, he met the Game Warden, who, on seeing the trout, said, "You know that it is not trout season that is an illegal fish, and I am going to have to take you to jail." On the way to the jail, they passed our house and the Game Warden stopped and apologized to my folks for taking Grandpa to jail, perhaps hoping that my Dad would pay the fine and grandpa would not have to go to jail. Grandpa would have none of it, he said, "No, I knew it was illegal fish but it was the one that bit, if I threw it back it would just die, and I would go hungry, where's the sense in that? I will go to jail and take my medicine." So Grandpa spent some time in jail for catching a trout on the day before the season opened.

Many years later, my Aunt told me the rest of the story. She said that sometime after the jail incident, Grandpa went to the river one day to fish, and when he got there the Game Warden was there and asked to see his license. He said, "I ain't fishing, just looking," and headed down stream, the Game Warden following, after about half an hour he stopped to rest and the Game Warden again asked for his license, again he said, "I ain't fishing, just looking." After a couple or more stops with the same conversation, Grandpa set down his tackle box and said, "Now I'm fishing" and showed the Game Warden his license. The Game Warden was then a couple of miles downstream from his car. He was not happy. He would probably like to have taken Grandpa back to jail that day. Jack Adair was a respected Game Warden in the Onaway area for many years.

The Bear Who Bit the Tree

Onaway was my home for 17 years and I have many happy memories of Onaway and the people there. My earliest memories are of the depression years, as I was only three when it started so I don't remember anything of the good years before the depression. Being poor was just normal for me.

We relied on wild fruit for a lot of our winter food, and every year picked a lot of wild berries and canned them. One summer day we were going berry picking with the horses and wagon, we were headed down an old logging road and the horses were getting very skittish, there was a spruce top lying in the road and my dad got out to move it out of the way and

wondered what had broken it off. We had not had any big wind, when he picked it up; he noticed that it had moisture in it and bear hair. He looked around and there was a spruce stub beside the road broken off about six feet above the ground, when he took the top over to the stub, it was the top of the stub, and there were bear tracks beside it. The tracks were the same size as his tracks and the tree had been bitten off about six feet from the ground. He decided that if there was a bear that big in the area it was no wonder the horses were skittish. He turned the wagon around and headed out of there, the horses were more than willing to hurry out of there.

We knew there were bears, in the area but never had any trouble with them getting into the livestock; we always had a good watchdog.

My Dad always kept a loaded shotgun in the corner behind the kitchen door for hawks and coyotes, which were a big problem for the chickens and sheep. Any disturbance from the chickens or sheep and he grabbed the gun in one hand and the doorknob in the other. By the time he was out the door the gun was aimed and ready to shoot.

✓ Living Up North
By Janet Watts of Hartland, Michigan
Born 1947

I had just turned eight years old and was almost halfway through the third grade when I learned my family would be moving to Alcona County, a rural community located in the northeastern part of Michigan's Lower Peninsula. I had been born and raised in Saginaw and although I enjoyed visiting my grandparents' farms in northern Michigan, I couldn't imagine living there.

In 1955, Saginaw was a thriving city. The public library and post office both looked like castles and the downtown stores had wonderful things like decorative tin ceilings, pneumatic tube systems to return one's change from an unseen office and elevators operated by real people. The operators would call out the floor number... mezzanine—glassware and fine china... second floor—ladies wear. And then, best of all, they would adjust the level of the elevator with a lever to meet the floor and manually open the doors, the inner door looking like a hinged golden gate. There

Janet and Tommy Campbell in 1956

couldn't be anything so fine Up North.

Of course, northern Michigan had its own charms. We would live only a few miles from Lake Huron where we would swim in the frigid water and have family picnics on the beach and I would soon discover the car ferry which would carry us over the Straits of Mackinac to the Upper Peninsula—the Mackinac Bridge not yet a reality. And there were acres of Christmas trees that scented the very air. I had lived there only a month when I learned more about those Christmas trees.

A few days before Christmas, my class was given a list of supplies to bring to school the following day. Those of us who lived in "the country" were told to bring extra to share with the kids who lived in town.

I wasn't familiar with most of the names on the list. My father helped me to recognize and cut the boughs of cedar, pine, spruce, and balsam. In class, we turned those raw materials into fresh corsages for our mothers and I learned my first lesson about nature.

Not every lesson was so pleasant. We lived on a dairy farm and my parents expected my brother and me to drink the milk produced by our cows. This milk tasted nothing like the milk we were accustomed to having delivered on our doorstep by the milkman. We were sure we could taste the bacteria in it and told our parents that we didn't like cow's milk. We wanted store milk. My mother tried to trick us into drinking it by hiding it in cartons from the store but we knew the difference. We compromised when she agreed to heat it on the stove and then cool it in the refrigerator. This was our first lesson in pasteurization. Much better but not great.

I still missed downtown Saginaw but found things to like about the village of Lincoln. On Saturday evenings the people of the community would do their weekly shopping. Popular music would be played over a public address system as they met and visited in the streets. The merchants would combine resources to have a weekly drawing and we always knew the winner. We knew almost everybody in the town. I was related to half of them and went to the school with the rest. The town was only three blocks long and safe enough to be able to run off with my classmates and enjoy the evening. I was young enough to be innocent to the possible downside of living in a place where everyone knew each other.

I had two best friends in the fourth grade. One was just like me. She was quiet and not too adventurous. The other was the third of seven children and was the exact opposite. I slept over at her house one night and had the time of my life. Clara's mother was a beautiful and vivacious woman. She was also the most relaxed mother I had ever met. Maybe that happens when you have such a large family. That evening she brought out some polka records and taught us to dance. We twirled madly until we were a sweaty mess then dressed in the warmest clothes we could find, everybody wearing things that belonged to somebody else. There were large hills in their backyard. That was new to me too. Saginaw is flat as a pancake and you can see for miles in all directions. We tobogganed down those hills until we had enough and then Raymond, the only boy in the family and the oldest, cooked bacon over an open fire and we had a feast. Maybe I would like living Up North after all.

Thank Heaven for the Two Seater
By Ralph Smith of Rogers City, Michigan
Born 1925

There are many tales of the "2 seaters." some recall the little ford coupe of the '30s, a beautiful little two seater, while others think of the early airplanes with one seat in the front and one in the back, also a beautiful two seater.

But to me the words "two seater" brings back memories of the greatest two seater of all. That little shack that sat on the back of the lot, cursed by many on a cold winter night but a relief for many, regardless of day or night, summer or winter.

Although our mother was Irish, I'm sure she had a little gypsy in her as we moved often, thus gained a vast experience in "2 seaters." in the early thirty's my mother got the notion we should move to the farm where we could "live off the land." so we moved about 7 miles from town to an old shack that had half the windows boarded up, a wood

Stove, no electricity, no running water and of course the old"2 seater" in the back of the lot right next to the cornfield. We did have a garden, we got milk from the neighbors, had chickens and ducks, so it wasn't all that bad. For a boy of 7 it was heaven, no shoes to wear, no nightly baths, we had a small creek close by, a great swimming hole and good fishing.

Once or twice a month, a friend form town would pick up the folks and take them to town for supplies. So it was on one of these days that my sister and I, who had heard that corn silk was good for rolling your own smokes, thought we would give it a try. With a handful of dry silk and some matches we took to the "2 seater" where we planned on using

The brown sheets out of the sears and roebuck, as they were the thinnest. So we rolled some pretty hefty smokes only to find the paper burned faster than the silk and soon got to your fingers. About this time, we thought we heard a car, so down the ole with everything, and started fanning the smoke out, only to see flames coming out of the hole! Luckily the horse trough was nearby and the milk pails sitting by the backdoor. Grabbing the rails and running to the 2 seater, we somehow got the fir out. Other than a horrible smell, no apparent damage. Oddly enough, nothing was ever said, we had escaped a disaster worse than the Chicago fire! I guess for me this put the fear of smoking in me and to this day (heading for 88); I have never smoked, not even during my tour with Uncle Sam in WWII. I found that the black market or trading for candy was a better way to get rid of your cigarette ration.

Soon we moved back to town, with a little 2 seater in the far corner of the lot, very prone to being tipped over by neighborhood ruffians. So soon, we moved to an upstairs apartment where we shared the 2 seater with the landlords, an elderly couple, who regarded their 2 seater as part of the household, scrubbed every Saturday, painted yearly and woe to anyone leaving a mark on the seats. From there we moved to a small, buy fairly new house. I mention small for a reason, this was still during the depression and were aghast one day to see my mother's family drive up, hoping to find work. With e kids, (two in diapers) and now we found what it was like to stand in line for the 2 seater. They stayed for the summer and though it was very hectic, we got along fine, the grocer soon cut off our credit, can't blame him. But we fished, picked berries, ate applesauce by the gallons, and all survived.

We recall moving 1 5 times in 1 5 years and the old 2 seater was always there. on a summer day maybe you would just sit there and meditate or look through last year's sears and sawbucks (as we called it) look at the cowboy boots you never got last Xmas, look at the jack-knives, check the price of the 20 gage you were going to buy. I skip the stories of cold winter nights running with the lantern, or the horror of ever having the diarrhea.

But I must relate one more part of the 2 seater, and that is of the gentleman who dug the holes for these 2 seaters. Coming home from school one noon-hour we found our 2 seater moved off the hole and this old man digging a new hole, tossing the dirt into the old hole. As it was lunchtime he sat on the edge of the hole, calmly having a sandwich and a cup of coffee, he got the "makins" out and rolled himself a smoke, oblivious to all. I have often wondered just what his thoughts were. Probably wondering how long it would be before some damn fool would think of some way to eliminate his job. This was soon to come, buy the old gentleman had already passed away. God Bless him.

√ **Life Time of Memories**
By Jerry Rehage of Cincinnati, Ohio
Born 1952

It was a hot and very humid Sunday afternoon, that 1st week in August, 1957 in Cincinnati, Ohio. As mom and dad, my older brother, two sisters and I gathered on the back porch in the shade trying to find relief from the mid 90 degree temperatures.

We wanted to plan some sort of vacation being summer was winding down and I only being 6 years old ready to start my first experience with school.

Mom sitting in her lazy chair, reading the Cincinnati Post and Time Star, came across an ad in the classified, it read, Come to Northern Michigan, get away from the Cincinnati heat and enjoy the cool summer nights along with daytime breezes from our cottage on Clam Lake. Everyone agreed how refreshing it sounded; we could sense the clean air immediately. As mom dialed the number in the paper, as it was a local number, a man answered the phone and said, "Hello this is Gene how can I help you".

Mom stated our situation; we were looking for a cottage that would sleep two adults and four children. To our luck, it had two bedrooms and a pull out sofa that would be perfect for two of us kids. Gene said he had the last week in August available and with no hesitation mom reserved that week for our first trip to Michigan.

We were all excited about the trip, we were going to fish every day, but the next two weeks took forever. As our week finally approached and dad knowing how anxious we were, decided we would leave a day early. With his deep stout voice he said, "I want to be on the road by 5:00 A.M. since it is 500 miles to Clam Lake from Cincinnati".

We were not exactly sure how long the trip would take as we had to travel route 27 most of the way since 1-75 was not completed yet, so we all packed in the 56 Buick and headed north.

As the directions read, we had to pick up the keys at a Dewitts Marine at Clam River and the swinging bridge, which meets Torch Lake. As we found our way up thru the pine and birch trees of Northern Michigan, we finally arrived at Dewitts. It was so rainy and extremely foggy that afternoon we could barely see the shores of Torch Lake. Needless to say, our expectations were deflated.

The man at Dewitts had our name from Gene, but stated we could not get into the cabin until Saturday but recommended Fetz's Lodge across the way if we needed a place to stay for a night. Not wanting to sleep the six of us in the Buick, we decided to spend the night at Fetz's. It was the perfect northern lodge with a huge fireplace, which was actually burning due to the cold rainy day. We had to get adjoining rooms to hold the six of us and the bathrooms were down the hall, but that was no big deal for us kids we were on vacation in a Northern Michigan Lodge.

As the next morning arrived, we were all up early only to witness more rain and heavy fog across the lake. Mom decided to pick up some groceries across the road at Dingmans IGA, known as the Clam River Superette, which was a typical small village market connected to Stan Orr's Bar which is all now the famous Dockside.

As we made our journey to the Clam Lake Cabin we planned every day of fishing and swimming, we just knew the rain had to stop. Tuesday came, Wednesday came, but no luck, all of our planning was starting to diminish. But as gloomy as the weather was we made the best of things, we would find a game to play or do something to keep us busy as there were no TV to watch in the cabin and never heard of a computer.

As we came familiar with the surrounding area we would go into Bellaire and eat at Buds Diner which is now Toonies or just go up to Stan Orr's and get a burger and play shuffle board as long as there was an adult with us or between rains just sit and watch the boats go thru Clam River as the bigger boats had to wait for the bridge to open to get thru.

Yes, it sounds like a very simple and at times somewhat boring vacation, but we made the best of it and just enjoyed being together "up north".

After we arrived back home in Cincinnati, back to the hot and humid weather, the cold and rainy week we just had, didn't seem so bad.

After a couple days being back home, Gene called stating how sorry he was about the weather we had and if we wanted to go back next year he would rent us his cabin for half price. He said the weather could not be that mean 2 years in a row. Well needless to say, it didn't take long to decide, we all wanted to give Northern Michigan another chance and another chance we did.... Year after year we would make the journey north, taking along friends, as we grew older showing off the beauty of the clear blue waters of Torch Lake and the fresh clean water of the surrounding lakes. We even bought a board and placed our names on it when they renovated the docks in 1981 along Clam River, wanting to be part of the area.

Well 55 years have now gone by, mom and dad have both passed away, Gene and Phyllis, no longer have the cottage on Clam Lake, and moved to South Carolina, after many years of living on Torch Lake. The swinging bridge has been long gone, Fetz's Lodge, which became Mico's, has been lost to a fire, and Dewitts Marine is now Butch's. But thanks to the heavens above, we can proudly say we have a place of our own in Northern Michigan to enjoy with our children and their children, the cool summer nights and the daytime breezes, and reminisce the memories of the past and enjoy the ones yet to come.

P.S. We are very grateful to Phyllis and Gene (Flash) Heizer for giving us a second chance, back in the late '50s and most of all their friendship throughout the years.

Brian Peters

✓ The Little Elto Engine that Could
By Karen Peters of Charlevoix, Michigan
Born 1943

In the early '80s, our family purchased a small cabin on the South Arm of Lake Charlevoix. Our 10 year old son quickly discovered the joys of fishing. Since the only boat we owned at the time was an aluminum 17" Grumman canoe, he rigged it up for fishing and perfected his skill of paddling to the closest and best fishing spots, where he readily caught pan fish and small mouth bass. Since we and his sister spent the entire summers on the lake, with Dad coming for the week-ends, he had lots of wonderful time on his hands - and the pure joy of being a boy on a beautiful lake. Brian was soon spending a good eight hours per day fishing, irritated by those friends who might come by to check out his activities. One of them had an almost identical canoe, and he would often inadvertently bang their aluminum canoes together, scaring the fish away with the reverberating clang. Between the limits of mobility due to having to paddle to and from his fishing spots, and my fear of him being out of my sight or over the deep waters of the

middle of the lake at his young age, he did not travel far from our own dock.

Brian learned a lot about paddling a canoe, becoming as skilled as any old timer who had no other mode of water transportation - and about fishing: how to rig the line, what bait to use, the types of spots where fish like to spend time, and how and when to reel a fish in. Then one day his Dad brought out of the well house an old black box. None of us realized it at the time, but Brian's world was about to change forever.

Out of the box came a little 1.1 horse power outboard motor, an Elto, made by Evinrude. The engine was built in 1941. Brian described it at the time to friends by saying, "It is an antique - silver, covered with black oil and grime, with the red and gold labeling barely visible. A tiny gas tank was built in at the top, with a small, two-bladed propeller at the other end. The whole contraption resembled a giant egg beater." His Dad told him, "This was used by your Paw-Paw (great grandfather) and your Pop-Pop (grandfather) to go fishing on the lakes of northern Wisconsin, including Plum Lake and Razorback Lake, during the 1940s and 1950s. In the 1950s and 1960s it was used on Intermediate Lake, not far from

196

here in northern Michigan." He added that he would try to get the thing running again in order to keep the tradition alive.

As Brian wrote, "after some cleanup work, putting in a new spark plug and adding fresh gasoline, we attached the Elto to the back of the Grumman canoe using a special wood bracket. The starter rope was literally a three foot long nylon rope with a knot at both ends that was wrapped around the flywheel on the top of the engine. After setting the carburetor adjustment, you had to depress the primer needle (a process which automatically dripped gasoline on your fingers), adjust the throttle, and then pull as hard as you could." We all remember to this day the miracle that allowed that old motor to fire up on the very first pull of the rope!

This was no whisper quiet engine like today's modern ones. When this motor started, it sounded like a seaplane taking off, only louder, due to its above-water exhaust system. I can recall still the response this produced among our neighbors. Everyone who was home came running outside to find out what the ruckus was, only to see Brian and his Dad proudly steering the boat along the lake. When the motor was running, it was running only forward, much as old SeaDoos did, for there was no reverse nor was there a neutral. Its top speed was about that of a brisk walker or a slow runner, but that outdid any boy's paddling, no matter how adept. The severe vibration in Brian's left hand was, however, well worth the thrill of freedom, according to him. This little motor changed his fishing by allowing him to quickly get to the places where the Northern pike could be caught!

As it happened, the same neighbor boy who had a nearly identical Grumman also had a little Elto in his father's garage, which had been long forgotten. Brian's escapade convinced his friend's father to put his family's old Elto into service as well. There was never any doubt in our cove just when the boys were using their Eltos to find a good fishing spot! Many impromptu community fish fry dinners were enjoyed when the boys came home with a stringer of bass and pike. The two boys were the talk of the South Arm.

Our son's early fishing experience led him to later outfit a 13' Boston Whaler for salmon fishing, complete with a downrigger and a fish finder. Before Brian was 16, I would trailer the boat to Lake Michigan, where he and his buddies would happily catch plenty of salmon and lake trout, catching the attention of the charter captains who shared the same space. Later, there were a few summers when I met my son at our dock nearly every morning at 5:00 a.m. to make the 45 minute trip by water to Lake Michigan for fishing. For Brian, there was no activity more exciting or more relaxing.

As often in life, one experience leads to another. Brian skipped one week of his senior year in high school in order to take the classes and pass the rigorous test to become a Coast Guard licensed charter captain, the youngest on all the Great Lakes at the time. For four summers, Brian ran a charter service for bass, pike, lake trout, and salmon, helping him to pay for college expenses and filling him with wonderful memories he will take with him throughout his life.

This coming summer, we plan to once again take that Elto out on Lake Charlevoix, attached to the very same Grumman canoe, and fire it up for what will be the fifth generation of users, our grandson (Brian's son and fishing buddy). I wonder who else might be inspired to do the same thing.

A Perfect Childhood
By Ann Reynolds of Sun City West, Arizona
Born 1936

What fun recalling some memories from life growing up in Oscoda. One special memory is of the skating pond in the park around the Township Hall. The fire department would freeze the pond every winter. They would string lights in the trees and we could go there to skate every winter. It was a drawing card for the kids in Oscoda (adults too.) There was something magical about putting on our skates and gliding around the trees in the evening.

Another special Oscoda treat was going to Silver Valley. There were toboggan rides if you wanted a thrill, a skating pond, good sledding hills, and ski runs. My favorite Saturday would consist of spending the day there. When you got cold, you could go into the shelter to warm up with cocoa and a snack. It was a special treat to be there after a heavy snowstorm. I recall much more snow when we were growing up then we get now.

The roller rink in AuSable rink was another favorite hangout for kids when I was growing up. Every weekend I put on skates and spent the day spinning around the rink to music! Do kids ever have that much fun now? Probably. But I wouldn't trade my childhood for anything. My brother and I talk about our "perfect childhood." And it was!

Then we had the river across the street from our house. Since we were free to roam as children, we spent many hours by the river, either swinging off a rope into the river, taking a canoe down the river to see what we could discover, swimming in the river, and fishing. We also had a big sand bank that was wonderful to roll down.

We had a centennial parade that I will never forget. Parades were big when I was a kid and I recall my Mom making dresses for my sister and me so we could walk in the parade with our big, black Newfoundland dog named "Shandy." Boy, did we feel like a celebrity being part of a real parade!

The beach was a special part of my childhood. We were within walking distance from our house and I swam nearly every day of the summer. I recall many hours there with friends and family, picnics on the beach, long walks up the shoreline, sunrises and sunsets and the calming sound of the waves. Water has always been soothing to me because I was blessed to grow up by the river and the lake. I grew up in a family with a sister and two brothers. My Dad was the one who left for work in the morning and returned in the evening. My Mother was the center of the family as she was always there when we returned from school. We came home to home-baked cookies, Mom busy in the kitchen planning the evening meal and there to listen to reports of our day at school. We had a lot of freedom as we roamed the neighborhood as we wished as long as we were "home by supper." We had a sense of stability in our home situation and a lot of freedom to go where we wanted to go…no "structured activities." I'm understanding what a blessing that was as I see my grandchildren's scheduled activities with very little free time.

We lived near a family with six children, all ages available to play games with. We always made up our games and they were so much fun. We had a secret hideout in the lilac bushes that grew in the neighborhood. There was always someone available to do things with. The family gathered in the living room at night to listen to our favorite radio programs. One the weekends, we went to the movies and that was always a special treat. Saturday night was bath night and we had a four-legged tub! We were not much aware of the war, as my folks didn't discuss it much. But I do recall seeing my Mom mix up the little colored spot in the "margarine." It was probably lard with color mixed in. I recall seeing rationing stamps also. My Mom did a lot of sewing for us. I recall milk being delivered and it would freeze on the porch and raise the lid on the bottle. That was fascinating to me. We especially looked forward to snowstorms as we had a horse and cutter. When we got heavy snow, we hooked up the horse and took everyone in the neighborhood for rides. That was so much fun and so beautiful with the snow blanketing the trees. How many kids have a memory like that?

We always had animals around as my Dad ran a Mink farm in addition to his job as a banker. We had mink, red fox, beaver, right in our yard. And we always had at least three housedogs! Looking back, I don't know how my Mom handled all this, but she did. As a result, I grew up loving all kinds of animals. We spent time walking in the woods with our Dad when he went hunting. We saw deer and other animals on these walks. I especially loved seeing the ducks and swans. I wonder how many city kids never have these adventures. I grew up with a real love for nature and all the wonderful lessons it teaches us as we observe the animals and birds.

We lived in a big, old house with my grandmother. We lived upstairs, she lived down. She was a pioneer for her time. She would tell us stories of traveling by horse and buggy to visit the five banks that were scattered around the area. She did this in all kinds of weather. She was a widow, left with this responsibility when her husband died young. She raised her son alone while handling this huge responsibility by herself. We were fascinated by her stories of Oscoda and the things she remembered about the building of this community. She always knew the Generals at the base and they found her to be a good source of the history of the area.

So I had this sense of history through my Grandmother, security and freedom from my parents, siblings to share all this with, and a beautiful natural environment to grow up in. Many people say that seniors tend to sugarcoat the past but I think that fact that these memories remain says a lot about all the things that were "right" in those times. I am thankful every day for the wonders of my childhood.

✓ A Wonderful Life on the Farm
By Josephine DeYoung of McBain, Michigan
Born 1920

I am an old lady and I can't believe the many things that happened in my 92 years.

I started school when I was 4 years old and I graduated from elementary school at age 12. We went to a one-room school and we had some good teachers. There was one teacher that still stands out in my mind today. I remember him telling me and my friend that "he used to think we were pretty good girls but now I think you are not worth a 'hill of beans'. We still talked about that at a recent funeral we were both at.

We could not afford to buy dolls from the store so we made our own. We used a block of wood from our woodpile. We nailed thinner sticks on for arms and legs. We used white birch and drew faces on them for eyes, nose, and mouth. We used yarn for hair and dressed them in old baby clothes. We had a good time.

We also built our own playhouse out of old boards and put sod on for the roof.

We had very little for Christmas. I can remember we had a buffet in our living room and stored all kinds of things in there. One Christmas my present fell out of the buffet. It was a small yellow mirror. That was a good present for me because I always wanted to look nice.

My Ma would walk to her folks, which was about two miles away. I would love to go along. One time she told me, I had to stay home and cook dinner for my Dad. I was not very happy about that. I even had to pour his coffee for him. He was kind of mad at me and said, "Pour it"! I can still see him sitting there and wiping his glasses on the curtain.

My father was a farmer but also had a side job of butchering cows and pigs for other farmers for their winter meat supply. He would hitch the horse to the cutter and drive around to the people who needed something butchered. He charged $1.00 and sometimes $2.00. They would give him some extra pieces for pay and sometimes it would be either a tail, the heart, tongue, liver or cheeks. Sometimes it would be the whole head to make headcheese or the lower parts of the leg for soup. He enjoyed butchering but it was hard work.

While we were having breakfast one morning, our house roof was on fire. When there was an emergency, we had to put a long ring on our telephone that would ring into about five or six other people's homes. Our nearby neighbors were milking cows and came with pails of milk to help put out the fire. That was the good thing about the old party line phones. It was also a place for all the neighbors to catch up on the news about everybody in the area. Our ring would be a sure way for all the neighbors to run to the phone and "just listen in a bit" to see what was going on at our house.

My invalid father was at our house for the day so I could care for him. We got a big snowstorm and the weather was bad. He wanted to go home. They got about a half mile down the road and were stuck in a snow bank. My husband walked back to our neighbors, about one half mile to get help. They had to find the toboggan and get some rope and lots of blankets. It took a long time for him to get back again pulling the toboggan thru the storm and my Dad thought he was going to die in the car. They wrapped him in blankets and tied him on the toboggan and pulled him thru the cold and snow banks and finally got him pulled up into the house. His eyes were as big as dollars when they unwrapped him in the house. He was glad to be alive and back inside the house.

I worked for a family when I was out of school and still very young. They had a boy that was 12 years old and a little mischievous. The kitchen table was in the middle of the room and he would chase me around the table and try to catch me. I was supposed to be working. I remember I had to scrub the floor, which was made of old flooring, until it was almost white.

We also had a big patch of strawberries. People would come and pick so we could earn some money. One lady came and picked in a pail and put all her little quart boxes in a larger box and then dumped the pail in her boxes so they would be heaping full and running over. She got a lot of free berries. I did not think this was right. At age 16, I worked at the B.F. Goodrich Rubber Co.

When I went to meetings at night, I was supposed to ride home with my brother. When I came out of church, one night there stood a handsome, good-looking young man. I knew who he was. He asked me to go out with him. I said "sure" I would be glad to. I told him I would have to tell my brother. My brother got mad at me and said, "I'm going to tell ma on you." When I came home, my dad was standing on the porch. He was not very happy with me. But the dating kept on for four more years and I married this man.

There was a 100-acre farm for sale just up the road for $4,500.00. We could borrow money so that is what we did. My husband's parents gave us a cow for our wedding gift. We also bought eight cows and two horses. We used other people's farm tools at first. I canned a lot of food. Hundreds of quarts of fruits and vegetables. We canned our own meat. I baked six loaves of bread twice a week and lots of cookies and cakes. Some special treats were "long Johns." This was bread dough dipped in hot grease (lard) and then frosted.

At Christmas time, the kids could only have one gift. Dad planted a big garden. We also had pickles and beans to sell. After we sold them, we could go to the candy store and buy a 10-cent bag of candy.

As the family grew up the boys got into more mischief. One of them tied a rope high in a tree and anchored it at the bottom so he could have a fast ride down. That resulted in two broken arms.

Some years went by. We now have six children. They all went to a Christian School. At times, we were concerned about paying the tuition but somehow the money was always there. We lived together for 69 years. My husband was 93 when he died. We had our ups and downs but it was a wonderful life on the farm. I am very thankful I am still living in my own house.

Saturday Evening Ritual
By Nancy Ann Priest of Lake Leelanau, Michigan
Born 1934

I was born in 1934 in my Paternal Grandparents farm home on Popp Rd, one mile west of the Village of Lake Leelanau. My grandfather Roy Anthony Howard owned and operated "The Leelanau Dairy" at that site. He farmed the land with his horses and along with raising food crops for the cattle and horses, my grandma cultivated a very large garden of vegetables. Together they sold from the back of his Classic Wood Sided Ford Wagon the dairy produce, the garden goods and the chicken fryers that grandma killed and cleaned by the gross every week during the summer months especially for the Indiana Woods people who vacationed in the hills along the Lake Michigan Shore Line every summer.

Very few of the farm homes had electricity in their homes. Outdoor toilets and iceboxes were the rule. Often the tray under a neglected icebox would not be dumped in time and melted water would run across the kitchen floor! Oil chandeliers hung in the center of the living room ceiling and oil lamps were carried about, as light was needed from room to room.

My Grandma Mary's kitchen had a wood burning stove, an indoor water pump, and a large pantry to hold foodstuffs and her dishes, pots and pans. There was only the kitchen table as counter space for preparing meals. She did make the most wonderful home make noodles and poppy seed kolaches that we enjoyed with much enthusiasm! Chicken Dinner every Sunday was the rule with family and neighbors coming by after church services to enjoy the camaraderie. A good game of cards and a piece of grandma's chocolate cake with seven minute frosting and a glass of grandpa's homemade cider would finish the evening off, with good wishes and hopes for a happy week to come before meeting again.

In my grandma's home, dish and laundry wash waters were thrown out into the yard, there being no sink with drain in the kitchen.

Six families owned and maintained the primitive telephone system. I remember during my growing years watching my dad and Mr. Bill Popp climbing the telephone poles to fix the wires. The Central Office was in the Village of Lake Leelanau. The Plamondon family operated the office. I remember trying to call our grandma's house from our home with the code and having Marie Plamondon at Central telling us kids to "Get off that Telephone"! In 1954 while my husband was in the U.S. Army in Germany, I received a call from him. With several curious neighbors wanting to know what was being said, the transmission was so weak we couldn't talk. The overseas operator asked me if I could get to a private phone. I went into the Village and called back to Germany and the operator re-connected us. The transmission was much better. However, with the oceanic cable moving as it did under water, the words sometimes came across garbled, even then!

In my parent's time, before my birth, The Great Depression caused much hardship. Work was scarce. The W.P.A. and the C.C.C's conservation camp efforts did put some young men to work for a few dollars, which they would mostly send, home to the parents to support

Nancy's grandpa, Roy A. Howard in 1962

the homestead. Many foods, gas and tires for cars and tractors were rationed. Ration Books were issued to each family. With the stamps, one could buy the limit allowable per each member of the family. I remember that fruits were canned without sugar. Jams and jellies became almost nonexistent, except perhaps for occasional celebratory dinners!

Our family moved to Ypsilanti just before World War II. Dad worked for Mr. Henry Ford at his Auto Plant. When it was retooled for the War Effort, it became the Willow Run Bomber and my parents both became Airplane B-23 and B24 builders. As my grandpa was aging, he asked Dad to come back to the farm.

We moved home, Dad bought the Norman Gauthier house next to the Leelanau Trout Rearing Pond. He then worked the farm with my grandpa on shares for some time.

The M.&N.E. train ran daily across our land. My maternal grandparents the Ernest Wise's would board the train in Traverse City where they were living and the conductor would stop the train at our home and leave them off. That was a delight to my mother and to us kids. We would sit at grandma's knees listening by the hour to the stories she would share with us. We always wanted to know more about her life in what we considered the "long ago days"! We would picnic in the woods, hunt mushrooms in the springtime, go fishing in the pond, and make popcorn balls together. At the end of their visiting, they would stand on the railroad grade and wait for the train to stop on its run and pick them up and off again they would go as the train clacked its way down the French Road, back to Traverse City. We would wave at the conductor and he would sound the whistle with long toots, much to our delight!

Mothers and grandmothers, like pioneer women, were excellent seamstresses. They made clothing, and quilts. From flour sacks, they made dishtowels and baby diapers. One winter my mother made for us three girls each a new coat from older coats that my aunts had worn. She laundered them and turning them inside out, they made beautiful new garments! She trimmed them with colorful new wood flannel for front panels, cuffs, and collar trim. How we did love those coats!

While Dad (Arthur) was helping grandpa on the farm, my mom (Bernice) would be working in the dairy with Grandma Howard doing the bottle and equipment washing, the bottling of the milk, the separating of the cream and emptying the iceboxes twice a day. And I, then about 11 years old was responsible to watch my younger sisters and brother for a few hours every day. I would get my "work" done in the morning while I listened to the radio. I did love the soaps! Fibber Magee and Mollie, Young wider Brown were favorites. The soap ads, Ivory, 99and 99one hundredths pure, La France and Satina and Marvelous Vel. I can never forget them and the jingles that went with them. Lux radio theater was also a favorite. My dad on Sunday evenings would have us settle down for an hour with Amos and Andy and Mrs. Buffington and the Henry Aldritch Program.

Some water from the reservoir or on the laundry stove, which would be heating the dining room; would warm the clothes washing water, which would be done in the wringer washing machine. Two number 2 galvanized tubs would be filled with cold water for rinsing everything. Then the clothing would be hung on clothes lines in the yard. In winter months, it would hang frozen until mother would bring everything into the house to be hung around the dining room to finish drying. Then because everything was made of cotton, all garments would need to be sprinkled and await ironing. It would take several days of hard labor for mother to complete the week's laundry. She would heat the irons on asbestos pads over the kerosene burners of her kitchen stove.

And, it is true! The weekly Saturday night bath in the laundry tubs in the middle of the dining room floor was the usual! The youngest child went first, each followed until Mom and Dad had their turn. Polishing of the Sunday Shoes followed and getting the Church Clothes ready for the early morning Services ended the Saturday evening ritual!

A Farm Boy's Life
By W.T. Diemond of Alpena, Michigan
Born 1934

Our farm was located ten miles west of Alpena near the junction of Werth Road and King's Settlement Road. We worked around two hundred acres of land and usually had about fifty head of cattle and two dozen hogs.

In addition to a large flock of chickens, the farm housed a few goats, some rabbits, and even a flock of sheep for a short time.

I had two brothers and a sister, all younger than I, but I was mostly a loner when it came to play time. The main school of my youth was the Beyer School on the corner of Hubbard Lake Road and Marwede Road. It's still there but appears to be a dwelling now. It was a mile and three quarters from the front door of our house to the school house—up hill both ways, as they say nowadays, but a long cold (most of the time) walk capped off by the heat of late spring and late summer. I have very few good memories of this citadel of education, which usually contained around thirty-five students. I distinctly remember each and every one of the five teachers employed during the six and a half years I attended it. My favorite was Margie McCoy, mostly because she was tall and pretty and because she opened every day by reading a chapter of "The Adventures of Tom Sawyer." This imbedded the love of reading in me for life. They tell me she's still around somewhere and that was seventy some odd years ago. Bless her heart.

Upon conclusion of her reading, I disliked just about everything else. I inherited a temper from my mother's side of the family and I was constantly in trouble with the German-Russians that dwelled to the South of Wolf Creek and had only one friend—Richard, who was also a distant relative. His dad, Edgar, became our teacher (the fifth) and he used Richie and I as examples to the rest of the students—bad examples, that is. To this day, I do not understand how he could hold each of us by an ear and knee us both in the rear end at the same time. For quite a while, he'd put Richie in the cloak-room and stick me under his large desk. This went on until I took advantage of the situation to eat his lunch. It was the only time he gave me a ride home from school. I had to face the stern frowns of my parents' faces until 01' Edgar left, at which time I fully expected to be over their knees for a good spanking. They both broke into hysterical laughter instead. But I did get a good chewing out for it, which lost much of its effectiveness because of the giggles.

In the summertime, I operated the horses for raking hay, cultivating or just plain riding. My dad or one of the hired hands would harness ol' Queen and Lou and I would put them to work. We had anywhere from one to six hired hands during the work season, which was from Spring Thaw until about Thanksgiving. I don't remember much about some of them but I do recall Willie, Clubfoot Al, and OF Lyle. I remember The Old Man (my dad) firing one hand for mistreating the horses but the rest are just names that occasionally crop up in my memories, Tomato Face, Horrible Harry, and so forth.

One of my chores (all of which I detested) was cranking the Cream Separator. It was terribly difficult to get it up to speed so somebody else would get it started and then I took over until the milking was done. On Fridays, we would go into town and take the cream cans to Bedard's Creamery. We'd get a few cents, usually a nickel, or a dime, to splurge on pop (soda) or a handful of loose candy. Candy bars were too quickly disposed of and the ones we liked cost a dime, thus deemed beyond our means.

Occasionally we'd get to ride our bikes into town to go to the Lyric Theater to see the latest double-feature Westerns. My mother took me to my first "good" movie—"The Wizard of Oz" at the Maltz Theater (The Old Maltz Opera House).

After supper we'd usually hook ol' Queenie up to the buggy and ride down to Wolf Creek, which was a quarter of a mile past the Beyer School. It was here that I first learned to swim. I knocked Billy Timm on his kiester and Wilbur Timm, Norman Timm and Billy Timm threw me off the bridge. I usually got what was coming to me.

At the beginning of the school year, I got a new pair of bib-overalls, long-handled underwear and a new pair of sneakers. When the cold weather came on I also got a flannel shirt and a warm coat, complete with cap and mittens. My old clothes were given to Brother Bob and his were, in turn, given to Brother Bill. By the time they got to Bill, they were pretty well patched to keep his elbows, knees and rear end from hanging out.

We had an out-doors Burper (or Throne Room, as we like to call it) and it was located about fifty yards from the house. It had two holes on the upper level and one on the lower level for the kids. Needless to say, there were a lot of indications of closer emergency areas from whence came the saying, "Don't eat the Yellow Snow."

On Sundays, after Sunday school and Church, The Old Man would stop by Dege's Store and buy the Detroit Times. He'd build a nice, warm fire in the Living Room, then set down on the rug in front of it and read us the Comic Sections: "Maggie and Jigs" and "The Katzenjammer Kids" were the favorites. At that time, the only Radio Station available to listen to was WJR Detroit, which on Saturday nights we listened to "The Hermit's Cave," and "Inner-Sanctum Mysteries" and other Hair Raisers. Then we couldn't fall asleep until very late. On Sundays, it was "The New York Philharmonic Symphonic Orchestra" and we became very fond of Classical Music as a result. Upstairs was a crank-up Victrola and dozens of records, some of which I can still remember very distinctly: such as "The Fate of Floyd Collins," "The Mississippi Flood," "The Ohio Prison Fire" and many others.

Late in March, 1947, The Old Man came home and, instead of putting the 1937 Ford Panel Truck in the garage, he left it parked between the house and the barn. It took us ten days to find it again. During the night, the worse storm I can remember struck and the snow drifted off the roof of the barn and piled up all the way to the house. A twelve-foot snow-drift buried the entire yard for several weeks. The snow plows had to cut through our fields to get back to town and, finally, the county sent an outfit we'd never seen before called a Snow Blower to cut a track through the snow that was piled up from bank to bank on the roads. Needless to say, we had a ball— no school during that time and the only thing that I remember was hooking up our wonderful dog "Collie" to a sled and cutting across the fields to Dege's Store, about three miles away, for the few items we didn't grow on the farm. Sugar, Coffee and Salt with maybe a few other items thrown in to get us by until we could drive or run the horses again.

The following fall we were awakened to the sounds of violent coughing and found out that our mother had contracted Tuberculosis. That was a death sentence in those days and we listened to The Old Man and Ma discuss the options available to her. They talked about moving to Arizona, of going to faith healers and, finally, to having her committed to the Gaylord Sanatorium, where she remained for nearly two years. I remember sitting in the car while they checked her in, and wept myself sick. It is one of the worse days of my life and it would remain so for nearly a half a century until the death of my dad, The Old Man, then in 2002 when Ma died, then little brother Bill, then my wife and the latest one, sister Sal. It was necessary to sell the farm and move close to town when Ma was committed, and thus ended my youth.

With the death of my beloved wife, my life ended for all intents and purposes. Now the only reasons for my existence are my two fine children who are no longer children but, really, the only two really good things I ever accomplished, with the help of God.

John's mother, Gertie with his older brother

The Homestead
By John A. Elzinga of Charlevoix, Michigan
Born 1932

Just a country boy story of my early life on the old homestead farm in the little town of Atwood, Michigan. Our home in Atwood was a hand hewn log house, which in later years had siding put over the logs. I came into this world right there in that house. After many years of living there on that old homestead farm, you can sure bet we had many great experiences.

The farmhouse was built in about 1860. It was a two story with four bedrooms, built on land that was mostly woods, purchased from the U. S. Railroad Company. In 1998, the farm became a Centennial Farm, after 3 generations in the same family.

The log house was torn down about 45 years ago after the State of Michigan bought the house to widen U. S. Highway 31. We purchased the house back from the State for $ 1.00, with the agreement to have it all removed from the site. We then took everything out of it that we could salvage. We were thinking of bulldozing it in, or even burning it down. A man came along and said he would tear it down for us if he could have all the lumber that was left in it. We thought that was a terrific idea, so we made that deal with him immediately. After two days of him tearing the siding off and exposing the hand-hewn logs, a man from the Traverse City Woolen Company stopped and said he would like to buy the logs. The T. C. man ended up buying

the logs for $ 2,000.00 from the first man we had "given" it to! That was a lot of money in those days, but he just put it in his pocket and walked away smiling! We only received a big "Thank You"! We then built our new home 100 feet behind the old house.

The Depression years on the farm were tough. My father was born in the United States. My mother came to the United States from the Netherlands, at age 11, with 9 other brothers and sisters. There was no money in those days, but we all learned to live happy and enjoyed our early farm life. I had 3 brothers and 2 sisters, so there was always lots of noise and excitement.

I still remember the days when my younger brother and I had a bedroom upstairs, with no heat (at all!) so in the winter, it was very cold and "drafty," snow would seep thru the windows. In order to stay warm, we would heat a blanket on the old wood stove down stairs, then hurry up and crawl into bed with that nice warm blanket. We had no inside plumbing, just a little 6x6 back house building, which had lots of stories to talk about in later years. My 2 sisters were petrified to go there after dark by themselves, so it would be a hurry up "line up."

Walking to our one room school, about 3/4 mile every morning and night, was something I did thru 8th grade. I can still remember the times we would walk half way, and then turn around. We would tell our parents there was no school that day because the teacher was sick! Then we could play at home all day! I did start school when I was 4 years old. My sister was the teacher, and pretty tough at times!

As soon as we were old enough, we had to help on the farm. I remember milking cows, by hand, when I was just a teenager. Yes, also memories of Pat and Rock, the last team of horses that did all our farm work, before our first John Deere tractor. They are the ones that turned me against horses! Our job as teenagers was to drive those horses, pulling an old steel wheel wagon, with our first hay loader behind. The horses would either be going too fast or come to a complete stop, making us have to hang on for dear life.

Lucky, our farm collie was the best and smartest dog you could have on a farm. He would help us bring the cows home every night from way over the hill and down the long lane back to the big red barn.

The first barn my father had, burned to the ground the day the threshing machine was filling the barn with fresh oat straw. The threshing machine was run by a steam-boiler

John's dad, Albert with all of his farm horses

tractor, which took wood and coal to heat the water to make steam to run the machine. My father told us the story of one little spark coming out the stack and landing in the straw - starting the fire. No one could do anything. There were no telephones to use, and no fire departments to call. The threshing crew just stood there helpless, watching the barn burn to the ground. Another barn was built and used for a few years, and then they built the last big barn. It was a huge barn. The basement walls were built with stone that my father hauled one whole winter from off the farm. The walls were a good two feet thick with all cut stone on the outside.

It took over two years and many, many

hours to finally complete in 1915. The beams were all hand hewn logs put together with wooden pegs. The peak of the barn was nearly 60 feet high making the haymow big enough to hold enough loose hay to feed 30 - 40 head of cattle and 4 horses all winter long. I remember my older brother telling about the winter the well quit. It took all winter to drill a new well. He hauled water in big barrels all winter with horses and a sled. The water was taken out of the creek nearly 2 miles away. That was more of the "Good Ole' Days"! The barn blew down after a 80-mile windstorm on Maunday Thursday in 1979. The storm blew in from the east with tornado like winds. This was very unusual because most of our storms came from the northwest. On that early morning, we were standing in the kitchen window and saw the east side being blown in. Only a few seconds later, the wind lifted the whole roof off and carried it 100 feet west into the field. Some farm machinery was stored upstairs, and when the big beams started coming down, nothing was even scratched! Hard to believe, but true!

A blind date, with a small town girl, changed my life over 55 years ago. We were married in 1957, and blessed with 2 Lovely daughters and 1 Delightful granddaughter.

All those "Good Ole' Days" certainly still do hold lots of good memories! From trying to farm with a team of horses, and lots of old farm equipment, to finally owning a John Deere Diesel Tractor with over 100-horse power.

From milking over 20 cows by hand, with my younger brother, while still attending Ellsworth High School, to planting the 200 acre Centennial Farm into over 2,000 tart cherry trees, 500 sweet cherry trees, 30 acres of apples, plus pears, peaches, plums and apricots.

From selling our first apple crop on a table in the front yard (self-serve), while my wife and I picked our first apple crops, to now a modern Farm Market with a bakery, lunch room and gift shop.

From pressing 15 to 20 gallons of fresh cider, with a little hand press, after a hard day's work, and selling it on our self-serve table, to now where the new owner can press 1,000 gallons of cider in a day's time.

From starting out in a tent in 1950 for my first deer camp, with 7 other guys from the Atwood area, to buying an old log cabin, about 10 miles east of Grand Marais in the U. P., to this year—the 62nd year I have gone to "Camp Atwood" to hunt deer. What memories!

From playing the piano at age 14, in our little country Church, to now being a Church organist for over 65 years, and still going strong.

And, now, as I am retired, with old age creeping up on me fast, I can still take time to remember those "Good Ole Days"! The days we spent at our own swimming hole, a big old dirty pond of water over the hill, on the farm. The days we would sneak in to the East Jordan County Fair, saving our money for the rides. Those were certainly the "good ole days"!

Did She Really Know a Horse from a Cow!
By R. Michael Shaft of Williamston, Michigan

I was about ten when Melody galloped onto the farm. I rode her a little bit that first summer. She wasn't ridden that winter, and it was late spring before anyone rode her again. Dad realized that Melody was a bit too frisky for my younger brother Roy and me to ride. One Saturday afternoon while we waited at the edge of a freshly plowed field Dad took a break from plowing and drove the tractor up the lane to the barn. There he saddled up Melody, mounted up into the saddle and rode our spirited mare back down the lane into the newly plowed field. Walking on newly plowed soil is not unlike walking on the sandy beaches of Lake Michigan. Running is even more strenuous. When Dad urged Melody into a gallop in that field, she was rearing to go. Before long, her legs felt the strain

of running on plowed turf. She lathered up mightily before she had had enough of a run. Her vigorous gallop had become subdued to a trot. Dad cooled her slowly in her walk back to the barn. We began riding her daily and she became a good horse for us kids to ride.

By summertime after school let out, if we weren't splashing in the swimming hole next to the river's bridge, Roy and I took turns riding our horse Melody all over the farm. I coaxed her into the river and though she didn't relish it she did walk down the stream, stopping occasionally for a drink. In the woods, I taught her to jump over logs. When it came time for milking, I took her back to the fields where the cows were grazing and rounded them up and led them back up the lane to the barn for milking.

I associate pleasurable pain in two special memories. The former involves a classmate of mine, Bill Philo, age eleven and who lived on a small farm next to the Looking Glass River southwest of our farm. Bill came over one day and we decided to ride our horses west from our farm along the Looking Glass River over to his place, rather than ride west on gravel roads. Unknown places fancied our imaginations; we sought adventure across the farm on trails less traveled. It was a bright sunny day as we rode down the lane, beside the river and into the woods. The warm breeze carried the shrill trill of red-winged blackbirds singing atop fence posts and cattails. Occasional moos of cows drifted across nearby fields. We entered the woods and continued along the river to the far end of our farm. Here the woods were filled with a jungle of prickly brush and vines. Part of the time, we had to step out of the saddle and walk ahead of our horses. As usual, Melody needed a lot of coaxing to walk our horses downstream. She was okay once she felt the gravely bottom. Doubting that we could weave through the entanglements in the untried river we at last reached Warner Road. The scratches, scrapes, and thorny pokes of brush into our flesh mesh the memory of our great adventure. It was just one of those awesome days that had to do be done at least once! We determined finally that riding on lanes through the woods and along fields were less bitter acorns to chew.

Melody always sensed that we were heading back to the barn to be unsaddled and fetch some grain. All I had to do was head

R. Michael's dad instructing him on riding Melody as his brother, Roy watches along with Curley the dog

her in that direction and let up on the reins. In full gallop, she sped up the lane across the barnyard then slammed to a four-legged stop right in front of the gate. Her promptness to gallop full steam at any given signal up the lane leads me to the second illustration that harbors my mind about the thrills of riding a horse full speed across the farm. It shows even more how companionship with like species is mighty important to a horse too. Melody I found out, does understand she is more a horse than a cow. That is to say that when she did see another piece of horseflesh, she knew what it was! Most times in the summer, I rode back to the pasture to round up the cows for milking. Along with the saddle, on this particular day for a bridle I substituted a rope halter for my ride. Earlier that day I had removed her bridle and hung it on a tree branch and didn't think it that necessary to retrieve it to control my horse. I always say we are not supposed to think, we are supposed to know; little did I know what was in store that day!

It was on this particular sunny afternoon I took my routine ride back to an alfalfa field to round up the cows for milking. At the end of the lane that runs from the sheep barn south to the first bend is a fork in the lane. The main fork angled right down to the bridge over the Looking Glass River then into fields on the southwest side of the farm. The other fork turned abruptly and went up hill right next to a fence where the upper strand of barbed wire

runs along it. At the side of the lane opposite the fence lane, the hill slopes steeply down parallel to the river. Continuing down the hill the fence stops to turn back north and the field opens up on either side of the lane and veers down near the river's bend where white sandy ground with thin green grasses lay before going straight on away from the river through a gate and into the alfalfa field.

By now, Melody was easy to ride and reined effortlessly with rope and halter to each command to trot, or canter. I had circled around the herd and started them back out of the field. Heading up the lane back to the barn, the cows were lured to the barn by the taste of ground up grain flavored with a dash of salt scooped into their mangers. These thoughts no doubt kept the cows moving steadily along. I was in no real hurry myself to get the cows back to the barn. I dismounted from the saddle and with the rope and halter walked along beside Melody for a spell. Just as I started to remount calm clarity blurred into a calamity of whirlwind dust!

Far on top of the hill of the lane, there came into view a four-legged creature with a school friend by the name of Larry Beers riding his horse, Babe. Melody's ears shot forward. Her nostril flared to a snort. Larry called to me, "Hey Mike!" That did it! With my foot in the stirrup I had started to swing my right leg over the saddle, Melody lurched forward in full gallop. I pulled on the rope and I yelled whoa for her to stop but she wouldn't yield to my command. There was a greater calling up at the top of the lane - the draw of a similar kind of creature such as her lonesome self-surpassed any pull on the rope of a halter could command. Running full speed up the lane, I had one hand on the pommel; my stomach thumped on the saddle and the other hand on the back of the saddle. I hung on for dear life and as she reached the narrow lane, I continued to hang on for dear life with my stomach bouncing along on the saddle in full flight. My rear-end neared closer and closer to the barbed wire atop the fence; visions flashed of my pants and flesh ripped by the barbs. Oh what potential pain!

Well, I only remember unsaddling Melody in the barn. Then my next recollection is walking up the hill from the barn into the house and lying down on the davenport. I felt weak and sickly. Later I asked Larry what happened. Larry informed me that I had fallen off head first from Melody to the ground. Melody continued running to the top of the hill towards him and introduced herself to his horse, Babe. I had groggily raised myself up off from the ground, walked up the lane to Melody, climbed back into the saddle and rode her back to the barn. Of these events, I remember nothing.

Would such adventures ever measured up to the journal written by Gene Autry with his horse, Champion, or Roy Rogers with his horse Trigger, or Hopalong Cassidy with his horse, Topper, or even Straight Arrow with his horse, Fury? No.! But in some ways, bloodshed from bullets and dynamite in the old west does prove to be more dangerous for cowboys and Indians. The absence of the searing pain of a bullet from a six-shooter zinging lead seems quite kind.

However, the real lesson, which could have averted the mishap, concerns the bridle. If I had taken the time to go back and retrieve the bridle to rein in Melody instead of using the rope and halter I might have averted the mishap. The GPS—global positioning saddle ride on my stomach instead of my seat will long be remembered.

Just as Joshua said to the Israelites in Chapter 18: 3—"How long will you wait before you begin to take possession of the land that the Lord God of your fathers, has given you?" I say, how long next time shall I procrastinate before returning to the tree to grab the bridle and reins and properly equip my horse for riding? I think my GPS: Global Procrastination System is one to be removed from horsemanship skills 101.

I taught in Indian River 1968-1972 and ran the Straitsland Resorter weekly newspaper 1970-1971. This story took place in Shaftsburg, Michigan in the early 1950s.

Too Young to Enlist

By Joseph D. Variot of Mancelona, Michigan
Born 1927

My father was a supervisor at the main post office in Detroit MI. It was nearing Christmas and he could not get the help required to move the mail and requested that I return to Detroit. This was my first time to lie about my age. In so doing, I had earned enough money to pay for my bus fare home, and buy some new clothes. I also gave my mother some money to help with the bills. In the summer of 1942, I returned to Detroit again lying about my age. I took a job catering food to war factories that were just starting up. I was die ripe old age of 14, driving a truck to several different factories and selling lunches to the workers. I got the bright idea to join the Navy. I told my father of my intentions, changed my birth certificate and talked to the recruiting officer who took no more than a minute to tell me I was caught. A few months later, I ran across my older brother's birth certificate. I told my father I was going to try again to join the Navy, using my brother's birth certificate. Everything seemed to work. I was accepted.

I reported to Fort Wayne, Michigan where I was to board a train for Great Lakes Naval Training Center. When a Chief Warrant Officer called my name (my brother's name), he asked me a few questions, what is your mother's and father's name and address, what is your birth date, where do you five, etc. He then told me that the person I was pretending to be was already in the Navy. He also told me that if he ever saw me again he would put a boot so far up my rear that it would never be found.

It took me some time to try to figure what happened. When one day, I went looking for my father. I was told that he was across the street at the Federal Bar. When I approached him, he was talking and drinking with a couple of Navy Recruiting Officers. Things started to come together. I believe my father blew the whole thing about my enlistment In October 1943 a buddy of mine, Bill Myatt and me were talking to a couple of our friends who were soon to be 18 years of age and did not care to be called to serve in the military. We got the bright idea to use their identification and enlist in the Navy. We followed through with this plan and it worked. We asked if we could stay together and it was approved but we would have to wait until our buddies identification showed that they had reached 18 years of age. Two months later, we were sworn in, and soon were on our way to Farragut, Idaho Naval Training Center. This time no one knew I had joined the Navy.

After recruit training, we were sent to Bremerton, Washington. Upon our arrival my buddy was assigned to the Battleship

Joseph D. Variot

USS Massachusetts and I was assigned to the Battleship USS West Virginia which had been sunk at Pearl Harbor with 7 torpedoes and 2 bombs. She had been raised and temporarily repaired. We put the ship back in shape with new super structure, radar, and new guns of all calibers except our 16-inch main battery, which was kept completely repaired; we were put back to sea July 4, 1944 for shakedown and gunnery training. We received orders to get underway to Manus Island in the Pacific By the time we arrived the operation was completed. Our next assignment was Leyte Island in the Philippines. We were to bombard enemy positions and clear the bay for landing troops to begin the invasion of the Philippine Islands. The Japanese had other plans. They were determined to hold onto the Philippines at any cost The Japanese put together the mightiest fleet they had ever assembled to stop the invasion, and also put into effect a new operation using aircraft on suicide mission to dive into our ships while loaded with bombs and gasoline. Jap pilots readily volunteered for the operation called Kamikaze. We witnessed several suicide planes hitting our ships. This lasted a few days when we received word that the Japanese were sending several fleets from different directions to halt the bombardment and the landing of allied troops. The bombardment group to which we were assigned consisted of old battleships and several cruisers and destroyers. All were rushed to intercept the fleet approaching from the south, through Surigao Staits. We waited in line in hopes the Jap fleet would fall into a classic naval maneuver of crossing the "T." Most of our armor piercing ammunition had been dispersed during the previous bombardment Still we waited in hopes we would have the upper hand in our surprise attach and maneuvering of Surigao Straits. Our ship was credited with the sinking of the Japanese battleship I.J.N. Yamashiro and assisting in the destruction of several other ships. We were recommended for the Presidential Unit Citation. Later we were sent to the New Hebridies Islands where a floating dry-dock was in wait for us as repairs had become urgent I had been boxing since I was 14 years old and had joined in with a few others in exhibition boxing. I had three bouts in the short time we were in dry-dock and lost two, and won one

We were sent to Mindoro Islands for preliminary bombardment for the landing of troops to take over the Japanese held airfields. During the operation, we witnessed the sinking of the aircraft carrier, USS Ominey Bay and a destroyer. We took on survivors and within forty-eight hours buried 60 men, some of them at sea. There were a few other vessels destroyed by suicide bombers that same day, adding more survivors. After securing the island, we were sent to Lingayen Gulf to clear out any opposition in preparation for the landings on Luzon and the recapture of the city of Manila. We destroyed many gun batteries and encampments. We also sank a tanker and several smaller vessels. After securing several landing positions on Luzon, we were sent to Ulitha Islands for repairs and replenishment We were there very briefly when we received orders to get under way for the Island of Iwo Jima where we stayed until the campaign was complete We were sent a message from Admiral Nimitz for a well done job and to return to Ulitha to finish repairs. While there, the battleship Pennsylvania was torpedoed some one-hundred yards from our anchorage. The Kamikaze pilots were more plentiful at each new campaign and captured islands and mooring sites.

After replenishing and repairs, we received orders to get underway to the island of Okinawa. We had several days of bombardment before the landings began. On April 1, 1945. Our luck had run out We caught a Japanese dive-bomber loaded with a heavy bomb and a great deal of aviation fuel on the after port side of the ship. It crashed into a quad 40mm tub, killing several and wounding many more crewmembers. We stayed on site repairing our ship with whatever was on hand. This was the longest campaign we had encountered. It lasted from the end of March through August. It seemed that every day we would lose a ship to the kamikaze pilots. The Navy suffered more losses at Okinawa than any other campaign. Toward the end of this struggle, we were ordered to get underway to meet the mighty battleship Yamato that the Japanese had sent out on a final suicide mission. Before we got there, our aircraft had sunk her. While we were in Okinawa the Japanese had agreed to surrender. Our orders were to get underway to Tokyo Bay. When we arrived, word was received that 500 volunteers were need to go ashore I believe the reason was to test the population's response to the surrender. I was in one of the parties. We were told no weapons would be allowed and to visit every major building. I went into a library, a museum, and a couple of other government buildings. When we approached military personnel, they would lay down their arms and bow. It was kind of scary at first, but we were accepted. A few days later the surrender terms were signed aboard the battleship, USS Missouri.

After the battle of Surigao Straits, I realized that the shoe could have been on the other foot with the Japanese winning the battle. I thought had I been killed my friends (whose identification) I was using would have been notified of his death and my folks would have no knowledge of my passing. I approached the Chaplain of the ship and told him I had something to confess, but he must promise not to leak it out if it didn't fly. He said I do not know if I can fill your request, but he would try to help if he could. I told him of my concern, my insurance and etc. would go to the people I didn't even know. I also told him I above all, wanted-to stay in the Navy and remain aboard ship. He then proceeded to tell me that I had committed a General Court Martial Offense, by enlisting in the Navy under false pretenses during wartime He also told me

he would see what he could do. A few weeks later he called me to his office and informed me I could stay in the Navy, that I was now 17 years of age, my parents had consented to my staying in. I was told that until my records were completely straight, I would have to get by with a substance allowance of $6.00 per month. That lasted for five months. By then I was smoking heavily but only shaving once or twice a week. Cigarettes were five cents a pack, razor blades about fifteen cents a pack. I really didn't need any more in the way of money as we were still at sea for another year. I felt blessed, it was official Now, I am myself and still in the Navy. I had a total of eight years, nine months of active duty and about two years of reserve duty. To this day, I wish I would have stayed in the Navy for twenty or thirty years. There were many of us, who later regretted taking a discharge

After my discharge, I took an apprenticeship program as a sheet metal worker under the GI Bill The company that I worked for was contracted by General Motors. General Motor employees decided to go on strike It was the longest strike in the history of TJ. S. bargaining as I recall In any case, I had to find a new profession. I reenlisted in the Navy. I remained doing so through the Korean conflict I served on several destroyers, first mothballing WWII ships then replacing some back to the fleet for service in Korea. Later I served at a Naval Air Station until I was discharged in June 1954. I later went into business. I semi-retired in 1980, and moved from the Detroit area to our present location in Northern Michigan. I had five children and three stepchildren. My wife Margot and I live alone in a house much too big for two people We have many friends and love to have company. If you are ever up this was give us a call We would enjoy seeing and visiting with you.

The Railcar Roller Coaster
By Brian Davis of Oscoda, Michigan
Born 1950

It must have been about 1955 when my dad took our family to camp at the rollaways overlooking the Au Sable River. We had an old surplus WWII canvas Army tent that took at least two people to put up. We would rent a boat to go fishing. In order to get the boat down the 300-foot hill to the river below, they had a homemade railcar, which ran on railroad tracks and was lowered down and pulled back up by a cable on a pulley run by a gas motor. The front wheels were on eight-foot pipes while the back wheels were on one-foot pipes. This kept the car level and we would ride up and down with the boat. It was just as fun and scary as a roller coaster. The tracks and everything were all removed around 1960. I would always imagine what would happen if the cable broke.

✓ Silver Valley Queen Contest

By Elvira LePard of National City, Michigan
Born 1951

A few miles outside of East Tawas was the greatest place to spend winter weekends: Silver Valley. My father volunteered there during the late fifties and worked the toboggan hill. They had two railed lanes with extra-long toboggans that people stood in long lines just to experience the thrill.

There was a great hill for skiing with a lift, a wonderful hill for sledding, ponds for skating, and horse-drawn sleigh rides. Also available was a log cabin with a concession stand and a cozy blazing fire that was always buzzing with laughter.

One day my family and some friends of ours were having a picnic. Burgers and dogs over coals on the grill, snow gently falling, you know, the usual, when Mort Neff of Michigan Outdoors came and asked if he could film us and put us on his program. Oh my gosh we were going to be on TV! What I wouldn't give to be able to see that again!

Every year there was a Silver Valley Queen contest held. The contestant who sold the most tickets to the Silver Valley Ball was crowned that year's Queen. That year my father entered my mother because to him she was the most beautiful woman and he just wanted to show her off. Plus he just plain liked to have fun! Mom on the other hand wasn't amused. She never felt special, but at 30 years old and the mother of 2 girls aged 2 ½ and 8, she said if any tickets would be sold he'd do the sellin'. Dad enjoyed that entire time!

In 2002 Mom and I visited the Iosco County Museum in East Tawas, a wonderful place. We looked through the news clippings of all of the Silver Valley Queen contests… all but the 22nd Silver Valley Carnival that she was in.

Mom passed in 2008 and while my sister and I were gathering photos there it was, perhaps the one and only photo left of the occasion. Soon it will take its rightful place at the museum.

There's no finer place to live than "On the Sunrise Side."

In loving memory of Fred and Hildegard LePard.

✓ Memorable Foods

By Robert Merchant of Traverse City,
Michigan

Home was 3 bedrooms and a ½ bath (no tub or shower). Baths were taken in laundry tubs in front of the kitchen stove. We also had a coal stove in the living room, which later was oil and then gas. Home was located across the street from what is now "F & M" (Florida and Michigan) Park.

Hope Street was our playground. It was paved with gravel and had little or no traffic. In the summer, we played baseball and in the winter, it made a cute ice rink. We lived just a block away from Sunset Park where as a family we would swim and have a picnic or go fishing in the back of the Cherry Growers Plant. Now the Maritime Academy is there.

Saturday mornings were spent cleaning the bedroom I shared with my 2 brothers. After cleaning, we would get our 15-cent allowance and go to the movies downtown at the Tra-Bay for a double feature. It was usually two Western movies with Gene Autry and Roy Rogers, etc., and often the main movie there was cartoons, plus a news reel showing worldly events, mostly on the Korean War and the Cold War.

Saturday afternoons sometimes, I went shopping for groceries with my mother at the A&P store. There were plenty of local neighborhood stores then: Jack's Food, Roman's Food Store, Merchants Market, and Vets. If you went shopping for clothing and shoes, the place to go was Perry's or Montgomery Ward's.

Thanksgiving, Christmas, and Easter were family gatherings. On Thanksgiving, we ate turkey, cranberries, stuffing, mashed potatoes and gravy, and homemade pumpkin pie. On Christmas we ate turkey (and with luck venison steak) mashed potatoes, hubert squash, and homemade pies. Easter we ate good old ham with mashed potatoes, sweet potatoes, home canned beans, and for desert yellow cake with white coconut frosting. Of course, all meals were served with homemade bread and Mother's favorite strawberry jam. The ham bone and turkey skeleton were saved for pea soup a couple days later.

On Friday nights, we would eat popcorn, fudge with walnuts, and have a cold drink made from orange or grape syrup from the Watkins door-to-door salesman. We would sit around the radio listening to shows like the Shadow, Jack Benny, Sky King, and others as we read comic books and the *Life* and *Look* magazines.

We went to school at Boardman Grade School, which was 3 blocks away. We got up at 6:30 to have breakfast, make a lunch, and head out the door rain or shine. We would eat a bowl of Kellogg's Cornflakes and drink a glass of orange juice and take a vitamin pill.

My (Not) First Day of School
By Morley Kellogg of Presque Isle,
Michigan
Born 1928

In the fall, before I was five years old my family elected not to start me in school, I guess because it was a one-mile walk to the country school. Sometime in the mid to late September, a little neighbor girl around my age was also not attending school, probably for the same reason, we decided that we wanted to go to school. Together we started down the road toward the school. We hadn't gone far when looking back my friend's mother was following us. The roadside had tall growth of vegetation, mostly sweet clovers to a height of probably four feet. Knowing that she would be unable to locate us, we ducked into this cover. However, she walked right up to us and pulled us out. I don't know what punishment my friend suffered however in my case; I was led back to my house. My mother was about eight months pregnant with my brother and she was doing ironing. She got a long rope 10 or 12 feet long. Tying one end around my waist and the other to a post on the porch. In time, I begged for a drink of water, hoping she would turn me loose. She responded by untying the rope from the porch post and led me to the kitchen for a drink of water, then back to the porch, securing the rope to the post. This ended my adventure of what turned out not to be my first day of school.

The Wagon on the Roof
By Mary Lyon of Traverse City, Michigan
Born 1933

Snow plowing in the late 30s on the side roads was very difficult. The plows had a huge blade that would cut the packed snow from the banks. Some of the snow banks were taller than cars. People would place a red cloth on the cars antenna so they could be seen nearing intersections. We would walk the banks to get to school when roads were not plowed. Our family of 16 children would enjoy the long winter months with snow forts and ice-skating rinks.

During World War II, my brother Alfred was in the Navy. Often he would send candy bars home to his brothers and sisters. We were not able to purchase candy due to sugar rationing. Each family was allowed a book of stamps to be used for sugar, meat, and gas, which were all rationed to be used for family needs. The rationing lasted until the war ended.

My dad, Frank Clous farmed 80 acres at Hannah, near Kingsley. Our main cash crop was potatoes. Every year during the October harvest, the local schools would close for two weeks to allow the students to help in the potato harvest. Picking up potatoes was back breaking work. My grandfather used to run a produce farm. His wife Frederika Clous used to drive a horse and wagon into Traverse City with fresh eggs and produce. One day she was crossing the 6th Street and was struck by a car and died. Frederika was the first woman to be killed by a car in Traverse City. She was hit and killed in 1918.

The Clous Family in 1955

My favorite teacher was Sr. Patrice, a Dominican nun who was a true nature lover. She used to take the class to the local swamp to hunt for rare birds. By the time school year ended, we knew the names of all the birds, color of their eggs, and their habits. We used to collect bird cards, which at that time were given by Arm & Hammer baking soda. I would like to hear if anyone still has any of the colorful keepsakes.

The local boys would tip over the outhouses on Halloween as a prank. One time they took the wheels off of a wagon, put it on a shed roof, and put the wheels back on. The next morning the farmer, who lived near Kingsley, was very upset to find the wagon the roof.

Doing the Wash in Winter
By Harriet Ellwein of Oscoda, Michigan
Born 1934

Growing up in the small village of Grand Marais on Lake Superior was a challenge for our family. The winters were bitterly cold and the ground covered with lots of snow. Winter washdays were a chore for my mother. First, the Maytag washer was moved in place next to the kitchen sink. Then it was filled with hot water. Next came the most important part. The Fels Naptha soap would be shaved just so and then added to the hot water. After the clothes were put in and swished around for a while came the dangerous part! Women had to be extra careful when putting the clothes through the wringer. We all knew of women that had caught a finger, hand, arm, or worse yet their breast in a wringer. After the clothes

were rinsed and went through the wringer one more time they were hung on the outdoor clothesline to dry. What a sight it was to see Dad's long johns frozen solid on the line! The best part of washday was the smell of the clothes thawing out next to the stove in the house.

A Walk Through the Woods
By Ruth Moyer of Buckley, Michigan
Born 1916

This evening I went for a walk along the road that winds back over our farm. Each time there are interesting things to see and hear and smell. As I followed the road through the cornfields that are already knee high, some killdeer flew up, startled, crying killdeer, deer, deer, deer trying to lure e away from their hidden nest, with the broken wing ruse, that they always use. I walked on, leaving the killdeer to return to the duty of caring for her eggs in the nest. The feathery heads of the brome grass is beautiful and the clover has such a sweet odor, rain and sunshine has hastened the growth and many fields have already been cut and stored in the barn for next winter's food for the farm animals.

The beauty of the woods is almost breathtaking. Maple, elm, beech, and ironwood blended together in their majesty. The new trees growing make the woods appear almost impenetrable. I could walk within a few feet of some woods animals and they would feel safe from my intrusion into their domain in the thick tangle of brush.

The blackberries are all in blossom! In a few short weeks, the berries will be hanging luscious sand juicy. If I can get to them before the birds find them, they will make some delicious pies. I reminisce of other years while picking berries and I am assured that God has provided enough for both the birds and me. A feeding partridge flew up from a few feet away, we were both started, he because I had wandered too close to his feeding spot and I because his swiftly beating wings carrying him to safety was like sudden thunder so close. I stopped to pick a few honeysuckle blossoms, bringing the wood back to someone at home who loves the woods, but is unable to get out and walk in them.

The woods road goes on over a hill, there

might be a deer, but no, they are all safe under cover of the heavy foliage. Here is the wheat field. It has already headed out, by the time I come this way again the heads will be starting to turn gold, promising a bountiful harvest. The road takes me thought he neighbors woods on the other side of the farm. The trees form a canopy with now and then a chance to see the sun shining through. The white violets have grown so tall in the rich damp soil.

As I emerge from the woods, I am treated to a gorgeous sunset, a deer bounds gracefully away, his white tail flying high behind him. I am almost home. A pair of bob-o-links is perched on a swaying grass stem. As I walk past, the male bird bursts into the sky with his song bob-o-link, bob-o-link, spink, spank, spink, and his mate answers from far below, chee, chee, chee, these lines spring into my thoughts from poetry I learned as a child. I reach home refreshed and renewed renewed in the promise that God gives us for a pleasant tomorrow.

Generations of Sewing
By Betty J. Marks of LeRoy, Michigan
Born 1926

It all started in a one-room schoolhouse, first grade through eighth grade, in Ashton, Michigan. Our teacher was Mrs. Esther Sprague and our 4-H leader was Mrs. Mildred Schachtele. Together they taught us to cook and sew. To this day, I still make the chocolate pudding recipe I was taught in 1938. I don't remember all I sewed, but I did sew a dishtowel and an apron. Then in high school, I continued with home economics class and more sewing. I always thought I ripped out more than I sewed. I believe during high school I did make a skirt, but don't remember what else.

After marriage in 1946, I had my own treadle sewing machine, which I used for mending and sewing clothes for my children. In later years, I did get an electric machine.

Over the years, I made my youngest son, Steve, two leisure suits with an extra jacket. I had a hard time putting the pockets in right.

In 1976, my youngest daughter, Pat, was married. I made her wedding dress, two flower girl dresses, and my own dress.

Betty with her daughter, Pat the bride in 1976

They all needed to be completed at least two months ahead of time, because of a planned trip to Germany to visit my son Bob in the military. The two-week trip would get us back to LeRoy the Wednesday before the wedding.

Later years, my granddaughter Sarah and grandson John were active in 4-H. During those years, I made an English Saddle Seat suit that included two pairs of pants, vest, and jacket. Sarah used these when showing Tennessee Walking horses for her school Equestrian team and 4-H. The suit has been passed on to other 4-H kids. I made Western shirts for John, with one that looked like an American Flag being a big hit. I also sewed a pilgrim outfit for my granddaughter MaryAnn, for a grade school party/play, and a wedding dress for granddaughter, Erica. The majority of the time, I would make the article out of old sheets, before completing the REAL thing. Many times the grandchildren would make funny comments about the sheets used, such as, flowered Western shirts or polka dotted wedding dresses.

As great-grandchildren were starting to arrive, I decided to sew a quilt for each grandchild. I chose a theme that fit each grandchild's life: soccer balls, horses, etc. I explained to each grandchild that I was making one quilt for each of them, for their firstborn, and the quilt was to be used for each of their children.

This past month, (April 2013) a granddaughter, Monica, decided she would like to learn to sew. I had taught her mother Pat years ago. (Even back then, we had many long days of ripping out, crying, and laughing). Great times together. Monica and I were together for 7 - 8 hours sewing patches on jeans, cutting off slacks to make shorts, and taking up straps on tank tops and dresses. It was a good day for both of us.

So I guess you could say that what I learned in grade school and high school in the 1930s has carried on for two more generations.

The Police Go After the Guy Who Continues to Race
By James Chereskin of Traverse City, Michigan
Born 1943

I was born in Iron Mountain, Michigan in 1932. At the age of eight we moved to Chicago and then to Brookfield, Illinois, a suburb of Chicago. While growing up my family would always go back to Iron Mountain to visit family and friends. I had a cousin, Bill, who was my age and we would go off and do crazy things.

Now my story begins the summer my dad drove his 1959, stick shift, Ford Galaxy 500, two door hardtop, 300 hp, dual exhaust, tachometer on the steering wheel, white, new car to visit the gang in Iron Mountain, Michigan. While hanging out with Cousin Bill, he said, "Can you get your dad's car and we will go cruising the main drag." I was so surprised when my dad said okay, but told me to be very very careful. "Ya dad, I will." So now, we take off in this shiny white Ford, looking very tuff with the fender skirts and tach. Well as fate would have it, while cruising the strip, some of my cousin's friends thought they had a very fast car and wanted to race

the kid from Chicago. Well, I couldn't say no, I had to defend my Chicago gang. So my cousin suggested where to go, north two miles out of town, where the highway was divided, two lanes, grass, and two lanes. At 11:00 at night, we went out, against a 1956 Mercury Coupe. We raced from a rolling start at 10 miles an hour to 100. Now, all looked clear and off we went the Ford with my cousin and the Merc with his one passenger, for weight control. After going through all three gears and beating him to 100, and seeing red lights flashing behind me; since we raced right past the Michigan State Police, which my cousin had not told me, I backed off, but the Merc kept on going fast and faster, maybe 110-115 mph. I was desperately trying to get off the highway to hide. Sure enough, the police always go after the guy who continues to race.

To make a long story short, they got the Merc and brought the boys into the station. Meanwhile, my cousin and I hid in the back woods until about 3:00 a.m. thinking is it safe to go home now? I was never so cared. Will the boys in the Merc tell the police about my cousin and me? What will my dad and mom say? Nothing ever happened to me. The driver of the Merc got a big fine and lost his license. It was 20 years after that I finally told the story to my mom and dad, thinking it was safe after all that time, and it was. Things could have gone so differently.

I now live in Traverse City, Michigan where no one races on the street anymore. Back then it was cars and how fast. When we were negotiating a race, one would say to the other, "So, how's it running?" and his reply would be, "Healthy" or "It does keep up with traffic."

Schools, Baths, and Theaters
By Nancy Gould of Millersburg, Michigan
Born 1932

At age 6 I started 1st grade in a one-room school for grades 1-8. I don't remember a kindergarten. I do remember we all drank from one dipper and one pail of water. Whooping cough was prevalent that winter and I got it. Mothers took turns in the winter bringing hot meals, especially soups, to school. Food was kept warm on the side of a large wood-burning stove. I liked honey sandwiches, as the cloakroom was so cold the honey became crunchy.

In 2nd grade we consolidated to the "big" school in town, population 200, which went to 10th grade. Now we had buses but still outdoor toilets. I don't remember where or if we washed our hands. 11-12th grades went to the next largest town to graduate.

We finally got a phone in 1962-63. It was an 8 party line. One neighbor let us know loudly when he wanted the line "right now." All 8 rings we heard which was handy when one family was waiting for a call from a son in the Army and they couldn't be home to take the call, so they asked us to listen for their ring. Later we became a 4 party line and finally private.

Our chamber pot was in a little alcove under a stairway with no ventilation. We must have had toilet tissue but I always remember the grandparents' outhouse only had a Montgomery Ward catalog.

I don't know how we ever stayed clean as Saturday night the galvanized tub was filled with warm water from the cook stove. The littlest went first, then in order up to Dad, last. The rest of the week we just washed up in a wash pan, including washing our hair. Our home didn't get running water until 1956. The well was out by the barn where we hand-pumped for all the animals until then.

I do remember after our Saturday night baths and with clean beds and clean pajamas; we listened to "Your Hit Parade" on the radio. I still know many of the words to those songs.

One Saturday night a girlfriend stayed over, took her bath turn, and then backed into the hot stove, resulting in a blister on both butt cheeks. While running at recess a week later my friend yelled, "One of my blisters just broke!"

During WWII we were unloading wood into a basement window when a plane flew over which we were sure was Japanese. I still have a problem seeing Japanese names on products.

Every Saturday night included a trip to town to take in the cream for cash. We each got 5 cents, which bought us either an ice cream cone or a bottle of pop, but not both. We enjoyed seeing neighbors and running the streets (2 blocks long) with our school friends. Summers often had a movie shown on a screen put up in a parking lot.

Later a theatre opened 6 miles away. We had to make a choice. Saturday night was usually a western with Gene Autry, Roy Rogers, or Hopalong Cassidy, etc. Sunday night was a musical or drama, such as George Raft or Jimmy Cagney in "Yankee Doodle Dandy."

Eventually we got bikes and could ride to the swimming hole in the river 2 miles away. A neighbor boy kept trying to drown me but my sister said it was because he liked me.

Fresh Warm Milk
By Sharon Fewless of Kingsley, Michigan
Born 1947

I was born in 1947. We lived at Long Lake. My parents moved my siblings and me to Hoch Road where they bought a farm. There were six children. Both parents worked. My dad had a milk truck; he picked milk up from farmers and delivered it to Kraft in Cadillac. He drove school buses for Sabin School in Traverse City. Of course, he drove the bus that we rode on, so he was stricter with us, and then he was with the other kids, so we didn't get away with much. Our house was the first stop.

When we got home, we changed clothes

Sharon Hoch Fewless with her sisters, brother, aunt, and cousins

Sharon's parents, Eva and Ray Hoch

drink fresh warm milk as soon as my mother separated the milk from the cream. She used the cream to make butter.

When we got sick, she cut up onion and put them in a big cup, put a little bit of sugar in it and set it on the register on the floor and kept stirring and mashing the onion. It tasted pretty good. Our oldest brother would put my sister and I on his shoulders and run to the bus stop, which was about two blocks, town wise. We could make it to the bus stop on time. We had cows, pigs, and chickens, so we had our own meat. My youngest sister and I would get on our cows and ride them because we couldn't afford a horse. We would get bucked off in a cow pie and get right back on. We had a great time. I am proud to write about this as my parents have both passed away.

and had a slice of homemade bread and fresh churned butter from the cream of the milk from our cows. We had to have the chores done when our dad got home from the bus route. We also had to help get dinner ready. Our homework always came in last. Our mother always made homemade bread and cookies. She spent $15.00 a week on yeast and things she couldn't make. We had a big garden that we all helped work in it and pick when it was ready and it was so good. Our oldest sister was born with heart problems, so she couldn't help. She was in a hospital bed in the house when she was not in the hospital. When she was in the hospital, we spent Christmas with her as a family.

There were enough of us to play baseball on the farm when there was time. My sister and older brother found a nest of hen's eggs that rotted. My sister and brother were throwing them over the woodshed. I was in front of the woodshed, but they didn't know it. The eggs landed and busted on my head. What a stinky mess. My mother made my sister wash my hair.

We collected eggs every day and kept track on a pad of paper how many we had. We had an outhouse and we had to wipe with newspaper until they started making toilet paper. Our mother made her own soap for laundry. When we became teenagers, we would have barn dances in the part of the barn where the haymows were. We would

Flash Gordon and the Bean Girls
By Wilma Pauline Bean Cook Stafford of
Kingsley, Michigan
Born 1931

Every Friday night in the summer months of 1939-40 the merchants of the small town of Honor, Michigan, would sponsor free shows, sometimes called movies, for anyone who wanted to come. Marilyn, I, and our older brother, Phillip, would pile into the back of Dad's old Ford pick-up truck with some blankets for us and a couple chairs for Mom and Dad to sit on. The movie was projected on the side of a storage barn under the summer sky.

Mom made us popcorn to take from home and Dad would give us each a dime to buy candy or a coke. I often passed up the candy and pop to purchase instead a bottle of racy red nail polish or a lip stick, that Mom wouldn't let us wear except for play, or a bottle of Evening In Paris perfume that I loved because it came in an exquisite tiny blue bottle that spoke to me of glamorous faraway places and only cost a dime. We shopped and ran around with our friends who were there till the cartoons came on just at dusk. Then we settled down on our blankets to wait for our hero, Flash Gordon, to come on.

Our hero was a very muscular blonde man who was super smart, and so handsome even in black and white. We only knew he was blonde from the comic books our brother had that were in color. His T-shirt was red with a lightening flash across his chest and his tights looked like skin with no pockets. He wore snazzy black boots that came up to his knees. His short blonde hair always had a lock falling on his forehead and no matter what exciting thing was going on in or out of the rocket ship, our hero was always immaculate.

Dale Arden was a beautiful brunette with long black hair, a spectacular body, and wore very racy clothing for that time, a bra top with straps around her neck that crossed on her back, little boy type shorts that stopped midway to her knees, and tall black boots. Dale and Flash always wore the same clothes in every movie we ever saw them in.

Dr. Alexis Zarkov was a good guy, a space scientist always on the lookout for space danger as the crew rocketed through the sky. He had a cape and bushy eyebrows. He was in many battles with their archenemy, Emperor Ming the Merciless, who looked like a very big Chinese man with a thin mustache on his upper lip, always in his black cape with the standup collar.

On a summer day, Marilyn and I decided we would make our own space rocket ship and play Flash Gordon. We went into Dad's granary that was also his repair shop and helped ourselves to his hammer and saw as well as a couple old window roll up car handles, a few nails, nuts and bolts and gear cogs. By sunset, we were happy and inspired with the rocket ship whose entire control panel was nailed to the side of the barn. We were exhausted with the effort it took to handle a 12 oz. hammer and a saw with two feet of teeth. Our rocket ship was complete and would have awed Flash, Dale, and the crew.

When our dad came in the house in the morning after milking the cows, he questioned our motive for nailing all the junk on his barn. He was pretty upset about his hammer and saw spending the night in the dew and damp.

Two little girls spent many exciting hours zooming through space for a couple of summers with me as Flash and Marilyn as Dale.

I can't remember Dad ever taking the junk down. Over the years, it just fell off as the nails rusted.

The Three Lives of a Dog Named Ricky
By Loraine Becker of Atlanta, Michigan
Born 1934

A dog with beagle/blue tick mix came into the lives of Carl and Doug Becker when they were first hunting, at ages 13 and 11. His name was Ricky and he had a passion for running rabbits. He wouldn't leave the scent until they either shot the rabbit or caught him as he ran by. A time or two they had to leave him in the woods because he refused to come when they called and it was long after dark. They would leave a jacket on the ground for him to come back to and sure enough he would be curled up and waiting for them.

One evening Carl and Doug walked south of town to hunt and right away Ricky got on a track. He headed east and was soon out of earshot. They trailed him as fast as they could but only knew the direction he was going. It grew dark and he still wasn't coming back. Carl knew that rabbits usually circle around so he and Doug got on either side of the swamp and waited. After a long while, they could hear Ricky coming and Carl could make out a rabbit fleeing the dog. Even though it was dark, he could see whiteness coming. He shot before it got between him and Doug so he'd not be putting Doug in danger. He picked up the rabbit and they waited until Ricky came howling and tackled him.

Ricky was with the family for many years and through many mishaps. He was hit by a train and lived to run rabbits again. Carl and Doug had been hunting by Beaver Lake marsh and were trudging back home beside the train tracks. They tried to get Ricky to walk with them but he wanted to run down the middle of the track. He was too far ahead of them when they saw the train coming from behind. Carl ran as fast as he could but he couldn't get to Ricky in time and the train hit him, catapulting him into the air, and sending him about 40 feet. The boys raced to him, sure that he was dead, but his tough little heart was still beating. They wrapped him up, carried him home, and placed him behind their wood stove on a blanket where he stayed for three days without eating or drinking. They gave him water every now and then but he was reluctant to even take that. Then he was up and about and ready to hit the rabbit trail.

Another near disaster of Ricky's was

trying to join the kids having fun on Dad's trailer. They had made a teeter-totter of it: running back, making the tongue come up, then running to the front to lift the back. Ricky dashed underneath the tongue just as it came down, hitting him hard on the neck. Again, they thought his number was up, but they took him and put him behind the stove once more where he stayed for three days, without eating.

Ricky often trotted between Grandma's and home, having to cross the road and one unfortunate night he was on his way home, within a couple seconds of being in the driveway, when a truck purposefully swerved off the road and hit him. Carl could tell by tracks in the gravel that whoever had done it had made an effort to do so. He survived the train and the trailer tongue but this time, because of maliciousness, his strong little body was lifeless. The family felt bruised themselves by such an act, and mourned the little guy.

Carl took him carefully and placed him in the basket on his bike and with shovel in hand, took him on his last ride to a hogback knoll a little east of the schoolhouse. There he buried him on high ground but within sight of the marsh where there just might be rabbit or two to chase.

Some Memories Are Best Forgotten
By Donald Jones of Indian River, Michigan
Born 1930

As I try to recall the days of my past life in Indian River, I am reminded that those were indeed, the good old days. Although my recollection of my childhood in northern Michigan began much earlier in 1934 when my folks camped along with other families at what was called the Goerke farm on Scott's Bay Mullet Lake, our family and I moved to Indian River in 1942. My dad bought what was known at the time, the old Bell home where Doctor Bell once practiced medicine, which was located on the corner of US 27 and Floyd Street.

World War II was going on at the time and my dad was unable to enlist and being a tool and die maker, had a cement block building erected on the back of our property and equipped it with the necessary machinery to manufacture war materials. I of course began

school and was enrolled in either the 5th or 6th grade. Time has erased the names of my teachers, but I do remember being disciplined when I got out of line and was hit over the knuckles more than once with a yardstick. I remember playing "Anti-Over" when we would throw a ball over the roof of the school and someone would try to catch it before it hit the ground. In the winter when the snow was on the ground, we would sled down the hill toward the river. Unfortunately, in those days there were no organized sports so we made up our own games. I went to the Indian River school until the 9th grade when I had a choice of being bussed to Cheboygan or go to Petoskey High and for some reason I chose to go to Petoskey.

I do remember some of my friends during that time, but most of them have passed away. I remember Donald Goerke who lived down the street from the school and was a good friend of mine. His dad, Carl, was the golf course superintendent and we got permission from him to pick night crawlers for ourselves to sell to the vacationers. The best place to pick the crawlers was on the greens, but we were forbidden to go on them. More than once I confess that we disobeyed that order because the shorter the grass, the easier it was to see them and pick them.

I remember the Fisher boys and Harold Hallopeter, a farm boy who lived north of town. I knew the King boys well and hung out with Rich, better known at the time by "Smokie" much of the time. His older brothers, Bud and Wilbur were also friends of mine. As time rolled on and us kids got older, we played independent basketball in the town hall, which was right next to my house. Rollie Dagwell was our coach and we would play other independent teams and anyone who would play us. I remember we had a pretty good team, but must admit I didn't help the team much.

During the spring and summer, I, along with most of the kids, spent our days on and in the water. I remember those of us who were brave enough – or dumb enough who would jump off the Indian River Bridge. The public bathing beach was always a popular place for us to gather to swim and horse around. Of course, being rowdy kids, the boathouses across the river from the beach were too inviting a place to pass up as a place to jump

219

from. I'm sure the folks at Columbus Beach never looked at it with approval, but we never got caught, as I remember.

I had a boat and motor at the time. Smokie and I would race up and down the river making the residents with boats docked along the river upset. Needless to say, I was quite rowdy during my youth but never got into any real trouble by God's grace. I might interject here that after leaving Indian River, and after returning 45 years, Fay Martin remembered me as "a little rascal." I'm looking at the notice requesting people to share their experiences and as I look down the list of suggestions, I can relate to all of them. I guess that declares my age.

During my years in Indian River, I held several jobs, when it didn't interrupt hunting. One of the jobs I had was working as a security patrol for the Little Sturgeon Hunt Club. Rollie Dagwell, who oversaw the club, hired me. It was my job to report anyone who sneaked onto and fished on the stream. Luke Cahill was a good friend of mine and guess who I caught as the first violator? Yup, good old Luke. I told Rollie about it, but I never heard anything else from it. I also got a job sand blasting the Indian River Bridge. They put my buddy Rich on one scaffold on the south side and me on the north. We found it was good fun to aim the blasting guns at each other across the river. Of course, the stones never reached their target, but we had fun anyway. I also remember shoveling sand in dump trucks and getting paid $1.00 per hour. The blisters on my hands prevented me from staying too long at that job.

You may have noticed that I've mentioned the name Dagwell several times. Indian River was a very small place during the years I lived here as a kid. The bulk of the town's people were either the Dagwell's or the Martin's. The Dagwell's were always feuding and fussing and most were not as high class as the Martin's. Bill Martin ran the only grocery and general store here in town and he lived just across the river with his wife Alice. The post office was just to the right of the store and Gronseth's Drug Store was on the other side. All of these old places have long since changed much through the years all but Gronseth's Drug are still here. The other drug store in town was Nelson's Drug Store, which was run by Hugo, the owner and his wife Thelma. Racking my brain to remember the different stores that have come and gone over the years, I do remember some such as the A&P grocery store, Oosting's Gas Station, the Hi-Speed gas station, the Dutch Mill restaurant adjacent to the train depot and next to Oosting's Gas Station and Garby's Garage located next to the A&P. Anna King also ran a small restaurant, which was in the line of stores on West 27. There was also a Gulf Gas Station, which burned to the ground around 1943.

Now, about the trains. The high light of each day especially in the winter was the trains that came through. It was common practice for the town folks to gather around the depot and share the news of the day and visit. The passenger trains were the most interesting, as everyone would strain to see who was getting off the train.

I remember one of my favorite things to do in the winter when the roads were covered with snow and ice. Some of us boys would hide till someone would come out of Nelsons Drug Store and when the time was right; we would grab the bumper of the car and hang on for dear life as the car drove away down the street. Of course, this was dangerous to say the least, but at the age of 13 or 14, I thought I was invincible and like Superman could leap buildings in a single bound and stand unhurt in front of, and stop a moving freight train. I thought life was grand and never got bored due to some very hair raising experiences that about drove my parents crazy, many of which my parents never knew about. Another of my pastimes in the summer was fishing. I caught the largest rainbow of my life under the "old" Sturgeon Bridge, which weighed in at over six pounds. The "old" bridge has been replaced sometime in the past but you can still see the remnants that are left just to the west of the new bridge. Another thought I have concerning fishing was seeing the lights of the fishermen at what we called the walleye hole. This favorite spot was located at the mouth of the Sturgeon. At night, it looked like there were hundreds of lights out there. The fishing in those days was real good and most of the time you caught your limit in short order. I remember working when I was about 14 at French's Restaurant as a bus boy and dishwasher. My future mother in law, Mel Dagwell must have gotten me the job as she worked there as a waitress. The job didn't pay much, but at least the food was good, which I had plenty of.

My dad died of a heart attack in 1944 and my mother began selling off the properties that my dad had bought over the years. At some point, she decided to go into the real estate business and became the only woman to sell real estate in Indian River, up to that time. She had a rough time breaking into the business, as I remember because A.K. Smith was the sole realtor here and had been here for years. Mom's office was just to the south of what is now a lighting store, but in those days, it was a gas station owned and operated by the Vincent's. Of course, the only clothing store here was and still is McClutchy's, it is a little pricey for some town folk, but they sold good merchandise. Sam McClutchy used to be the school principal here, but he and Donna Beth ran the store as well. Sometime in the mid 1940's Sam became principal at the school in Pellston.

My dear wife went on to glory on the 21st of March 2010 after several years battling Dementia. This "old" man still is hanging on to life by God's grace, and living on Oakhill Street. I am blessed to have two of my four children living close by. Tom, the eldest, lives in Alanson and Cliff and his wife, or Kip as we call him, live just around the corner from me. This provides great comfort to me, as I get older. My daughter is in a rehab and convalescent center in Ft. Lauderdale, Florida. She is suffering from the same disease that took my wife. My youngest son and his wife live in Lynchburg, Virginia.

So that's about the extent of my memories concerning the days of yesteryears here in Indian River or Squaw Creek as we kids used to say. There are no doubt many, many things that I can't recall, but some of them probably are best forgotten.

Determination More than Skill (But That, Too)
By Dennis Villeneuve of Hillman, Michigan
Born 1950

This is a story of a young boy who wanted to play Little League Baseball as a youngster. A story of hard work, ethics, and living by your means, being determined to pursue what I wanted with a set goal and having the will to

Dennis Villeneure and friends

do so and gaining a lifetime of memories to cherish.

I lived approximately 8 miles north of the small village of Hillman, Michigan. I was born into a traditional Catholic family. My father and mother lived in the family farmhouse. There they raised 13 children on that 80-acre farm. I was born the 11th child. As we grew up on the farm, everyone had chores: milking the cows by hand, slopping the hogs, or maybe gathering the eggs, but I made sure my chores were finished. I wanted to play my last year in Little League Baseball. I was 11 years old and was signed up for Little League.

Knowing that this would be difficult, meaning that there would be no ride to and from practices or games, I was still determined that I wanted to play baseball. I had not made it to any of the practices before the first game but I still decided to set out for the village of Hillman for that first game.

One sunny day I started out our long driveway and headed for Hillman. I knew this was going to be a lengthy walk as it was 8 miles from the farmhouse to the Little League Field in Hillman, Michigan. As I continued my walk, I was three quarters of the way to town when a lady (Mrs. Mary Cadieux) that we knew from our church passed by me and stopped on the side of the road, and asked me if I would like a ride. Knowing that I was very tired, I thought that this was a great idea. Well, I guess she did not hear me say yes I would like a ride and or I did not run fast enough as she sped away in her car, leaving me on the side of the road.

Continuing to walk to the game, I finally

made it to Hillman. Not really sure how the day would play out, it was my turn to bat. Feeling kind of low after that 8-mile walk I was determined I would try my hardest to have a great game. Because I had not made it to any of the practices I also did not have a uniform to wear that first game of the season, but that did not stop me from playing as I was allowed to play in the game. Holding that bat in my hands the ball was pitched to me and I swung at the ball and hit a long ball deep into the outfield and the ball bounced over the fence to make it a stand-up double and later in the game also hit for another single. WOW what a game.

After the game that day, the local Sheriff of Montmorency County (Doc Eagle) congratulated me and gave me a quarter. Mrs. Mildred Godfrey also congratulated me and gave me a dime. In those days, receiving 35 cents was a large sum of money. This was a very memorable moment in my childhood and also that day the coach, Mr. Bernard Ripley, told me that he would pick me up and give me a ride for every game after that.

I will never forget that walk nor the experiences that went along with the day. There were tough times raising a family of so many children and memories that will last a lifetime. Memories that I have cherished and passed down to my children and grandson.

What is Home Economics?
By Ruth Westphal of Houghton Lake, Michigan
Born 1934

We walked 1-½ miles to school. Bullies would chase you home with a dangled snake; others teased you about your buckteeth, until one got her thumb in my mouth. My buckteeth almost bit it off in a homeward fight outside the school zone sign. Truant officers spanked more than one. We took pint jars of food to put in a huge pot of water on the school stove for hot lunches. There was one room with three or four grades. Misspelled words would make one write the word 100 times on the board. Today I'm a pretty good speller. We walked through many rain and snowstorms to learn school was closed. We couldn't see hardly to walk. When we graduated from 8th grade to a city high school, we never heard about half the classes that city kids had. We were farther ahead in English, spelling, and math. We never heard of civics, home economics, gym, mechanics, etc. We could play good softball and were taught the pledge of allegiance. In college, I never needed to take a test to enter. Coming from Midland County assured my entry.

October would produce tipped over outhouses. Some toilets made it to the barn roofs. We raised rabbits during WWII. The pens were built on the back of ours. They didn't tip ours. We used roughed catalog pages and old newspapers to save regular toilet tissue for nighttime pots.

My dad hoarded foods during WWII - sugar, flour, and spices. We canned vegetables, fruits, meats, and cream from the farmers to make butter. Our little arms were so tired pulling up and down on a pole that fit a cake tin, centered hole, placed on the top of a big pickle crock. WWII had food stamps and gas stamps. Often stamps were traded. *The Lone Ranger* came on while we were doing dishes. Radio gave excellent music with words one could understand and sing along, there was no slang or swearing permitted.

During the depression dad dug ditches with a shovel to support us. Butter was $0.10 a pound. Homemade bread, pies, cakes, and cookies were common. Ice and milkmen delivered with horse drawn wagons. Used clothes were handed down and shoes were stuffed with paper until you grew into them.

My mom made fulltime use of the party line phone. Neighbors would get upset most of the time. TV's were snowy, round pictures, but we didn't complain. We still used treadle sewing machines. My sister crawled up to the wringer washer, her arm rolled into the wringer to her elbow. Our bird dog caught many pheasant's dad shot. Dad loved to tease the DNR. They would spear fish in deeper ditches and hide in the culverts till they gave up looking for him.

We always had a Christmas tree. We made all the trimmings; strung popcorn and Santa would bring a set of blocks, dolls, etc. That was it for the year. One big box of chocolates divided to all. Our home was hand built for $2,200. My sister was born in the front bedroom. Doctor came to the house. I stayed at my aunt's that had a new Eureka vacuum. Noisy!

We were afraid to be naughty. The whip or a belt kept you in line. We went to church every Sunday and throughout the week when there was something going on. Today I love God and Jesus Christ with my whole heart and very being.

✓ Prying Eyes, Chores Undone, and the "Back Brush"
By Carol E. Bogucki of Reed City, Michigan
Born 1939

It was 1946 and the last day of school at the Rehkopf School in Osceola County, Reed City, Michigan.

It was our big picnic day at Lincoln Township Hall. The best thing, and what caused all of us to be so excited, was the fact we got to eat *all* the ice cream we wanted. The Hall was just across the road and down a ways.

Our school had inside toilets, the kind that each day one of the kids got the job of carrying pails of water to pour down them.

The Hall had the good old-fashioned outhouses with an opening in back. And that's what caused this 6 year old's big problem.

After eating lots of goodies and ice cream, I needed to go. One of my classmates saw me go in and thought he'd be real funny and peek up the hole.

Well, as bad as I needed to go, I wasn't about to sit down and let him see me. Guess what? Yep! This kid's big fun day was over and I had to go home to do my business. Some way to end a school year.

We lived in the country during the era of outdoor privies. You've heard the saying, "We didn't have a pot to go in"? Well, we really didn't. Ours was a pail covered with a newspaper. To be emptied, it had to be carried out and around the house to the outdoor john, which was a little distance.

Sometimes, it was set out on the porch until someone had to make a trip. Then we killed two birds with one stone.

I was thirteen and had a babysitting job that Saturday night. When the gentleman came to pick me up and I answered the door, what a shock for me. There sat the throne, proud as could be, full to the brim. Someone had not emptied it. I could have died!

Off we went and there it sat. I think, after that instance, I made sure it was promptly emptied so I'd never have to relive the most embarrassing moment of my life.

It was September 1958, and I was so proud to be enrolled at Ferris State College in Big Rapids, Michigan. It is now Ferris State University.

I was going to share the upstairs with 6 other girls. The home was just a half block from campus. Very convenient! There were 3 girls in my room, 2 pharmacy gals across the hall, and 2 very lucky girls who had their own room.

Our living space consisted of the four bedrooms, a kitchen, and a bathroom. We had a meeting to decide who would get what duties. I got kitchen duty.

My first meal was to be a lovely pot roast with all the vegetables. At home, I always put mine in the oven at 350 degrees, like my mom did. However, one of the older girls knew better. I ended up doing it on top of the stove.

Well, this was not a good idea, especially when everyone had classes, including me, the cook. When I opened the downstairs door, the smoke was rolling out the upstairs.

I don't remember what we ate, but it wasn't what I'd planned. I was immediately switched to cleaning the bathroom.

Now, to fully understand my circumstances, I'd lived in the country in the small town of Reed City. No bathroom did we have. You might say I was from the "sticks." Therefore, I had no experience using or cleaning one.

Friday nights my boyfriend, Bob, always picked me up to take me home for the weekend. I was telling him about the nice inside toilet and how wonderful my back felt after using the back brush.

He laughed and laughed. That's when I found out the "back brush" was to clean the stool.

After nearly 50 years of marriage, we can still get a good laugh about the good old days.

✓ You Better Not Forget Your Lines!
By Frank Krajnik of Posen, Michigan
Born 1935

I remember when stamps were 3 cents for a letter and gas was 25 cents a gallon. You could drive a week on 5 gallons because Dad had a 1936 Ford.

Frank's brother, Casimer, Uncle Louis, Frank, and his brother Ace in 1954

I remember you had to have 2 pails for the cloth diapers: one to clean and one to soak until wash day. You washed on a washboard with a bar of soap before we got a wringer washer. Then you had to watch so your fingers would not get caught in the rollers. Women had to watch out for their long hair.

We did not get any electric until 1953 or 1954. We then had lights in the house, barn, woodshed, and a yard light. Boy, it was nice and we did not have to do homework by kerosene lamp.

In our one room schoolhouse, there was one potbelly stove. There were 6 of us kids that went from 3rd grade through 8th grade. We put on a Christmas show for our parents; that was fun. You better not forget your lines! When we came to school in the winter, the room was cold. My brothers and I had to walk 3 miles. It was rough and cold. Then we had a school bus.

We had no TVs. We would get all the news by radio, hooked up to a car battery. We listened to the Lone Ranger, Dark Shadows, and the Grand Old Opry.

Stores would close at 7 pm on weekdays and 4 or 5 pm on Saturday and did not open until 9 am Monday. If you did not do your shopping, you were out of luck. There was no crime and we would leave the door unlocked.

We had no phone because we had no electric. We had windup record players. You just had to watch that you wound it up when you put on a record.

Boy, blizzards in northern Michigan were bad. When it would snow sometimes, we could not get out for a week because we lived

½ mile from the main road. So we had to plow our road with horses or shovel our road with snow banks as high as 5 feet. Posen had some real cold temperatures and blizzards.

We did all our farm work with horses: plowing, grain planting, cutting hay. It was hard work. We had our own garden. We had lots of vegetables. No freezer, so all the meat we used was salted in a big barrel. In the fall, we would cut cabbage and put it in a barrel, and the youngest boy had to get in the barrel and stomp it down. You had to wash your feet before going in.

We had an old hound dog. If he would see you with a gun, he would get all excited, because he knew we were going hunting.

Farm chores were bad in the wintertime. You would try to carry a fork load of hay to feed the sheep in winter and a gust of wind would blow the hay off your fork. To water the cows we had a small pond behind the barn. You would take an ax to chop the ice so they could drink some water.

In the summer, we would go to Grand Lake in the evening to wash and swim to get clean. The outhouse was behind the house with a Sears catalog for toilet paper. In the winter, you had lots of clothes to take off before you could sit down, with long johns on and a drop back seat.

We had a hard life, but we all made it. Kids today don't know what life is all about. Like, I did not see a black person until I got drafted in 1958 and went to Detroit for my

Frank in 1948

224

physical. And we all got along all right.

We were farmers and made our toys from potatoes and played Hide and Seek. In the fall, we used to have parties with the neighbors and play records or they would play the fiddle, clarinet, guitars, and drums. We would drink, eat, and dance until midnight. That was fun.

✓ Grandma's Hands
By Judie Sprague of Cadillac, Michigan
Born 1937

The most poignant memory I have of my grandma are of her precious hands; busily knitting, crocheting, baking, leafing through her bible, trying to braid my hair, but first and foremost folded in prayer. My earliest recollections of her were from visits when my folks would make the long drive from our residence, in Chicago, to Michigan. It was in the 1940s and there weren't the freeways available to us as we now have, which made for longer, less frequent trips. My grandma lived alone in a small white house whose most redeeming quality, for a child my size, was the porch swing just waiting for a little girl with an apple in one hand and a book in the other.

To me, a child of probably eight or nine, grandma was old. She had steel gray colored hair, sparse, but always neatly curled by old, metal rollers fastened with an attached metal wire with a little round piece of rubber at its center, which clamped across the curler to close and hold it in place. And, of course, she kept the stray hairs in place by the thin, wirehair pins used by most women during that era. She dressed in cotton housedresses covered by a button down sweater, which she kept darned and patched and most always, covered by an apron. She wore cotton hosiery and always, the black, thick heeled, laced, sturdy shoes.

Her day started in the kitchen with arranging the kindling and lighting a fire in her cast iron cooking stove with large wooden stick matches, which were kept in a small tin container on the wall behind the stove. A trip to the back porch to fill her blue and white speckled metal coffee pot with water from the water pail came next and if the pail was empty, then a short walk to the corner of the block was necessary to fill the pail at the neighborhood water pump–a job readily assigned to the grandchildren, when visiting. She had modern plumbing complete with running water, but back then, what came out of the kitchen tap was not used for drinking. In those days, there was a pump on nearly every neighborhood corner, which brought forth cold, crystal clear well water used for drinking and cooking.

Once the coffee was started on the back burner of that old cast iron stove, she went about her ritual of preparing breakfast with her homemade biscuits, whatever fruit was in season and some hot oatmeal. She would never have dreamed of switching on a stovetop burner, or for that matter, popping open a microwave oven to heat a cup of water and add a packet of instant oatmeal or coffee. Those short cuts were to be far in the future.

Once her personal needs had been taken care of and she was dressed for the day, it was her daily ritual to sit in her rocking chair by a large space heater, which filled a prominent spot in the dining room, offering comforting warmth while she opened her Swedish bible for her morning devotions. I think those devotions were her lifeline. Grandma needed a strong faith in her God to keep her physically and emotionally steady. As a young girl of 16, she said goodbye to her parents and family in Sweden to brave a strenuous voyage by ship on a courageous venture to a new world called America. This was a giant step to willingly explore a new life in this faraway place, to live with an uncle whom she barely remembered from childhood. A brave, yet frightening course for such a young girl to take both then or now. Grandma never returned to her native land, after arriving at her destination, a small lumbering town of Clam Lake, now Cadillac, Michigan, and worked as a housemaid to earn her keep. She soon met and married my grandpa, a worker in the lumber camps whom she met through attendance at the small community Swedish Lutheran Church. With grandpa, she bore and raised four children. Grandpa died soon after the children were raised, from complications of an accident, leaving grandma to maneuver through middle and old age on her own. Her native tongue being Swedish, she wrote and spoke this language fluently with others in this small, heavily populated Swedish community.

Her greatest pleasures were the infrequently received letters from her homeland telling of her family and touching her heart with a great sense of loneliness for those she loved and would never see again. Her treasured letters were tenderly read and reread, as she sat in her rocker, with memories pouring through her mind and heart of those she had left behind and often a tear or two slipped down her cheeks while reading as she endured the separation from her parents and siblings.

By the time of my visits, her children were grown and had families of their own. Three of the four located outside of Michigan in the state of Illinois. One son remained in the hometown of Cadillac and he and his family was her closest source of loving relationships and sole source of reliance for any problems or tasks for which she needed assistance. Their loving support was a constant in her life and enabled her to live independently. Visits from those out of town were infrequent but cherished. Their cards, letters, and occasional monetary assistance were received with a grateful heart.

The church and its activities became the social life for grandma, as well as the source to nurture her soul. She lived only two blocks away from the Lutheran Church and found such solace there as she walked up the hill each Sunday morning to worship, dressed in her very best clothes, completed by matching hats with veils, as were the style at that time. She carried her white gloves and pocketbook, which held her "widow's mite," faithful in supporting the church with whatever she could possibly afford from her modest budget and whatever extra money she managed to save from babysitting jobs she frequently took to make ends meet. She also kept a stash of peppermints in her purse, just in case of a cough or to settle a restless grandchild who might occasionally accompany her.

As grandma grew older, many hours were spent in her rocker, reading and re-reading her letters from Sweden, the Swedish newspapers, and exercising her arthritic hands by lovingly and laboriously knitting mittens for each and every one of her 10 grandchildren, to be given as Christmas gifts. Letters and phone calls were exchanged with the families to inquire which colors would match the yearly purchased snowsuits and winter coats. Yarn and knitting needles found their home daily, in her lap, as she sat in her rocker, knitting and rocking, deep in thought.

In the quietness of her home, during the days and months and years, I believe that with each stitch created by those loving hands, a memory passed through her mind and heart of family past and present. As the stitches linked the yarn together with such perfection, so did the memories link together the gentle and deeply meaningful life lived by this wonderful woman.

Clothesline Blanket Tents
By Susan Smith of Gaylord, Michigan
Born 1958

When I was a child, we lived in the projects due to my dad having brain cancer. While living in the projects we were poor, but those were some of my best years there. I had many years of happiness there and these are just a few.

My parents had a station wagon and I remember they use to lay down the seats in the back. Us kids would get our pj's on and mom would pop lots of popcorn and put it in a paper bag and away we would go to the dive in. When we got there, my dad would go to the indoor concession stand and buy foot long hotdogs. Those movie nights were very special nights out.

My friends and I would go across the street and dig in a field with spoons and look for what we called "Gold sand." If you found some, you were considered lucky. We also had an ice cream truck come through everyday all summer playing his music. We would all race into the house to get some change so we could get an ice cream bar for $0.10-$0.20.

As kids, we all walked to school, which was probably about eight blocks. After it rained, the mud puddles dried up and cracked. They looked like huge puzzles and me and my friends would sit and play with those mud puzzles for hours. My mom would have to send my older brother or sister out to find us.

Another thing we did while living in the projects was make clothesline blanket tents. You would get two big blankets and mother's clothespins. You would put one blanket end up on the line with clothespins to hold it and then another blanket on the other side and then pull the blankets out at the bottoms each way and put rocks on the ends of the blankets to hold the blankets out so we could play inside. Another favorite pastime was walking up to the railroad tracks and putting our ears to it and listen for the train to get closer. Then we would put a penny on the tracks and go and hide until the train was out of sight. Then we would go look for the smashed up penny.

Farm life for 10 years meant lots of work, but also lots of fun. We moved from the city to a farm after my dad passed away. Here are some of my fondest memories of some of the work and fun we had as "farm kids." Kids think they have it so hard now; well they should have lived on a farm like we did.

My younger brother and youngest sister and I all had chores to do, winter and summer, along with homework and all. I was in the 3rd grade and they were younger and we would have to go and hand pump water into a big water trough and take turns pumping it until it was full. For us that was a lot of work being so young. When we were done with chores, we ate dinner then did homework. By then it was time to go to bed. On weekends, we had time to play outside or in the house in between chores. Some of the fun things we did were go back into the woods with our ice skates and skate in and around the trees. When our friends came over, we would walk to the "Valley." This was just a big hill, but to get there we had to walk two fields away through snow that was up to our knees. It was all worth it to get to the top of that hill and get as many as we could on a big tire tube and fly down that hill. Then came spring when we had a fast snowmelt. My brother and I built what we thought was an awesome boat, so we could go out in the water and float around. That boat sank and we were left walking home in knee deep-freezing ice-cold water, wet from head to toes. Also during that melt, our front yard and driveway and parts of our road were flooded so we had to wear knee high rubber boots to get into the school bus and then change into our shoes after we were on the bus. Also in the winter, my older brothers and sisters and friends would take an old hood off a car and hook up a rope to it with the tractor and pull the hood down the road as a big sleigh ride.

A&W was around and that was really special when we got to there. We would get those thick frosty glasses full of A&W root beer. Mom and dad got big glasses and us kids got smaller ones. That frosty cup was the best thing, the food didn't matter it was the frosted glass cup. For fun on Sundays, my parents would once again load us up in our station wagon and take us for a ride out in the country. We would get out of the car on the side of the road and pick apples from a tree in the ditch. Sometimes my dad would find cows out in a field and go and hop on one just to see us kids laugh. After all, we were city slickers then.

When I was young, my oldest sister graduated high school and got herself a job as a phone operator. She actually plugged wires in and out of a board, just like you would see on TV. We had party lines then, which meant that you could pick up your dial phone and listen in on your neighbors' phone conversations. You had to pick up the part you would talk into and set it back down very carefully so that the people on the other line couldn't hear you. If someone was talking on the phone too long you could pick up the receiver and say, "When are you going to get off the phone, I need the line." Phone booths were fun too because you could call people for free by telling the operator that you had put money into it but you didn't get connected. She would send you your change back. That was pretty cool back in the good ol' days.

Homemade clothes were made by my mother who would make my sister and I western style shirts and pants by us laying out newspaper, cutting out the pattern she had drawn and would sew up us our western clothes. Needed to show our horses in western pleasure classes. She sewed us up our outfits every summer and you would think they were bought. Imagine making patters from old newspapers. She was very very talented to say the least. Blizzards were almost an every winter thing. I remember one storm we got, the snow drifts were so tall we could climb on top of them and get on the roof of the two-story house we lived in. In order to get down to the barns to do chores my brothers had to hollow out the snowdrifts in order to get through them to get to the barn.

Living 10 miles out of town meant we only went once a week and that was on Friday after dinner. Our allowance was $5.00 per week for us kids, but back then, that could get you a lot at a dime store. Couldn't wait for Fridays so I could get my new baby doll bottles and clothes for her. Some of the games we played were playing on the swinging rope in the old barn. You had to go from one side of the barn rafter to the other side and jump off in time or you would either be hanging on for dear life or slide down the rope the hard way. We use to also have corncob fights in the old barn. Boys on one side and girls on the other side. Sometimes on a hot summer night, we would catch those lightening bugs and use the part off the bug that lit up and put it on our fingers as rings. We also played Red light, Green light, Mother May I, and use to twirl in circles until we could no longer see and then try and walk. So much fun.

✓ Mother's Nerve-racking Discovery
By Marie Louise Cournyer Schanck of Mio, Michigan
Born 1933

I have lived in Mio 77 years. We came to Mio when I was 3 years old.

I was born in Rose City and when I was three my grandpa and my father traded the Rose City newspaper for the *Oscoda County News*. I have lived all of my life in Oscoda Co. except for 10 years. My husband John and I lived in Midland.

In 1967, we bought the Dairy Ace from my brother, Jack Cournyer, and our kids and I moved back to Mio. Johnny worked at Dow for 33 years.

I have been in everything that has ever happened in Mio since 1935! I have been called a legend and a lot of other things in my time, but never lazy! I was one of the "ladies" that stopped the cattle by climbing in the pen with them. In 1978 and 1979, they were going to dig nine pits and the people of Oscoda County declared war on the government, and we stopped them at two pits! I guess that's about the most famous thing I have done.

I sing gospel music. My husband and I have sung in every church in Mio and all over Michigan. We belong to the Northern Michigan Gospel Music Association. In fact, we were part of the group that founded it. I sang my first solo when I was 3 years old in the Mio Methodist church where the minister died on the furnace.

My brother Bayard John Cournyer II,

Marie Cournyer, Bayard John "Jack" Cournyer, II with their dog Rip

known as Jack, was 22 months younger than I, and his nickname besides Jack was "Squeaky" because when he was about 2 years old he ate a fuzzy caterpillar and it did something to his throat and he couldn't talk right until his voice changed as a teenager.

I had an older sister, Barbara, and Jack was the baby.

Anyway, my dad had this big hound that he had sent to Kentucky for, and they sent it up on the train to West Branch and we had to go get it. West Branch was 30 miles away. Well, when he went to work in Bay City, Jack and I took over the dog (Rip was his name). He was always tied because he was valuable! But he had a nice house and we played in it.

One summer day Jack was outdoors and for some reason I was in the house and my mother was baking and she said, "Where's Jack?" and I said, "Outdoors," and she told me to go get him.

So I went out and called and he didn't answer and so that's what I told her. She told

228

me to go see if he was at Grandma's, which was 2 blocks straight north of us. I went down there and he wasn't there, so I stopped at the newspaper office which my grandpa owned, one block North and one block East, on Main Street. He wasn't there. I went home. By this time, my mother was worried someone had taken him.

We started calling and she went to the jail one block east, and the sheriff, Geo. Marsh, Sr. came home with her. We were all upset and everybody in the neighborhood was looking for him. They were about ready to call the State Police in West Branch when he came crawling out from under the doghouse where he was taking a nap.

I think he heard us and was playing a joke on us! Barbara and I were both older, but he could always find a way to get our goat.

Rip was a special dog. He was pedigreed. When I was a child dogs were dogs. You got one usually when your friend's dog had a litter, usually of the Heinz 57 variety. Another tail, another day!

I was 8 years old in 1941 and my dad Keith Cournyer left our newspaper office and went to Bay City to work at the Dow Chemical's plant there because he couldn't pass his physical to join the Army.

He and my grandpa owned the *Oscola County News,* a weekly paper, from 1935 to 1975. My grandpa's name was Bayard John Cournyer. My brother Jack was named after him, B.J. II.

In those years you were frozen to your job seven days a week and he lived in Bay City and Mama (Mildred), Barbara, Jack, and I, lived next to the old Methodist church on the corner of 10th and Deyarmond.

In 1939 to 1940, they dug a basement and moved the church over on the new basement. In 1940 and 1941, Reverend W. L. Jones was pastor. He was a carpenter too, so he worked finishing the basement.

During the war years, my mother kept herself busy by baking for the stores and restaurants. One day she baked a lemon pie for the pastor and his family and was going to take it over to him while he was putting a register in the sanctuary floor. When she got to the door, she smelled a strange smell and called to him and he didn't answer. She went to the front of the church and looked down and he was lying on the top of the furnace,

dead!

This was a terrible shock to my mother! I can remember Dr. Smith had to give her some nerve medicine for quite a while.

My father Keith Cournyer with Vern Dockham a Conservation Officer rediscovered the Kirtland Warbler in 1950.

✓ Shenanigans and Electricity
By Monica Urban of Howell, Michigan
Born 1957

I loved it when my mother would tell stories of growing up in a large family on a farm in rural Posen. One of my favorites was when in 1938, thanks to President Franklin Roosevelt; electricity was made available in the rural communities of northern Michigan. A big topic of conversation among the twelve excited Pokorski children was what would be on their Pa's list of things to purchase that used "electricity." They almost couldn't believe it when Pa came home with strings of electric lights for the Christmas tree. Pa was not known for wasting money on frivolous things! Now it wouldn't take half an hour to light all the candles on the giant balsam fir tree! They could gather round and sing more than one Christmas carol before having to carefully extinguish the candles. They enjoyed every evening of the Christmas season, gathering in the living room, enjoying the soft glow of lights on the big beautiful tree. It was a Christmas to remember!

All too soon, it was time to take down the Christmas tree. The older girls in the family were in charge of taking down the colorful glass ornaments, carefully wrapping them in tissue and packing them away. By the time they got to the lights the older girls had chores to do and Theresa, age 8, and David, age 9, were given the very important task of taking the lights off the tree and putting them away. Well, they just puffed with pride at such an important task being given to them. Everyone scattered and Terri and Davy were left alone in the living room with their very important job!

No one was familiar with the dangers of electricity, least of all Terri and Davy. They decided to get all the lights off the tree before separating the cords. Carefully they laid the great big string of cords all around the living room and started unplugging the cords from each other. It never entered their minds to unplug the lights from the socket in the wall. The first two cords came apart easily enough but the next two just wouldn't budge. Davy pulled and pulled, and then Terri tried her hand at it, no luck! They each grabbed one end and pulled, nope, now what? With everyone else out of the house and not wanting to admit they failed at their very important job they sat there scratching their heads. All of a sudden Davy said, "Go get me a butter knife." Terri scampered to the kitchen and grabbed a knife out of the drawer, ran back and sat on the floor next to Davy. Heads together, Terri hanging on to the cords, Davy wedged the knife in between the two plugs!

Holy Cow, their bodies jerked, Davy dropped the knife and the cords came apart! They looked at each other in a state of shock and then looked at the knife on the floor. It was a ruined!

Now, Davy and Terri, being close in age, were often partners in crime in the Pokorski family. Between them they decided it was in the best interest of everyone if they simply hid the knife. After all, they surmised, the cords were apart, the lights weren't broken, it was just an old butter knife, and hopefully it wouldn't be missed. They had to give some thought to how they would get rid of the knife. They decided the snow covered stone pile out in the pasture was the perfect place to bury the knife.

Ma and the older girls were in the kitchen getting supper on the table and Pa and the older boys came in from doing chores. It was starting to get dark and Pa told Martha to turn on the lights. Nothing happened, and poor Martha thought she had done something wrong! Pa went through the house checking all the lights and then shaking his head, checked the fuses, replaced them, but still no lights. He went outside and in the clear, wintry night he could see in the distance the twinkling lights of the neighboring farms.

In the morning Pa went into the village where Presque Isle Electric Co-op had an installation office. He demanded they come out to the farm to find the problem. They sent out an electrician. He took one look at the main pole and gasped and said," My God, you blew a transformer!" He and Pa went through the house and found a singed spot on the wall by the outlet in the living room.

Pa called the entire family into the living room questioned them and the electrician talked to them about the possible dangers when using electricity. Terri thought to herself "Too bad we didn't know that sooner."

After the man from the electric company got done talking she and Davy looked at each other and knew they were the culprits. They told Pa and the man what had happened. Pa told them to go get the knife! The man looked at the knife and told Pa they were lucky they didn't get electrocuted!

I suppose that was why for once in their lives they didn't get in much trouble for their shenanigans!

Grand Sailing Adventure on Houghton Lake
By Mark A. Mitchell of Dearborn Heights, Michigan
Born 1950

Hello. My name is Mark. I'm 63 years old and I have lived in southeastern Michigan my whole life, but the Houghton Lake area has always been my home away from home. My grandparents, Hilda and Herman and three sets of great aunts and uncles all built cottages on Houghton Lake. I started coming up to my grandparents' place with my mom and dad when I was two. I always loved it up here and always looked forward to coming up.

When I was eleven my cousin Gary and I were staying with my grandparents and my great Aunt Elsie and Uncle Art who are Gary's grandparents. Their cottage was off of Old Trail Drive near Greenbriar Ave. We were staying for about eight days. For the first three or four days, Gary and I were content to swim, fish, and just mess around on the property. We were having a great time. There was an old fourteen-foot speedboat made out of wood by the garage. We were absolutely forbidden to use it but we kept pestering everyone specially my grandfather. They finally gave in and agreed to let us use the boat. We were restricted to the area right in front of the cottage. We had to wear our life jackets at all times and we could only use the oars. There was absolutely no way we could use the outboard motor that was hanging on the wall in the garage. Nuts!

After a day or so of rowing, I came up with the bright idea of rigging a sail and using one of the oars as a rudder. The rudder was no problem but finding something to make a sail out of and supporting it was a little tougher. Then I spotted it. An old picnic table top standing against the back wall of the garage behind a bunch of other stuff. Gary and I dug it out and drug it through the main door. The garage was a long way from the lake and the tabletop was way too heavy for the two of us to manage. It was time to ask Granddad. Somehow, we had to convince him it was a good idea and at the same time not let anybody else know what we were up to. I explained to him our plan to use the top for a sail. He said, "No!" immediately. He said," It won't work. There's no way to stand it up in the boat and there's nothing to tie it off to." So I kept whining and pleading until he finally gave in. He said, "Ok, I'll help you drag it down there but I'm telling you it's not going to work." He probably figured it wouldn't work anyway so there's no harm in it.

The three of us carried it down to the lake and laid it in the boat. My grandfather took off for the house. I think he had enough of us for one day already, but the day wasn't over yet. The boat was floating in about two feet of water. Gary got on one side and I got on the other. We lifted the end of the tabletop that was at the back of the boat. Then we pushed it straight up until the bottom end slid down between the front seat and the bow. When it leaned forward, it locked itself into position.

There was a light wind. It was about ten or twelve miles per hour out of the west.

We climbed aboard and off we went. It actually worked, not very well, but it worked. We were able to go with the wind and even go crosswind, holding our course with the makeshift rudder. We made several runs going away from the shore but drifted downwind a short distance. We would turn around, row back and go again.

Anyone who is familiar with Houghton Lake knows that a storm can come up on that lake in an instant. That's exactly what happened. We were at the end of one of our runs and a strong wind came up out of the west. The boat took off toward the east bay. Gary and I tried to pull the table top down but the wind was holding it up. We weren't strong enough to overcome the wind. All we could

do was ride it out and try to keep the boat from getting too far from shore. The wind took us all the way to the east end of the lake. We jumped out and turned the boat around. The tabletop blew down by itself.

Now we had to decide what to do next. Should we leave our uncle's boat and try to get help from one of the cottages? That would have been the smart thing to do, but no, we decided to stay in the shallow water along shore and pull the boat back with us. The sky got very dark and it started to pour. The wind was blowing like crazy and there were large waves with white caps. I can't remember if there was lightning but there probably was.

I don't think I was ever afraid that we would be injured or would drown. Gary kept saying things like "I don't think we're going to make it," or "I don't think I can go any farther." I assured him that we would be just fine and we didn't have much farther to go. I knew we were in big trouble and that everyone would be worried about us. I can imagine what my grandfather must have been thinking.

After about two or three hours we made it back to the front of home base. Standing on the dock was my great Uncle Charley. He had driven up from Saginaw to help look for our bodies. We tied the boat off and climbed up on the dock. He didn't yell or anything. He just told us that he had stayed behind just in case we showed up. He said that everyone else was out looking for us and that the State Police had been called. My grandmother and great Aunt Elsie were sure we had drowned. They were probably trying to think of a way to break it to our parents. Finally, everyone returned home and they were glad to find us safe.

So that was my big adventure in Northern Michigan! My wife and I own a vacation home near Houghton Lake. I hope that my grandchildren don't get in as much trouble as I did!

Papa and the Blizzard of 1947
By Jessica Helfmann of Howard City,
Michigan
Born 1983

During winter break, when I was a child, I would go and stay with my Papa and Honey (a.k.a. Grandma and Grandpa) for the week. My siblings and I used to beg Papa to tell us the story of the big blizzard of 1947. As Papa told us the story every year, we would all take turns looking at the photo she has of the 15-foot snow banks. It is one of my favorite stories that she tells us, so now I am going to share it with you.

The story starts in mid-January 1947 in Posen Michigan with Papa and her sister meeting their match... Mother Nature.

Papa's sister Bernadine Pokorski (now Robinette); was a freshman; and Papa, Theresa Pokorski (now Donajkowski), was a junior at Posen High School (a.k.a. St. Casimir High School, which was operated by the Sisters of Mercy and Father Szyper [Sheper]). They had mid-term exams on their minds that morning.

Before the girls left the farm, my great-grandpa wished them luck on their exams and as they walked out the door, he said to them, "Looks like a snow storm. You girls better stay home." Papa and Bernadine told him that if they missed the exams today they would have to either make them up after school or go in on a Saturday, which

Jessica's grandma with her dog in 1947

neither of them wanted to do! Plus, then this would leave my great-grandpa having to milk the cows and do their chores on his own, so skipping their exam today was not an option for Papa or Bernadine.

Since the girls made a valid point about leaving my great-grandpa to do their chores and milk the cows if they skipped their exams, he said, "OK, I've got to go to the office in the village anyway, so I'll drive you to school today." My great-grandpa dropped off Papa and Bernadine at school and then he headed off to his office in downtown Posen, where he collected property taxes for the township.

As soon as Papa and Bernadine walked into the school, they got busy taking their exams and were unaware of the developing weather conditions outside. Before they knew it, it was noon and Fr. Szyper came

into the school and interrupted the class. He announced to the school "No one is to leave the school premises because of the blizzard conditions."

Apparently, all of the roads were closed except for the one between the village and the school. The one village plow had just come by so the Father was going to drive those students who lived in the village, home. Those that did not live in town, which Papa and Bernadine did not, were ordered to stay the night at school until the storm stopped and the rest of the roads were clear.

She was panicked because she knew that her dad would not be able to make it home and the farm would still have to run! If Papa did not go home, the only people that could take care of the animals would be her mom, her mentally challenged brother, and her bed-ridden grandmother. Knowing that they would be unable to milk the cows, feed the horses, and take care of the pigs and chickens she knew that she HAD to find a way home!

So that is exactly what Papa did. She grabbed her lunch and headed for the back door so the nuns would not see her. On Papa's heels was Bernadine. She cried and said, "You're not leaving me here!"

"OK." Papa whispered back. "But you must do as I say and you can't whine or else I am going to whack you over the head!" Bernadine agreed and the girls were on their way!

Scrambling through the blowing snow, they hurried through the cemetery so the nuns would not see them. When they reached Grand Lake Highway Papa started to have second thoughts. The five-foot high banks that were on the edge of the road this morning were now filled in and there was no end in sight of the snow stopping. The highway no longer existed. Papa knew at that point that the only

232

way to make it home would be to walk on top of the five-foot banks that were growing rapidly, since the road had disappeared. Since Papa and Bernadine were walking the top of the banks they had no coverage from the storm so they were walking directly into the wind, making it difficult to walk and even to breathe. At that point Papa decided that they needed to walk backwards all the way home.

Walking down the banks backwards, Papa and Bernadine were not only exhausted and cold, but they were hungry too. Papa knew they had to find shelter to eat and rest. Papa had a feeling that Bernadine was going to start whining if they did not stop soon and then she saw it... a semi-truck stuck in the middle of the highway. The truck was abandoned and Papa and Bernadine hopped in! They devoured their lunch and enjoyed the break from the blustery wind whipping around them.

Once they finished their lunches and warmed up Papa and Bernadine abandoned the shelter of the truck cab and once again began walking backwards in the direction of home. Surprisingly, Bernadine still was not whining! Papa was happy about that!

At 4:45 p.m., snow covered, frozen, and beaten up by the wind, they arrived home. They had successfully walked backwards for three miles in a Michigan winter blizzard! The best part of the story was that my great-grandpa came home from his office at 10 am and was not stuck in town like Papa had thought he was!

Meanwhile, back at the school, Fr. Syzper was angry that the nuns did not notice that Papa and Bernadine had left. He had no way of knowing if they had made it home or not, so he kept going to the village to ask if anyone knew whether the Pokorski girls made it home.

I would always ask Papa why the Father would not just call on the telephone to see if they had made it home safely and Papa would laugh every time and say "Jess we did not have a phone in our house back then".

Papa and her family ended up being snowed in at the farmhouse for two weeks! The snow banks ended up being 15 feet high by the end of the blizzard. They even had to bring bulldozers down from the Upper Peninsula to help open the roads.

I will always remember this story that my Papa has told me. It helps to remind me how loving and caring that she is. She took care of her sister, walked 3 miles in a snowstorm backwards, just to make sure that her family's farm was taken care of. She will always be a hero in my eyes, but this story just proves that point.

✓ Winter Sports Park Antics
By Peggy Schmidt Olsen of Grayling,
Michigan
Born 1935

Grayling was a sleepy little wonderful town to grow up in. Summer time was magic time, and your bike was your magic carpet, as soon as your chores were done. After breakfast Mom gave us our list (I had four sisters) and we went right to work. As soon as you were finished, you could go play. One of my standard daily chores was emptying the water pan under the icebox, which was tougher than it sounds. There wasn't room to maneuver it, so it always sloshed. Then I had to mop. This was World War II time—there were no refrigerators, only iceboxes.

Breakfast was usually toast and oatmeal with raisins made on the wood stove. But then it was off to play, and the fish hatchery was always a good starting place. The conservation officer that worked there was great to all the kids. He always had something to show us and let us help feed the fish. Another fun place was Mr. Atkins' Riding Stable in Karen Woods. He also let us pet the horses and showed us how to feed them apple pieces.

Somewhere along the way, we would stop and have our lunch, which Mom packed for us every morning. Then we had to be home in time for supper. After supper and the dishes, we would be out in the street, playing kick the can, hide and seek, Annie-over, hopscotch, and jump rope, with all the neighborhood kids. At dark, we all turned into pumpkins. We had to be in the house, take our bath, and then gather at the dining room table to write our letters to our uncles and cousins that were fighting overseas, in the war. We had to use "onion skin" paper. It was so thin you could see through it, and you had to be careful, as your pencil could poke a hole through it.

The envelope was the same. By keeping the weight so light, the planes were able to carry more mail to our soldiers. The planes were not jets then.

One of those wonderful 1940s days that I remember so well, started with myself, my sister Phylis, and Marlene Sorenson. We rode out to Grayling's very famous Winter Sports Park, and there we met LouAnn McEvers and Bob McClain. In our wandering around, we saw a "flatcar" that they used on the railroad tracks. It had wheels that fit the tracks, and a hand pump, that was used to get them up and down the tracks. We had no idea why it was at the bottom of the toboggan run, but decided it would be great to push it up to the top and ride it down.

We managed to push it half way up, then found stones to prop the wheels, and all headed for home and supper. Everyone was there the next morning and we finally made it to the top, and with no hesitation, we all hopped on and away we went. Grayling was noted then for the fastest toboggan run in the state. We had no idea how fast we were going, but when we hit the first dip, five kids flew in five different directions. Phylis broke her glasses, Bob hurt his shoulder, and we were all sore and shaken up. But as I said, this was the type of town that we kids could go anywhere, but everyone knew us, and without us realizing it, we were watched out for. Of course, someone drove by just as we were riding the flatcar down, realized we were not seriously hurt, and by the time we arrived home, all our parents knew about it. So the winter sports park was off limits for quite a while.

So we went back to another favorite haunt, on the main stream, just out of town, and we would ride past the house and back to the river where there was a big gazebo. It was a great place for our lunch and a wonderful spot for swimming. One day a gang of us were going there, all racing to see who would make the turn first and win. Phylis and I were in the lead. We turned in, and someone had stretched a wire across the drive, which we ran right into, and kids behind piled into us. Phylis broke her glasses again! It was about 40 years later that I found out that house just out of town was a house of ill repute! It wasn't there very long, so we got one of our favorite river spots back.

Another one of my very favorite memories was our local candy store. Mr. and Mrs. Bugsby owned and operated it, and what you could buy for a penny boggles the mind. There was no hurry—you were allowed to look and look to your heart's content. The wonderful smells were as satisfying as eating your candy.

The 1940s were tough years too. Everything was rationed by the government, so our soldiers were taken care of first. We had stamps for food, clothes, shoes, gas, etc. You had to be really careful of your shoes—no going through mud puddles—because you were only allowed one pair a year. Flour came in 50-pound bags only, but the bags were made from cotton with all different designs, so many dresses were made from those. It cost a nickel to go to the Saturday afternoon matinee at the theater. And we had the radio on Saturday night. We all sat around the radio and listened to the Amos & Andy comedy show, then Big Town, a mystery, the Green Hornet, and many more.

Probably half the homes had a phone, but most were "party lines," so when you picked up your phone, your neighbor was probably talking. We had lots of three-way conversations back then. How safe and secure everyone felt. No one locked their doors. If a family had a problem, everyone quietly helped. We had a "Poor Farm" on M-72 West where those without family would go if they couldn't take care of themselves. Most of the dads in town hunted and fished, and would share their catch with the Poor Farm. We were very patriotic. We did not complain about all the things we couldn't have, we just made do with what we had. Everyone was in the same boat, so it did not seem to be a hardship. Looking back, I guess we couldn't be classified as angels, but we were sure respectful kids. It never entered our minds to damage anyone's property. All in all, we could not have been raised in a finer city or time.

Speaking of our winter sports park, it was known then as the finest in the north. The trains came in every Friday afternoon, from Chicago and Detroit, filled with passengers, that in turn filled the hotels, restaurants, and bars, and they spent Saturday and Sunday enjoying sports at the park. We had some great local skiing talent such as Mr. Millikin, Mr. Isenhower, and others. They would slide down the ski slopes standing on their head, on a shovel—truly amazing!

Surrounded by Good Music
By Jerry Francis of Lowell, Michigan
Born 1941

I got my start during November 1941. They called me a Pearl Harbor baby because I was only one week old when the Japanese bombed Hawaii. I still have Depression coupons that my family used for me to get goods from the store (sugar, shoes, etc.) as everything at that time was rationed.

My earliest memories of life are in a big three-story house with six other brothers and sisters and a hard-working father who sometimes worked all day for one dollar. Somehow, he managed to pay the rent and feed us. The neighbors were close-knit people who helped each other and everybody knew each other.

I remember skipping school in kindergarten. The school was next door so I would hide behind our house until noon. Some little orphan girls from St. Johns Orphanage ganged up on me. They called me names, stole my treats, and bent my fingers back. The teacher called good ole Mom and asked why I was missing so much school. The next day she watched. Darn lilac bushes fashioned switches that stung on the back of the legs. I swore I'd never whip my kids when I grew up. I had seven kids just like Mom and Dad but the lilacs were never used for punishment.

My mother baked in an old black firebox of a stove. The boys had to keep the wood box filled up, as the old stove was very greedy. She baked our bread, pies, cakes, beans, stews, and the family favorite: pancakes on the old iron griddle. Eventually the modern electric or gas stove was introduced into her kitchen. Food was often burned and meals were just not the same until Mom learned to use the modern stove.

My brother and I loved sloshing barefooted in the creek with our pant legs rolled up. We often caught frogs and put them in a wicker fishing basket. The biggest one he used for frog jumping contests on the Showboat and the rest were battered and fried alongside the trout he caught for our supper. He was the fisherman and I carried the equipment. As I got taller, I was allowed to carry his golf clubs and chase balls for him. He eventually built his own golf course but I never played on it. I'd had my stomach full of that stuff as a child slave.

In the colder months we skied, ice skated and played cards. In warmer weather, we played baseball and cut up wood for the upcoming winter months. A hot dusty job in the summer on the farm was cutting and drying hay for our jersey brown cow, Tag. Tag had a cow bell that told me where to find her. Usually in the meadow, she had to be driven to the barn for nightly milking. The hay was cut and dried in the fields, then loaded on a wagon and thrust into a square cut window to be stacked dry inside our barn. My job was packing down the hay standing on the top of the wagon and again packing it inside the barn so more could be stored.

On warm summer nights, several of us children slept on the hay in the barn. Every year we tied the forbidden rope swings in that barn and slid down the hay. Tag never told on us. She ate her hay and gave us plenty of rich milk to drink. Any excess butter, buttermilk, and eggs were sold to the neighbors. My sister and I had a regular walking route in the country and were allowed a profit to earn our first two-wheeled bike (shared between the two of us). With occasional new tires, chains, and a large front basket, that bike lasted more than 40 years and eventually gave rides to my own children and grandchildren.

We had an old player piano that played hole-punched music rolls. Our legs got plenty of exercise pumping the bellows for that wonderful music. We also had a Victrola Cabinet as tall as I was that played Al Jolson Records. "Mammy, how I love yah, how I love ya, my dear ole Mammy." Whoever figured that years later we'd be singing that and many

Jerry's dad, Byron Potter

235

other songs on an old fashioned minstrel "Lowell Showboat" as it came down the river to dock in front of thousands of people? It happened one week in July every year in an outdoor arena. My whole family loved being part of the chorus to sing background music for six endmen. Several local talent contests picked different acts to perform on stage with a well-known artist. My older brothers and their friends did water ski tricks and the youngsters had frog jumping contests to entertain the crowd until the boat arrived at the dock to unload all of us. We marched off the boat singing, "Here Comes the Showboat."

Jerry Ford was present several years as a young congressman long before he was President of the United States. Hobnobbing with well-known musical groups was a small town girl's dream come true. Pearl Bailey, Sanchmo (Louis Armstrong), the Harmonicats, the Everly Brothers, Bob Crosby, The Letterman, Gary Pucket, B.J. Thomas, Loretta Lynn, the Moderaires, and the Mamas and the Papas were just a few of

Jerry's mom Mary Euzefa Potter in 1956-57

the greats that were part of our Showboat Celebrities. Eventually the show was moved to a week in June but too much rain caused the show to lose money and it was shut down.

My brother-in-law claimed his Indian mother gave him cow patty tea when his family was sick. If he was not sick before he sure must have been afterwards. Yuck. I also remember having a bad cough and my mother's cure for that was a batch full of fried onions folded in a clean cloth and slapped on my chest. It stunk, but worked. Years later when my own son got pneumonia, I used the same remedy out of desperation to give him some relief. It took a whole night of repeated applications but by morning, he could breathe and fell into a gentle sleep. I got a needed nap myself and when I awoke part of the onions had disappeared (he woke up and ate them).

We did not have a TV so we listened to a lot

of radio. Music, news, and weather during the day and evening programs included Charlie McCarthy, The Shadow "Knows", Fibber McGee and Molly, and George Burns to name a few. Eventually Dad brought home the first black and white television. We watched shows starting from Jack Benny right through the Lone Ranger and everything in between.

Sitting with big bowls of homegrown popcorn covered with fresh churned butter melted just right, we washed it down with some of Mom's homemade root beer. One year she did something wrong in the recipe causing it to blow up all over the attic where she stored it. After listening to the bombs of root beer explode, we mourned the loss of our precious treat while watching it drip down through the ceiling and right onto the piano. After that, the piano played the "Beer Barrel Polka" on many a summer night through Mom's talented fingers. She was good at playing any song by ear.

I wasn't as talented growing up and had to have lessons from the nuns. Three older brothers kept my fingers skipping through boogie woogies. An Irish Tenor, Dad sang in a barbershop quartet S.P.E.B.S.Q.S.A. If we wanted to win great prizes at the parties, we had to sing solo at their music gatherings. As shy as I was, I eyeballed a net stocking full of Christmas candy and had to sing a whole verse of Jolly Ole Saint Nicholas to fill my sweet tooth. After that, I couldn't be shut up. Many years later I'm still singing: weddings, parish funerals, Sunday mass and have toured twice in Europe with the Bishops choir (including an appearance before Pope John Paul II).

Wringer washers took over the old scrub boards and wash tubs. We still had to grate up Fels Naphtha to make our own soap flakes (my job of course). Keep in mind there were nine of us so that wringer washer got a lot of use. It got so much use that it sometimes cut loose and swung around cracking Mom a good

Gerarda "Jerry" Joy Potter in 1959

one. We had heard of women getting their hair and arms caught in the wringers and even one instance of an old woman's breast. Thereafter my smart aleck brother referred to the machine as the "booby trap"! He "milked" his humor as far as he could get away with.

During the Korean War, my two older brothers served our country. My job at that time was to mix the yellow food powder with the white margarine to make it look yellow like butter. We used oleo when the cow was dried up for a rest period and before she would freshen again after dropping a new calf.

Mom had many talents. She made a lot of our clothes on our old treadle sewing machine. Homemade quilts used up a lot of outgrown shirts or skirts, they were made into squares or triangles for her log cabin pattern quilts. If I promised to be careful around the needle, I could sew all the strips we made ripping up old sheets or fabric outdated in style or size. The strips were crocheted into round rag rugs "Little House on the Prairie" style. They were colorful and kept your bare feet off the cold winter floor when getting dressed in the mornings. Dad used his talents to make a large wooden crochet hook for Mom to use. Years later and long after my parents had passed, I made a handful of crochet hooks and taught 4-H girls how to make the clever rugs. One of

them took a grand prize at the county 4-H fair for hers.

I remember baths in the round wash tub with my knees tucked up under my chin. Lord, I'd never fit in one now and would probably be crammed into the sides like a cupcake in an ungreased pan. Dad used that same tub to put the beer bottles in or the homemade ice cream churn, which was made at family picnics. Best tasting ice cream you ever had but it was a long wait to enjoy and a lot of cranks on the handle.

Summer time tramps looking for the first pussy willows and yellow dogtooth violets for a Mother's Day bouquet, I hopped from one swamp mound to the other. Sometimes I fell in the water (but it was all in fun). Mom made wine out of the cowslip and dandelion blossoms (using my grandpa's old recipe). She also made wild grapes into the stuff. We made a lot of jam out of wild or tame berries that we came across. Strawberries and red raspberries were supplemented with rhubarb, wild black caps, mulberries, elderberries, or any excess fruit that came our way.

The local fire department flooded the indoor 4H arena in the winter to make a skating rink. We were country kids but snuck in anyhow so we did not freeze shoveling off our frozen, snow-laden ponds. Sometimes the Grand Rapids figure skating club came out and taught us a thing or two like how to look more graceful when we fell flat on our posterior. One of the older gents was flinging my older sister around by one ankle and one wrist. He let her go when they were wound up really good. She broke her new wrist watch as she splattered across the ice. They never got me to do that trick. I figured if God wanted humans to become helicopter propellers he could have made us into steel, not soft flesh with brittle bones. Oh well, time to leave that one alone.

Sewing on Rainy Days
By Jessie M. Battenfield Tallman of Fife
Lake, Michigan
Born 1935

I remember one Sunday in winter my sister and I walked 2 miles to our friend's home (the Haskins) to slide downhill. We were using enamel covers to slide with and we'd had an ice storm so you really went far and fast. We

237

were to have started home at a certain time but we decided to take one more slide downhill as it was so much fun. The youngest Haskin girl, Jeanie, went so far she hit a fence and cut her lip terribly. So after that we went home when we were supposed to. She still has the scars.

When I was young we walked 1 ½ miles to church. The preacher came from Manton and one Sunday he brought his nephews with him. Andy was about 9 years old and I can still see him sitting on the front seat holding Pastor, Ali Jarmen's son. I never saw him again until I went into Manton for high school and there he was. The Pastor had given us a ride home to our corner and he told Andy, "Those are 2 of the nicest girls." Well, halfway through the 8th grade he had won my heart. It wasn't easy. He made me so mad at him for teasing me all the time at first. But we were married almost 59 years when he died.

My home is also the one from "Have a Cup of Tea with Mrs. Murphy"—not the one here as we moved it off and built a new home in 2000. Mary Murphy was supposed to have murdered a dozen people. Maybe the title was "Murder by the Dozen"? They write it was haunted but my sister and I slept upstairs for 16 years and never was afraid.

Being farmers we always looked forward to rainy days in the summer, for the crops and as we didn't have to go to the fields or work in the garden. On those days Mom would sew my sister and I a new dress or shirt out of pretty print cotton grain sacks. Then after the rain was over Dad would pile us in the car and we'd go look the field over to see how much good the rain had done for the crops. I still find myself wanting to sew on a rainy day!

I remember in 1941 when they were putting the electric poles down Shippy Rd. knowing they'd be up our road soon. We were so excited.

My dad trucked cattle to Detroit every week that he would buy at auction in Traverse City. That was one way my dad made extra money besides farming. My grandparents lived and worked in Detroit and they sent us up a used electric stove and refrigerator on the cattle trucks. I can still see them unloading them and setting them in the yard. We were so thrilled to have them.

Also, my mom would send an egg crate full of eggs to my grandparents by the truck and then Grandma would send us goodies back. When sugar was rationed, there was sugar and candy from them.

My sister Lloy and I had to walk a mile and a half to Maple Hill Country Grade School. When winter was too bad, we walked on top of the fencerows. If a car came, it would be too dangerous to be on the road.

One morning Mom sent us off to school in a blizzard. We got half a mile down the road and our aunt stopped us, saying Mom was coming after us. She hadn't realized how bad it was until she went to feed the chickens. She came and walked us home.

I remember one winter we had a terrible ice storm and Dad backed the team of horses up to the sleigh and put Mom, my sister, and I in and covered us up with horse blankets and we went right across the fields over the fences to Fife Lake to get groceries. The long way there (by the road) would have been about 3 ½ miles.

We haven't had a winter like that since. It must have been the middle '40s or before.

We had a big windmill that Daddy rigged to pipe water up to the house to a big crock in the corner of the kitchen and we just had to turn a switch when we needed to fill the big crock. Well, if we had an electric storm we had to stay out of the kitchen, as lightning would come in the party line phone across the kitchen and down the water pipe.

I remember one Christmas Mom sent Dad to town to buy my sister and I a doll for Christmas. It was to put under the tree for Christmas morning as she always made us beautiful clothes for Christmas and wanted a big surprise for us. Well, Dad brought the dolls home and gave them to us. Mom was so disappointed that there wouldn't be a nice surprise under the tree and that has stuck with me all my life. I do not want to know ahead of time what I'm getting for Christmas. I love surprises.

I always told my children if they snooped and found out what they were getting I'd take it back to the store. Well, we took our niece in to live with us and I told her the same thing. Well, she snooped and my kids tattled on her. I had gotten her a new coat so I took it back and Christmas morning she was looking for the coat but she learned her lesson the hard way.

When we were little, Daddy had a 1937 Chevy Coupe and we'd go visit my grandparents in Detroit. My sister and I would take turns sitting on Mom's lap. The other one had to lay up on a ledge by the big back window. Couldn't do that today!

We always had horses to work the fields with until Daddy purchased our first 1946 Ford tractor. Then when my sister and I were old enough we cultivated the corn. One would drive and the other sat on the fender because we had to uncover the corn when we went around the corner.

We had free shows in Fife Lake on Saturday nights. Dad and Mom would take us and they would sit on my grandparents' porch until the show was over. One Saturday night Dad didn't get home until late and we knew he had to milk the cow before we left, so my sister decided to go milk the cow in the barnyard. Well, guess what? The bull came around the barn and she left the pail sitting under the cow and ran for the fence.

One night at the free show someone had a pack of cigarettes and they were all taking puffs. So my sister and I took a puff and all the way to my grandparents' house we were blowing in each other's face to see if we thought Mom and Dad would smell it. We were scared to death they'd find out. Needless to say, my sister and I never smoked again. I don't think they smelled it as they didn't say anything.

The Land of Grace
By Grace Jean (Emerson) Langea of Garden
City, Michigan
Born 1941

I was born to John Henry Emerson and Margaret Sophie (Badenhoop) Emerson at the University Hospital in July 1941, in Ann Arbor, Michigan. My parents were both from large families: 11 kids on Dad's side and 12 kids on Mom's side. Dad was from Harrisville and Mom from Barton City. My four brothers were all born in Alcona County. My one and only sister was born in Detroit. Our family kids would have been nine, except my mom had two miscarriages, one set of twins.

We stayed with my grandma and grandpa Emerson on Everett Road just west of Harrisville. It was a dead end road back then. One of my dad's sisters and her two kids at the time stayed there also, I guess our dads were

Emerson farm at the end of Everett Road in 1943

in the service. My dad was in the Mounted Calvary at the same time Mickey Rooney was in. Mickey Rooney being a movie star, he got to drive the officers around in the military vehicles. I am related to Mallorys, Dellars, Dorrs, Hakeses, Kuenzlis, Rzepkas, Emersons, Badenhoops, Miks, Coseos, Argyles, Bellhorns, Bauers, Nashatkas, Rosses, and Dolneys, through my aunts and uncles.

When I was about four, we moved to our own 40-acre farm on Miller Road, near Hubbard Lake Road. Our neighbor to the east was Nellie Martin, who lived to be 102 years old. In 2000, I visited the old farm and there was a building that had a sign on it, "The Land of Grace." I saw the pine trees we planted in the '40s along Miller Road. I first saw a picture in the *Alcona Review* that had a location of a shooting on Miller Road, and in this picture were the trees we planted. The picture was taken at the top of the hill a few hundred yards from where our driveway used to be. A lot of the roads changed from when I was a kid. The hilly roads were flattened out and new roads were built.

My dad was good at building and while we were on that farm, he built two cabins on opposite corners of the 40 acres. One was in an apple orchard and the other was a wooded lot.

Then he built a large building with an A-frame roof that we were going to use for chickens. I remember all the neighbors and

Grace and Johnny on a snow drift in 1946

friends came to help erect this building. First, a frame had to be built where they bent two by fours into the beams to hold up the roof. They were glued or nailed or something, and maybe wet down to bend them. There had to be maybe three to four boards wide. It took months to build the beams. That building was still standing along with a log barn that we used to keep our cows in. There was no electricity at first and we had lamps, kerosene lanterns, a big old fashioned radio, and wood burning stoves for cooking and heating. When we did get electricity we were at the end of the line and our transformer would blow out during bad storms. One time the electric fence was on and I had rubber boots on so I knew I wouldn't get hurt, but little did I know a blade of grass was touching my leg above the boot. I got a jolt.

We had a well and had to pump our own water for drinking, cooking, and baths. Our bath day was on Saturday night and we would use a metal wash tub in the kitchen. After our baths, we would listen to the radio shows such as Gun Smoke, The Green Hornet, Gangbusters, The Creaking Door, The Shadow Knows, etc. Mostly any other time the radio was tuned to WSM Nashville, Tennessee, and The Grand Ole Opry. (Minnie Pearl, Hank Williams, Roy Acuff and others).

We grew our own crops and Mom canned up everything imaginable for the winter months. We would sell the excess to the neighbors. We'd pick wild blueberries, blackberries, strawberries, and gooseberries for jams and once in a while, we'd have strawberry shortcake or a pie. We had the usual outhouse with the Sears or Montgomery Ward's catalog for paper to look at or wipe with, you had to crunch it up for a while so it was soft. At night, there was an enamel pot with a lid in the house.

I went to school in Harrisville, K through 3rd, then 4th through 8th in Lincoln, then back to Harrisville for the 9th and two months into the 10th, then we moved to Detroit. Sometimes the roads were so bad that the bus couldn't make it the mile and a half to get me so I'd miss school. I only went about 1/2 a year in kindergarten. We used to have to take naps on those old picky Army blankets. The next years when the roads were bad my dad used to drive us the mile and a half to catch the bus on Hubbard Lake Road. In the afternoon, the bus dropped us off and we'd walk the mile and a half. I remember one really bad winter when it drifted so bad that there was a snowdrift at least one story high between the house and the building we kept the tractor in. My brother and I would climb up on top of it and slide down toward the house.

There are a lot of memories that happened on the farm, like when we were being punished for something we'd done wrong, we would have to cut our own switch to be spanked with. Like taking a day and going fishing from a small stream, to a larger one, then on to Sucker Creek and then end up at Hubbard Lake. That day I remember because I saw a snake swimming across the water. By the way, I hate snakes. My mom chopped one up with an ax one day because it was all curled up ready to attack. Another day at about 3 in the afternoon it got as dark as night, the a couple hours later it got light out again, we thought the world was coming to an end. Later we heard that there was some huge fire somewhere in Canada.

By the time we left the farm, I had three brothers and Mom was pregnant with another one. My dad sold the farm and took off with the money and we had to move in with my grandparents in Barton City. At least they had an indoor bathroom and plumbing. A washing machine was better than a washboard. While at this farm, we helped in small ways by helping bring in the hay, weeding the garden, and chasing the cows home for milking. My aunt and grandpa would milk the cows. I tried to do it once but couldn't get the milk out.

During deer season, Grandma had a bunch of hunters that came up from the big cities to do their hunting. They paid her to stay the two weeks, brought groceries, and stayed at the house since she had lots of beds after having such a large family. They would hunt during the day, and Grandma, Mom and my aunt would have a big meal ready for them about six o'clock. After that, the guys would sit around and play cards.

This one year I ended up having pneumonia. I ached from one end to the other. I was out of school for two weeks, thought I was better after the first week and got ready for school, then walked down the lane and turned around and came back and stayed in bed for another week. This was during deer season and the regulars would check in on the sick kids, (there were three of us that were sick) slipping us a silver dollar every now and then. We had all the childhood diseases: chicken pox, measles, and mumps.

Grandma used to make my school dresses from chicken feed bags. They used to come in prints and she would add a little lace around the collar.

We stayed at the farm west of Barton City until Mom got on ADC, and then got a house in Lincoln. I hung around with new people that lived around town. We'd go swimming in Brownie Lake, or rent a canoe and paddle around the lake. One girl and I would walk about two miles to where her horse was boarded and then go riding. I would go strawberry picking with the town ladies to make 10 cents a quart. Sometimes I would use my earnings to buy some of the berries for the family. My mother always made homemade bread, usually 7 or 8 loaves at a time and a few pans of cinnamon rolls. The kids around town used to come by for slices of warm bread and butter. To this day, they remember that warm bread.

Life was good, and then my dad came back and begged my mom to take him back. That was when we left Northern Michigan. I would love to move back up there.

The Newaygo Dam
By Gary Versen of Newaygo, Michigan
Born 1946

I was born in 1946 and my story is about the Newaygo Dam. When I was a child I used to fish the dam all the time. There was mainly fish that stayed in the area around the dam. During the spring the fish would swim up to the dam to spawn. There were many different types of fish such as Walleye, pike, bass, trout, etc. In or around 1958-1960, sometime in that era, they took out the dam, then they made a bridge over it to make it easier travel from Newaygo to Northern Michigan. The bridge was 4 lanes that connected to US-37 that ran up north. Just across the dam you could go to Fremont and could go to Croton dam.

Wartime in England Boyhood Memories
By Frank Hurst of Tawas City, Michigan
Born 1928

My friend, Eric and I loved the countryside and its ever present opportunities for adventure. One day it was suggested that we should learn the art of rabbit catching to supplement the meager meat ration. This was not simple, especially for two 13 year old boys from a rural area. There were at least two ferrets to buy. Ferrets were feisty little animals, about half the size of a rabbit but without fear of anything. Then there were nets to buy, pegs to secure them to catch the rabbits as they hopefully flew in terror from their warrens. Here I must explain that rabbits in Europe make their homes in warrens dug from the hillside. The rabbits in the US are actually hares.

Everything being in order and the ferrets being secured by means of a simple collar with a long thin line attached, the ferrets were eagerly set off down the last remaining hole, which was left uncovered.

Needless to say, we progressed from one rabbit to three, or even four, which were snapped up by friends and neighbors much to the advantage of our pocket-money.

One day whilst busy with our nets, we were interrupted by the noise of an aircraft. This wasn't unusual in those days, but boys being boys we stopped what we were doing to see what kind it was to add it to our aircraft spotters list. As we watched, a plane broke through the cloud layer and began to circle overhead. It was a Liberator of the US Air Force and we could tell it was in trouble because the engines were intermittent.

Suddenly as it circled, we saw parachutes blossom from the plane and drift slowly out of sight. Meanwhile the Liberator with the pilot still at the controls coughed and the engines died. The next thing to our horror the aircraft did a complete nose dive into the ground about half a mile from where we were. There was a terrific explosion with a sheet of flame, and where the plane crashed, it formed a crater about a mile from the village it seemed to avoid.

The pilot was a very brave man, but not only did he save his comrades by giving them time to jump, he saved the lives of the villagers by avoiding their homes. I don't know his name, someone in America does, and God knows.

Later, one of the village ladies came forward and the police helped her down into the crater, where she laid a bunch of daffodils. A tribute to the unknown airman I can never forget.

✓ I Was Roy Rogers When Other Girls Played With Dolls
By Jacquelyn Beebe of Marion, Michigan
Born 1946

1957—4th grade, Patty Kundinger, WOW! She was Norwegian; very pale skinned, raven black hair and green eyes. I was a very chunky 10 year old, but oh how I loved her. So much, that she came to my mom and dad's for lunch, we had 45 minutes. Also, on TV was, Search for Tomorrow, Guiding Light, both 15 minutes and As the World Turns, first ½ hour soap. Wow, what days they were, and what a great teacher.

1958—and still I am now 66 and so is Beverly Kay Haine-Knodson, grew up next door neighbors and Joan (Snookie) Sloiter Sutton, all pals in 60's, now. We all went to Lincoln Elementary K-7th though Bev left after R1 and went to St. Anns Catholic School, but all together again in 8-12th. They both graduated in 62. I quit at end of 11th kind with child, but got diploma after I got GED in 82-diploma for 12th grade. Engo, my oldest girl graduated in 87.

First ever new car—a 1959 Chevy Impala, Ice Blue, I was going on 13. I stood on a snow piled bank in front of house looking down at the car. It looked the size of a matchbox car and I an elf "Good Ol Daze."

52-59—Carl Swartwood owns Swartswood's Dairy. I remember his white truck. He delivered to us for years. I don't remember, also and my grandparents too. I set out milk bottles quite often. Wow! How times have changed.

5-11-55—mischief I might have gotten into, I was always Roy Rogers when other little girls want fancy, smancy dolls, and the like. In kindergarten, I wanted two gun holsters and cowboy boots and at one time, the sheriff's office (Dad's fishing shanty) held my big sister's new model doll buggy. I lit it up and all that was left was the frame of (sheriff's office/fishing shanty and doll buggy frame, was my butt warm.

1958—I will always consider my Gramma, Amanda May Jackson, an idol and ideal mother. I just loved her. I spent much time with her as I did at home. There was 4 years between Biggs and me and 7 years between me and youngsters. Guess maybe I got more 1 on 1 from Gramma, and was jealous of sisters.

✓ I Remember Pearl Harbor
By Phyllis (McGillis) Babel of Traverse City, Michigan
Born 1931

It began as an ordinary Sunday in Traverse City, Michigan on December 7, 1941. My sister Marilyn and I were nine and ten years old respectively, at this time. We walked to Mass in the morning (no car). I was really excited, as we were going to our grandpa and grandma's for dinner. My aunt and uncle were going to be there along with my two cousins, Don and Bob, who were also our ages. After dinner, we walked downtown to attend the movie playing at the Michigan Theater. There was no TV at that time, so movies were a real

Phyllis's Grandpa and Grandma McGillis in 1953

242

treat! The movie playing was "Keep 'Em Flying" starring Bud Abbott and Lou Costello. They were a great popular comedy team.

After the movie, we began to walk home. When we were across from the post office, we heard boys yelling and running with extra newspapers. We asked them what had happened, and they yelled that the "Japs" had attacked Pearl Harbor! They told us to get home as quickly as possible. We looked at each other and began to run as fast as we could to Grandma's house, as we believed the "Japs" would be in Traverse City soon! We arrived home and everyone was sitting and attentively listening to the radio. After hearing about the many casualties, we knelt down and prayed for the victims and our country. I will never forget Sunday, December 7, 1941, "a day of infamy."

Phyllis and Marilyn in 1941

Life's Hard Lessons
No Childhood, No Prom, and No Graduation
By Alma Leist of Traverse, Michigan
Born 1939

My father walked away from a farm where he was born and raised, with 11 brothers and sisters in Northern Michigan. He hitched rides and walked to Flint, where he got a job as a short order cook. He was 14 years old. From there he worked his way up to a job in the Buick plant. He fit right in; moonshine, parties and fights with the Union, where he was badly beaten.

He then, met my mother, the youngest of three daughters, sheltered and raised by a widowed mother. There my oldest brother and sister were born.

My father saved for a down payment on a farm. Then the Depression hit. He used to say he was one of the lucky ones, always having a couple of days work at the Buick plant. He had to walk a lot, because of the gas rationing during the Depression. Finally, he had enough for the down payment on the farm. My mother was slow getting my brother and sister dressed to come north, so my father went two blocks away to get money from the bank, then, picked them up. When we went back past the bank again, it was closed. That was how close he came to losing all his money.

So, they moved to Horton Bay and bought a farm. Eight years later, I came along. My earliest memories were of being poor and working hard. My father saved almost all he made, so we didn't have much. He said after walking back and forth to work in Flint and seeing grown men digging in garbage cans looking for food to feed their families that he would save enough so we would always eat.

Eight years later I was born. My parents did not want any more kids, so they named me so that my initials spelled A.L.L. That didn't work. I always told them that was what they got for giving me a terrible name. They had three more after me. Three families really, she was 18 when my older brother was born and 53 when my youngest sister was born. This was before birth control, as you see.

`People are really spoiling their kids now. I never had a toy when I was little. My mother made me a rag doll. My best Christmas was one year I got a sled and a pop. It was usually socks and underwear. The only doll I ever had was when I was seven. My older sister lied about her age and got a job at Cary's. Then she bought me a doll. My older brother threw it down the stairs and smashed its head. He said there was too much work to do, to play with dolls.

I remember when I was 3 or 4, playing in the sand with stones for people. Why didn't I develop the pet rock? That guy made a million off of it!

Oh yes, kindergarten! I was sick half the year with every childhood germ, measles, mumps, strep throat etc. The house was always so cold. I remember getting out of bed in the morning with snow on the foot of my bed, running downstairs and standing in front of the wood and coal stove. First, your butts roasted, then you turn around and your front roasts. We never had warm clothes. My mother would take apart old coats and make me a coat. My older sister told me she had a new snowsuit from Sears & Roebuck every year! All I can figure out is, they must have been sick of kids when I came along.

Walking to school was real fun! Freezing! Then, when you got there, there was another wood stove. Sometimes we had boiled potato for hot lunch. I had to wash my own socks, because if my mom did them I would have one pink and one white. I hid them and washed them by hand.

I hated school. Some of the kids thought they were hot stuff. One little girl came to school with a bag of candy. Her parents owned a store. She would never give me any. She called me a rag-muffin. I probably was. My mom made my dresses out of feed sacks.

The next year, first grade, I was told I failed kindergarten. They said I didn't have enough days in. Lucky for me, the first grade teacher let me stay in first grade.

On the farm, in summer we were barefoot. One time I stepped on a rusty nail, bad times! My mother took the shovel and got fresh cow manure, put it on my dad's sock, and tied it over my knee. She changed the manure every day and my foot got better, but no one came near me for a week or so.

We used to go to town once in a while to get groceries. My dad would sit in the bar. When Mom was ready to go, she would send me in to get him. That was fun. He would get me orange soda and if he wasn't ready to go, he'd give me a dollar to go to the dime store. That spent real fast, and sometimes I went back and got another dollar. Sometimes he would just come to the car where Mom was waiting. Good thing there wasn't much traffic then. I would sit in the middle and help drive the car. He would go from the right shoulder to the left shoulder if I didn't steer.

Then my father planted about 30 acres of contract green beans. That meant growing for the canning factory. We had to pick them. I was probably 6. My older brother would pick in the row beside me. If I slowed down, he would take his foot and kick my butt. I would

fall face down in the hot dirt, with sand in my eyes, nose, and mouth. I hated him then. He made me pick as fast as he could. I really got even with him one day. Mom asked me if I wanted to go and fix lunch. I was glad to get out of the hot sun and dirt, so I did. I put a big kettle of water on the wood stove, went out, picked, and husked sweet corn. I put it in the kettle to boil while I got out the rest of the lunch. When I went to take it out of the kettle, it was full of worms. So I took it out, put it on plates, and called them to lunch. No one didn't even notice I didn't eat any corn.

Right after that, my older brother lied about his age and enlisted in the Army. That meant more work for me. Like helping my dad, castrate the pigs, YUCK! Leading the cow to the neighbor's farm to breed, YUCK! Always watching cows, which meant taking them to fields to graze that didn't' have fences, for hours, then, chasing them back. One time I was chasing one that tried to get away and I stubbed my toe, cut the whole end off! I can still see all those wash dishes full of blood. Sometimes when my older sister was still there, we did it together, that was fun. She had a big yellow cat. We would pretend we were fighting and that cat would get after me. What a loyal cat. Once in a while, maybe on Sunday, I was allowed to play. There was a neighbor girl three years older than me, I used to play with. She was an only child, so she had lots of toys and clothes. Her dad worked on the boats, so he was gone a lot, and it was just her and her mom. She let us do anything we wanted. Our favorite thing to do was to play store. We took everything out of the cupboards and played store with it. Her mom would always make us a really good lunch. Then, her mom got TB and went to a hospital for a long time, so her dad was always there. I went with them to see her mom a few times.

My grandmother lived about 15 miles away, and sometimes we visited her, (rarely). I used to stand and admire her cupboard full of antique dishes. She used to let me play her old pump organ. That was fun. Sometimes Mom would say, "Go ask your dad if he would take us to see grandma." I would run and ask him and he would say, "Don't that old woman know how much work I have to do?" I took the brunt of his yelling, a lot.

We used to have a daybed in the living room beside the table that the radio, operated by batteries, was on. When "The White Shadow Knows" would come on the radio, it would cause the table to vibrate and the light on the ceiling would dance from kerosene lamps. I can still feel how scary that was.

We did not get electricity until I was eight, so we had a back house with Sears and Roebuck, and ice on the seat in winter. We would have to pump water by hand, carry it, and put it in the reservoir of the wood stove to heat and take a bath in a metal washtub. We took turns, from the youngest to the oldest. Lucky for me, I was the youngest for 7 years.

One time the church people were there and my older sister tripped over someone's foot. My mom said, "What do you say?" My sister said, "Get your damn big foot out of the middle of the floor." Boy; that was never forgotten.

I had a dog that was mine for a short time, a little black terrier. I really loved that dog. One day I came home from school and he was gone. I used to get down on my hands and knees every day in the snow and pray for my dog to come home. A few years later, my mom told me he got rabies and my dad shot him.

My mom used to sew a lot for us girls. Bags cow feed came in made dresses. They were cotton with flowers on them. She would take apart coats and make coats for me. I sure hated the mess. When she sewed, nothing else got done.

I was always cleaning as a little kid. Even after I got married, when I would go out there, she would dump all that sour milk she saved to make cottage cheese, and I would wash all these jars.

You can imagine what a job laundry day was, with the old wringer washer in the middle of the kitchen, pumping and carrying all that water in and out. I always hated to come home from school when my mom did laundry. Water running down all the windows, wooden clothes racks in the living room in front of the wood stove, what a mess! Dad used to say Mom could make enough mess in one hour to take six women six hours to clean up.

I don't know what I would have done without my friend, Pat. She worked at a dry cleaner's and kept my clothes dry-cleaned for me, bless her.

One night my friend and I were riding around, pouring out part of a 7-Up and putting whiskey in the bottle, so we could drink as we drove. We ended up in Gaylord. By then we were hungry, so we stopped and bought some pickled bologna. Boy, did I get sick! I really learned young what blowing chunks was! That was the end, and only time I drank whiskey.

When I was almost fifteen, I quit school. I got a full time job at Alice's Coffee Shop. She made the best banana cream pie! Then, I got an apartment right down the street. It was really nice and only fifty dollars a month! My job was right next door to the place my boyfriend worked, so he was there all the time.

When I was sixteen, I got married. He was twenty-one. My daughter was born four days after I turned seventeen.

To anyone who is thinking of doing what I did, don't do it! I missed out on so much. Not only did I not have a childhood after age eight, I didn't have any teen years, no prom. No graduation, just a lot of hard work! A (G.E.D.) works, but not like all of high school and college. The less education you have, the harder the jobs are that you will get. DON'T DO IT!

I Remember
By Betty Edman of Ann Arbor, Michigan
Born 1930

When my sister, Joyce, and I were little, Grandma and Grandpa Wilcox would spend summers with our family in Petoskey. I remember grandpa with his watch fob and candy corn in his pocket. During evenings, he would sit close to the small radio listening to world news, followed by Amos & Andy. On a nearby table was a rotary phone, and our number was 47. Since we were on a party line, we often would have to wait to make a call.

Our town of 5000 was classy with fashionable shops. We used to laugh about the names of two—I.M. Reinhertz and M.I. Fryman.

Grandpa Wilcox's brother, Great Uncle George, came to Northern Michigan for one day every July to sell funeral supplies to the undertakers there. He arrived in a huge jalopy filled to the brim with merchandise, with a lady friend in the front seat. On this day every year,

Jack Edman in 1930

Grandma would cook a scrumptious dinner of white field corn on the cob, baked potatoes, and her specialty, "floating island" for dessert. The lady friend was never included.

One summer I developed Scarlet Fever, so a red sign was placed on our front door. I was quarantined, which meant that no one could come in. Grandma came into my room with the news that my friend, Noel Feather, now wore glasses. I thought she said, "An old feather wore glasses." This brought laughter into my life, much needed.

My other grandma played the piano. She hired a dance instructor to teach tap in her home. Miss Merry came all the way from Gaylord, 35 miles away, and Grandma was the accompanist. At age 3, I performed on the large stage of the Bay View Auditorium, and the newspaper reported, "Little Betty Bailey received a standing ovation for her dance number."

Winters were cold and snowy. We little girls clad in bulky snowsuits would trudge up the hill daily to school. A few years later, we would walk to the Winter Sports Park every day after school for skating or jumper riding. A jumper was a low-to-the –ground seat on one runner invented in Petoskey. It has a different name now (bump-jumper). There was a toboggan slide, which was torn down later due to several accidents. We all learned to ski on the hill with a simple rope tow.

A highlight of the seasons was the Winter Carnival at the Winter Sports Park in February.

I remember a beautiful ice throne designed by a local artist, Stanley Kellogg. The Queen was always crowned by a celebrity. One year it was Tom Harmon, star football player from the University of Michigan. Figure skaters of all ages performed and speed skaters from all over Michigan raced. Eric Heiden, Olympic star and localite Gary Ross competed.

My family owned Bailey's Newsstand, a hangout for high schoolers when pinball machines were the rage. The store was located in Pennsylvania Park, and my dad, who loved baseball, had a radio broadcasting Detroit Tiger games as well as a blackboard with a running score. Resorters would gather on benches in the park to listen to the game while reading the newspapers.

Growing up in Petoskey in the '30s and '40s and '50s was innovative in that we made our own fun; it was healthy as we enjoyed the out-of-doors; and interesting as we had the opportunity to meet people from all over the country coming to Petoskey for relief from hay fever or to enjoy the beautiful lakes.

Michigan Wonderland
By Ed Barnes of Kewadin, Michigan
Born 1931

We never went hungry. We didn't have anything, but our dad kept us from going hungry. Our dad built our house from recycled lumber. The Buick Company tore down some old houses to make room for a new factory. The wood was available free for the taking and a friend loaned us a big truck to collect it. The house was made entirely from that recycled lumber. We had no electricity, no water well, and no indoor plumbing. We carried water by the bucketful from relatives nearby who had a well. When I was just a little fellow, I got pneumonia. This was before the era of antibiotics. I missed my whole year of kindergarten, home in bed slathered in Vicks. It has made a marvelous excuse when my grandchildren ask for help with their schoolwork. I just point out that I'm the one in the family who flunked kindergarten. Our shoes were saved for school. At the start of every summer, we were real tenderfoots, walking gingerly on the sharp gravel of the roads. By the end of the barefoot summers, we could run on the gravel without even noticing the roughness.

246

We lived between two farms and did all sorts of farm chores there. We did the tending of the livestock, milked the cows, disked and plowed the fields, and brought in the hay. We didn't get paid in money, but we did get well fed in return for our hard work. Sometimes there were hand-me-down clothes that we would not have been able to buy that we would get. I remember how exciting it was to drive the new Alice Chalmers tractor provided by the government during the war years. What competition there was among us boys to see who would drive and who would follow along doing the handwork on any given day. Our home was on about one and a half acres, an acre of which was the vegetable garden. My big job at home was to keep the garden weeded, watered, and free of bugs. My favorite nemesis was the big green tomato worm. I had to stomp those gooey monsters into fertilizer with my bare feet, their innards squishing up between my toes. With that kind of chore, it isn't any wonder that on a hot sunny summer day, I left my hoe and went to the swimming hole with friends. Boy, was my dad upset with me when, getting home from his hard workday, he discovered that my chore had gone unfinished! With my dad's work, we moved for a time to Chicago. What a culture shock that was! In rural Michigan, people were friendly and caring, helping one another whenever there was need. In the big city, kids my age were selfish, callous, and abusive. I was very happy when my family was able to return home to our Michigan wonderland.

✓ **Grandma's Fur**
By Irene E. Ensing of Houghton Lake, Michigan
Born 1940

As a child, much time was spent at my maternal grandparents' (Robert Towne, Sr. and Altha May Towne) home. Our home was only two miles away. Dad worked in Flint, and commuted back and forth, first by bus, and then later by car. My grandparents heated and cooked with wood. Their small home was always warm and cozy. They did not have luxuries such as running water, electricity, telephone, and bathroom facilities. A large rain barrel provided water for household chores. Drinking water was brought in by cream cans that were hauled from my Aunt Mildred and Uncle Lewie Spink's farm a mile away. An icebox sat in the dining room and light was provided by kerosene lamps. Bathroom facilities consisted of a two-holer outhouse. They used an outdated mail-order catalog to wipe with. Neither the outhouse nor the catalog pages were user friendly. When someone was ill or Grandma needed something, an article of clothing was hung on the mailbox. She did that until she hung out her under slip and was teased by my cousin, Don. After that, a small American flag was used. My grandpa was a snort man who had a game leg and several fingers missing. For that reason, he signed his name with an X. he enjoyed reading "The Grit" and reading aloud "The Song of the Lazy Farmer" from the Michigan farmer. As he tended his garden, he carried a can of tea with him, moving it from fencepost to fencepost as he worked. He hunted, fished, and trapped. His sense of smell was gone, so many a skunk found its way onto the drying board. That begins the gist of the following story.

Grandma was petite and had long hair, which she braided and wound into a bun at the nape of her neck. She baked many delicious goodies in her Dutch oven. She was always a meticulous housekeeper and had certain days to do household chores. The one day she always kept was the Sabbath. Church was a quarter mile from their home. She never missed a Sunday. On Sundays, she donned her church hat, apple scented toilette water, and her jewelry. A treasured possession was a fur coat. Before Sunday, she would hang it on the outdoor line to freshen it up. However, this week, Grandpa had a successful catch: you guessed it—an odiferous polecat! Grandma never gave it a thought and arrived at church thinking she smelled of apple blossoms. Halfway through, she was nudged by the lady next to her. The lady whispered in her ear twice, "I smell a pussycat." Grandma realized it was her, but managed to sit through the service. After the "amens," she made a hasty retreat. I never heard what transpired, but I imagine that Grandpa got an earful. I've never seen any family member wearing that coat, so I imagine that it met its demise. The stress or trauma on Grandma evidently did not affect her health, as she lacked two months of being 102 when she passed on. Many descendants of Grandma and Grandpa live in this area, including 14 families of grandchildren, great-grandchildren, and great-great-grandchildren.

19th and Early 20th Century Washing Machines
By Ron Hamlin of Farwell, Michigan
Born 1936

I was born on a farm near the town of Shepherd in Isabella County, Michigan. This farm has been in my family since 1879. My grandfather was born in 1880 in a log cabin on this land. This log cabin sat just back of a large, white pine tree. The front of the cabin was about 20 feet by 20 feet. That area served as kitchen, living area, and a small bedroom. There was a loft overhead for more sleeping area. They used straw ticks to sleep on. There was a wing on the back that served as a pantry and for storage. My great-grandmother had to haul water from a flowing well in the field north of the cabin to do the laundry. The washing machine was a galvanized tub and a scrubbing board. My great-grandmother raised four children under these conditions. My grandfather was the only boy in the family and he stayed to help farm the land. His son, my father, was born in 1905 and my Aunt Irene was born in 1912 in the same log cabin. They lived there under the same conditions, but with one improvement to the laundry equipment—there was a hand-operated wringer that would squeeze the water from the clothing. It consisted of two rubber rollers with a crank on one side.

Sometime after that, more land was added to the farm and with it became a nicer home. However, there was still no electricity or running water. The Maytag Company produced a gasoline-engine-powered, agitating washing machine that worked real well. It had a kick-starter on it, but because it used gasoline, it had to be used outdoors or in a well-ventilated area. They still had to haul drinking water, but got other water from a cistern that collected rainwater from the eaves of the house.

Our parents were married in 1928 and lived in this newer home. There was still no electricity and they still utilized the same water supply. My three brothers were born in 1931, 1933, and 1935. I was born in 1936, and brought electricity to the farm with me. Along with electricity came a new washing machine.

It had an automatic agitator and a wringer on top. The squeezed-out water would then run back into the tub to be used again. The one thing wrong with it was that when a three-year-old boy (me) got a tall stool, he could get his fingers caught in the wringer…and I did! It tore my thumb loose, and pulled my arm in up to my shoulder, spinning all the way. I guess my mother heard me screaming and got me out. I wore a sling for a few months. The skin all grew back and there were no lasting effects. I always suspected that one of my older brothers had something to do with it. You know how they are. The farm is still in our family after 134 years.

Aunt Linnie Payne
By Neil Frisbie of Rose City, Michigan
Born 1937

This story tells of Linnie Payne. Linnie Payne was a life-long resident of Maple Rapids. She and her husband, Arnold, lived next door to my folks, and did so for as long as I could remember. I can't recall what Arnold did for a living, but I do remember him as being an old grouch. He died at an early age and I dare say that Linnie was better off without him. Linnie was best remembered as being "Aunt Linnie" to all the kids in town that I grew up with. When you went to visit her, she always managed to have two or three cookie jars full of homemade cookies—none of that commercial stuff for "Aunt Linnie's kids!" Aunt Linnie had a dark interior in her house because Arnold liked it like that, and she didn't change it even after he died. Aunt Linnie didn't drive, but would walk down to Grandpa Son's store and get what she needed. Of course, after she became too infirmed to walk, some of us kids would go to the store for her. We also did a lot of other errands at the same time.

Now, this is the best part of being one of Aunt Linnie's kids. All of the door casings in her house were painted a bright white—the reason being was to measure kids! Somehow or other, Aunt Linnie decided she would measure all the kids in Maple Rapids. She did so on her door casings and even the walls near the end. During our birth month, we were supposed to report to Aunt Linnie's home, and she would record the necessary information.

She measured our height for the year and also added our weight, as she had a medical scale at the house. She kept records so far back in time that most of our parents were on her casings or walls also! Most usually, when we were done with the measuring, we stayed for milk and cookies and a lively discussion of some sort. Also, another item of interest that Aunt Linnie was proud of was her outside toilet! It was painted a sparkling white on the outside and had a bright green door with the windows trimmed in a light green. The inside was painted a soft pastel yellow and had fancy magazine holders mounted. Aunt Linnie probably had the first pay toilet around because it was the first one where you had to pay a nickel to pee and a dime to poop. It was on the honor system for payment of services rendered! We kids used it as often as we could because she always had the latest comic books to read. In those days, your word or handshake was all you needed to complete the transaction. Even our moms used it from time-to-time because Linnie always had the latest Sears Catalog! I don't know of anybody who ever cheated Aunt Linnie out of her "P & P" Toilet money!

✓ A Mischief-Maker's Growing-up Days
By Elizabeth Betty Dembny of Gaylord, Michigan
Born 1930

I was born on September 15, 1930. I was the seventh child. My parents had 12 children. We lived on a farm in a very small village. I went to a country school. We had to walk two and a half miles every morning and afternoon, no matter if it was raining or two feet of snow on the ground. We only had thin mittens, so our fingers were frozen when we arrived home. We could tell that our parents felt sorry for us walking in the winter months. One day, my neighborhood boy rode a bike, and I sat on the bike farm bar. I think my behind hurt me for two days. I never rode that bike again.

Yes, we had an outhouse 90 feet from our house. "Brrrr," it was cold! We had one small radio and always listened to the polka party hour every Sunday morning. That was special. We didn't have electricity until 1940. Spankings were always in action. It didn't matter whether you were a girl or a boy; you still got spanked with an old leather belt. The punishment in school was to stand in the corner with your nose touching the wall. My mom told my dad to spank us with that leather belt at least once a year. When Dad spanked me, I always wet my pant, that's when I even got spanked more. My oldest brother was in the Korean War for two years. I had two more brothers that went to war. They all came home safe, thank God. The Depression years were really bad and sad. It was hard to feed 10-12 kids every day, but we lived on a farm, so we had our own food. We had chickens, eggs, beef, pork, ducks, rabbits, and a large garden. We did okay.

We had two horses to do farm chores. We butchered a chicken almost every week for our Sunday dinner. My dad was a hunter, so every year; he'd kill bears, deer, rabbits, and wild ducks. He'd go fishing a lot. That was his escape from the full house. We never had any toys. For Christmas, we little kids would only get an orange and some candy. One year, my brother and I hid in our parent's bedroom. I was afraid of Santa. Mischief was fun for me. My younger sister and I teased each other, and she would get so angry for a few minutes. Six of us would play ball and play with used tires, rolling them down the driveway. We had no TV, but we listened to records. I was the mischief maker, no matter what it was about, and I still am today. It's fun; some people love me, and others are just jealous.

The girls took a bath in the afternoon; the boys hook their bath in the evening in a wash tub. We had the wringer washer. When I was 11, I had to iron all the clothes every week. One day, my little sister was watching me iron, her nose just above the ironing board. In anger, I touched the hot iron on her nose. She never came around when I was ironing again. My mom sewed our nighties, slacks, and aprons. We also renewed many used clothes from so-called "richer" people living in bigger towns. I was in a one-room school house from grades one through eight. Then I went to high school to the tenth grade. I didn't like school.

My memorable people would be my parents and then my first husband, who died on a ship in 1965 in an accident with another ship. He was only 36 years old and had five beautiful sons. I remarried two years later, and my second husband died in 1988. What a loss it was for me. I also lost a baby.

✓My Dream Place: Northern Michigan
By Terry Bohlander of Cincinnati, Ohio
Born 1949

I will never forget as long as I live. It was the summer of 1956. It is hard to believe that it has been 56 years, but I was seven years old then and I'm 63 now! Being from Cincinnati, it was a typical steamy, hot, and humid summer day. My parents were reading the morning newspaper, the *Cincinnati Enquirer*, and noticed an ad that read, "Escape from the heat and humidity and cool off in the mild climate of Northern Michigan to a cozy cabin on the lake." That was all they needed to hear. They called the number instep to check availability. (My parents hated the heat so much that one time they took a long awaited trip to New Orleans and ended up driving to Michigan after one day!) A few days later, they loaded up the car with all four kids and headed north on Rt. 27 to Clam Lake, Michigan. Interstate 75 wasn't even completed yet! We were all so excited. Little did I know this would make such a positive impact on my life, as well as on my sister and brothers!

Being overly anxious as we were, we arrived in the rain to find out that the place we rented wasn't going to be vacated until the next day. Even though it was late, we were able to find a place for the night on Torch Lake called Fetz's Lodge, which was a bit rustic to say the least! My Dad always tried to make the best of things, so we spent the night there with only one bathroom in the entire lodge of 20 occupied rooms and bare light bulbs hanging from the ceiling! We still had fun and laughed ourselves to sleep. We awoke the next morning with the bright sun shining through the windows and walked across the street after breakfast to one of the most beautiful beaches on Torch Lake! I couldn't wait to get in the water (not knowing it was ice cold in July!) My Dad noticed that I was actually shivering, and proceeded to rescue me and put me on his shoulders, wrapped in a beach towel. It may sound strange, but this memory on Torch Lake beach has stayed with me my entire life and has calmed me through many difficult and stressful situations!

We finally got into our cabin later that afternoon and had dinner that night at a restaurant nearby called "Trout Creek Inn," who at the time was known for their fresh Lake

Clam Lake boat trip in 1959

Michigan perch. I must have been starving and ate too fast because I got a perch bone stuck in my throat for over 2 hours! It seemed like two days. My parents and the staff there tried everything, and finally made it go down after several attempts of Coke, root beer, and lots of bread! Needless to say, I have never had perch since then! We stopped on the way back to the cabin to get gas at a station across from Torch called Steiner's. Mr. Steiner would wait on you personally, pump your gas, clean all your windows, and strike up a conversation. Those were the days! I will never forget what a kind and wonderful man he was. The next day, we rented a small fishing boat from DeWitt's on Clam Lake. My mother got very excited to find that she had only caught a large, snapping turtle! Since we couldn't eat our catch for dinner that night, we took a ride to Bellaire that evening and had dinner at a place called Bud's Grill and had the 21 shrimp basket for $1.99. As I said, those were the days! After dinner, we went to a movie and saw "April Love" with Pat Boone and Debbie Reynolds. It was wonderful and so romantic! That night definitely made up for the perch bone episode.

I could go on and on about all of the wonderful memories that will stay with me forever! Every time I am there, I feel that my parents are there with me! Needless to say, we have spent every summer returning to that area, and now our children and grandchildren can't wait to go up north! My parents ended up buying a mobile home on Lake Charievoix, which I have taken over. My sister and her family have a five-bedroom home across from Mt. McSauba and a block from Lake Michigan. My nephew has a house he is remodeling next to theirs, and my brother has a beautiful home overlooking Torch Lake where it all began! My dream has always been to spend the entire summer there, which I am working on right now. Whenever I think of northern Michigan and all of my wonderful childhood memories with my parents, I smile! I strongly believe that when you find a good thing, stick with it!

My First Kiss, for Only a Penny
By Priscilla Bennett of Cadillac, Michigan
Born 1927

Outhouses-the perfect place to go to delay doing the dishes or other jobs we were supposed to be doing. Accidents happened out there quite often and I guess the most often was dropping your hat, mittens, and etc. in that extra hole. Of course, we didn't have toilet paper and I do believe that must have been where catalogs got the nickname of "Dream Books."

There were six of us kids. My mom or dad would put the washtub near the stove and fill it about ¼ full. My older sister would be first to get her bath, then my mom would go down the line until we were all bathed. I was lucky, because I was second–I sure would have hated to be the sixth one in there. We had a reservoir on the stove and she added a pan of warm water after each child, so it ended up with about ½ tub of water. Only one bath towel and wash cloth for all.

WWII and Korea—World War II was a different life-boys from our high school classes got drafted. We waited daily for the paper in hopes that none of our friends were missing in action or killed. It happened more often than we could imagine. So many things were rationed—sugar, flour, butter, meat, gasoline, and so many others—shoes were two pair a year. It was common practice to exchange ration coupons with neighbors or friends; like maybe a pair of shoes for a gallon of gas. My folks were very poor, so they couldn't afford to buy shoes, so they often traded shoe coupons for food ones.

When we ran out of coal my dad gathered corncobs from the local elevator (in gunny bags) and that was what we burned in the kitchen stove and we burned wood in the living room. I think my parents missed coffee more than anything during the Depression years.

My folks were so very poor, but during the Depression, my dad got a job mowing lawns for a man who ran the bakery. Instead of getting paid by money, he got the day old bakery items. Aunts, Uncles, and neighbors came every morning for coffee and rolls. It was real fun for us kids as we were too young to realize the Depression was causing this.

One-room schools—I went to three different country schools, grades kindergarten through high. It was great! I learned from hearing classes of the older kids, so my grades were easy. There was no "bullying" there as the older kids always looked out for the younger ones. We were all neighbors and good friends. We did not have slides or swings, but we made up games and recess was always fun.

Rumble Seats-My dad always had old cars—most of them were Model-T's. I can remember a couple where my sister and I rode in the rumble seats. If it was cold or rainy, that was a nasty ride, but we would cover our heads with a blanket and sing. The worse was on Sunday nights after church—that got pretty cold.

Tales from parents-My mom used to tell us about when her sister was born premature—they kept her in a shoebox on the oven door (Their idea of an incubator), also, about when one of her sisters was stillborn. How they wrapped her in blankets-decorated a shoe box and buried her in the garden. Also, she told of walking to school when the snow came up to her waist.

My dad loved his horses. He told about after being on a date with my mom, he would go to sleep and the horse would go home and into the barn and then wake him up with her noises.

Trips to town—Every Tuesday night we would get all cleaned up and go to the free movies (silent). We would take a blanket and sit on the ground. The movie would be on the side of the old town hall. I'm not sure if it was a screen or just a sheet. On Saturday night, everyone went to town and parked on the main street. Us kids each got a penny to buy candy. People would walk up and down the streets and stop to visit to ones sitting in cars.

My first kiss was on the way home from school. One of the boys gave my brother a penny to talk me into letting him kiss me—I was thirteen years old.

Icebox-We usually couldn't afford to buy ice, so the milkman used to bring ice in off his truck and put in with the milk. My dad sometimes pumped cold water in jars or bottles to keep things cold.

✓ Summers in the Northern Cabin
By Bonnie Salmon of Cadillac, Michigan
Born 1943

When I was eight years old, I lived in Livonia, Michigan. Every summer we would go up north to Gaylord, Michigan to a cabin in the woods. The cabin consisted of one big room that had a sink, a Cold Spot refrigerator, a wood stove to cook on, and a couch that pulled out to a double bed. A room off this room had a single bed and one double bed. The back porch had an icebox where we got ice every two weeks. Outside, we had a shed outhouse and a red pump where we pumped our own water. I remember we hung a metal cup on the tree so we could have water throughout the day. It tasted so good and so cold.

My dad would drive us up north (Mom did not drive) after we got out of school. We would spend the whole summer there. We all piled into a '49 Ford. It was myself, my mom, my brother, my dog Bootsie, a cat, a bird, and a fish bowl of goldfish. It took all day, as there weren't any expressways back then. My dad only came up for his vacation of two weeks, one week at a time. Mom was in charge. My grandma (whom I called Cookie Grandma) lived down the hill from us. She would take us to town

Bonnie on the horse in 1950

shopping every two weeks. In between that time, we would walk about one mile to Arbus Beach store and get a few things like milk, bread, and whatever else we could carry.

My mother gave us chores to do every day. Mine was to empty the pee pot (which I hated) every morning. My brother's chore was to get up early in the morning to load the woodstove and start the fire. We were told not to use the pee pot for bowel movements. We had to go outside to the outhouse for that. My mom was very good in cleaning the outhouse with bleach throughout the week. I didn't like the outhouse because it was dark inside and I was afraid I'd fall through the hole. Another chore that we had to do was the laundry. My mom had a big tub where she heated water to put into the tub to wash our clothes. She used a scrub board with soap. We rinsed them and hung them on a line in the woods. It would take us a long time, but we had good teamwork.

Our biggest thrill of the day was when my brother and I would hear the train whistle. We would see who could get down there first. Then, we would wave to the front engineer and the caboose. It was neat seeing that black smoke. One of the fun things that we did was to go swimming on Otsego Lake, which we could walk to. It was called Pleasant View Beach. Lots of times, we would spend the entire day. My mom always went with us. She also would rent a boat and we'd go fishing for sunfish and perch during the day. Then, at night, we'd fish for bullheads.

When I was a little older, around 13, my brother invited his girlfriend up for the weekend. We decided to go horseback riding at AuSable Ranch. They gave me a very slow horse, but my brother and girlfriend got two horses that were spunky. They took off on me and were way ahead. I came around the curve and his girlfriend had

Bonnie and Larry McCall in 1951

fallen off the horse. He put her back on and was walking the two horses on foot. He told me to go back to the ranch to get help. I took off and to get the horse to go faster. All of a sudden, the horse realized the shortcut to the barn. He went through the woods and I kept saying to him, "You can't go this way!" He still kept running. There was a large branch across the path that the horse ran me right into and knocked me off the horse. He didn't miss a step, and went on his way back to the barn. I got up with tree limbs and dirt all over my body. I ran by foot back to the ranch and into the clubhouse. I told them that there was a girl who fell off her house that is on her way back there. They took a look at me, thinking I was that girl. I looked a wreck. In the meantime, my brother and girlfriend came back and they checked them out. We went home and I realized my glasses were gone. We went back to the ranch where I was thrown and found them on the ground. My mother was really upset over the whole experience, but it turned out okay. It took me awhile to try horseback riding again.

One time, a bat got into our cabin. It was flying around and we couldn't get him out the door. Finally, my mother got a broom and knocked it down. Then she placed a towel over him and threw him out the door. It was quite an exciting experience. We used to play tag and hide and go seek with a few friends up there in the evening. This one time, my brother was heading toward home base for tag, and he ran into the pump and knocked himself out for a little while. It left a big knot in the middle of his forehead. After that, Mom said that we could no longer play tag at night. We played hide and seek until to mosquitoes came out. They were eating us up with bites!

All in all, my experiences up north were fun. One more experience I had was when we were out picking blackberries. My brother said to me, "Run." I thought he was crazy, but I did what he said. Once we got far enough away, he explained why. There was a bear nearby that he smelled. Somehow, he knew that smell. The bad thing is that we left all of our berries. We went again and got some more. With the blackberries that we brought home, my mother would put a little sugar on them and we would eat them up. They were so big, good, and delicious. They don't taste like that anymore. I always loved it up north, and that is why we bought a place in Cadillac.

Born On a Hill
By Don Franklin of Harrisville, Michigan
Born 1942

The little town of Lincoln, Michigan is 5 miles off the Lake Huron shoreline, 200 miles north of Detroit.

I was born in 1942, the youngest of seven kids. First, came three sisters, (Virginia, Elaine, and VanDeita) then three brothers, (Robert, Richard, and Theron) then me. We lived 1 ½ miles out of town and our house sat on a hill about 500 feet off the road.

I attended kindergarten in the basement of the Baptist Church, 1st & 3rd grade in the little red school house, 4th & 5th grade in the basement of the Memorial hall, 6th grade in the "Chicken-coop" which was a small school newly built near the hall, then back to the hall for 7th & 8th grade. I skipped the 2nd grade for reasons unknown to me, but that's what the teachers did if they thought you could handle it.

I attended Harrisville High School and the city of Harrisville is 5 miles east of Lincoln and is a small beautiful city right on the shore of Lake Huron. I only attended Harrisville High School for my freshman year, because the next year they opened the spanking new Alcona High School, near Lincoln. It was there that I completed my other 3 years of High School and will always be a member of the very first sophomore class.

We had a very small farm where we had a cow or two, a few chickens, a couple pigs, and lots of strawberries and raspberries. My dad, Leonard Franklin was a member of the local berry growers association and we had to transport the berries about 35 miles to greet the truck about 3-4 times per week during the season.

I picked many, many thousands of quarts of raspberries both at home and at the Louis Barger farm, 12 miles away. One time Mr. Barger told my dad that, "your youngest son has picked more berries for me than anyone." At 10 cents per quart, I always tried to pick 50 quarts per day so I could get a crisp, new $5.00 bill, which I often did. I can remember waiting for my next older brother to get home from school when he was in kindergarten and I was too young to go. I always waited on the front cement porch with our dog Jack who lived to be 19 years old. Our cat's name was Tabby. I can't remember her age, but she lived a long time.

We used to listen to the Lone Ranger on the radio and my mom, Julia Franklin listened to Helen Trent in the mornings. My mom was of course, a stay at home mom and she cooked everything and baked the greatest sweet rolls. It was chicken and dumplings on most Sundays with apple pie. About once a month, we would have roast beef, but chickens were cheap and in abundance, so we ate it a lot.

My oldest sister, Virginia graduated from nearby Oscoda High School before I was born. She got married and had a daughter, Judy who is my niece, but she is older than me.

Growing up was the best, because even though we always had to do our chores, my parents made sure that we had a lot of playtime. No one in our family was much for swimming or boating, but we lived across the road from Trask Lake, so we did a lot of bluegill and bass fishing. Dad used to take us out in the middle late at night sometimes to get bullheads, but we always had to agree to be tied to the boat so we didn't jump in.

When I got to about the 6th grade, we got our first TV that was a 21-inch Philco. We could only get one channel and we thought we were rich, because about that time we got our first telephone.

My dad always worked hard and even though we never had much money, he and Mom made sure that we got to keep a lot of our earnings to get to the local movie theatre at least once a week. The shows usually started playing on Thursday for 3 days with 2 showings each day. On Sunday, a new movie came to town and played Sunday, Monday and Tuesday. The theatre was closed on Wednesday. Mr. and Mrs. Thorn owned the theatre and they charged 12 cents for kids and 15 cents for adults. We usually spent about 40 cents on the night, after popcorn, RC cola and maybe black crows or milk duds. We always sat down front with other kids, and most always had girlfriends. Dad would drive us to town for the movies and then come back to pick us up unless one of our older brothers would pick us up. Myself, and my brother, Theron closest to me were always in town together and always looking for mischief. We knew every rooftop and the few alleys that were in our small town, and we could escape from the "big guys" whenever they got mad at us for antagonizing them. There was one time when a buddy of mine, George Parent whose parents owned a bar in town, and I were razing a couple older guys playing pool, and they started chasing us. Well, we went into this alley, jumped up on the fuel tank and launched onto the roof. We then sprinted in the dark across the rooftops, but we didn't know that a guy, Charlie Culberson that owned a hotel had put up a TV antenna, and we hit the guide wires. When I came to, one of the "big guys" whose name was, Glenn MacNeill was standing over me, threatening to beat my butt.

We had a party line on our phone, and I still remember the phone number was 2067. It later became RE62067, which stood for Redwood 62067. To this day, the prefix is 73 (RE). Our ring on the phone was 1 long and 2 short rings, so if the phone rang 3 short rings and then a long ring, we didn't answer, because that was for someone else on the line. My dad and mom didn't allow us to listen in on people's conversations, but of course, we did anyway.

The same hall that had some of our classrooms also had a gym floor and on Tuesday nights, it was open for basketball, wrestling, and boxing. On Tuesday, we would walk to town and about ½ mile down the road was a small incline and when we reached the top, we could see if the 8 large windows were lit up, so we'd know if the hall was open. If it was open, it was a 1-mile sprint from there to the hall. Of course, another reason for hurrying was because there was a cemetery we had to pass. My mom, dad, 2 sisters, and 2 brothers along with in-laws are buried there now, and all that is left is my second oldest sister, my brother next to me, and myself, but I have all of these great memories.

My mom always checked my knuckles, my neck and my ears before I left for school, because she didn't want a kid that wasn't clean going out in public. She always was sewing our clothes, mending the heels of our socks, washing clothes on our wringer washer or canning vegetables, venison or fruit.

My dad always dug what were called, apple pits, in the apple orchard to store them for winter. We would dig it big enough for, maybe 10-12 bushel; cover it with straw, then dirt, then more straw and then boards. In the middle of December, we would break into one of the pits and get a bushel of the crispy apples. We had about 30 kinds of apples including crab, greening, Arkansas black, kings, sweet, wealthy, transparent, russet, and some I can't remember.

Our road to town was a dirt road with high banks on both sides and when bad storms hit in the winter, the road would blow shut. One time around 1948-49, the road was blocked so Dad took my brother and I with him with the horses and sleigh. He decided to take a short cut across Lincoln Lake, which is one of the small lakes in town. The horses got buried in the snow on the lake and Dad had to go get another guy, Milt Somers with his team of horses to pull our team of horses out of the deepest snow.

We had two swimming holes in town. One was a regular one and the other one was called BAB for obvious reasons. Even though we hardly ever went swimming, one day when I was about 7 or so a local older kid took me out to the last dock, which was surrounded by water, much deeper than I was tall. Another older kid came up behind me on the dock and pushed me off. I would have drowned, but for the quick thinking of Kenny Lemke who was a son of the Lutheran Minister. That experience finally convinced me that swimming was not for me, and is not to this day.

We had a family of twins, Ray & Fay, older than I, and a younger sister Ruth, that lived ¾ mile away. There was another younger brother, Roy, but he was too young to play baseball with us. It seemed like we played baseball every day at least for an hour. It would always be my oldest brother Rob, Ray, and myself, on one team along with Ruth. My two brothers, Rich and Theron, along with Fay, were the other team.

My first girlfriend was Betty Buchanan, and we mostly met at the movies on Thursday nights. When she got older, she married Jack Throop, they still live today about 3 miles from me, and we are good friends. My first kiss was Marianne and her older sister Marie became my sister-in-law when she married my brother Rob. My brother Rich was the one always looking out for me when I was younger. We had a Saturday night drawing in town and sometimes Dad would let us sign the merchant's ticket. I was watching the movie one Saturday night, when Mrs. Thorn shut off the movie sound and announced, DON FRANKLIN FOR $100.00. I bolted from my seat and out the door to cross the street. My brother, Rich had heard the announcement and was waiting outside the door. He grabbed my arm, or I would have gotten run over. Dad let me buy a new, $27.00 bike and, of course, I had to give he, and Mom the rest.

Halloween night was always a big night and boy could we ever find mischief. We put machinery in the streets, we set straw fires in all the intersections, we threw water balloons, we played the suitcase trick, we tipped over toilets and one time mistakenly tipped over a machine storage shed. It took about 15 of us to do it, but we got it done and wow, what a racket.

We had an outhouse and at the time, it wasn't pleasant, but now I'm glad we had one. It was especially bad in the winter, but it smelled worse in the summer.

I had a lot of memorable people in my life and outside of my parents, I really loved my brothers-in-law, and I loved to talk to them because they seemed so smart. I always thought my sisters were beautiful and they tolerated me being around bothering them and their boyfriends.

Living in the country outside of a very small town, we didn't have milkmen because we had our own milk from our cows.

We played "hide and go seek", "kick the can" and "hunt the grey rabbit" at night all year. We played ball or fished during the day in the warm months and went sleigh riding or ice-skating in the winter.

I could write on and on about my youth and what a wonderful time it was.

I now live on the site of our old drive in movie theatre and serve on the Senior citizen board of directors in the very room where I attended the 7th and 8th grade.

The house on the hill is gone now, but the memories will live forever.

✓ War Times and Hailstorms
By Marion V. (Fabera) Neely of Tebbetts, Missouri
Born 1937

When I was born in 1937, our home was one room—probably 14 feet by 28 feet. We also had a basement. One would enter through a back porch. Four steps led up to the house. Another set of steps went from the porch to the basement where our homegrown food was stored. The house was built by my parents. It was located a few miles north of Prescott, Michigan. We were crowded, but my family of seven (two parents and five children) were grateful for the wood heated, dry space. The sleeping area was separated from the kitchen/living activities by a curtain that hung from one of the exposed rafters. Clothing for the family hung on wire hangers on spikes above the curtain. One army cot served as a bed for my sister and me. Each of us had a small pillow at our individual end of the cot. Two brothers shared another army cot in similar fashion. The youngest brother slept in an iron crib until he was nearly five. Our parents shared a double bed. Typical of that area, our home had no electricity. Kerosene lamps provided light. Use of our battery-powered radio was very limited. Familiar voices were Walter Winchell and Lowell Thomas. Saturdays we heard some of the Grand Ole Opry and Judy Canova. Sunday might include a baseball game. I was very young, but was aware of Franklin D. Roosevelt and World War II and rationing.

During the war years, our one-room school was closed for one day each autumn. The children were taken out to pick wild milkweed pods from road ditches and uncultivated fields. It was a joint project between Civil Defense and the local theater. We were paid in theater tickets for the number of burlap sacks of milkweed pods we picked. The pods were processed at a plant in Petoskey, Michigan and used in life jackets for the military. Metal was very limited during the war. During that time, much of the cookware was granite or enamel, which was a brittle covering firmly attached to the interior and exterior of metal. Sometimes these pans would chip and eventually the exposed metal would rust through, causing

Marion's mother and father, Marie and Robert Fabera with their children in 1941

a leak. A product called Mend-its was available. Each package contained a flat pointed tool with a square indentation cut out of the other end, Also there were several cork washers, metal washers, and tiny nuts and bolts. Instructions showed how to use the pointed end to make a smooth hole. Then, an arrangement of bolts, washers, and nuts were attached by using the square cut out area as a wrench. Pans repaired in this way lasted a long time. Another metal saver was the 63 jar lid flats and rings. These were manufactured by Ball and Kerr, the two companies that sold most of the canning supplies during that time. They were similar to, but smaller than, regular size jar rings and flats. Some coffee companies sold their coffee in jars that had lids the same size as 63s. These coffee jars were used for canning. This was before pressure cooker canners. White pennies, instead of copper, were another memory of war years.

The year is lost to memory, but I remember the day when our little farm was hit by a hailstorm. It was on July 1, my twin siblings' birthday. A family tradition was to have homemade ice cream for our birthdays, as the rest of us had winter birthdays. The year of the hail, my parents scooped up hail by the buckets full and were able to make ice cream on the first of July. This hailstorm destroyed our garden, crops, and much of the roof of our house. Three cows of our eight-cow herd were sold to pay for roof repair. This was serious for our family, as most of our cash income came from the sale of cream. The garden was destroyed. There was no time to replant in time for harvest before winter weather set in. At that time, navy beans were a major income crop for local farmers. Dad went to the nearest elevator and got many bags of "culls" normally used for hog feed. These bags were stored in our granary where oats would normally have been stored. Every Sunday, one of our parents would bring in a big dishpan full of these culls. A good size pile would be put in the center of our round kitchen table. Our parents and the four older children all sat around the table. We would each reach to the center pile and drag back a handful or two to within easy reach in front of us, Then, we removed the good beans from the rat turds, rocks, weed seeds, etc. We would sort enough beans each Sunday to feed us for that week. Navy beans were all we ate that

entire winter. The following spring, relatives from Indiana visited us. They brought quart jars of home canned tomato juice. Some of this juice was mixed with the beans. That was the best tasting food ever. I still like navy beans.

My dad raised a small flock of sheep sheltered in a simple structure he called a straw shed. As I recall, there were wooden fence posts at the sides. Longer poles went across the top. Woven fence wire was stretched over the horizontal poles and fastened. When grain was threshed, some of the straw was blown on the flat fence wire, making a roof for the structure. Throughout the year, Dad would pull straw from the roof for bedding for the sheep. This structure was too short to stand up in, but the sides were open. It worked for housing sheep. When my parents bought their farm, there were many stumps left after the harvest of the virgin pine forest. Dad chose to use dynamite to remove the stumps. He had a local craftsman make him a tool using a five-foot long rod with a two inch by two-inch scoop at the end. With this shovel, he was able to dig deep holes and place the dynamite far under the stump. Using this tool, he was able to get the job done with fewer dynamite blasts. Every penny had value in our household. Dad also trapped and sold the furs. The fat that was removed from the fur was rendered for use in making soap. Mom made lye soap using that fat. Fat from butchered calves and hogs was used for food preparation.

Perhaps the most memorable event of my childhood happened when I was seven years old. That was the year my mother received a yellow telegram, informing her of the memorial service/funeral for Wendell Willkie. I had heard of him from the previously mentioned newscasts. Wendell and my mother were cousins, growing up in Indiana. I had no idea that she was important enough to receive a telegram!

School Days
By Harriet Scheller of Hillman, Michigan
Born 1923

In the 1930s we, who lived in rural areas went to a rural school within the township. It was heated by a center stove where those who sat near it were cozy and the children in seats further away were chilly. It contained a crockery water container and we brought telescoping aluminum cups to drink from. Two outhouses were placed in the back of the woodshed, which was attached to the school. It usually had six windows, three on each side, but in the later '30s the government placed one window facing east and several windows on the west side. While this repair was being done, we were housed in a crowded old house belonging to a school board member where we literally froze our lunches in pails until we placed them all around the stove! What a chore for the teachers to teach under those conditions, but one memorable teacher we had, made taffy to pull on Valentine's Day, and we had a great time pulling it and eating it even if we were in an old house. We walked to school with neighbors, cutting across fields, one behind the other forming a hardened path. To slip off the hardened ridge, you were up to your knees in snow. We wore shoes and galoshes and heavy homemade mittens, and heavy scarves covered our faces. We had an iced rink in a nearby field at the school where the teachers allowed us to skate during noon hour. Other things we did at recess were, playing "Anti-over the school with a ball and catching the ball, and hurrying around to the opposite side to tag the others. In warm weather, we played softball and hopscotch and jump rope. We revered the teacher who was strict with discipline, even on some older students who were sometimes unruly.

Our one teacher whom I remember well, always opened the day with the Pledge of Allegiance and a patriotic song. Then she would read "Little Women", "Little Men" or "The Rover Boys" for a half hour. This increased my love for reading.

She also devoted a session of the day to music. We sang from the Golden Book such songs as, Old Black Joe, (a no, no now) Way Down Upon the Suwannee River, Long, Long Ago, Santa Lucia, America, and many others. Depression Years—we lived on a farm and had a huge garden and orchard. We canned everything in sight. Dad killed a hog and a beef, so we always had canned beef and salt pork, which Mom parboiled to remove excess salt, and then fried it up nice and crisp and yummy. We had apples far into the spring stored in the cellar and we'd have apples and popcorn, which Dad grew too, nightly. We always had cream and milk from our cowherd and chicken from the flock Mom raised. Our house was heated by a wood stove in the living room and the cooking range in the kitchen. It had a big reservoir attached for hot water. We had no electricity, so we used kerosene lamps. It was my job to clean the sooty chimneys each day. We'd use hot water bottles in bed, as bedrooms were chilly.

Childhood diseases were prevalent, chicken pox, measles, and scarlet fever. When my brother got the fever, we were quarantined 5 weeks, so I studied at home. A placard (scarlet fever) was placed on our house during that period to warn others. We had a blind doctor and nurse come to give us a shot to all, but Mom and Dad. We reacted to it and were very ill, more so than my brother, who had the disease! Later, before going back to school, our home was fumigated with sulphur canisters burning in each room to kill the germs. Our textbooks had to be laid out in rooms to be fumigated also.

We entertained ourselves at night with the family playing card games, checkers, and singing. Mom played the organ and we'd sing hymns and other songs. We also had a battery powered radio and listened to Amos & Andy and Dad listened to boxing fights on it. Mom also read to us.

Our clothes were often homemade from old coats. Most women could sew. Mom made us all new dresses for the Christmas season when we had programs at school. Those were a big event. All the parents attended, sometimes standing room only to hear their children recite. Then Santa came and gave out the presents. For the stage, the teacher used sheets strung across on wires to be pulled back and forth between scenes in the plays.

Farm chores were labor intensive. My brothers and I hauled hay from the hay barn to the stable to feed the cows. It was loose hay, so we carried it in cloth like tarps. It took many trips in all kinds of weather. In the cellar, we also chopped mangles, a root vegetable much like sugar beets to give to the cows in addition to the hay. When the cows heard us come in with those, their old long tongues came out in anticipation for that succulent treat.

Christmas was a big day. We went to Mom's folks on Christmas and had a bountiful meal, and fun with our cousins. I can still remember Gram's Jell-O. It was a special treat. After dinner, we and our cousins would go upstairs and slide down the bannister. What fun! What a slide!

WWII was on in 1940. By that time, I had reached 17 and had gone to high school and County Normal School, a one-year preparation to become a teacher in rural areas. I began teaching 37 children at 18. That was in 1941-42, when the Pearl Harbor attack occurred. That year I had a patriotic Christmas program with lots of flags and drills and patriotic songs.

In 1944, the war was still on and they needed women to relieve men for overseas, so my sister and I joined the WAC, going to Fort Oglethorpe, Georgia for our basic training. We were assigned to the 146th Base Unit at Selfridge Field, Michigan. During that time, 15 friends and neighbors lost their lives in WWII. Three neighbors we knew well would never return home. There were few men left in our neighborhood.

During my time teaching in rural schools, my children and I collected iron and tires, and picked milkweed fluff for kapok life preservers, sugar was rationed as well as coffee, so honey was often used as a substitute. The rural teachers made out the ration cards. We were given a day off to work for the government.

Trips to town were few and far between. Since we were almost self- sufficient for foods, all we needed were staples. We'd go in with our cans of cream to take to the creamery and get the check and buy what we needed. Mom and Dad would treat us to jelly filled bismarks from a nearby bakery and we'd eat them in the parking lot in the cart—no fancy restaurants or McDonalds for us, and how we relished them! It was such a treat.

A memorable person in my life was my grandma. She had come to America alone at 14 from Germany, paid passage by a cousin. She traveled in a hold of the ship. She was seasick all the way across. She settled in Ohio area and worked for a Jewish family as a maid. I admire her courage and stamina to come to a strange country, knowing only her cousin. I wrote a biography of her in a college course, I took later.

Looking back on those days memorable, full of love of a close family and though considered "poor" now a days we were close knit, taught to take responsibility early for the good of the family, without allowances. It really shaped our lives to assume responsibility with a can-do spirit, in later life.

After service in WACS, I went to college to get my degree in teaching on the GI Bill and taught 39 years in Alpena schools.

Coming back home after service, was difficult. I worked summers as a waitress and went back to teach in the fall. I transferred from rural school teaching to a city school and also taught teachers one year in the County Normal School, as a Critic teacher. The County Normal Schools were a boon to young people in 1940, giving many a job with only one year of training.

Kids Games, "Boys Will Be Boys"
By Mike Madden of Alpena, Michigan
Born 1935

Place: Cheboygan Michigan, 1943

At the age of 8 years old, my grandfather (a blacksmith) found me a job peddling papers for Detroit Free Press. Every morning, 7 days a week, before school started. I met the train at the depot to pick up the newspapers. The big steam engine would pull in and the conductor would throw my paper bundle to the deck. My job started as the papers were folded and packed into my delivery bag, walked the whole 60-customer route, then off to school.

The summer was different; instead of school, I would run to the horse and wagon to peddle milk. This was fun, because as the horse, Maud pulled the wagon up the street, I was the runner, from one house on the right side of the street, back to the wagon, picking more milk to deliver on the other side. The horse knew the route and its owner, Elmer Wing would hand me the milk. The milk sitting on the porch in the winter would expand and the cream would pop out the cap.

During summer season, the kids I played with would help the war effort by picking up wagons of scrap paper, then put the papers in bundles and deliver to the news.

Spending time with my grandfather, Ceph Dove in his blacksmith shop was fun. He was a tobacco-spitting guy who always was working on making shoes for a waiting horse. He would have me hold the horse's tail while he shod them. You see, the tail would keep flies away and also hit my grandfather in the head. The shop was full of iron horse shoes and tools to shape them. There was a

Mike's grandparents and parents with their children in 1944

stagecoach sitting behind the shop we would play in.

My father returned from the war in 1945 and took up sailing with the ships of Calcite in Rogers City. We moved to Rogers City that year.

At the age of 12, I joined the Boy Scouts group from Church down the street. The group got involved in building kayaks and so did I, with two fellow scouts. We built a kayak from scratch and it was a good one. It was built to save our life, if need be, with air pockets at each end. The finished product had to be tested, so the day that we graduated from eighth grade, the 1st of June, we took our kayak to the big Lake Huron. One of the scouts was not a swimmer, so decided not to go. George, my dog and I, paddled out to deeper waters, big test was costly, as being out about ½ mile, a big wave flipped us over, and the water was very cold. We stuck to our capsized kayak, till help came. Our dog swam to shore. A man walking on shore saw us and called for help. A good size speedboat picked us up and put us back to shore.

We made all the newspapers, because we stayed with our safe kayak. The dog got home before we did.

Rogers City, Michigan, 1945: (Sand Lot Baseball) It was the summer activity for the gang in our neighborhood. After a morning of peddling papers, baseball was on! All the gang would meet at the field, the bat was tossed to the captain and it was "hand-over-hand" till there was no bat left and the last hand got first draw of player. The teams were picked every day in this manner. Sometimes we would play with 14 players, but no less than 10. The game would go on till lunchtime. Then we would change players around and have a new game. This would last most of every day. The weather or Sundays would keep us from playing.

Winter was a time for winter sports, skating and snagging for us guys. To do the snagging, the street would have to be icy or heavy snow. You and a couple of buddies would hide on a street corner and wait for a car. The car always had a slow start from a corner, we had time to grab its bumper, go for a ride, our boots sliding on the snowy street. It was dangerous; we had to know how to get off safely. We all were doing it, and having fun, without getting caught.

The skating part was, pick a team to play hockey. We made our own rink and played after school. One of my best friend's back yard became the hockey rink. Seems the most of our sports was mid-shift, to make it happen.

(Bird hunting with my best friend in the fall, after school) We took the highway towards Onaway, Michigan and turned off on a two-rut road. We hunted in an area until we were lost. Now, we stopped hunting and started to find our way out. We walked for about an hour, but we seemed to be going deeper in the woods, and not locating our car. We found a high area and decided to spend the night in the swamp. We had started a little fire and were keeping warm (shooting the bull). At that time, I saw a flickering light deep in the woods. We headed toward the light and about 100 yards we walked up on our car. Wow! And the flickering light was my best friend's father out looking for us. We were lucky, as the next morning we were walking to school in 4-5 inches of snow. The area we were in was called, The Onaway Swamp.

The Cream Separator
By Leeland Wilson of Okeechobee, Florida
Born 1932

I remember the day the DeLaval Cream Separator was delivered. The truck dropped it off at a nearby John Deere dealership. My father hitched the horses up to a "stone boat" and went to get it. It was crated in a real ragged-looking wooden box put together with bolts. They slid it on the stone bolt and headed for home.

I could hardly wait to get it uncrated to see what it looked like. Finally, when we got it out of the wooden box, there it stood. I thought it was the most beautiful thing I had ever seen.

It was painted a dark blue with a black stripe around the edges, and it had a little vine-like pattern all around the edges in a brilliant gold. It had a big shiny bowl with a valve that could be opened and closed with a shiny handle. There were two spouts that protruded out, one for skimmed milk and one for cream.

There was a little bowl that the whole milk was poured into before it went on down to a series of disks that rotated at a very high speed, separating the cream from the milk. There was a hand crank with a hand piece made of polished oak. As the crank was rotated, a bell would ring. When the bell quit ringing, it was time to turn the handle on the valve, letting the milk flow downward through the rotating disks. There was a round platform that a pail was set on to catch the cream. The skim milk went into a can that sat on the floor. The separator had to be bolted to the floor with four lag bolts, as there was quite a bit of vibration.

There was a strainer that fit on the bowl. Strainer pads could be bought that fit into the big funnel that the milk had to pass through. The strainer pads were made of a cotton cloth-like material about a quarter of an inch thick and six inches in diameter. The used pads were always thrown out and the cats would devour them. Sometimes two cats would try to eat the same strainer pad. After they chewed on a pad for a while, it would get like a piece of rope about eight or ten inches long. Then, it would turn into a tug of war and sometimes a fierce catfight would develop.

After the milk was separated, the bowl, all the disks and the two spouts had to be washed, dried and put back together. I had the job of turning the crank, taking the disks apart; drying them and putting them all back together. I would always wash down the entire separator and polish it with a dry cloth.

My job was milking one cow, but when the separator came along, I volunteered to milk two cows, so that I would have more milk to run through the separator. This went on for a while. Then, electric power lines came into the country. This was a big change. We no longer had to use the kerosene lantern to see while doing the chores. And we no longer had to use a hit-and-miss gasoline engine to pump water. I no longer had to use a kerosene lamp to see to do my homework. It was just a new world!

I could now see things on the separator that I hadn't known were there. There was a little brass plate riveted on it with a serial number and a model number and the word, "DELAVAL" that I polished with brass polish.

The big change that took place with the separator was that an electric motor was installed on it. So, my job turning the crank was eliminated. All I had to do was pour in the milk, throw the switch, wait for the bell to quit ringing and then open the valve. And when all the milk went through it, I shut the power off. My grandfather would just stand and shake his head. He would say kids nowadays are going to get as lazy as a bunch of pet coons with all these new fandangles. He said, "The whole world is going to go to pot!

Now I think, maybe he may have been right!

Living in a Lighthouse
By Paula Van Wagnen of Alpena, Michigan
Born 1949

Little did we know that when my husband graduated from Indiana University Optometry School that we would be living in a historical monument. Jim was offered a job in Alpena, Mi. located in northern Michigan on Lake Huron. Just north of Alpena is a small village, Presque Isle. It is home of a library, post office, general store, church and two lighthouses. When we first moved to the area, we rented a house on Grand Lake and were not aware of one of the lighthouses—the Old Presque Isle Light, built in 1840 and had been designed by Jefferson Davis prior to the Civil War. We had a friend visit the fall of 1973 right after we moved and we visited the old lighthouse. I had seen an ad in the local newspaper looking for caretakers to live in the lighthouse for the winter. I asked the young man who was there if this was the lighthouse they were talking about. He looked at me as if I was crazy and said it was for the one at the end of the road. That was the first we knew that the road didn't continue all the way to Rogers City.

261

We drove out to the end and found the New Presque Isle Light that was built in 1870 after the old one was abandoned. We learned that it is the tallest light on the Great Lakes and the Coast Guard had automated the light and left the station earlier that summer. The property was turned over to the township for their use as a park and they wanted someone to live in the house for security. So we contacted the township supervisor and put our names on the list.

For one reason or another, the township board got down to our names and we were asked if we were interested. So, in November of 1973 we moved down the road to the lighthouse. We paid rent and phone through the winter and the township paid for heat and electricity. The light House sits on a point in Lake Huron and has 93 acres of land around it.

The winters were great with lots of snow and ice blows along the lake. It was fun to explore the land and we had our personal night light. The Coast Guard had left two old dumps that people liked to look over for old bottles. There were a lot of deer, snowshoe rabbits, and even a cougar. At night, we could hear sounds on the front porch and it would be the local porcupines eating the porch. The Coast Guard told us that they use to crank ice cream on the porch and porcupines were after the salt. We had two beagles and a house cat that loved the open areas.

Come spring, it was evident that we needed a lawn mower for all the grass areas on the 93 acres. Township meetings are a good place to go to raise your blood pressure. To get anything accomplished at the Light House, it had to be approved by the board, but the public can put in their two cents worth. When we were trying to get a lawn tractor—one suggestion was to use the old push mower that the Coast Guard had left—another suggestion was to get a goat. The lawn tractor finally passed and Jim's favorite pastime after work was mowing.

With added responsibility at the Light House, the township did away with the rent, but we still had to pay telephone expenses. The township wanted to start the park so we put in grills at different locations, picnic tables, and garbage barrels. Luckily, we had an old utility trailer that we could haul the trash down to the dump when needed.

Our second winter at the Light House, our first child was born. We had become really good friends with the township supervisor and his wife. They became our daughter's God Parents at the Presque Isle Chapel the spring of 1975. Most people, who drove down the road, still thought the Coast Guard was still there and didn't bother us. It was a great time to live there.

Since that time, the township has bought the land from the government and they have turned our old house into a museum and no one lives there. My Girl Scout troop completed their Gold Award remodeling the upstairs and provided furniture and curtains of the 1870 time period. There are no more snowshoe rabbits because of the increase of coyotes, and no more deer because of clearing and making trails. The lake levels are at an all-time low, having uncovered old pilings from piers they had used to build the lighthouse. It is still one of our favorite places to visit, but we lived there during the best years.

✓ **Work and Play of the Old Days**
By Delores Troupe of Herron, Michigan
Born 1938

I grew up on a small farm in Herron, Michigan. We didn't have any inside plumbing in our house. We carried our water from a well that was a ways from our house. We had a two-seater outhouse with newspapers and magazines for toilet paper. My mom always made homemade bread, which she cooked in the oven of a wood stove. If my father didn't know Mom had bread in the oven, sometimes he would throw more wood on the fire and Mom's bread would burn on top. Either way, we would have to eat it anyway. We burned wood and coal to heat our home. The walls would get black from the coal. Every spring we would have to clean our walls, which all had wallpaper on them. We used wallpaper cleaner, which was the consistency of play dough. We would wipe it on the wall and it would pick up the black coal dust. You would have to keep working your cleaner and wipe the whole wall and ceilings. This is how we did our spring-cleaning. At nighttime, the fire would go out and. I remember one winter when we had a glass of water setting on the windowsill in our headroom and it was frozen solid by the morning.

I went to a one-room schoolhouse. I walked about a mile to school. We had about 15 cows to milk, so I had to milk two to three cows before I went to grade school. Our school didn't have any inside plumbing either. We also had an outside well. It had a big coal and wood furnace in front of the room. All the heat came out the top. You couldn't get around the stove to get warm. In the winter, the school was still cold when we got there because the teacher had to start the fire every morning. I remember keeping our snow pants and coats on all day to keep warm. We didn't have any playground equipment like swings or anything. We had one ball and one bat. We played games we made up like "I send" and an inside game called "Clap in, Clap out." Of course, in the winter we had snowball battles. In the game "Clap in, Clap out," the boys and girls took turns. First, the boys would all take a seat at their desks while the girls would all go out of the room to the entryway. Each boy would pick out one of the girls. Someone would write down their names till all were chosen. Then, the girls would come in and have to think of who might have chosen them. They would sit with the one they thought chose them. If he chose her, the boy would let her sit with him; if not he would clap his hands. The girl would have to get up and keep trying until all girls found the one boy who chose them. Then, it was the boys turn to go and the girls would choose a boy. In the game "I Send," everyone picked sides. Each side had a captain. One team stood by the front of the school and the other by the road. Your team captain sent one of his players to tag a player from other side while they ran to get to your side. If you got caught and tagged, then you were on their side. They took turns. The side that finished with all players on their side was the winner. The object was not to get tagged.

There was a big drain ditch through the woods, not far from school, that was full of water. In the winter, it froze over and some of the kids would meet there and ice skate up and down the ditch. One of the older boys built a bonfire for us to get warm by. One year, we were snowed in for two weeks. Of course, we didn't go to school for two weeks. Growing up on the farm was a lot of hard work. My father raised potatoes when I was

Delores in a berry patch with her sisters and brother

little. I remember picking up potatoes. Then he also had cows to milk. There was also the task of putting up hay in the summer. I was always feeding the cattle and cleaning out the barn. My father sold cream in Alpena to at a little creamery. My mom made homemade butter. We raised pigs and chickens. We had our own eggs and meat. Dad butchered his own pigs, cows, and chickens. When I was little, I was gathering the eggs and one day our rooster chased me. I was carrying a little pail of eggs, and I fell and broke some of them. In haying season, I drove the tractor at age nine. I was driving the car by age 11. My father sold the cows and started raising strawberries. My sister and I stayed home two days from high school and helped plant 75,000 strawberry plants. The first year, we had to pick off all the blossoms off the plants so they would put out runners instead of fruit, plus they all had to be hoed.

My mom's job was hot and tiresome too. She always cooked on a wood stove, even in the summer. She had a wringer washing machine. We had to carry water from the well and heat it on the stove for Mom to do the wash. All the clothes were hung on the clothesline to dry. My mom never had a lot of fancy appliances to work with, but I don't ever remember her complaining. My brother, who was always curious about how things worked, got his arm caught in the washing machine ringer all the way up to his armpit. He was just two or three years old. Thank God, he didn't lose his arm. I remember when we got our first TV set. My dad said, "Wouldn't it be nice if you could just sit here in your chair and have something you could change the channels without getting up?" He never got to see it, but look at what we have now!

263

When I got married, my father gave us a lot on the roadway. My husband-to-be, at age 18, built us a house to live in. It was just a shell when we got married—no inside plumbing or running water. As we could, our home was finished, and we never had a mortgage on our home. I had a wringer washer all the years my children were young. My babies wore all cloth diapers. The milkman delivered milk to our home every week when kids were little. Once in a while, he would give the kids a small carton of chocolate milk. Our first telephone was a party line. There was no privacy to your calls, so if you didn't want everyone to know something, you didn't tell anyone on the phone. The worst thing was when you needed to make an important call and someone was just gossiping on the line. Sometimes if it was an emergency, you would just politely ask them to hang up so that you could make your call. It was a blessing when we finally got our own phone lines.

✓ The Old Icehouse
By Lee Schrader of Houghton Lake, Michigan
Born 1931

This memory, though centering on the family farm, was also a wintertime example of neighboring. We happened to be the keeper of the icehouse that served the locals with ice. That lasted well into the summer. Most of the neighbors had iceboxes, and their need for ice in the summer was very important for cooling fresh milk and produce from the garden. Our icehouse was an area with a building that sat a few feet away from our back porch steps. Nearby was the winter wood supply that served for fuel for both the cook stove in the kitchen and the two other heating stoves that heated the rest of the house.

I don't mean to stray from my story, but not all of the house was heated, mainly the upstairs where my brother and I slept. I can still remember when Mother would yell up the stairs when it was time to get up. After carefully calculating how to crawl out of bed without unmaking it, we would thunder down the stairs full throttle, clad only in our underwear. We would each choose a vacant spot behind the kitchen range to dress. Of course, it never occurred to me at the time that some heroic person got up much earlier and warmed the place up while cooking breakfast! I thought we suffered at the time, but what we really had was the chance to experience a world much more peaceful and real than it seems today. I suppose by measure of material things, we had very little, but how wealthy we were of non-material things!

Meanwhile, back at the icehouse, the area that held the ice was built with two inch by six-inch studs for walls, and then covered with a layer of one-inch boards. This left a vertical area space between each upright. This area was filled with sawdust from the local sawmill for insulation. There was also a six-inch layer of sawdust between each layer of ice. This method of insulation would keep ice until July to early August. Homemade ice cream, made nearly every Sunday, was very important. Anytime in February was the time that we had to put up the ice.

The Cass River bordered our property on the east, a peaceful river and basically pretty flat. This meant that there were very little currents. That made for thick ice. Most years the cakes were 12 inches to 14 inches thick. Pop (my dad), with our horses and sleigh and a few neighbors, would scout out a fairly level approach to the river. That's when the fun would begin. This always seemed to be a very lighthearted project. I guess it was a welcome break in the winter months. It was quiet work with the one man ice saws cutting a thin line, making not much more than a whisper. The work left lots of opportunity for small talk among the crew. Most of my small talk centered on Pop telling me to get back from the hole so I wouldn't fall in. I felt big, but I guess I wasn't. The loaders and the people who sawed switched jobs regularly. Usually, the project lasted only a day or two.

The final year we put up ice was exceptional. The Rural Electric Association (REA) had just run their lines through the neighborhood and electricity was available. Some of the neighbors still had iceboxes, so this was to be the last year that we would do it. This year, the horses were left in the barn, and we loaded up on the neighbor's Model-A Ford truck. To top it off, after the truck was loaded, when we were about halfway to shore, the ice gave way and the truck sank up to the windshield. Two more days were spent rescuing the truck. After that, the operation was history.

Strangely enough, a few years later, I again put a truck through the ice on a river north of Chunchon Korea. This time, the truck was loaded with ammunition. I was trying to get to a gun position during a push on the front line. As I sat with my feet in the water, I couldn't help but think of how many people had actually sunk their truck twice through the ice—and 12,000 miles apart! I guess each person's life is unique and special in many ways.

The ice house stood empty for many years. It finally gave way to years of weather and time.

✓ Lumber Industry in Cadillac
By Mayme Guthrie of Cadillac, Michigan
Born 1922

I am 90 years old, having been born on October 13, 1922 to Finnish immigrants, John Ramo Williams and Lempi Pulkkinen Williams. My father didn't have a middle name, and his name was only John Ramo when he came to the United States. When he married my mother, he added the name of Williams to his name since his father-in-law in Finland had a first name of William. Most of the Swedes had taken their dad's first names and added "son" to the end to make last names like "Carlson" or "Johnson," etc. my father wanted to be different than the Swedes. My parents came to the United States in 1912 and

Popcorn John's horse drawn wagon in 1878

1913. They came on other ships, so barely missed being on the Titanic, which sank after it hit an iceberg. They came to Jennings, Michigan, a small town near Cadillac where the lumber industry was booming. They met each other for the first time in Jennings. My father was boarding at my mother's aunt and uncle's home. When my mother came in December of 1913, they became acquainted and married in August of 1914.

My father worked for the Mitchell Brothers Lumber and for Joseph Murphy who was also in the lumber business. George Mitchell the founder of Cadillac, Michigan. He is the man who began the lumber industry in the area when Cadillac was nothing but a forest with huge trees. Huge logs were cut and floated from Lake Mitchell through the canal, separating the two lakes into Lake Cadillac, which was that time called Clam Lake. After the lumber had all been cut in the area, the people who lived in Jennings, Michigan moved to Cadillac, leaving Jennings a ghost town. Most of the businesses also came to Cadillac. Now it has a population of over 10,000 residents. There were lumber mills on the east shore of Lake Cadillac and huge piles of lumber stacked on trams by the lake. The lumber companies sold lumber and hardwood flooring for building new homes and buildings. Most of the homes in Jennings were moved to Cadillac on Acme trucks that were manufactured in Cadillac. These homes were owned by the lumber companies, and after they were moved to Cadillac, they were sold to various people.

After the lumber industry went down before 1920 in Jennings, the Swedish Lutheran church was sold to the Finnish people since all the Swedes had moved to Cadillac. The Finns had it moved with an Acme truck that was manufactured in Cadillac to a location on M66 Highway south of Lake City. It was then called the St. Johns Evangelical Lutheran Church. My parents were charter members of that church, having been married there when it was still in Jennings in 1914. My mother, Lempi Ramo Williams, was the last charter member to pass away. She lacked four months of being 99 years old.

When I was three years old, in about 1925, we rented a house on North Shelby Street from the VanderJagts. They were grandparents of Guy VanderJagt, who was a United States Representative in Washington D.C. for several years. He was a great orator, and donated to and supported the Miss Michigan Queen contest.

Big blocks of ice were cut from Lake Cadillac and were loaded onto wagons pulled

Mayme Guthrie's family in 1957

by horses to a huge icehouse on the shore. It was then stacked and packed with straw to keep it cold and stored. Since no one had refrigerators in those days, only iceboxes were in their homes. A horse drawn wagon delivered ice to homes. Also, horse drawn milk wagons delivered milk to homes in Cadillac. When I was eight years old, I recall seeing a horse drop dead from the summer heat in August while it was pulling a milk wagon.

When I was eight years old, there were no homes on the east shore of Lake Cadillac. We used to pasture a cow there south of the trams where the lumber was stacked. One day when my brother and I were taking the cow to the pasture, we heard a train coming. The cow ran across the tracks and tried to jump the fence. It got caught on the fence and hurt its udder. We made it across the tracks before the train came. My girlfriend and I used to pick huge wild strawberries in that area. In later years, a man by the name of Holly Johnson bought and developed all that property where Holly Road now is. There are many new homes there now. My brother owns one of them.

The first car my father purchased was a Model-T Ford from the Flynn Ford Sales in Cadillac. Michigan Senator Felix Flynn of Cadillac owned the Ford Agency. We drove to Ironwood, Michigan in that car when I was a baby in the year 1923. Since my father was just learning to drive it, a friend of his who was familiar with it was driving it in the Upper Peninsula, and he drove into a lake when he missed the road. After we were pulled out, we went to Ironwood where we sold the car. We took a train back to Cadillac, and my mom and we kids sat in the city park while my father went back to Flynn Auto Sales and purchased another car. In 1931, my father purchased a 1931 New Model-A Ford for the sum of $500.00, also from the Flynn Ford Agency.

There was a popcorn wagon automobile parked on the main street of Cadillac, and a man we called "Popcorn John" owned and operated the business. He made and sold popcorn. I was eight years old at the time, and Senator Felix Flynn bought me a bag of popcorn. He noticed I was standing there wishing I had money to buy some, so he treated me. He was a very nice man and was well respected.

We lived on Pollard Street, and there was a large hill we called Bunker Hill by our house. During the depression in about 1929, we couldn't afford sleds since there were eight children in our family. We used cardboard as sleds to slide down the hill. At the bottom of the hill, there was a frog pond that would freeze over in the winter to make an ice rink for ice-skating. We would skate with clamp-on skates. In the summer, the pond was open, and the chirping frogs would put us to sleep a night.

I graduated in 1941 from the old Cadillac High School, and after graduation, I worked as a stenographer at the St. John's Table Factory. That was the largest table factory in the world. I worked for the Petrie family who had began the operation in the early days of Cadillac. I was the secretary to Earnest J. Turnbloom, the Secretary of the Company. They made quality dining room furniture, which was shipped all over the United States and the world. They had been in business for many years, and employed as many as 400 people. There was also a chair factory next door. Jobs were plentiful in those days. There was also a chemical plant in Cadillac, as well as many other industries.

In 1961, I purchased 20 acres east of Cadillac, and my son and his friend and I tore down an old three-story house. I used the old rough lumber to build a new house. My 15 year old daughter held one end of the 26 foot two-by-four while I sawed them into eight foot lengths to build the walls. My husband had left home to marry another woman, so I was raising three children myself. I am a carpenter, and built my own house. The property I bought was the old Swartwood Dairy farm from years ago. The big barn had been torn down and I had the old barn beams to string in the basement to hold up the floors. Some of the two-by-fours were in one piece up above the third floor.

Grandma Wille's Legacy: The Farm
By Judith A. Benner of Sleepy Hollow,
Illinois
Born 1940

In the spring of 1915, my great-grandparents, "Maggie" and Oscar Wille, along with my not quite seven year old mother, Bertha (Peggy) Feid, traveled from Chicago, Illinois to Higgins Lake, Michigan in a wagon borrowed from the upholstery business my great-grandfather worked for. Their dream was to have a farm. The wagon carried furniture, kitchen utensils, linens, and tools. The entire trip took them eighteen days. We're never too certain as to the circumstances of their purchasing the land. My mother thought they had seen an advertisement in the Chicago Tribune, but there are also indications that because her grandfather was a veteran of the Spanish American war, he was entitled to some of this land. Nevertheless, they arrived and moved into the very small, already old house on this land and settled in.

On account of the house not being set up for year-round living, they would travel every year in April to the farm. They would then leave again in October to go back to their Chicago apartment and jobs. During the time they would spend at Higgins Lake, my mother would attend the one-room schoolhouse, and then upon her return to Chicago, she would attend the city school. A few years later, my mother's mother and my mother's step-father moved permanently to the farm to raise their family and farm the land. They were very hard years for this family, as the winters were harsh, the land wasn't good for growing crops, and as the story goes, my grandfather was not much of a farmer. Two of their children died at very early ages and are buried at the cemetery in Roscommon. Eventually, the family moved back to Chicago, but my great-grandparents and my mother kept their yearly ritual as before. In 1928, my mother married Chris Konow of Pullman, Illinois and spent their vacation at Higgins Lake every summer with her grandparents. During the depression, my mother, on some occasions, baked pies from berries collected on the property. My dad would sell them to the cottagers on the lake to pay for the gasoline to get them home. Thinking this beneath him, my mother told us that he would clean up, shave, put on a white shirt and bowtie, and sell in this manner, so as not to look like they needed the money.

My brother was born in 1931, my sister in 1935, and I in 1940. This special place still remained my great-grandmother's farm, but was our regular vacation spot and we spent wonderful summers there. Chickens were delivered in the spring, and on many occasions, we were there when they were delivered by mail. I can remember the small little chicks scrambling all over the kitchen floor while I sat and let them climb over my legs and held them in my lap. My sister and brother have other remembrances of the chickens, such as my sister holding the string attached around the grown chickens' necks while my brother held the legs and chopped off their heads. My only memory of this ritual was the chickens flopping all over the yard with no head! On account of Grandpa Wille having died some years earlier, our Grandma Wille moved in with our family in Dolton, Illinois. This was in 1942, and until her death in 1949, she continued her yearly trek to the farm. My mother told her when she was 83 that she could no longer be up there alone because she had one leg amputated during the winter. Mom said that they would not be driving her up there that year. Her response was, "Fine, then I'll take the bus!" My mother, knowing her so well, knew she would, so they drove her there, made arrangements for someone to help her out with things like chopping wood, getting groceries, and whatever she needed. Grandma Wille died at a friend's home on Higgins Lake, near her beloved farm on May 21. 1949.

Our road, which is now W. Pine Dr. had only two houses, the farm and its outbuildings, a white ice house, a green chicken coop, a log barn, and a two-hole outhouse! The only other house on the road was a large frame home with many outbuildings and an outhouse. There was no electricity. We had a pump behind the house and; to many of our friends' amazement; this remained so until the late 1960s. This was the best part of the farm;

even our children remember brushing their teeth around the pump, while one of us would pump. Kerosene lamps were our only source of light, and of course, we had to use the outhouse. During World War II, we were not able to go up one year because of gas rationing. That was one of the only years we ever missed spending the summer at the farm. However, the following year, my mother took we three children on the bus. A friend of Grandma Wille's picked us up in a horse and wagon in Roscommon and drove us up to the farm.

The most wonderful part of this legacy is the amount of wonderful memories shared with cousins, aunts and uncles, family friends and, of course, our magnificent lake. At that time, it was pristine with so few cottages. The marvelous State Park was there with its screened in area and the bath house. The little store built during World War II was positioned at the bottom of our hill. I still remember Markey Church where our parents would take us on Sundays, and having tea with Mrs. Sharp in her house behind their small store. I remember walking the dirt road to the lake, walking back for lunch, and then making my way back down to the lake again for the rest of the day. Mrs. Zulauf let us use her dock and raft if their renters weren't using them. Darryl used to let us use his rowboat if no one else needed it. The memories are so many and vast, but forever cherished through our family. Now into the 7th generation, we are sharing this wonderful legacy of a remarkable woman, Grandma Wille.

In 1993 after the death of our father, our mother divided the property between we three children. In 2002, my husband and I built a larger new home in the meadow. One of our sons maintains the small house and opens up the little house when our house overflows with family and guests. Our tradition is, if you can be at the farm on July 4th, we'll be there! In 2011, our children surprised us with a 50th anniversary party attended by 53 family and extended family members. We all always keep in mind that we have so much to be thankful for, and we never forget Grandma and Grandpa Wille. Our great-grandchildren now walk down that dirt road to the lake, spend days at the state park, roam the woods, and pick berries. They enjoy sunrises from our large front porch and evenings by the campfire, just as we did as children. "If I can just get to the farm, things will get better!" That has been our mantra through wars, depressions, and deaths. It has over these generations proven to be true. Thank you Great-grandma and Great-grandpa Wille, Grandma and Grandpa Leader, Mom and Dad Konow, and our children and their children, for keeping the tradition alive!

The Old Days in Cadillac
By Shirley Fauble of Cadillac, Michigan
Born 1942

I was born on Colfax Street in Cadillac, Michigan in 1942. I was delivered by two midwives, which was common back then. My father served in World War II as a cook, but he wouldn't discuss the war with anyone. Our outhouse had morning glories and hollyhocks growing around it. My oldest sister Betty told me that one day when I was three years old, I had a new outfit on, and I fell through the hole. She came and pulled me out and said, "What a mess!" When I was in grade school, I got a round, hard butterscotch candy caught in my throat. My mother grabbed me by my legs and shook me upside down, and the candy popped out. Once in a while, my mother would give my sisters and me a teaspoon of castor oil. My sisters would gag on it, but I just loved it. My mother baked delicious bread, and we would mix a packet of coloring into a substance, and it would make butter. Before we reached school age, we had a large washtub that my sisters and I would take a bath in. One day, I got out of the tub and ran right into the hot coal stove, burning my stomach. I didn't do that again!

Our family didn't own a car, so every Friday evening sisters and I would walk with our parents along the Clam River to the giant super market to buy groceries. We had a large garden at home, plus a large garden planted on property we owned on Cotey Street. We also had an outdoor pump, which pumped clear, clean water. My mother wouldn't let us cook on the gas stove unless she was home to help us. My mother had a wringer washing machine, and one day, her long hair got caught in the wringer. Thankfully, she got herself out of it right away. Also, one day when she was sewing my sister and I clothes, the sewing machine needle went right through her fingernail. When we were

Shirley's parents, Loland and Opal Jacobson with their children

in grade school, the mailman didn't' deliver to every house. We had our mailbox by our other neighbors in front of Powell's Store on Burlingame Street. I can remember the horse and buggy bringing ice to our home to put in our iceboxes and the milkman delivering glass bottles of milk to our home. Our pets growing up were goldfish, guinea pigs, parakeets, and rabbits. My mother was scared of lightning, and when it stormed, she would move the furniture away from the walls and bury her face in a pillow until the storm was over.

My younger sister Maryon had her appendix taken out when we were in grade school. I was supposed to go to a Brownie Scout meeting that same day after school, but I was so worried about her that I didn't go to the meeting. My younger sister, some friends, and I would buy look-alike clothes when we were in grade school. Maryon and I had hair so long that we could sit on it. Every Saturday night, my mother would use rags to wrap our hair in to make in ringlets for Sunday school the next day. Sometimes, we would sing on stage in front of the congregation the song *In the Garden*. We were given 25 cents to put in the collection plate and 10 cents to spend on candy on our walk home. Instead, we put the 10 cents into the collection plate and spent 25 cents on the candy!

On Saturday afternoons, my father would buy us chocolate stars candy from HL Green Store or Woolworth's Store. Almost every Saturday evening when I was in grade school, my sisters and I would spend the night at my Grandma and Grandpa Hoel's farmhouse in Lake City. We played in the barn, helped bring the cows home, and picked berries. Almost every Sunday afternoon we spent at my Grandma and Grandpa Jacobson's house in Hector. They would let us order sweet treats from Game's Store and Willis' store. Everyone dressed in their Sunday best.

In grade school, my classmate Mary and I had the same birthday. One year, our classmates bought each one of us a pair of light blue anklet stockings. My sister Maryon's birthday is September 2nd, and her best friend Donna's was on August 2nd, so one year, our friends, and I bought them each a beautiful cornflower blue sweater, which both of them just loved. We would play treasure hunts and scavenger hunts at our parties. I can remember my parents giving my sisters and me money to buy a Monopoly game. We also played a lot of rummy, bingo, and checkers. For Christmas presents, my sisters and I would buy mother a bottle of Blue Waltz cologne and my father a white handkerchief. Maryon and Donna took baton lessons, and were in a group called "The Glow Worms." In grade school, my sisters and I would go door to door selling Cloverine Salve. Whoever sold the most would receive a large glossy picture of Jesus or a landscape scene. One year, my friend June and I sold Tums at the fair. We ate so many of them that we got sick.

During Paul Bunyan days in the early 1950s, my sister Ardie worked at the Chamber of Commerce. We helped her get ready for the parade. After the parade, music would be played in the city park. The 21 Gun Salute was done at the cemetery. Ardie belonged to a group call "The Rainbow girls." All the girls in the group wore different colored formal dresses. Sometimes on weekends, my friends and I would wade in the city park cement wading pool, bringing a picnic sack lunch with us. My sister and friends would also go to the matinees, paying 10 to 12 cents. We would ice skate at Lincoln School and Diggins Hill, and would also slide down Diggins Hill. We stayed so long that our fingers and feet were frozen, so we crawled home. We would make toast and hot chocolate when we got home. I still have my ice skates. In grade school, we roller-skated at Lincoln School wearing rented clamp-on skates. In the seventh grade, my parents bought me a pair of precision roller-skates that the wheels didn't make any noise. I still have my roller-skates and case. We would skate Friday and Saturday nights at the Park of the Lakes, known now as Carl T. Johnson Museum. Sometimes on Sunday nights, we would skate at a place called "the spot." I can also remember my sisters, mother, and I in the summertime would walk up town so my mother could get her check cashed. We would stop in the city hall building to get a drink of water. I can remember the room where older women would meet to crochet and knit. My mother never wanted us to learn how to swim because my sister Ardie almost drowned when a babysitter took her to the beach. In high school, we would go to Dayhuff Lake, which people would say was bottomless.

As teenagers, my sisters and I would have slumber parties and made fudge and popcorn. I remember my father listening to the Detroit Tiger ball games on the radio. My sisters and I would gather around the tall, round, wooden radio and listen to "Amos and Andy," "Sargeant Preston of the Yukon," "Roy Rogers and Dale Evans," and "The Lone Ranger." I always wished my mother would be chosen to appear on "Queen of the Day." We also had a record player that we had to wind up. Years later, we bought a more modern one. When we got TV, I can remember my father watching "Groucho Marx," "Art Linkletter," and "Ed Sullivan." We would also watch "I Love Lucy" and "American Bandstand." My younger sister and I took piano lessons for three years when we were in grade school. We walked from Maurer Street to Lincoln Street every Saturday morning for the lessons. At one of the piano recitals, I played *Snug as a Bug in a Rug* and *Mr. Popcorn Man*. Mother told us that she was going to sell the piano if we didn't want to practice anymore, so she did.

I can still remember party line phones. Our number was 1323J3. I can still remember some of my friend's phone numbers. No wonder I became a telephone operator! In grade school, there was an assembly, which all the grade schools attended. They didn't tell us beforehand, but after the assembly, I was presented with a silver dollar because they said I was the quietest girl there. The quietest boy was also awarded a silver dollar. When Whittier School closed, some of the students were transferred to Cass School and some to Lincoln School. Lincoln School had the best track field in Cadillac, and so all of the schools would come there to run. One day in the winter in high school, some friends and I decided to skip school. We drove over to the Lake City School to see some kids that attended that school. We got stuck and the principal came to help us shovel our way out. He never called Cadillac School.

During my years in high school, I worked at Cunningham drug store. I worked many weekends by myself, having to clean the grill, sweep the floor, and wait on customers coming from the movies. One evening, someone ordered a hamburger and I didn't put the meat in it. Someone else ordered a banana split and I didn't put a banana in with the ice cream. The customers were surprised; I was embarrassed. People's Stephan's and Wooley's were also good soda fountains that served Cherry Cokes. We would also go to Johnny's Restaurant to play the jukebox and to the Hillcrest for hot powdered doughnuts. We also went to dances at the high school, Armory, and the YMCA.

My mother bought a 1954 blue and white Chevy so my sisters and I could learn to drive. The police officer who gave me the road test was also the associate pastor of our church. We ran out of gas over by the high school and had to call someone to bring us gas. I hated to parallel park, and so he said he was going to watch me when I came to work the next day because the police station was located across the street from my workplace. On account of me knowing that he was looking out for me to park, I parked in the back so I wouldn't have to parallel park.

I still have my diary from high school. I still keep in contact with some of my grade school and high school friends. In the summer of 1958, my father passed away. I was babysitting at a home on Pine Street on a Sunday afternoon, and my father was admitted to the hospital. I can remember him lying there with the large oxygen tent over him. The following Tuesday he died. My mother passed away in 1985. I'm so fortunate to have had such wonderful parents. They always put our family first. My husband and I have been married for 52 years. We have two children and two grandchildren.

Crazy to Climb
By James Wyatt Cook of Grawn, Michigan
Born 1932

Although I lived in Detroit, Michigan, from the time I was three years old until I reached my late twenties, every summer my mother, my father, and I journeyed south to visit my widowed grandmothers. My father's mother lived in Hickman, Kentucky, and my mother's mother in Selmer, Tennessee.

As my father never owned a car, we always took the train to Chicago from Detroit, changed trains, and traveled overnight to Fulton, Kentucky. From there we took a cab for the remaining seventeen miles to Hickman, a pretty town on the banks of the Mississippi River. Then, after a week or so, we continued south by bus to Selmer. Once my father's two or three weeks of vacation were over, he would journey back to Detroit alone, and my mother and I remained for the rest of the summer in Selmer with my invalid Aunt Blanche, her brother, my bachelor Uncle John, and their mother Irene.

Selmer is a small, thriving community near Shiloh National Park and only about seventeen miles from the Tennessee-Mississippi border. Now, as an aging adult, I have become such an acrophobe that I develop a severe case of what Mark Twain called "the fantods" if I even see a child nearing the edge of a precipice. In my boyhood, however, I was a fearless and compulsive climber, and no tall structure or tree escaped my attention. If I thought I *could* climb something, I climbed it.

Near the high school in Selmer sits the town's water tower. Some 90 feet tall, it has an enticing ladder running from near ground level to an encircling parapet some 12 feet below its top. Up that ladder I one day decided to climb—not merely once, but twice. My ascents occurred in full view of the students attending summer school and their horrified teachers, many of whom shrieked at me to come down.

This I eventually did and, well pleased with my day's adventure, went home in a warm self-congratulatory glow.

Later that afternoon, however, my mother and I received a monitory visit from the McNairy County Sherriff. From him we learned that, not only had my daring exploit been too foolhardy and dangerous, it had also been illegal, and that, if I did not want to see the inside of a reform school, I would thenceforward desist from such folly.

Impressed by the warning and relived not to have been arrested, I took the Sherriff's good counsel. I have desisted ever since.

Running on Top of a 6 Ft. Snow Bank to School
By Inez Pletcher Wagner of Fairview, Michigan
Born 1918

I was born in April 1918. I started school in Fairview but because of space in the 2 room school, my sister and two neighbor girls were sent to a one room school about 1½ miles south of our farm. There was a South, East, and North Fairview school, all one room, with one teacher that was also the janitor.

There were 7 or 8 non-Amish and 7 or 8 Amish children that went to our school. The Amish children talked Dutch so we could not understand them, but they talked English to the teacher.

Our classroom looked east so the western states are still north to me.

We usually walked to school except in the winter when it was too cold, when my dad or the neighbor would take us in the sleigh. I was in the 1st and 2nd grade.

The school finally had enough room for us to go there so we walked 1½ miles the other direction. Finally, the school had a bus built for us, an oblong box with tiny windows, and one door in the back, 2 benches, one on each side with a walkway in the middle. If you had long legs, you bumped knees!

This box was mounted on a truck chassis, which was pretty narrow, and then in the winter the driver put skis on the 2 front tires so we could ski to school. Sometimes we rode in an open sleigh to school.

One time we had so much snow we couldn't get into the schoolyard, so the driver stopped out in the road and picked me up and stood me on a 6 ft. bank of snow so I could run on top to the schoolhouse.

The school finally built more rooms and the 11th and 12th grade went to Mio to graduate from a bigger school but I didn't have to go to Mio, because we had become bigger at

Fairview.

I graduated from Fairview High School and so did my three daughters.

✓ Adventures of a Shy Farm Girl
By Mary Jane Allgaier of Traverse City, Michigan
Born 1934

My hometown is Traverse City, Michigan, the cherry capital of the world. My parents were Francis and Anna Allgaier. My family's farm was located a few miles west of Traverse City on M72. There is a road named for my family—Allgaier Road. It leads off M72, circles past the old house, and reconnects to the highway. Whenever anyone says to me, "What an honor to have a road named for you," I say, "It is appropriately named for me because, like my life, it goes nowhere!" I was the last of seven children, coming along seven years after the sixth child and 20 years after the first. My first years forever influenced my entire life. We moved to town when I was about eight years old. When I am being a little silly now, people say, "Mary, you are in your second childhood." I reply, "No; it is my first. I never had a childhood; being born on a farm I was put right to work!" As soon as I could walk confidently, I became adventuresome. I even learned to run quite soon since my older brother teased our rooster and it would chase me and fly at me. That's also when I became a loud screamer and had nosebleeds. One time, my grandfather was visiting and witnessed it. That evening we ate a rooster supper—no one enjoyed it more than I did!

In winter, my mother would bundle me up in leggings, snow pants, boots, coat, hat mittens, and scarf over my face. She took me out on the porch and told me to go play in the

Mary Jane with her mother, Anna Allgaier and Pal

Mary Jane's father, Francis Allgaier

snow, that it would be good for me. After a while, she would come out and tell me that I must be tired and cold and need a hot lunch. Actually, I had never left the porch. With all those clothes, I was sure that with one-step I would fall face down in the snow and die there! My mother began taking me along as she did all of her many chores. I watched as she milked the cows. I never wanted that job, and I never drank milk! I also went with my mother to the chicken yard with a pail of feed to spread around. Inside the hen house, we gathered a few eggs for the day. Later, she sent me to get a few more, which she needed for baking. I was terrified when I saw only two. That meant that I would have to reach under the hens for more! Hens cluck and peck at you! Mother took me with her to the family garden to hoe weeds and stir up the soil. She taught me to pick off potato bugs and put them in a jar of kerosene. I also remember that when she could see that I had some pinworms in my system from playing in the dirt, she would give me a teaspoon of kerosene. I bravely swallowed it because I trusted her so much. For other medical ailments, Mother ordered things from a catalog. I still have a little container of pills for fever and urinary tract infection and half a jar of liniment from the Humphries Company in New York. I wanted to keep those little pills and keep the aroma of the liniment just to remember...

Soon, I became interested in chasing butterflies—especially monarchs. So, my mother found a caterpillar and put it on a stick inside a jar with air holes in the cover. She told me to watch each day, and eventually I would see how the butterfly comes into being a butterfly. However, she also taught me that butterflies must be left free to do the job they were created for. The wooded hill north of our farm began calling to me. So, I ventured off there, walking through the trees and looking for interesting things. I discovered what looked like green onions; they tasted good. Whenever I ate them, I didn't need to go to school—at the teacher's request. Was it leeks breath, or what? Needless to say, I did not like going to school in a one-room schoolhouse. The main reason was that I was very shy. When you come along seven years after other siblings, people just tease you instead of talking to you. I liked the little desks with the lift-up covers. I stored my one pencil and tablet in it. With the cover up, I could laugh a lot. Recess was not fun for me. I was not used to playmates, nor all that screaming! One day resulted in a fight with a boy, and my tooth was knocked crooked. When my second tooth came in, it was also crooked, and still is. So, anyway, I just wanted to be at home where I could help with important stuff!

Growing up on a farm instills a real love and appreciation for animals. I wanted to help my brother put hay in the mangers. We had two workhorses, Chub and Fred. They pulled the wagons, plows, and cultivators. They liked me, especially when I brushed or curried them, even though I couldn't reach up very high. Once, my brother put me up on top of a load of hay and said to drive it back to the barn, enabling him to bring the cows in for the evening. I didn't have to worry—the horses knew where to go and exactly when to stop. It was my mother who went into shock after finding that the driver was me! My brother was never afraid to have me do those "important" things. I liked to be friendly with all the animals and pet them and talk to them. But, when I went with Mother to take leftover food and vegetable peels, she cautioned me to not reach in to the pigs or be friendly. She told me that pigs think that they are supposed to eat everything that comes their way. She only needed to tell me that one time!

We picked cherries at my uncle's orchard, which was down the road from us. We got up at 5:30, took a lunch and tea, and worked all day. I was told that after picking eight lugs, I could stop. Naturally, it took me all day. At 5:00, my uncle came with his homemade tractor to pick up the lugs of cherries from the day. He called it a doodlebug. To my surprise, he said, "Mary Jane, I want you to drive ahead and stop when I say." My brother had told him that I understood about the gas and brake pedals and could save time. I did it, to the amazement of my mother. That was a real big happening for me to have such trust and confidence placed in me! After that, when I was with my brother at his own farm that he was buying and hauling in hay with his car and trailer, he told me to drive the car ahead as needed. He just told me to not "lurch." I said to him, "But my feet don't reach the pedals." He said, "Well, we can't wait for your legs to grow!" He just moved the seat way forward!

A real early memory is of our old model car, which took us to church on Sundays. That was fun. However, on our return trip, we needed to drive up the long dirt road and up the hill. Halfway up, the car would not go any farther. Everyone, except me, would have to get out and push it up. At the top, everyone would get back in and the car took us on, putting down the road. I had enjoyed coasting down the heel, but the way up was scar, and I feared going backwards down it.

Soon after, we moved into the city of Traverse where this little farm girl had quite a few adventures in getting used to city life and school. Just imagine all my experiences and adventures in the 70 years since!

✓ **Winning the Greased Pole Contest**
By Allen L. Lawson of Boyne City,
Michigan
Born 1937

I remember the Greased Pole Contest one summer.

The pole was 12-14 feet long, 8-10 inches around, and extended out over the lake (Lake Charlevoix) down by the docks in Boyne City.

It was greased all up with axle grease. They tacked a $10 bill to the end of it, and the idea was to get that $10 bill in your hand!

The bigger, older boys had bathing suits. I didn't and was wearing a pair of corduroy pants, which I simply rolled up. They got us all in line and put us out there, on the pole, one at a time. There were three or four boys ahead of me, and then it was my turn. I didn't get very far out before I fell in. I swam over to the side where other boys helped me up onto the dock. When they pulled me up my pant legs came unrolled. I hurried back to get into the line, again, dragging my feet and pant legs in the sand and gravel. As I waited my turn, I saw that the two boys ahead of me could take one-step and slide half way out the pole. The boy ahead of me just missed getting the money!

This time, I knew I had to get out there before one of the bigger boys made it out there. When I stepped onto the pole, I noticed my sandy/gravely feet and pant legs kept me from sliding, and I was able to walk the pole almost to the end. Then—I slipped—but I was able to reach for, and grab, the money on the way down!

And, by the way, I was the smallest boy at that event.

Before the Mackinac Bridge Opened
By Diana Green Hudak of Rogers City, Michigan
Born 1938

It was August 1957, the last summer before the Mackinac Bridge opened on November 1st.

I was going to be a sophomore at Central Michigan College (not yet a university) in the fall, but at this time I was a waitress at the Glass Kitchen on the Ferry Land in St. Ignace, Michigan. You see, before the Mackinac Bridge, in order to go from the lower or upper parts of the State of Michigan, you had to take a car ferry from either St. Ignace on the north, or Mackinaw City at the south of the Straits of Mackinac. This is a body of water that joins Lake Huron and Michigan. There were five car ferries, the Vacationland being the largest, and the Straits of Mackinac, the smallest. Even with the boats churning across the straits, during the summer and deer hunting

Building the Mackinac Bridge

season, the wait could be as long as four hours or longer. So everyone was anticipating the opening of the bridge.

That summer, my roommate Barb and I were always walking the mile or so from our rooming house to watch the construction of the bridge in progress. One day when we walked to the site, we noticed that no one was working and the approaches to the bridge were empty. Since the bridge was almost complete, we climbed around a little fence (security was lax in those days), and we walked out to the first bridge tower. It was windy, the scenery was beautiful. On the way back, we encountered no one and to this day, we always say, "We walked the Mackinac Bridge before it was opened."

Pet Goats and School Bus Rides
By Rosemary McCracken Bean of Charlevoix, Michigan
Born 1947

I grew up a country girl out on Phelps Road. It was a nice farm with several outbuildings which included a barn, a chicken coop, a grain shed, a sawmill, and an outhouse. It also had a small orchard with five apple trees, two cherry trees, a plum tree, and a pear tree. We also had a big vegetable garden and clotheslines. In the winter, we could see our neighbors across the fields, but not in the summer.

One summer, our cousins, who had been out of the country for a few years, came to spend two weeks with us. They had five children at the time. The older girls were fascinated with our outhouse. I don't know that they enjoyed using it; however, I do know they enjoyed playing in it. Their favorite game was drop the clothespin. My older sister and I watched them do it, but we didn't tell. My mother wasn't happy when she sent us out to hang the laundry and we only hung part of it. When she asked us why, we had to tell her that that we ran out of clothespins. It wasn't until a few days later that she discovered they were gone. But the fun didn't stop there. The same cousins decided to drop their father's shoes down the hole. When he went looking for them, his girls had to confess. He was disgusted, but he went out, moved the outhouse, and went searching for the shoes. That is where they discovered all of the clothespins, too. We thought it was hilarious. One last memory about the clothesline is the time when my sister Sue stood under one of the lines, thumb in mouth, hanging on for dear life to her security blanket. She never went anywhere without it.

Our grandparents lived down the road about three miles from our house. Grandpa used to drive what we called the Lake Road to visit us. Two of the goats he had given us recognized the sound of his car and would race down to the corner to meet him. He would stop the car and open up the back door. The goats would hop in, and he would give them a ride back to our house. We also raised goats for milk and food, but played with them and made them pets as well. We understood that one day some of them would be butchered.

Beaver was our favorite. We used to take him out to the road, which back in the day was where everyone in the neighborhood came to slide. We put him on the sled and he would ride down the hill, lickety-split, with us. We would then hook him to the sled, and he would pull it back to the top of the hill. We had hours and hours of fun with him until he got too big. In the end, he became wonderful Beaver burgers. That was just the way of things. We also had an old long building that I think had been a chicken coop that wasn't being used any more. At some point in our life, Peggy and I, and the girls in the neighborhood, turned this building into our clubhouse. We cleaned it as best we could and then started to decorate it. We pasted wallpaper on all the walls, and even hung curtains on the windows. We played in there for hours at a time, and even had sleepovers in it.

I had to learn to spell my grandparents' last name before I could get off the bus at their house, so I did. I could spell Strohschein by the time I started kindergarten. Oh goodness, the joy of riding the school bus. I remember snow banks pushed up higher than the bus windows, older boys always getting kicked off bus for causing trouble, and being called "Skeeter" because I was so small. One day that stood out is when there was a storm so bad that the bus could not even get through. It turned around and took us back to school. We had to spend the night unless our parents came for us. Our neighbors picked up and offered to take us home too. My older sister thought it was cool to stay, and wanted to spend the night, so she told them no. They wouldn't take me because she wouldn't go. I didn't like it; she thought it was great fun. We ended up having dinner there and then slept on the gym floor. There were lots of cots, but I don't know that everyone had one. I didn't think there was any reason to stay at school, especially overnight.

There was a railroad track at the bottom of what we called Phelps Hill, and the bus always had to stop for it and check for trains. On a good day, that was all right, but when the roads were bad, Mr. Foster had trouble getting up the hill. He would make it up about halfway, and then have to back down. The bus always seemed to slide to the right side, which had a bit of a drop off. Sometimes, he tried as many as three times. I am of the opinion that some of us prayed him up and over the top of that hill. Since then, the hill has been cut down quite a bit, and there is no longer a railroad track at the bottom. Another memory of getting on the bus was when I first started riding; the bus driver had to get off of the bus to help me get on. That first step was just too tall for my little legs.

Just walking through the kitchen can bring back memories. I was told that I could walk underneath the kitchen table until I was at least five without bumping my head. I also remember the kitchen being a great place to dress in the morning because I could stand in front of the wood cooking stove and stay warm. We would open the oven door and lay our clothes on it to warm before we would put them on. The rest of the house was really cold because we heated the house with wood, and it would be pretty low by morning. At some point, we turned to coal, and later oil. Currently in use is gas and wood. I also remember standing at that same stove and helping Mom make donuts. She made the best ones ever. Many Saturdays, Mom and I would walk around the neighborhood with them. For most of my life, I thought we were sharing, but later found out that we were selling them for a little extra money.

One crazy memory is being in bed asleep in the room above the kitchen and hearing loud popping noises. I went downstairs to see what was going on, and found my aunt, uncle, and mom sitting at the kitchen table laughing. They had spent the whole evening hanging wallpaper on the ceiling to change the look, and now it was popping and falling off!

There used to be a wooden bridge that crossed over the railroad tracks on Lake 26 Road. That was a meeting place sometimes for the girls in the neighborhood. We would stand on it and wave at the conductor as the train went under us. Sometimes we climbed underneath on the bridge supports. The one scary memory I had was the day my sister Peggy decided to walk on the rail of the bridge. It was only a foot wide, and the bridge curved up and then down, as most bridges do. If that wasn't scary enough for me to watch, she did it as a train was coming! Thankfully, she was off the other end before the train got to the bridge. I can still feel the shaking of it every time I think of it!

A Flint with a Rumble Seat
By Dorothy Damm Gruschow Zboyan of
Maple City, Michigan
Born 1918

I was born in October 1918 in Chicago, IL, and grew up in Oak Park, IL. I moved to Michigan in 1965.

Our first phone was a four party line-- Euclid 3434J.

We had an icebox with an opening onto the back porch for the iceman who had a horse-drawn wagon. While he delivered ice, we children would reach in the wagon to grab shaved ice and eat it.

Our first radio was a crystal set, and my dad had to find the right spot for us to hear. A Dempsey/Tunney fight was one of the first events we listened to.

During the Depression, "bums" would come to our back door and my mom always fed them. I think there was a sign on the curb that meant this is a good place to stop.

We had a wringer washer in the basement.

I walked to Oak Park and River Forest High School, because I did not have the nickel

Art, Dorothy, Lucille, Elsie, and Roger in 1946

for a bus. I made my graduation dress in 1936, and also my wedding dress in 1940. My boyfriend whom I married, Warren Gruschow, had a Flint with a rumble seat.

The garbage man would come through our alley with his horse-drawn wagon calling, "Old Rags and Old Iron," and we would sell to him.

There were five children in our family. My dad had a seven passenger Packard with running boards. There were two seats that pulled down from the front seats, and the five children sat in the back.

Dad would drive (my mom did not drive till she was 65, and they retired and moved to Port Angeles, WA) to Cedar Lake, Indiana, to our cottage which had kerosene lamps (I still have one), a well with a pump, an outhouse, a kerosene cook stove inside, and a big one outside.

It was a good life. I am healthy at 94, take no medicine, live alone, and still drive. Thanks be to God who put me in Christ at age 65. Joy, Dorothy Z.: Under the Mercy.

Farm and Work in the War Days
By Dorothy Stein of Traverse City, Michigan
Born 1921

My family consisted of 15 boys and four girls. My father and first wife had four children—three boys and one girl. My sister Marcella was the only one to survive. His wife died in 1904, leaving him with a small child. Then, Pa married my mother and there were 15 children born. One baby, Lawrence, died in infancy. One other died at a young age. I was born in 1921 after eight boys, so I was pampered a little. We had carbide lights in the days that I remember. One of my brothers persuaded my dad to buy a wind charger. We had at least 12 batteries in the basement, so together with the wind, the energy that those sources provided gave us lights in every room in the early '30s. Leonard installed these, plus wired the house with a line to the barn. We enjoyed these until electricity came through. Leonard and Raymond also were two of the men who started the Old Engine Show in Buckley. It has become quite large, and the patrons came from all over. Also, they have an old train that had rides during the show. There were food courts and bake sales. There was also a large flea market.

My father had a team of oxen, and I barely remember them. They pulled a stone boat to load stones on from new ground after it was plowed. The first year we always had huge potatoes from the field. It was also used to haul sap in the spring, as the boys would tap the maple trees. There was a syrup shack in the woods and a dugout fire leveled off with stones. These held two large pans to cook the syrup on. One was to start it and the second was to finish it off. The syrup was delicious, and it lasted the year, as my mother canned it in two-quart jars. My parents had a large garden and we grew cabbage, which Pa had us make into sauerkraut. It was shredded, and some of us took turns with a special wooden block with a handle to stomp the slaw down. Salt was then added. This was done in two huge crocks. It was weighted down with a wooden board that was used only for that purpose and a heavy stone. Then it was covered with a cloth from flour sack material. Enough kraut was saved and canned for the family, and my dad hauled it by horse and wagon to town to sell to Maxbaurs. When he went inside to get the owner, the horses pushed off the cover, and had a midday snack. My dad was mortified, but Mr. M. said, "Ach," pulled off some of the top kraut, and said, "This is 'goot.'" All ended well.

One of the neighbors had a threshing machine and he went to the farmers who raised wheat and oats to help out. It was a daylong job with about ten men assisting with the various jobs. It separated the wheat from the straw, and a fan at the end would blow out the chaff or debris. Men would be holding gunnysacks to catch the wheat as it came

down some sort of shaft. It was loaded by others on a wagon and hauled to the granary in the tool shed. The shed had a special room partitioned for wheat, oats, and corn. It was well sealed to keep out the vermin, with windows for ventilation. When noontime came, the men hurried to the house for a good meal. My mother was an excellent cook, and usually had two kinds of meat, tomatoes, green beans, cucumbers, and homemade bread that she made. She made about 12 loaves a week. As girls, we had to help with the preparations and cleanup. We also had a butter churn, and after the cream soured to the proper stage, the kids had fun pushing the staves up and down. This caused the barrel to go round. When we heard a "plop, plop," we knew we had butter. Mother then drained off the buttermilk and finished working the butter. We enjoyed both the buttermilk and the butter.

My dad was an excellent meat man, and in the fall, we had a butchering and processing day. He made several kinds of sausages and roasts. My mother and those who were old enough to help would cut up cubes of beef, and Ma would pack this in sterile two-quart jars with salt, pepper, water, and a seal. Then it was put into the oven for three hours. We always looked forward to roast beef dinners. Lots of soup from the bones was also preserved in two-quart jars. To do all the meat processing, Dad had a sturdy bench with a large meat grinder, sausage press, and a large mixing pan. Mother cleaned and scrapped the casings and sterilized them. These held the sausages. Also from the pork, the chops were fried down or baked. These were preserved in the hot lard rendered from the pork. They were preserved in a closet off a room that extended to the north. We also enjoyed those pork dinners. Dad had a smoke house, and all the shoulders and hams were smoked in a smudge fire inside the smokehouse. Bean and pea soups were made from the bones.

We harvested the corn in the fall. Some of the corn that was immature, and so the stalks would be blown into the silo with the machine and packed down by the boys as it was filled to the top. This was fed to the cows in the winter. We also had a corn sheller and grinder for chicken and animal feed. Lots of corn was stored in a corncrib to dry out. After the corn was all used, the girls and neighbors would use the corncrib as a playhouse. Other games were "anti-hi-over," "fox and geese," and the boys had their own baseball team behind the barn in the hayfield. Also, there was ice skating and sledding in the winter. We also had enough snow to make large snow huts.

We walked to school at Hannah, St. Mary's for about eight years until we shared bus rides with Kingsley School until St. Mary's purchased their own. My sister Teresa was about six or seven, and we were walking to school after a huge snowstorm. We lost her in a snowdrift. After a few minutes, she came walking out the other side. It was shaped like a cone. Another time when we were walking, my elastic broke, and my underpants fell to the ground. I sat right down, and some of the boys teased and said they would stay until I got up. Soon afterward, they left, and I hurried on home. These were called bloomers in my time. My mother made most of our clothes, and she taught me to sew, quilt, and bake. I learned how to make my own clothes. We had a touring car, which we used in the summer. We used an ice cutter (like a buggy) in the winter. The family would pile in and go to church

Dorothy's family in 1926

on Sundays. There was a long barn north of church, which was partitioned off so the horses would have some shelter during Mass.

In the summer, Kingsley merchants hosted an open free movie on Saturday nights. The folks would all go downtown to see it. We also had a group of school friends who would get together and go sledding and tobogganing. When we tired of that, we walked to Ockert's, and Mrs. Ockert had cake and hot cocoa for us. Some Sunday nights my brothers were able to take the car and we

could go to Traverse City to see Gene Autry and other western stars—all for 25 cents each. We listened to the news on the radio and also Amos and Andy. That was our treat for the day.

I graduated from high school in 1940. There weren't many jobs in Traverse city, so I went to Detroit and found a job at Cunningham's drug store doing soda fountain work and serving sodas, coffee, and sandwiches. I even did some cooking on the stove and grill. I was soon called to Cadillac Motors during the war and did some surface grinding for several months. Then I was recruited to try out welding. At first, I worked on a small jig and had the unfortunate piece fall out of the jig and cut my big toe, almost in two. They took me to the emergency room and the doctor sewed it back together. My boss brought me to work and back, and eventually everyone had to get steel-toed shoes. Guess who got the blame? I was transferred to another department to weld armor plates. It was quite a process. One needed inspection at every different weld. We had to make sure the plates were always level and had to use a huge jig to turn, which happened after each procedure. One could only do a plate and a half a day. When the war was nearing the end, I was asked to work inside the tanks. I learned how to do vertical, overhand, and down hand, plus the regular thing that I was already doing. While working at Cadillac Motors, they came around and took some pictures of us. I was the one from Cadillac Motors chosen as a candidate to have my picture in the paper as a Victory Girl. Someone else was the winner from another factory.

I was approached by my foreman to take

up a collection for our boys in service for money for cigarettes. They were asking for one dollar. He told me to make sure I stopped at the repair area and ask for a donation from a young man who had a special gift. When I located him, he proudly took out his billfold and cockily handed over a $2.00 bill. I told him that he didn't have to be so cocky; as I had one also that, I had donated. He started coming to my workstation during breaks and a friendship started. Eventually we were dating, and the rest is history, as we were married for 58 years. Edward loved the North Country and we eventually moved to Traverse City. Life was hard, as we were still in a type of recession and layoffs were common. I am the mother of five living children, 11 grandchildren, and 12 great-grandchildren.

When my oldest daughter Marie was three years old, she came looking for her dad. When she asked me where her daddy was, I told her that he was next door shooting the bull. She ran out the door and found him talking to the neighbors. She said, "Daddy, Mom said you were out shooting the bull. I don't see any bull." This cracked up the neighbors.

I just have to add one more story. My youngest sister married a cherry farmer and moved to one of the most beautiful places on the peninsula. Both of us used to enter our baked goods in the county fair. She (Mary) made all kinds of baked goods and won lots of ribbons. I baked only bread and cherry pies, and won blue ribbons on all. Mary never won on her cherry pie. I received the Gold State Award for mine one year. The joke here is that I always received my cherries from Mary and her husband. We have a running joke about all this. My family was very good to us, and we were close knit, always getting together several times a year. There are seven of us living still, ages ranging from 78 to 95.

✓ Grandma… Laughed?
By Patricia P. Sullivan of East Tawas,
Michigan
Born 1945

We were just two kids, 11 and 12, trying to find things to do during a summer visit to our grandparents' home in Grayling, Michigan, back in the 1950s. Grayling then was a village. The most significant things about Grayling were that the Au Sable River ran through it and the Michigan National Guard summer camp was located there. Not much else going on from our vantage point, in other words, pretty boring. We wanted a little more excitement than grocery shopping with Grandma. We rarely spent time with Grandpa, who was still working as an electrician on the railroad at that time and was away during the days and some overnights. So we spent much of our time with Grandma, a stoic, no-nonsense woman of few words. She smiled rarely and we never heard her laugh.

As 11 and 12 year old pre-teens, we were just getting interested in attracting boys. And, it just so happened, that our grandparents' home was on the flight path for take-offs and landings. We could actually see the guardsmen in the planes as they passed overhead and fancied ourselves that they could see us as well. Well, we decided one hot day while we sunbathed in the back yard to wave at them and try to get their attention. When they tipped their wings as they passed over Grandma's house we were convinced that they saw us as we waved our arms and beach towels. We thought it was great fun. Grandma did not. She'd call us inside for the day whenever she saw us waving at them, or decide that we needed to go to the grocery store.

Grandma didn't drive, so we would all walk the several blocks to the grocery store. On one occasion, we convinced Grandma to purchase a watermelon, and she told us that if we did we would have to carry it home in our arms. Well, the watermelon we bought was way too bulky for me to get my arms around so my older sister was elected to carry it. The three of us started the journey home with Grandma quietly walking and my sister and me making jokes about carrying this huge big melon home. The watermelon was not only big and bulky, its skin was slippery and soon slipped right out of my sister's arms, splitting open on the sidewalk. Our Grandma was in shock and appalled at what happened.

To our unbridled surprise, she laughed harder and louder and longer than we'd ever experienced our Grandma do before. We, too, were embarrassed but laughing so hard we could barely contain ourselves. In the midst of her laughter, Grandma told us we had to pick up the pieces and carry home what we could salvage. And, we did what she told us to do. We carried home the bigger watermelon pieces, with red juice staining our shorts and tops, laughing so uproariously that we dropped more of the melon on the way. By the time we arrived home, we had about a third of the melon left and our clothes were dripping with red juice. But we had had some excitement and experienced our Grandma in a way we had never before or ever would again.

✓ Surrounded by Eyes Reflecting the Lantern Light
By Claribel Mason of East Jordan, Michigan
Born 1925

We still lived on the old homestead in 1937 and our farm, which is now the Gaylord Golf Course, was bordered on the west by a section of virgin timber that was owned by the Antrim Iron Company.

This was the last section of virgin timber to be cut in the lower peninsula of Michigan. Twenty-five new shanty houses were built around the west end of Horning Lake and soon twenty-five families had been hired and moved in to harvest that great stand of maple, elm, and white pine trees.

The camp was about a half mile from our place and as the lumbermen cleared the forest away new grass, fresh and green, sprang up everywhere. The section of land had six small lakes and wild game was everywhere: logging roads run in all directions.

This area became known as the "slashings" and we were allowed to let our milk cows run and pasture for free which during those Depression years was a great help to our very strained budget. Every morning after milking the cows we drove them near the lake and let them go all day. Then my sister and I would go and hunt them at evening. Several of the cows wore bells around their necks to help us find them.

One Sunday we had all been away and came home later than usual so my sister and I took the lantern and matches so we could light it if darkness fell before we would get back.

We hurried along one logging trail after another, every few steps listening for the tinkle of the cow's bells. The crickets hummed their monotone choir hymns, frogs provided the bass, and the red cardinals, the robins, and blue birds, sang soprano. Still we listened for the bells.

The sun's long arms of late evening lingered longer through the scattered treetops but slowly retired into her golden boudoir. Darkness came and we lit our old kerosene lantern.

As we kept trudging on in the darkness with only our one little circle of light, moving deeper in the slashings and into the night, a hoot owl in a tree just above our heads sounded a warning to his family to let them know we were there. We were so startled we both jumped, and then threw our arms around each other for whatever protection we might afford each other. Ignoring our goose bumps and the owl's warning we hurried on, ever listening for the bells.

Then in the road in front of us and on all sides of the road we realized, bright eyes were shining by the reflection of the lantern light. Such fear as we had never known gripped us and held us frozen in a vice of panic. I could feel the hair stand up on my neck and had almost stopped breathing when I felt my sister slip her hand into mine and she whispered, "We'd better pray!" She didn't need to tell me for I was really praying!

Then we heard old Dinty's bell. It was the eyes of our herd of cows and the bells, which had remained silent while the cows were lying down, now became a merry din and joined our laughter over our fear of our imagined danger.

✓ An Enchanting Melody of Peace
By Valerie Murden of Bellaire, Michigan
Born 1950

Clam Lake is one of the Chain-O-Lakes that lie nestled between the tips of the little and ring finger of Michigan; winding and sparkling like a strand of dew-dropped spider's web. It was here, as a child, I felt close to God and dared to dream dreams.

Grass River, a shallow, snake-like, and grassy river, paralleled on either side by gently swaying, whispering pines, is the source from which Clam Lake originates.

Clam Lake, shaped like a bucking kidney bean, with a straight tail, is approximately three miles long and one-quarter mile wide. I considered it my favorite aunt and uncle's back yard.

It is surrounded by rustling pines that seem to hold up the sky, all hiding cozy, little-

The old boat houses in winter

windowed cottages at their feet.

White, sandy paths run down from the cottages to the edge of Clam Lake and out onto tongue-like docks that stick out into the water.

On a lazy summer's day, it was a common sight and sound to see and hear what started out to be a deep-voiced fly, turning into a lazily driven motor boat, sputtering along and pulling a fan of rippling water as it filled the air with the pungent odors of oil and gas.

As I looked across the lake, it was only an illusion that the water appeared to be sky-blue as it wrinkled and glistened with the dancing of sun diamonds. Actually, its depths held many colored and awesome secrets.

Climbing into a rowboat, I could hear the steady, gentle lapping of the waves as they washed the shore. Near the shore, as I looked into its depths, I could see that the water was as clear as it could be, but turned brown by the mucky bottom, if slightly touched. It was covered with sunken and abandoned clam shells, snake grass, long, flat fingers of slimy seaweed swaying gently with the under currents, and tall green, slender poles reaching up and balancing lily pad plates that held white-pedaled flowers.

Occasionally, I would see a turtle's head sticking up amongst the lily pads, trying to camouflage itself against the not yet opened buds. I might have even seen a snake gliding under the water or a striped perch suspended between surface and the bottom of the lake; so still except for the whisper movement of a lacy gill.

The further out I'd row into the lake, the greener and more eerie and captivating the waters would become.

Near the beginning of the approximately five-hundred-foot long Clam River, which leads into Torch Lake, on either side of the ever narrowing lake, were old, long, some old and some new, half moon-shaped boat houses that displayed a haunting reflection of patchy lights, dancing on the water and their ceiling, combined with a rhythmic bumping of boats against their berths, as the water rippled in from the passing motor boat.

All of this seemed to be echoing a ghostly tale of a different world, long ago, of sun-filled, easy-going days filled with laughter that floated lightly across the water and played an enchanting melody of peace to my ears.

Mom Sat on the Porch and Looked at Her Day's Work
By Mary Carolyn Brown of Central Lake, Michigan
Born 1937

When we could have a new dress, Dad took us to the co-op to pick out feedbags from those with pretty stripes, flowered, and polka dot patterns. Mom made our slips and dresses on her Singer treadle sewing machine. She never had a pattern. She measured us and cut out a pattern from a newspaper. When our dresses were made, she sent for us new shoes from Montgomery Ward catalog. We could hardly wait for the mailman to deliver our package! On Saturday, shopping day, Mom got us new socks and ribbons for our hair to match our new dress.

On special occasions, Mom did my hair in rags. She tore strips from an old sheet. They were then tied around some strands of hair next to my head. With half of the strips, she wrapped the hair around, then she took the other half and wrapped it around the hair. Then the two ties were tied in a knot. She kept going around until all the hair was wrapped and tied. They were not easy to sleep on!

But in the morning, we put our new dress, new shoes, and new socks on. And Mom took out the rags. I had ringlets all around my head. Then she added new ribbons in my hair. Oh, how pretty we were. Mom and Dad looked so proud.

Washday was an all day chore. Water needed to be carried by pail in the summertime and a sled in the winter. The well was about

281

70 feet from the house. The pitcher pump always had to be primed to get the water to come. Filling the tub in the wintertime seemed to take a long time. Then on the way to the house, if the tub slipped off the sleigh, the water was gone, back to the well to get more water. Getting it to the house, the tub was carried and put on the stove to heat. Then back to the well to get rinse water. When the wash water was hot, Mom shaved a bar of Fells Naptha soap and blueing was put in the rinse water to make the colors brighter.

Mom was so happy when she got her first "Gas Maytag Wringer Washing Machine." Dad filled the gas tank, Mom put the exhaust hose out the door, and the machine was started. Anyone near our house knew it was laundry day. The exhaust had a muffler on it, but it was still loud. With the rinse tub in place, Mom added the hot wash water to the washer. Adding the clothes, she turned on the agitator. And then she timed the time to be washed. When done, she turned on the wringer rollers. Mom had a stick she used to pick up the clothes out of the hot water. Then she put them through the wringer. If the clothes wrapped around the roller, you had to hit the release bar and take them out. The washed clothes then went into the rinse water and the wringer turned around to wring out the rinsed clothes. She kept adding the sorted clothes to the washer as needed. She shut the motor off. The wash and rinse water was emptied by pail and dumped. Then the hose was brought in and everything was put away.

Then came hanging up the clothes on the line outside or upstairs on the line in the winter. Mom mixed up starch and starched her aprons and collars. When the things were dry, some needed to be ironed. She sprinkled the clothes with water and rolled them up and put them in a towel to be ironed later.

Mom had a gas iron. She filled it with white gas. When she lit the iron, flames came out the sides. She turned down the flame and waited for it to get hot. She wouldn't let me iron with that. I had to use the flat irons that were heated on top of the stove and put into a jacket with a handle.

When the washing on the line was blowing in the breeze, my mom loved to sit on the porch and look at her day's work. She always had a good-looking washing on the line. The smell of the dry washing smelled wonderful.

Haying, Grain Binding, and Cleaning the Outhouse
By Marlin F. Schmidt of South Bend, Indiana
Born 1935

I was born and raised in Flint, Michigan, but spent most of my summers working on the family farm in Cheboygan, Michigan. I will soon be 78 years old and have many memories of my time on the farm.

It was important for my brother and I to be in the North Country because we both had an allergy to ragweed. Many people in those days fled north to escape the pollen of giant ragweed that did not grow in the north or at least did not get ripe enough to inflict pollen on allergy sufferers.

My first memory at age five was being made a water boy, to take water to the relatives that were working in the fields. My first real job was shocking hay, taking the hay that was raked in rows by a horse-drawn dump rake and putting it into piles to help it dry and be available in piles to pitch up on the wagon. The hay was then driven to the barn by the team, and either put in the mows by pitchfork, or if possible drawn up into the mow with a large fork that hooked into the hay wagon and drew up a large bunch of hay with ropes and pulley drawn by the team. Hot, dusty work and we were always glad to see the bottom of the wagon. Near the end of my time on the farm, my uncle purchased a hay loader. The hay loader was hitched on the back of the hay wagon, and the whole thing was pulled by the team.

We would start the team down the hay row and work the hay off the loader onto the wagon. As the load got bigger and bigger the horses would go faster and faster and we would need to run up and grab the rains to slow them down. One day it was about 100 degrees out, and while working fast and hard to keep up with the flow of hay, we both fell off the wagon. When the load of hay was put in the mow, I would run to the house, into the pantry, spread some soft butter on a few squares of soda crackers, shake on some extra salt, and run back to the wagon to head out to the field to get another load.

Another job was to follow the grain binder that would cut, gather, and bind the stalks of grain. You would pick up two and set them up in shocks to dry and wait thrashing day.

There was no way one could cheat on the job of setting up shocks of grain. One could clearly see how well and how much you had accomplished. It was a very long day when you had to set up a 10-acre field by yourself. One day working alone, along came my dad's brother. He was very happy to help me and relive some of his early farm days as he lived in Detroit and enjoyed his vacations on the farm. I was only too happy to share this task with him as the grain beards and barbs would get down in your clothing and make you itch.

My uncles had a grain separator that they would haul to neighboring farms to separate the grain from the straw. We would bag the grain and carry it on our shoulder to the granary and the straw was blown into a pile or blown into the barn to be used for bedding in the cow and horse barn. Sometimes my job was to mow away the straw as it was blown into the barn. A very hot, dusty, and really dirty job. The one compensation for doing this job was it entitled you to a shot of whiskey to cut the dust.

Thrashing day was always an event. The neighbors would gather to do all the necessary jobs: loading the wagons in the field, hauling the wagons to the separator, load the grain sheaves into the separator, operate the tractor and separator, and sack and man haul the grain in sacks that weighed up to 100 lbs.

The highlight of the day was the great food for lunch as wives gathered to help make the meal. There was a wash pan, comb, and mirror outside for the crew to freshen up for lunch, and then it was back to work.

My last year on the farm my uncle did not want to take the separator on the road, but the neighbors needed to have their grain separated. So, I took the job. I needed to purchase gasoline, grease, make up a schedule, and go on the road. The work and weather went well and I got all the neighbor's work done. The problem was getting paid for my work. Most all the farmers said they would pay me when they sold their grain. I needed to get back to school, and needed to get paid. A rude awakening for a budding businessman.

Another great job on the farm, one done on rainy days, was cleaning the outhouse. The outhouse was a two-holer, and kept clean by putting wood ashes on business to keep down the flies and smell. But, it needed to be cleaned. We dug a hole in the field and wheeled the material out to the hole. Before we could cover up the material, the dog jumped in to do a good roll and then wanted to be our friend. The outhouse door faced the road, and if and when they would plant corn in the field between the outhouse and the road, one could enjoy the experience with the door open. A real treat when treats were hard to come by. At that time, there were no women on the farm, and when my uncle did marry, things were a bit different. For instance, one early morning I did not want to get up for a nature call, so I did my number one out of the window. Well my new aunt was working in the kitchen sink and saw the stream coming down. My uncle was requested to make sure that did not happen again. When there were no women on the farm, we boys would go out on the porch roof to water the lawn. New brooms sweep clean.

You took a slop jar with you when you went to bed in case you got a nature call in the middle of the night, because it was a long cool walk to the outhouse. You took it down with you in the morning to empty and rinse and set it aside for the night. When we visited in the winter, I was always in wonder that the liquid did not freeze overnight. The heat stove in the living room did not do a real good job of giving heat to the second floor rooms, through the one-foot square hole in the ceiling above the stove. On the other hand, I always felt sorry for my aunt on a hot summer day working over the cook stove. It was bad enough in summer without having a fire in the stove in the kitchen. Things were even worse when she was having hot flashes.

As my dad used to say, we took a bath every Saturday night whether we needed it or not. We washed our feet every evening, but the bath was Saturday night.

We needed to pump water into a double copper boiler, put it on top of the cook stove to heat, and then carry it into the bathroom and tub. That old saying, "don't throw the baby out with the bath water," makes sense when you figure by the time the baby got into the tub last the water was so dirty, you could not find the baby in the water. Then you put on your fresh clean cotton J.C. Penny oxcloth blue shirt and cotton denim pants and it was off to town for the Saturday night band concert, and people watching. It was my joy to take my aunt to town on Friday to buy groceries. When I came up in the early summer, the old '41 Plymouth was a real pig from my uncle's slow careful driving. By fall, I could spin the back wheels on shifting and really make that old car fly.

We had a twelve-party line phone. The phone was on the wall. You turned the crank to generate a ring that was your signal to answer the phone. Our ring was two longs and a short. When my grandmother was ill, my uncle rang our own number on the phone, and when he was sure all the parties on the line hooked in, as he knew they would, he told them of her condition. Early E-mail? If you needed to call out of the twelve-party line group, you called downtown and asked them to connect you to your party.

My grandfather came to Cheboygan and built his barn in 1873, as that date was carved on one of the main wood beams in the barn. The story was that he fought in the Franco-Prussian War and tossed all his medals in the ocean on the way over. He needed to build a corduroy road for well over a mile to the site of his log built home. The site was selected as the highest point on his plot by the surveyor. Most of the land was quite low, covered with trees and stones. Michigan is known for its variety of stones because of the glacier, and firms in that area were covered with large stone piles, picked, hauled, and piled by hand year after year as the stones came to the surface with each year's frost. When one reflects on slavery, land settlers in those early days were slaves to their own aims to be free and self-supporting for themselves and their family. It was not uncommon for farmers to work in the woods for lumber companies in the winter to earn money to purchase farm equipment. My dad who was born in 1888, the third of nine children, told me a story that I did not appreciate until later in life. A farmer in those early days lost a newborn child. His neighbor in an attempt to console his neighbor said, "It could have been worse; it could have been your horse." In today's thinking, this statement seems very crude, but in those days where money was hard to come by, if you lost your horse it caused a real danger to the family.

On hot summer evenings, we could talk the adults into taking us to the lake to wash off and cool down. It was a great departure from farm chores. Often we would have neighbor kids to join up.

My mother and aunt both from the farm in Cheboygan moved to Flint to be in service. My mother worked for a physician and did the housework, laundry, cooking, and care of the three children. My aunt worked for Walter P. Chrysler during the time he worked for General Motors Buick Motor Division. She also worked for a Mr. Strong that was the manager of Buick. They knew most all of the early movers and shakers in the budding auto industry. While in Flint, my mother met other young women who were in service. One of the women was from East Leland, and my mother was engaged to her brother. He was killed in WWI in October of 1918. My dad was from the farm 1/4 mile down the road from where my mother was born and raised, and moved to Flint in 1912 to work for Buick. This was very common in those days for the farm people to move to the big city for work.

You Gals That Smoke Keep Your Butts Out of This Car
By Claude (Harriet) Hubert of Hillman, Michigan
Born 1926

Mr. and Mrs. (Fred and Eva) Hubert lived north of Hillman, Michigan, on a farm. They raised eight children: Barbara, Cyril, Clare, Vincent, Clement, Bernard, Loretta, and Claude.

Money was tight. The boys had two pairs of bib overalls, one for school and church, and one for play. Eva was kept busy mending the play clothes, as the boys were rambunctious and not too careful. There was only one bike and it provided play for the family as well as the neighbor kids too. It was in repair

The 1917 Model T

practically every day.

Vincent had polio and was unable to walk far and had a very prominent limp. Often the boys would carry him on their backs, as he wanted to be in on all their activities. His loyal dog Amos pulled him back and forth to school with a four-wheeled cart that Mr. Hubert had made. The teacher did not want Amos in the school but he barked and barked so she let him in. He stayed right by Vin's desk. There was a dog that lived on the way to school. Amos hated that dog and one day he took after that dog and upset Vin and cart end over teakettle right in the middle of the road.

Up behind their field were hills. The boys and Loretta would carry water up the hill to make ice slides. Vin was inventive and came up with ideas to make fun ways to descend. He asked his brothers to mount a bench to sled runners. They had lots of spills on that contraption. They also made a high ski jump by rolling up a huge snowball and icing it down. But they were all afraid to try it out. So a brave neighbor boy said he would give it a go. He did and he ended up end over end with arms and legs flying.

One 4th of July, Mr. Hubert told Bernard and Claude that if they finished plowing the cornfield they would go on a picnic at Long Lake. Their horse was plodding along ever so slow. Bernard wanted to speed him up and stuck firecrackers in the cooper strap. The firecrackers went off before Bernard got back. Claude was dragged kitty-corner across the field. He got up a cryin' and spittin' sand. Bernard brushed him off and said, "Oh, you'll be alright." The horse began plodding along slowly again.

The boys would play "bombs away" by placing a cork in a bottle and putting it in a fire. When the water boiled, the bottle would shoot the cork out. Claude was to watch so no cars would get bombed.

As the boys got older, they began to drive. Their grandpa gave them a Model T 1917.

They wrote funny sayings all over it like "Capacity 4 gals" and "You gals that smoke keep your butts out of this car." They drove it in many parades in Hillman. They used to race from Alpena to Rogers City to Hillman. There was only one sheriff in those days and very little traffic.

One day a neighbor man who was known to imbibe a bit was weaving all over the road.

The Hubert children

Bernard and Claude were adjusting the brakes on the Model T. Claude was on his hands and knees and they were distracted. Anyway, the neighbor zigged when he should have zagged and they hit him square on. He rolled up on the car, his eyes rolled back and he let out a heck of a grunt. Claude said, "I think we killed him." Bernard said, "Naw, he's alright." And he was.

Vin was living at home on the farm. Barbara was working downstate at Ford's. She had a friend that told Henry Ford there was a crippled boy up north who wanted a job. Mr. Ford said, "If he's a farm boy, hire him." Because of this, Bernard and Claude were always loyal to Fords.

Claude is the only living sibling. He will be 87 this year. He still tells many wonderful stories regarding his family.

Playing Music at Grampa and Grama Baldwin's
By Roger L. Baldwin of Glennie, Michigan
Born 1941

I had trouble in math and Mary Cordes had a store in Barton City, MI. She was also the substitute teacher. She would have you work in the store running the cash register to help make it easier to learn. Like most boys, I got into my share of trouble. The teacher used her razor strap on our behinds. Mrs. Coleman donated the razor strap. If we got a spanking in school or the neighbor's we got another one usually at home. When the neighbor told my parents and it was pretty bad, the spanking was in front of them.

Grama gave us castor oil to make things run smoothly. She would pinch our nose and make us open our mouths. I can still taste it today when I think about it.

We loved Roy Rogers and Dale Evans and Gene Autry so we made sure our chores was done so we didn't miss these programs. My dad brought us kids home a comic book every week.

The party line phone in Glennie was more fun than the one in Barton City. A whole crank was two turns and two cranks was a long. To get the operator you did a long turn on the handle. I think the operator listened in most of the time. We had a lady in Glennie who always listened in and we knew who it was by the old grandfather clock that we could hear in the background.

We took baths the old fashioned way: a big tub of water and all us kids used the same water. Our baths were always by age, oldest first, and I should have been second but it didn't always work out that way.

When it was wash day, we boys had to carry water in ten gallon cream cans from the well house next to the barn. We each had to carry two cans each.

I was born about the time of the Depression. Times were hard and I helped Grampa pick up the culled potatoes. My mother canned fruits and vegetables so we never went hungry. We ate lots of lard and sugar sandwiches. We carried them in our lunches to school.

Mom and Grama made most of our clothes. Grama had ten kids so she was a good sewer. My mom learned to sew and made some or most of her clothes also.

My favorite teacher was Jim Basselman. We had a one room school so one teacher was all we had and one substitute.

I always wanted a car with a rumble seat and never even got to ride in one. Now at the age of seventy I finally had the opportunity to buy one. It is in my garage and needs lots of work. I bought two old cars at the same time: a 1930 Oldsmobile and the 1931 Chevy with a rumble seat. I hope to one day get it fixed up so my wife and I can go for a ride in it. I fixed the 1930 up first cause it ran. I had the interior all replaced and then painted. I am still working on things as money comes available.

When my uncle came home from the service, we had six feet of snow and it was so hard the road grader could not break the crust so they (the road crew) cut the fence in Vonfentls field (comer of Stout Rd. and Trask Lake Rd.) and made the road go around.

We had a collie dog. His name was Buster. He liked to protect everyone and he went with us wherever we went except to school He walked us to the corner and went back home. He was always happy to see us when we got home from school.

We had trouble with the dog and the porcupines. We pulled out many quills more than I like to remember. It never seemed to make the dogs remember to stay away from those critters.

Grampa made us our first handmade sled and a wagon. We pulled each other around in the wagon. We lived on a hill so we would sleigh ride down the hill and keep climbing up to give our bodies a ride down.

We bought a farm in Glennie in 1955. We had 240 acres and so had milk cows and since Dad worked in Bay City we all did chores. Haying was a big job and hot too. We grew grain and there were always fences to mend. We had to carry water to the cattle. When it was too cold, the cows stayed in the barn.

We fed the cats with cow's milk and sometimes we squirted milk at them.

We went to Bliss Lake to cool off and one time Berniece, my wife now, came to the lake with her parents and I was swimming in the buff so I had to swim across the lake. Bliss Lake was the lake of choice back then but now it's the Au Sable River back waters.

The McGregors were our good friends and the Shultz's.

Mischief always found me. We put a skunk in someone's mail box on Halloween, and we caught live coons and put them in a school bus. The driver was suspicious about who did it but couldn't prove it. There were several of us guys who caught the coons.

In the winter, we played Fox in the Snow in the hay field. We would go to Busch's and ice skate and sleigh ride. We had lots of fun with them.

We hauled ice from the Barton City store, for the ice box. The ice was kept under a saw dust pile. It would keep all summer and never melt.

Mr. Cordes would get a group of men and go to the lake in Barton City and cut out hunks of ice.

We had our own farm so we milked cows twice a day and sold the milk. We had all the milk and cream we could use.

At Grampa and Grama Baldwin's we would get together and bring our instruments and play music. We had organ, piano, guitar, harmonica, and violin. The rest were those who wanted to sing. Some even danced to the music.

We had an old crank phone. That was in the days when everyone seemed to like to listen in on other's conversations. That was the gossip line as we called it.

Sometimes I think we would be better off if some of the things today were like they were back in the good old days.

The Family Cottage on Van Ettan Lake
By Richard Griese of Oscoda, Michigan
Born 1930

It was in the early 1920s that my family first arrived in Northern Michigan. They lived in Detroit and they went on a steamboat excursion on the Great Lakes run by the Detroit & Cleveland ship line. They docked in Oscoda and were taken to a lodge a few miles from town to Van Ettan Lake. The lodge had fifty rooms at a rate of $4.00 to $6.00 a day. Adjacent to the lodge were thirteen cottages with range of $20 to $30 per week. After spending some time there and viewing the area they decided to buy some property on the lake. It was still the early '20s and they had a large summer cottage built and all the family was more than welcome. The property was quite remote and they had to cut a half mile trail through the woods. When they traveled from Detroit to Oscoda by auto, it was a two day trip to travel the 200 miles.

Now my memory goes back to 1936; I'm six years old and this will be a start for me spending summers in Oscoda on the lake along with the sandy beach, romping in the woods with the pine-scented air. I figured that there was no better place on earth. We had an outhouse with two seats. I could never understand why because when we went there it was always one at a time. There was a problem though because at night using a flashlight it sometimes ended up down the odd hole.

Dick and Peter in 1946

We didn't have a refrigerator and used an icebox. Ice was cut out of the lake in winter and stored in an icehouse.

There was a bird in the back woods called a Pewee. Its voice call was much the same as their name. I had a whistle that gave the same kind of sound. I would go back into the woods and blow the whistle and they would answer me. Wow! I couldn't believe I was talking to birds.

There were great years ahead to come in the north, but in 1941, the U.S. went to war. It was four years before we returned. I was so sorry that all those years were gone. Then I thought I should not feel bad because what about the guys fighting for us that never came home.

In 1945, the war was over and we came back. The family had a dog named Peter I, he was an English Cocker Spaniel, and we became great pals. He would follow me like a shadow. I had a rope swing in front of the cottage in a big oak tree. I would swing back and forth with him running alongside. When I went swimming, I would swim out to deep water, raise my arm, and call for him. He would swim out to me, then he would take my hand in his mouth and swim back to shore. I know that he thought he had saved me.

The lodge that I mentioned before burned down in 1942. The thirteen cottages were moved to different lots around the lake. One of them ended up just a few lots from the family property. After about 30 years had passed many of my family were gone. The remaining children lost interest in the property and it was sold in 1985. I wanted to buy it but the property value was too high and I couldn't afford it. I ended up buying a cottage next to the old family property.

My wonderful wife Sue and I are living there all year round now. As we stand side by side looking out the window at the old family property, I think she can see the tears in my eyes. My by-gone days are gone. Peter is long gone. Gone is the sound of silence because of the high powered boats on the lake.

Some vacationing Ya-Hoos come here to blow off fireworks on not just the 4th of July, but all summer long. Gone is my rope swing. The big oak tree is still there and if you look up you can see a small piece of chain still there after 68 years hanging over a limb where I had my rope attached. The Pewees are gone because the air base expanded their property cutting down most of the woods, plus taking out our nice trail through the woods.

I know that I do not have many years left and I'm really not ready to go but when I do, and if I was good enough to make it into Heaven, I sure hope there is a place there like Northern Michigan.

✓ Winter Outings on Hog's Hill
By Berniece Baldwin of Glennie, Michigan
Born 1944

I was born and raised in Glennie till about the age of fourteen when I went away to a private school for my high school years. I do remember my mother would make us girls wear the undies that came down to our knees in the winter and I hated them so when I got out of Mother's sight I would pull the legs up as high as I could get them (Mother never knew till I was older and told her).

We had an outhouse when we were young and at nights, we had a pot or "owl" as we called it. It took a leak and my dad patched it with gum. My dad swore that I picked the gum off and chewed it 'cause the pot leaked, but I don't think so. Those outhouses were so cold in the winter you got in and out as fast as you could, believe me.

We had a-party line phone and everyone on our line it seemed would listen to everyone's conversations. We knew it, so we would talk about them once in a while just to hear them hang up. My grandparents had a rotary phone that they hooked up between them and a neighbor so they had a private line way back in the forties.

My father always told us if we got in trouble at school, we were in trouble at home too. I tried very hard to be good but one time my teacher accused me of something I did not do and sent me out in the hall with my work sheet. It made me so mad I ripped the paper into pieces and when she came out; she got mad and grabbed me by the hair. Well that made things worse and I grabbed her by the hair too. I had to deal with Dad when I got home and needless to say, I got the belt on my behind. I never got in trouble again either.

We always took our baths on Friday nights and Mom would heat a washtub of water on the wood stove. Then Dad would put it in the washtub for us. All four of us kids had to use the same water. Kids today wouldn't dream of using the same water. We had an inside bathroom but it wasn't finished yet.

When Mom did the laundry, she had to heat all the water on the stove and in a tub of hot water washed all the clothes starting with the whites, then lights, etc. We had milk cows across the field at our grandparent's farm and so Mom needed to go milk the cows. She left the washing machine set up in the kitchen till she got back. I was cutting peppers and went into the kitchen. My brother turned the wringer on the washing machine on and I got the scissors caught in the wringer and it pulled my hand in, set, and slid on my hand till Paul shut the wringer off. It broke my little finger and messed up the fingernail on the finger by my thumb. I know have three part fingernails on that finger. What a bummer to keep it short so it don't snag on everything.

We didn't have much money so my mother made our clothes and we wore many hand me downs. I was always bigger than my sisters so Mom remade things for me. One year for Christmas my aunt and uncle bought us girls new dresses. We were in seventh heaven, we thought. Christmas was nothing like today. We got a dolly between us three girls and one year we got a sled for all four of us kids.

Us kids all worked in the pulpwoods with Dad when we got old enough. In the summer, Dad cut Popple trees down and cut them up in four-foot lengths. He made peeling bars for us out of car springs because they had the right curves to them. We hand-peeled every one of them then later we would go back over them and make sure they weren't laying in their bark and restick in them. One time in the evening Dad and Paul was turning them over and out came a rattlesnake. They got it and killed it and cut the rattlers off. I believe it had six and a half rattlers. It was pretty scary because we still had to go to work out there. Dad would set a goal of three loads of wood a day, and when we were done, he would take us to the lake (Bliss) with our washcloth and soap to get cleaned up and have fun cooling off. We sure looked forward to that. My father always made work as fun or pleasant as he could. I prayed many times that it would rain so we didn't have to work but God knew we would starve to death if it rained every time I prayed for rain.

Dad had an old model A and every time we would get to the Four Corners section of town it would get hot and blow the wood cork Dad had in the radiator. Quite frequently, I had to get out and retrieve it. How embarrassing.

My mother was our milkman (woman). She usually did all the milking and brought it home after she strained it and separated the cream from the milk. She made butter, which sometimes us kids churned, for her, and she made cottage cheese, which was so good with the fresh cream on it. Amazingly, the cheese and milk do not taste good to me in the raw form anymore.

We had the best family time any kid could ask for. We worked very hard but Dad always made sure we had good times also. He was a kid at heart. In the winters, we had a lake behind our house and Dad would check the ice to make sure it was safe. Then he would shovel the lake off and build a bonfire to warm up by. We would gather all the neighbor kids and have a skating party, oh what fun we had. Until one time I was hanging on the back pockets of the neighbor guy's pants and he tripped and fell and stuck the blade of his skate through my lip, I never did that again. On other Saturday nights, Dad would build a fire on top of Houg's Hill and again we got the neighbor kids and had sleigh riding parties. If we could catch Carl Kirbits heading home up the hill we could hitch a ride on the bumper and get towed up the hill. Other times my dad would take the tractor or model A and tie a rope off the back hitch or bumper. Then

we tied sleds and shovels on the back and jumped on them. We would go down through the plains. Oh, what fun we had. Cold never seemed to bother us till we got home and our toes and fingers would sting. When Dad would mention a winter outing and we were always ready to go.

We had the best times and best dad and mother any kid could ask for. The neighbor kids always enjoyed our fun times and got to do things they might not have been able to do otherwise. Dad is gone now but the memories will always be there. Love you Dad and Mom.

Lupton Lumber Camp
By Juanita Walt of Rose City, Michigan
Born 1934

This is Don Mathew's story, recalling his early days.

"After supper, Pa would push back his chair from the table, cross his legs and light his pipe. We knew it was story time." Don said. The boys listened while the oil lamp flickered and cast shadows on the wall.

"Well, boys, life in camp was hard but we had a pay check; lots of people didn't."

"I was twenty-two, your Ma was eighteen, when we married and moved into camp three." He told stories of how the shacks were built by the lumber company; thrown together, encased in tarpaper and dirt piled up all around the shack to help keep out the cold. A forty foot well was dug by hand but produced little water. Water was carried from the springs in fifty-gallon barrels by horse and dray. The families living there got along with next to nothing, a stove, a bed, and a place to sit and eat. Sheets were hung on wire to divide the place into areas.

"Families were allowed to have a cow and a garden spot. Winters were long and hard. When spring arrived, the women and children waded through the melting snow to search for budding saplings for the cows to eat because cows were vital for the families' food supply.

"Summer brought opportunities for the women and children to put away food for the long winter. They not only preserved the food from the garden but they went to the woods to pick blackberries, blueberries, strawberries, and currants, which were canned for winter meals.

There was no way out except by horse and buggy. If someone was sick, they were treated with home remedies and if they got sick enough to go out by horse and buggy, they usually didn't come back. "

Don leaned back in his chair and said, "Pa told of a man that got sick in camp and nothing seemed to help." He rapidly lost weight and got weaker by the day. His frail body was wrapped in quilts and laid in a buggy. Rocks were heated and wrapped to help keep him warm. They stood and watched the buggy go out of sight, only imaging how rough the ride must be for the sick man. They never saw him again. Don speculated that they sent his body back to his family, who could have been from Marlette, since a lot of workers came from that area, as did his parents' families.

On another occasion, Don's dad witnessed a logging accident that took place near him. A tree fell on the worker, eviscerating him. "Ma said that Pa didn't speak for several days."

Pregnant women delivered their babies in the camp shacks with the help of family members and other women living there. Don's mother delivered two sons, Lawrence in 1911 and Oliver in 1913, in camp three.

Camp three was also known as the Ashe Camp because one of the camp bosses was named Hank Ashe. It had 25-30 men living in the bunkhouse. Bosses had their separate places to live but close enough to keep an eye on operations by day and the men by night.

"The house would cool down and Pa would get up to stir the fire in the Beckwich wood stove. We knew when it got cold; we had to go to bed."

Hank shared the boss's job with his friend, Elf, who told this hunting story:

After a short time hunting, Hank shot a rather large deer and slung it over his shoulders. They walked on for a while and finally Hank said they might as well go home empty handed. His friend reminded Hank he was carrying a deer on his shoulders.

A lot of the men drank and played cards when they went into town but no alcohol was allowed in the camps. Some of them drank to the extent that they didn't have any money left after payday.

"Pa let us know he didn't think much of that, but they were good men and looked out for each other." Don said sitting at the table, listening to his dad, was how he learned how to live his life. "We did as he said and we never talked back to him."

The men crawled between two feather ticks to sleep on boards that lined the bunkhouse walls. They were up at daybreak to go to the cooks' quarters for breakfast. They ate breakfast and supper there, and a chore boy brought them lunch at the work site at noon.

There was never any talking at meals in the cooks' quarters. It wasn't written, it wasn't spoken, but the men knew it wasn't allowed.

They went to work at daylight and could go home when they had ten carloads of logs. That was about 30,000 feet of lumber. If they had ten carloads at four p.m., they could go home but if it was dark and they still didn't have ten carloads, they stayed until they had their quota.

After supper, someone would build a campfire and the lumberjacks began to gather and tell lumbering stories. After a while, they brought out their instruments and began to tune them up.

"Pa played the banjo," Don said. He then pulled out an old hand-made banjo. "Pa played this. He said it was made by a black man but that's all he said about it." The banjo is still in perfect shape and the hand-carved pieces look as if they could have been made yesterday.

Lumber camps were set up in areas. Bosses and superintendents had fifty to sixty men in their camp. Groups of men had different chores to do and they all had their names based on what they did. The cooks were the cookies, the skidders snaked or dragged the logs over ground, ink slingers, or pencil pushers were people who kept the company books. Jammers hooked on the ends of logs to keep them in line to prevent a jam. Working in teams of three to four men, they moved the logs into position so the teams of horses could lift the logs to a railroad car. Don said his dad told him how impressive it was to watch the large horses work, seemingly as well-trained as the men to do their job. Chore boys were groups of workers who did whatever needed to be done such as having the horses ready to go to work when the men got to the barn. They had pine torches ready to use for light so the workers could see to get to the work site and go to work at the crack of dawn.

In the winter, the sprinklers were men who sprinkled the trails down to freeze so logs and skids moved rapidly over the ice. Horses pulled barrels of water. Jobbers were groups of independent lumberjacks who traveled from camp to camp to bid on the timber that was left behind by the lumber companies. Don said that some jobbers could make money from what was left behind and some could not.

If the lumberman cut a tree with a hole in it, they left it behind. Oak and other hardwoods were considered worthless and if it was in their way, they cut it and left it behind. If a pocket of lumber was too hard to get to, they left it behind. The lumberjacks stood straight and cut the trees with a crosscut saw, leaving stumps waist high and up to four feet across.

Cruisers were men who traveled alone or sometimes with a partner to look for large stands of white pine. They took with them maps, a compass, and enough provisions to last for months. If they were lucky, they made friends with Indians, who helped the cruiser locate the largest stands of white pines. The lumber barons, who many times never saw the area, depended on the cruiser's calculations of how much white pine could be harvested from an area and then they set out to buy the land with the most white pine that could be harvested.

A round acre meant that the lumber company went outside the acres that a lumber baron bought, and cut surrounding white pine.

The California gold rush and the search for white pine occurred about the same time in 1848 but the gold grabbed all the attention and left the stories behind even though the white pine industry brought more money.

Eventually, the trees were gone and so were all the workers. The railroad company pulled up their tracks and left.

Don sits at the table alone, his wife, Dorothy, now in a nursing home. I visit as often as I can and listen to his stories. I began to take pencil and paper to Sunday lunch. Telling his story becomes more and more important to him. We eat, talk, and wonder what the next sought-after natural resource Michigan has. Could it be water and will we do a better job managing it?

"Ma and Pa left the camp and bought the yellow house on the east side of Deckerville Road," Don said.

"Ma said Pa ran out of hay and drove the cows to grassy slopes where snow had melted. He came down with pneumonia and was sick for a long time. During this sickness, his hair turned white overnight. They couldn't pay the taxes so they just moved out of the house and into a place on the Reasner farm," Don said.

Don's sister, Ione, was born on the Reasner farm and wrote her account of her early life.

They moved from the Reasner farm to a place on Heath Road. Don's not sure just how long they were there but they built the log house on Deckerville Road in 1921, when Don was two years old. Don's dad soon added a barn to his forty acres.

"Odie Rakestraw was a real estate man when Pa was young. He said 'Melvin, I'll sell you land at a cheap price. It's twenty five cents an acre.' The land was the Jewett property which is now Rifle River Area."

Pa leaned back in his chair and said, "What would I do with it? It's all swamp and lakes."

"Ma took cream, butter, and eggs to the store and they told her how much money she could spend. She bought the staples, but most of their food was from the garden. Once she fell and broke her ankle. She got a stick and went on to the garden," Don said.

Don said he heard this story many times from his mother. She said that his Pa was working away and just got home on the weekends. He was exhausted from the long hours, hard work, and the trip home. Early Sunday morning, she went into labor and stepped into the bedroom to tell him. He was sleeping soundly. She delivered the baby, wrapped it up, and took it to the barn with her to milk. She put his sister, June, into a manger and milked seven cows. When she got back home, she cooked breakfast and woke her sleeping husband to come and eat. Don considered this the greatest love story that could ever be told.

"Ma ordered a mailbox from Montgomery Ward catalogue because they were going to start bringing the mail to Deckerville Road, which was then called Vaughn Road. The box arrived and Pa put it up, ready for the mail. The mail carrier was Julius Rank. We could see him coming with his horse and buggy. He was dressed up with tie and jacket for this important occasion."

The same mailbox still stands today.

"I'm glad to be here with Dorothy and my

dog. I'm glad to be in Michigan and I'm glad to be here in Ogemaw County, where I've spent my life."

Pa played the banjo

X A Christmas to Remember
By Florence Erdman of Bellaire, Michigan
Born 1920

My folks lived two miles from Casselton, North Dakota and twenty miles from Fargo, North Dakota. I was eleven years old at the time. It was the day before Christmas and a beautiful day. Many people went to Fargo for last minute Christmas shopping. But a snowstorm came up and many started for home in Casselton but ran into a ditch.

My brother took a team of horses and a sled and went and got people out of their cars and brought them to our house one and a half miles from the highway. My brother kept on going back to get people and bringing them home. One little old couple didn't want to leave their Model A Ford. My brother carried them to the sled and brought them home also.

Many of the people had frozen feet and legs. My sister and I brought snow in to thaw out their feet and legs. We had thirty-five people at our house that night. Mom had baked many things for Christmas: bread, cinnamon rolls, and other things, and it all disappeared quickly!

Our old doctor in town used to do house calls. He had a horse and buggy. I used to ride with him sometimes. He came out and took care of the people who had frozen legs and

hands. He heated a razor and told me to cut the blisters on one lady's leg, which I did. It was awful.

The weather cleared up, so my brother helped the people get their cars out of the ditch and sent them on their way.

That was a Christmas to remember. I am now ninety-one years old.

X Delivering News of Lindbergh's Baby
By Joyce A. Leslie of Cheboygan, Michigan

My husband, Quincy Leslie, passed away in 1993, but one of his stories about early Cheboygan was about the day the Lindbergh newborn (Charles Augustus Lindberg, Jr.) was abducted in March of 1932. At the time, my husband was carrier for the Cheboygan Daily Tribune.

When all the paper carriers were gathered to pick up their Tribunes for delivery that day, they were detained with the hope that there would be news before going out. They waited until suppertime and after and then through the evening.

Finally, the news came that they could print about the news of the boy, and the newsboys would be able to deliver the papers at about 2:00am. So they sent the boys out at about 2:30am with the important announcement, the body was discovered on May 12, 1932 within a mile of their home. Quincy's route took him across a bridge over the Cheboygan River, which included a narrow bridge over the narrow falls behind the paper mill.

So off they went at 2:30am to deliver the Tribune!

√ Lining Up to Use the School's Stools
By Doyle Eckhardt of Brethren, Michigan
Born 1925

When I was in grade school, I went to a K-12 school in a small town. This was in the '30s and nearly everyone was poor, but they managed somehow to get along. There was no electricity except for the townspeople. I lived on a small farm 3 miles from town. Many of the students at the school lived on small farms and they walked to school.

The school had one bathroom for the use of everyone. Consequently, in the wintertime when you got to school you headed for the bathroom, as it was much more comfortable than the outhouse at home. There were two urinals and two stools. The stools were the target, and there would be a line up to use them. I've often thought of this and how there was no cutting-in as I think would not happen today.

✓ **Making New Coats From Old**
By Nancy Chapman Thompson of Bay City, Michigan
Born 1929

I was born and raised in a small town called Onaway beginning in 1929. I am the youngest of eight children. I recall standing by Mother's old treadle sewing machine watching her make new coats from old ones. She would take it apart, wash it, and use the wrong side of the material where the nap would be new looking. All the wool pieces left over were used to make wool quilts for the beds.

After WWII Dad would buy printed feed sacks from the grain elevator and Mother made short sets and broomstick skirts for my older sisters. I remember Mother unraveling old sweaters and knitting me bobby socks to wear with my Penny loafers. I was in the tenth grade.

I remember Mother telling of her mother making baby bonnets for Marshall Fields in Chicago. I guess I inherited their sewing talents as I've done much of it over the years.

✓ **Houghton Lake in the '40s**
By Robert L. Uhan of Higgins Lake, Michigan
Born 1933

I am not much of a writer but I can remember a couple of things about Houghton Lake when I was eight or nine years old.

My grandfather was building a cabin on Maple St. in Prudenville at Houghton Lake, MI. We didn't have any electricity so all sawing was done by hand and the logs had to be peeled of bark with a drawbar by hand.

We stayed in a homemade trailer. For lights my grandfather ran a wire from his car battery to a couple of little Christmas size bulbs, and would yell at us to get in bed quick, so the battery would not go dead and the car would start the next day.

I also remember what was called a sand sucker on the lake. They would suck sand from the lake bottom to fill in low and swampy land onshore so they could sell it.

Also, the Detroit Tigers would come to Houghton Lake and stay at Johnson's Resort (now gone) during the All Star break every year.

✓ **We Never Heard of Milk from a Store**
By Darlene Groff Meske of West Branch, Michigan
Born 1939

When I was a kid, I walked to school, two and a half miles one way. Then I got out at 4:00pm and had to walk home. Kids now days need a ride to the end of the driveway. At school, there was one room, eight grades, and one teacher to do it all. It was not like now days.

I had to milk fifteen cows before walking to school at that time. Now they milk one hundred and twenty-five.

So I had to use the outhouse during the day. It had two holes. If I had to go at night, I had to use the chamber pot. Then I had to make sure I emptied it out the next day.

We never had a phone in them days. We was too poor to have a record player.

I never got spanked at school, but I remember getting sat on a wooden chair until my dad came home from work. Then I got it with his belt that he took out of his pants. Ma would never hit us. She just scared us with words, like "wait until your dad comes home."

We had baths on Saturday nights. Four of us, one at a time, used the same water. By the time the last person got to wash, it wasn't very warm. Then we got to go to town and get a penny candy. We thought that was great.

Ma washed clothes in a wringer washer, and it took her most of the day. She made our clothes from feedbags bought at the mill. The bags came with chicken feed in them.

I remember a bad storm in the wintertime. I had to go to the mailbox after a few days. It was half a mile away. The drifts of snow was six feet high. I rode the horse with only a halter on, as plows did not do side roads. The horse got stuck, as the snow was really deep. The plows didn't come through for weeks.

Our swimming hole consisted of a pond in the neighbor's woods.

My first love was a guy on a horse who rode three miles one way. I only seen him on Sundays.

We never had an icebox. My mother used to use the cellar to keep things cold, and we drank milk from our cows. We never heard of milk being in the stores or a milkman.

√ No More Navy Beans
By Elaine Zielaskowski of Alpena, Michigan

The sun was shining so hot as we were in the middle of the navy beans hoeing for hours. My dad had 30 acres in the "thumb" of Michigan. Since I was the second child of 14 children, we marched to the fields daily during the summers to help. Our suntans made us look like Mexicans. My mom was back at the farm tending to the younger boys. There was always someone in diapers and babies to feed. We felt like the rows of beans would never end. It was more like a punishment than a job. I never wanted to own a farm when I married; too much work for girls and no breaks. In the fall, back to High School. We were laughed at from other students because there were so many of us. We were called the "Tribe."

Our family finally moved to upper Michigan when I was a senior. My sister and I attended a Catholic school and had to make new friends with no trouble on the bus.

Two years later, I married. My husband and I had four children and built a big home on three lots. Every summer we grew tomatoes, corn, and green beans, not navy. My kids hoed the gardens when old enough.

They had no idea how hard I worked as a teenager in the big fields like slaves. I did enjoy canning dill pickles and tomatoes. We all enjoyed our harvest after all the work.

√ Mrs. Badger's Class
By Bernice (Bee Houghton) Macy of St. Petersburg, Florida
Born 1938

I went to school in Ironton. My brother took me to school on horseback and picked me up too.

I don't remember much about when I came to my school. My teacher was Mrs. Badger.

I worked for summer folks that stayed up late until October. I worked for them after school and got their night meal. They were old folks. I worked all summer for them, and cooked for sometimes 12 to 15 people, 3 meals a day, and did the housework. And I played shuffleboard in the afternoon to make the fourth member.

When I was growing up my dad drove a cream truck and I rode with him on Friday when you handed out the cream checks.

I listened to records with my neighbor; they were 45-rpm records.

I can't remember too much more. I lived in St. Pete, FL, for the last 20 years or more. I enjoyed what I did; I worked for a coffee plant for nearly 20 years and love it here.

That's all I can remember about my childhood. I'm going on 75 years old. I lived in Prospect Valley.

√ A Child's Life on a Farm During the 1940s
By Katie Rittershofer of Roscommon,
Michigan
Born 1939

What is inside plumbing? I did not know until I went to the third grade in a nearby town. I used an outside toilet (out house) with a Sears Catalog for what others knew as toilet paper. Inside plumbing didn't have farm animals sticking their heads in to see what you were doing. I was never lonely.

Later in life, I helped my father dig the hole for our septic tank. I was very young when my father put a faucet in the house instead of the hand pump in the yard. We never had to worry about not getting enough exercise.

We may have had a faucet but not a water heater. We had a pig stove to heat the water. I never knew why they called it a pig stove. Maybe I didn't need to know.

As I think back, many memories surface. The homemade dresses my mother made out of used feedbags. I remember attending the county school, which we walked to, with two grades in one room. It also had a coat closet. That is where the teacher did the spankings with a wood paddle. You didn't see anything but you heard a lot.

Katie age 2

When I pick up a bag of oranges at the store today, I cannot help but to remember that there was always an orange in the bottom of my Christmas sock. That was the only time I had an orange. It was always better than a toy.

When I drive by the old farm today, there are never bad memories only good ones. It was a good life.

✓ The Way I Was Brought Up
By Mary Jo Sobleskey of Petoskey, Michigan
Born 1927

I grew up on a farm on Greenwood Church Rd. There was always something to do, for instance laundry.

Washing clothes took all day just to wash them. We had no electricity. Our washing machine was started by winding a rope around a wheel, then pulling real fast that would start the washer. It ran on kerosene. We had two tubs of water for rinsing, and then the clothes were put through a ringer to get out the excess water. The ringer had a crank you had to turn to make it work.

Outside we had five lines to hang the clothes on to dry. Worked great in the summer but winter was a different story. The clothes would freeze while sitting in the basket waiting to be hung on the line. They were left to hang for a couple hours then they were brought inside to dry.

They next day was ironing day, so even if it was eighty degrees outside we had to keep the cooking stove burning because we had to heat the irons. We had one handle (used to remove the irons from the stove) and three irons. As one got cold, it would be replaced with a hot one, put the cold one back on the stove, so you always had a hot iron. In those days most everything was starched, that was done before putting them on the line to dry. Before ironing the clothes we would sprinkle them with water, roll them up to keep them damp, then you were ready to iron.

Another great memory is, well it may not be great, is toward the end of August and the beginning of September the flies got in the house, they were looking for warmth. That's when we had to get the towels out. We started in the dining room and two or three of us would start waving the towels chasing the flies towards the open door, most of them went out.

When Dad got up in the morning, we could hear him swatting flies that were still on the ceiling. Sometimes we would hang those fly sticky things from the ceiling that got rid of a lot of them. This lasted about two weeks. Everyone had this problem you just had to deal with it.

Even with all the work we had to do, we still had time for fun. Lot of times the neighbor kids would come over and we would play baseball, hide 'n seek, go swimming or fishing. There was always something to do. In the winter, we would go bob sledding right down the road in front of our house. Sometimes we would play Fox and Geese a game played in the snow. You make a big circle in the snow, make a pattern in the center of the circle like a cut pie, the geese must run the path made in the snow while the fox tries to catch you. If you go out of the path or are caught by the fox, you become the fox.

Another fun thing in the winter was ice-skating, we had one pair of skates size 13, and we took turns wearing them. We had to stuff them with socks to make them fit, it was great fun.

Sundays were great fun in the winter, if there were icicles on the house us kids would knock them down while Mom mixed up some eggs, sugar, and cream, in the ice cream crock then the icicles were packed into the outer crock to keep the mixture cold; keep turning the crank until you get ice-cream.

One winter we were snowed in for a week, there was so much snow it took a day and a half to plow a block. All the farmers were in front of the plow with picks, axes, and shovels because the plow couldn't do it alone.

I could talk for hours about my life on the farm but space is limited so in closing, it made no difference what we did we had lots of fun, we worked very hard. I never regretted any of my life. The way I was brought up I learned the meaning of respect, appreciation, and love.

Building Our Cabin a Family Affair
By Bert Doser of Atlanta, Michigan
Born 1937

Our entire family loved hunting and fishing. Not only were they a challenge but our success helped feed the family. Unfortunately, though, as time passed our neighborhood in southern Michigan became too crowded to continue hunting. The folks decided to look for some property, build a cottage, and use it for our new base. Shortly after World War II ended, they were able to acquire 60 acres in a place in northern Michigan located approximately 150 miles from our permanent home. The property located in Montmorency County had recently been logged out for timber and consequently was crisscrossed by old railroad beds and logging trails which provided relatively easy access to the site.

The folks drew up their own plans for the cabin. Due to the war construction materials (basically cement and concrete blocks for the foundation and lumber for the enclosure), were very difficult to obtain locally and instead had to be purchased downstate and hauled in by trailer. This was a rugged trip for the road was only paved about half the way and where it ended, the gravel stretch was anything but smooth. While this was taking place, we began the chore of clearing the site for the building of trees and brush. These had to be removed in total. We had no electricity and chainsaws hadn't been invented yet. Armed with a pick

axe, grub hoe, double bit axe, a crosscut saw, and a lot of muscle and determination, the job was completed in a relatively short time. The trench for the foundation, about 2 feet wide and 2 feet deep, had to be dug by hand; another strenuous chore. One should understand that this site preparation and later construction could only be done on weekends as my father had a job in a factory at home and we raised a substantial amount of fruit and vegetables on our property as extra money for the family. Of course, it required a lot of work to take care of them.

With the building shell finally in place, Dad decided we should have a fieldstone fireplace but not with plain stones; they had to be split to reveal their colorful interior. At one time in the past a farmer had cleared a small area on the property removing the trees and stumps and stacking the stones in a pile. If you carefully examined the rocks, you could find an obvious grain in them. By placing a pointed sledgehammer along this grain and striking it with a regular sledge, we split the rocks revealing their vivid interior. After the rough splitting had been completed, we loaded them on the trailer and hauled them back to the construction site where Dad completed the final fitting with a 5-pound hammer and a stone chisel. Once the piece fit just right, it was cemented in place. Occasionally while he was chipping away at the rock, it would split the wrong way. Fortunately, the windows hadn't been installed yet for in exasperation he would hurl the reject out that opening.

It should be noted that not only did we not have electricity, we didn't have water either. Water, required for cooking meals, for mixing cement, mortar, washing up, etc. had to be hauled from the neighbor, about a 1/4 mile away. Armed with a 5 gallon container we drove there, pumped (no electric pump there either) it full and tried to get it back without spilling too much. Occasionally when Mother Nature provided some rain, we were able to take much needed showers. If there was no rain, we could always hike to Barger Creek (1/2 mile one way) to scrub up. Unfortunately, by the time we hiked back, we were generally as dirty and sweaty as before we left.

While all this activity was taking place, we slept in bunk beds in a cedar slab shed that had been erected as a temporary shelter and which later became the wood shed. What a joy to wake up at night, turn on the flashlight, and stare at a big wood spider about a foot from your nose. Summer was particularly bad when the mosquitoes and black flies had their piece of you. No matter how much insecticide was spread around, you still wound up sharing the space with them. Many nights were spent with the covers drawn up over your entire body for protection.

Today we take a lot of everyday things such as heat, electricity, water, etc. for granted. If they stop working, we just call a repair man or run down to the local hardware store, get the parts we need and fix it ourselves. Sixty years ago though, things were a whole lot different. When the cabin was finished and we moved in, we had a wood stove for heating and cooking, which, of course, meant we had to have a ready supply of dry wood as fuel. Coleman lanterns utilizing white gas provided light and ice blocks were purchased to keep the refrigerator cold. Toilet facilities were available via a three-sided outhouse, located some distance behind the cabin, open to the panoramic view of the ravine below, nice in the summer if you ignored the mosquitoes and black flies (a spray can of repellant was provided) but it could be extremely uncomfortable in the winter when the north wind blew directly into the open side of the enclosure. Visits at those times were short especially when the snow blew in on the seat (broom provided). The porcupines also had a penchant for chewing on the stool walls so one of the first things you did was look in the hole and check to see if there was another occupant. That basically took care of the most necessary utilities except for water. That turned out to be another story.

Hauling water from the neighbor's well for our use soon became a very unpleasant chore. With the structure now closed in and habitable, my dad directed his efforts toward getting a suitable supply of drinking water. The first problem he encountered was that while the location of the cabin on top of a hill made for a picturesque view, it also meant you had to go deeper for water. He started with a well point that was driven into the ground with a sledgehammer. The wellpoint consisted of a section of pipe about 4 feet long. A fine screen was located in the walls of the point to filter out any solids in the water when suction was applied by the pump. This section was reinforced to handle the shock of the hammering. As the section went into the ground, additional lengths were added as required. Unfortunately, these sections came in 8-10 foot lengths, which meant that at times you were swinging the hammer from a ladder, hardly the most stable work platform. Unbeknown to him was the fact that 28 feet down there was a clay layer 5 feet thick and once the wellpoint entered it, the point became stuck, moved neither up or down, and the whole system had to be abandoned.

His next effort was to drop dynamite down the hole to try to blow through the clay. This unfortunately was doomed to failure for the clay layer merely quivered a little and stayed in place.

Still my dad was stubborn and he wasn't about to quit. His last effort consisted of using a rotary type post hole digger. As the hole progressed downward, additional lengths of tubing had to be added to the shaft forcing one to operate the digger off a ladder. At 28 feet, he once again incurred the clay layer. Not only was the sticky material difficult to drill through, a foot or two of ground water unfortunately not of drinking quality lay on top of the clay and washed out any material captured in the digger. Thus ended another attempt.

Finally, out of sheer desperation he and my brother picked a site in the ravine on the opposite side of the hill from the outhouse. Here they dug a hole six feet deep and six feet in diameter. This was filled first with gravel and then topped off with sand to act as a filter for the water. They then installed a short length of vertical pipe, screwed a pitcher pump to the top and this became our water supply (actually surface water that ran down the ravine) for many years. Contaminated water was not a concern at that time. To obtain water one wetted the leather in the pump, primed it with more water, began pumping by hand, and filled your container. Easy to carry the pail up the hill in the summer; a real problem as you climbed the hill in winter slipping and sliding in the snow trying not to lose it all before you got to the top.

Good thing Dad didn't know it at that time for years later when he finally had a well drilled by a professional; he had to go down 116 feet for good water.

During the winter, the quarter mile

driveway into the cabin was invariably drifted shut preventing us from driving in. This was long before snowmobiles and trucks with 4wheel drives. As a consequence, when we visited all the supplies, spare clothing, and food had to be carried in. This frequently turned out to be an ordeal. All the goods were loaded on a toboggan and we dragged it in often wading through drifts up to our hips. The terrain was very hilly which meant the sled hit you in the rear on the down slope and dragged like an anchor on the upslope. Of course, the cabin was located on the last and highest hill where the pull frequently used up the last of your energy. Upon arrival, the first chore was getting a fire going since the place was not insulated and had bare wood floors. If possible, our arrival was planned for early in the day as it took almost 24 hours to heat the entire place through and through. If you arrived in the evening, the beds were ice cold and stayed that way through most of the night. Also, someone had to get up frequently during the night to keep the fire going. The first few hours would be miserable as we huddled next to the fire trying to stay warm. Of course, those with chores such as unpacking supplies, shoveling a path to the wood shed, bringing in wood for the fire, etc. had less problems staying warm. In the morning when the bed at last was nice and warm, the fire had died down and the place was again freezing. With no carpeting, those wood floors were icy cold. There were times as a kid I lay in bed, the covers over my head with just my nose sticking out, praying that someone would get up and start the fire before I had to get up.

It seems it was a lot colder in those days. It was not unusual to incur temperatures 20 to 30 below zero. Sometimes the sap in the trees would freeze and rupture the tree with a sound like a rifle shot. On one occasion when we returned to the car where it was parked on the county road, we found that the oil in the engine was so thick, thanks to the temperature that the engine would not turn over. Dad built a small wood fire under the oil pan to heat the oil. Oh boy, if there had been any gasoline leak around! It worked though for in a short time we were on our way home.

While I must admit that I enjoy all the modern features that exist now, I have to say we did have a lot of adventures and fun times over the past 60 years.

My First Attempt at Washing
By Shirley Fosmore of Alanson, Michigan
Born 1954

I helped my mother after school. I cleaned the house, made supper, and did the ironing while Dad was working, and Mom got a part-time job at the Sears Catalog office in Petoskey.

I thought, "Well, I am going to help Mom just a little more." We had an ole wringer washer in the basement with the matching rinsing tubs. The washing was piling up, what with the folks both working and having five kids. There were a lot of clothes. I started supper and took a big pile of clothes down the steps to the basement and to the ole chug-a-lug, as we all called the wringer washer. Of course, at nine or ten, I had never done any washing before, except to hang up clothes on the line, take 'em down, and fold 'em, or iron sheets and pillowcases and of course Dad's uniforms for work.

I filled up the washer with nice hot water and plenty of suds and took a big pile of clothes–every color in the book, whites, reds, and blue jeans. I stuffed 'em all into the washer, packed it real full, so proud of myself. I went back upstairs to tend to my supper, listening for the sweet sound of chug-a-lug, chug-a-lug, doing a fine job washing the clothes. I thought I sure was helping out.

Shirley and Jim

The washer stopped. I thought I had burnt up the motor, but the wringer still worked even though the suds were going over the side. I faithfully rinsed each one and hauled the basket of clothes out to the line and hung 'em up. What pretty colors–red, pink, and blue. But no more whites? Oh, well! I brought 'em in freeze dried as we called the clothes that froze on the line.

My mother came home and, to say the least, was horrified at the stack of multicolored clothes and her poor washer, still full of suds in the basement. By this time, they had spilled over on the floor of the entire basement. Dad eventually got the washer to work again. I cleaned the basement, after getting a stern warning never to touch the washer again. And then we all broke out and howled with laughter at my first attempt to do the washing.

From Hamburg to Posen
By Sharon Miller Grulke of Posen, Michigan
Born 1942

On April 1881, a ship called Cimbria left Hamburg, Germany for America. After six long weeks, the Mullers arrived and settled in the Gaylord area, where August worked for the railroad company, making firewood for the steam engines.

In 1884, the Mullers moved to the Grand Lake area and homesteaded an eighty-acre parcel in Krakow Township. After meeting the requirements of clearing some acreage and planting a fruit orchard, the United States granted the Muellers ownership on January 7, 1890.

August was to live only until the age of 56, with seven children to raise. William was a teenager at the time. He stayed with his mother. William was 32 when he married Martha Frederick. They farmed until their deaths. He died in 1960 and she died in 1985. Martha spun wool, knitted socks, and mittens, made butter, and baked bread.

My dad worked for G.M. My dad built a house on Maplerige Street in Southfield, Michigan. There was one boy, Allen Kirluk, who lived down the street. His dad had a paving business, which Allen now has. He now lives in Bloomfield and has a summer home in Lewiston.

We moved up to Krakow in 1945. I walked to Rock Valley, a one-room school, with Marvin Hunt, my cousin. He stayed at his grandmother's, as his father was killed in a car accident. He now lives in Hillman.

We tried to listen to radio programs, but they would fade out. There was no TV picture. My grandmother had a wind-up record player. I believe that was shipped to her son in Nebraska. My mother had a wringer washer. We sold it for $25.00.

After one snowstorm I can remember, the snow banks were so high we could touch the electrical wires.

We have three iceboxes used for papers and magazines. We have a rocking cradle that used to be my dad's. It is from 1913. I used it for our son and daughter.

I have a wool baby quilt made in 1948 that my mother made. I have another one from 1948 that my mother made for my sister. I have made several quilts. I made a log cabin, double wedding, and a cross star. I make one when the grandchildren are confirmed. I made one for my grandson when he was born in 1965. It now looks like a rag because he and the dog sleep with it every night. In 1971, we won the family costume in the Rogers City Festival, wearing costumes, which I'd sewn.

My cousin, Robert Hastener, has written ten books about Alpena: The Town in Bits and Pieces; The Town that Wouldn't Die; Alpena Gleanings; Stones from Her Granite, Parts I through VI; The Town that Went to War; Stories the Red People Told.

1993, we made a Baunmuchen for our daughter's wedding. This originated in Pomwereu, Germany since 1885. In 1964, I had plucked chickens for my wedding.

If I could change the world in just one way, what would that be? I would make everyone a Christian.

Fond Memories of the Good Old Days
By Ardath Norton of Alba, Michigan
Born 1920

I've lived in Alba all my life. I am ninety-two years old.

Alba was a lumbering town, a thriving community with a lot of businesses. It had a bank and a jail. The lumberjacks would come into town on Saturday nights and get drunk, cause trouble, and end up in jail. The next morning, they would go back to camp. After the timber was gone, it was like a ghost town, with a lot of empty buildings. People left and the ones who stayed had to go to other towns to work. The old buildings are torn down now. We have a township hall, library, post office and a fire hall.

I lived in the Depression years. My father was a carpenter and there was not any building being done. He picked up odds and ends of jobs. One job he had in the fall was working in a potato warehouse. We got our winter potatoes that way. They were called culls. They had little slices taken out by the digger, but the potatoes were still good.

My mother worked for the merchants, doing washing and ironing and cleaning houses. She canned everything she could. My brothers hunted and fished, so we had meat on the table. Mother was a great cook. She cooked venison and rabbit so it was really good.

On Saturdays, my sister and I cleaned house, and my mother baked for the week. She baked bread, cookies, and pies for Sunday dinner.

My mother washed clothes by hand until her brother from Muskegon brought her a washer with a wringer. She took in washing then.

We didn't have water. We carried our drinking water from my grandparents' house, which was close by. There was a reservoir on one end of the cook stove. We had hot water to cook with and do dishes. We had a cistern that had rainwater in it. It was used for washing and cleaning.

We had an outside toilet. When my mother's sister and her family came for a visit, my mother scrubbed the toilet and papered it with wallpaper, and she put a piece of linoleum on the floor. She bought toilet paper. It's true about the *Sears Catalogue*; that's what we had. We didn't use the colored sheets. We took the black and white ones and scrunched them up to make them soft.

What was called chamber pots we called slop jars. We emptied them and rinsed them with Lysol.

In the winter, we had house parties. We played cards, and if the house had a big room, we squared danced. I learned to dance at the parties. We had a late night potluck supper.

We had a radio. We listened to the *Grand Old Opry* and *Fibber McGee and Molly*. On Sunday, we listened to the *Hermit's Cave*.

My mother was a great seamstress. People gave her clothes, and she made them over for our clothes. My favorite outfit was a skirt and vest. It was made out of a man's suit.

I look back on the good old days with fond memories. I never felt we were hard up. We had enough to eat and clothes to wear.

Meeting Bob Seger
By Mary Rinke-Mogle of Petoskey, Michigan

This picture was taken in 1986 at the Mitchell Street Pub in Petoskey. I was working there, just finishing my shift around 11 pm, when you took a seat at the end of the bar. I was the only one who recognized you and asked you quietly if you were "Mr. Bob"? You acknowledged that you were indeed and when I said that no one else noticed, you said, "Let's keep it that way." We had a couple of drinks and after about an hour, people began to question your identity. You left to go to the Reunion Bar up at the Holiday Inn. Shortly after you left, Mr. Keiswetter, told me I was crazy, that he could call Punk to prove that you were elsewhere, and he bet me $100.00. With

Mary and Bob Seger in 1986

a little liquid courage on board I said, "I'll go get him (you)". Mr. Keiswetter continued to bet other people to the tune of about $500.00. I got the cook to drive me to the Reunion.

When I found you at the Reunion, I asked if you were coming back to the pub for last call. You said probably not. I dropped my head. You asked me what was wrong. I said I had money riding on you. You threw back your head laughing and said you would be happy to come back. I called the pub to tell them you were coming back and then waited by the door for you. Five minutes later, you took me by the arm and away we went, in your jeep, back to the pub.

That night you were so cool when truthfully you could have been totally the opposite, Thank you. I have told this story a hundred times and it still seems like only yesterday. An incredible memory that I will cherish a lifetime.

May God continue to bless you and those you love."

√ Big Black Cast Iron Pot Full of Popcorn
By George Erickson of Whittemore,
Michigan
Born 1929

I attended a one-room country school from Kindergarten through 8th grade. It was about 1 ½ miles from home across the fields. When I was in the 6th grade, I had a trap line set for fur-bearing animals. I checked the traps on my way to school. One morning I had a skunk. I didn't think I had picked up any odor from it but I guess I did. As soon as I walked into school, the teacher told me to get home and not to come back smelling like a skunk.

We didn't have electricity at our house until I was 10 years old. But I can remember the neighbors came and listened to the news and programs such as "Gang Busters" and "The Hermit" on the battery operated radio. My mother would make a big black cast iron pot full of popcorn. I think we had more fun than the kids now with all of their electronics!

When I was 8 years old, my dad gave me a steer calf. I broke him to ride and drive. We made a dray for him to pull and I used him to haul stones for a barn we were building. I rode him in a 4th of July parade in West Branch and several times to Prescott, about 3 miles. The

Kenneth and George riding Buck

bar owner gave me an ice cream cone when I rode there.

"Buck" grew faster and stronger than I did, so I had to sell him. That was a sad day and I shed a lot of tears. I used the money to buy bikes for my brother and me.

When I was a senior in high school, I was sitting in the seat behind our school bus driver. I mentioned that I bet I could drive the bus. He said, "There's only one way to find out." So we traded seats. I drove on to my house. There are still kids (adults now) who call me their bus driver.

√ Never a Dull Moment
By Mary Johnson Pearce of Manistee,
Michigan
Born 1926

I was born in 1926 in Manistee County on a farm near Chief Lake. My parents were married in 1922. My folks had seven children. We all had to work hard to help outside with harvesting the crops to sell. I remember pickles and beans the most. That was all summer until frost.

We went to a one-room school with eight grades. I would get my grade ready for the next day and listen to the other classes. We walked about one and a half miles each way. The county consolidated the one-room schools into the larger ones and we had bus service part way, so after the fifth grade our family all went to Kaleva through twelfth grade. We walked one mile to the bus stop on the main road. That was always plowed but we had to make our own path to the bus, and when the weather was really cold and stormy, my dad would hook up the sleigh and horses and give us a ride. He kept hay and an old horsehair blanket in the sleigh all winter.

We had no car at that time, but the side roads were never plowed or kept up like they are now. We had about a half mile of swamp to go through and spring time it was always red muddy and wet. When our neighbor girl met her husband-to-be, he would leave his car on the main road and carry her through the swamp road on their dates. That was close to a half mile. They would wait until her folks were asleep and take the horse and buggy and go for a ride. Her folks didn't want her to date him, so this one night, they went to town, about four miles away. They took the horse and buggy without permission. The horse dropped dead on the main road. He lived six miles from her parents' farm. They asked him to buy them another horse. I don't know if he did. They found a way to keep in touch and married after he got out of the service.

My father liked to tease and pull jokes on us, and I was only five feet tall at age sixteen. Well, a six foot two inch guy wanted to take me to a dance hall a couple of miles from our home. I was embarrassed to go, but my folks knew him and his family, so I went. When we got back to my home, my father had put a six-foot ladder by the outside door. I could have crowned him. My dad explained the ladder. I would need it to say goodnight. We never necked on the first date. And I never went with tall guys again.

Another time, our neighbor came to see my older sister. They were both about eighteen and when she got up to leave, she took her jacket and put her arm in the sleeves and let out a yell. My dad had taken tissue paper and crumpled it up and pushed it up from the bottom. So when she pulled it out of her sleeve, out came a creek crab. My brother had them in a pail to keep them fresh until he could go fishing. The crab got a hold on her fingers and wouldn't let go. There was never a dull moment.

My brother was a tease just like Dad. He took the candy and nuts and a big navel orange out of our Christmas socks and put potatoes and onions back in the stockings. It wasn't funny to the other six kids, but he emptied the stockings and put the goodies back.

We never had money for gifts, just the stockings. My grandma always bought me black underwear or black stockings, and so did my other grandmother. My mom always peeled the oranges and made candied orange peels. They were better than the hard candy.

After I got about fourteen, I wouldn't wear the black underwear, and a girlfriend found some extra that was given to her. They were light colored so I took the black underwear and put it under the sub-floor in the unfinished attic. My mother noticed when it was gone in the wash, so next Christmas, one grandmother gave me a nice homemade knit hat and mittens and the other gave me a small purse with a dollar bill. I was not only happy but rich that Christmas. Those were real gifts. We never had toys. When I cashed that dollar, I bought an all-day sucker for one cent each for each family member. That was the longest I ever stretched a dollar bill.

Homes were at least a half a mile apart. We had one real old couple for neighbors, and he died. I could hear her yelling for help, and my dad and mother went across the fields to see what was wrong. After a couple of days, she wanted me to come and stay overnight, as she was afraid after dark, so I did. One morning on my way home, I saw a large animal with two small ones coming over the hill behind my folks' house, running. I didn't know if I should go back by the old lady or keep running for home. I ran home. It was a bear and her cubs, and she turned and went into a small woods about a fourth of a mile from the folk's building. Dad said, "That was a cow." Later, he went and saw the bear tracks and quietly told my mother, "Yes, she did see a bear, but don't tell the other kids or the old lady, because she will want someone there all the time."

My grandparents came from Sweden when they were teens on the same boatload of immigrants. Grandmother spoke some English and Grandfather could but needed improvement. They had nine children and three stayed in the area. The rest left for work in Chicago. My folks were about six miles from them and the other two worked in factories near Manistee and were about three miles from the grandparents.

302

ral. I could have them all. I stayed after I
done at work and helped her clean up the
en. Then I had a ride with her.

y folks saved enough for their first car
8. They had no electricity until 1949.
sband wired their house, barn, and
for them, but buying the electricity
the neighbors was a big item. It was
0 or $4,000.00 at the time. That was
money back then. They never got a

her grandfather on my mother's side
umber camp of pneumonia in 1929.
est child was about nine, so some
r children had left to go to work.
was the oldest girl. She was 27
ther passed away. I know there
children in school yet. They had
ors. They brought fresh fruit and
d other food, and even canned
nd gave the kids work so they
Grandmother kept her home
n for forty years. She passed

sed away in 1990, at 96 years
1993 at 92. My mother came
thirteen children, nine boys,
e of the boys were in World
War II. All home safely, and one got
ere two-hundred and eight
ndents when grandmother
ge of 93 over 350 relatives
amily reunion.

nsgressions at Sixteen

iser of Grand Rapids,
higan

was rough to the touch
with the initials and
ing to go over the car
dered what the next
upe thought when seeing
ce of past passengers.

The car jump was a natural indentation in
the earth, bowl shaped and off center in a field
so far out in the country that the nearest farm
when last occupied, needed a generator for
power.

Our illumination was the moon. A full one
signaled making our way out of town to jump
and establish whose car landed the farthest
distance.

G
Gr
in a
my
brou
furni

M
She a
me. E
from n
goods.
and I h
to my h
when I
baked go
first taste
I have. I c
it.

I left s
the 11th gra
go back the
wore my gr
got teased s
the-ankle 2-in
old woman's s
first thing I di
a pair of saddl
anklets on cred

I worked sev
for $8.00 a we
were real scarce
of pennies or a
was lucky, becaus
about three block
she offered me he
He had been drafte
was alone. I just
had to help her keep the housework done. I
was so glad, because she had clothes from
her married daughter. I guess they didn't fit
her, so I could have anything because she
was going to give them away to the Salvation
Army, even the shoes and a beautiful winter
coat. I had never had a purse and there were

The high school seniors passed down the tradition of jumping cars to the juniors usually at the time when most of us got our driver's licenses and could now legally drive.

The first thing you did after arriving was to check the bowl for litter. Sometimes a fender, bumper, taillight, or errant outside mirror were left behind. Next, the necessary speed had to be estimated for the size and weight of the car including its occupants. Then a decision was made where to start in order to gain enough speed to drive down one side into the bowl, across the bottom and hit the farthest edge in order to go airborne and hopefully, exceed someone's previous line in the dirt.

My classmate, Steve, was the best driver. Steve, who was serious, focused and determined to land the farthest from the bowl's edge. The coupe had a wall between the front and the trunk cut away so passengers could lie down in this section. Usually, there were six of us including the driver.

Measurements were visual. No one used a tape measure but I'm guessing the bowl itself was forty, possibly fifty feet in width and with a depth of ten to fourteen feet.

Our family's motel was 200 feet long. The distance we landed was maybe less than half that length. I still use that visual measurement when estimating how long something is or how far away.

As the only girl who would go over the jump, did I scream the entire time? I'm sure I did though I don't remember it. I do remember laughing and being willing to take the risk again.

The spectators were those who wouldn't ride with us. They stood on one side and cheered as we landed fortunately always top side up.

Phyllis, Jan, and Richard in 1957

The last time I looked for the bowl many years later, it was filled with tall grass, weeds, and several wooden boards. I stood at the edge and thought of it as a common grave for my classmates who lived life at full momentum: Steve, Frank, Mike, Jim, Sid.

All have died except for the writer of this memoir.

Epilogue: We called the car jump "Southfield." It was south of town and it was in a field. I don't know that I could locate it today approximately fifty years later. I do know this. If it were possible, I'd like to take one more ride with Steve driving his Ford coupe.

Rag Curls Just Like Shirley Temple
By Betty (Lee) Bordine of Alpena, Michigan
Born 1927

"Ouch!" I yelled.

"Just hold still while I finish this last curl." Mother retorted. Mother had a vivid imagination and she greatly admired Shirley Temple. If she could create curls like Shirley Temple on her two little girls, she would be one up on Mrs. Temple. And she knew how.

After shampooing our hair, out came the curling rags, pieces of soft white cotton material cut about one inch wide and about eighteen inches long.

"Ok, Joan, you're first. Now get up on the high chair so I can work on your hair.

"Tomorrow is the Christmas program at church and I want you girls to have Shirley Temple curls. Now sit still while I tie up your rag curls." Mother told my impatient, wiggly, and younger sister.

About an hour later, she started on me. By now, my hair had to be soaked in water again. After combing it, Mother picked up a few strands of hair and tied an end of a rag around it tight to my scalp. Then she wound the hair tightly around the rag. When the hair length was finished, she wrapped the rest of the rag over the curl and again knotted the end tight to my scalp. Finally, she finished. Joan and I with our heads covered with rag curls slept that night while the curls dried.

The next day Mother untied the knots at our scalps and gently pulled off the rags.

There in her eyes were her two little Shirley Temples. As the years went by Joan

304

and I graduated to pin curls instead of rag curls.

Many, many years later, I received this phone call.

"Hi, Gramma! My coach for the Color Guard wants us to have Shirley Temple curls for our competition Saturday. Do you know how I can get them?"

I paused a long time trying to remember how my Mother used to do this. "Maya, come over Friday night and I'll see if I can remember how your great grandmother curled my hair." To this day, Maya is using rag curls on you three year old daughter.

I spent a lot of time thinking back on how the curls were done. I could remember the rags, but I had never curled anyone's hair with them. I bought a yard of soft white cotton material and cut the rags, so I was ready when Maya came on Friday evening. She shampooed her hair and we started.

"I think this is how it goes." I told her, as I tied a knot around a bit of hair at her scalp, wound the hair, and wrapped it. She went home with a head full of white rag curls, about six inches long bobbing from her head; happy as could be, confident she would have Shirley Temple curls. I hoped she was right.

The next day my husband and I went to the Color Guard competition. When the Clayton Valley team came out, we couldn't find Maya. Then suddenly this girl with all the Shirley Temple curls turned to face us and it was Maya. She smiled and winked at us. The curls were perfect and her team won the competition.

✓ Near Calls on the Ice
By Walter Zelony of Interlochen, Michigan
Born 1922

In the year of 1932-1933, we had 10 acres of potatoes, 1400 bushels that we stockpiled in the fields covered with potato vine and straw, waiting for the prices to go up. The price at the Farmer's Market in Pontiac, Michigan, was 29 cents per 100-pound bag. We went to that market many times with a Model T pickup loaded with garden goods that we grew on a 2 ½ acre garden. We would barely make enough money to pay for the expense. My parents never gave me a nickel to buy ice cream. I stayed on the farm until 1942.

I then joined the Navy and applied for submarine duty with 11 other sailors. I got rejected because I was then 19 years old. I had passed the age limit for submarine duty. So I kept in touch with my sailor friends and after their training, they went out on their first trip in the European theatre of WWII, got attacked, and all perished. I guess the man upstairs was on my side. Thank you Lord.

I am one of seven children. Mom and Dad came over from the Ukraine, formerly Austria. Mom was 15 years old, Dad was 18. They met on the trip to the USA. It took 14 days to cross. Dad worked in a coal mine and Mom did housework for a dollar per week. They had seven children, Tony, Paul, Mary, Anna, Walter, George, Helen, in that order. Tony passed in 2002, Paul is still living at 96, Mary died at 91, Ann died at 89 3 or 4 years ago. I will be 91 in April 2013. George is now 87, still living, and Helen is 81. We are all relatively in fair shape. I walked the great Mackinaw Bridge 16 years in a row, it's 5 miles long. My last walk was in 2005. After moving from Detroit, Michigan, at birth, one year later we moved to Vermontville, Michigan. We spent 7 years growing sugar beets then moved back to Detroit. One or two years later, my parents bought a 96-acre farm in White Lake Township in SE Michigan. We worked hard there, plowing fields of potatoes, 10 acres of corn, and many acres of hay, grain, and a 2-acre garden.

After the war I took machine shop training and became a tool and die repairman.

Back to my teenage years on the farm, one day I and my two older brothers were ice-skating on a small lake behind our farm. It was near spring when there was open ice. I was skating as fast as I could with my head down when I heard my brothers yell to me. I was no more than 20 feet toward the open water—another close call.

Now the most interesting call was when I was about 12 or 13 years old walking home from school, again in the near-spring. With two of my neighbor buddies we stopped at a neighbor's pond and I fell through. Screaming for help, the farmer came out and pulled me to safety, then drove me home, and I got the beating of my life to teach me not to go out on bad ice.

God was with me again. Thank you Lord.

We Thrived on the Farm

By Virginia Jean Smith of Atlanta, Michigan
Born 1927

This is the story about how my parents, Hans and Mary Peterson, originally from St. Joes Island, Canada, came to live in Atlanta. We came from Flint, Michigan in an old Chevy truck. My parents and us six kids, ages from one year to nine years. My dad had been laid off from the Buick Plant in Flint and wanted a better life for his family. He worked with a guy, Floyd Downing, and his parents lived near Atlanta. They had heard that the government was looking for families to homestead property here. So Dad came here with Floyd to find out the details. The rules were to pay for the paperwork, which was $4.00 and you must live on the property for two years and improve it, and then it was yours.

My dad was overjoyed to come and have a home for his family. We moved in the old truck in April of 1931. My baby sister, Joann, was a year old. The old truck had a wooden platform and sidewalls, and we put the furniture we had on the back and left a space near the cab for us to sit. My dad put a heavy canvas over the top and it was a cozy little space for the four of us older kids. Joann and Jacqueline (we called her Honey because we younger kids could not pronounce her name) sat in front with my parents. I was thrilled to be able to sit with Joy and the boys, Fred and Norman. It was a long ride for all of us, and we slept off and on and played games. When it was mealtime, our mother made peanut butter sandwiches and apples and passed them through the back cab window, along with glasses of milk. It was a fun trip for us but I'm sure my parents were so glad to get there.

I remember getting out of the truck and Freddie running around the yard and looking at everything and we followed him. There was an old log house that looked forlorn, but it was waterproof and had windows and doors, so we had a home. It also had forty acres to grow a garden and fields of corn, potatoes, and even grain. My dad was thrilled, since he had worked on a big farm in Canada, growing grain.

We eventually bought a team of horses, built a small barn, bought several cows, and raised chickens and pigs. We were well situated and ate very well.

We went to Atlanta to school and had an old guy, Mr. Ralph Wyllis, driving the bus. We never knew what time he would come, so we went early and walked out the lane to Kellyville Road. I remember one time it was raining so hard, so my dad carried old blankets out to meet us and cover us. The bus driver, not knowing who he was, drove right by and brought us to our door! We laughed about that for years.

We thrived on the farm. Mother took a job cooking for Claude Mowery in his hotel. Dad bought an old Ford and would drive her to work and work the farm and then pick her up. She liked the work and made $5.00 a week. Then Mr. Mowery told Mother that if she would sweep and mop the floors after work, he would pay her $5.00 more. She was so thrilled to have more for things we needed. I remember her saying one time when she was sweeping she found a cigarette package with a $5.00 bill in the cellophane, and it was like Christmas for us.

She always bought flour sacks and sewed all our dresses. I still have school pictures of me in the dresses.

Later, my dad got a scoop shovel and dug a basement under the back of our house. He made shelves for canned foods Mother canned and bins for potatoes and apples, etc. to last the winter. We picked every kind of wild berries. I remember Mother telling us she canned 300 quarts of food one year. My dad also learned to butcher a cow every fall, along with chickens and pigs.

One of the things I remember most is that in the summer we had a lot of flies in the house since no one had screen doors for a while. After supper, our mother would do up the dishes and cover everything with sheets and newspapers, close all the windows and doors, and spray the house with bug spray. I don't know what this was but it killed the flies and bugs. We would go outdoors and she would come out, and we played or my parents talked about the day. After an hour or so, she would go in, open windows and doors and sweep up all the dead flies. We bigger kids took towels and waved them all through the house to air out the smell of the spray. It would be nice and cleaned out by the time we went to bed.

Many years before, when we lived at Kellyville, we got to know our neighbors and only the Valentines had a phone but invited us to use it if we needed to. Then my oldest sister, Joy, got sick when my dad was still working in Flint. Mother asked Fred to go to the Valentines' to call Dad home. He called the only doctor Atlanta had at the time, a Dr. Lister, who lived on Main Street, near where the Credit Union is now. The old doctor came out to our house and treated Joy for pneumonia, I think. Mother gave him canned food for coming. Joy got better in no time, and Mother was so grateful. I don't know how the doctor treated her then, but I remember her coughing a lot, and I would cry when she couldn't breathe well.

We also knew a family of Jimmie and Doris Smith who lived with their Grandma Smith there on Kellyville Road. She was the nicest old lady and we played with Jimmie and Doris for years until Grandma passed and the kids went to live with their dad and new wife. The new wife was Ethel, a sister to Fanny Secrist, who lived on Manier Road. We also got to know the Maniers, Fanny and Lawerence, who farmed acres and raised three children, Larry, David, and Mary Larue Manier. Mary still lives in the old farmhouse there.

Everyone, including us, went to church at Big Rock. When we got there, the church had been closed for a few years due to lack of finances and participation, so we went to the County Farm for Sunday school. The Secrists, William, Nora, and their family, ran the farm for the government for poor people who had no home. We walked from our farm, about a mile, to have Sunday school classes with them. A family named Dundas lived on the way, and the father came out and asked us if Elsie could go with us. Elsie in later years married Ben Valentine. They were grandparents to Kristan Peterson Cheedie.

My dad was a very good handyman and fixed everything he needed to. He was also good at carving things out of wood and made us a sled for fun in the winter. He would sleigh ride with us. We still have the sled today.

We didn't have a well, so we had to take the sled to the creek and fill five-gallon cans for all our water needs. We also used Freddy's red wagon to haul water in the summer. We all had jobs to do. Honey and I had to haul water up the hill to our house. Like normal kids, we would argue and disagree, and we would do

this and spill the water and have to go back for more.

Mother made butter, and she would put it in the creek in a large crock to keep it cold and fresh until she needed it. Dad built a box around it to keep any animals out. We also sold cream from the cattle and a truck would come every week from Remus Creamery to pick it up. Dad bought a cream separator so we could sell the cream and have plenty of milk to drink and cook with. I still have a cream separator here just like it. We had to crank the handle and keep it up until the milk was all through. The one I had a few years later was electric. How nice that would have been for us then.

I also remember in the summer we used to occasionally see and hear an airplane. We would run out to the open field and wave and yell, "Give me a ride!" We would pretend he did. My dad found out it was a man from town called George Commings, who owned and operated the dam in town, south of the Thunder Bay River. It had some type of big engine and furnished electric to the town before the R.E.A. came in in 1937.

Later, my dad bought a car so we could go to Alpena for groceries about once a month. One of the boys would stay home with two of us girls and the others went with them. Then the next time, the other boy and the other two girls would go, so we all had turns going. We shopped at the A&P store, and Mother liked to look at the dishes in the dime stores. I remember Dad taking us for a Coney dog, and it was so good! One time, when we went and Norman was home, he found a nest of turkey eggs in the edge of the woods. He took them to the house and made us lunch with the big bunch of scrambled eggs. As it turned out, Mother had set the eggs with an old clucking hen so we would have some turkeys to raise. Needless to say, she wasn't happy when she found out. And we had no turkey for Thanksgiving that year.

We usually had a big Thanksgiving dinner. It was new to my parents, since Mother was from Canada and Dad was from Norway. We all liked it, being Americans now. Our dad's birthday was November 21st and my brother, Fred, and mine was the same day, November 26th, so we always had a big cake and usually celebrated on Thanksgiving. We had a very happy home life.

Later, my dad took a job in the Great

Lakes as a Merchant Marine and worked there every summer. He sailed summers and did taxidermy at home in the winter months. After we sold the farm, eight years later we moved to Big Rock. My mother was offered a job in Lewiston, cooking at Eddie's Restaurant, so she worked there and at Barstows for a few years, too. We were all pretty grown then.

The boys joined the military, Fred in the Army for three years and Norman in the Marine Corps for four years. We girls were in high school, still in Atlanta, and working summers at Gassels Lodge in Lewiston. It was a busy time for all of us and soon it settled down and the boys came home. My dad got sick and passed on and our lives were sad. I met and married my friend, and all my sisters married also. We had our families and happy lives. Our mother passed in 1975. Our lives were changed forever but good later.

The Cabin at Houghton Lake
By Mary E. Grba of Roscommon, Michigan
Born 1940

Many happy memories were made visiting a dear friend's cottage at Houghton Lake, Michigan. The cottage was an original log cabin built sometime in the 1940s out of logs from the nearby forest and later sold by the original owner to my friends, Loren and Irene Ryseise, who are both deceased. They sold it to the present owner before that.

My first experience to the north was when I was about fifteen. That was before I-75 was the main route north. It seemed then that it took forever to get there, and most of the time we left in daylight and got to the cottage in the dark.

The cottage was one large room at the time, with no indoor toilet or shower. So when nature called or it was too cold to bathe in the lake, there was an old semi-trailer box behind the cabin with a toilet and a shower. It even had lights for at night. However it had no heat, so in the winter, forget taking a shower. Finally, after several years of complaints and freezing potty time in the winter, an addition was made to the cabin of a bathroom and a shower. Also, the cabin needed a lot of repairs. The original caulking between the logs was falling out and little creatures were finding their way inside.

Mary at age 18

My friend was very adamant about keeping the cabin clean so before we left to go back to the city, we had to scrub the walls and floor so that when we came back up everything was clean. Today, the cabin still stands and inside is still as it was fifty years ago, but the outside has been sided.

Once we arrived at Houghton Lake and the car was unloaded for our stay, it was time to head down the road and across M-55 to the lake. From early April to October it was lake time, weather permitting. In the evening, a huge fire pit with a big bonfire was used to cook hot dogs and roast marshmallows. This was our time to relax and plan for the next day's activities. My friend who was an adult used to go to the local bar at the end of the road and would invite everyone home to the cabin to enjoy more drinks and the bonfire.

As a teenager, we sometimes went to The Music Box in Prudenville, a place to meet boys, especially from Camp Grayling, listen to some great music, and maybe find a new friend. The Music Box is long gone, but it still brings back a lot of wonderful memories for those who were part of that history.

Many places have disappeared over the years in Houghton Lake, with businesses moving from one building to another or just going out of business. The old Conservation Fire Tower on Tower Road is gone, but if we were lucky enough when it was still there and the ranger was on guard looking for any signs of fire, we could climb all the way up and into the tower, where we could look all around Houghton Lake and beyond.

Also gone is the county dump where one took their garbage and also looked for other people's treasures that they discarded as junk.

As I grew older, we used the cabin for deer hunting. It was then that I discovered that yes there were bears in the area.

Two children later, we still visited the cabin for fun and vacation. Their favorite place to go as soon as the car was unloaded was to Chief White Bird's store to get some beads and to see the Chief. That store still stands and is open in the summer.

Ron's Restaurant in the woods is gone now but was a favorite place for breakfast and their fish. While waiting for our food, we could enjoy looking at all the old license plates and the giant airplane that hung from the ceiling. Ron's still sits in the original spot but has been closed now for many years.

The last place that has changed for us over the years but still is there is Reedsburg Dam. Now there is still a place to go fishing below the dam, but being able to jump off the bridge and go swimming above the dam is now closed for swimmers. The water is still cold and iron-colored and the campground area has improved, but the fun was jumping off the bridge into the cold water!

I will always treasure my early memories of Houghton Lake and Higgins Lake, but now it is time for new memories, as I no longer have to make that long drive up here, because I live here.

✓ I Am So Blessed
By Lela M. Sydow of Brutus, Michigan
Born 1930

My dad was Louie Bonter, Sr. My mom was Addie Ruby Monroe. Dad had five brothers and five sisters. As a young man, Dad came north to Michigan with all his brothers and sisters to the Pellston "Camp Ten" area from Lebanon, Missouri with horses and a wagon. They worked in logging camps and saw mills.

Dad and Mom met and they started their own family of nine children. I was very young so I hardly remember two of my brothers, Everett and Edward. Mom and Dad were farmers in later years on a 160-acre farm. We had milking cows, two large draft horses, mean bore pigs, sheep, chickens, a mean roaster, barn cats, and a large yellow collie who ran the farm. My brother would squirt milk into the cats' mouths. The draft horses were western and very wild.

With my dad, Teddy was very protective. He worked hard and was very loving. In those days, cows ran wherever so about five o'clock, Dad would say to Teddy, "Go bring the cows home." It wasn't long before here they came. He put them right in the barn to be milked. What a smart, wonderful dog. He was so great.

I first went to country school in Pleasant View, about one and a half miles from home. I walked there. Then in fifth grade, I went to the same place to catch a bus to Pellston. For one year after that, I caught a bus closer to home. It was about a half mile to walk to go to Hardon Springs from sixth grade to graduation. I was a 1949er.

My uncle and aunt bought two new outfits for me for school every year. They also bought me a coat and boots if I need them. They had no children so they did a lot for me. They were so generous. This was Dad's brother.

I remember the old days and loved where I lived. We never had any money but we still had a good life. I just never knew that until now.

My mom had a hard life as a child. She had a stepdads and moms. They sent her to homes to work for people. When she was older, she waited tables and that's where I got my name, from a very good friend of hers.

I had four brothers and four sisters. Two younger ones passed away. When I was in high school, my brother went to the service for two years. My other brother and sisters were gone to work or got married so I was left at home to help. I drove the tractor for Dad, shocked corn, stacked hay in the field, and drove horses to haul hay. I helped Mom pick milk pails of berries when they were in season. We also had an acre of strawberries and an acre of cucumbers. No wonder we had bad backs.

Men went out and got two and three washtubs full of smelt. We cleaned smelt all day. I don't like smelt anymore. Mom canned them in mustard sauce and catsup sauce. She canned pickles and vegetables, meat and fruit. We had a root cellar full of food, large crocks of sauerkraut, chunk pickles, smoked ham, and bacon. Yum, was it all good.

Mom and I worked in the kitchen together. She was always singing, so we would harmonize together. That was fun. Sometimes we danced a little, too.

Mom and I also took our little blue coupe with a rumble seat in back to haul drinking water from a good spring up in the hills and also wash water for washing clothes from the cows' spring.

What I did was nothing compared to how hard my parents worked. I never appreciated what they did enough. Dad and Mom worked so hard all their lives, and now that I'm older I realize that. How much they did for their family to have a warm home, a lot of good food, warm clothes. We had a lot of fun together, also.

Many weekends, our neighbors would just drop over, so Dad would kill chickens. Mom started cooking and baking pies. She worked all day while others played baseball in our field. But that's the way my parents were, always ready to give to others. They got a lot in return also.

We had neighbors with three older men who played violin, guitar, and banjo. We had a piano in our living room, so we square danced and round danced. That's where I learned to dance. Then we would have lunch. I still love to dance; I just can't dance as long.

I really loved to sit and listen to my dad tell stories about the olden days, about his family and people he knew. It took him a long time, as he was from Missouri. Dad used to tell me about spirits and then I didn't understand but now I do. I believe those because it happened to me.

My husband, Harold, still works hard at 82. We have two special sons, Tim and Rob, and a daughter, Kathy, who works so hard and does so much for other people. We have two of the best daughters-in-law anyone could have. Their children, our grandchildren, work very hard in school and in college and at home. They all treat us with so much love and respect and would do anything to help us always.

Our second son and his wife, Rob and Dena's first child died when she was two. She was very ill. They have a son who is twelve and very healthy. Our oldest grandson, Michael, is in his third year of college. His sister, Taylor, will graduate this year. Our youngest grandson is twelve and is in seventh grade at Harbor Springs, where my picture is on the wall. How great is that for me? Our daughter, Kathy's oldest daughter graduated from Pellston and went to college for one year at Marquette. She is now in the National Guard to finish her college. Her sister, Karly, is an eleventh grader at Pellston.

I am so blessed to have this family. They are all very special, hard-working people. They are loving and respectful to everyone. They love each other unconditionally always. How lucky can that be?

We started going to Pellston Friendship Center to play Yuker and eat dinner a couple times a week. It is the best thing we ever did. I have never been treated better anywhere. The people are so loving and friendly. They want to be kind and do something nice for us always. We have so much fun with everyone. We love them all.

Thank you for your kindness. May God bless you all.

✓ Dad was my Mentor
By Helen Hemmingson of Herron, Michigan
Born 1935

When I was growing up, girls wore dresses all the time, below the knees. There was no standing on your head. My mother made all my dresses. She made three a year, one dress for Easter, one for a church picnic in August, and one for Christmas. Mom also taught me to sew by hand and with the Singer treadle sewing machine, which I have and still use.

I learned to darn socks when I was eleven years old. Socks were all cotton back then. I would put a ball in the heel or toe and weave a patch with thread.

I was in 4-H Club at age eleven. I learned to make towels and hem them. I still have

Helen's father bringing in a load of wood

them. I also made a slip and a very nice dress, which was aqua blue. I made buttonholes and covered the buttons with material. I also made a belt. I won a blue ribbon and was in the country dress review. I wore the dress to church.

Mother had a Maytag wringer washing machine and used it once a week, when she did six loads of the dirtier clothes. The girls did the nice clothes in a tub. The clothes were all hung outdoors to dry on clotheslines. It was a pretty sight!

I learned to iron clothes with a flat iron heated on the cooking stove. It didn't stay hot too long and would have to be exchanged for a hot iron. I started learning on handkerchiefs and dishtowels. Everything was cotton then and needed ironing after going through the wringer washer.

Our kitchen always smelled so good. We would just finish the dishes, which were done on the table in a big dishpan. There was another pan to rinse them in, and we would dry them with a towel and put them in the cupboard. Then Mom would get started on the next meal in the oven, meat and vegetables, bread and pies. There were two boys, five girls, Mom, and Dad in our family.

This was berry country. There were wild blackberries and blue ones. My dad had an acre of tame raspberries down by the river. Dad taught me to love and enjoy picking berries with him. He showed me the biggest berries to get my baskets full fast. We earned a penny a pint then. One farmer had one hundred acres, and people from town came out to help pick them.

My dad often would surprise us by saying, "Who wants to go fishing?" I'd always go with, "I had Dad all to myself." First, we'd dig up some nice, fat worms, and then we would go to the river and catch minnow fish to use for bait for the great northern pike. Next, we'd get in the homemade rowboat that Dad had made. It leaked some, so I needed a can to bail out the water. We fished with bamboo poles with a bobber. When it went down, we had a fish. We would just bring the pole up and the fish would come right to us. Good eating.

Dad was a great friend and mentor for me, and I loved doing things with him, like going to the woods in the winter with the team and sled to get a sled load of long poles (cut trees) of firewood. He would put them in a big pile

and then in the summer, he would cut them into cook stove sized pieces.

I learned to make fires in the stoves at home, and when I was eleven years old, I got the janitor job at my rural school. There was a school every two miles, and children came from all directions. I had to go by myself and get the school warm. School started at nine and ended at four. Then I had to bank the fire, clean the blackboard, sweep, do whatever needed doing, and lock up. My pay was $10.00 a month. With the first check, I bought a nice, warm woolen shirt. I must have done a good job, because I had the job until I graduated from grade school. I lived almost a mile from school.

Helen's sisters and brothers

Why My Last Name is Bushaw
By James M. Bushaw of Wellston, Michigan
Born 1927

About 1900, James and Nelle Bushaw, Frank and Emma Bushaw, and Joe Bushaw (wife's name unknown), moved down from Canada to Mesick, Michigan. James Bushaw bought about 80 acres in what is now the Northwest part of the village of Mesick. Jim and Nelle built a big barn and a home and they started raising beef cattle. They had a holding corral with a loading chute so they could load cattle on the train. Most of their beef cattle were sent to Chicago.

Frank and Emma Bushaw bought a house on the west side of Mesick. Great Uncle Frank worked in the logging of the big pines. After the logs were in the river, he floated down the stream on them, with a tool called a PeeVee. It was like a big cant hook and his job was to use the cant hook to keep the logs from jamming up and stopping the logs from floating down to Manistee, MI, where the big sawmills were.

Joe Bushaw and wife didn't stay in Mesick very long. They left with a horse and wagon and their belongings and no one in Mesick knew where they went or ever heard from them again.

In the year 2000, we (Jim and Elfa Bushaw), were down to Scottville, MI, to see our daughter and son-in law, Jock and Judy Drier. While Jock and I were looking at their garden, their neighbor, Big George Wilson came over to get some tomatoes. Jock introduced me to George, and George said he knew a Joe Bushaw, and that Joe had raised him as a foster child down south of Custer, MI.

Now we knew where Joe Bushaw went when he left Mesick.

Frank Miner and wife Lidia came up from Cassopolis, MI so Frank could work in the logging business. He drove oxen skidding logs to the roll-aways on the river. There is a Miner's Roll Away on the river north of Mesick.

John Miner and wife Nora moved up to Manistee, MI, and built a two story home. They rented the lower story and lived in the upstairs.

Lew Miner, a bachelor, worked on a farm near Glenwood, MI. Frank, John, and Lew also had a sister named Etta, married name not known, but she lived in Glenwood, MI.

Hank Miner, another brother, also a bachelor, lived near Glenwood, MI, and made his living fighting bare fisted. He rode a horse from southern Michigan up north, stopping at saloons that would have set dates for fights. Bets were made and money was held by the saloon owners, to be paid out to the winner.

At this time, Frank Miner was a bartender at a saloon in Yuma, MI, on a night when Hank was going to fight a man who thought he could knock Hank down in the fight. Hank hit the man in the head and the man went down and was out in the middle of the dance floor. Hank walked back to the bar to get his money and while he was standing at the bar, waiting to get his money, someone yelled, "watch out, Hank!" Hank turned around and saw the man he had knocked down coming at him with a knife in his hand. When he got close, Hank grabbed him and threw him on the floor and landed on top of him. Turned out the man had fallen on his own knife and it stuck him in the stomach. Blood started running out on the floor, so Hank left in a hurry, got on his horse, and rode away from the saloon and nobody ever saw him or heard from him again.

Frank and Lidia Miner had a son born in 1906. The baby was named Frank L. Miner. Two years later, Lidia died in childbirth. Frank Miner had business to take care of back down in Cassopolis. James and Nelle Bushaw said they would take care of the baby until he came back up north. Frank Miner was gone one month and when he got back to Mesick, the Bushaws had paperwork made out saying that Frank Miner had abandoned the baby and they had adopted baby Frank. Frank Miner thought about this for a while and as he was a single man, he decided to let James and Nelle raise the boy. The baby, Frank L. Bushaw (my Dad), grew up on the farm and married Edith Corning. They had three children, James M. Bushaw (me), Helen M. Bushaw and Donald L. Bushaw.

When I (James M. Bushaw) was about ten years old, I went with my dad (Frank L. Bushaw) out to the Deer Horn Inn (a beer joint) and while we were there, Joe Cole came in and he asked my dad how his dad was and my dad said, "Joe, my dad's been dead for ten years," "No, I mean your real dad," Joe said, and then my dad said, "what in the hell are you talking about?" Joe then told my dad that his real dad was down in Southern Michigan and that Dad also had an Uncle John in Manistee, MI. My dad looked in the telephone book and found an address for John and Nora Miner.

We got in the car and left Wellston and went to Manistee (17-mile ride) to see dad's real Uncle. Uncle John gave Dad Frank Miner's address in Glenwood, MI. Dad took a vacation and we went to Glenwood where my granddad (Frank Miner) was running a big muck farm, growing mint plants and steaming the juice out for Wrigley's Gum Company. Dad saw a small man working from one of the buildings and walked over to meet him. Dad asked if he was Frank Miner, and he said yes. Then Dad told him there was a guy in the car who wanted to see him. When Granddad Miner saw my red hair, he turned to my dad and said, "Are you Frank?" and Dad said yes. After that, we got out of the car and gave

Grandpa hugs and went into the house and got more hugs and kisses from Grandma Ida.

And now you know why my last name is Bushaw!

Around Rennie Street in Traverse City
By Marilyn J. (Carder) Scheck of Traverse City, Michigan
Born 1933

This "Good Old Days" story was taken from a letter I wrote to a photographer, about a picture published in the *Record Eagle* this past fall, which stirred up so many memories...

Back in the mid '40s my father managed a Standard Oil Gas Station in Detroit. One of his customers, Mr. Ed Harroun, was planning to retire in a couple of years. Their daughter and son-in-law had moved to Traverse City, where their son-in-law, Lee Brannock, was teaching in the Traverse City Junior High. The Junior High School was just upstairs from Central Grade School; and TC Central High School was at the east end of the building.

The Harrouns had decided to buy the Pine Lane Cabins, so the Brannocks could live in the adjoining house and take care of the cabins until the Harrouns retired and moved up here. The house and cabins were facing Rennie St. at the corner of W.14th St., which was the main highway that came into Traverse City from the south.

Just across Rennie St. from the cabins, on the corner of W. 14th St., was a closed Mobile Gas Station. Mr. Harroun knew that my dad was interested in leaving Detroit and suggested that he come up to Traverse City with them, and see if he would be interested in managing that gas station.

The gas station, owned by Rennie Oil Co., included the station building and the separate "Lube" room building. The station faced the corner, with the driveway cutting across the corner. The "Lube Room" with a "lift" for working under the cars; faced Rennie St. Also included was a two-bedroom house facing W. 14th St., for the manager's family to live in. My dad liked the setup and accepted the job as manager.

We moved from Detroit in April of 1944. As we finished loading the car, my dad told me that, in Traverse City I could eat all the cherry pie I wanted! I was ready to go! (Of

Marilyn's father, Everitt Carder

course, he didn't tell me that I had to pick and pit them first).

After a long trip, we and our moving truck pulled into Traverse City at night on the highway down the long Rennie St. hill that ended at W. 14th Street. Directly ahead of us, across W. 14th St., was a large, lighted billboard. To the left were the Pine Lane Cabins owned by the Harrouns; on the right was the Mobil Station and our new home. We spent the first two weeks in the Pine Lane Cabins, while the house was being readied for us—new linoleum floors and refinished walls. The house had recently been moved from somewhere else; and soon it was also settled onto a whole new basement.

Beyond the big billboard across 14th St. was a railroad track that ran west to Division St., and east to Boardman Lake. To the right of the billboard was the Conservation Department. And back of the Conservation Department and railroad track, was Thirlby Field, where I enjoyed many winters of ice-skating on the football field.

At the west end of Thirlby Field was a large empty field that was sometimes used for playing baseball. And, at least two or three times, it was the Circus Grounds! I can remember the Circus Train backing west on the railroad track, and the circus people unloading the big tents and setting them up. Because elephants were too large to stay on

313

the train, I saw them walking south on Rennie Street, and up Rennie Hill to the Traverse City School Bus Garage parking area, where they stayed for the night. And saw them walking back down for the circus. What fun!

Eventually the billboard across W. 14th Street was torn down and a big building went up in its place. The Grand Traverse Tractor Company moved in. They sold those neat blue Ford Tractors!

As I said earlier, Rennie St. was the main highway into Traverse City from the south. From Rennie St. the highway turned right on W. 14th St. and then left/north on Union St., past Union Street School, where I arrived in the middle of 5th grade. The highway continued north on Union St. to Front Street, where it turned right and continued east to Munson Ave; and then on north.

North of the downtown area, Clinch Park Zoo was located between the Boardman River and the bay. A favorite sight there was a really neat model of Traverse City with a little train that ran around it. Also there were free wandering peacocks all over, which would occasionally come across the Cass St. Bridge and wander along Front Street. I loved hearing them "calling."

For some time after we moved here, Division Street ended at W. 14th Street, where 14th St. became Silver Lake Road. South of 14th Street was a huge field with several "islands" of trees, scattered around. Much later we heard that a new highway was coming to town right through that big field, to be connected to Division Street.

The Harrouns finally moved up to the house at Pine Lane Cabins and their daughter and son-in-law moved a few blocks away. A few years later the Brannocks left Traverse City and the Harrouns sold the Pine Lane Cabins to a family with a son and daughter. The son was among the first students at the new Northwestern Michigan College; and was in the first graduating class.

I also became one of the first students at the new Northwestern Michigan College, where I met my husband, Al Scheck. After two years at NMC, Al also graduated and was drafted into the Army. A few months later we were married and moved to the West Coast for 2 years.

We returned to Traverse City for a summer and then headed to Michigan State College in Lansing, which had just become Michigan State University! Just before we left, my father Everitt Carder died. Carder's Service Station was closed and my mother moved to an apartment.

There is now another service station at that corner. The building sits about where our driveway was. The current driveway is about where the station and Lube Room were; the car wash sits about where our house was. My folks loved gardening and had a big vegetable and flower garden across the back of both lots.

Al graduated from MSU and became a public school teacher. I finally completed my college education at WMU; and we both taught in public schools as our children grew up. When we moved back to Traverse City in 1996, I learned that Rennie St. had been renamed to honor the US Veterans; but to me it will always be Rennie St.

✓ A Family of Dry Hill
By Edward Howard of Arcadia, Michigan
Born 1933

Hard to imagine now, but the empty, homeless high ground bordering Arcadia on the north and running far eastward was once a thriving farm community, known by early settlers as Dry Hill. Local dinner conversations in the '30s and '40s rang with Dry Hill names like Van Loon, Bunker, Riley, Chalker, and Baird. Even then, some names had long left the area. As a youth, hearing their stories told over and over again, it seemed those families had been up there forever and always would be.

Ren, Mat, Addie, and Gertie

314

But things and folks are not always, as they seem. One Dry Hill family, the Bairds, came to make that very clear. For as long as this farm boy could remember, brothers Ren and George Baird had lived as bachelors on Dry Hill with their spinster sister, Gertie. Besides raising their own crops, they made a living planting and harvesting for other, off-the-hill farmers like my dad and the Putneys. When I remembered, their average pay was two dollars a day. Of course, when hired men came to work, wives like my mother were obliged to feed them. Since none of the Bairds could drive, my dad was also obligated to pick them up and take them home, too. So around the dinner table in those days of only radio, young folks would, and must, eat quietly while the old folks talked. One learned a lot.

I soon learned that Ren and George were not the boring, old stay-at-home farmers I presumed. Dad would encourage Ren, deaf as he was, to talk glowingly of his early excursions west. He'd been in Texas and many Southwestern states before settling a while in Pomona, California. There, he worked the citrus orchards. Pomona was so nice; he was always "going back someday."

Younger brother, George, had also gone west, sometime before 1910. In that year, he was a fireman and part time engineer on a mining train in Ely, Nevada. He'd been a member of the Elks Club in Ely and still had many friends there. He talked of his fellow workers, the dangers of the job, his friends, and his many hunting ventures. George, like Ren, was yearning to go back someday.

Well, the winds blow and the sands shift, especially on Dry Hill, and it seems "forever" changed direction up there. Ren and George never did make it west again. They both died in their late eighties, some fifty years ago. Most of their final days were spent on their Dry Hill farm. Gertie lived to be ninety-seven and passed away in the early 1970s, shortly after turning the farm over to the Consumers Power project.

I like studying those by-gone days, so I feel fortunate to have purchased things from the Baird estate, shortly before they tore down the old house and barn. Now and then, I paw through the stuff and admire things, like the billy club George probably carried on the mining train or the brand new Elks tie pin he never wore. Then there's Ren's rough, hand-sewed traveling pouches, still holding old razors and straps. What a trail drifter he must have been. And thanks, Gertie, for saving all those letters, scraps, and photos that help paste together the stories of Dry Hill.

Dough Dodgers and Sink Baths
By Ethel L. Schultz of Alpena, Michigan
Born 1929

I was raised on a farm. My parents had a three-room house, and my folks had eight of us kids. We had an outdoor toilet with two seats in it. We carried our water from a pump outdoors. We washed clothes in a tub and had wringer washers. We had a big garden, and apple orchard, and farm animals.

When I was growing up, us kids had to get up early to do the chores. We had to feed our animals and water them. We had to pump water and fill things for them to drink from, clean the barn, and milk the cows. When that was done, we had to change our clothes, eat, and get ready for our walk to school.

When I went to school, I had to walk two miles to school and two miles back home. We had no car to drive us kids. I remember going to school when we got older. We had to change our clothes and go out in the fields and pick stones and stuff until dark.

We had to go get groceries with a sleigh and a box to put our stuff in. We had four miles to walk for groceries.

My mother made most of our clothes. I had some pretty dresses that I wore that she made. I loved them.

My mother was the best cook. I remember the homemade bread and dough dodgers, as

Ethel's parents

315

Harold and Ethel's wedding in 1949 with her sister and twin brother

she called them. She made desserts, too.

My father had to dig pits in the ground to keep our apples and vegetable in the winter. He covered them with straw to keep them from freezing.

For entertainment, we had an old wind-up record player. We went to movies about once a month when we could get a ride with someone. We walked two miles to play ball with other schools. It was fun.

When I was sixteen, I had a terrible accident. Our stove exploded and I caught fire. I was burned from my waist up to my head. I spent over three years in Ann Arbor in the hospital for skin grafts and operations on my burns. I had 33 skin grafts. After I was finished with hospitals, I was glad to be home.

I had a nurse from the hospital hire me to babysit and do housework for her. I worked for her for about three years.

After I was done working for her, I met a guy on a blind date. It was Easter Sunday. Six months after that, he proposed to me with a ring. We were married six months after that.

We lived with my in-laws for six years while we built a two-room garage. We lived in there for the time we built our house. We had our three kids while we lived there. We had a two-hole toilet outside and had to pump our water, too. I gave the kids a bath in our kitchen sink. Our bath was a sponge bath. We had a wood stove for heat. I cooked on a wood stove, too.

He worked at Huron Portland for thirty-five years and retired at 58 years of age. After he retired I found out he had Parkinson disease. He had it for 28 years. It was no fun either. We had three children, seven grandkids, and nine great-grandkids. My husband died on September 17, 2005, eight years ago. Many things have happened since then.

I am still a widow. I babysit a lot and my hobbies are sewing, oil painting, quilting, and gardening flowers. I love flower gardening. I play bingo. I love housework, because it keeps me busy.

I had five sisters and two brothers. One, Clarence, was my twin, but he died. They are all dead except me and two sisters. My two sisters and I do a lot of things together. My baby sister lives in South Carolina, so I don't see her much, maybe once a year. I can't wait to see her again. Maybe we will go mushroom picking in April. My son, David, keeps me plowed out in the wintertime, bless him.

Kid getting a bath in the sink in 1960

√ Grandma Mae
By Donna L. Groulx of Linwood, Michigan
Born 1937

William and Mary Fox were married in August of 1897. Shortly after they were married, William and Mary traveled from Sanilac in a covered wagon. The roads were so rough that one of their children, Edna, bounced right out of the wagon. Along with Edna, there were seven other children: Mae, Cleo, Eva, Audley, Ovid, Jay, and Johnny. Grandma Mae always used to show me where Great-grandpa would stop on Campbell Road to water their horses.

William and Mary also purchased eighty acres on Deckerville Road in Lupton, Michigan. This is where they not only raised their eight children but raised William's son, James Perry Fox's five children as well. These grandchildren were Nada, Virginia, Lela, Vera, and Sid. All of the children used to help out with the family farm. After all the work was done on the farm, the children were allowed to run and horseplay. But only after the chores were done.

Grandma Mae

Mae came from Marlette, Michigan to Rose City in 1896, at the age of six years old, traveling one hundred miles in a covered wagon with her parents, sisters, and brothers. The trip took one week, and after living in the Rose City area for a year, her mother, Mrs. Fox, wanted to return home to Marlette. Her father loaded them back into the wagon and they returned home.

One year later, Mae's mother decided she wanted to live in Rose City, so they made the long journey once more. "There were no roads or trails. We just traveled through the woods," she remembers. "We once hit a log and the wagon tipped over. My mother was thrown from the wagon while holding my sister, Edna. Luckily, no one was hurt."

Mae's father was a lumberman, and he found work in the area. Mae has lived here ever since. She remembers traveling from camp to camp, living in one-room shacks, having a bed, a trunk, and a small table. This was home to her family. She remembers everyone in camp eating off tin plates all at one big long camp table.

At age eighteen, Mae met Melvin Matthews, also a lumberman, and they were married. Their first home was a converted sheep shed. "From front to back, the roof pitched to the ground," she remembers. "My husband, Melvin, cleaned it and the sky all lit up," and she thought the world was on fire. It was the Rose City fire of 1910.

After they were married, they purchased eighty acres right down the road from her mother and father. Unfortunately, Melvin wanted to purchase the land that was right across the road from Grandpa, but at the time, he couldn't afford it. So his brother, Floyd, purchased the land. Mae and Melvin had six children together: Lawrence, Oliver, Ione, Don, William, and June.

Mae remembers the birth of her first son. She was in labor for three days when Mae's father, Grandpa Fox, put on his cowhide coat and walked to town during the snowstorm to get a doctor. The date was July 24, 1911. "That's right," says Mae. "It snowed in July that year."

Everyone claims Mae raised two families because she had two boys and one girl, and then six years later she had another two boys and one girl. "I have no recollection of what happened during those six years," she says.

Melvin would work for only twenty-eight dollars per month. He loaded logs onto trains that would go north from Lupton to the water hole switch and then onward to Yurk Homestead. After saving enough money, Melvin started buying cattle to bring to the farm.

Mae recalls going to see her first movie in 1938 at the movie theater in West Branch. The movie was *Gone with the Wind*. "On the way home, we got stuck in a snow bank, and it was a mile and a half to get home. When we got home, Dad went to the barn to check his cow and found a newborn calf, which we all named Gone with the Wind."

Mae remembers washing clothes on a scrub board. After that, she used a wooden washing machine, which operated by hand. Mae's son, Oliver, hated doing laundry, so he hooked the washing machine to a gas engine with a belt. "We called him the engineer of the family," Mae says.

"I made all the clothes from cloth, burlap bags, and flour sacks," Mae recalls. Ione and June Matthews remember wearing gathered skirts made from flour sacks. "Mom made us wear long johns under our dresses to go to school. When we got out of sight of the house, we would roll them up so no one could see, and then we would roll them back down just before we got home," they say. "Everyone was equal in those days," says Mae. "No one was rich or poor. We were all the same."

Mae remembers when she was a child dreaming of owning a pair of colored shoes, but her father told her she would have to wait until she was married to get them. He father always bought her boy's shoes, because "they last longer and they had better last at least a year," he would say. He dream came true when her husband, Melvin, bought her pair of tan

Oxfords with white lace cotton socks of her own, Mae remembers. She also remembers buying black stockings for ten cents a pair.

After many years of farming, it had become too much for Melvin to handle, since his six children were starting to leave home. So he ended up selling the farm to Don Matthew, who still has the forty acres of land today.

When Mae and Melvin sold the farm, they also rented a small restaurant where they lived until Melvin built the rest of their home in Lupton. Once they had built the house, they moved their sawmill to Lupton Road. Then, after a year went by, Melvin ended up selling the sawmill to Lawrence, their oldest son. Melvin helped out with the sawmill every day by sharpening the saws for Lawrence. While in the kitchen, Mae and Cleo baked fresh cakes and made coffee every day for the workers. Mae was such a great cook.

In June of 1978, at the age of 87, Mae did something incredible. She was working out in her garden near a pond, which was fed from a natural flowing well. Two neighbor boys came by, one only three years old, to watch her working. All of a sudden, she heard a splash. One of the boys had fallen into the icy cold water. Even though she had a bad leg and with little regard for her own safety, Mae jumped in and pulled the drowning boy from the mucky bottom of the pond. She managed to get him to shore and began "pumping him" until he regained consciousness. Two days later, Mae was in the hospital fighting pneumonia. Mae has several plaques hanging on her walls commemorating her heroic act.

Mae has survived through six wars: the Civil War, World War I, World War II, the Korean War, Vietnam, and of course Desert Storm. When asked how many Presidents she can remember, she said, "I remember when Teddy Roosevelt was President. But my favorite President was George and Mrs. Bush. He is the greatest."

Mae lived on her own and drove a car until she was 91 years old. Her happiest thoughts are of her husband, Melvin, and their six children. The children are home in Ogemaw County and have never left. Mae says, "I would live it all over again just the way it was." Her advice to everyone is to "live a good clean life, enjoy yourself, and never fight with each other."

Growing Up in the Upper Peninsula
By Lola J. Lawrence Sell of Indian River, Michigan
Born 1935

I was born April 13, 1935 in my grandmother's house in Germfask, Michigan. My dad couldn't get my mother to the doctor in time, so the lady across the street delivered me. This lady was Lolah Losey and a midwife. My parents decided to name me after Lolah, but they removed the h in her name.

I attended the Germfask School, kindergarten through eighth grades. The school was big and square and had very high ceilings. I remember the lights hanging down on long chains. The classes were often together in the same room. There was kindergarten and first; second and third; fourth, fifth, and sixth; and seventh and eighth. I remember listening to the higher grades and learning from them. We had inkwells and pens to dip in them. They were messy.

I lived right on Highway 77 with my mother, my dad, and three sisters. I could walk to school every day. It was on the back road, and I could see it from my house. The school bell was used to start school and to end recess.

Lola's mother, Clara and her sister Irene

318

Our family of six used outhouses for a few years, before we got running water and added one inside bathroom. We also had pots with covers so we didn't have to go out if it was cold. I hated those pots. I always felt I was going to tip over. We always had catalogs to clean up with. The sales catalogs were always best. They were thinner and softer.

We used to haul water from the back road near the school. There was a fantastic flowing well there and excellent water. We also had a garden and raised chickens for food. To this day, chicken is my favorite meal.

We had an old wood stove in the kitchen. It had a reservoir to keep water hot. Mom would let us peel potatoes and slice them and lay them on the stove to brown. They were delicious. It was an awful mess for Mom to clean after though. We kept soda crackers in the warming oven. They are my favorite snack today. I remember taking a stack of crackers and reading comic books. We didn't have pretzels or potato chips back then.

We always had potatoes at our house because of our garden. We would fill the big bin under the basement stairwell, and they would last us until spring.

Something else that is a vivid childhood memory is my mom killing a chicken or two for our dinner. It was especially vivid when there was snow on the ground. When Mom got the block and the hatchet ready, she would make us girls go in the house. My bedroom faced the backyard and my grandma's house, so I would go up there and watch my mom when she grabbed the chicken's legs and wings and lay the chicken's head on the block. She would chop the head off then throw the chicken out in the snow. It would flop around for a long time, and of course, the backyard was quite a sight with the white snow and the blood everywhere. My mother was not yet finished. She would dip the chicken in boiling water so the feathers would come out easier. Then she would roll a newspaper up in a cone and light a match to it. This fire would singe any hair or feathers left on the chicken. My mother was very good at cutting a chicken up. She was spot-on when hitting the joints. Mom cooked the chicken a lot of ways; roasted, in soup, or fried. It was all good and we always had fresh eggs.

Just down from my house was St. Theresa's Catholic Church, built of small

Lola's dad, Romeo with Irene, Mary, and Lola in 1936

stones from Lake Superior. In the early years, we had mass only once a month. The priest had to travel from Grand Marais. I made my first Holy Communion, confirmation. I later married Harold G. Sell in 1958 in the church. The little church burned to the ground years later.

Radio wasn't much good where we lived, but we had an old phonograph with records. I remember how real the sounds would be of creaking doors or storms, and the suspense was as good as watching TV.

Our house was heated by coal and I remember a Thanksgiving when my mom had to put the turkey roaster on the end of a shovel and put it in the furnace because the electricity went out during a storm. We often had to cook on a little gas burner camp stove rig because electricity would be gone for days.

In the early days, we did not have phones. I remember the first time I ever talked on the phone. I was around ten. The only phone was at Morrison's General Store.

I was spanked only once at school. It was in seventh grade. The principal made a few of us bend over a bench and cracked us three times with a board that had holes in it. To this day, I don't remember what I did.

A bath was a real treat at our house. It was

319

once a week if we were lucky.

I remember when World War II ended. My grandmother rang the church bell. I think I was around ten.

Wringer washers were very much a part of my life, also washboards. I remember my mother's knuckles would bleed from using them, and my grandmother made homemade soap.

I saw my first movie in seventh grade. A man named Mr. Beach came once a week to show us movies in the community building. He charged twenty-five cents. We sat on benches. We couldn't wait for the continuation of the serial; they were cliffhangers. So often, the film would break and we would patiently wait until Mr. Beach fixed it.

We lived during the Depression years. I remember needing stamps to buy things like sugar and meat. I also remember my dad saying, "We were so poor we didn't notice the Depression."

My mother did not sew, but I never wore new clothes or shoes. They were handed down from my sisters. We were only one year apart and then my youngest sister was five years younger than me. We called her spoiled.

My favorite teacher was probably Mrs. Mercier. She was pretty, and she played piano and loved music.

The only rumble seat I remember was the one on my boyfriend's car. I think it was a '40 or '42 Ford with a Cadillac engine in it that he had restored.

We had some very bad storms years ago. I remember my parents driving us kids out in the country to see five huge workhorses dead in a field under a tree. They had been struck by lightning. The owners were cousins of my mother. I remember everyone crying. Those horses were their livelihood.

We didn't have pets. We didn't think we could afford them. Besides my mom was alone a lot to take care of us girls. My dad worked road construction and was gone for months. Sometimes we would be entertained by a little mouse. We wouldn't tell Mom, because she would trap them.

We didn't have homemade toys, but Mom sent our dolls out to a farm where my dad was staying in Dafter. The ladies made clothes for our dolls, and they were under the tree for Christmas. My folks could not afford to buy us new dolls. We always had a nice Christmas. I believed in Santa until I was quite old, because I knew my parents couldn't afford to buy all those presents.

The Manistique River ran behind our house. We were forbidden to go there because the boys would swim in the nude.

At school recess, we played marbles a lot. If the weather was bad, we loved to play jacks on the wood floor. We also threw a big ball over the roof and the kid on the other side had to catch it. We yelled, "Ante I over" before throwing it.

My sister, Mary, and I stole some cigarettes from my mother and went out to the chicken coop to smoke. We got caught and got the hairbrush on our backsides.

My mother kept us very close to home. My sisters were my playmates. My two older sisters and I did a lot together. My youngest sister was five years behind us, so it was hard for my mother to leave the house. My dad was not home very much when we were growing up. Grama lived down the path and we visited her a lot. We used to play card games with her.

By seventh grade, when Dad was home for a weekend, we would drive to Manistique to visit my grandma, his mother, for an hour. Then Mom and Dad would take us to theater to see a movie and buy each of us some popcorn. When we visited Grama, she would pass the box of candy to all of us, and then she would talk in French to my dad for an hour. I remember her as being very kind and loving.

We had a lot of family time. My mom's family lived nearby and my dad had three brothers who lived in Germfask. One had a grocery store and the other had gasoline. So we had cousins.

I remember when rotary phones came into our lives. I still like the part we held to talk through. The party line, however, was a nuisance. I don't ever remember iceboxes or a milkman, though.

The small town where I was born is located in the Upper Peninsula. Germfask got its name from the first letter of the last name of the first eight settlers.

G = Grant
E = Edge
R = Robinson
M = Mead
F = French
A = Ackley
S = Shepard

K = Knags

Growing up in the Upper Peninsula was good. It certainly made me appreciate the better things in life. I wouldn't give up those days for anything. They were some of the best days of my life.

Henry Ford, My Pet Alligator, and Walloon Lake

By Marilyn Stockwell Colestock of Petoskey, Michigan
Born 1937

Back in the late 1800s, my great-great-grandmother had a farm next to Henry Ford's father's farm in Dearborn. It was fall and all the men were going out on wagons to harvest the hay. Young Henry was riding on one of the wagons when Grandma Hellner spotted him and called to him, "Henry, I have a clock that stopped working. Can you help?" Henry hated haying and was glad to escape. He tinkered with the clock all afternoon out in the barn and got it going. The clock has worked perfectly ever since, over one-hundred years, and my brother now has it.

It was winter, 1944, and I was seven years old. A small box with air holes unexpectedly arrived in the mail from Florida from a friend of my Dad. We carefully opened the box and found a wad of seaweed containing a baby alligator, six inches long. He was mostly tail. He hissed and flashed his sharp baby teeth at us. After three days in the mail, we quickly put a small piece of meat on a toothpick that he hungrily chomped down. Then we built him a little pen in the basement in front of the furnace, where it was warm. The top of a birdbath became his swimming pool. Mother's eyes were rolling as Dad named him Caspar Milquetoast, after a 1912 comic strip, The Timid Soul.

I adopted Caspar as mine and carried him around the house, often kissing him on the mouth. Caspar doubled and tripled in size. Twice a week, I'd ride my bike down to the butcher shop, where I'd buy a nickel's worth of hamburger for his dinners, wrapped up in brown butcher paper. In the summers, we moved his chicken wire pen outside, where he'd grin and happily float around in his pool. He was more than two feet long when he disappeared. I asked all our neighbors to be on the lookout for him but to no avail. After two years, Caspar Milquetoast was gone.

The Great Lakes Theatre on Grand River was built by my grandfather and great uncle just before the 1929 Depression. It was way out in "the sticks" of Detroit and had a huge, tall marquee – a landmark seen for miles. It was a beautiful building with a stage and dressing rooms for vaudeville shows, which my dad often MCed. There was a fantastic theatre organ to be played during silent movies. Later, there were double features, a Movietone newsreel, and a cartoon. Adult tickets were thirty cents, and children's tickets were fifteen cents. There were uniformed ushers to watch over us. My parents often dropped my brother and me off there for afternoons of free babysitting, because they knew we were safe there. The films never showed anything suggestive; the word "pregnant' was banned, and of course there was no swearing, and a married couple in the movies never shared a bed, they always used two twin beds.

I grew up in the northwest Detroit area in the 1940s, back when Detroit was a great city.

The Great Lakes Theatre

321

Our grammar school, Edison, was on Grand River near Southfield. I remember all us kids rode our bikes to school and put them in the bike racks. No one had a bike lock. When we came out of school at the end of the day, our bikes, totally unprotected, were still there.

In the 40s, going to the J.L. Hudson Co. store was an event. Mother and I would walk four blocks down to Grand River and take a streetcar downtown. After checking out the beautifully decorated store windows, we would go inside with all the bustling people. There were floorwalkers dressed formally in suits to direct us and elevator operators in uniforms. My tiny mother in a loud voice would demand, "Where are all the chubby clothes?" Those were for me! Everything Mom bought was left there and Hudson delivery trucks freely brought our packages to our home later that day. Delicious lunches were served on the 12th floor. And, of course, who could forget the wondrous Hudson Thanksgiving Day parades.

My husband and I had just moved up north to the tiny village of Walloon Lake. We went to the post office to see about getting a post office box. A very polite young man at the counter was advising us. Then he looked out the front window behind us, apologized, and excused himself. He came out from behind the counter and hurried out the front door, leaving us alone. We watched as someone in a car was dropping off a disabled man with a cane. Our clerk helped the man out of the car and assisted him into the front door of the office. I grinned at my husband and blessed the day we decided to move here.

Johnson Lake Ranch, a Vacation Paradise
By Eleanor Ann (Finger) Harkey of Prescott, Michigan
Born 1935

My parents came to be part of the pioneers of the area. My father John Finger, Jr., was born in Ottawa Lake, Michigan, in Lenawee County to William and Lena (Miller) Finger and moved here in 1887. My mother Ortensia Ann Mogg was born east of Prescott to Samuel and Catherine (McLeod) Mogg in 1897. My parents were married in 1916 and purchased the farm of 160 acres. This farm has been

Eleanor's husband, Charles Roland Harkey in 1956

in the family since 1908 and was declared a centennial farm in 2012.

These folks were self-employed. They raised sheep, cattle, hogs, horses, and chickens. We had 8 to 10 milk cows and sold cream and used the skim milk for hog feed.

My father did custom work for the neighborhood and surrounding area. He drilled water wells, sheep sheared, wood buzzing for firewood, butchering, and kept an icehouse year round. He cut off the lake, as we didn't have electricity until 1948.

They ran a campground on the lake for renting, four cabins, and boats, for many years. My father knew a lot of people in cities as far away as Detroit, Flint, Saginaw, Bay City, and even out of state in Ohio. They could not afford a vacation of any great expense.

He purchased an army tent and set it up in the spring for all summer's use free of charge. It was large enough to accommodate a large family. The tent didn't have a floor in it, so he laid a tarp down and covered it with loose straw and another tarp on top. In the middle of the tent, it made a good bed. They used picnic tables and gas stoves to cook on. This large tent was used by several families. At times one family moved out the back as another family moved in the front. Boats were rented for 50 cents a day. These boats were wooden and built by my father and maintained in good order.

One family from Saginaw, Henry and Edna Butzin, came and was staying there. Edna was pregnant and gave birth to a son early at our farmhouse. The baby came a month early so she wasn't prepared for him, so he wore my sister's clothes as she was newly born at the same time. People with children enjoyed being on a farm and gave a helping hand when it came time to harvest hay or crops we raised at the time. We raised potatoes and fruit for sale.

I am the youngest of seven children born to my parents and raised here on the farm. I was born in 1935 and married my husband in 1954, Charles Roland Harkey. We moved to Missouri for 3 years and moved back to Michigan in 1957 to help my parents with the farm activities and campground. My mother died at age 72 in 1969 and my father died at age 84 in 1978. I am at the age of 78.

We raised our family here on the farm also and still own 43 acres of the original 160. We have two children, four grandchildren, and eight great-grandchildren. Our grandson Andy Burr farms our property at present.

I've kept in touch with a lot of the folks who camped at the campground years ago. They all wish they could camp there again and tell me, "Eleanor, rent me a cabin and a boat."

My parents had the forethought to sell the township a 66' right of way for public access to the lake for fishing. So the lake stayed open to the public.

I know I'm partial but it's one of Michigan's best lakes for fishing, I kid you not. I, along with many former campers, have pleasant memories of fishing and good catches on the lake as a kid and as an adult.

Eleanor in 1949

My parents helped to raise several extra children who lost their parents at an early age. My mother knit socks and mittens, hats, and mended clothes for all of us. The neighborhood kids knew where the table was for meals and all were welcome. They referred to my mother as Our Mom. My father was a good provider. He hunted and fished and fed us all well. I count it a blessing to have had all of God's gifts to enjoy. I pray for a few more years and to pay forward all these blessings.

My grandmother on Mom's side was a midwife for years. She did the area quite a service as people called for her to come help with the delivery of a new child. Catherine (McLeod) Mogg and her horse Nellie and buggy traveled the area back roads. My grandfather Samuel Mogg and two sons Max and Albert were cemetery sextons for over 100 years at Richland Township's cemetery east of Prescott on Sheffer Road.

I am a retired Rural Mail Carrier from Prescott Post Office. I served for 21 years. I traveled a lot of miles on bad roads. My husband is a retired machinist and drove back and forth to Bay City and worked 18 ½ years at American Hoist until they moved out of state. He then worked at a small shop in Whittemore till he retired at age 62.

We praise God for all our family and friends. We are members of the Judson Baptist Church of Prescott.

"Kindergarten Babies!"
By John L. Flitz of Lake Ann, Michigan
Born 1928

My mother and dad, Phylus and Harold, met in New York City at Flower Hospital, where they both worked. Mom was a dietician and Dad had some kind of an office job. They got married in New York, I think about 1926. Through a mutual friend, Dad got a job offer from Ruemelin Manufacturing Company in Minneapolis. Since it paid more Dad took the job. Mom was all for it since it got her much closer to her hometown of Bayfield. So I was born in Minneapolis in August 1928.

I don't remember anything of my first two years of course. In 1930 Mr. Ruemelin moved his business to Milwaukee, so our family made the move too. Dad got along real good with 'old man' Ruemelin, who acted as

Jack Flitz

Dad's mentor and taught him all aspects of the business. I always thought Mr. Ruemelin's first name was 'old man,' because that's how Dad always referred to him. Dad idolized 'old man' Ruemelin because he started and ran a very successful business and was a self-taught engineer who learned the profession by reading books. He had dozens of patents relating to the products he made and sold. These were sand blast, fume, and dust collectors.

So my earliest recollections were of life on 33rd street on the south side of Milwaukee. Those were happy years with lots of little playmates, both boys and girls. My closest friends were Buddy and Shirley Tess, right next door. One day I had a spat with Bud and I threw a small rock at him. It hit him on the leg and raised a big welt. He ran in the house crying and came out with his mom who really yelled at me and told my mom what happened. So I was confined to the yard for a few days. After that we were all good friends again.

We had an industrial dump about two blocks from our house so we would troop over there and bring back all kinds of neat stuff (junk). The older boys would erect sheet metal forts and have stone fights between the forts. No anger, just fun. I was too young to participate so the older boys would seat me behind the sheet metal where I wouldn't get hurt. I can remember the stones banging on the sheet metal.

One time I got lost and a policeman took me to the station. The policeman played with me until my mom came to pick me up. Was I ever glad to see her.

Two other friends were Joan and Elaine Reed from down the block.

Joan was the oldest and she was o.k. but Elaine was sort of obnoxious and weird. Sometimes she would sit in the street and play with horse "apples." There were a lot of horse-drawn vehicles then so plenty of opportunities for her. Sometimes, we would tell her when the fresh horse apples arrived and laugh when she ran to the street to play with them. One time, when I had some kind of altercation with Elaine, I was looking for a way to get even. So, I picked up a can, filled it with horse apples, and smeared it on one side of the Reed's freshly painted garage. Needless to say, that did not endear me to the Reeds so I was confined to quarters again.

Another way we had of getting even was to inflict pranks on Halloween to families we didn't like. This consisted of shooting split peas (with peashooters) against their windows at night, sticking pins in their doorbells (so they would keep on ringing) and soaping windows. If it was a family we really didn't like we would use wax on the windows since wax was so much harder to remove. These were the days before there were treats on Halloween, only tricks. No parents were involved either.

Still, our families stayed friends in spite of us brats. I remember corn picnics at the grounds of a roadhouse. Corn was boiled and all kinds of other food were to be had. The biggest treat was when Dad gave us nickels and we went in the tavern to play the slot machine. When the machine spit out a few more nickels we thought we were rich.

Once in a while the Tess' invited us to their cabin on Booth Lake. This was really fun. Bud and I would go fishing in a leaky old rowboat and we always came back with bluegills and sunfish. We dug our own worms for bait in the cow pasture behind their cabin. We also had air rifles and would go hunting for gophers in the cow pasture. Loads of fun, no adults involved. They were having their own fun. A big treat was when Mr. Tess would lug his outboard motor to the beach and put it on one of the leaky old boats and we went flying across the lake. This is where I learned to love boats (fast boats) and lakes and anything to do with them.

Back in Milwaukee, the Tess' would ask me over for breakfast when they were having blood sausage. I loved this stuff. They got the pig's blood from their relative's farm and congealed in into loaves and then sliced it and fried it. It was really good with syrup. I've never had it since.

Mr. Tess ran a small Whadams gas station (the flying red horse).

Bud and I loved to hang around there. I thought it was the neatest place. I loved the smell of gasoline, new tires, and grease. When I grew up I knew I wanted to have a gas station. Next door to the gas station was a movie theater where Bud and I would go in and watch Tarzan movies. I thought Tarzan was great and I wished I was like him, but knew this was not likely since we did not live in a jungle.

This time was before electric refrigerators, so we had "ice boxes" to keep food cold. The iceman would come around every day to deliver ice. We put a sign in the window saying how much ice we wanted, 25 pounds, 50 pounds, or 100 pounds. We would hang around the back of the ice truck and beg the iceman for slivers of ice, which we would suck on to keep cool on hot days.

Mom learned to drive then and I remember this as a time of terror. I would cower on the floor in back while Mom lurched and jerked the car learning the clutch and gearshift. Of course this was twenty years before automatic transmissions. Dad was so patient with Mom. She was so determined to learn but it scared the crap out of me.

When I was three the twins were born. Mom was so busy with them she no longer had much time for me. I was called "the big guy" at three. I remember Lois didn't like to eat and would pinch her lips shut when Dad tried to jam in pabulum. Ken was a crier, especially when Dad and Mom went out in the evening. He would jump up and down on the sofa and scream his head off. It drove the babysitter nuts but she stayed because she needed the money. When Dad would reprimand Ken, Ken would back up. Dad called him a backer-upper.

One time Ken got so sick he almost died. Our family doctor didn't have a clue what was wrong with him. So Dad took him to another doctor (Dr. Bauman). He diagnosed Ken with pneumonia and saved his life. Dr. Bauman was Dad's hero after that.

These were the Great Depression days and families were really poor since so many men had no jobs. Dad was always employed but he only made $40 per week. We were one of the few families that could afford a radio. Before Christmas our favorite show was "Billie the Brownie from Shuster's." My little friends and I would crowd around the radio about 4:00 P.M. and listen to Billie cavort around with Santa. We were entranced. And then when I went with Mom to the basement of Shuster's, I was gaga at the toy train sets. I didn't get one until I was older, about nine or ten. I loved trains from then on and still do. There is something awe-inspiring and wonderful about trains.

When I was six, Mom started me in kindergarten at Greenfield Elementary. At first I was a little scared, but then I learned to love it. Our teacher's name was Mrs. Brown and she always wore a brown dress. I guess she thought she had to because of her name. I remember we had to line up in the hall before the bell rang. On the other side of the hall the first graders were also lined up waiting for the bell to ring. They would taunt us by hollering "kindergarten babies." I hated this but the next year when I was a first grader I enjoyed taunting the kindergarten kids by hollering "kindergarten babies," at them. I guess I had a little mean streak in me.

When I was in first grade I excelled at

A 17 year-old with his 1937 Harley

reading and the teacher called on me a lot to stand up and read out of our little books.

I never knew what Dad did all day at work. When I asked him he told me he sold doorknobs. He knew I couldn't understand what he really did.

I was fortunate to have very loving parents. After the twins were born, Mom was so busy with them that I was pretty much on my own. When I would get sick or hurt I couldn't wait for my dad to come home because he would sort of pamper me and make me feel better; he was strict but a really good dad. None Better.

I remember I would go around the house with a screwdriver taking everything apart that had screws. I had to see what was inside. Sometimes I had trouble putting it back together and Dad would help. He never bawled me out for doing this. He thought curiosity was a good thing and that's when he decided that I should be an engineer someday, and that's the way it turned out.

Dad did have a habit of swearing when he was aggravated. I picked up on this and started using swear words at a very young age. This shocked older people but of course my parents couldn't bawl me out because they knew where I learned it.

In closing, I just want to say that our three wonderful children and four grandchildren have added an immense amount of joy and satisfaction to our lives. I can't imagine life without them. We are also grateful to our two son-in-laws for being good husbands and fathers. Our girls picked really good guys.

Dad passed away in 1975 and Mom in 1981. I miss them both so much and think of them every day of my life.

Outhouses
By Eileen Pulido of Benzonia, Michigan
Born 1952

When I was young, we used to have an outhouse. My mom and dad had a double-seater. When it was cold, we would make a mad dash outside, do our job, and then come back in. Summertime wasn't bad; we would sit and read a paper while we did our job. My great grandma didn't have toilet paper. We used Sear's catalogue pages to wipe up with. The bees were pretty bad in the summer. We were lucky we never got stung. One day, someone tried to take my great-grandmother's toilet but mom and dad caught them. We never had an actual bathroom until Mom and dad moved in town when I was 13 years old. Wow! We were so excited to have toilets that actually flushed!

Snakes, Worms, and Oatmeal
By Hazel Phetteplace of Curran, Michigan
Born 1924

One sunny day, when I was about nine years old, I went to my favorite spot to meditate. It was located on a hill about 40 rods back of the farmhouse. From there, I could observe the house and area around without being seen on a nice sunny day. As I left the spot to go back to the house, I somehow decided to look into the hole in the middle of a huge stump left over from the original logging days of late 1890. I approached the stump and looked inside. I instinctively jumped back as the longest garter snake I had ever seen came over the outside edge of the stump straight toward me! I turned and ran as fast as I could for the house, never looking back to see if that snake was following me! It had probably had a litter nesting in the stump.

During those Depression days, Mother served oatmeal for breakfast cereal, and alternated with corn meal on some days. One morning, my younger brother looked at the bowl of oatmeal and said, "Not this stuff again!" Mother responded, "Eat it and be darned glad you got it!" At least we actually had food. Christmas gifts were homemade out of wood. Usually they were little wagons, jumping jacks, and hand toys. Sugar and flour came in 50 or 100 pound printed cotton sacks that my mother used to make garments, table scarves, and curtains out of.

My younger brother's habit of sucking his thumb had to come to a stop before entering Kindergarten that fall. Big Sister could stop that! I took him into the well house where Dad kept an opened can of tar. I just knew that he wouldn't suck his thumb with that nasty stuff on it, so I promptly tarred his thumb. Problem was, when we tried to wash it off, it wouldn't come off! We went crying into the house for help.

The boys often dug for angleworms to sell to fishermen. One day, my brother was using a hoe to move the soil back; I would then look into the hole to see if there were any worms in it. This time, since we had not seen any worms, he had decided to give an extra hit with the hoe. I was already leaning over the hole, looking for the worms, when the hoe came down directly on my head! I am 88 years old now, and I still carry the scar! Today, looking back, I'm glad I was raised on the farm in the country and can reflect on such memories. They were definitely rough years for the parents, but we had a respect and family closeness that isn't as evident today as it was back then.

✓ Paper Dolls and Radio
By Agnes Moraitis of Whittemore, Michigan
Born 1925

Since there were no cars or buses, we had to walk to school. We would walk the two miles to school, go home for lunch, and then go back to school for afternoon classes. For amusement, we used roller skates, which we put, together with spare parts. We played outdoors a lot. Mother would gather my sister, me, and several other girls on our front porch to teach all of us to crochet and embroider. On Saturday mornings, Mother would give my sister and me five cents for the theatre plus two or three extra pennies so that we could buy goodies. We had no snow pants, gloves, or boots, long underwear, or long stockings. Girls just didn't wear blue jeans. We would put a pair of socks on our hands to keep warm. The Detroit newspaper would have a paper doll in the Sunday paper with dresses. I had fun cutting them out but it was very tricky.

In 1937, my dad bought a brand new Chevy for $800.00 cash. We had nine people living in our two- bedroom house. Three adults slept in each bed. Money was scarce, but we survived. Saturday was bath day. Mother would gather up three of us to bathe together. The hot water we used for bathing was warmed up on the kitchen stove. I can still smell the soap she used for bathing and washing hair. We didn't have shampoo, just the bar soap.

We didn't have a television, only a radio. I remember one radio program that was very scary. It opened with the sound of a squeaking door. Mother always listened to soap operas. On Saturday mornings, a kid's show called "Let's Pretend" came on. We also listened to "The Green Hornet," "Tonto," and "The Lone Ranger."

✓ The Milkman
By S. A. Tolan of Alpena, Michigan
Born 1949

It was a frosty morning as the sun slowly rose on that beautiful day. We were eating breakfast while the coffee was brewing for Dad. We appreciated our mom's early chores, making the house smell good and feel warm. We three kids were getting ready for another school day while Dad was gathering his lunch box and heading out so that he could get to work early. We could hear those famous familiar sounds of the glass milk bottles in their metal containers headed to the back door to be sat out on the porch. Mom had already placed the empties out to be replaced with full new ones. She was still organized even with the morning rush. She had asked for chocolate milk as a treat that particular morning! What a gal! We knew we had better hurry to get our daily ride on the white milk truck from our friendly driver, "Speedy."

Speedy was waiting patiently for a few more minutes for us in his wagon near the garage. The ride down to the end of the road was a special treat just for us. We could walk, however, the "taxi" was a tradition and much appreciated during bad weather. As he drove, we smiled, thinking how lucky we were to have such a wonderful friend that had his wits so early in the morning; we were blessed. When he finally retired, we were very saddened. No more friendly smiles or advice. We had to go to the store for milk and also had to walk to the highway to catch the school bus. We knew he missed us also. Some family friends stated that he had enjoyed our many talks. We saved the milk tops for years for Saturday movie giveaways. It was a double pleasure.

✓ The Old Victrola
By Louise Kane of Traverse City, Michigan
Born 1928

When I was growing up during the Great Depression, I spent all of my summer, Easter, and Christmas vacations at my grandparents' farm. It was about 30 miles from where I lived in the city. Their farm was a couple of miles from the nearest town, off the graveled county road and on a two-track lane with woods and swampland on both sides. It was a typical farm in the 1930s. There was no electricity, no running water, and no rural mail delivery. Alas, I loved spending every moment there with my grandma and grandpa. Nothing inside the house or outside was forbidden me or taboo, although I did have a healthy respect for the two horses that my grandpa and bachelor Uncle Frank used in the fields.

There was just one thing in the old farmhouse that really fascinated me— probably because I wasn't able to understand at first how it worked. That item was the old-fashioned Victrola record player that stood in the parlor. The cover opened up on little brass hinges and about six heavy black records were stacked standing up in the bottom of the cabinet. My grandma showed me how to carefully lay a record on the turntable, making sure the spindle fit in the little hole in the center. To make it work one had to slowly turn the crank on the side of the Victrola to "wind it up." After a switch was released, the record began to slowly revolve around; an arm with a needle was swung over and gently placed on the edge of the record. What happened next was magic! There was music—Jeanette MacDonald and Nelson Eddy singing "The Indian Love Call" to each other or Enrico Caruso singing something in Italian from the operas "Fedora" or "La Vuive."

I had yet to develop an ear for classical music, so I had little attention span after I had played a couple of records. I was more interested in the mechanics of the Victrola, especially changing the needles that wore out after a few songs. However, for a few years I just recycled them, using the same six or seven needles over and over again.

One day I thought I had broken the Victrola and was almost afraid to tell my grandma. I had put the record on the spindle, carefully placed the needle, and stood back to listen. Unfortunately, the sound was awful. It was so slow and slurred that it didn't make any sense. My grandma tried to get it to work as well. She changed the needle, but that still didn't make a difference. The problem was finally assessed at noontime when Uncle Frank came in for dinner. He reminded us that we had both forgotten to turn the crank on the side! This experience was a good one in teaching me to do things in "counted steps." After that experience, I would look at something, know that it took perhaps four or five steps to

complete, and would count to myself as I did them. I have followed this rule all my life: in cooking, cleaning, farm chores, schoolwork, and even years later in my nursing career. It also taught me to own up to a problem that might be my fault, no matter the consequences. Lots of times, there was hardly a problem at all.

✓ Trips to Kalkaska
By Foster McCool of Kalkaska, Michigan
Born 1916

When I was a child, we had no television, just radio, and it was a fairly new concept. WLS, WKAR, and WGN are a few stations that I remember. There were a couple more; I just can't remember them. We listened to Amos & Andy and Lum & Abner every night.

My sister, brothers, and I walked ¾ of a mile to our one-room schoolhouse. We had deep snow and our roads were not plowed as they are now. There were small country stores scattered around where people could usually get to them. They were usually within four or five miles of anywhere. Our store was called Sigma and it was about three miles away. Kalkaska, the county seat, was ten miles away. It was an all day experience to make the trip. We would go shopping and have our wheat made into flour there. When the entire family went, we filled the sleigh with loose straw and covered up with heavy cowhide robes. It took about two or three hours to go just one-way. When we arrived, my dad put the team up in Hainstock's livery barn and gave them hay and oats. We children were given some money to do our Christmas shopping. When we arrived home, the team had to be put in their stalls and fed. Afterwards, the other farm chores had to be done and the cows had to be milked. It was a long, cold day as I remember it.

Growing up, I recall that we were better off than most of our neighbors. We had hot and cold running water, a bathtub, and an indoor toilet. We lived in a two-story house with an attic. There was a large water tank located in the attic, which piped water to the lower floors. Water was pumped up to the tank in the attic with a gasoline, one-cylinder engine. Baths were taken every Saturday night and I don't ever remember taking them any more often than that. Occasionally, the water tank in the attic would run over and water would cascade down through the ceiling! That was always such a disaster! We had a big box telephone and each party on our line had a distinctive ring. Our ring was four short rings. Our mail was delivered by a mailman with a horse and buggy or sled. Electric power did not get to the farm until about 1938. Before that, our lighting was pretty bad—by kerosene lamps and lanterns. When electric power arrived, it was such a joy to be able to flip a switch and have light!

I began high school in 1930 and drove a Model-T Ford car until the roads were blocked by snow. Before I graduated from high school in 1934, my dad bought an Essex sedan. What a big improvement! I did not participate in school sports because I had farm work to do. Graduating from high school did not mean we went off to college. The great depression was in full swing. We had no money. I had decided to continue doing what I knew how to do, farm! Only two or three of my classmates went on to college. Only one of them is still living. The two of us held a class reunion in 2012.

Since we did not have much money, I learned frugality early. I married at age 25 to a lovely girl I met at the Grange Hall square dancing. I still love her and we will celebrate our 70th anniversary on Feb 15, 2013. We have six children. Right now, I am 96 years old and have never been sick.

I can thank our God that I was born to grow up and live in the great, GREAT country, the United States of America. We enjoy freedom and liberty that people all over the world yearn for.

Adventures on (and to) the AuSable River
By Cindi Strong of Traverse City, Michigan
Born 1954

In a small cabin in the deep woods of the Huron forest surrounding the AuSable River Valley, I woke to the gentle but firm hand of my father, shaking me. It was my turn to go fishing with him. It was still dark, the sun hadn't risen yet, and we had to get going so we could make it to the river before sunrise. I carefully wriggled out from between my sisters who were sharing the same bed me, trying not to wake them. I quickly and quietly grabbed some sweat pants, sweatshirt, and jacket, and then followed my dad to the car.

I then watched, still half asleep, as he loaded the car with fishing gear. Uncle Sonny was doing the same thing over at his cabin: getting ready. Our aluminum boat was already waiting for us at the landing owned by the resort.

The ride to the river, down the old two track lower landing road, is one of my favorite memories. It twisted and turned, went up and down the lay of the land, and cut through high banks. Roots stuck out that scraped the car, making that high-pitched scraping sound. There was one part of the road that split and then came back together again. It was there that my dad and uncle would revert to a couple of kids themselves. There was a long-standing bet that my uncle could split off and beat my dad to the end of it. I remember the keys shaking and jiggling in the ignition as we bounced our way to the end of the split. My dad was the more cautious of the two. I know this because I had been in my uncle's car on many occasions over the years. Sure enough, as the roads edged closer and closer to becoming one again, I caught a glimpse of my uncle's car through the trees, just ahead of us. He merged in just in time to take the lead. I believe that most times, they staged it for the passengers on the edge of their seats, but once in a while, I could sense that edge of reality to the race between them.

By the time we pulled up to the place that the boats were tied up, I was fully awake. All senses were firing on high alert. It was understood that we went about our business with a stealth and respect for the quiet hush of the early day. As my father carried poles, tackle, and sandwiches to the boat, I was free to explore the shoreline in hopes to find a tiny toad or any such creature that would amuse my love of such things.

The steam was rising off the river. The anticipation of the catch was thick in the air as my father and uncle discussed river conditions. "It's like glass," they would say, "perfect conditions for fly-fishing!" When it was time to get into the boat, I could hear the banging noises echoing across the river and bouncing off the shoreline as I balanced my way into the seat, magnifying every little move I made. After rowing a few feet offshore, Dad started the Johnson and we were on our way. In my mind, I can still smell the river, feel the cool moisture in the air, and see the menacing look of trees bent over the banks in front of the thick, dark forests. The boat lifted slightly at the bow where I sat (the best seat in the house) as we motored and navigated our way upstream. I felt the light prickle of a dragonfly on my knee as I sat very still to keep it there. My senses were 'drunk" with input. The dawn sky was lightening from deep reds to pinkish-oranges and the riverbanks had their beckoning trees-stumps with holes of who-knows-what that lived there. There were high, sandy banks that were riddled with holes of the tiny birds that nested there. The AuSable held all the jewels above and below the surface that could keep a kid like me mesmerized for hours. It was then that I learned to bait a hook and to hold a fish as to not get finned. I was occasionally subjected to a string of profanities, as the "big one" would get away from dad or Uncle Sonny. These memories stay alive in me just like the AuSable runs through me in my blood: with no separation. A part of me is still fishing with Dad on the AuSable River.

✓ The Mastodon
By Stephen M. Remenar of Roscommon, Michigan
Born 1936

In 1942, my dad bought a farm up north in Michigan. The farm and four other farms surrounding ours had a drainage problem. In 1944, the farmers involved collectively hired a dredging company to clean out an overgrown ditch that was causing the problem. While dredging the ditch, the operator dug up the skull of a mastodon! My dad was at work at the time, but the farmer whose farm adjoined ours was on the site. The operator said that they needed to get the skull washed off, so he went to another farmer's house to get a trailer. When he came back, he loaded it up and took it back to the farm where he was staying. He then washed it off and locked it up in a shed, thinking "finders keepers!"

Since the ditch was on the border of two farms, a surveyor was hired to determine whose farm it was actually located on. It was determined that it was on our property. All digging stopped, and archeologists from the University of Michigan came out and did their own digging. They found about 75% of the bones.

My dad had to get a lawyer and take the operator to court. The judge ruled in our favor. A few days later, my dad came home from work, hooked up the trailer, told me to jump into the car, and he drove to where the skull was stored. We waited until the sheriff came. He took a hammer and chisel and knocked the padlock off. Then we loaded the skull into the trailer and took it home.

When word got out, we had a lot of people stopping by to see it. My dad wanted to give it to the university but they said that they would rather buy it from us. So my dad figured out how much his share of the dredging cost was and that was the amount he asked (and got) for it.

One day, my friend Harry came running to the house and told me to come with him. We went to the ditch that now had running water; he jumped in and started walking around. The water was about a foot deep. He said, "Come step here." There was a bone! We thought we would bring it up to the house like a couple of safari hunters, but we were unable to pull it up. Sadly, we had to tell my dad we couldn't' do it. He came and pulled it out. It was the shoulder blade. That mastodon is still on display at the University of Michigan Natural Science Museum.

The Mastodon

✓ Strawberries
By John Duerr of Ann Arbor, Michigan
Born 1947

I am in the produce section of my local supermarket. I notice the strawberries packaged in those clear plastic cartons, the ones that are almost impossible to figure out how to open without some sort of tool. The berries themselves are beautiful. They are a rich, deep red color and come in an interesting variety of irregular shapes. They are huge; the larger ones would take at least three bites. I turn over the carton and discover that they are a product of Chile; they could just as easily have come from Argentina, Mexico, California, or Indonesia. While I admire their appearance and marvel at the transportation system that brought them to me, I will not to buy them. You see, I have had *real* strawberries. I remember real strawberries and I don't want to cheapen that memory with these tasteless monsters dressed up to look like real strawberries.

Real strawberries were grown by a woman named Francis Durance in my hometown of Charlevoix in northern Michigan. Francis maintained a strawberry patch on her Centennial Farm about a mile from the neighborhood IGA grocery store where I worked during the summers of my high school years in the early '60s. Beginning in late June or early July and for two or three weeks thereafter, Francis would bring in two or three crates of strawberries every few days.

Most of our produce was delivered by truck to the back of the store and placed in a walk-in cooler until it was ready to be put out. Not Francis' strawberries. Francis would arrive around ten in the morning in her old station wagon and park near the front door. Francis was a slight woman, maybe 5' 2", thin, and wiry. She could have been in her sixties or seventies; it was hard to tell. She never seemed to age—even many years later when she celebrated her 100th birthday. She would be wearing a sundress, sometimes overlaid with an apron, sometimes not. She always had her straw hat with the frayed brim atop her silver hair, which contrasted, with her craggy nut-brown face. Overall, her appearance was that of a ten year-old boy's ideal grandmother. When she lugged her berries into the store, she always had a smile on her face and a twinkle in her eye.

I would take the berries from her and set the crates of berries on a couple of wooden pop crates near the front door and adjacent to the checkout counter. If I had time, I would grab a magic marker and make a one-word sign that just said "Durance" and tape it to one of the berry crates. Word would get around the small store quickly. It was not long before the makeshift berry display was surrounded by shopping carts piloted by anxious women who were impatient for their turn to select two, three, or even four quarts of Francis' berries.

Inevitably, the news of the availability of Francis' strawberries would spread throughout the neighborhood and there would be an influx of folks, all hoping that they were not too late. Those that didn't make it within 30 minutes were usually disappointed. On one occasion, Helen Meggison who lived just a block down the street was in the store when Francis arrived. She quickly snatched up two quarts of berries for her family and left for home. On her way, she saw her neighbor, Lucille Bergmann, outside her house watering her flowers and hollered to her that Durance berries were in at the IGA. Moments later Lucille came puffing in the front door just in time to see another neighbor claim the last quart. From that day forward, Helen and Lucille maintained a pact. If either one was in the store when the berries arrived, they were to grab four quarts—two for each of them. I never knew either of them to fail to keep the bargain.

Because of my privileged position working in the store, I was almost always among the first to know when Francis had arrived and I developed my own modus operandi. I would quickly grab two quarts and set them aside. I would try to get ones from the bottom layer of the crate that still had dew droplets glistening on the sides of the berries. Just before my lunch break, I would grab a pint of Maxbaurs half-and-half from the diary case, ring up the berries and half-and-half on my mother's charge account, and jump on my bike for the quick two-block ride down the alley home. I would slice up one of the quarts of berries, being careful to capture the precious juice that oozed out during the slicing. Berries, juice, and half-and-half (no sugar needed) would go into one large bowl and become my lunch. Those lunches were so wonderful that even the memory of them still tastes good. I'd leave the second quart in the fridge for the rest of the family to share. Mom never complained about the spurious charges I left on her account. I guess she figured it was a good trade.

Yes, I will pass on the Chilean strawberries at the supermarket. I will avoid the disappointment hidden beneath their magnificent appearance. I will, however, look at them and remember when life was simpler and the world was a little fresher and a little sweeter.

Shanties and BB Guns
By Ron Heinz of Oscoda, Michigan
Born 1943

When a child of nine years old endures the winter winds howling around his/her ears, recreational pursuits seem rather limited. How did we ever survive back in the day? Television was a brand new technology and extremely austere. Back then, the Internet, cell phones, Blackberries, and satellite technologies in all forms were not even a shadow on the most distant horizon. However, we did have BB guns and six-pronged fishing spears—both of which played a major role in two of my following recollections.

It was a blustery day when my pal Hammie and I exited the shackles of the old three-story schoolhouse. The same designer must have drafted all of those early 20th century school buildings that appear throughout small town mid-America. They were always rectangular in shape, three stories high, and of brick construction. This particular penitentiary of higher learning was but a block's walk from my house and twice that distance from my cohorts, so our nefarious activities were confined to a rather limited range. Directly downhill and but a stone's throw from my parents' home was a backwater bayou that connected to the Au Sable River. This bayou proved to be a popular ice-fishing spot for the local anglers. At that frigid time of year, it blossomed with a dozen or so fishing shanties.

This particular recollection centers on after-school free time, me, Hammie, the frozen shanty-covered bayou, and my prized BB gun. I would not want to imply that I was reckless with that BB gun since the standard barrage of parental warnings regarding its appropriate use was always on my mind. However, I was always quite willing to demonstrate the gun's penetration capabilities whenever a challenging target caught my eye. Soon, one such opportunistic target did just that.

I can still recall my boastful diatribe as we crunched along the frozen surface and came upon Chris Grable's apparently vacant tarpaper fish shanty. It was obvious that Chris was not in residence since there was no flume pouring from the fragile structure's smoke stack. "I'll bet I can punch a BB completely through that old shack," I huffed while bringing the gun to bare. Hardly had the slap of BB striking tarpaper faded before the shanty door sprang open and a very agitated and red-faced Chris Grabel appeared. Six long strides brought the enraged octogenarian down upon us, an ungloved hand rubbing the growing welt on the back on his neck. Frozen in our tracks like terrified rabbits, we could neither flee nor speak as old Chris snatched the offending BB gun from my trembling hands. "Tell your Dad to pick this danged thing up at my house," Chris fumed as he stalked off the ice toward his home on the hill.

It was only a day or two later when my dad asked me, "Ron, where's your BB gun?" "I left it at Hammie's," I lied. Dad did not reply. A week went by before the question came up again, and once more, I pinned the disappearance on Hammie, only this time I somehow knew that the trap had long since been sprung. It seems that good 'ol Chris had called Dad to spill the beans on my indiscretions within moments of having been gunned down (so to speak). Eventually, I earned my BB gun rights back but it took a while.

That same ice-covered bayou comes to mind during another poignant miscalculation. Again, Hammie was my accomplice, and in this case, the victim. It was an incredibly cold mid-day Saturday when we decided, once again, to go ice fishing. We were using an aluminum-framed and canvas-covered fishing shanty in the hopes of warding off hypothermia in the sub-zero temperatures. Our quarries were the large northern pike that prowl beneath the ice; our means of conquest involved long, six-pronged fishing spear. A small, live sucker bait was suspended beneath the ice while we would watch for an approaching fish form the warmth of the shanty.

The shelter was assembled and erected in record time and the only remaining task was to use an ice spud to chop a rectangular three foot by three-foot hole through the eighteen inches of solid ice. I began this arduous endeavor outside while Hammie hunkered warm and comfortable inside next to the shanty's blazing stove. My chop, chop, chopping was progressing well when it occurred to me that I was shouldering the bulk of the grueling work for our mutual gain. With that realization, I summoned my partner to do his share of the work. We traded places: him doing the chopping, and me warm and toasty inside. Initially all went well as I listened to the thump, thump, thumping of the spud against the ice. The next wound that reached my ears was a muffle crunch, followed by an unmistakable splash!

Apparently I had come very close to penetrating the ice during my term with the spud, and Hammie, not realizing my progress, had stepped into the center of the soon-to-be fishing hole. As I emerged from the shanty, only his wide-eyed and startled head appeared above the slushy water. The only good news was that the large block of ice had been shoved beneath the remaining ice rather than sliding back into the hole above my partner's submerged body. As I recall, I took advantage of the finally realized fishing opportunities while Hammie shuffled off for the long walk home—more like a medieval night sheathed in a rapidly forming coat of ice instead of a suit of armor.

✓ **Life on the Cherry Farm**
By Arthella Dickerson of Boyne City, Michigan
Born 1933

On July 29, 1933, I was born to Elzada and Arthur Erfourth on the Millspaugh Cherry Farm. The farm was located north of town on Wildwood Harbor Road. My father was caretaker there for almost 20 years. Mom told me about how the cherry pickers filed in at the door of our large back cement porch into the bedroom just to see me, the new baby. They would come in, one by one, take a look at me, and then exit out the other door. I'm sure many will remember picking cherries there. I know my brother and I did. This is how we earned money for our schoolbooks and clothes. Would you believe that uncle Jim wanted to name me Cherry? I'm so glad that he did not get his way.

Wildwood Harbor Road used to have a very sharp curve that connected right into our driveway. Since then the road has been reconstructed to make it a more gradual curve. Back then, the snow would blow across the field and really drift there. I can remember a time when we could have walked off the snow bank there and walk right on top of the bus. That's when we used to actually get a lot of snow. This was also a meeting place for the bobsledders to start from and go all the way into town. I can remember watching them from my bedroom window and hearing lots of screaming and laughter. Of course, this also was a good spot for my brother, Ray, and I to get on our hand sleighs and ride down to Park Street. We would then hurry back up the hill before Mom and Dad got done shopping; we were already forewarned that we were not allowed. It was so much fun though, and we always hoped we wouldn't' meet a car on the way, especially our parents'! Many times, we got to go to town on Saturdays and go to the movies while they shopped. This was a big treat for us. We also used to ski in the orchard; we always ducked the limbs to make it more challenging.

I remember being baptized in the Tainter School/Church, whatever it was being used for at that time. The ladies used to have a quilting bee there, too. My folks used to have a lot of house parties on Saturday nights. Mart wicker used to call square dances, and his wife Alice would play the piano and Mr. Anderson played the fiddle. We kids would fall asleep on piles of coats on beds usually upstairs. I remember one time we were at the Leist farm and we were all snowed in. The men helped do the chores and the women made breakfast for us all. We didn't leave till the plows came through.

I had a Shetland pony, King, which we kids really enjoyed. We would pick up rocks in the orchard with him and the stone boat that Dad had made for him. I remember one day Uncle Jim got the idea he would ride King to check out the cherry trees. Well, King had other ideas about an adult riding him; he stopped quickly and Uncle Jim flew right over his head onto the ground! King just galloped right back into the barn. I remember that I got my first store-bought coat from the money that we sold him for. I liked my new coat, but I missed my pony.

I remember our first telephone. Naturally, it was a party line. Our number I've never forgotten: 298-F22, two long, and two short rings. Often we would listen to the radio, a big one that stood on the floor. Usually Dad controlled it. We would listen to the news at breakfast time and Frolics at suppertime. The Grand 'Ol Opry was our favorite program to listen to on Saturday nights. That is when I would make fudge or popcorn. When it was my turn to use the radio, I would turn it to my favorite station, WMBN in Petoskey. All the latest hits of the

Hit Parade would be playing on that station, and we learned the words to all the songs.

In the winter, we went to Smeltania on Ice. So many shanties would be there, with lights strung all around. It literally looked like a city on ice! In the spring there would be smelt dipping. They filled whatever they could find with the fish: buckets, baskets, tubs, and pails. We had lots of good smelt dinners. Makes me wonder: what happened to all the smelt? That river then curved around behind the old Eagle Hall where we used to go dancing and to dinners. Seems there was always something going on there. Mom and Dad were members for years; Mom was a charter member of the Women's Auxiliary.

In the winter, Dad would groom our horses, Duke and Dugan, and braid their tails and manes. He would then put on the fancy harnesses with ivory rings, connect them to the sleigh, and take hayrides all around the town and countryside.

I remember the old clock on the co-op. It would chime out the time; I can remember counting out the bongs. I also remember our Chamber of Commerce building now at one time was a little restaurant. I also remember the nighttime curfew at 10:00 pm. My boyfriend and I were reminded of the curfew one night while observing the moonshine on the water at the dock in Veterans Park. The curfew whistle still blows after 65 years but now at 10:25 pm.

I loved our old school across from the library. I recall that our school nurse was Mrs. Geiken. She was always there for anyone if they had problems or didn't feel well. I went to that school from Kindergarten through the 11th grade. We moved down to the Flint area in 1950, so I wasn't able to complete my schooling there. My dad had gotten a job on a farm in Swartz Creek. I lived in the Flint area for 44 years until my husband, Jim, and I bought 20 acres in Elmira in September of 1994. I was glad to be back in the area again. It was nice to see all of my relatives that live in the area and old classmates of the class of 1951. After I showed Jim my pretty old church in Boyne City, First Presbyterian, we decided to become members there. We have been going to that church ever since. I'm very happy to be back in Boyne!

Hanging Out Downtown
By Steven Webb of Fife Lake, Michigan
Born 1951

I have so many memories growing up in northern Michigan. I have lived here all of my life and wouldn't trade a day of it for anything. My grandparents raised their children here, as did my parents, our children, and grandchildren. Right now, my great-grandchildren still call northern Michigan their home. My home was in Kalkaska where we lived a simple life with simple pleasures. Dad was the breadwinner and Mom was a stay-at-home mom. That was the norm in those days.

Kalkaska was a different place back then. The village was much smaller and everyone seemed to know everyone. Downtown was abuzz with many a shopper. The buildings were all occupied by grocery stores, bakeries, restaurants, shoe stores, clothing stores, and hardware stores. For entertainment, our family would drive there and park in the parking lot facing Main Street. We watched cars go by and would see what all was happening. We paid attention to who was with whom, and what they were doing. As we looked around, we noticed others doing the same. Nowadays we have a lot of cars driving through, not a lot of people walking on the main street

Steven's father holding him in 1951

334

of town. Most of the shops that offered so much back then have all closed their doors. I miss those days. The big hotel was on the corner where you could rent rooms. On Saturday evenings, the hotel would open up the basement so that people would have a place to take their sweetheart dancing. They served up spirits and food as well. In years prior, you could try your hand at bowling. Now, all that roams the halls of the hotel are *real* spirits, according to the local newspaper.

As a youngster, I did some funny things. One day at school, I played sick so that the teacher would send me home. On the way home, I decided to stop and play. My mistake was that I didn't walk far enough away from the school and therefore my teacher saw me playing. She informed the principal who tried to give me a ride home. I refused to get into his car because I was told not to talk to strangers. I ended up running the whole way home. When I arrived, the principal was at my house talking with Mom, filling her in on what had happened. She decided that if I was sick then I should see the doctor. An appointment was made. The doctor told me to drop my pants. Meanwhile, he was putting on his rubber gloves and told me to bend over. Apparently, my mom and the doctor thought I needed to be taught a lesson! Needless to say, I never lied to my teacher again!

Another time I was walking home from school with other neighborhood kids when along the way we passed the local funeral home. Being the curious kids we were, we thought we would go into the funeral home to take a look at the bodies. We would walk in file past the casket as we looked down at the lifeless body. One of us would wander into another room and holler to the others, "Hey! There's another one in here!" We did this routine a few days until the funeral director asked us if we knew the deceased. We admitted to him that we didn't, so we were asked to promptly leave.

As I got older, I had a paper route. I sold 115 "grit" papers for 15 cents per paper. I made five cents per paper. It took me two days to deliver all my papers on my bike. My customers looked forward to their paper each week and it was my job not to disappoint them. I delivered on my bike whether it was raining, snowing, or scorching hot outside.

I rode my bike all over and put many miles on it, especially in the summer. I would ride

Steven's father with his boys on a coon hunt in 1963

to Log Lake for a swim or to the mill pond to go froggin'. I used the bike to ride to school as well. In those days, they held all grade levels in one building. Now, Kalkaska has four school buildings to accommodate all of the children.

As I grew older, I had more chores to do. Our home was heated with wood and it was my job to keep the wood box filled in the basement. It was quite a job for a young boy but I was up to the task. Dad was a coon hunter and sometimes he would take me along. I would find myself walking the banks of the river at 4:00AM wishing that dad would hurry up and get his coon so that we could go home to bed. Come Sunday, our family would drive to the country to have dinner with Grandpa and Grandma. They didn't have electricity or running water. Grandma had a wood cook stove. It was the kids' job to take the bucket outdoors to collect water from the pump for grandma to use for dinner and for washing dishes afterward. She would heat the water on the stove for the dishes. Grandma would always announce her dinner guests in the local newspaper, just as so many did back then. I felt that we were lucky to have a hand pump at the kitchen sink inside our house. It made things much simpler.

Grandma had an outhouse to use, when necessary. I remember that one day my cousin bolted out of the outhouse, announcing to all of us that he had been stung by a bee. He was rubbing his bottom at the time. I'm sure it wasn't funny to him, but we all laughed. Grandpa raised honeybees to collect honey. Maybe one of those bees lost its way back to the hive and ended up in the outhouse.

I have been married for 40 years now. No, things are not the same as the years that have past but you know what? Our present will someday be our grandchildren's "Good Ole Days," so not all is lost.

✓ Shanty Days
By Lindsay Paul Abraham of West Branch, Michigan
Born 1950

I was 12 years old on that cold February day of 1962 in Pigeon, Michigan. My dad, Sylvester, his best buddy, Al, and I were preparing for the drive to Saginaw Bay to go ice fishing. The temperature was about -30°F. We had 24 inches of snow on the ground and 6 inches of fresh snow, that came overnight. By noon, the roads were clean and we were finished with our church duties at St. Francis Borgia Catholic Church. Father Kerchman was planning on coming along with us but he needed to be with his family that afternoon in Saginaw. He always made our Sunday brighter. Every Sunday, without fail, he preached a sermon more suitable to a Baptist preacher than a Catholic priest. Consequently, he kept everyone on the edge of their pews rather than falling asleep. He was my inspiration that prompted me to eventually go to the seminary. However, that is another story; let's go fishing first!

We hurried home so that we could change out of our suits and ties. Yes, you heard right: suits and ties. Those were the days when folks (kids included) dressed nice, especially on Sunday. We would wear a suit, tie, white shirt, and have our shoes shined. Women wore hats, lipstick, and high heels. They always smelled real sweet, too.

We had all of our 'necessities' packed in my dad's car: matches, two wooden boxes of kindling, charcoal, tuna fish sandwiches, salt water taffy from Florida, and plenty of bourbon and coffee for Dad and Al. Everything else that we needed was already at the shanties. I had the clothes that I had planned to wear for the trip already laid out. The articles of clothing consisted of long johns, thermal socks with bread bags to water-proof them, two pairs of jeans (one pair of my own and one bigger pair I stole from my brother to go over the top of mine), a tee shirt, a wool sweater, a sweat shirt with hood, an old winter coat, a scarf, a stocking cap, and wool mittens. Those wool mittens were very warm. Once you had them on, the best way to get them off was to stick your hand in your mouth, bite down, and pull it off. The texture and feel of the wool in my mouth was maddening; for the likes of me, that yucky imprint will forever be negatively etched in my memory. I loaded the boxes into the car while Dad got the sandwiches from Mom in the kitchen and kissed her goodbye between the laundry room and garage door entry. We jumped into the car and headed over to pick up Al.

When we arrived at Saginaw Bay, everything was white. The ice was three feet thick, so we simply drove out onto the bay and parked beside our shanties. Some of you may recall the movie "Grumpy Old Men." That was a close representation of the way it was at Mud Creek that day. There were at least 50 shanties scattered about the ice there. It was a small, cozy city on the water. All the shanties were unique and colorful. They were all hand-made of wood and tar paper with sled runners attached to the back side. You could simply tip the shanty over onto the runner, hitch up to your vehicle, and away you would go! My shanty was about eight feet by six feet on the inside. There was a two by two foot opening with a trap door in the corner floor.

Once I was inside with my supplies, I shut the door and light a lamp for light. It became like a darkroom inside once the door was closed. My first job was to put a fire into the small barrel stove. Once the fire settled in, I would toss in a few pieces of charcoal and the temperature would jump from below zero to 65 degrees in minutes. In no time, I would be stripping down to a tee shirt and one pair of pants (sometimes down to just my long johns.) Then I would be comfy and cozy. When the fire was hot and all was organized, I would open the trap door. There would be a thin layer of ice in the opening and I would spud it out and put the ice in a pot on to the stove for tea; my favorite was named "Constant Comment."

With water ready for tea and fry pan ready for preparing fresh fish that I would soon catch, I waited. If I did not have a catch, I would eat the tuna fish sandwiches or candy bars left behind on the shelf from earlier trips. I had a stash of at least six Almond Joy bars left behind from the last time. Once all this was done, I would blow out the lantern. Within seven minutes, my eyes would adjust and I would look down into the bay through the window into the water. I would drop my decoy, a carved wooden fish. It had a lead weight inside, was painted to match a fish, and shaped so that when you would lift up on the rope and release it, the decoy would swim in a circle. Hopefully it would attract a large Northern Pike so that I could spear it with my Uncle Adam's fish spear. If not a pike, then maybe some perch would swim by; in that case, I would drop down a Russian hook on a small pole and hope for them to take the bait. There is nothing better than pulling up a fair sized, freshly caught perch, cleaning it, and throwing it on the pan with butter. With the fire ablaze, wind howling around the shanty, subzero temperatures outside and the smell of fresh-caught fish on the inside, I was in pure bliss.

Before long, the three-foot-long pike came slowly into the window. I had my small pole with Russian hook in the water. As I attempted to pull up the line and grab my spear, the pike drew back from the window because of the upward movement of the Russian hook. I stopped, put the small pole in my mouth, and reached for my spear with still one eye on the pike. She moved back into the window and I eased the spear into the water a few inches and then propelled it down and into the huge pike! She was a monster fish; at least 36 inches long, fat, and full of eggs. Pulling her up and into the shanty was a struggle, as she was not wishing to come aboard! I clubbed her to unconsciousness, took her off the spear,

and opened the door. Blinded by the light, I threw her out into the cold to freeze instantly.

It was just then that I heard a commotion, a holler, a call for help. I stuck my head out the door, eyes still straining to adjust to the bright light. Some 50 yards to the south and 15 shanties away, stood Henry Gruber, from Bay Port, out of his shanty, in his underwear, calling for help to come save his shanty. It seems he had fallen asleep smoking and caught it on fire.

Dad and Al, who were just next to me on the ice, had heard the call and were gathering their wits about them. I had heard them earlier laughing in Al's shanty enjoying a drink and a short story. They were quick to respond. The trouble with this picture was that all of us had no bigger a container than a coffee can full of water to take as a fire extinguisher to tame the inferno! So, the picture I witnessed was about 50 men and half a dozen women running toward Henry's shanty, all with about eight ounces of water to fight the fire, to no avail. It was full ablaze. Henry was desperate, so he "whipped it out" and peed all he had toward the blaze, and so did the other men! The women watched in amazement. Some peed longer than others, some peed higher, and others failed to have an offering because of the cold temperature. Henry's shanty burned down to the ice. We all watched as he lost everything, left with only the shirt on his back. I look back at it now and realize that it was probably the worst disaster to occur on Saginaw Bay ever at that time, except for maybe a car falling into the thawed-up bay from waiting too long to collect his shanty.

Dad and Al offered to take Henry home because he was starting to freeze. There was a storm on the way, so I knew that school would be called off again on Monday. When Dad and Al were leaving to take Henry home, I asked my dad if I could stay the night. He agreed to leave me there to fish, read, and contemplate the great Lake Huron. He knew that I'd be safe, warm, and feeding on the eggs of that monstrous pike.

Late that night, about one or two in the morning, the snow started coming down gently and the wind had pulled back. Everything was very quiet; I think I actually heard the snow falling. I was reading a good book entitled "Hot Rod" when suddenly it sounded like a gun went off and my shanty rocked! I almost pooped my pants! The ice had, for some reason, fissured straight through and under my shanty! Mother Nature sure has her way! This was a first for me, so I stepped out of my shanty for safety and to look around and see if we were all sinking. The rest of the shanties were okay.

The snow ceased at around three in the morning and the sky cleared to reveal a full moon. Strange sights and sounds surrounded me. I could hear my boots "squeak-crunching" on the cold, fresh snow and the sounds of the shanties with their fires crackling into the subzero air. Every now and again, I'd hear a chuckle, a big laugh, some low conversation. Someone had their transistor radio playing low and I'd catch the quiet tones of a polka playing. The bright full moon created shadows of the shanties on the pure blanket of fresh snow. I looked to the north and the sky was shimmering. It was the most glorious display of the Aurora Borealis that I have seen to date. They always say, "Hind-sight is always 20-20." Because of that, today I always carry a camera with me. I wish I would have had a camera with me that night to capture its brilliance. My mind snapped shot after shot of my beautiful surroundings. The display of the huge moon, the smoking shanties and their shadows, the star-filled sky, and the shimmer of the northern lights are still stored in my heart to this day. It was an once-in-a-lifetime experience that I can only share now in words. I stood out there for a long time, just taking all of it in. I had a feeling of gratitude. I felt fortunate to be watching all this happen around me. It was a gift. From that day on, I realized how blessed we are to have this majesty constantly around us. I replay that evening in my mind's eye from time to time, for "mind candy." My plan, my dream, today 51 years later, is to build another shanty with runners, and pull it out onto our local lake, Peach Lake, and spend a night or two. I want to recapture that feeling just one more time.

My Childhood Memories
By Geri Moody of Glennie, Michigan
Born 1946

My mother, Nora was born in Boston, Massachusetts and attended twelve years of Catholic school. She was a city girl and never had any intentions of leaving. Shortly after her graduation in 1934, she and a friend went to a

Geri's parents, Nora and Al with Carol, Rita, Geri, Marge, and Butch

fortuneteller: something that would never have been allowed in her family. The fortuneteller told her that she would leave Boston, meet a man in a white coat, and have ten children. Of course, my mother did not believe her and just laughed. She was one of seven children, with three older in college and three younger still in school. One day, my mother's Aunt Anna from Michigan came to visit. Mom's mother asked if she would take Mom back to Michigan with her because times were tough. She had heard that there were many automotive jobs available there, so my mother left. While in Michigan, she met my father, Albert. He was a barber and was wearing a white coat. Yes, they married and had ten children. She raised nine; one was stillborn.

I was born in 1946 with three older and five younger siblings. My mother was the strongest and funniest "Irish" person in the world. Her faith was strong and she took in ironings and cleaned a hair salon in town for extra money. She graduated with honors and was by far smarter than any of us kids. My father was a barber by trade, but built three homes, fished, hunted, and farmed on top of that. His love for music made for fun times when we all got together. He taught himself to play the piano, violin, and the harmonica, and taught me to play the piano during late-night sessions in my youth. He always played "Irish Washwoman" for my mom. We played together whenever we got together up until he died at the age of 97. We had our own beef, venison, chicken, eggs, and garden vegetables of which my mother canned on the wood stove in the garage. The cellar held the potatoes, onions, and canned items. We also always had a freezer full of food. Mom made the best molasses and raisin bread. White bread and white sugar were never allowed—only wheat bread and brown sugar. We were also forbidden any type of pop or carbonated beverage. We drank KoolAid sweetened with honey or brown sugar. We never had Oleo, only real butter, and never had deep-fried foods. We had a basis meal every day and creamed tuna with biscuits on Fridays. We also ate lots of fruits: canned blueberries, strawberries, apples, pears, and applesauce. When spaghetti was served we were asked, "Would you like red or white?"

I always remember walking to town to go to the dentist. Once, with an ear infection, I went to a doctor's office, which was located upstairs in his home. In 1953, shortly after my brother, Frank was born; he got pneumonia and was laid under a tent that was placed over his bed. Mom signed the doctor's name for all of my school shots. I never received any shots or vaccination. I had my first doctor appointment was when I get pregnant in 1967. My parents treated all of our cuts, scrapes, or stepping on nails with kerosene, which never hurt, just smelled. They made their own butterfly bandages themselves.

I spent my young years going to the store

Geri's mom with her children

for a cardboard box to use to sled down Wards Hill near our home. I also went ice-skating with my older brother, Butch. I remember once, he and I were on our bikes going down a hill and he promised me a Dairy Queen if I beat him; I did, because halfway down his hat blew off and he stopped. All three homes that I lived and grew up in had a basement. Many younger years when it was raining, we would roller skate in the basement. I remember playing checkers and card games with Dad. He had so many card tricks, and he remembered them up into his older years. Once I had my very own Halloween party in our basement. It was great until Mom found two of my friends making out in one of the bedrooms and one girl smoking.

Before age ten, I remember waiting and hiding in the closet for Dad to come home from work. On Fridays, he would bring us ice cream. Grandpa Wenzel also lived with us and was sick in bed. Each morning we had to kiss him goodbye before leaving for school. Dad owned 80 acres out in the county with a small, one-room cabin. There were no utilities, but the woods were nice and it had a small creek on it. It was a Sunday tradition to go there and we loved it. We would walk over and visit our other grandpa, who owned the 80 acres adjoining. He would bring us a candy bar that he bought on his way home from church in his Model-A. After his death, we got the Model-A and I remember riding in the rumble seat and going to town to get something from Dairy Queen. Once an airplane crashed on that land and we had fun searching the woods for the wreckage. On one occasion, while I was in the outhouse singing my heart out, a bee flew into my mouth and stung me! Dad took us out trout fishing on occasion, but we could not make a sound. We also went perch fishing at the mouth of the AuSable River where it meets Lake Huron. We loved it. We would find the worms for bait underneath cow pies! Yuck! I remember that when grandma visited from Boston she would walk with all of us to the Lake Huron to swim. We always had a horse, a cow, chickens, ducks, and a dog in my earlier years. We went for many horse and buggy rides.

We never missed Sunday mass; during lent we went daily. My mother would walk there and my brother, Butch would ride his bike with a couple of us on handlebars or in the basket. All of us were baptized, had communion, and were confirmed. During any bad storms, we all knelt and said the rosary. If any of us acted up during praying, we would start all over. I remember Mom and Dad arguing about how the church always preached about love but not much about the devil. Dad seemed upset. Mom, on the other hand, stuck up for the church, stating the nuns taught her well and with much respect, even though they were strict. She also told dad and us that she was taught that the good Lord had twelve apostles and one turned against him, therefore, one out of twelve priests may not be perfect. Dad would always reply, "Well, did we have to be blessed with all of them here in Oscoda!" They both had a lot of faith but I know that Mom had the most. Over her 86 years of life, she proved many times just what a lot of faith can accomplish.

Discipline for the younger years was a time-out—standing in the corner facing the wall. Once, my sister, Marge had to push a peanut with her nose on the cement floor in the garage and spend the night in the root cellar. In the teenage years, I received Dad's 'ol razor strap—a lot. I remember that I used to talk back and argue a lot. In school, we could only wear pants on Friday, therefore the welts on my legs. I was always embarrassed of it. Once after coming home from a date, I climbed into bed with my sister, Marge to discuss it. I suppose that we were laughing too much and making too much noise because Dad kept telling us to be quiet. When we did not obey him, he proceeded to throw a glass of water onto my hair, which was up in rollers for work the next day. We did not have a hair dryer, so that definitely shut me up. I never held it against my dad, knowing that he was a strict German. He raised nine children who never went to jail or got into any trouble.

At a very young age, I was taught of the importance of work. My sister, Marge and I sold garden vegetables out of our little red wagon, going door to door. I also peeled potatoes for a restaurant that was next to my father's barbershop. From the time I was 11, I helped my brother, Butch with his paper route. When he left to spend his 12th grade year of high school at Green's Barber College in Detroit, I took over the entire route. I had 54 customers, with daily deliveries of the "Detroit Times." At the age of fourteen, I would walk to and from my job at a local grocery store. Actually, all my brothers and sisters worked there at one time or another over the years. In between working and going to school, I did a lot of night babysitting. The money that I earned was kept by my mother. I was not allowed any of it during my teen years and while living at home with my parents, I paid them five dollars a week. I did not mind because my mother cleaned our room, picked up our clothes, and had an outfit ironed daily for school and/or work. It was worth it.

I had home chores along with going to school and working at the grocery store. I weeded the garden the thinned the carrots early in the morning before the sun was too hot. I also had the job of sweeping out the garage, washing all the garage windows, mopping down the basement stairs and hauling out the wash from the wringer washer in the basement. Once I had to hold down the chicken while my brother, Butch chopped off his head. Then I picked off all the feathers. I also remember helping my father nail down the sub floor for our new home in 1956. Also during the junior and senior high school years, I helped dad on his day off to go to the eighty acres in the country to cut down trees for lumber. Many hours were spent buzzing up the logs, running through a planer, and making huge lumber piles for another larger home to be built.

I never spent the night at a friend's house and never attended a school function or football game. I had to quit band in the seventh grade because of my working schedule. I graduated in 1964, had one day off, and then started a new job working at the Base Exchange at the Wurtsmith A.F.B. I was very excited. My boss at the grocery store offered me $1.15 an hour if I would stay, now being old enough to sell liquor, but I refused and went to work at the base for $0.98 per hour.

To my surprise, my parents had saved $2100 of the money I earned all those years; with that money, my father had purchased me a 1964 blue Ford Custom. It was a new car but it sure was ugly—with no white walls or radio. I talked dad into getting the radio. In 1966, and engaged to be married, I took the car back to the dealership to sell; they offered me $750.00. I almost died, but learned quickly how cars depreciate. I finally sold it to the person with the best offer of $850.00: my father. That car was in our family, from one brother to the other, then finally to an old man in town who ended up having it for years.

The Old Gravel Road
By Barbara Rosso of Traverse City,
Michigan
Born 1924

In my eighty-ninth year, I look back to early days visiting in Traverse City. In the 1930's, my father drove our family from Grand Rapids to Traverse City in his Buick. We spent a week at one of the little white cottages on the Bay, near Three Mile Road. The four of us walked across Munson Avenue, which was a gravel road, for meals at a farmhouse. Now, whenever I visit my daughter and her family on Elk Lake, I remember the old gravel road which is now a five lane highway going north. I am blessed to have early, happy memories!

Stuck On a SnowBank
By Richard S. Kler of Mancelona, Michigan
Born 1938

When I was about eight years old, we lived on Satterly Lake Road. That's about three and a half miles north of Mancelona.

Winters back then, were quite harsh and the county didn't plow our portion of Satterly Lake Road. They used the snow blower on Doerr Road, which built a snow bank across our road. The road was clear, on the other side of the Bank.

My dad had a Model-T Ford at that time, and he thought he could make it over the bank and then drive the quarter mile to our house. The car stopped on top of the snow bank and wouldn't move, so dad left it there and three days later, he was able to drive it off the bank, and home.

The Old Icehouse
By Laura Greve of Traverse City, Michigan
Born 1929

When I was a child, I lived with my mother and father in a house near Portage Lake in Manistee County, Michigan. Across the county road that ran past the house, there stood an icehouse, which belonged to a neighbor. It had been built into a hillside, and was used to store blocks of ice, which had been cut from the lake during the winter. When my friend

and I were about ten years old or so, we took great pleasure in sneaking, unnoticed by the owner, into the icehouse on a hot summer day to climb the stacked, sawdust-covered blocks and sit on the topmost block to enjoy the cool, half-light within. We did this until, somehow or another, the owner sensed our presence and came out and chased us out. The icehouse is gone now is was no longer used, but the memory of it and this exciting childhood adventure still remains some 70 years later.

Pennies From Above
By Chuck Cornell of Levering, Michigan
Born 1932

It was the summer of 1937. My parents worked in town, and each day would drop me off at Mosswood Park, which covered many blocks with woods, playing fields, gardens, plus jungle gyms, swings, and exercise bars. Pete, Howard, Ronnie, and I were 5 and 6 year-old "regulars" who hung out there on a daily basis.

The park refreshment stand sold soda pop at 5 cents a 12-ounce bottle, Hostess cupcakes, 2 for a nickel—with ¼ inch of real chocolate frosting, licorice sticks a foot long, plus many other goodies for a penny. It was Wonderland itself. Once in a while, one of our parents might supply a couple of pennies, or maybe even a nickel! The rule was; lucky ones had to share with less fortunate buddies, but usually trips to the refreshment stands were only to ogle or imagine.

One day we spied some "big kids," maybe 14 or 15 years old, showing off on the exercise bars. Suddenly, Pete blurted, "Betcha can't hang by your knees from that bar and touch the ground without falling off." "We can too!" "Naw, Never!" "Well, by gosh, Ya' did it. You guys were pretty good!"

Soon after they left, Ronnie spotted a shiny penny in the sawdust under the bar. Suddenly, we all were scrambling around sifting sawdust through our fingers.

"I found a nickel!" "Here's two pennies!" "Wow, a dime!"

We marched triumphantly to the refreshment stand. An, ya' know, it wasn't planned the first time, but we used that trick a couple more times on other big kids with equally rewarding results.

My Special Hometown: Traverse City
By Marge Lipp of Traverse City, Michigan
Born 1925

I was born and raised in Traverse City, many moons ago. Although I did not wear a grass skirt or a tiara, made of prehistoric bones, I am still a true native. Ask the other natives—they know. Every day growing up here was a miracle to me because hanging from a large tree in my neighbor's backyard (being Tarzan at times) along with roller skating and shooting marbles could potentially be hazardous to one's health. There was only one Tarzan, but many aspiring Janes. My dear friends and I were much more knowledgeable than the kids are today. We also obeyed our parents with little resistance!

We made our own entertainment. We were born before television, before penicillin, before polio shots, before ballpoint pens, and before peashooters. No electric blankets, credit cards, and air conditioning did we have. We never knew of McDonalds or instant coffee. We made do with what we had. We survived. Do you remember Blackjack, Howdy Doody, and S&H stamps?

Neighbors were friendly and nice to know. Car keys were left in the ignition and unlocked cars in the driveway. Honesty counted for everything. We remembered to love thy neighbor. My wonderful friends and I are all grown up, and times have certainly changed. To me, Traverse City, my hometown, will always be remembered as the Four Seasons Playground, spring summer, fall, and frosty.

Our beaches are nice, our schools are special, and so are our teachers. Plans are being made to make our waterfront even nicer. Soon, east and west bay will simmer with our most welcome vacationers, young and old. Summers are delightful! Come and visit our area; you may decide to move here someday. The sunshine and sand will be waiting for you. We also accommodate skiers. Friends, we hope to welcome you soon!

Marge in 1939

Driving on the Railroad Tracks in my '58 Fairlane
By Fred Putnam of Redford, Michigan
Born 1944

Driving on the railroad tracks became a local fad in the early sixties with the teen boys who were always seeking new adventures and exploring the possibilities of what they could do with their cars. The rural and small town boys discovered that their full-size American cars had wheel spacing that matched the railroad gage. No modifications to the cars were needed to drive on the tracks. The tires would take a profile with the tracks centered on the tires. The point loaded tires caused them to bulge slightly on either side of the rails and allow for hands free driving. All one had to do was find a suitable highway and railroad intersection, line the car to the tracks, and begin the journey.

Safety is not a trait normally associated with young boys and somewhat newly minted drivers. We were, however, aware that trains are too much of a match to meet on the tracks. We knew that the rails were used only during the daytime, so stealth driving our cars on the tracks after dark would not conflict with train traffic. As the popularity of riding the tracks grew, we began traveling with our parking lights on to avoid a head on collision with another car in the dark. The railroad that we used had many driveway crossings. These crossings provided a place to exit the tracks and allow other cars to pass. The driveways also provided opportunities to abort the unlawful endeavor if you suspected detection. Most cars traveled 30 miles per hour or slower. Some braver individuals claimed to travel 50 or more miles per hour.

Driving on the tracks was always done in the darkness of night, with headlights off and no hands on the wheel. We could drive with our friends in the car, drink a beverage of choice, listen to the radio, and have the background sounds of the tracks going "clickety clack" under the tires. I never heard of any accident or mishap while this stealth driving was occurring on the railroad tracks. The feeling was eerie with no hands on the wheel and moving in total darkness. It was fun!

Life Savers Candy and Everlasting Love
By Ila Bredahl of Manton, Michigan
Born 1920

I was born in the country, no plumbing or inside toilet, so we had to go outside to the outhouse (toilet). I was 38 years old before I lived where I had an inside bathroom. I remember at Halloween time some of the bad boys would tip the neighbor's outhouse over. One neighbor had prepared the walls and hung a corncob on the wall.

My dad had a battery radio and we would listen to boxing matches and stories on it. Of course, we listened to the old barn dance music too.

When I got married, I live 6 miles from town. We didn't have a telephone. Finally, they laid a wire on the ground and when the animals chewed it or the men that mowed grass by the road, it would get cut, then, we would be without again. There were eight people on our Party line. Everyone could hear everyone's ring, maybe 1 long and 2 shorts; whoever picked up could listen in. One lady had a big clock by her phone and when she would listen in you knew it was her. When they finally buried the line in the ground, we were very happy.

We had a wind up phonograph and several 78 records. A group of us would get together, play records, dance, and have lunch.

My mother had a washing machine that had a crank handle on the side we had to turn until we figured the clothes were clean. Then, we had to put them through 2 tubs of rinse water, then hand wringer 2 times to get the water out, then outside to hang them on the line to dry.

On Saturdays, farmers for miles around went to town to see the free show. The stores, about 5 of them, and the 7 gas stations, would all stay open until the movie was done.

My mother made my sister and my dresses, also our own quilts; even made what we called mattresses. Mom would sew thick material for them and we would fill it with thrashed straw, the only thing with that is after a few nights it would smash down.

My favorite teacher was the Glee Club teacher. She would take each one at a time in the room to see if they could sing. When I went in, she asked me if I could play the piano, I said, "A little." She said she would help me. Then, I played piano for two years for the Girls Glee Club. I never went to a country one-room schoolhouse, but my husband did. I think they learned more than we did, because they could hear all the other classes.

In bad weather, their dad would take the horse and covered sleigh when there was too much snow to walk.

I met my first and only love one Saturday night when at the free movie. His two sisters and I were friends. They asked me to stay all night with them; he was in the car when we went to their house. On the way there, he gave me a roll of Lifesavers candy and 7 years later, I married him.

Living in the country and having no neighbors, when we did get together in the winter we went sledding down the hill, played dog, and deer, made snow angels and played cards. In summer, we walked across 80 acres to friends and over 40 acres to go swimming in the creek.

In the summer, we had to work on the farm. In the winter, before the plow came by our house, we would leave our pickup at my Dad's, and take our team of horses out there and put them in his barn, then take the truck into town to take the cream and eggs to sell to the store. We didn't go to town very often in the winter.

The blizzard I remember most was in 1935. The main road, 131, north of Manton was plugged. Snowplows couldn't get through. The school bus couldn't go on the side roads, so some of the kids stayed at our house. My folks had a 10-room house. Some people got stuck and came to our house. Good thing my dad had cows and chickens for milk and eggs. My mother had lots of canned food, potatoes, and a crock of sour kraut in our Michigan basement. We were happy when we saw the big road truck come from the North and made a trail thru.

Our favorite pet was a dog we called Buster. Buster was a lot of help bringing the cows to the barn. He was not a housedog, but we all loved him.

Living on a farm all my life, we had chores. I was the oldest, so I had to help my dad; my brother was 4 years younger and my sister stayed in the house. I had to help milk the cows. We had horses for a few years before we got a tractor. I drove horses with hay rake, hay wagon, and disk, but turned too short and tipped the disk on edge, so that ended that. One day when my dad was driving out of the field to the farm the loose hay slid off the side and me with it (I was riding on the top of hay). I tried to plow with one horse, but couldn't hold plow in the ground, so didn't have to do that anymore.

When I was 19, I married a farmer with a horse, so I drove horses; later got a tractor and big truck and I helped with it all.

My mother told us about good times at Haire Siding, a little town by the railroad tracks where the train stopped. There was a store, post office, washing machine factory and a Grange Hall where the families gathered, danced, and had fun. Also a church, the preacher baptized several of my family in the creek.

We had an icebox, so we had to cut our own ice for it, at a millpond close to us. We put ice in the shed we had and covered it with sawdust for our sawmill.

Our family time was at Christmas when my sister, brother and my family would get together taking a turn at each home, exchanged gifts, and had potluck supper with oyster soup.

We put up a 100' windmill that worked when the wind blew and had batteries in the garage, and when the wind didn't blow, there was a gasoline engine.

We had a 32-volt radio, washing machine, lights in 2 houses and big barn. Was married 9 years before Consumers ran electricity to our house. My husband hurried to town, bought a refrigerator, radio and a record player.

We had to have our mailbox about 1 ½ miles from our house in the winter and the kids had to walk to the main road to catch the bus until the county started to plow our roads. Then the bus and mailman started to come down our road.

As a kid, my school bus driver lived on 131, across the road from us. The bus was small and we sat knee to knee, then they made seats so you sat behind each other, 2 on each side of isle. It held more kids. The buses was red, white, and blue. I don't remember when the color changed.

As a freshman, I played basketball (only 1 team) and played 3 courts. I was jump center and a guard, so never got to make a basket, just gets the ball to our end, to the forward. Then they changed to 2 courts. I was still Jump center and guard, but one night they put me in as a forward and I was high point and got my name in our town paper. The girls only had 1 team; the boys had 1st and 2nd teams and when we went to other towns, all went in one bus. Our girl's suits in 1935 was like one-piece bloomers, was orange, and black number. The next year they changed to shorts and shirts.

The Milkman
By Donald Akers of Tustin, Michigan
Born 1938

As the song goes, "Milkman, Keep Those Bottles Quiet!" It was the 1940s, and clinking of the bottles in the metal carrier was a sound I knew well. Winter mornings it was quiet, but the milk was there when you woke up. The glass bottles were covered with a cardboard cap that popped up an inch or so when the pasteurized milk was frozen. Plastic was not too common in those days. They did come up with a wrap over the cap that kept the neighborhood cat from feasting on the cream at the top of the bottle.

Before the advent of milk cartons, milk bottles had a five-cent deposit. The bottles were placed outside for the milkman to collect, clean and reuse. My first job was washing those bottles that were returned to the dairy.

It was January in the 1960s that I took the job of milk delivery. (I had a cold for a month, but never got sick after that, even though I was out in every kind of weather.)

I soon realized the complications of milk

Don in his modified truck in 1943

delivery. In to work at 3:30 A.M. to load your Divco truck and start delivery at 4:30 A.M. Milk boxes, now insulated, were sitting on the porch. Many had notes ordering extra milk, butter, cream, or cottage cheese. About 30% of my customers left the door unlocked and a note on the kitchen table. I would fill their order right to the refrigerator while they slept. The newer product was placed to the rear. At the end of the billing period (some weekly, some bi-weekly), I would leave the bill on the table and collect the next time I delivered.

Saturdays were the longest, driving 152 miles standing up! It was a country route and the drive was enjoyable. By 7:00 in the morning, many of my customers were up, expecting me and insisting I have coffee, a sweet roll and conversation. Needless to say, even though I lengthened my day, it meant a lot to know customers as friends.

Those memories recall one of my finer times in life. I met a lot of great people and filled a need, especially for those who could not get out.

I think, not many milk men who delivered to the door are left in the area. As a teen, I had other delivery jobs. In those days, ice, coal, and newspaper came right to the door. Work can be fun!

The Bubble Gum Tree
By Sally Kay Ragan of Harrietta, Michigan
Born 1937

Having been raised on a small farm in Northern Michigan, I remember the Good Old Days when it was pickle-picking time in the summer. We would get up early to start our picking; wanting to get as many sacks picked, as many as we could, because we were going to get a little change for each sack full.

Later in the day, Dad would load the pickles on a trailer, pulled by our Ford tractor and we would head into Harrietta, to the Pickle Factory. Now, the factory was located on the south-west end of town, down by the railroad tracks. I always looked forward to going into the building and helping myself to a big salted cucumber that was held in big vats. They were big, deep and filled with brine, but the pickles were so tasty.

This particular day, one of the workers was there and he said to me, "You know, a dirty old railroad bum fell into that vat this morning and we haven't had time to get him out. He is still in the bottom of that vat." Well, needless to say, I spit out that pickle and that put an end to my pickle eating, at least from that vat.

After getting our change from picking, I would head to one of the local stores. I preferred to go to Tony's, where he had several flavors of ice cream, which cost five cents for a cone. We made our ice cream on the farm, so this was a special treat for me to have store bought ice cream. After dwelling over the candies and gums, for me, I usually bought the big Hubba-Bubba bubble gum, and of course, my ice cream cone.

When Dad was finished at the pickle factory, and that was not only business, it was a time for all the old timers to sit around and chew the fat; we'd head for home.

After arriving home and the hubba-bubba flavor was all gone, I'd head for the "Bubble gum tree" where I would deposit my gum. I'd turn my gum into a work of art of some sort, another way of entertaining myself.

I guess those were The Good Old Days, when you had to invent ways to entertain yourself and didn't depend on a screen or buttons!

"Foxfire", It Lit UP Our Tents
By John J. Murphy of Marysville, Michigan
Born 1931

Last week I turned age 82, but this is an experience, 70 years ago, when I was 12 years old and I can remember it like it was yesterday. I was a Boy Scout in the Village of Roseville, a suburb of Detroit. It was 1943 during World War II, when we were told we were going on a 2 week camping trip in Northern Michigan. It would be the first time I would visit the big North Woods. It was near the small town of Mio.

We camped in tents out in the woods. It was very exciting. We would roam the woods stalking deer. Every time the deer would start to eat, we would take a few slow steps, trying to see how close we would get. As we had been trained by the NRA, we had 22 cal. rifles, which we shot red squirrels, which we skinned and cut up, even a porcupine, which we cooked up in a large cast iron pot, along with vegetables. It seems like we were always hungry.

I remember one day we ran across this beaver dam on the trout stream. Oh, boy, a swimming hole, off came our clothes and in we went, then, whoose, back out we came. How could such a small stream be so cold? We later, watched the beavers early in the morning working on their dam.

Then, one night after dark we were in our tents, and as we again quite hungry; I remember eating raw potatoes, also some wild blackberries. We got thirsty, so we got our canteens and started walking down this hill where there was a small pool fed by a spring. Walking in the dark, I noticed a small spark of light on the ground. Wondering what it was, I gave it a kick. It turned into a bright green spot, glowing brightly. It turned out to be wet rotting roots of trees. Some of them were about 2 inches thick, glowing green all the way through. You could read a book by the glow. We turned up a lot of the hillside, putting some of them in glass quart jars that lit up the tents. We found out they lost some of their intensity if they dried out. None had any idea what this was; even our adult chaperones.

Several days later, we walked to town, spotted this real old man, and asked him if he knew what this was. He said it was "Foxfire," saying he saw it long time ago. We never found out it was—to this day. Then, I thought it could be anywhere, as who goes out digging after dark.

Like I said, it was 70 years ago, but I remember it clearly, like it was yesterday.

The Two-Track
By Irma M. Schwartz of Traverse City, Michigan
Born 1918

Rolling the calendar back to 1918, it was late in the afternoon when the good doctor, his horse, buggy, and his little black satchel were ready for the six-mile drive out in the country where he would assist with a birth. How were the roads? Well, there were no road commissioners in this area at the time, just farmers and workhorses that pulled a special scoop to move the ground and design the "two-track" that would be the highway through the hills and valleys. The way the land laid would determine if it would be a sandy area, contain some gravel, or dark, heavy soil. Very seldom was a car seen in this area at this time. Farmers kept the road open and mainly it was used by horse-drawn vehicles.

One older man, a bachelor, was always willing to help and was often out on the "two-track" with his horse and buggy. He related his connections, saying, "John, pay the taxes. John, do the roadwork. Toot, toot. John, get out of the way." It was not an easy task on a two-track. This was beautiful country with much area left to be cleared. I'm writing of Leelanau County in Northwestern Michigan. No electricity had been established here yet. Kerosene lamps and lanterns were used. They required attention in keeping wicks trimmed. Also, the glass globes needed washing frequently to get the best possible light from them.

My brother, who was four years older than me, was mechanically inclined, and put together a nine-volt system to work with

The Model T in the snow

346

regular car batteries. Now we had a nine-volt iron, which was great compared to heating the flat irons on the old wood-burning range (also called a cook stove). Many of these ranges were built with a reservoir, which heated water. It was not at all like today's wash and wear! Not all homes had water piped in at this time. Our water supply came from a well located on the property. This supplied the house, barn, and chicken coop. Some folks had windmills that pumped water, but they still had to carry water into the house. Outhouses and chamber pots were very popular. Ours was a three-holer. It was very deluxe, but not popular.

We had woodsheds where wood would be stored to dry out. The dried out wood provided a quicker start for heating the oven on the range for bread-baking and other cooking. Some new ground was always developed in those early years. We were just learning to live and thrive in those early pioneering days. Power was horsepower, and men, women, and children all provided whatever would be helpful at the time. Electricity was used in the Grand Traverse area before it was available in Leelanau County. Cherryland Rural Electric made its way as soon as feasible, which never seemed soon enough!

✓ Poison Ivy, Rooted in my Memories
By Jean Smith Riggs of Commerce Twp., Michigan
Born 1935

My first memory of the Tawas area was when I was four years old. My father had been on a fishing trip to Houghton Lake with his buddies, and on the way home they came across "For Sale" signs at the top of the hill (Lake View Drive) leading to Douglas Drive. I think that they paid $100.00 for the 50 foot lots, and two of them bought adjoining lots—R. Vard Martin and my father, H. A. Smith. When my father got home, my mother insisted on seeing his purchase, so he took us up to the Holland Hotel in East Tawas so that he could show us his wonderful lot on the beach. My mother, an amateur botanist, was unhappy that he had selected a lot that was not even walkable, because of the poison ivy that was everywhere. My father and Mr. Martin decided to burn the underbrush to get rid of

the ivy and clear the way for a driveway—not a really good idea, since poison ivy sap is carried in the smoke and both of them got really bad cases of the dreaded stuff.

I remember that they contracted with Herman Fahsault to build log-on-end cottages, although because of the War, there was no electricity for a few years. I developed a love affair with the lake that lingers to this day. The water level was low enough that there was this an aspen tree on the beach that offered shade on sunny days. When we were going fishing, we caught our own bait, shiners, by using a net that looked a lot like a badminton net, and we had the fresh perch for dinner that night.

I remember the Dime Store and the Drug Store on Newman Street. They were on the south side of the street then. The Drug Store had a hallway that led to the parking spaces in the back that was lined with the heads of the animals that the owner had shot on his hunting trips to Alaska and out west—wild sheep, bison and elk and more. I hated that hallway, and I always ran through it. The Dime Store was the source of our entertainment on rainy days, and paper dolls cost 10 cents a book and the puzzles cost a quarter. The movie theatre was right where it is now, but we only went there on special occasions. Sometimes we even went with the next-door neighbor to the theatre in Oscoda! And after the movie, we had ice cream cones or milk shakes from Marion's.

Back then, the lighthouse was actually at the tip of the Point, and was on every night. On foggy nights, the foghorn would blare the warning to ships. When the Port Huron to Mackinac, sailboat races were run, the boats that could not make it to Mackinac would come to the big dock for refuge and repairs.

When the Gypsum Mine in Alabaster was running, we would feel the earth shaking when they set off the dynamite blasts. And after Wurtsmith opened, the jets would fly just above the trees along the beach line. We hit the ground more than once because they were so loud and scary.

Our neighbors on the beach included the Keiths, next door to the south. Mr. James Keith was the news editor of the old Detroit Times Newspaper. Mrs. Betty Keith was a proper southern lady from Kentucky who was a lovely lady. Their son, James Keith Jr. was a brainiac who had a full scholarship to

MIT and became a Nuclear Physicist. They sold their cottage to the Johnstones. Mr. Harry Johnstone, owned a tool and die shop in Detroit, and they had one son, Freddie. Freddie rode his bike up and down Douglas Drive and one time he had to "pottie" some distance from the cottage, and he used poison ivy as toilet paper. He spent a couple of weeks in the hospital for that. His father was a friend of Chris Craft's owner, and Freddie got his first speedboat for his eleventh birthday. He pretty much terrorized the beach that summer. Just south of them were the Schonfield's—Walter and Josephine—who lived off of the land mostly. He was a carpenter who did all of the finish work in our cottage, and they were the only ones on the beach who had a phone for emergencies. Just south of them were the Coashes—Art Coash and Josephene Shonfeld were brother and sister. Mr. Coash was a Justice of the Peace in Tawas. Both the Coashes and the Shonfelds had huge gardens that include lots of flowers for the ladies, and the vegetables to be canned for the winter months.

Eventually, they all started going to Florida for the winter months, and Mrs. Shonfield's little white terrier lap dog got eaten by an alligator! She always called the Atlantic Ocean "The Pond." Both, Mr. Schonfeld and Mr. Coash got their bucks from their garage windows in the late fall. When Mr. Schonfeld passed away, Mrs. Schonfeld married a Tawas area farmer.

Our neighbors to the north were the Martins. Mr. Martin and my father both taught Industrial Arts at Fordson High School in Dearborn. They had one daughter, June. Next door, to the north of them were the Cotters. Mr. Cotter taught shop in Wayne, and Mrs. Cotter taught third grade in Dearborn. He built the cottage himself, with very little help.

One summer Mr. Cotter decided to get a small sailboat, and he bought one from Jerry's Marina on the Point. He started to sail it across the Bay, when it flipped over—he had no experience at all with a sailboat or sailing, and couldn't swim! The Coast Guard was called by someone who saw him and they rescued him and towed the boat to his cottage. I don't think that he ever sailed it again. Mrs. Cotter had a small organ in their cottage that she played loudly every day.

We did most of our grocery shopping at Martin's Grocery in Tawas City. They didn't have much of a meat counter, as I recall, but they cut the meat that you ordered while you shopped for other items.

One time they offered bear steaks, but they were very greasy and strong tasting and not to my mother's standards.

We also shopped at Slaven's Grocery, and the Slavens just lived up the road from us on Douglas Drive. Their adopted daughter, Janet, had her own horse that she rode up and down Douglas Drive, although she kept it somewhere else. The Capstraws' owned Capstraw's Cottages that they rented out. They had 12 children, and a goat for a pet. Mrs. Capstraw always said that even though one child took all of her time, what more could 12 do? She did have live-in help too.

My mother heard about the Kirkland Warblers, and she made my father plant a couple of rows of Jack Pines near the road, hoping to get them to nest where she could watch them. She never met a plant, a butterfly, a moth, a bird, or anything natural that she didn't like—they all had proper names, and we were taught to use the correct name to identify them. Except, of course, poison ivy. She did not ever curse—she said people who used bad language did so because they didn't have a good command of the English language, but she did have a couple of doozies that she called that poison ivy!

I learned to ride horses in Martin's Riding Stable that was on 23, at what is now called Blair Rd., and I rode a little black mare named Babe. My future brother-in-law, Al Worth, rode with me on a horse named Sam. Al and my sister Patty built a cottage across Douglas Drive, on a lot that my father gave them. That cottage is still there, and my nephews still own it and spend vacation time there.

Oh, the wonderful memories!

Making it Through the Winter
By Anita M. Armstrong of Honor, Michigan
Born 1940

During World War II, my sisters, Delores and Bethany, and I lived with our Grandparents, John and Ethel Webber, on their family farm at Wallin, Michigan. At that time our parents, Wayne and Leora Trumbell, were living and working in Muskegon in

The Trumbell sisters enjoying a tea party
Delores, Anita, and Bethany

wartime defense plants. They had tried getting babysitters for us, but to no avail. Our mother was one of the original "Rosie the Riveters." Our parents stated that the factory owners would send buses into the southern states and returned with workers, dropping them off by the factories and telling them they could try to get housing nearby. We were always happy to see our parents when they visited. They always brought extra groceries and candy.

Even at a young age, we were aware of the war going on and the sacrifices everyone had to make. This included shoe rationing, so we kids went barefoot during the summer months. The rationing also included sugar, gas, tires and other items needed for the military. Each family had their ration cards and had to plan accordingly. Our grandfather boiled maple syrup and looked for wild beehives to have a supply of sugar. Every day, my sisters and I would walk to the farm next door to pick up a quart of milk. Every family enjoyed the fruits of their victory garden and traded with neighbors for extra produce.

In August 1945, The Trumbell family was reunited, as dad and mother were able to save enough money to buy five acres of land in Honor and have a house built. Because of lumber rationing during the war, my grandfather cut all the trees, processed the logs at his sawmill, and built our house while our parents were still in Muskegon. This was the first time we had lived in a home with electricity and running water without having to pump water from a well and running outside to the outhouse.

Growing up in the little northern Michigan town of Honor during the 1940s and 1950s

had its perks. We were able to walk to church and school, there were other kids to play with, and we participated in 4-H, Girl Scouts, cheerleaders, baseball, and basketball. All the neighborhood kids would gather downtown and play kick-the-can until dark when it was time to go home. Neighbors looked out after other neighbors and their families. My brother, Wayne was born in 1947.

Summers always meant preparing for winter. As a family, we all pitched in with the canning and processing of food. I can still remember one summer's day in August while our father was working, Mother and us girls went over to Grandma Webber's farm. Grandma had picked bushels of corn, and we all pitched in to husk the corn. Mother and Grandma would cut the corn off the cobs and then process it over the very hot wood stove. Every year, Mother would can hundreds of quarts of fruits and vegetables. In the fall of the year, Dad would always buy about six bushels of potatoes and another six bushels of apples. The apples would be individually wrapped in old newspapers and stored in the basement. In the fall of the year when all the prepared food was in storage, our dad would always say, "Well, I think we can make it through the winter."

The Big Fish Tale
By John Gordon of Fife Lake, Michigan
Born 1954

It was a foggy August morning. Dad and son Matthew put in at Boardman River site after meeting, Miles at 7 am. We trolled around the mouth of the river for about an hour, marking numerous fish, but coming up empty handed, so we headed north along the Peninsula.

About 9 am, the sailboats started racing. The sun was bright and the wind filled their sails. We pulled our gear up and headed north to the White Walls. We began trolling in 150 feet of water. Matthew had on his favorite Gold & Green Spoon (monkey puke) and we all had several other colors out. Our gear was out at 60-80 feet deep. The time was beginning to drag, when all of a sudden, the line began to scream! Dad grabbed the rod and handed it to Matthew saying, "Here's the king you've been waiting for." The line continues to scream. Matthew was convinced it's a snag. "Just keep the rod up." With little line left, the decision was made to rig down other rods and turn the boat towards the beast. Big brother Miles rigged down 4 rods in record time as Dad turned the boat and got on the throttle and about threw everyone out. Gaining composure and throttling down, we started to slow the fish's retreat. Matthew began to gain line and thought the fish had gotten off, but to his surprise the line again screamed and the fight was still on. After two more 100 yard runs, we worked the fish directly under the boat. Matthew moved to the bow and started pulling the fish from the waters depths. "Look at the size of that" we shouted spontaneously. We stood there shaking in shock and knew we had to get this one in the boat. Miles stood ready with the net, but the fish took one more, deep dive, straight down. Matthew gained line quickly and we soon saw the fish's side.

We netted the fish and both Miles and Dad had to lift it over the side of the boat. Knees week, we all sat and stared in amazement at the 41 inch, 29# 10 ounce King Salmon.

Then, all of a sudden, the silence was broken by the screaming drag and Miles shouts of "Fish On!"
With only one pole in the water and barely moving, the fight was on. The fish seemed to be stronger than the last. As Miles fought the fish, Matthew stowed his fish and Dad got the boat moving. We all dreamed of a twin to the first. Twenty minutes later and several runs, we landed the second fish, a respectable 36", beautiful King.

Three hours of fishing, followed by 35 minutes of fighting fish is a most pleasing way to spend the morning for a Dad and his two sons, and to think; all this before noon!

✓ The Diamond Club
By Rozanne Curley of Oscoda, Michigan
Born 1949

It all started on a cool, sunny, March morning. After breakfast, the "Diamond Club" began making plans for another grand adventure. The "Diamond Club" consisted of my sister Sylvia, who was twelve, my brother Frank, ten, me (Rozanne), eight, and the baby of the family, Mary, who was six at the time. Sylvia was our leader most of the

time, but on this day she had strep throat, so Frank, being the next oldest, took charge of the day's plans. Sylvia had to stay in bed at home. We were from a large, poor family and we were pretty much on our own for fun and adventure. By then, Mom was just plain tired of keeping track of kids. On that day (just like anytime we could) we left the house first thing in the morning. We would normally always make it back home on time for Mom's wonderful home cooking at suppertime, but it just wasn't to be this particular day.

We got dressed and made a jar of lemonade and three peanut butter and jelly sandwiches. We lived next door to our grandparents' farm by Cedar Lake Elementary, so we walked from there toward town and turned onto Hull Island. Back then, there was just a wooden bridge to get onto the island. There were no houses or roads; it was just a grassy kind of woodsy area. It was a place where we grazed our cattle during the summer, so there were a lot of cow trails, especially along the bank of the bayou. We crossed the old wooden bridge and started down the trail. Frank was leading us, armed with a stick. Mary was in the middle to keep her from getting too far behind. (We had to watch out for bears, wolves, and attack deer, of course.) I would bring up the rear with supplies in tow.

We walked most of the day, stopping only to look at Mother Nature's beautiful gifts: evergreen trees, rushes along the shore, and birds flying overhead. When Frank said it was time for lunch, we found a spot by a big, leafless shade tree. After lunch, the three of us laid on the cold damp ground, looked up at the fluffy clouds, and pointed out the pictures they made. Then we continued down the cow path.

After a time, the wind started to pick up, the sun was getting low in the sky, and we were getting into thick brush and cattails. It was beginning to dawn on me that we should be heading home, so I yelled up to Frank, "Let's get going; it's time for us to get back." When he turned around, I could see by the look on his face that we were lost, and he didn't know what to do. We all looked at the chunks of ice floating in the bayou. I suggested we follow the path back to the bridge and get home from there, but Frank said it was getting too dark to find our way, so we would just go until we could see the lights from the farmhouse and go across the bayou there.

It wasn't long before we could see the farmhouse with a police car out in the front. Frank said he would take Mary across first, send her to the farmhouse, and then come back for me. I waited in the muddy ooze and the cattails. It was very dark and really scary. I could hear the search party yelling for us, but the wind was blowing their voices around, and I couldn't tell where they were coming from. I could also hear Frank right across from me yelling for me to go down farther where it wasn't so deep, but I couldn't wait another second. I jumped into the water and swam the only way I knew how, the dog paddle. I moved through the icy water to the other shore. When I reached the other side, I grabbed Frank's hand. We ran together to the farmhouse, where our Aunt Angie wrapped us in blankets and put our feet and legs in the wood stove oven to get us warm.

We found out later that Sylvia had been one of the searchers, even as sick as she was. We also found out that Mary would not tell the police where she had left us because she thought Frank would go to jail for getting us lost. Even Mom could not convince her to talk.

The next day, Frank, Mary, and I went down to the bakery for lunch where all the locals met for coffee, doughnuts, and gossip. Just then, I heard a man at the next table say in a loud voice, while looking right at us, "Did you hear about those kids that started a Polar Bear Club?" Then, the whole table of men laughed a big friendly laugh. The three of us finished our tuna sandwiches and milk and walked back to our family-owned paint store behind Cec & Eeb's IGA. I went right up to Mom and asked, "What's a Polar Bear Club?" She answered, "That's what you are; you are like polar bears. They like to swim in icy water, too." From that day on, I knew the only club I wanted to be a member of was the "Diamond Club."

✓ Toughing it Out, Not Stuffing it Out
By Nedra Wagar of Elk Rapids, Michigan
Born 1927

There are many comments and jokes these days about getting children dressed for winter outdoor play. First, the cozy super stuffed snow pants, then the super stuffed jacket, then super stuffed gloves (never mittens, heaven forbid) and then come the superhero boots. Are they actually ready after all of that? Depending on the weather, the hood may be pulled up, and this is super stuffed too! However, shortly after all this, the child has had enough of this "winter play" and is ready to come in and get at the TV or video games! Oh, the frustration of taking it all off again after maybe only fifteen minutes (or less) of outside wonderful winter fun!

Being a child of the Great Depression, getting ready for "winter play" was a bit of a challenge! First, there was the struggle into long underwear. Then, more tugging and pulling to keep the underwear down under the stockings. Then, the stockings were pinned to the underwear (no garters of any kind) with a few arrant ouchy stabs! Hopefully, they would stay down in place! Then, a rather well worn hand-me down coat with stringed mittens through the skimpy sleeves was put on. This was a must so they wouldn't get lost like the Three Little Kittens' mittens did. Then a Gramma-made stocking hat, maybe too large or maybe too small was capped onto our heads! To finish it off, we wrapped

Nedra's father holding her

351

a scarf that was long enough to be wrapped twice around the neck. We did not have boots! The whole process was fairly quick, and we weren't bundled up so we couldn't move.

Move we did, and without all that super stuffed clothing on and stuffed boots (that light up no less). Regardless of the temperature, we stayed out for hours! Well, maybe not hours but at least an hour. No coming in after fifteen minutes or so to be glued to a flashing TV monster! Such creativity we had—snowmen with the coal eyes, nose, and buttons for a smiling mouth. He sported clever sticks for his outstretched arms or possibly one waving at the passer-bye! Many of the sled rides were belly floppers or possibly, on only cardboard on which you felt every bump on your bottom or tummy! With thoughts of just maybe there would be a sled under the Christmas tree this year. We made grand protective forts for our threatening but fun snowball fights! When we, reluctantly did come in, we were cold and sopping wet of course! The dripping wet things were hung all around the house—over chairs, lamps, and even over the stove pipes (fancy dryers did not exist back then!). Then we were all snuggled in blankets around a glowing potbelly stove. If lucky, maybe with the rare treat of a cup of hot chocolate! Brothers, sisters, and neighborhood friends were all there. Even shivering and wet, what wonderful memories all of us had!

✓ Big Dad's Grocery Store
By Robert Bucklin of Zephyrhills, Florida
Born 1936

He spat chewed shreds of the dead cigar into the sawdust covered floor. His apron was red and brown where he had wiped his bloody hands. The sawdust was polka dotted with bits of chewed cigar, the leavings of a morning behind the meat counter. The man; short, wiry, thin, wispy gray hair, stern, but gentle with baggy pants that did not fit the waist and the ever present butcher apron; my grandfather.

The time was the early 1950s and the location was the first block on North Third Street in Marquette, Michigan. The grocery store/meat market was 30 feet wide and 80 feet long. There were two long shelves, one down the side wall that displayed a variety of canned goods. The other, down the middle of the store, displayed various dry foods such as breakfast food, dried beans, and crackers among other foods. Cookies, candies and other sweets dominated shelves near the check-out counter at the front of the store. Two large bay windows bracketed the single front door. The ringing phone was answered by a clerk who took orders by hand on an order pad with a carbon sheet to make a duplicate copy.

The meat coolers dominated one side of the store, my grandfather's domain. The refrigerated chest had a base about three feet high and a slanted glass front that lead to a sturdy ledge. The sliding glass doors, facing the butcher's side of the chest, made it easy to reach fresh lake trout, meats, and cheeses that were prominently displayed for the customer.

My grandfather knew all of his several hundred customers by name, and their preferences for the delicacies in the meat cooler.

"What can I do for you Mrs. Miller?" my grandfather said, as he leaned over the meat counter. "The T-bones look especially nice today" he said as he reached into the cooler and picked out a choice steak with a small square of paper, so that he did not touch the meat. He held the steak in the palm of his hand, over the counter, so that it could be inspected by Mrs. Miller.

"That marbling looks good today Mr. Williams, I would like three." A square of paper was placed on the scale; each steak then placed on the scale separated by a square of wax paper. With some adjustments of the scale, the price per pound was introduced and the price was calculated and displayed. The white paper for wrapping the meat was on a large roll under the cooler counter. My grandfather grasped the paper and pulled; with a squeaky sound, the paper unrolled. He lifted the paper as he pulled and with a screeching sound, it was cut by a sharp blade attached to the roller. The paper was placed on the shelf behind the counter, shiny side up and the meat was placed on it. The left corner was folded over the meat, followed by the right, the lower corner next and finally, the top corner. My grandfather's hands moved as fast as the eye could see. A strip of white tape was pulled from a holder and with a flick of my grandfather's wrist; the tape was cut on the serrated edge of the tape holder. The tape was placed on the intersection of the folded edges. My grandfather turned over the package, took a pencil from behind his ear, checked the weight on the scale and the price per pound and the total price, and wrote each on the package of meat.

"Will that be all Mrs. Miller?" he asked. She answered, "I think that will be all Mr. Williams, I have some other groceries to pick up."

As she turned to continue her shopping, my grandfather said, "Thank you, Mrs. Miller."

✓ **Growing Up On Tawas Bay**
By Charles M. Noel of Tawas City, Michigan
Born 1942

Being raised in the lakeside city of East Tawas, Michigan was an experience that produced many fond memories. The earliest of which, was playing Cowboy and Indians after watching matinees of Roy Rogers, Gene Autry or Hop-along Cassidy at the local Family Theatre, but the biggest thrill then, was having my picture taken upon a life sized stuffed bucking bronco.

Being on Tawas Bay, there were many opportunities for water sports, mainly fishing and swimming. The numerous docks in the bay were visited frequently by our family, using a trusty old cane pole, we caught perch by dozens. My favorite docks were, Lixey's

Riding the bucking bronco

and Capt'n Mac's each had boathouses. During this time commercial fishing was a big industry in the winter, as ice formed on the bay, crews would hand cut large blocks of ice to be stored in saw dust lined buildings that were constructed along the shoreline. This ice was used to fill local home iceboxes and to keep fish cold while shipping downstate. The Bay had three party boats that took fishermen out daily returning with good numbers of perch. Sadly, as the perch population declined, so did these businesses.

In the early 1950s, we had a two party shared phone line that we answered on the ring. Our first TV was a black and white screen, Zenith. I watched such shows as Howdy Doody, Sky King, and Soupy Sales. My first pizza had end crust that blistered up from being baked just right without being burnt; it came from Nino's small shop on Newman Street. Cherry phosphates from Dimmick's soda fountain were the greatest and the malts at Marion's Dairy Bar were the best while their bumper pool table and pinball machines were always a challenge. The Roller Dome became a regular meeting place, as did the American Legion Post, who hosted square dance lessons by Mrs. Pierce.

Fishing on the dock

353

Who could ever forget going to Silver Valley, riding the twin toboggan runs using a saddle ski, and drinking hot chocolate. Then there was Perchville starting with a parade and ending with a little city of shanties on the frozen ice of the Bay.

During my teen years of the '50s, the golden era of 'Rock and Roll', when being cool was having a 'DA" with a water-fall haircut. Cruising the Mid-Way Diner and going to the Drive Inn Theatre were the norm. In the summer months, the streets were busy and stores were filled with tourist. The big event was the dances at the State Park Community Building, where there was a good chance of meeting a girl from the adjacent State Park Campground. If the building was crowded, my closest friend and I would take a RCA 45rpm record out on the State Dock, spin Rock and Roll records with the sounds of Bill Haley, Chuck Berry, Buddy Holly, Eddie Cochran and Little Richard. That always gathered people and new friendships were established. There also were the beach parties and the unauthorized parties on Grenades Hill.

After Labor Day, the campers and tourist left and to some it was a welcome sight. I recall someone saying, "You can shoot a cannon down Newman Street and not hit anything." But for me, there was the wish of a short mild winter and the return of another tourist season. Growing up in Tawas was a "Blast" and I have many more memories to tell...

"Good Old Days" In Northern Michigan
By Susan R. Grutsch of East Jordan,
Michigan
Born 1946

My parent's father, Otto Axel Jacobson and my mother, Virginia Clifford Kime, were from Boyne City, Michigan. During the Depression, they moved to Saginaw to find work.

I remember the stories told by my grandparents on both sides, my mother's and father's parents. As a child, I remember the long drive to come up north to visit the grandparents. On my father's side, he was 100% Swedish. His father, Carl Axel Jacobson, came from Sweden; it is believed

that he had once lied about his age to either go to sea as a cabin boy aboard a square-rigger or to join up with the American Navy in the Spanish American War. He sailed around Cape Horn three times. He settled in Elk Rapids and he was a border in a boarding home. That is where he met my grandmother, Jennie Marie Lawson, who was also Swedish. Her mother ran the boarding home.

After they married, they moved to Boyne City where he built a house into the side of a hill that overlooked Lake Charlevoix, across from the Tannery Manufacturing Company. He worked at the Tannery. I remember the stories they told about my grandfather, that when they would make him mad he would pile the bales of hides so high on the rack, no one could move it. The home he built is now gone and so is the tannery. They had ten children, seven boys, and three girls.

My mother's parents moved to Boyne City from Breckinridge when my mother was nine years old. My grandfather, Grant Oland Kime, sold school supplies and later was a security guard on the mail trail that came into Boyne City. My mother's sister tells when she was growing up in Boyne City (she was five years younger than my mother), a few houses down the street from them, there would be a lot of fancy cars that would come there. One time they invited her over. That is where she had her first taste of beer. She found out that the people that came there in their fancy cars were gangsters from Detroit. When my mother was a teenager, she worked at Menonaqua Inn, in Harbor Springs. I have letters she received from her mother while she worked there. They had to stay right there at the Inn when they worked there. It was a summer job.

I remember my father telling when he was young, he would walk and meet up with Ernest Hemingway, and they would go fishing. That is the first time he ever heard the name, Carol for a girl. That was Ernest Hemingway's sister's name. My father liked the name so much he named his first daughter Carol.

The story that sticks in my mind the most is the one both my mother and father told about when they were dating. They had gone on a date and my father had been to the pool hall earlier before the date. While on the date he found out, he had lost his wallet. They went back to the pool hall that night, but no one had seen it. They told my mother's parents about it the next morning, and they told him to go see Ol' man Behling. He was an Indian that lived in a tarpaper shack outside of town, and was able to "see things." My mother, father, my mother's mother, and my mother's sister, all went to see Mr. Behling. When they got there, he was sitting in a chair at the table. He asked them what they wanted and my dad told him he had lost his wallet and wanted to find it. Mr. Behling started to make some noises and went into a trance. He looked at my Aunt Phyllis (my mother's sister) and put his hand on his head and cried, "Trouble, bad trouble, tragedy for you." He looked at my grandmother and said, "Strong, very strong." He told my mother he saw her standing over a grave, she was young. He told my dad to look on cover over table; "wallet there!" During this time when he was in his trance, he was grasping for breath and my dad thought he could not breathe, so he ran out to tear some of the tarpaper off the door and window to get air in the shack. Mr. Behling came out of his trance and did not know what he had told them.

My dad went back to the pool hall and in the cover they used to cover up the pool tables at night, was his wallet. It got folded up in the cover. My Aunt Phyllis had a hard life. Her only daughter, Christy, had diabetes and was a hand full, and Christy died very young. My mother was standing over her husband's grave at age 45.

Looking Back, Things Sure Have Changed
By Joyce Oliver of Alpena, Michigan
Born 1934

My hometown memories of the good old days began last Saturday, as our local newspaper wrote about a place my mother lived in the early days of the 1900s. It's a place called Isaacson Bay, which lies on the east side of Lake Huron. The two trees my mother had a swing rope and old tire on, still stood two years ago.

Depression which was part of my era, as she used to tell me about walking to school in the cold without mittens, putting her hands in her brother's pockets to try to keep warm. But, still she had an education through the eighth grade.

Joyce's Uncle Max holding Joyce and having fun with the children

Then, in 1934 I was born, the only child. We lived in a tarpaper shack that later had a lean too added on. Outhouse with Sears catalog, well outside. For a while, my dad would bring our water in cream cans from someplace in Alpena, so water was sparsely used. We would have to use only a small amount for washing on a washboard and then wringing our clothes on a hand wringer.

Heating our water in a side boiler then, was connected to our stove. My dad worked for the W.P.A. Money was so scarce for entertainment, we had a battery radio so we could have some music or listen to stories like the Inner-Sanctum. My mother would wait for a certain time of the month when the people would get in line for nylon hose, then, flour, sugar, rice, raisins, lard, and peanut butter. Each person got just so much.

We had a Model-A, to travel to town in, when it would run. Gas was 25 cents a gallon then.

Going to school having a kerosene lamp to do your homework by, there were kindergarten through eighth grade in one room. A big kerosene heater to heat the whole school, when you got there in the morning it was so cold we had to leave our coats on until the big guys got the stove going. There was commodities given to the school kids, like beans for a snack and small containers of white or chocolate milk. We had ball games during recess and everybody participated. Everyone helped each other during the day. If the school bus got stuck in the snow or went in the ditch everyone got out and helped get on the road again.

On Sundays, it was a day to go to Grandma's house for dinner. She lived on the Naylor road. Her house was made with logs and surrounded by a hill. She had a roof of tarpaper and a tin chimney coming out of the roof. Chickens were everywhere. My grandma had a big old range, always wood inside. The coffee was always boiling on the back of the stove and the aroma of it was like a welcome hello. She always had peanut butter or homemade bread. It always tasted real good. If we were lucky enough, she would have real cream to spread on the bread. Life on Sunday at my grandma's was great. All my mother's sisters and brothers would come and visit. There was eight of them.

My uncle who drove an old truck with a snowplow would tell us all kinds of tales in each day's work. He would take us to a small lake; he and my aunt lived in Bolton, and go bobbing with the fishing pole. He had one daughter too, so we had a lot of fun doing that. We always caught fish.

One thing I remember doing in their house was going down to the root cellar. There my aunt made the most delicious dill pickles. Those days were happy and sad times, but families were very close. I remember going to the Lyric Theatre every Friday night to see, they were called serials. Each week there was different episodes, mostly westerns, Roy Rogers, Gene Autry, and a lot more. Admission, I believe was 25 cents. I baby sitted for 25 cents an hour so I could go to the show and football games. Popcorn was 5 cents, and with a lot of butter, 'so good.'

I recall the coal trucks that would load coal on the truck by hand and then deliver to homes and businesses. Most everybody would burn coal or wood to stay warm in the wintertime. We used to have snowstorms where it would be so deep we would have to stay in for several days.

I believe this is the end of my early days experiencing many different situations. Like fishing for perch having the water up to 23 South. Cars used to be lined up enjoying catching fish, now, no water, no fish, no fun. You can look across the south end of Partridge Point where there was water on the beach, but now dry. The cement plant used bags for the cement. If there was no money for the families, they would use the bags for clothing

On the farm I remember seeing my sister-in-law milk 25 cows by hand with the old tiger colored cat nearby, dipping his paw for a drink of milk in a small, low pail. This was milk they disposed of after the cow had her baby.

On telephones, you had to wait on the party line, then, came dialing the party line you wanted.

This is the end of my story during the Depression. Now we live in a technology world. I believe everyone is so thankful for the many ideas and inventors who made life a better place to live in, even though it is expensive.

✓ The Old Khaki Tent
By Doris Badgley Barrett of West Branch,
Michigan
Born 1931

Let me tell you a story about an old khaki tent, which six generations of our family have enjoyed on their summer vacations. Oh, if that old tent could talk, it would have so many bedtime tales to remember, as we camped in so many beautiful Michigan campgrounds. My great-grandparents purchased this tent from the Sears and Roebuck catalog and immediately loaded family, food, and tent into their car and headed for their northern destination: Traverse City State Park. Years later, my grandfather and grandmother took their newly adopted five year old daughter to this same park. They set up camp, went swimming, picked cherries, and had a great Michigan vacation. Then, in the late '30s, my father and mother took by brother and myself and the "old khaki tent" to Tawas State Park. We set the tent up next to the railroad tracks and my brother and I jumped for joy when the train and engineer went slowly by each afternoon. He blew his horn and waved to us.

Camping in Traverse City State Park in 1936

When our two sons became boy scouts, the old khaki tent went to Scout Camp where several boys got to sleep in it and smell that "old tent smell." It had a screen room zipped to the front and it held the table, chairs, cook stove, pots, pans, and food. There was always ice from the iceman to keep our food safe to eat. The old tent was just for sleeping, playing in on rainy days, and changing clothes for swimsuits.

Our youngest son has a daughter and a son. Our oldest son took the tent to Canada to fish and celebrate graduation from C.M.U. They too set the tent up in our backyard for over-nighters. Now our grandson has a five year old daughter, and our granddaughter has a two year old son and a six month old son. They all plan to take "the old khaki tent' and go camping.

I doubt that my great-grandparents ever dreamed that their Sears and Roebuck purchase would bring so much fun, laughter, and memories. "The old khaki tent" has made many beautiful Michigan State Parks its temporary home. Now it is patiently waiting to be set up again for our seventh generation of fun and memories!

✓ Our Prosperous Life
By Ruth Warren of Baroba, Michigan
Born 1920

In 1943, my husband Alton Warren, little daughter Glenda, and two young sons moved from Benton Harbor, Michigan to Fremont, Michigan, the home of Gerber Baby Foods. We bought a 20-acre farm with an old house. It was hardly livable. There was no electricity, and had an outside toilet. We carried our water in after pumping it by hand from a well. The purchase price was $1200.00 with $50.00 down and $15.00 payments per month. We sat on a small hill surrounded by higher hill on the north. Joining our farms was a small lake with lots of blue gills and bass. On the east, there was another lake about the same size. In the front of the house, across the road, was a swamp that was full of big, black bullfrogs. We all loved to fish and go frogging. How we enjoyed the frog legs and fish fries.

My husband had gotten a job in a defense plant in Miskegon making big money. He started the trial period making $0.50 per hour and soon increased it to $125.00. There were four young families we had left behind that we were very close to. They had from two to four children. They were always eager to get out of the city on weekends and come to our house. We had made three bedrooms available, and we put blankets on the floor for the kids. We had a ball! My husband played accordion. His brother Wilson played the mouth organ and my cousin beat the big tablespoons. Sometimes, someone strummed to the tune on the old washboard. The kids would dance and sing or just go out and play hide-and-go-seek. However, it was a great busy simple life. What did I do to entertain? I baked chocolate cream pies, did dishes, and really enjoyed the noises.

The following March, along came another little baby son, Kenneth. He was such a cute, chubby little guy, and to my husband's pride and joy, he was a boy! He was to be another hunter and fisherman. The following open season, we would bundle the little guy up on weekends when the weather permitted, and I'd put a warm bottle of milk in the boat and leave it in the sun to keep it warm.

As time went on, the families grew up and moved in different directions. Seldom would we all get together at one time. Wilson and Jean Pharma and family moved to Kentucky, but came up once a year. By that time, we had become more prosperous. We had a truck and a big tent, therefore, when the company came, we'd plan a camping trip. This time, the Pharms and their son Jimmy came for a week vacation. My husband took off that entire week. We decided to go to Wilderness Park to camp, and also we were to visit Mackinaw Island, which is very remote. No cars of any kind or motor vehicle are permitted. We crossed the river on a ferryboat. There are buggy and wagon trails, all horse drawn, and also bicycles. It is beautiful!

We got our tent all prepared in Wilderness Park. Our bed was a bale of straw, which was divided and put in each corner of the tent with blankets over it. We did have electricity available in the park. We really had an enjoyable day on the wagon trails.

At the end of the day, a storm came up and it turned so cold on the way back to Wilderness Park. We had no way to warm the tent. Our only way to cook was on the two-burner camp stove. We couldn't pack up and go home; it was too stormy. Our young son Ken and their young one was being very brave. They were jumping around and saying that they were not too cold, even though we knew that they were.

About that time, I got a brainstorm. I went to the store and got electric cords and a couple of the strongest light bulbs they had. I put the lights up in the tent, and believe it or not, it kept us warm enough through the night. The next day, the sun came out nice and warm and we enjoyed the remaining weekend.

God has been great to our family. Even today, our reunions are not as active as it used to be, but I often lay at night and thank God for family and friends that are left. Many are gone one before me. Michigan is a wonderful state!

Welding, Sunday Drives, and Drive-ins
By Joyce (Robarge) Konwinski of Posen, Michigan
Born 1946

I grew up on a farm three miles south of Rogers City. My father Howard and my grandpa William were welders and blacksmiths. They had a welding and blacksmith shop in Rogers City. My dad worked with Grandpa and bought the shop around 1953. He and Grandpa made cultivator teeth, wrought iron railing, spears, boat docks, plows for trucks, and basically anything else that anyone needed. In the winter, some people had water pipes that would freeze, and Dad had a portable welder in his truck that he would hook up. It would thaw them out. He also used it to go to jobs that couldn't be brought to him. We would get to go with him at night and on Saturdays. Since I grew up on a farm, but my dad wasn't a farmer, it was rented out

Joyce and Tony Konwinski on their wedding day in 1965

and the buildings weren't all used. We used one to play house in. There was an old stove and some cupboards in there. My favorite memory about my dad

happened one summer at his shop. A family came in that was on vacation with a camper. They were about 75-100 miles from home, and something on their trailer hitch broke. Dad had to make a new hitch. The bill was about $30.00, as he had spent most of the afternoon on it. That's all the money the father had, so my dad just charged him $15.00 and told him to go buy the kids some milk. Dad knew they needed it to get home even though we could have used the money.

I went to Heslip School, which was a two-room school with about 50 kids. We got a ride to school with Dad in the morning, but didn't have a bus yet, so we had to walk home about three miles. Our lunch pail usually would have a sandwich, and a fresh fruit like an apple, orange, or banana. Sometimes we would have canned fruit that my mother would can in the summer and a Hostess pink snowball. At school, we had a bookmobile that came every two weeks. We read a lot of books. The bookmobile was a van type truck with shelves on each side. A class or two would go out at a time to check out books. We would have a Christmas program for school. We would practice at school and then a few days before the program, we would go to the Belknap township hall and practice with all the props. We would exchange names, and the night of the program, Santa would come and pass out gifts from whoever had drawn our name. They were only $0.50 to $1.00 gifts. We would also get something from our teacher. We also had a Christmas program at church and exchanged names for gifts as well; we also got a gift from our baptism sponsors. At home, Christmas gifts were put under the tree when we went to bed on Christmas Eve. We opened them in the morning at church.

One summer, they were putting an addition onto our St. Johns Hagensville Church, so we had church in the woods at someone's farm. Dad made some of our toys—the big ones. He made us swings—not the kind you can buy today. They were much larger and sturdier. They were cemented in the ground. He also made a swimming pool and some bikes from parts of other machines. Some things we did for fun were trying to find four-leaf clovers, catching June bugs, playing Cowboys and Indians, Kick-the-Can, and Ante-I-Over. We would pick sap pickles from the trees in spring. In the winter, we would go ice skating and tobogganing on the field when it would freeze over after a thaw. One year, we had a large slide off the barn. When I got older, I would go to the skating rink in town. In the house in the winter, we would play paper dolls cut from the Aldens and other catalogs. Other games we would play in winter were Fox and Goose, make angels in the snow, and play cards, put puzzles together.

We had a restaurant near our house, and when Dad would come home for lunch in the summer, he would give us a dime or quarter as he was going back to work. We would use the money to buy candy or ice cream. In the summer, we would take Sunday rides in the afternoon and stop at some little store and get a ring of pickles bologna and crackers and bottle of pop. Sometimes, we'd just get an ice cream cone. A favorite sandwich of ours as teenagers was Velveeta cheese, onions, and mustard on white bread. Mom, Hannah would take everything outside in the summer to clean the house—even mattresses. She would can berries, pears, peaches, carrots, beets, and beans since we had such a big garden.

When I was about six years old, we were on one of our Sunday drives, and it was raining real hard. They were working on the road and maybe getting it ready to blacktop. It was really muddy, and some car passed us, going way too fast. We had a panel truck at the time. A few miles after he passed us, he was way in the ditch in the mud. I think he learned a lesson that day.

My grandpa once spent his time building his own three-wheel car that he drove around town for a time. They finally told him he couldn't drive it in town anymore, but people came around all the time to have a look at it. A story that everyone that grandpa worked for knows is that when it was time to pay and they asked him how much, he would say, "Fifty cents." If they

didn't hear him and asked again, he would say, "A dollar," and then "A dollar fifty." He would keep going until they quit asking.

The restaurant near our house burned down when I was a kid and was later rebuilt. I was home from school sick the day it burned down, and all I could think of was all the candy getting burnt. That restaurant was the North Star, and was where my husband asked me out on our first date. I was working there as a teenager. We have now been married for 47 years. My husband Tony and lots of high school kids hung out there. At the restaurant, in the summer, they also had a family stay there in a trailer that showed movies outside and went around the area showing them. People would bring their families and sit on the grass to watch them. We would walk since it was only a block from our house. We also went to a lot of drive-in movies with Mom and Dad in Alpena. We went to the Alpena Fair to watch the daredevils. There was never time to be bored. Life was fun in those days! I wouldn't change a thing about growing up then!

Fishing and Having a Good Ole Time
By Laurel E. Mason of Arcadia, Michigan
Born 1945

When I was eleven and my brother was eight, my Dad wanted to take us fishing. Dad was a wonderful man: patient, kind, and rarely irritated. His work allowed him to be home only on weekends when he really enjoyed his time with his family. There were just two children in our family, my brother and I. Our mom was forced to be a liberated woman long before the term became popular as she took over the responsibilities of head of the house in my father's absence. We thought going fishing with Dad was a wonderful idea. Dad had saved money for some time to purchase a new fishing pole and was eager to try it out. We had a number of old fishing poles good enough for me and my brother. Our summer cottage was not too far from a pier jutting out into Lake Michigan, and fishing for perch there was always a lot of fun. However, on this particular fishing trip, Dad was going to rent a small boat and we were going to fish on Spring Lake—a lake connected to Lake Michigan by a channel. We were so excited!

We arrived at the boat livery and Dad rented a boat with a small outboard motor. He cautioned us to sit still and not move around as we found our way to an area that Dad thought might prove to be a good fishing site. We had three poles, one of which was the new pole Dad had saved enough money to purchase. Being the ages we were, sitting still was not easy, especially for my brother. Besides, he always thought he was so smart and didn't have to mind 100 percent. (I always did exactly as I was told and suffered for being so obedient as my life progressed.) After sitting for what seemed like hours, my brother decided he needed to move around. As he stood up and started to find another seat in the very small boat, his foot hit the handle of the new fishing pole, and over the side of the boat, it went. Dad looked a little disgusted, but as was his nature, he did not get angry. In an all out effort to make the situation have a happy ending, by brother and I jumped in the water and attempted to locate the pole. We dove and dove down to the spot we were sure the pole had gone. We had no luck. Our fishing trip soon ended with no fish and minus one new pole.

A few weeks after the doomed fishing trip, a friend of mine called to see if we would like to go out on her family's boat. My brother was invited, too. We were thrilled, and they picked us up in front of our cottage on Lake Michigan. What a wonderful day! The water was warm, the sun was shining, and there was lots of good food on the boat. My friend's father captained the "ship" and we sure to have a wonderful day. As time progressed, we headed towards the pier and down the channel finally arriving at the lake where we had gone fishing a few weeks before. We had a picnic and enjoyed seeing land from the water.

As the boat made its way around the lake, not too far from shore, it seemed to me that we were near the spot where the fishing pole had been lost on that fateful afternoon a few weeks before. I told my friend's parents what had happened and explained that I thought we were in the area where my Dad's new pole had been lost. I also told them it was my brother's fault because he didn't do what he was told. The Captain of the boat we were on produced a magnet connected to a long line. He explained that it was possible to bring up all kinds of treasures by throwing the magnet over the edge of the boat and hauling up whatever attached itself to the magnet or was snagged on the line. We had a lot of fun "fishing" with the magnet and managed to bring up a number of items, none of which were of much value. The Captain announced that it was time to head back. He said we would go to the marina where the boat was kept and they would then drive us to our cottage. He told us to throw the magnet overboard for one last time. My brother got the honors and threw the magnet as far as he could and then started hauling it in. As the magnet and rope got closer to the boat, we could see a fishing line was wrapped around the apparatus. He continued to haul in the rope and there at the end wrapped around the line and the magnet was a fishing pole— our dad's fishing pole! It was a miracle!

We couldn't wait to get back to the cottage and present Dad with the prize. Our friends dropped us off in the parking lot and we ran through the woods to the cottage. We gave the pole to Dad and as was his usual manner, he quietly thanked us and proceeded to take the reel apart and clean the rod and reel. As the pole had not been in the water for too long, it soon looked like new and ready for another fishing adventure.

Oh, the "good ole days" when cottages were not palatial houses, but seasonal dwellings— rustic, wonderful places to spend summers with the freedom to explore and prowl around. Sometimes we were gone for hours at a time with no one worried about where we were; when cottages were opened up in the spring and closed in the late fall, the family working together to get the place in shape and then, months later, preparing for winter by boarding up the windows and draining the pipes so they would not freeze over the winter months. Yes, I remember the "good ole days" when money was saved to buy items like a fishing pole, as credit cards were rare if non-existent. If one didn't have the money, it had to be saved before a purchase could be made. Fishing trips taken in a rented boat were experiences to be treasured and valued with no electronic devices on board, participants talking to each other, or just enjoying the scenery and the experience of being with Dad. Will these days be the "good ole days" someday? Who knows? But, I do know that my memories of the "good ole days" in my life are very good, precious memories that helped form the person I am today, and for that, I am grateful.

✓ The Simple and Mystical Life
By Cindy Vezinau of St. Clair Shores,
Michigan
Born 1953

I was born in 1953 and named Cindy Lou. Yes, Cindy Lou. A good Michigan French Canadian and German combination named Cindy Lou. Thanks Mother! Mother's family was German (Prussian), and she had seven siblings. Her parents were founders of Roseville, Michigan, and built the first hotel there. Grandmother's parents were Hoteliers, too, along with my great grandparents in Presque Isle, Michigan. That made three generations. Grandmother was originally from Rogers City and only came south to find her husband also from a Rogers City family. Grandmother and many other Prussian dependents lived in Rogers City, a quaint small U.S. Steal Great Lakes sailing town in northeastern Michigan. Roseville is where I grew up. Rogers City is a large Polish community as well. Depending on whether you were German or Polish determined where you went to church, where you shopped, and which tavern you were most likely to be seen in.

Cindy Lou

Okay, so enough with the history of what took us to this up north paradise. Back then, marriage between Catholic and Lutheran were greatly discussed, and the offspring between the two were called Kasubs, whatever that means. I was caught somewhere between a good Lutheran girl with parents who wanted to have good fun times, like those they were then seeing on TV. Of course, they always lived within their means. With seven in the family, someone was always making the trek five to six hours at that time to reach Rogers City. I-696 and several of our current freeways were not in place. Mother had to see Grandmother,

quarterly it seemed, but in the summer, watch out! A great time was to be had by all. Many times, several cars would caravan, swapping cars, passengers, and especially children. Some family member would drive up with one and back with another. Sometimes I wonder how they kept track…or did they?

Okay, so I survived. No seatbelts, no sunscreen, and even the multitude of stops in these cars made at bars. I'd hear them talk about how long it took them and how many stops they had made. Stops, right, stops. There was always beer in the trunk and after the halfway point of the drive, all bars were welcome spots. It seemed one car would make the turn in and Dad would have to follow. Well, it was shuffleboard and jukeboxes and pop for the children. I didn't know fear, nor did I know that they were affected by alcohol. I only knew we were headed to a place where the simple pleasures in life abound.

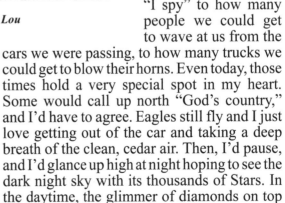

I believe I was conceived in Rogers City. I'd say Cousin Cathy was, too. We would chime, "Rogers City here we come, two little stinking Roseville Bums." Yes, we were creative. We'd have every drive game thinkable from "I spy" to how many people we could get to wave at us from the cars we were passing, to how many trucks we could get to blow their horns. Even today, those times hold a very special spot in my heart. Some would call up north "God's country," and I'd have to agree. Eagles still fly and I just love getting out of the car and taking a deep breath of the clean, cedar air. Then, I'd pause, and I'd glance up high at night hoping to see the dark night sky with its thousands of Stars. In the daytime, the glimmer of diamonds on top of the crystal clear fresh water called me near.

It was the summer of 1969, and I was caught in the coming of the Aquarius. I walked from church that spring and heard about nearby family boys being sent home from Vietnam in a box. I worked at a donut shop near my church, the Sugar Shack. I was too young to know the potential evils that lurked there, but my mother and father were not. On the way up north headed toward Rogers, I was seated in the back seat, with Mom and Dad in Front, begging to find "my" music. When we stopped at our breakfast spot in Standish, Father said, "We have decided to stay until Tuesday." I said, "No way; I have to be at work Monday." Father said, "You don't work there anymore. I called the owner for you, and it was not the right crowd, honey." The table was still. The King had spoken. I stayed for a majority of time in Rogers City that summer. It was an amazing summer. I earned money by taking the bus a few times out to help migrant workers pick strawberries. I learned to whistle, so others could hear me and respond back with a whistle. I learned to swim with Cousin Ron, Cousin Tom, and Cousin Cathy. We rode on their handlebars to the Lake Huron and swam out to sponge rock. It was just over our heads and every time we reached it, it was the same joy of accomplishment. The best things in life are free.

Our families would always rent a cottage at a lake during the summer. It was so much fun. That was when I first met Oreo cookies. I loved the smell of the fishing boat motors going out. At night, we would go to Dad's car and try to find CKLW radio so that we could hear something other than Polka and news. We were so cool. Honestly, the best nights were the nights my cousin Tom would take me to the dumps to watch the bear. I love bears and wish the hunters would leave them alone. I remember berry picking with Grandmother when a bear and her cubs came up. Grandmother just walked me away calmly saying, "They only wanted some berries too."

Life was so simple, so mystical, and so youthful. It was the summer I first met "him." He was so handsome, so sweet, so shy, and so right. Ah, we were young. The kiss, the French kiss. The bonfires and the thoughts. I was one of many in line for this innocent young man. They nicknamed him Fox. I thought they called him Fox because he was so handsome, he said it was because he could run like one. I smile today to think of those times.

Thirty years later, I, with a broken heart, drove to Rogers City to find some pleasure.

The annual festival was on. That is where all those who wished they could find work and live in the Norman Rockwell town returned to. Across the room, I could see Fox standing there. He looked at me and I said to myself, "You are in trouble." Now, 14 years later, I still call him "my" handsome fox.

My experience and fearlessness still fight to preserve this up northern empire. I fight to preserve our natural assets there. My grandest quest is to help children who have never seen the jewels of the water, the fragrance of cedar, and the diamonds in the sky. I'd love them to feel the safety as I did, and to experience nature's best: Rogers City. Thank you, God, for Northern Michigan. By the way, stop up sometime on Memorial Day and visit the city's Purple Martin Mania, celebrating this endangered bird. This bird represents the help needed, as with children, to survive.

Lost in the Woods
By Sharon Purkiss of Mesick, Michigan

Thirty years ago, my husband and I would spend several evenings after dinner picking wild blackberries in the beautiful, rolling hills east of Yuma, Michigan. Doing this over several years, we had become familiar with several acres of the woods and hills and the sprawl of brambles. One cloudy evening, we parked farther to the east, entering the woods just on the edge of "our territory." After picking berries for a while, we realized dusk was quickly approaching. We came out of the woods at an unfamiliar path. I felt certain our truck was to the right just beyond a stand of trees. My spouse was just as confident we needed to go left.

Being a woodsman and hunter, he had found that by making left-hand turns every little while he would always came out close to where he went in. Following a short discussion, we turned left. We trekked with quickening steps through hard woods, down open slopes where ferns grew taller than I am, past stands of tall pines, and it was all a view of an expanse of misty hills that I did not recognize. My experienced hunter assured me if we'd keep turning left we'd come out okay. As the dusk thickened, it seemed like we'd be spending the night in the woods. However, just as dusk was beginning to turn into blackness, a sandy path opened up in front of us. It kind of glowed with the last bit of day light. We turned left, as usual, and eventually came out on the main road about a quarter of a mile from our truck, much to our great relief. That husband of mine was quite right about the "left turn trick." As we saw on our next visit there, our vehicle had been only a few yards to the right from the path we had come to first where the fateful discussion was made. I'm sure I said, "I told you so!"

✓ Making a home on Pincherry Road
By Glenda (White) Reinhardt of Boyne City, Michigan
Born 1942

At some point after my mother and father married, Dad bought a farm formerly owned by his Uncle John. The house where they had met had burned, but further back in the property was a barn and shack with a shed roof. It was not considered livable. Mom and Dad camped there in the summers and rented here or there in winter. During the winter of '37/'38, they lived with Grandpa and Grandma White. Quin was two, Irene just a baby. Dad's sister Ida and her husband moved from Petoskey also, as Ida was "expecting." Ida and Ken Jefferson had the upstairs, Mom and Dad had the front of the house, and Dad's parents used the back. Diane Jefferson was born that winter.

During World War II, Dad rented the Tillotson place for us while he was gone. After the war, it became the "Zipp's" and Dad moved his wife and four children to the

Glenda in about 1946

three room shack further south on Pincherry Road. I was very young, but I watched Mother wash with water hauled from Horton Creek in barrels on a sledge pulled by the "doodle-bug," a homemade tractor. The Baker's across the road had a well with a pitcher pump. They let us pump drinking water, hauled in a cream can. Grandpa White bought the property next to the Baker's.

The roof on our old place needed to be repaired. Dad tore off the shed roof, giving it a four-foot pitch. We kids could stand in the center. Of course, it rained halfway through the job. All four kids were (out of necessity) shipped off to Grandma White. Mom and Dad took blankets to the barn. I remember watching lots of extended family, men with muscle, dig a basement, and pull the old house onto it. They used that doodlebug and chains hooked to a huge scoop with handles like a wheelbarrow. Then they made wooden frames to hold poured concrete walls. The cement was made in a machine powered by a belt hooked to a wheel on the doodlebug. There was no R.E.A. here yet. No electricity! They poured concrete floors, too. They hauled water to do all of that.

A well soon followed, with a pitcher pump right next to the basement door. It had a shed over it that was attached to the house. That meant there would be no more hauling water—at least not very far! Didn't even have to go out in rain or snow! We lived in that basement. How warm and cozy! It was our kitchen, dining room, and living room.

Glenda's grandma, Ethel White in about 1918

*Quint and Bonnie's family with
Glenda, Irene, Quin, and Quinton, Jr. in 1951*

The land naturally sloped east, and Dad dug a "sump hole" several yards from the house, concealing a drain from the basement sink. No more hauling out dishwater! We took our baths behind a couple of kitchen chairs draped with a sheet, the galvanized washing tub cozied up to, but not too near the old pot belly stove. In summer, water in a tub was heated by the sun for us kids or we headed for Horton Creek. There was a lot more water running in it then than there is now. Usually, in summer, we tumbled into bed after washing our dirty bare feet, Mother insisted. I was about eight when we no longer resorted to kerosene lamps and battery operated radio. Though still in the cozy basement, Dad converted the hand pump to electric and gave us running water. At first, it was just cold, and then we got hot as well. I was 12 by the time the phone lines were strung. It was a three-way party line.

In my sophomore year, we moved to Petoskey, while Dad and his friend Al Leist "tore the place apart," adding onto the little three room shack. They made a new kitchen, living room, bedroom, and bathroom. Two existing tiny bedrooms remained of the original. They left the cozy basement intact, complete with homemade bar, sink, and apartment-sized gas range. Mom continued to do a lot of canning in the basement.

Grandpa and Grandma White and Mr. and Mrs. Baker were our closest neighbors. Our driveway was set away by almost a quarter mile from the gravely two-track we called Pincherry Road. I was Grandma's sidekick.

She is the inspiration for my garden today.

I also spent a lot of time at the Baker's who lived across the road from our driveway. The Baker's grandkids were older than I, and quite often, one or the other or two would be visiting. We were allowed to go to the attic, and it was fun! An old wind-up record player dominated the space. We learned the old Sousa marches by heart. "Grandpa and Grandma" Baker were typical country folk, proud and poor, just like us. And hard workin', just like us.

There was an old corncrib on the place as most of the old places had. Some still do. The Baker and Bailey girl cousins were just like all the girls I knew. We all wanted a playhouse. Grandpa Baker let them clear out the old crib. The girls had raided all the dumps in the neighborhood to furnish it. Orange and potato crates served as furniture. A dishtowel, with some holes carefully folded under, was a tablecloth. Then for fun, they cleared out the inside underbrush in one of two interconnected and hugely overgrown lilac clumps. It made for a cleverly concealed "cave." I "visited" often on my way home from school, or when picking up the mail. And now I wonder who cut down those wonderful old lilac bushes. They were already very old—at least 75 years, and had been left unchecked and un-pruned. In the name of progress, they were destroyed to widen the road. I never did get a playhouse of my own. The closest was catching Dad building a "just the right size" building that turned out to be for pigs! I hate pigs still today!

Pincherry Road in 1940 beyond Price's was literally a two-track. Grass grew in the center. There were four houses, Southwood's, Mcclellan's, Zipp's, and the Price farm between Murray Road and Stolt Road. From Price's it was a little more than a mile to our neighborhood. I mentioned the decreased water flow in Horton Creek. Every spring, the melted snow in the hills west of Pincherry Road would flow down any ravine or avenue it could follow, overflowing the road. Culverts were unheard of, necessary for a week to ten days of the year. The children in my family raced our stick boats. The mud for this period was horrendous. Dad would leave his car near Bay Shore to walk home. Grandpa White's old Model-T would usually go through it. If not, Peanut, his old workhorse would. We all waited for the Spring break-up. Those runoffs simply don't occur anymore. These run-offs eventually made it to Horton Creek. The springs are drying up or are being destroyed by building sites, or carelessness.

I'd been to school before with my parents because of my siblings, but I sure do remember my first day. I wondered why everyone was making such a fuss. I walked in with Mom, and she anxiously pointed out Sandy on the other side of the room. Sandy and I are cousins who were raised together. So I just took her for granted she was here. Murray School was as what is known as a one-room schoolhouse. With grades kindergarten through eighth, one teacher presided over anywhere from 18 to 28 pupils and was responsible for housekeeping. When I began kindergarten, there was an outhouse. The girls and boys had separate cloakrooms with shelves and hooks. The cloakroom also had a sink with a drain. There was an open tank above the sink. The tank had a tap and spout. Our drinking water was just outside the door of the girl's cloakroom. The big kids filled all the tanks from the hand pump outside. Within a couple of years of starting school, each cloakroom was separated off to allow a chemical toilet. So you hear of horror stories of what happens in school today? Well, Quinton Jr. was held by his heels over the boy's toilet, lowered into it, brought out, and then threatened by what would happen next time if he "tattled" again. He told Dad many years later. Heads may have rolled if it had been sooner.

The room was heated by a massive coal furnace that took up a twelfth of the big room. There was a shed off the back of the school, which was filled with coal in the fall. The coal room was dirty. Of course, the boys were in charge of keeping the furnace stoked after the teacher had started it in the morning. In winter, after recess, we hung our wet things behind the furnace.

Our school boasted a kitchen about six feet by six feet and contained a gas stove. If you had something to heat for lunch, you were allowed to. The state issued "surplus" to the schools, and older students used class time just before lunch to make instant potatoes. They then dished it out with butter for everyone who wanted it. Another time, it was boiled carrots that they had had to peel. We also had them with butter; I think there was always butter!

In the fall, during recesses and noon, the younger kids had lots of fun playing on swings, slide, teeter-totter, and the merry-go-round. To operate the merry-go-round, one or two kids stepped over the seats into the frame of the thing to push. Going fast enough, the pushers hopped up onto the framework to ride. There was much woe to any of the pushers who slipped and fell inside the framework! We girls owned jack knives, too, and carried them to school. We played mumble peg during recess. Sometimes when one of the first kids out the door yelled, "I'm going to play on the bars!" we would all run for a place on the iron rail fence that ran the length of the west parameter of the school lot. We used these rails as a kind of a primitive monkey bar.

In good weather, recess for the older kids meant work-up baseball. We "called" positions as we ran out the door. The pitcher's mound faced the road. The catchers spent a lot of time running down the bank of the ditch because usually one out of eight pitches was a wild ball. A home run was a ball put over the fence and into Griffin's pasture behind the school. We did not, however, have an umpire, so I do remember there were a lot of "you're out!" cries followed by rebuttal, "I am not!" During recess in winter, when it was too stormy to play outside, we played with jacks, perfecting our coordination. Even the boys played and got quite good at it. Younger kids rolled marbles down the hardwood aisles. We talked to each other. We listened. I can't ever remember once hearing "I'm bored." I don't think we knew the word. We had books, games, and each other. After the noon recess teacher would read to us, our favorite part of the day.

Today, Murray School is a little brick house located on the corner of Murray and Upper Bay Shore Roads.

My Northern Michigan Childhood Memories
By Nelson Louis Kirby of Central Lake, Michigan
Born 1917

I was born on January 5, 1917 on our family farm, which was located a few miles north of Central Lake, Michigan. My parents, Richard L. and Ethel E. Kirby were married in 1916 and lived on the family farm in Antrim County. I was the oldest of four children. My younger brothers,

John Wesley Kirby (deceased) and Lloyd George Kirby (86 years old) were followed by my sister, Beatrice Kirby (deceased).

My brother, Lloyd Kirby, was nicknamed "Buster" by one of my aunts, because he was a rough kid. My earliest recollection while on the farm was when I was about three years old. My mom and dad took me to visit Grandpa Louis Kirby who was dying from cancer. I remember being scared when Grandpa Kirby tried to talk to me even though he had no voice box. My father tried farming for a few years and after several failed crops, gave it up and became a carpenter. His carpentry work was mostly done in neighboring Charlevoix County. Our family moved to the City of Charlevoix and lived there for a short time. We soon moved to the village of Norwood in Charlevoix County, on Lake Michigan. My aging grandparents (mother's parents) lived in Norwood and our family relocated there to help care for them.

I was six or seven years old at this time. We lived in a house in Norwood that was about a block away from the schoolhouse and Methodist Church I attended. I started my education in a one-room schoolhouse in Norwood, and attended there from the first through the eighth grade. My only teacher for the entire time attended there was Mrs. Lashbrooke. She taught first through eighth grade curriculum to approximately 25 to 30 children each day. Mrs. Lashbrooke was paid $75.00 per month, which was considered a very well paying job for the 1920s and 1930s. I remember our classroom had rows of wood desks and a wooden bench up in front of the teacher's desk. Mrs. Lashbrooke would bring groups of students by grade level up to the front of the class where she would teach individual lessons. The other kids were given assignments to do at their desks. Our teacher would walk up and down the aisles carrying a wood ruler, and anyone caught talking without permission or misbehaving would be the recipient of a rap across the back of your hands with the ruler. I recall getting hit with the ruler on more than one occasion. Another form of punishment was standing facing the corner while wearing a "dunce" cap for about an hour. All the other students would laugh at the kid in the corner. I remember being in that corner and having to wear that dunce cap more than once. I soon learned that being laughed at and suffering the humiliation from my classmates was not for me.

Every school day started with the ringing of the bell at 8:00 A.M. and you had to be in your seat by 8:15 A.M. Mrs. Lashbrooke would pray, and then the entire class would stand and recite the Pledge of Allegiance. We would have class until 10:15 A.M. when the whole class would have a 15-minute recess. All students were expected to use the boys and girls four hole outhouses during this time and still have time to play before resuming class. At noon, class would stop for lunch. Since I lived close to school, I always went home for lunch. After lunch, we played in the schoolyard until the bell at 12:45 P.M. All of us had to be back in our seats by 1:00 P.M. School would last the rest of the afternoon, and we would be dismissed at 3:30 P.M.

Because our school was located in a rural/farming community, all school classes were suspended for a week during harvest time in the fall so that the children could help on the farms and in the orchards. I can remember picking beans and potatoes for one cent per pound and cherries for a quarter per lug (30 pounds). I was able to pick five lugs of cherries a day. Some of my buddies could pick more than I could, but I thought that 150 pounds was enough! When I was 14 or 15 years old, the farmers would allow my friends and I to camp out in the orchards during the summer picking season to make some extra money. Me and my buddies would get a large mason jar, fill it with smashed cherries, add some sugar, and make our own wine. We would hide the jars in stone piles near the orchards and let the summer heat ferment the juice.

Soon after the Stock Market crashed in 1929, my dad lost his carpentry job. Our family went through some very tough times during the Great Depression. My dad worked for local farmers and fruit growers and was never paid cash for this work. He was "paid" with fruit, vegetables, dairy, and meat to feed our family. As a teenager, I took on the job of part-time janitor for the Norwood school I attended. I cleaned the school after class, did miscellaneous odd jobs, and made sure the wood burning furnace in the basement of the school was always going and well stocked with firewood. The job paid $5.00 per month, which I turned over to my mom and dad. For several years during the Depression, this was the only cash income our family had coming in. My mother would use part of this money to buy Christmas presents for our family.

During my teen years, I fondly recall many hunting adventures with my 20-gauge shotgun and my dog "Ring" by my side. Many a rabbit, partridge, and pheasant were hunted to help feed our family. On more than one occasion, my dog grabbed a rabbit or bird and I didn't even have to shoot. Ring was my trusted hunting companion for 12 wonderful years. My dad insisted that I never waste a shotgun shell on target shooting, as they were far too valuable, and needed only for game.

My mother, Ethel, possessed a very strong faith in God, and insisted that the entire family attend the First Methodist Church of Norwood every Sunday. I attended Sunday school prior to each worship service with approximately 10 to 12 other children, ages six to 15. I remembered having to take a student aptitude test with 50 or 60 other kids after I completed the seventh grade. The testing was held in the Charlevoix High School gymnasium. The test was difficult, and to make matters worse, there was a time limit. I failed the exam and had to repeat the seventh grade at Norwood school. This was a big disappointment at the time, but looking back now, it was probably best for me.

After graduation from the eighth grade and passing another tough aptitude test, my family moved to the village of Central Lake so that I could attend high school there. My Grandma Kirby already lived in Central Lake, so I already knew some buddies there from earlier visits to my grandmother. Central Lake was a great place to live while I attended high school. During the summer, my buddies and I would swim in Intermediate Lake and take turns diving off the lift bridge on old State Road. We would all try to impress the girls who came down to the lakeside park every day. Sometimes my buddies and I would get bored and would think up various pranks to play on other people. Sometimes we would tip over outhouses in the village and surrounding area. Once on Halloween, we climbed to the top of the Methodist Church belfry in Central Lake. We tied one end of a 400-foot clothesline to the bell and then strung the line through the trees to a remote location in some backyard. At 11:00 P.M. on Halloween night, we began ringing the bell from our remote hiding place. When townspeople ran to see who was ringing the bell, all they saw was a "ghost" pulling the rope up and down inside the church. We were never caught. One of the best pranks me and my buddies ever pulled off was on our high school Superintendent, Mr. Alexander. We had nicknamed the superintendent "Corky" because my friends and I didn't like him too much. My good buddies were Jack Knowles and Jimmy Aenis. One night, we decided to borrow a neighbor's cow, bring it into the school, and tie it to Mr. Alexander's office door. One of us climbed up a tree next to the school, came in through an open window, and then unlocked the main door. My buddies and I had a heck of a time getting that cow to go up the steps and into the school. We had to twist that cow's tail to get her into the school that night. Once the cow was tied to the Superintendent's door, we fed it some corn stalks, and by morning, there was a big mess waiting for Mr. Alexander. The school janitor, Mr. Robertson had the unpleasant task of cleaning up the mess. Getting caught meant that all of us would have been expelled from school. We laid low and were never caught for pulling this prank!

I met the love of my life while attending Central Lake High School. Her name was Fern Roberts and she lived with her family on a farm about two miles south of town. I used to walk her home every day after school. She was two years younger than I was, and was one grade behind me. After I graduated from high school, I heard that a plant in Pontiac, Michigan was hiring workers. I left Central Lake with $70.00 in my pocket and headed south. I stayed with a friend's aunt and uncle in Pontiac while I searched for a job. The Depression was beginning to ease its grip on the country, and I was very fortunate to land a salary position at the Yellow Cab Manufacturing Company (soon to become General Motors Truck & Coach).

Six months after Fern graduated from high school, we were married in Pontiac, Michigan. While earning a salary of $76.00 per month, we started our life together. We lived in Pontiac, and raised three children. We had one son named Raymond, and two girls, Linda and Gail. Fern, the children, and I came back to Central Lake to visit family on vacations and during the holidays. After working for General Motors for 38 years, in 1973 we retired and moved back to Central Lake. We enjoyed our retirement years and the wonderful people of this community have been so good to us. My dear Fern passed away in October of 2002, and I currently live in Central Lake with my daughter, Gail.

Friday Night Home in the '60s
By Susan Floer of Hillman, Michigan
Born 1953

One year my Dad decided to surprise my Mom for Christmas by buying her a living room group of furniture. He searched all over trying to pick out something to really get her excited. He picked out a Mediterranean motif complete with a burnt orange L-shaped couch that came complete with a tall fake green plant in the corner of the sectional. Two dark gold velvet-like swivel chairs complimented the couch. We went to Joshua Doore, where we bought a Spanish-looking electric fireplace. He wasn't done yet. Topping off the furniture selections, Dad bought a wall mount that was half of a candelabrum made out of heavy black chain links with gold candles around it. Dad was so proud of his purchases. Mom hated it! My folks bought rust colored carpet that was extra thick had a tightly weaved loop. It was so tight that any lint stayed right on top of the carpet. When we vacuumed all the lines showed in the carpeting. I loved the thickness because it was great for practicing my cheerleading jumps in the reflection of the door wall.

It was Friday Night at the Rathbun house. We lived in a middle class subdivision, where everyone lived in a similar three-bedroom style ranch home. Dad worked full-time, which required him to be on his feet most of his busy eight-hour day. Mom worked a part-time job in a department store to help pay the bills. With four kids in school, it was a busy house, but everyone did their part to help out with chores. By the end of the week, we would look forward to sitting down together to watch some of our favorite shows on TV. There was never a question of what we were going to watch; it was McHale's Navy, Andy Griffith, Jackie Gleason and Red Skelton. It was an all-American memory that I hold near and dear to my heart. Dad would always lean back in his black nauga hide leather lazy boy. Mom sat on the couch with her feet on the coffee table. Sally sat in the rocking chair, which gave her a space of

Susan and her sister Nancy in 1960

her own to knit where the yarn would flow freely over the arms of the chair. Nancy and I usually sat with Mom on the couch, and my brother Jim enjoyed the thick carpeted floor.

In the excitement of the Friday family togetherness, I would jump up and say, "Hey! It's Friday night! How about a party?" Without hesitation, I would head for the kitchen while the family cackled away at the comedy shows we were watching. I riffled through Mom's cupboards in search of anything to put together a tempting snack tray. A common staple in our house was saltine crackers. That was always how my tray of goodies started. I began spreading the "ho-hum" crackers with peanut butter, jelly, liver sausage, cream cheese, bologna, and American cheese. To dress-up the tray, I would slice up some olives and place a slice on a few crackers. Now I had a tray full of beautiful crackers that spelled "presentation" all the way. Before unveiling my party surprise, I would go around the room taking drink orders. The choices were always the same, Pepsi, root beer, or water. (Of course I took a pad of paper with me to play out the waitress duties; as to not to get anyone's drink wrong!) I poured all the selected drinks and put them on a tray. Once I delivered all the requested drink orders, I'd pass out napkins to each member of the family.

The big unveiling was about to happen. I had everyone on the edge of their seat. I never allowed anyone in the kitchen while I prepared my saltines. After all my hard work, I proudly brought out the big tray off delectable delights. Everyone "oooed and ahhed." My expertise in party planning was worth every sliced olive.

One would have thought I was serving shrimp cocktails and sushi. It wasn't long before the once boring saltines were gone with nary a crumb left. Oh, to bring those days back again when life was simple. We didn't have much, but what we did have was very special. Better than that, it was great family togetherness on a Friday night in the Rathbun house.

Grand   Vacation

When I was a young girl, my family and I vacationed on Lake Michigan in Grand Haven. It was my first experience swimming in one of the Great Lakes. Some friends of the family invited us to stay with them in their trailer on the beautiful shores of southwestern Michigan.

My Dad loved to swim. The water was such a relaxing change for him. He worked in a busy airport where his days were full of stress. He was like a kid; he would splash through the waves and swim out in the deep blue water. I watched his artful stroke and hoped that someday I would be able to look as graceful.

I carefully walked out onto the dock that had a bench on it. My sisters weren't afraid of the water. With each step I took, I could see the mighty water dancing back and forth. Then there would be a plank of solid wood. I felt safe on the wood. Then there would be more water in the cracks of the wood. I was getting a little dizzy. My Mom sat on the dock and let her feet hang in the cool water. She was kicking one foot at a time. I finally made it up the dock and sat alongside my Mom. I looked out into the distant sun going down over the water and caught a glimpse of a giant boat in the distance. Mom told me that those were called freighters. My Grandpa sailed on those big boats for many years. Closer into the shoreline, there were smaller boats bobbing over the waves. They were trying to catch fish from the boats.

I couldn't believe how big the sun was as it got lower and lower in the sky. The lower it got the deeper shade of red it turned. At night, the moon shined over the huge body of water. We had a bonfire on the beach. We all sang songs together. I watched the fire reflecting in everyone's face. When the fire died out, it was time for bed. I got to sleep in a top bunk. There was a tiny window where I could watch the waves roll into shore and back out again. They never slept.

I woke to the sound of seagulls swooping around the tall pier. They must have been in search of fish. Dad couldn't wait to take us swimming. He took my sister and by our hands and slowly walked out into the lake. The waves were rushing right by us. As soon as one would come close, Dad would lift us out of the water so we wouldn't get swept away by the strong current.

After lunch, Dad took us out fishing on the big red pier. We had long cane poles made out of bamboo. My sister and I each wore our new skorts and, of course, sunglasses. I sat next to an old man who looked like he was catching a few fish. Just about the time I got my line in the water…SMACK! I got hit in the face with a fish! The old man was pulling a fish and it happened to come right in my direction. I didn't like that, but he didn't do it on purpose. We actually caught a few fish. They weren't real big, but back to the trailer we went with our long poles over our shoulders and a stringer full of perch. Mom was excited when she saw that we actually caught some fish and I told her my "fish-in-the-face" story. We had a great time in Grand Haven. I'm glad to have experienced Lake Michigan.

Sanitary   Sam

In first grade, while living in West Virginia, my teacher's name was Mrs. Wetzel. As class was just to begin for the day, we were all asked to go to the front of the room and stand in a semi-circle. Above the chalkboard, there was a big picture of cartoon character whose

Susan's dad with Susan's daughter in the '60s

369

name was "Sanitary Sam." He was as clean and well-dressed as any young boy you could imagine. The purpose of having this picture for us to look at was to teach us to be a reflection of his cleanliness. The year was 1958. I think it's safe to say that he has retired by now. He had a hanky pinned to his pocket. His face was clean. His fingernails were cut and there wasn't a trace of dirt between his fingers. His shoes were shined. His hair was combed. His clothes were pressed. His teeth were brushed. Mrs. Wetzel would inspect us, one-by-one, and make sure that we were a mirror image of "Sanitary Sam." This was a daily ritual. The importance of proper cleanliness was a healthy reminder that was drilled into our heads. If we had one unsanitary item, our teacher sent a note home with us to give to our parents.

My Mom and Dad were responsible for making sure that they didn't send us off to school with soiled clothing, or mussed up hair. Back in the '50s, most parents took pride in what their children looked like as they sent them off to public school. Throughout my life, I'd have to say that personal hygiene was constantly preached. My family life was great. I have two older sisters and one younger brother. My parents had to teach these good habits repeatedly four times a day, day in and day out. We wanted to be just like "Sanitary Sam," after all.

In Junior High School, my home economics teacher taught me how to iron, sew and cook. I even learned cleaning tips on polishing cupboards and proper cleansers to use in different parts of the house. We learned how to press a wool sweater and how to do a wash.

Once I got to high school, playing basketball and being outside was more important to me that cooking, cleaning and primping. I learned the word "procrastination." I hated taking the time to wash my hair and shower. It was too much work. I was always too tired to go through all the fuss. Mom would say, "Quit procrastinating and get in there!" I learned my lesson in the tenth grade. One day when I was on the fourth day of procrastinating. That day, the school photographer showed up for class pictures. When the yearbooks came out, I saw what procrastination looked like. It was a lesson learned the hard way!

Tonight as I was getting ready to retire, I picked up a table napkin that had not been used. I began dusting off my coffee tables with it. As I went to throw it away in the office trash, I looked around and couldn't help but notice how many art projects I had lying in the room. I began putting them away. Finally I got to my nightly ritual of hygiene, which is about four steps. I decided while I was at it, to clean the toilet. I had to or I wouldn't sleep.

It's hard to believe what I go through because "Sanitary Sam" stared at me every step of the way. I am thankful to everyone who had a hand in teaching me to live a healthy life. I've passed the same traits onto my daughter, who is now busy teaching her three sons the same lessons. By using that goofy looking picture of "Sanitary Sam" my house is clean today.

✓ Adventures with the Family
By Jane W. Smith of Shaftsburg, Michigan
Born 1936

Our first house on Wolf Court was a bus body with an addition off the back of it for our bedrooms. We heated it with a pot-bellied stove. We lived in that for several years until Daddy built us a new house. We had a kitchen, bedroom, living room, and an upstairs. Our beds were upstairs. It wasn't finished off up there, so in the winter, the frost would build up on the nails that stuck through the roof. We would lay in bed and eat the frost off the nails. My grandma used to sew a lot, so she made a lot of quilts out of our old clothes. At night, my sister and I would look at the quilts and we would point out the different squares and tell each other who wore which one.

I started school in East Lansing when I was four years old. I used to play with the toy phones and build houses out of the blocks in kindergarten went through the fifth grade at East Lansing, then we moved up north. We always had an outhouse on Wolf court East Lansing. We had a neighbor boy who came over to our house. Our dog had puppies, and they were about six weeks old. He threw them down the toilet hole. Poor puppies! Daddy saved them all and Mom gave them a bath.

We used pots in the winter so that we wouldn't have to go outside to the outhouse at night. If we had to go at night in the summertime, we just went out to the outhouse. Saturday night we had a washtub to take our baths in. We started with the oldest of the kids and went down the line until we all had our

Jane W. Jenks Smith in 1950

baths. We had a bathtub given to us, and they put it in the corner and the piano sat front of it. We hooked a hose to the drain to run the water out the back door. We had a curtain across from the piano to the wall for privacy.

We used to sit around the radio on Sunday nights and listen to the Lux Video Theater with James Mason. We also listened to the Sunday funnies. We also listened to Hashknife Hartley, Hop-a-long, Lone Ranger, and many more. When we moved to the farm up to Clare, there was an Edison hand crank record player and some records, too. Grandma Bell brought us some old thick Edison Records. When we moved from the farm, Mom gave it to the neighbor. It is still in their attic. We had a party line phone. If you picked up the phone to use it, you might end up talking to someone already on the line. You would have to wait until they got done using the phone before you could use it.

Grandma Bell had a green Plymouth Coupe, and us kids would lay up in the back window to ride. Daddy had a big Buick. It was in the 1930s, so it had the spare tire on the driver's side built in to the front fender. We were getting ready to go to Indiana, Ohio, and Kentucky. My brother slammed the car door on my middle finger. It split it open. While Mom was putting a bandage on my finger, I reached out and grabbed a bee with my other hand. My grandma had shown me how to grab a fly and catch it, so I guess I thought it was a fly. After we sold our big Buick, Daddy bought a 1931 Model-A. We drove it for a while and the engine had to be fixed, so Daddy took the engine out of the car. He carried it into the house into the living room. There, he took the engine apart and put it back together. He would tell me what part he wanted, and I would hand it to him. When he got it all back together, he carried the engine back out to the car and put it back in. He paid $40.00 for the car, drove it for 12 years, and sold it for $40.00. I always wished I had bought it.

At Bawsley School in Clare County, they had a razor strap that the teacher would spank the kids with. The teacher threatened to spank my sister with it. Other kids actually did get spanked with it. If we were bad at home, we would get spankings. Our mother would spank all three of us, even if she knew which one of us had done it. I got a lot of spankings that I didn't need.

My father had a trap line, and he would catch muskrats, minks, and weasels. I always liked to help skin them. One time, he caught a large mink and he got $40.00 just for the mink. That was a lot of money then. Mom and Daddy talked about that money for the mink and wished he could have caught more of them. I still have the bullet from the first deer Daddy shot when we moved to the farm.

We went fishing a lot at the Farwell Mill pond, and I used to always catch a big bass before the season was open. I cut what they called a sucker off of our apple tree; was it a very straight branch that would grow straight up. I cut it, and put a hook and line on it. I put a big worm on the hook and threw it in the water. That's how I caught that big bass. I took it and showed my Mom. She said, you have to throw it back. I told her "No. I have to show it to Daddy." I ran down the bank and showed Daddy. He said, "You have to throw it back." I said, "No. I have to show it to Grandma." I ran on down the bank to show Grandma. I told Grandma, "I have to throw it back now." She said, "No, Give it to me." I gave the fish to my grandma and she took off her undershirt, rolled the fish in it, and put it in her pant leg. It was 19 ½ inches long and weighed 4 ½ pounds. We had a good fish supper that night! We used to fish a lot, at least three or four times a week with my sister, and then on the weekends the whole family would go fishing. I still love to fish.

I remember World War II with the air raids, blackouts, and sirens. It was really scary. We had to cover our radios and phones so that no lights could be seen. Then, we would gather around the radio to hear what they were saying. Sometimes, we would go outside to watch for the planes. My father had to go to Detroit for a physical, but he didn't pass. I had three uncles (two were my father's brothers, and one of them my mother's brother) and some cousins who had to serve in the war. I had cousins that served in the Korean War, too. Some were wounded, and we lost one cousin. We used to have a single tub. We used a wringer washer, but the wringer was wearing out, so my folks and Grandma went to Saginaw to buy a double tub Dexter wringer washer. That made it much easier because we didn't have to stomp the clothes by hand to rinse them. They used to have free movies. They showed on the side of a building, and we went to the drive-ins, too.

During the Depression, my mother cooked a muskrat and told us it was rabbit. It was the most awful tasting stuff you could have ever tasted. We ate my chickens, Polly and Molly. Daddy said, "Can we eat your chickens. I said, "No." Daddy asked the next day and said that we didn't have anything for supper. I told him that we could eat one, so we ate Polly. Then, a few days later, we ate Molly. I had two red New Zealand rabbits, and we ate them, too. We also ate blackbirds and sparrows with homemade noodles. I thought it was so cool to have a whole bird to eat. We used to catch a lot of frogs and eat their legs, too. We ate turtles as well.

We used to get printed bags of cow feed. One of my favorite dresses was made out of feedbags. It had bubbles with real pretty rainbow colors on them and a beautiful background. Grandma put a piece of organdy in the neck. I just loved it. Chicken feed came in plain feedbags, too. Our mom made us pajamas and underwear out of those. I hated my underwear, so I wouldn't wear them when I wore jeans. My mom told me I would get "blue crotch" but she would never tell me what that was, so I never wore them with my jeans. I thought that if she wouldn't tell me what it was then it couldn't have been that bad.

I loved all of my teachers, but I think my favorite teacher was Mrs. Lee. I had her in the fourth grade at Central School in East Lansing. I moved to Clare in the '40s. We went to school at Bawsley one-room school. It was so different. There were only 17 kids in the whole school, from beginners though the eighth grade. There were five of us in the eighth grade. I started out in the sixth grade there. We would toast our sandwiches in the furnace in the winter. When Sno-Snake Mountain opened, they invited all of the country schools to a big Valentine's Day party. Cornwell ranch brought a stock truck to the school and backed up to the window, and all of us kids crawled through the window into the back of the truck. They took us to Sno-Snake and we had a wonderful time skiing and tobogganing. We were treated to all the hotdogs, donuts, and hot chocolate that we wanted. It was one of the most wonderful days that we had. We had so much fun.

We had a springer spaniel that was black and white. He was my favorite dog. Also, we had a little tree frog. I brought some plants back for Florida, and when I took the plants out of the bag, a little tree frog hopped out. I fixed him an aquarium to live in and named him Freddie the Frog. We went back to Florida that spring and took him with us. I put him on my hand, went outside, and held my hand out to the bush, but he ran right back up my arm. I went back in the camper and put my hand in the aquarium, and he hopped down my arm and back into his safe little home. I had him for five years.

We were camping at Lake Magarite by Grayling at the State Forest Campground. There were 21 rattlesnakes killed in the park that year. I came out of our tent, and a rattlesnake was coiled up right beside my tent door. I had never heard a rattlesnake rattle before, but you could hear him above the two radios that were playing. I grabbed a shovel and killed the snake. He had eight rattles on his tail. We also had a woodchuck that tried to attack us once. We grabbed a hoe and killed it. We went swimming in the river one time, and a car stopped on top of the bridge. We had left our clothes in a pile by the side of the road, so the three of us girls hung on the girders under the bridge. Mother said that from then on we had to swim fully clothed.

✓ The Old Winter Sports Park
By Eleanor M. Jardine of Harbor Springs, Michigan

Back in the early thirties, Harbor Springs had a Winter Sports Park. It was located west of town, off from the Shore Drive and Ridge Road. The property was donated by Mr. J. E. Otis. There was a warming house, a ski jump, a toboggan run and a bobsled run.

I was a 9 year old in 1935, and considered a little kid, so when I rode down the big hill on the bobsled with my dad, I was allowed to stay on the sled and ride up to the top of the hill.

Mr. George Cook, a family friend, owned the team of horses that pulled the sled back up the hill. A few years ago, I conferred with Mr. Bob Cook (George's nephew) and we reminisced about the old Winter Sports Park.

Bob was a senior in high school that year. Using some of his senior knowledge, he pulled a toboggan up to the top of the ski jump. He laid down on it on his stomach and slid down the jump. The landing was such a jolt; it was his first and last time taking such a ride!

My parents took me to the park on Sunday afternoons. A lot of people attended the park on Saturdays and Sundays. Many families were there with their children.

Mr. Otis' daughter showed up one Sunday afternoon wearing a beautiful white snowsuit. She was also allowed to stay on the sled and ride to the top of the hill. But, this one day, Mr. Cook had overfed his team. When they arrived at the top of the hill, Nancy's beautiful, white snowsuit wasn't pure white!

Those were the days, and I can remember the Winter Sports Park with many fond memories.

✓ Inverness Dairy
By Christine McDonald from Cheboygan, Michigan
Born 1948

My first school was in Cheboygan, Michigan. It was Benton #7, located on Huron Shore Road or US23. Grades one through twelve were taught at that time, by Delores Kronkowski. She not only was a wonderful

Christine at the Benton #7 School

teacher, but smelled yummy!

At five years old, I remember going to the front of the classroom with other first graders and sitting at a long table with our teacher. We had Dick and Jane readers, and learned to read by sight (no phonics back then).

Every morning the Pledge of Allegiance to our flag was recited, and milk was furnished by Inverness Dairy (white or chocolate) in glass bottles.

I had a Long Ranger lunch pail to carry my lunch, and those that lived closer went home for lunch. A station wagon picked us up for school.

At Christmastime, a stage was built up at the front of the room and every student had a part in the program. Corsages were given to the moms.

I didn't attend this school for very long, but it is my happiest memories. I wish all children could start in a one-room schoolhouse.

✓ A Long Ago Snowstorm
By Geraldine Sturdavant from LeRoy, Michigan
Born 1919

This local area in the winter of January 1937 received the surprising news that one of their old-time residents had suddenly passed away. Her passing came at a time when the community also suffered the blows of a paralyzing snowstorm.

The nearest funeral facility was at Reed City, fifteen miles away. But the affects of the storm complicated the funeral facility from reaching her residence.

W.P.A. workers were sent to the location to dig out the farmyard and the half-mile of roadway that the residence was located on.

One snowplow served the LeRoy-Tustin areas on the main roads. It took three days of digging the W.P.A. crew to complete the farmyard the roadway, which connected up with an east and west roadway, which was more traversable.

When completed, the north and south roadways were traversable to automobile traffic and the cars that traveled down them resembled cars traveling down a tunnel as they moved along.

√ Halloween
By Martha Robinette from Alpena, Michigan
Born 1924

In 1947, there were still many homes that did not have indoor plumbing, including ours (my husband and I). We had an outhouse. Come Halloween, a couple of pranksters came after dark and moved it forward thinking we would fall in if we went to use the outhouse during the night. But my husband was the first one to go out in daylight, the day after Halloween, he moved it where it should of been.

The following year, come Halloween, the pranksters pulled off the same prank. My husband thought that "Enough is enough, I will fix them!" The next year on Halloween night, as it turned dusk, he moved the outhouse, same as they had done. Guess what? Someone came after dark again, and must have fallen in as they went to move the outhouse, because the next morning there were tracks leading away from the crime scene. Ugh! Needless to say, that was the end of anymore Halloween pranks on our outhouse!

√ Buried Alive
By Maxine Donajkowski from Alpena, Michigan
Born 1945

Have you ever nonchalantly begin an experience that you end up remembering for the rest of your life? I am somewhat adventurous, but my husband's trip to show me the cracks and crevices on his parent's farm, in Alpena County, Northern Michigan, nearly did me in.

First, we had to row our boat across the private lake and moor it among the rocks. Then there were bigger and higher rocks, which necessitated a fifteen minute climb uphill. And I am not as nimble as I used to be!

When we reached the largest of the crevices, he decided to descend and investigate any changes since he was a boy. Only after much negotiation did I agree to accompany him, but the minute I could not see the sky above, and felt the cold, damp, and murky horror of the underground, my terror began to nauseate me!

In the few minutes (which seemed like years), it took me to ascend back to daylight, I experienced the morbid sense of being buried alive. A terror I never knew existed took control of my very being. That feeling was so powerful and so frightening I don't think anyone could put it into words.

Don't misconstrue, this may never happen to you! My husband remembers only the beauty of the rock formations, the snow in July on the cave floor, and the excitement of exploration. For me a trip into any cave or crevice will be only a topic of conversation and then given only nominal attention. I've had my adventure of a lifetime!

√ Confession of a Cover-up
By Jack McGee in Lake City, Michigan
Born 1947

During my twelfth year of life, the local creamery ceased butter production and closed its doors forever. My father, like many other small farmers in our area, sold our small herd of milk cows and we started receiving our milk, butter, and cheese from the McDonald Dairy delivery truck.

My very best friend at that time was a ragged-haired, flop-eared, red dog we called Babe. His mother was the local junkyard guard dog and his father was of unknown and questionable character.

My mother realized that Babe and I were kindred spirits with the tendency to find mischief and trouble far too often. Along with my daily chores, Mother would often say (in a scolding voice), "...and pick up all those empty milk cartons that YOUR dog has dragged into the front lawn!"

Our country neighbor, retired Preacher Smith, and his wife lived about a mile from us. Old Mrs. Smith, who found happiness elusive and made complaining her long suit, would constantly grumble about the milkman to my mother on the seven party phone line we shared with our neighbors. One of her many complaints was that he regularly shorted them one quart of milk and then had the nerve to charge them for it.

One morning, after rising a little earlier than normal, I saw Babe happily bounding across the hay field from the direction of the Smith place. With smiling eyes and ears flopping in the wind, he carried a quart carton of milk in his mouth. When he arrived in our front yard, he promptly grasped the carton in his front paws, rolled onto his back, chewed off one bottom corner and sucked the carton dry (like a baby holding its own bottle). While I was hiding the evidence in our private farm dump hole, I noticed that many of the other cartons were also missing a bottom corner.

I didn't fess up to the crime until well after both Babe and Mrs. Smith had gone to the hereafter. Until her dying day, Mrs. Smith never stopped accusing the milkman of overcharging.

✓ Newton Maid Washers
By Wilbur Garrett from Glennie, Michigan
Born 1924

When I was a boy, I remember helping my mother with the wash. The first task was to get water into the washer. The washer was filled using a hand pump that brought the water up from the cistern located in the basement. The cistern was filled with rainwater collected from the eaves system. If the cistern was too full, an overflow spigot was turned to allow the water to drain out. If the water level was too low, we would fill it with lake water. The water was heated on the old cook stove and poured into the washer and the first rinse tub. The second rinse tub was filled with cold water. We had a washing machine, but it did not have a wringer on it. The round wooden tub was on legs with a gear on the lid. It was my job to move the handle back and forth so the gear on the lid would agitate back and forth cleaning the clothes. The agitator looked similar to a round milk stool with four legs. We had to wring the clothes out by hand and hang the clothes on the line to dry.

In 1935, the men who wanted electricity to their farms went to the swamp to cut tall cedar poles. These poles were set and readied for Consumers Power Company of Michigan to run the appropriate wires. After we got electricity, my mother got a new Newton Maid washing machine made in Newton, Iowa. It was a round metal tub with a roller wringer attached. We would take the washed clothes and run them through the wringer into the first rinse tub. The wringer would need to be adjusted to swing so the rinsed clothes would be run through the rollers into a second rinse tub. Again, the wringer would be swung around so the twice-rinsed clothes could be squeezed through the wringer rollers one last time into the awaiting basket, which would be used to carry the laundry outside to the clothesline.

The wringer would then complete a 360 degree circle and be returned to the first position over the washer. My mother used this washer until the mid-1940s, when running water was installed in the house and a more updated model was purchased.

✓ Ice for the Summer
By David Kent from Atlanta, Michigan
Born 1946

Have you ever wondered where we got our ice before they had icemakers? Most people probably have never even given it a thought.

I'm not sure what they did in the warmer climates, but up here in northern Michigan, it came off the frozen lakes in the winter. My dad, James Kent who was pretty handy, built his own equipment for harvesting ice off the lakes. He had a buzz saw rig mounted on sleigh runners that could be raised or lowered. It had handles similar to a plow handle to guide it. They would set the depth so it would not cut all the way through the ice, so they could still walk on the ice after it had been cut. They would then cut a large area in a checkerboard pattern making ready for someone to finish cutting the ice the rest of the way through with an ice saw similar to a loggers crosscut but with a handle just on one end. Since they were working in subzero temperatures, the blocks of ice would freeze together a little and would have to be popped apart with an ice spud. Using a "pike pole," which was a long pole with a metal point and a hook, they would float the blocks of ice to a conveyer that was submerged in water that went up to a dump truck. The conveyor had metal plates about three feet apart that carried the blocks of ice up. There would be a guy on the truck with ice tongs to take the blocks of ice off the conveyor and stack them on the truck.

The ice was then delivered to the various places of business that sold ice. The ice blocks were stacked in their icehouses and covered with sawdust between the layers and about two feet over the very top.

After all the customers had been supplied, we would fill the icehouse at our home. In the summer time, it was my job to wait on customers who wanted ice. I had to shovel the sawdust off the ice and then wash it off with a garden hose. I got ten cents for every block of ice I sold, which I spent quite wisely. I would walk about a mile up the road to a little grocery store and spend it on (you guessed it!) Ice Cream!

✓ My Favorite Teacher
By Audrey Davis from Reed City, Michigan
Born 1928

I was born and raised on a farm and went to a one-room country school. We walked one mile in snow, sleet, rain, or sunshine. Our teacher was from Hersey and fresh out of County Normal in Evart. His name was Bruce Wanstead but we always called him "teacher."

There was no electricity so we had two outhouses, one for the boys and one for the girls. A hand-pump outside filled a pail of water, which the boys carried inside, and we all drank out of the same dipper.

The county nurse came several times a year and she upgraded our cleanliness. We averaged between fifteen and twenty students each year.

We had 4-H sewing for the girls and handicraft for the boys. Naida Wanstead, Bruce's wife, was our 4-H leader and Bruce taught the boys and Naida taught the girls. We had exhibits at the Evart High School and also took our things to Cadillac to the Northern District Fair. Our teacher and some parents took us to the Northern District Fair in Cadillac almost every year. What great fun!

We played games and "teacher" joined us at lunchtime and recess. Pom-pom-pull away, red light-green light, prisoners goal, baseball, and red rover were some games. Our school

Henry, Leslie, Norman, Audrey, and Bruce in 1941

was on a hill, so we had a good place to slide in the winter.

Our Christmas programs were awesome and Naida played the piano for us. We always had a good crowd. Halloween parties were held at our teacher's house and other parties too. Their house was small but we were always welcome.

Many Box Socials were held and we used the money to buy materials for our 4-H projects. We also raffled off an Indian blanket every year. We sold the tickets for five cents each.

I graduated in 1941 from the 8th grade with three boys in our class. Several area schools joined together and we went on a day trip, by school bus, to St. Ignace. What an experience! Some of us never had been further than Cadillac or Reed City.

On the last day of school, we would have a picnic for all the families. It was potluck and we had lemonade, which was a treat. Those were the "good old days" in Osceola County, LeRoy, Michigan.

✗ T. C. Natives
By Cheryl Morgan by Traverse City, Michigan
Born 1944

I was born and raised in Traverse City and come from a long line of T. C. natives. I was fortunate to live most of my childhood on East Bay, two houses outside the city limits on Birchwood Avenue. There weren't many houses there at that time and I remember the time the water rose and covered that road by Milliken Park. When it receded, it trapped large carp in the road and in shallow puddles. Sheriff Weiler had to come with deputies to shoot them to remove them.

My next-door neighbors were the Straubs. They ran the concession stand at the zoo, which was then where the Farmers Market is now. There was not a highway between the Boardman River and West Bay, only the railroad track. My cousins and I would go to the Railroad track by Darrow Park on Bay Street, and wait for the train so we could wave to our Uncle who was the caboose man. My Uncle, Ken Darrow, owned Darrow's IGA on Bay Street and in the winter, ice would be cut from West Bay and stacked by the store, covered with straw and sold to residents for their iceboxes.

There was a roller rink/dance hall on Front Street beneath the Michigan Theater named "Moonlight Gardens." Twice a week, there were dances and if you wanted a snack, you ran across the street to "Stacey's Restaurant," where Julie would take good care of you. You could even use the cash register yourself to pay your bill. Cunningham's Drug Store was on the corner of Front and Cass Streets and had a great soda fountain. There was a wonderful Ice Cream parlor named the "Tic Shoppe" farther down Front Street. On Union Street just off Front Street was "Nick's Chili Pot"...Great food and memories!

Milliken's Department Store was on the corner of Front and Cass and had a great little restaurant called "Milliken's Tea Room." I waitressed there as a teenager.

When I was a pre-teen, we didn't have a T.V. set but there were great programs on the radio: "Sky King", "Fibber Magee & Molly", "The Shadow", and "Inner Sanctum" to name a few. We also had telephones with operators, no dial, and party lines. We were on an eight party line and often had to wait for someone else to finish their call before we could use our phone.

Traverse City was, and still is, a great place to live and raise a family. I am a life-long resident and my children also live here with their families.

The Popular Inn
By John Renauld from Hubbard Lake, Michigan
Born 1931

It was 1965. My wife and I lived in Trenton, Michigan and I worked in Flat Rock, Michigan. We had a restaurant called the "Popular Inn," located at Riverview, Michigan. It was an old Railroad Bunkhouse, under a 100-year lease to the restaurant operator, with no repairs allowed. It leaked when it rained, some boards were missing on the porch, and there were only steps to the main entrance door. There was a floorshow every night in front of a potbelly stove, a worn linoleum on the floor. Dinner was served in your own room, which really had been a bedroom at one time. There was a spider web in an upper corner and the walls were covered with paper stained from rain.

One weekend my folks were visiting us from the U.P., Menominee, Michigan. My dad was a happy-go-lucky guy and liked to pull my leg. I decided to pay him back, so this particular night we told him we were going out to eat at someplace nice, not like the dives in the U.P. We made him polish his black shoes and my mother wore her good dress, jacket and gold open-toe shoes.

When we arrived at the Popular Inn, it was raining. Dad asked, "Where is the river?" (Flat Rock, Trenton, and Riverview, Michigan all were small towns in the area called Down River from Detroit.) I told him there wasn't any, just follow the tracks. Mother said, "The water is between my toes!" and dad said his shoe polish was being destroyed. Dad then asked, "Where is the sidewalk?" I told him, "Never mind, just go up the steps because the boards on the porch are missing. Just go and sign in."

I showed dad the floorshow, the worn linoleum, and he looked around bewildered. A waiter came and took us to the bedroom with a table and chairs. He had a red vest, white shirt and wore and tuxedo. Dad was still bewildered, and then asked for a menu. The waiter in the tuxedo said, "There isn't any. We have steak, chicken, fish and shrimp, all for $5.95 each and drinks are extra." We ordered, and mom couldn't stop laughing. Dad couldn't eat; he fell for my story of "someplace nice" hook-line-and-sinker. But after a few drinks, he checked the silverware and spider web, and he knew he had been taken. The food was fantastic and even dad admitted it was good. Back in the U.P., every bar in town heard of the Popular Inn!

Later a friend of mine purchased the building from the railroad for the liquor license. The poor maintenance of the building had caused its demise. In the attic, he found 50-pound lard tubs catching the rainwater. We were lucky it didn't cave in!

✓ $5 Monthly Payment Plan
By Joe Oyster from Lupton, Michigan
Born 1957

I grew up in a little northeast Michigan town called Lupton. Back 60 years ago, the town had a two-room schoolhouse, General Store, Post Office, Automobile Garage, Pallet Mill, Gas Station, and a Beer Garden named the Graceland Ballroom (which was a very famous landmark). But today all that remains is the Automobile Garage, and the schoolhouse. The government closed the Post Office, the General Store was torn down the mill is falling down, and the Graceland Ballroom burnt down.

I started going to school at the time when one and two room schoolhouses were being phased out. but I did attend Kindergarten through second grade at a two room school, then the school was moved to a town five miles away called Rose City, where they had grades K through twelve (the Lupton school was closed). School was very different back then. All the boys could carry a pocketknife to school, and there wasn't any bullying.

Now, let me tell a story! When I was ten years old, I wanted to buy a lawn mower so I could make a little money in the summer like the rest of the boys in town. So I asked my dad if I could borrow money from him to buy the mower. However, he didn't have the money at that time to lend me. I understood he was just making ends meet himself, working as an automobile mechanic and raising us eight kids. So, I got an idea. I went to the local Gambles store in nearby Rose City and told the owner the story about wanting to buy a mower. He asked me if I had any money to put a down payment on the mower I told him no but I could make payments on it from my lawn mowing jobs. He told me to let him think about it and come back in ten minutes. I went to the front steps of the store to count the minutes when all of a sudden, the front screen door opened and there stood the owner. He said to come back in to see what he could do about the mower. I had to promise to make

a five-dollar monthly payment to him until the mower was paid for or he would have to ask my parents to make the payments. I thanked him and left the store with a brand new mower and a gas can! By the next day, I had two lawns to mow and by the end of the summer I was mowing fourteen lawns ($1 for small lawns, $2 for big lawns), made my $5 monthly payment on time and had the mower paid off two months early!

By the end of the summer, the wheels were worn off, but the money I was making was all mine now, and I even had enough money that fall to open my first bank account at the Farmers and Merchant Bank in Rose City with a $25 deposit. I still have that bankbook today!

✓ Paper Routes and Mowing
By Dr. Hans Andrews from Ottawa, Illinois
Born 1938

Hans was involved in work projects from about the eighth grade forward. He had a paper route of 71 that grew to 94 over the time he peddled the *Bay City Times* newspaper. His brother assisted on the route for several months and cousin Roger had his own route. He also did gardening and mowing for several neighbors in Grayling. At the lake, he started a worm bait business for people renting grandmother Mathilda's boats. She provided coffee grounds to use in the worm grounds near the lake, as they were effective in drawing worms close to the surface for digging.

Hans Andrews in 1953
(In his Pure Oil uniform)

After his sophomore year in high school (1954), June Martin asked Hans if he wanted to work in her Pure Oil gas station. She and her husband had bought the station from Hans' uncle and aunt Earl and Alice Nelson. He had peddled papers to her for two years and knew him fairly well.

June pointed out that he was about three months short of age 16, which was the age necessary in Michigan in order to pump gasoline. If asked, he was to say he was 16. Those months passed quickly and he earned his first paychecks for 40 hours of work during those summer months. They amounted to just under $15.00 a week take home pay a week. During the winter, June kept him working every other night as her son Bill worked the other evenings. They also rotated weekend days.

Growing UP in the U.P.
By Marian Second from Traverse City,
Michigan
Born 1928

I was born in Laurium, Michigan in 1928. Growing up in such a magical place was my inheritance. I had a best friend named Barbara, with whom I traversed the surrounding areas. As soon as the top of the fences showed through the snow, we took our bikes out of storage and started to ride around the town to toughen our legs so we could take in all the hills of our summer adventures.

Our parents ruling was that we had to be back for dinner at 5:30pm, or else! Barb and I would take a jar of water, a peanut butter sandwich, and a piece of fruit, and we were off each and every nice summer day for our adventures.

Going to Lake Superior was one of our many trips in the summer, and it was a blast. The trip there had a hill about a mile long and we were able to coast down. Coming back, we had to push our bikes almost all the way up the hill. Our bikes were heavy with balloon tires and heavy frames...not at all like the bikes today.

Visiting my grandfather in Hubbell was another hilly adventure, but the rewards were worth the sore legs. Grandpa was known for his homemade donuts. They were crispy on the outside and moist in the middle. He fried them in lard (cholesterol was not a word in his vocabulary). He lived until 101 years old, and was alert and moving all four until the end. I guess all the lard he used must have preserved him and kept his joints oiled.

Once every summer, Barb and I took the scary trip to Houghton Douglas Falls. Scary because my mom told us never to go into the cave behind the falls because the cave could collapse and of course, we did. We would add a few matches and a small candle to our cache and off we would go. We would climb to the bottom of the falls and then climb half way up to explore the inside of the cave, scaring our self-silly.

Our ritual was to hold hands, and then make the sign of the cross to ward off any goblin or depraved person who might grab us. It must of worked because we never met anyone or anything.

Years later after I married Pete in Detroit, I showed him my many childhood haunts. We were both amazed that Barb and I never broke a limb climbing to the bottom of the falls. On our many trips to the U. P. we would visit with my cousin Jack and his wife. Jack was able to remain in the U.P. after college by obtaining one of the few good positions after the copper mines closed. The Houghton Douglas falls are still there. He said the cave behind the falls is still intact.

Mom lied, and of course, we disobeyed. But we never did find out with "Or Else!" meant, because were always home in time for dinner.

The Go Rounder
By Bruce Harlton from Suttons Bay,
Michigan
Born 1949

In the '50s, a road trip north from Detroit meant all day. To me, as a five year old, it seemed an eternity. Not so for my older brother and sister. They enjoyed unlimited opportunities for amusement at my expense. If you are, or have had, an older brother or sister, you know I mean.

We rented an old cottage on Long Lake near Traverse City. Your typical cottage of the day I suppose, except for one thing. In a sort of lean-to shed attached to one side, resided a monster. It made scary sounds, starting with a deep growl. This followed by a "crunchity, crunchity," then finally a loud "thwack!" I just knew a monster lived in there all right! Besides, brother and sister told me so.

As luck would have it, the monster house stood between me and the lake. A narrow path lined with dense pine trees on one side and you know what on the other. No other way to the lake and no escape.

Brother and sister weren't afraid. It never made noises at them. But when I approached, it made all those noises. I'd be back in the house before the "thwack"! I kept my eye on that thing. Easy enough to see from the safety of the kitchen window over the sink. It would never stir until I was just within grabbing distance.

Mom knew I was afraid of it. She tried to reason with me, but reasoning with a five year old? "It's just a pump," she said. "It gets water into the cottage." Well, we had water in our house back in Detroit, but not a pump. I wasn't buying it. So she gave it a cute, kid-friendly name: "The Go Rounder." This did not help.

I was put to bed early as usual, in a bed with bars to keep me in and a curtain so they didn't have to look in on me. As I drifted off to a fit-full sleep, I remembered dad yelling at brother and sister. Often my name was mentioned. Brother and sister snickered but said nothing. Oh how I longed for the safety of the streets back home!

Next day something amazing happened. As dad walked me to the lake, he assured me that the Go Rounder wouldn't bother me anymore. He was right but I still shook with fear whenever I passed it.

Over time, the Go Rounder lost itself in all the events of growing up. I grew bigger then my brother and sister. Besides, they moved off to college. I went to college, got married, and had kids. Now, my kids have kids. But that was not the end of the Go Rounder. One day at a family gathering, "He" showed up! Thanks to my kids, pestering uncle and aunt for stories about when I was a kid. My kids are still laughing at the vision of brother or sister standing in front of the kitchen sink, watching for me and turning on the tap at just the right moment!

Gypsies
By Phyllis Kilcherman from Northport, Michigan
Born 1933

There aren't too many of us left on earth today, who can relate seeing and interacting with Gypsies. This time takes me back to about 74 years ago, and is one of my many golden memories.

I was about six years old when the Gypsies arrived in town—two wagonloads. Little Phyllis had been warned by her mother that if Gypsies ever came to our small village of Grawn, Michigan that I was to be aware. She presented them as brightly dressed people, with a lot of jewelry and dangling earrings. The men were, no doubt, dressed the same way as the women. They would be driving a brightly colored covered wagon, not like our early ancestor's wagon, that were topped off from a white material. The tops of these wagons were more like wood, which had been painted bright colors. They were definitely bright enough, that even to the small children like myself; I would notice and start running to security in my home.

I had heard too many stories from my mother and other kids, and was frightened to death! They would steal anything that was loose, even small children. There was no way that I would be taken away from my family! I loved my parents and my brother (Clifford) and sister (Carolyn). The five of us fit just right in our home.

There was no way in this world that I would be joining a Gypsy family. At one look of them arriving in our town, I was instantly on the run. My mother checked to make sure that her three little ones were inside the house and then promptly locked the doors. What happened next was exactly like the stories I had been told!

Where did they come from? This time, they came from the village about five miles away, called Monroe Center. There was a fairly large group of them traveling in two wagons, with two horses offering the energy to pull their road homes. It was true that they exited the wagons and started to tour our town. We three kids were all on our knees, on the davenport, looking out the window in our living room. We knew that we were safe!

We watched curiously, as the Gypsies

Carolyn, Phyllis, and Clifford Bye in 1937

scoured our little town, taking things they felt they had ownership too. Our neighbor's garden attracted their interest, and they picked fresh lettuce, tomatoes, radishes, peas, and other vegetables. Although we couldn't follow them around town, we were sure they helped themselves to many other things.

After they left, my brother checked out the chicken coop, and YES, they had made a visit to his little project. Some of his chickens were gone, as well as every egg!

To this day, I don't really know a lot about the lives of Gypsies. I looked up the word on the internet and discovered that the first clan started in India in the 1400's. If you received the name of Gypsy, you had earned it!

✓ A Sledding Catastrophe
By Carol Glogovsky from Zion, Illinois
Born 1937

Being born in the late 1930s, it was a difficult time to enter the world because America was in the midst of World War II. I was seven years old when victory was announced. Even at that young age, I recall the day quite well, listening to our radio attached to a wire from a tall pole for reception.

My birthplace was in the Upper Peninsula of Michigan, a town approximately 31 people counting ten parents, four houses, a tavern, and a grocery store with one gas pump. My mother was a former teacher in the mid-'30s who stayed home to raise her family. My

father was a woodsman who expected his two young daughters to work alongside him when school wasn't in session. To keep us busy in early summer, we planted (on a government contract) a half acre of green beans. My sister and I kept them weeded and picked them when they matured and were taken to a cannery where our parents were paid a dime per pound. My grandparents had a primitive farm and were past 65 when I was born. When I was old enough, I loved to help out. My favorite chore was going to far-away pastures to bring the cows home for milking time. I learned how to milk (by hand) at the age of seven and Grandpa gave me the gentlest cow, and gave the most milk. My sister and I helped by tossing hay from the fields (with a pitchfork) on the hay wagon pulled by horses. Later, Grandpa rented a baler making the hay into bales, which were very heavy. It was hard work! We also picked potatoes by hand from the fields, putting them into a burlap sack to be stored in their dirt cellar underneath the house for food during the winter.

Along with the hard work, we found time to play too. Our neighborhood had five (sometimes six) older kids to play "scrub" in the summer. Scrub was a softball game with the two oldest brothers on one team and three of us on the other. "Pitcher's hand" was out if they caught the ball before the batter reached first base. We all played tag, touch football, hide-and-go-seek in the evenings, and caught lightning bugs in a quart jar after dark. In winter, our favorite was skiing or sledding on the "Big Hill," or playing Fox and the Geese (a game of tag played in a circle of fresh snow). On occasion, we walked a mile and a half to the river to ice skate, skating a mile and then back before walking home again. Strange, but we never felt tired.

My dad had a huge sled that his father built in the early 1930s. It was used when dad was a youngster living across the road from the Lake Michigan Bay, to haul huge cakes of ice cut from the frozen lake to be stored and used in their icebox. The sled was a source of delight since as many as five or six kids could pile on. One particular day, a most memorable day in fact, we pulled the sled up the "Big Hill" to slide down on the main road. The gravel was coated with snow and ice so it would be smooth sailing. My mother was game and had joined us, which turned out to be the funniest disaster I can recall. There wasn't a way to steer the sled except by leaning from one side to another, but with five or six of us piled on that didn't work too well. Soon, the sled began drifting to the right. With speed gathering, we couldn't stop and knew we were heading for a huge ditch that led into a wooded area. Down we went, mom at the helm, laughing and screaming we kept going down, and down and then over we went! We all flew in many directions but not one of us was hurt except our sides from laughing so hard. Mom lived to be over 100 years old, and not long before she passed away, she recalled that day, giving us some more laughs and good memories.

Growing up in the "olden days" has given me an edge over today's children. I lived with changes ranging from no electricity or running water in our home, an outhouse, riding in our 1932 Chevy coupe with a rumble seat on the back (outside of the car and no seatbelts), a crank telephone with a party line of twelve people, boarding my school bus with no heater in the winter for a 45 mile route to school each morning, making up our own games, riding our second and third-hand bikes over gravel roads, and playing in the "pollywog ditch", a tiny stream that flowed through a culvert underneath our road only in the early spring. Also, to watch and experience our world evolve into our current cyberspace age. How fortunate my generation is! I didn't appreciate my life back then, but I know now how much I would have missed if I had been born a decade or two later. I also know how much our current younger generation is missing out on, with few outdoor interests and making computer games and fancy phones something they "can't live without."

√ The Mighty Mac
By Newton Chapman from Onaway, Michigan
Born 1940

The time is mid-October 1957. Being a fourth generation Fur Trapper, I would like to share some memories that in my eyes were making history.

In 1956, my Father and I had made the trip from Onaway, Michigan across the Straits of Mackinaw to the Munuscong Bay Park where we stayed several days trapping muskrats for their fur and meat. You had to board a car ferry in Mackinaw City, Michigan and go to the docks in St. Ignace where you were now in the Upper Peninsula of Michigan.

We had a fun time and caught our fair share of muskrats. As we boarded the boat, taking us back to Mackinaw City and then home, Dad, and I were already making plans for the 1957 season.

Now when the 1957 season came, one of my younger brothers, Mick, wanted to go with us. We warned him that it would be work along with the fun, but even that did not change his mind.

We loaded 100 or more Number One Victor Stop Loss Traps, a canoe, Coleman stove, lanterns, food, boots, gun, and one cur dog named Polar into the old Pontiac. We were heading north to Mackinaw City where we would board the newest car ferry "The Vacationlander" and cross the Straits of Mackinaw to St. Ignace.

The "Mighty Mac" (as we called it) bridge was under construction and would be open for use when we returned. As we headed for Pickford, Michigan where we would eat our only meal in a restaurant, we bet Mick, that he could not eat a full order of pancakes at this restaurant. We knew how big they were from the year before. He managed to get one and a half down, and took the rest for his dog, Polar.

Newton's younger brother, Mick and Newton, Jr.
The injured Artic Owl is perched on the canoe

382

Truly an experience for a young lad.

We stopped at a local farm north of Pickford and bought two bales of straw that we would put in one end of the big tent to sleep on.

The day was spent setting up camp and cutting Tag Alter stakes for the traps. There were other trappers at the park also. Our good friends and neighbors, Gerald and Clara Northcott, also from Onaway, were just a campsite away.

I had to take Brother Mick to the top of the wooden Fire Tower (no longer in use) and from where we could see the many Muskrat Houses in the March and watch the freighters go up and down the St. Mary's River, which was about two miles across the marsh.

Daylight would come early and we had our traps loaded and ready for the opener. Our first couple of days produced over 100 rats. We were busy skinning and stretching, and making more sets. It was going to be a good year.

An Arctic Owl that had been injured showed up in our camp and hung around looking for food. I had shot a duck and laid it on the woodpile. When Mick's dog, Polar, was investigating the duck the owl suddenly dropped from the top of our tent onto the dog and sunk both talons into him. Polar was hurt but seemed to be okay. He died shortly after we got home.

I drove into Rudyard one evening and sold a bunch of rats to a local fur buyer we knew. It would pay for our trip back home and let us stop at "Castle Rock" and get a memento for those we left at home.

When we got to St. Ignace, my dad informed me that the Mackinaw Bridge would be open and we would be going back to Lower Michigan on the Bridge. I became more excited when Dad informed me that I would be driving across the bridge.

When we got to the middle of the bridge, there was a lot of yellow paint on the roadway where the Ribbon Cutting Ceremony had taken place two days before. There was a set of paint marks on the roadway where someone's shoes got painted. We later learned that Governor G. Mennen William's shoes were sprayed yellow while he was cutting the ribbon on the bridge.

After a few days of trapping, we were anxious to get home. It was Thursday and we knew that mom would have homemade bread and bean soup when we got there. Thursdays were washday at our house and homemade bread and bean soup always came with washday.

To me, at the age of 17 this was making history. We went to Upper Michigan on a car ferry and returned a few days later to cross into Lower Michigan on the "Mighty Mac," which had opened on November 1, 1957.

A Livable City
By Richard Whiting from Traverse City, Michigan
Born 1934

Recently, a national organization has named Traverse City as one of the top livable cities in the country. How amusing!

For some reason I believe that a few of us backwoods bumblers knew that this was a very livable place back then. No waiting at intersections, only crowded during the Cherry Festival, when it was re-activated after World War II, the beach had a large slide and a dock. There were three-dime stores on Front Street. Sleders had a market, with a sidewalk of tables with vegetables in the summer. Carol's Bakery on Union Street made the best Kolaches. Students could walk downtown at noon, or to Garlands Drug store for lunch or a pop. We had outdoor ice skating rinks and an outdoor hockey rink. The Fair Grounds were out of town, just beyond Garfield Road.

Tom's Red Hots was a favorite eatery, before pizza and all of the junk food came along. The Zoo had the miniature city, exposed outdoors, and had coin-operated music, mostly marches. The car dealers were all downtown so when the new models came out, crowds (of mostly men) gathered to look them over. Morgan's operated the cannery at the end of Union Street on the bay. You could smell the fruit, especially the apples. You could have your gallon jug filled with raw cider for a few bits. Fresh fish were served in local restaurants, taken right out of the bay. Students walked to school, unless you lived outside the city limits. The bay water was always clear, and we drank water directly from it often, especially while swimming. We had three theaters downtown, and a drive-in theater in Acme. The Coddington family also showed movies in the parks of small towns in the area.

We had recreation such as golf, bowling, shuffleboard, hunting, and fishing but mostly we had undeveloped woods and fields around the city, uncluttered scenery, and un-crowded beaches. We burned all our fall leaves at curbside and the smell of autumn was in the air. Winters were more harsh, but we survived and did things outdoors- no television for entertainment. The streets rarely had salt and sand so you could skate to the rink and back home. We could swim off the oil docks or in Cedar Creek in Greilickville, or the coal dock next to the power plant. There were noon and evening whistles at the Iron Works and the State Hospital so you knew when to get home to eat with the family.

Now the area has been "discovered." I wonder what Great Grandpas would say about it now, being discovered. What did those early settlers do, wander in the woods not knowing what they were doing No, the bays were discovered long ago. Native Americans knew of the benefits of the bays and scenic but protective hills. After the unfortunate clear cutting of the lumber, those that stayed had to make a living in a remote part of the state, with rail and water access before roads were suitable. The following generations discovered the city and area while growing up. Many moved away for employment, but many stayed and more have returned after careers elsewhere.

Too bad. The national news rating the city and area for livability and economic development will cause the death of those amenities that we so greatly enjoyed.

Caddis Hatch

By Gloria Gardner from Belleville, Michigan
Born 1945

Memories on the main branch of the Au Sable River near Luzerne, Michigan bring back a night of fly-fishing on the "Caddis Hatch" (Hendrickson Mayfly). This is a fond memory of my husband's. It took place when he was a freshman in high school.

Before leaving the cabin, Richard took his fly rod out of the green canvas rod case, put it together, and hung the case on the deer antlers over the cabin window overlooking

Richard Gardner with brown trout caught on the Caddis hatch in 1964

the Au Sable River (a stretch of water just above the beginnings of the backwaters of the Mio Dam). He put on the reel. He threaded the new line through the guides. He moved it from hand to hand, as he threaded it or the line would slip back through guides from its own weight. The line was a heavy, double-tapered fly line made heavy in order to lift back in the air and come forward flat and straight. This made it possible to cast a weightless fly. Richard opened his aluminum leader box, unrolled a leader, and tied it with a connecting knot at the end of the heavy fly line.

As he started down to the river, holding his rod and with his hatband full of Caddis flies tied that day from deer hair and a bit of yellow yarn, Richard could see the fog of hatching flies in the glimmer of the moonlight. He heard a trout suck in flies as they lit on the water's surface. He felt the shock of the river's icy water as he stepped into the Au Sable. He had his waders pulled high up around his chest to protect his legs from the cold river. Over his shoulder, he slung a green rubberized fishing bag for his catch. His waders clung tight to his legs from the push of the water. The water rose in a cold shock up his legs. His boots felt the gravel.

Near him in a quick circle, broke the dark smooth surface of the water as fly disappeared. A trout sucked it in. He pulled several yards of line from the reel and tossed his fly out ahead onto the rapid water. It floated down toward a logjam. Richard held the rod in his right hand and let the line run out through his fingers.

There came a long tug. Richard set the hook; the rod livened, bent double. The line tightened, came out of the water tightening in a steady pull. He knew the leader would break if the strain increased and let the line go. The reel ratcheted into a mechanical shriek as the line went out in a rush.

There was no checking it, the line rushed out, the reel sang. Richard had never seen so big a trout. The trout exhibited a power, which couldn't be held. The fish looked as broad as a salmon. Snap! The line broke and Richard's hand shook. He reeled in slowly. The thrill had been so great. He felt a tinge of nausea from the adrenalin rush and the loss of a magnificent trout.

The leader had broken where the hook was tied to it. He thought of the trout somewhere on the river bottom, holding himself steady over the gravel, under the logjam with the hook in his jaw.

There is a mounted head of an 18 inch trout in the cabin, above the door, with a caddis fly tied of deer hair and bit of yellow yarn it in its mouth. Maybe this is the fish that got away in May of 1960 or maybe the one that got away was even bigger. There was more than one brown trout in the river that spring.

✓ Mom's Life
By Nancy Birmingham of Alpena, Michigan
Born 1938

Martin Peter Trafelet was born December 17, 1871 and Barbara Devitt was born on February 15, 1873. Both were born in Canada. On October 30, 1899, they were married in Canada and moved to Michigan near the small village of Millersburg. They built a log cabin and later built a large home. They had their first baby in August of 1900. Every two years thereafter, they had a baby until there were a total of nine. They had six boys and three girls. Martin was a woodsman and a farmer of 153 acres. Martin was a strict disciplinarian; he made sure that all nine children graduated and went on to County Normal to be teachers. Mother never wanted to be a teacher; she wanted to be a secretary. However, she did what her dad wanted. They were housed in a small town about 20 miles from home. They traveled by horse and buggy and came home on the weekends. Mom loved being with her family. Mom actually wrote a poem to her brother and Aunt Mary about the outhouse. They used a catalog for toilet paper. Mom died at the age of 94 and most of her brothers and sister were in their eighties and nineties when they passed. One sister is still on the go at the age of 98, but she says that she now has to take a nap during the day. What a loving and fun family. We still have family get-togethers every year.

✓ Pearl Harbor
By Jean Hafner of Rudyard, Michigan
Born 1933

It was a Sunday morning on December 7, 1941, when Daddy was at his usual post baking pancakes. Mommy tended to the other things like the eggs, side pork, and oatmeal. My parents had already milked the cows and put down hay for them. They filled the cows' watering trough by hand pumping it from the well. We had no electricity. They put the cows out into the barnyard for exercise and water. Later, my dad and one of the six children would clean the barn and put down hay in the manger for the evening feeding. There were two young children, ages four and two. The rest of us, from ages eight to 16, were watching the youngest and setting the table.

The noise of the usual busy morning was invaded by a news bulletin. Japanese bombers had struck Pearl Harbor. The newscaster tried to tell more, but all I could hear was the drone of the diving planes. Then came the horrific explosions. I imagined all the military men, women, and civilians running for shelter. Then, the announcer said that the planes were bombing the ships in the harbor as well. I could only vaguely imagine how awful that was. Breakfast was forgotten. We listened as long as we could. Our radio battery ran low. We did hear President Roosevelt announce that we had declared war on Japan. Life became very different after that. Young men from the surrounding farms were either drafted or enlisted. They went away naive boys; those who came back were men. Many of us, even eight-year-old me, wrote to them. After that, the rationing came. Sugar, shoes, meat, gas, and many other items were rationed. Each person in the family had ration books. I don't remember other things that were rationed. I do remember that we had to walk a mile and a half to catch the school bus. To this day, when I hear the drone of a small plane, I sometimes remember that day in December of 1941.

A Great Place to Grow Up
By Linda Kelley of Mesick, Michigan
Born 1947

During my lifetime, I have lived in different places, but my fondest memories were from growing up in a little town called Thompsonville. There were three of us children. My sister is five years older than me and my brother is a year and a half younger than me. My folks bought our house in 1954. We lived two blocks from the grade school. Each classroom had three grades. Kindergarten, first, and second was in one; third fourth, and fifth in the second one; sixth, seventh, and eight in the third one. It was in the latter room that I saw the teacher (also the principal) take a book and hit one of the boys in the back of the head. It knocked him out cold! Yes, things were very different back then. When I was still in grade school, I fell off of my bike during recess and broke my left wrist. That same teacher wanted to teach me a lesson because we weren't supposed to ride our bikes during recess. She made me stay in class until the end of the school day, believing that I had only sprained my arm. The problem was that I couldn't do my penmanship in class—I was left handed! Needless to say, my folks were very angry and she got an earful from my dad. I was taken to the emergency room and my arm was set. Everybody signed my cast, even the doctor and nurses.

Our house was always spotless, we were always fed breakfast before school, and we always ate dinner together. We never locked our doors at night. We had a rotary phone and had a party line. In the summers, the town would have free shows, and we would take a blanket and popcorn. In the winter, my dad would make us a skating rink or we would go sledding. My sister tried out downhill skiing at Buck Hills, which is now Crystal Mountain Ski Resort. When we were a little older, there were dances held in different towns on different nights. The Copemish American Legion Hall held theirs on Saturday nights. It was the place to be if you loved to dance. My sister always had a partner to practice with because I loved to dance, too. We had a train track behind our house, and the trains ran daily. I loved to hear that whistle. Once when I was still in grade school, the passenger train took us to Grand Rapids for the Schriner's Circus. There were lots of Schriners for chaperones. It was lots of fun. At Halloween time, we would get popcorn balls or caramel apples instead of candy from some houses. Nothing was ever "bad."

We had great times back then and I never want to forget them. My brother and I had so much fun playing outside and using our imaginations. We could be anything or anyone. We made snow forts in the winter. In the summer, we would go exploring. We were never bored. We loved watching TV shows like *The Lone Ranger*, *The Three Stooges*, *Lassie*, *Zorro*, and others. They were all in black and white, of course. I'm sure if I asked my sister and brother, they would also say that it was a great place to grow up.

Incident Involving the Sheriff
By Jim Rasche of Ossineke, Michigan
Born 1956

One day when I was 18 years old, I was delivering fill dirt in the Hubbard Lake Area driving a Tandem dump truck when I approached the driveway of the Holiday Inn Bar and Restaurant. The local sheriff pulled out and smashed into the gas tanks of my truck. I don't know if he had a liquid lunch or not, but he was so red in the face. Both headlights busted on his car. He knew it was not my fault. I told him he was supposed to set an example for everyone else. He told me he would call it in, but I don't believe that he did. The fact is that he was not the one who dented my gas tanks.
Rides with the Stroh's Beer Man
As bored teenagers, me and some friends would walk around our small town to Black

386

River, Michigan. Sometimes a much older Stroh's Beer man would approach us in his retired cop car with a hemi engine. He would stop to say hi and we would ask if he could sell us six Strohs. He would usually relent and say, "Wanna take a ride?" As we got in the beast, he would go through the Black River Hills at 125 miles per hour. I would lose my guts at the crest and at the bottom. When he dropped us off, I would shake like a leaf and tell myself that I'd never ever do it again. The following week, there came Don again. We'd say, "Will you sell us six Strohs?" He'd again say, "Yeah; wanna take a ride?" He would enter a field, put on his spotlights, see deer eyes, turn off the headlights, and gun the engine. He was trying to run them down. Again, upon being dropped off, I had to thank God and check my pulse.

Our Gig at the Bar

At the age of 15, me and two brothers formed a garage band with a couple friends. One day at practice, a family friend stopped by. Marty owned the local bar. He told us that we had might as well play music at my bar and get paid, so we did. One night as it approached closing time of 2:30, Marty locked the doors and let his friends stay and party. Little Joe, who was a local alcoholic, was sitting nearby. As I looked over, Joe was diving under the pool table. As I pondered this, shots rang out. I too dove under the table. People screamed and Marty stood there with his pistol, shooting shot glasses off the bar. Finally, it stopped, and I came out from under the pool table and went to examine my amplifier. There was a bullet hole a sixteenth of an inch from my speaker.

Thanks, Dear Dad

My father, Leland Rasche, has a fence post business in Black River, Michigan. When I was 16, I would help with cutting trees, etc. one day, we were bringing the harvest up a huge hill. It was snowing and sloppy, so Dad could not climb the hill all the way with his bulldozer and skidder full of logs. He asked me to hook a big chain to the front of the dozer to see if my brother-in-law could pull him up. When he got to the top with his rig, we tried with no success. Dad then told me to unhook the big chain and wrap it around the hook on his blade. As I was doing this, Pa started sliding backward. He dropped the blade on my steel-toed boot and lifted the front of the bulldozer off the ground. I used words that 16 year olds should not know. Dad finally turned his head and lifted the blade. I bounded up the hill, plopped on a pile of logs, and pulled off my boot. A thin blue line was across my toes. I wiggled them and nothing was broken. After he got up to me, he said, "Well, maybe you should sit for a half hour." Well thanks, dear Dad.

Huge Snowball Wheels: A Phenomenon
By D. Elwin Hager of Williamsburg,
Michigan
Born 1927

I am in my 86th year of life, trying to remember the details of a phenomenon that occurred in my 13th year. We lived at that time on Woodman Road and U.S 131, which was in the process (or just finished) of being constructed. I remember it started with filling the swamp on Hart Curve, and doing the grading from the Manistee River, north of Mancelona in the fall of 1939. It was opened in 1941. Before it was done, sections were paved and used by local people. Sometime during this period (at least in the early 1940s or just before) the event I am writing about happened. It was never in the news. WTCM radio began broadcasting in 1941. There is no record I know of or any stories of this kind in any place that I have ever heard of.

The storm, as I remember, began in late winter on a warm, rainy Sunday afternoon. That night, we got three or four inches of wet, sticky snow on top of at least one or two feet of old crusty snow. The wind blew most of the night. I don't think it was still blowing in the morning, so I guess it was not a long period of wind, but it was still really strong from the west. In the morning, my two sisters busied themselves getting ready for school and trying to get me out of the bed to catch the school bus on time. As we were getting on the bus, we looked at the hayfield across Woodman Road from our house. Wow! It was full of snowballs! The field, a triangle of five acres before the highway, was bordered on the west by Shippy Road and Woodman Road on the north. Both had rows of big maple trees. There were no trees on the third side, which was bordered by 131 and the railroad track. The new snow stuck to the trees and the telegraph lines on the railroad. When the wind came, it blew snow in chunks from the trees, hit the ground, and just kept rolling along the crusted snow, propelled by the wind. If the ground was level, the snowballs, more correctly called wheels, were four to six inches wide and one to two feet in diameter. Some were smaller. There were hundreds of them! Where there was a slope or hill, the wheels at the bottom of the incline were as big as three or four feet in diameter. Some were even wider!

The school bus took you north on 131 and west on Larson Road. At that time period, on the north side of Larson Road there was a big open field of 40 acres, and a half mile long. At the end of that field, we saw more. Wow, again! Hundreds of snowballs were there, a few of them windblown down the long hill. They were four to five feet in diameter. Most of the really big ones were tipped over. The weather warmed again, and by ten o'clock, they had all tipped over. I believe this happened only in our neighborhood of three or foursquare miles. The only people that remember it are the people on our school bus—the Uitvlugh boys and Caroline and Manon Larson (Hart). I did talk to Les McCool about 15 years ago about it. He was the snowplow driver. Les remembered seeing them, but only for a couple of miles south of Boardman and along U.S. 131. I have been told of other storms of this nature, one in England with pictures recently. Donna Sears is my age and saw it happen at her home in Jennings, 30 miles out of my home in 1939. She also said it was in Ripley's believe it or not. My sister, Susanah Hansen, and friend, Manon Hart used to remember it, but I don't know if they still do. That's my true story and I'm sticking to it!

✓ The Unexpected "Train"
By Cloral Beeler of Beulah, Michigan
Born 1948

The following is a memory of an eight year old boy who will never forget March 27, 1956. We were having an uncommonly warm March. It was very hot and humid. Snow had melted early. It was suppertime, and usually we ate around 6:00 P.M. My dad was finishing up using the milk separator. He had milked four cows. Supper consisted of side pork (uncured bacon), boiled potatoes, and veggies. As we ate, we could hear the horn blowing on the B&O Train that was crossing over Zimmerman Road on its way to Beulah. As the crow flies, it was three

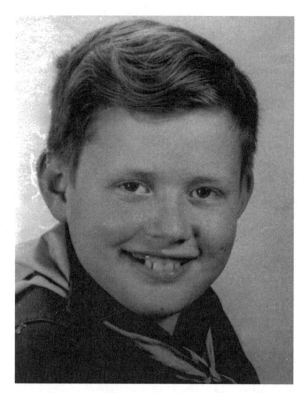

Cloral G. Beeler, II at age 8

miles away. Winds had increased; trees were swaying severely back and forth. Instead of the train noise fading away as it usually did, it was coming closer. My folks couldn't envision a train even close to our home.

Both parents got nervous, which scared me. Supper was forgotten. Curtains and pictures were falling off the walls. Mom went around closing the windows. We found out later that that was a bad, bad mistake. It could create a vacuum within the house. I was standing by the window watching things rolling past. I could see our barn and hill behind. The train was coming from the west/southwest, getting louder and louder. Then, just as quick as it started, there was no wind and all was calm. Trees stood still, and there was no haze in the sky. Our Irish setter was trying to get into the barn. It was two stories high with a basement. As I watched, the dog was lifted above the barn peak (around 70 feet), and flown down the drive (200 feet), still high in the air. Then, it was set down gently on Pioneer Road. He ran to the house, unhurt, as fast as he could. Then, I heard Dad say, "Van, take the boy to the basement. As we crossed the backroom, doors blew open. Dad told Mom to lie on top of me. He closed the entrance door, putting

388

his back to it, and braced himself. When the tornado hit, the house was shaking. Dad was tossed across Mom and me. Within the house, we could hear windows shuttering and plaster being blown off the walls. Half of the roof was gone. Some of the barn roof was also gone.

Then it was over. An eerie calm settled around us. Most of the interior walls were bare. Plaster covered everything. Glass from the windows was lying about. The dog stood by my side. We were lucky that our house was still standing. Our neighbor's semi-truck trailer, which normally sat behind his turkey barn a quarter mile away, was now sitting next to our house. His turkey barn was gone. Turkeys and equipment had been found up to 15 miles away. His tractor was set on his manure pile, about eight feet high. His home was shifted one foot on the foundation. Elm trees in our yard were five to six feet across. Several were snapped off at the base; on others, the limbs were broken. One mile west of us, a family's home was demolished. The mother died, and others went to the hospital. A visiting niece with her 14 month old boy was also hurt. At the crossing, a woman making supper had her house vanish around her, leaving the floor, her, and the frying pan that she was holding. Much, much damage was done. People in outlying areas didn't realize that anything had happened. From the time we heard the train till the tornado hit was only a matter of minutes, yet it changed so many lives.

✓ Guns and Stuff
By Wayne Bates of Terrell, Texas
Born 1942

I got my first gun on my eighth birthday. What a wonderful present! Mom had a big party for me, and the BB gun was the best gift ever in the history of gift giving. It was the Red Ryder with a wooden stock and even autographed by Red Ryder, whoever he was. The air rifle had a lot of power, and it got me into some trouble a few times. One incident by which I got in trouble was when I killed one of our roosters. By mistake, I nailed the old bird right in the head. I was aiming for his butt. Another time, I harassed the bull with the gun. He had it coming, as the beast used to threaten me every time I went to pump water for the cattle. When he would see me carrying the BB gun to the pump, the bull would leave me along. The most damage I did with the gun was to frogs. Some of the large frogs I kept, as Dad loved frog legs. It tastes like chicken.

My next gun was a 22 single shot rifle. This gun was my dad's and I believe Seth Bates has it now. It is a real antique. I was a very good shot with that gun, but not as good as my Dad. We hunted rabbits and squirrels with the weapon. I preferred the 22 to using the 4/10 shotgun, as I didn't have to watch out for small BBs when you munched down on the meat. When I would see a rabbit, I would whistle, and usually it would stop and put his head up. That was enough for me. I would bring a couple of them back and skin them out. We sold the fur and rabbit feet to someone downstate. They would attach a rabbit foot onto a key chain; it was supposed to be a good luck charm. It sure didn't work for that rabbit! The fur was used for lining gloves and hats. We didn't eat that much squirrel, as Mom thought it was too tough. She said it looked too much like a rat. She was right, as they are part of that family. However, she would sneak it into her stew with other meat and we didn't know the difference.

As I got older and became a good shot with the 22, it was now my chore nearly every Saturday to get Sunday dinner. Dad would select the bird and I would shoot it in the head as it walked around the yard. Those crazy chickens would run around for a while with a bullet through its non-existent brain. After a while, Mom thought it was too dangerous to shoot the bird, so we had to chase the thing around for dinner. After catching it, we chopped its head off and watched it walk around with no head attached. It was quite a scene to watch. Mom or Dad would bring out a pail of boiling water and put the bird in that for about ten minutes. The chicken was then taken out and its feathers were plucked. The feathers just came off in handfuls. Then, the naked bird was gutted out and made ready to eat. Mom would make baked or fried chicken with the meat.

When I was about 12, Dad taught me to use the single shot 20-gauge shotgun—a step up from the 4/10. I really liked that gun, as it had power and allowed me to hunt partridge and crows. I didn't have much luck with the crows, but partridge meat was one of my favorites. It took about three birds to make a meal. The partridge was something else. It would wait

389

until I just about stepped on it, and then at the last moment, it would take off right in front of me. Sometimes it scared the "juice" out of me. That surprise made me miss quite a few times. Still, I loved that hunt. I was about 14 when Dad let me use the big 12 gauge single-shot "long Tom." That baby was powerful enough even to use for deer hunting. Dad had warned me that the gun had a good kick, but I didn't realize how tough the recoil was until I first fired it. It knocked me backward and left me with a good bruise on my shoulder. I finally got used to it and loved to hunt with the gun. It was fired so many times that the barrel began to split; I had to hacksaw about eight inches from it. I think Brett still has it. That old shotgun sounded like a cannon when fired.

Sometimes when you hunt, especially when you are young, you can get bored if nothing is happening. So, one summer day I went hunting in the back 40 and was bored with no action. I saw a huge hornets' nest (about the size of a basketball) hanging from a tree limb about ten yards away and about six feet off the ground. Against better wisdom, I aimed the shotgun at the nest and fired. Big mistake! The nest exploded and a million bees were really pissed. They got down my shirt, in my hair, up my pants and nailed me in the face and hands. I got stung about 20 times. I dropped my gun and ran home crashing through the trees. They followed me for quite a distance. My face swelled up to twice its size. My dad said I looked like one of the monsters at the movies. I went back in a couple of days to recover the shotgun and never again fooled around with bee nests. I did have another encounter with the little warriors, but not on purpose. I had gotten bitten real good when I was plowing, and accidentally plowed right into an underground hornet nest. They also were very mad at me and attacked in full force. I just jumped off the tractor and ran. The little stingers got me good again. It was like someone had a hot needle and was poking me all over. From then on, I just stayed away from the little fellows.

My Pets

My first dog was a border collie named Bonnie. She grew up with me, as Dad had brought her home when I was around five or six. I really loved that dog and she was always by my side. One game we played was when Mom would keep Bonnie in the back porch and I would go hide somewhere on the farm. After a while, she would let her go and Bonnie would go find me. She always did, even when I climbed trees. It was a very sad day when she got ill. I think it was just old age, as she was near 14. Bonnie couldn't eat and would just whine all the time. She probably was in pain. My dad said she needed to be put out of her misery, so I said I would do it because she was my dog. So, Bonnie and I walked back to real pleasant spot in the backwoods where we went many times to hunt and explore. The site was in a small valley surrounded by large pine trees. Bonnie loved to chase the rabbits and flush out the birds in the area. That day, she followed me even though she was so weak. It took some time in that walk, and a lot of good memories went through my mind. Yes, it was a sad day. That final resting place in the forest also became one for other dogs.

After Bonnie was put to rest, my brother Bill, who was in college at the time, brought home a wonderful birthday present. It was in the form of a German shepherd puppy. That was very thoughtful of Bill, and I was totally excited, as I always wanted a police dog. He knew that I really loved Bonnie, missed her a lot, and I needed another good friend. I named him King. He grew up fast and became a friend that was always by my side. He couldn't wait until I got home from school. Mom liked him also, as she thought he was a great watchdog. He put up a fierce front when anyone came into the yard. German shepherds are not small dogs and they love to show their teeth. The visitors would stay in their cars until one of us would get King to back off. After a couple of visits by our friends, King would know that they were okay and greet them with his tail wagging. One day when I returned home from school, King wasn't there waiting for me. I called for him and he was nowhere to be found. Later that day around sunset, we heard his barking, so Dad and I went out to investigate. King was dragging himself on his chest coming from the orchard area. We found out later that his front shoulders were separated. To this day, we don't understand how that happened. Dad's best guess that he was running and both of his front legs went into a hole. I was sure my Dad was going to say that we should put King away. I would have been okay with that, I knew he was suffering. However, that same day, the veterinarian was called. We loaded King up in our car for the trip to Alpena. I remember Mom coming out with a blanket and a piece of pork chop for King. He stayed at the vet's for a couple of days. King was a sight to see, as he had a cast on his front shoulders down to his feet. Dad never told me how much money he paid the Vet, but it had to be expensive. I really loved my folks for that.

We made a special place in the barn for King. I attended to him morning, afternoon and night. The cast came off in about two months and King seemed to get around okay, but he was only able to walk, not run. Later that year he got severe arthritis in his front shoulders and it was painful for him to even walk. Dad said it was time to ease his suffering. I said I would do it. This duty was the toughest thing I had to do at this time in my short life. I had to do another death march to the woods. Here is how that sad event came about that fall day. I got the rifle, and we started the trek to the forest with King by my side. I was 15 at the time. It was a slow trip as King didn't walk very fast and it was painful for him and me. King just loved to take the walks to the woods, as it was a fun place for him. We walked to the spot, which was at least a quarter of a mile from the house. I got the courage to put my friend out of his misery, and to my horror, I forgot to bring any bullets. If I could kick myself in the rear, I would have! So, King and I walked slowly back to the house for the stupid ammo. I was in tears on that trip and on the way back. I remember Mom also had a few tears in her eyes when I told her why I came back with King. She said, "Once is enough for you! Let your father do it!" But, I decided to make the walk again. It was not a good day, but King was no longer in pain and he would be able to run again in Dog Heaven. I didn't want another dog, and we didn't get one until my wife, Shary and I were in Midland, Michigan.

Our Piece of Land
By John Diefenbach of Manton, Michigan
Born 1936

On October 1, 1869, 1,160,000 acres were set aside by the United States to the state of Michigan for the benefit of the Grand Rapids and Indiana Railroad Company to aid in construction of a railroad. This railroad was to go from Grand Rapids to Traverse Bay. The land not used by the railroad right away was available to homestead after the lumbermen cleared the large pine trees. Allen D.C. Waite homesteaded 160 acres on 33 and 8 Roads, in section 15 Greenwood Township in December of 1910. Muddy 10 Road was nearly impassable in the spring. There was a grocery store on 6 Road and 33 Road. The Greenwood township hall and school were at 8 and 31 Roads. The Waite family was large and several related family members owned parts of the property over the years.

In Greenwood Township, Wexford County, Michigan, Silver Creek is one of several long trout streams that have a confluence with the Manistee River that flows into Lake Michigan at Manistee, Michigan. In October of 1967, John and Ardys Diefenbach purchased 93 acres of the Waite property. We have two trout streams located here; one about a quarter mile long is Small Hower Creek that flows to the confluence of Silver Creek that flows along the half-mile length of our property. Both go next to our house. We have our own 42 by 12 foot covered bridge over Silver Creek and several walking bridges over the creeks.

We selectively cut trees for lumber. We used a chainsaw, utility trailer, splitter, and tractor to cut and haul our logs on four miles of meandering two track trails. We did this to do minimal damage to the woods. We preferred to cut trees that were leaning or starting to die. The large good parts of poplar, pine cedar, and birch trees were sawn at 104 inches for lumber. Usable remaining smaller wood was cut up for the wood stoves to heat the buildings. This is called using sustainable forestry, when a storm takes out trees, they are utilized if possible. This is still a practice that continues in 2013. We used a sawmill with a circular 46 inch blade to saw the lumber. In 1972, we constructed a 60 by 24 foot cottage with attached garage for farm equipment. We stayed there in the cottage while vacationing five times a year from 1972 to June 1987. There was no plumbing except artesian flowing well and a hose to a sink. There was also an outhouse. There was no electricity, so we used propane for the stove and used oil lamps.

Later in March of 1985, I retired after 31 years of working and started clearing 900-foot electrical easement and home site. Construction was done mostly just by the two of us. At the time, we were 50 years old. We had occasional help with the hard parts and an elderly neighbor helped us out. We constructed a story and a half home with three bedrooms and one bath. It was 30 feet by 60 feet including porches and attached garage. This was done using our 2x4s and 2x6s from the lumber from our own property, except for long roof rafters and floor joists. Diagonal subflooring was hand cut before we had a power miter saw. We had sawed the lumber, and then stacked and air-dried. Cedar was cut for the bathroom and poplar walls were in the rest of the house except there are pine tongue and grove walls. In the great room, there is a 17-foot cathedral ceiling.

We enjoy being in rural, sparsely populated northwest Michigan, nine miles from the town of Manton. We have mixed woods with balsam fir as the predominant tree, along with poplars, maples, pines, wild cherries, thorn apples, prickly ashes, tag alders, and very old apple trees. Numerous wildflowers are here to enjoy. We like watching many animals in the area. Deer and turkeys are often seen right in front of our house. They are not afraid of us, they just move off a short way when we go out the door. Coyotes howl, cottontail and snowshoe rabbits, opossum, raccoons, black squirrels, cougars, bears, chickadees, blue jays, and doves are also prominent here.

The Life Story of My Parents
By Phebie Pearce of Lincoln, Michigan
Born 1931

I am Phebie Pearce, the youngest of my parents' fourteen children. Alfred "Allie" Williams was born October 26, 1885. He died at 80 years old on May 5, 1966. He married Alta Taylor on March 1, 1905. She was 15 years old at the time. She died on July 15, 1963 in Lincoln Haven Rest Home where she had been bedridden for 11 years. She was born on May 27, 1890. She was 73 when she died. Allie only had two years in school, and then he went helping his dad in the woods cutting trees. Alta only went through the third grade in school, but they both could read and write very well. They had 14 children, 46 grandchildren, and 55 great-grandchildren at least. They even had some great-great-grandchildren. They

had twins and triplets in the 14 children that they had. Mother had only one full brother, but she had several half siblings. Dad had six full siblings and one-half sister. Most of these all had large families. Three of the girls only had one child, but one brother had 22 children; he was a preacher. Another brother had been crippled since he was a very young baby, but he had 15 children, drove a school bus, and worked for the railroad. All the while, he had to crawl on his hands and knees to get around.

Allie carried mail for 17 years from Harrisville to Curran with a pony and a mule. He never owned a car his whole life. He also never got a pension for carrying mail all that time—it was before pensions started. Allie's great-grandparents came from Ireland. Allie, Alta, and all of Allie's siblings with their whole families went to St. Louis, Missouri by train, and then went by wagon train from St. Louis to Colorado, twice. On this first trip, they had two sons, Tunis and Archie. Their first daughter, Augusta was born in Padrone, Colorado. While they were in Colorado, Archie died of typhoid fever. He is buried in Sterling, Colorado. Alexander "Zan" Stephenson was also born on this first trip in Padrone. Zan's mother and Allie's mother were sisters. The second trip out west, Robert was born in Winslow, Arkansas. David says that Allie and Alta's old homestead out there in Colorado is now full of gas wells.

Mother told of different things about these trips. Once they stayed in an outlaw cabin that was built over a river for a few days. Once they saw Frank James. He was an old man just living a normal life in a small town. Mother saw her first airplane while out there. She was home alone with Tunis and Archie as little kids. Dad and Mother returned to Barton City before May 6, 1914, when Frank was born in Barton City. In fact, all the rest of us children were born in Barton City. Dad got lost really easy, and one time in Colorado, he got lost. He saw a light in the distance, so he went toward it. A dog came running up to him, but he didn't know the dog, so he went to the door and knocked. Ma answered the door! It was his own dog greeting him at his own door at his own house!

Over the years of their lifetime, they had three fires. Their barn burned down. The twins and one brother was the cause of that fire. No one was hurt and no animals were hurt. Their house burned down and a brother and the triplet girl were the cause of that. Mother was burned quite bad, but she got the kids out safe. Then, my oldest brother was getting a barrel full of gas and he carried a lit lantern too close. It actually blew up. No one was hurt but people in Lincoln said they heard the boom and saw the light form the barrel on fire in the sky. These people were in Lincoln and the fire was in Barton City.

I moved back to Lincoln from Detroit in about 1955. Dad moved in with my family where he stayed the rest of his life. He died in May of 1966. He spent a lot of time with Johnny Jacques in his barbershop, visiting. Sometimes, they just sat at the shop and some days Johnny would close up and drive them all over just to visit people. Dad always smoked a pipe, the older the better, and he always had it in his mouth, even if it wasn't lit. He had a lot of old pipes; he didn't like the new ones. Dad worked a few years in a car factory in Pontiac, Michigan before he carried mail from Harrisville to Curran. Mother and one other lady were the first two patients in Lincoln Haven Rest Home when they first opened. Her funeral was exactly eleven years from the day she first became ill. Dad went to Lincoln Haven to visit Mother every day the whole eleven years unless he was sick himself, but that was very rare.

✓ Pure Michigan
By Dilla J. Miller of Adrian, Michigan
Born 1938

I grew up in Michigan, and thinking back, I realize how lucky I was to live in *pure* Michigan. A one-room cabin outside of West Branch is where my dad went deer hunting. Behind the cabin, there was a stream that was so pure and cold that we drank out of it. We gathered huckleberries for breakfast. I can still smell the bacon cooking in the kitchen. My father took me to see Bambi at the theatre in West Branch. He wiped his tears away as Bambi's mother was killed. I had never before seen my dad cry; I have never forgotten it. I remember that we used to have huge snowstorms that dropped four to six feet of snow. We were always housebound for days until we were able to dig ourselves out.

I met my husband of over 50 years at the Model Restaurant. Our children were born at Tolfree Hospital. We took our children every summer up to Grand Maris to go camping on the bluff of Lake Superior. One time, a summer storm off of the lake blew our tent over. Once there, it snowed on the fourth of July. Other adventures that we had there were going to the dump to watch the bears. One time, we also climbed down the bluff and it took us an hour to climb back up. For every step we took, we slipped back three steps.

My husband and I lived in an original log cabin with five tarpaper rooms. The cabin was located on a dead end street outside of Whittemore, Michigan with no neighbors for a half mile. We cooked on a wood range and did the wash with a wringer washer with two tubs for rinsing. We hung the clothes out on the line during the winter and they froze. When I saw them flapping in the breeze, I brought them in and laid them all over the cabin so the corners would unfreeze and dry. We heated the cabin with three wood stoves and flushed the toilet by pouring water in it. The bathtub was galvanized steel with a wood rim. We poured hot water in it for baths. Our water was from a pump in the kitchen, and the hot water was from the water reservoir on our wood range. We had what I call early attic furniture. My husband made us end and coffee tables for our home. We had this wonderful root cellar in our yard and stored all our canned vegetables and food in it. I wish that I had one of those today!

Our neighbors were so good to each other. We all shared our garden harvests and looked out for each other. We belonged to the Grange, and when someone was sick or needed help, everyone pitched in and did what had to be done. They did the chores, cooked them meals, and watched out for them until they were able to help themselves. No one had to ask for help, as it was given freely with no strings attached.

My husband worked at an elevator in town, and at night, he would plow the fields and hitch up the disk for me to disk the field the next day. I would take our children out to the field and put them in a playpen along with toys and our Collie, Lady. Each time I went around the field, I would wave and call to them. If they would cry, Lady would come bounding over the field to get me to let me know that I needed to get back to them. We would go on picnics across the street under a big oak tree. We thought it was so much fun. I sewed their clothes from feedbags that my husband brought home from the elevator. I would go into town and pick out the colors that I wanted and he would order them. It took three or four washings to get the feed out of them to get them clean enough to make the clothes.

My husband and I raised pigs, and one winter it was 30 degrees below zero. We decided that my parents would take the children back to Warren, Michigan to keep them for us. We could not keep the cabin warm enough for them. My husband and I slept in our clothes because it was too cold to take them off. I stayed because our pigs were furrowing, and I couldn't leave them. It was so cold that their tails froze off if they got out from under the heat lamps that we had in their pens. I went out every morning and helped my husband clean the pens and feed the pigs. One time, a sow had kicked the pen boards down. Without thinking, I put several nails in my mouth and went to put the boards back up. The nails stuck to the inside of my lips! My husband had to help get them off, that is, after he quit laughing at me!

I still have so many more wonderful memories. I still go up north and see my dear friend. I yearn for the good old days at times. I see how times have changed over the years. As you get older, the memories become more precious. You can only recapture them in your mind. Thank you for letting me share some of them.

Potato Harvesting and Deer Season
By Ann Hempel of Hawks, Michigan
Born 1943

Potatoes were a popular crop in this part of Presque Isle County. They were planted in May after the last spring frost; they grew well if there was enough rain. Then, by September, they were ready to be harvested, this time before the fall frost. Potatoes freeze very easily; if they do, they rot. My dad raised Russet potatoes till the new brand of Russet Burbank came out. They were less bumpy, and thereby a better seller. They are my favorite to this day. Many hands were needed to harvest the potatoes. Many of my school friends were hired. We worked after

school and on weekends, even on Sunday after church. We harvested together with my uncle, taking turns helping each other till all was done. The potatoes were dug with a two-row digger, which put the two rows into one row on top of the ground. Afterward, we picked up the potatoes and put them into crates with one person on each side, thereby picking four rows at a time. The crates had to be picked up and moved as you progressed down the row until the crate was full. After that, you started a new crate. When several rows of full crates were ready, three people were needed to get them into storage. One person drove the tractor with the farm wagon, one picked up the crates and set them onto the wagon, and the third person packed them on the wagon. Off they went to the storage area.

It was back breaking work. All worked together; even the younger ones could help pick up the potatoes. On Saturday, when we picked a full day, Mom would serve a full meal at noon. A big tub of water with soap and towel was available to wash before eating. After the meal, there were apple trees available to lie under and rest. Cold beverages and cookies were served in the field mid-morning and midafternoon. As a teenager, I had my own concerns, like Friday football games. "Oh, no! Dad is digging more potatoes. We'll be late for the game." However, it was good weather and farmers had to "make hay while the sun shines." I was aware of the need to get the work done when the weather was good.

Fall has its own activities, sights, sounds, and smells. That's why I like it so much. One of the best known activity and participation sport is deer season. Men, boys, and some women start preparations months before the season begins November 15th to November 30th. My parents owned 360 acres, much of it good woods, and the remainder was farm land. It was ideal for deer hunting because there was lots of food and cover for the deer. Unfortunately, my dad raised a lot of potatoes, and deer love potatoes. They could do a lot of damage to a potato field; but the deer were well fed, which meant healthy deer.

We lived in the house my grandparents built. They raised 13 children, so it was a big house. My dad was the oldest boy with four older sisters. I was the oldest girl with one older brother and three younger brothers and three younger sisters. We didn't have much money, as mortgage payments needed to be made and farming was a very iffy income. Much depended on the weather, especially for rain. Because of this, any opportunity for extra income was welcomed. We housed six hunters from Wyandotte. They would stay for 5-7 days. They really enjoyed my mom's cooking. She could stretch the budget like no one else, and still serve wonderful tasting meals. As a ten year old, I was expected to help Mom, especially to watch my younger siblings and help with cleaning after school. I kept the rooms of the hunters clean and the beds made. I was proud to be able to help that way. I was rewarded very well. Our guests paid me, and paid me well. I still have a two dollar bill from them. I could go to Pardike's store and buy six candy bars for twenty five cents total.

My dad had sold the potatoes to a distributor, who then sold them for potato chips. In the fall of 1953, my dad did not get paid for the potatoes. That put a tremendous hardship on us. Even at my young age, I could see and feel the results in my parents, especially talk about no Christmas gifts that year. One of our guests worked at a toy factory, and he was aware of the gift dilemma. Harry could get damaged toys for nothing. He made a special trip north with a lot of toys. What a wonderful surprise! We were so thankful. Deer season was very successful that year. All the guests got their bucks. My dad got two big bucks. Yes, there were hardships, but we worked together as a family. God has blessed us with a loving family.

Ann's father, Paul Claus

Omer, Michigan's Strange Civil War Legacy
By Marylou Bugh of Standish, Michigan
Born 1942

Omer, in the middle of Arenac County Michigan, is a small town that could slide by on a road trip up U.S. 23 without a blip. Once upon a time, it was an important part of the area—a thriving hub of the county situated on the Rifle River when logging and commerce were largely done by water. Once, Omer was the county seat and built an impressive courthouse in 1898. The county seat distinction was taken over by Standish a few short years later, but there were no shots fired, at least not any that have been recorded. Omer is still the smallest incorporated city in Michigan, although it has suffered two major fires and a couple of floods that should have put it out of existence altogether. However, Omer continued to survive in spite of everything that should have ensured its demise, as a hundred other boomtowns erupted in the logging days. The annual Spring Sucker Festival and the successful campaign that saved the historic courthouse, used for only a few short years, are not especially dramatic. Omer's last claim to fame was a national furor about free speech when the "cussing canoeist" made national headlines during one infamous fishing season. Omer's documented history is easy to trace, but its local legends go back even further, and are just as often told as the story of its historic survival. Everybody in the area knows the strange tales of the Witchy Wolf that have arisen around the Omer Plains, although none have been given any comment in credible historical documents. Many of the latest tales have been perpetuated by young people who have reported strange sights and sounds. Those stories could possibly be explained by a smuggled keg and a mesmerizing bonfire.

Omer stands on the fringe of the Omer Plains, a vast stretch of wilderness pierced by a few one-time Indian trails. The trails are somewhat improved, but are still largely uninhabited by 21st century America. It is no surprise that the Witchy Wolf legend comes from a cemetery located in the area, and dates back to the time of the Civil War and the Keeney family, one of the settlers on the Omer Plains. Homer, as Omer was then called, saw many families like the Keeneys attempt to carve out a homestead on the rough land. Some stayed, but just as many left. Life in the backwoods around Omer was not easy in the mid-1800s. At any rate, the Keeney's oldest son, Corwin, enlisted in the Union Army, as did many other young men in the area. Many returned alive, but Corey, stationed with the fifth Michigan Cavalry was taken prisoner and sent to Andersonville Prison in Georgia. He died there January 11, 1865 from scorbutus, according to Confederate records. Fred Vincent, a member of Omer's GAR chapter, worked to bring back the body of Corwin for his grieving family. His bodily remains were finally delivered to the post office, addressed to the local GAR, and simply labeled "Corwin Keeney, #12431." Although his remains came back to Omer in a container the size of a shoebox, Wilhelm Topp fashioned a full-sized coffin for the occasion. Corwin Keeney was laid to rest with full military honors. It was only right that his poor mother had that small comfort.

After those verifiable facts, the story gets less documented. It seems that in following May, a group of citizens from (H)Omer went to clean the cemetery's gravesites, something they did every year. But in 1876, their appearance was met with a she-wolf that had made a den over the Keeney grave. She attacked the men who approached her and, according to their reports, other wolves came out of the woods and sent them running back to town, afraid for their lives. Before long, their story had escalated into appearances by witches, warlocks, and vampires. Mrs. Gorrie, who had friends at Lone Star with relatives in Tennessee, offered an explanation for the strange happenings in the Omer cemetery. They had learned from the Indians that the damned Confederates had put a secret curse on poor Corey Keeney and other Union soldiers at Andersonville. When the bodies were sent home, they called the curse "scorbutus" to confuse the Yankees. According to Mrs. Gorrie, the curse had given Corwin Keeney's corpse the ability to reincarnate as a witchy wolf who could rise, reproduce, and do frightful damage.

Mrs. Gorrie actually approached Reverend Kay, the minister at Omer's Presbyterian Church and convinced him that a full-scale exorcism was in order. Fred Menzer, the undertaker, presided over exhuming the pitiful remains in the little box in the big coffin that Wilhelm Topp had made. Fred vowed that what he saw was not the remains of a human being, and Reverend Kay went to work exorcising the Indian curse that had been put on Corey Keeney. When the men finally left, after returning Corey to his grave, all felt that the Witchy Wolf curse had been put to rest. However, the following May, none of the women went to clean the graves, and the men went in a large group and took their guns along, just in case. After all, they knew that Keeney's Witchy Wolf had pups.

After the horrible World Wars, when other young, local soldiers were brought home in pieces, the Witchy Wolf stories that Reverend Kay thought he had put to rest arose again around the Omer Plains. Strange beings, neither beast nor human, were seen. Unexplainable cries were reported, not anything that country boys could identify, and so the stories live on to this day.

√ **My First Car**
By John J. Reilly of Tawas City, Michigan
Born 1925

A girl at school had mentioned that her dad had a Model-T Ford on blocks in her barn, and that he might be willing to sell it. That weekend, a friend and I went to talk to the farmer, and sure enough, there was a 1925 Model-T sedan in perfect condition (in my eyes). After getting some gas, checking the oil, and water for the radiator, we started it up. He showed us how to crank it without breaking an arm, as the car had no battery. I asked how much he wanted for it, and he said $7.00. I said, "Sold." I guess he could see how excited I was, and it was just taking up room in his barn. I said I would pick it up the following Saturday, and that whole week I spent talking my mother and dad into the idea of me buying the car that I had saved from my 50 cent a week allowance doing odd jobs at the family resort. I was 13 years old, and couldn't get a driver's license until I was 14. I would just have to drive it on the back roads that summer. A good friend of mine's dad had a barn on a back road a half a mile away, and he agreed to let me keep it there. Howard, my best friend's grandfather, ran the Bear Track Inn restaurant, store, and gas station that was

Jack's car

next door to my mother and dad's summer resort. That came in handy at that time.

That summer, we drove a lot of the back roads in Arenac and Losco Counties, and we always could get enough guys to push us to get started since we couldn't afford a battery. We learned how to set the coils, adjust and replace the brake, the first and reverse bands, and became experts on patching and changing tires. That winter Howard and I planned a trip for the next summer. We would take U.S. 23 to Mackinaw City and U.S. 2 to Sault St. Marie, and come back on the Lake Michigan shore to M 55, and to Tawas and home ten miles south. I got my driver's license in April, and after summer vacation started, we loaded the Model-T with tools and camping equipment. With a blessing from our parents and a promise to phone home each day (which we did), we left to go on our journey.

We made it to Mackinaw City without a problem, and we were the last car to load on the ferry. After parking, we went topside to look for girls. It got rough crossing the straits. We heard the captain over the loud speaker, "There is a Model-T rolling around bumping into cars. The owner of the Model-T, please get below and block the wheels." We hadn't put on the park brake! We raced down to the car and blocked the wheels. Since we were the last ones on, we were the first to get off. Wouldn't you know? We couldn't get the car started. We must have flooded the engine. The horns started blowing, and the captain wanted to know what the holdup was all about. Someone said that the Model-T would not start, and the captain said to just push it off. A couple of the passengers gave us a push, and

with a couple of backfires, away we went. The captain was probably glad to see us on our way, and hoped we would find another way home.

In going into St. Ignace, we had to go down a steep grade. The brake wasn't slowing us down, and we were picking up speed without an idea how to slow the car down. About halfway down, we were starting to get desperate, and began to use the reverse pedal to slow the car. Between both the brake and reverse, we were able to stop at the bottom of the hill. We unpacked our tools and adjusted the brake band. We made it to Sault St. Marie, to St. Ignace, and then back on the ferry. The captain gave us a skeptic eye, but there was no problem. The next leg of our journey was to follow down Lake Michigan shore to Manistee and M 55, cut across Michigan to Tawas, and home. We took a side trip up Traverse Peninsula to Old Mission. The engine sounded like it was getting a little noisy. When we stopped for gas, we mentioned that to the mechanic. He listened, and said for us to try using a heavier weight oil, around a 40 or 50 W. So, we drained the oil and put in a 50W. Boy, the engine sounded great after that. That night, it turned cold. The next morning we were ready to take off, but the engine wouldn't turn over. The oil that we put in the day before had thickened, and it took us till noon to drain that heavy oil and put in our regular oil that we had carried with us. Thankfully, we made it back home without any more trouble.

My bother worked in the paint department at Ford at the time, and would bring me different colors of paint. Each year, I would change the color of the car. I painted the doors one color and the body another. One year, after watching a Mickey Rooney movie in which he had a Model-T touring car, I

Dick, John's parents Joe and Gail, and Jack

397

thought to myself that it was pretty neat. So Howard and I got a couple of hacksaws and quite a lot of blades and made a touring car. However, we soon learned we had to cover the seats after the first rain. We had many happy days, and many small one-day trips until I turned 18. My Model-T was the same age that I was, and it was made in Highland Park, Michigan. Ford Motor Car Company was on one side of the Ford field, and I lived at that time on the other side with the Ford field in our backyard. I went into the service when I turned 18, and I thought my Model-T should, too. It went to the war effort for scrap metal. Just maybe it made it to the South Pacific with me in that 40 MM cannon of JEP.

Scary Cows and Snakes
By Carole Newlon of Oscoda, Michigan
Born 1937

I was born in Oscoda on Michigan Street in a tiny two-bedroom house. On my arrival on the family scene, it increased our family to six children plus our parents. That certainly made it a pretty tight squeeze. Thank goodness for Billy McCuaig, who was a lifesaver to many residents in the Oscoda, AuSable area. Billy approached my mom and suggested a house that was for sale in AuSable that would be ideal for our "little" family. He said that it was only $600. My mother's response to that was, "We don't have $600." He said, "I'll tell you what to do. You go to the bank and tell them you want to buy this house for $1200 and you already have $600. Tell them that you would like to borrow the other $600 from them." The bank allowed the loan, and this was the house I lived in until I got married. To this day, we don't know if Hammy McNichol (the president of the bank) was in on the arrangement or just looked the other way.

I attended Oscoda High School from kindergarten through 12th grade. My girlfriend and I walked to school most every morning. One morning, as we were walking along old US 23, we saw something sticking out the side of the road that raised our curiosity. At a distance, it appeared it could have been most anything. My friend, Rosy, said, "It's a turtle." We continued on our way toward the spot, imagining many things that it could be. Finally, we got close enough to see that it was Mickey Lynch, one of our town characters, sleeping off his nightly binge. What was sticking out in the road was his foot! Needless to say, there was no lack of conversation in school that day!

That house that we moved into had its good points and bad. First of all, it was at the top of a hill, which provided great sledding. In the winter, we would have "fake" accidents and we would even make "pills" out of vegetables. Of course, if you had a bad enough accident, you got a lot of "pills." We were all so poor, that's all we could afford to do. We even made potato chips out of slices of potatoes on our old coal stove in the house. You know, they weren't bad if you put enough salt and butter them. Nowadays, you have to buy liquid smoke to get that flavor. In the summer, we would still slide down the hill on anything we could find. Cardboard boxes didn't last long in anybody's houses.

At one point in my childhood, we had a cow named Peewee. It was neat that the grain we fed her came in cloth bags with real pretty printed fabric. I was treated with a new dress every school year from that fabric. We pastured Peewee down below the hill. Every evening she had to be brought up to the barn to be fed and milked. All that had to be done was to pull her stake, and she would run up to the barn. Well, I always imagined that she was chasing me, so I was afraid of her. That flat area where she grazed had holes all around from people digging for worms there. There were snakes curling in each of those holes. I was deathly afraid of the snakes (still am), and so it was a sight to see when I went down the hill to get the cow. I've thought ever since then that Mom had me do it because I looked so funny trying not to see the snakes and get away from Peewee. After we got rid of the cow, we had a milkman that delivered our milk in glass quart bottles. In the winter, if we didn't happen to be home, the milk would freeze and expand out of the top of the bottles. It looked funny.

At least once during the winter, we would have a visit from the Minnesota Woolen Mills man. He would make arrangements ahead of time with my parents to come to our house for an evening to show us his merchandise. It was quality stuff, and we certainly liked more than we could ever afford. It was geared more toward lumberjack type winter wear. He did have some pretty nice snowsuits and jackets, though. We always looked forward to the Minnesota Woolen man.

We had a wringer washer that we set up in the kitchen on washday. Because we used so much hot water, it overworked the water heater. Sometimes the roof would catch fire because of that. I remember that happening one time and my dad and brothers climbed up ladders and carried the galvanized tub of rinse water we were using to do the laundry up there. They dumped it on the roof to put out the fire. What a mess! The kitchen floor got a good cleaning that day. I don't remember if Oscoda had a fire station or not. I think if we had to wait for a fire truck, the house would have been gone by the time it got there.

I used to love listening to the radio while I was babysitting my little brother. My favorite shows were the scary ones like "The Mummy" and "Inner Sanctum." I would sit in the dark and listen to them. One night while I was listening to the radio, a man came up on the porch and tapped on the window with an ax. I went to the door and the man said, "I brought your dad's ax back that I borrowed from him." The thought never crossed my mind to be afraid. That is how Oscoda/AuSable was 75 years ago.

✓ Living in Long Ago Times
By Vera Sparks of Traverse City, Michigan
Born 1930

I am 82 years old, and I remember what life was like long ago. I grew up on a farm. We were five miles from a little town called Copmish, and three miles from a country store called Harlen. We had no electricity, no

Vera's parents, Clifford and Elsie Mae with Willard

refrigeration, and no running water. We only had outhouses to use. We had to use a slop jar a nighttime if we had to go to the bathroom. Lanterns and oil lamps replaced electricity. The whole family had to go out to the pump house to pump a pail of water. Everyone drank out of the same tin cup. Somehow, no one ever got sick from drinking out of the same cup. We had a wood stove in the living room, and a stovepipe going up the center of the house. This gave warmth to the upstairs rooms. Mom would get out the old galvanized tub for the family's Saturday night bath. Water was heated on the wood cook stove. Everyone took their turn in the same wash water, starting with the youngest member of the family and finishing with Dad. As I look back, he got the worst of the deal. He had to sit in everyone else's dirty water. I never heard him complain.

Bedtime was at 7:00 P.M. and Dad woke us up in the morning at 4:00 A.M. to help get the cows milked, the chickens, and pigs fed, and to separate the cream from the milk in the milk separator. It all had to be done before we walked a mile to school with a lunch bucket, wearing bloomers. At school, all grades were together. We had a potbellied stove sitting in the corner to help keep us warm in the winter. The same teacher taught all of the classes. Outdoors at recess time, we played red rover, tug of war, and threw the ball over the schoolhouse roof. Another game we played was wood tag. Our mother washed clothes on a washboard with two rinse tubs, squeezing clothes out by hand. The sun dried the clothes on the outside clothesline. Our house never had no insulation in it. The walls were wallpapered. The person who built it had just rolled roofing over cardboard walls. We had a root cellar to keep our stuff cold. Mom canned lots of vegetables from her large garden that she raised. We had a large orchard with every type of apples, peaches, pears, plums, and cherries. Mom canned all of these fruits. She also made jams, jellies, baked pies, cakes, and breads. All of this was done on the kitchen cook stove. The stove was heated by wood. Dad would make apple cider and grape juices. Everything went into our cellar to keep for the winter, including potatoes, squash, onions, cabbage, etc. Dad would butcher in the fall, so Mom canned beef, pork, and chicken. She also canned the fish that Dad would catch. We also never wore clothes that were bought at the store. Mom would make everything we wore. In the winter, she would make quilts. I used to help her tie the quilts. We had a pump organ. I learned to play chords on it. Soon, I found I had an ear for music. I could hear a song that I liked on the old battery radio and I could pick out the melody. I was able to play it so that it sounded really good. My closest friend and playmate at that time was my Collie dog named Buster. He was a beautiful show dog. My mother got him as a puppy and when I was 17 years old, he was still alive. He was my everything. I loved him so much and he loved me, too.

I remember that around Christmases long ago, dad would hook up the horse and sleigh and he would always put bells on the horses' bridles so that every time the horse trotted along, the bells would ring. We would cover ourselves with horse blankets to keep warm go down the trail to cut down that perfect Christmas tree. As the bells rang along the way, we would sing, "Dashing through the Snow." Since there was no electricity, we put candles and stings of popcorn on the tree. We would also make cookies. We would light all of the candles on Christmas Eve and let them burn for five minutes. Then, we would have

Buster Vera's dog with a neighbor

to blow them out so that the tree would not catch on fire. The gifts under the tree were all handmade. Everyone got just one gift. Children are spoiled today, getting so many expensive gifts. Besides the one gift we received, we got popcorn balls and candied apples. We were so happy to get what was given to us. We never expected nothing more.

When it snowed, the snow would pile up around the house. It got so high that it would come up over the windows. The snowplows would come once every two weeks. We would spend most of the time being snowed in. Dad would dig a trench trail in the snow to get to the outhouse. We used Chicago mail order catalogs to wipe with. Our windmill provided water as well for the cattle and horses. Living back then was at a much slower pace and more relaxing than it is today. We would go get the staple items once a month at the store. For entertainment, every Saturday night we'd roll up the rug in the dining and living room and move the furniture out of the way for a neighborhood country dancing. We had square dancing and round dancing, that was enjoyed by all. Food was served at midnight. Summertime, we'd got to the outdoor free show in the little town of Copemish. There were a few benches, but most of us sat on the ground. At that country farm, I really took the time to enjoy all of God's creations, the way our family worked together, and the simple things in life.

√ Moving to Michigan
By Shirley Bishaw of Boyne City, Michigan
Born 1924

I was born in Alberta, Canada on January of 1924. My parents were Susan Tyler Welsh and Henry Welsh. They had a farm on the prairie for years. They had eight children that were born. That dose include the three babies that had died. One died of the world flu, one died with pneumonia, and one died because it was born too early. All were buried there in Canada. We had a big house; nothing fancy, but it kept us out of the cold, and sometimes those winters were very cold. When we left Canada, our parents owned 57 heads of cattle, 27 horses, and a threshing machine. Dad and two sons would thresh grain for neighbors. They always had to have extra men, so they built a bunkhouse that went with them wherever they went.

As time went on, the weather got dry, and they couldn't make a living would go. So, my parents thought we should sell out and move to the United States. That's exactly what we did. We sold the farm, machinery, livestock, and bunkhouse. We still stayed there a little longer before we started out. Dad liked to drink, so he would go to town often. My brothers saw him in town and told Ma, "We should leave now while we have money. Dad is cashing the checks and buying everybody drinks." So, my parents bought an early model Chevrolet (about a 1925 or '26). They bought a Ford about the same model for two brothers, and also bought a lot of supplies. Then, we took off on our way to Michigan. We stopped several times to eat, sleep, and put up tents. We crossed the water on ferryboats. We went to my uncle's farm near Tourch Lake. Central Lake was the town. That was in the fall of 1929. There were fruit trees full of ripe fruit. That was something that we never had in Canada. We were glad that our uncle didn't stop us from eating them. We stayed there till spring. We liked our Uncle Willet's dog, Rowdy, because when Uncle Willet started toward the barn with milk pails in his hand, Rowdy would go round up the cows and bring them into the barn to be milked. Through the winter, my parents located a big farm near Central Lake to work on shares. The Walbright Farm had a big barn and silos, and a big house. However, the house was crawling with bed bugs. My family did all that was available at that time to get rid of them. My older sisters took newspaper covered with cooked flour, water, and lye, and papered the bedroom. That didn't stop them. They even took soup cans and put kerosene inside of them so they wouldn't crawl up the bedposts.

My two older sisters and I went to a one-room school, Grand View. Scarlet Fever was going around and people were getting vaccinated. My dad said that they weren't going to put that stuff in his kids' arms. The school kids told us, "Well, I hope you get it." We did. We were a big family, so we didn't get it all at the same time. We didn't have money for a doctor, but one did come out to check on us. He put a big quarantine sign on the front door. It lasted more than two months. Dad, Mom, and one brother were the only ones that didn't go to bed. They were sick too, but stayed strong to take care of the rest of us. The younger brother, 20 years old, died. They allowed the undertaker to come to the house and prepare him for burial. He stayed in the living room for three days. We had the funeral outside in the yard. People who attended stayed back from the house. He was buried at Central Lake Cemetery. My two older sisters were so sick that they were delirious. When this was over, the health department came out and fumigated the house before we were allowed to go back to school.

In the spring, the land had to be prepared for the crops to be planted. Dad had to hire a man to help him, but he continued to hire one man at a time. He kept one man to help out on the farm. We had beautiful crops, so much so, I imagine the neighbors were jealous. They had several young men on horses that would turn their cows out in our cornfield. We couldn't see the cornfield unless we looked out of the upstairs window. My brother, two older sisters, and a hired man would go to the cornfield to chase the cows out. My sister and I would have to keep checking the upstairs window because every day or so they kept putting their cows back in our cornfield. Dad got one, put it in our barn, and made them pay a quarter to take it back. Back then, that was a lot of money. After several times of us chasing the cows out, my Dad told the neighbors that if they ever let their cows get in his cornfield again, they had better bring a stone boat to haul the beef back home. Of course, he wouldn't have shot every one of them. I guess that was the last time for that.

One year, we had a big watermelon patch. It was the biggest one we ever had. That fall, they were big. There were different varieties: long striped, round, some all green. They were planted behind our corncrib, and they were fertilized good. They grew to the ripest peak. Dad kept watch on them. One morning, he went out to check on them and found that some had been stolen. The ones that they hadn't taken, they had cut and broken up beyond saving. I don't remember us having planted any more watermelons after that. I think my dad thought that it was the same people who put the cows in our cornfield. I was still quite young then. I don't think people called the police much in them days. I don't recall Dad ever trying to get even with them. We had some good times, too. We had many of neighbors that were

401

good people. My folks made a couple barrels of cider each fall. We had square dances at our house on Saturday nights. Dad called, and my older sister and brother played music. Other people played also. It was all free cider and all. Dad had a table full of men playing cards quite often. One night, the game got hot, and Dad threw the box of matches on the table. They caught on fire. Mom grabbed the box and threw it in the stove, along with the cards. That was the end of the card games.

The chickens and little pigs ran loose around the yard. There was a big cutout log of water for them to drink from. I thought it would be fun to see what the pig would do if I shut him in the chicken house. They went in and out as they liked, so when one went in and I shut the door, it just ran around and around. Some chickens were in there too. They ran to keep out of the pig's way. There was one window with glass in it, and chicken wire over the glass. Piggy jumped to the window to get out. Just when I thought it was time to let him out. Too late. He broke the window in pieces. Everyone wondered how the window got broke, but I never told. We lived on that farm for five years until the contract was up. After that, we moved to the other side of town. We still went to a one-room school, Lake View. My two older sisters got married while we lived there. My brother got married while we was on the Wallbright farm. All that was left was my sister and me. Dad didn't do much more farming after that.

Making Maple Syrup and Unfortunate Accidents with Cattle
By Donna M. Weber of Buckley, Michigan
Born 1929

In courting my mother, my father (Revella and Ed Nickerson) had a horse and buggy. He lived in Monroe Center, Michigan and my mother lived in Uba, Michigan. It was a long drive for a horse and buggy. Just before they were married, he bought a farm of 80 acres with a barn but no house on it. He bought a house in Grawn, Michigan, five and a half miles away. He cut the house in half and hauled it to its new location with three teams of horses. He put it on a new foundation with a small basement. After about ten years, he dug out with horses and a slush scraper next to the existing house and added a larger basement. He also added a new kitchen and three new bedrooms upstairs. At this time, there were three daughters. We still had no electricity, only kerosene lamps in the house and kerosene lanterns in the barn. The cows that resided in the barn were milked by hand, and the horses, claves, pigs, and young cattle had to be fed and watered. I remember milking and doing chores while the other children were at school playing softball. I always told my dad that I was never going to marry a farmer. The Monroe Center School was a one-room country school that was a short distance from our barn. When chores were finished, I hurried to the house, washed up, ate breakfast, and hurried to school before the bell rang.

When it came bath time, we had no bathroom. A big washtub was set up, and water was heated in the teakettle on the kitchen stove so that we could have a warm bath. It was then poured into the washtub for one to take a bath. When the next person went to take their turn, another teakettle of water was added to the existing water. This continued until everyone had taken their baths. Washday was another hard day for my mother. Dad had gotten her a wringer washer with a gas motor on it. She did all the washing herself, but we helped her hang the clothes on the line. A fair distance from the house, there was an outside toilet. There was always a Sears and Roebuck or a Montgomery Ward catalog in the outhouse that we used for toilet paper. My parents had no car for a long time; they went to town with a horse and buggy or sent for groceries and supplies with my grandparents. They lived about a quarter mile away from us if we took the route across the field. We did that quite often to see our grandma and grandpa. Once, when they brought groceries, they brought each of us an orange as well. My mother asked my younger sister, "What do you say?" She replied, "Peel it." I also remember my parents taking homemade butter or a couple dozen eggs to the doctor to pay for a doctor's visit.

When we were in the eighth grade, we transferred from Monroe Center School to Kingsley. When we came home from school in the afternoon, Dad would already have a horse harnessed for us. We would take the horse and stone boat and go to my grandpa's woods. There, we would gather sap to make maple syrup. The maple trees were tapped and a five-gallon pail was hung on them to catch the sap. We would go around through the woods and pour the sap into the barrel on the stone boat. They had a fireplace built that they put a three foot by six-foot pan on. We filled it with sap to boil down into maple syrup. We quite often took eggs along to boil in the sap. We would them eat them while we were watching the sap boil down. After it was cooked down, it was taken to the house in ten-gallon cream cans, cooked down a little more if needed, and canned in quart jars. Maple syrup sure tasted good on our pancakes and French toast in the summertime.

When it was corn planting time, Dad would plow and disc and I would drag the field. Afterwards, he and I would carry a long pole with chains on it for markers. First, we'd go one way, then another, until we ended up with a lot of figure Xs all over the field. Then, with a hand corn planter, we would plant in all the Xs until the entire field was planted. The corn planter had a fertilizer pouch on one side of it and a seed pouch on the other side. When the corn was four or five inches high, Dad would harness the horses, and my

Donna's parents on their wedding day in 1928

sister and I would cultivate the corn with an Ajax cultivator. We didn't always wear shoes, and sometimes we would run into a patch of thistles. That was certainly awful on bare feet! The corn had to be cultivated twice in each row. When we got all done cultivating that first time, we had to start all over again to keep the weeds down. When the corn was ready to pick in the fall, Dad had a long, slim stone boat that we put crates on and pulled with a horse. We each took a row on either side of the stone boat and threw them in the crates. When we got to the end of the field, we dumped it on a wagon to be taken to the barn at the end of the day.

As I was growing up, I remember my mother cutting hay with the horses to help

Dad out. He would be raking hay in another filed with other horses. When it came time to load hay, my younger sister and I would pitch the hay onto the wagon with hay forks. My dad would start to load the wagon so that it was loaded good. When it was too high for us to pitch it on, Dad would put us on the wagon to load. Then he would pitch it on until the wagon was fully loaded. When we got to the barn to unload, we used horses again to pull the hay up into the peak of the barn with hay forks. It swung over the mow and was tripped. Dad would then scatter the hay about the mow and scatter salt from a pail to help cure the hay.

One day one summer, my sister, and I went to get the cows to be milked. When we got where we could see them, there were dead cows laying everywhere. We chased the remaining cows to the barn. My dad, with the help of a neighbor, started drenching the cows with kerosene and milk. He told my sister and I to chase the remainder of the cows around the barnyard to keep them from bloating any more. It seemed they had lain in the barnyard for a long time and then went out and really filled up on our second cut of hay. The hay was wet because it had rained a little bit. The hay had swollen in their tummies. It sure was a bad summer for my folks, as they then had six children to provide for—four girls and two boys.

My folks had a cherry orchard that they had planted, and was a pretty good size. I used to drive the horses on the big sprayer that was filled with water and spray dope. We had one horse that was always pulling on the bit. One day, she pulled so hard that she pulled me off the sprayer and I fell down, straddling the tongue. It really scared my father because he thought I had gotten run over. He took the horses and sprayer to the barn and nailed a big strap of leather on it to fit across my lap so that

403

I couldn't fall off again. In the spring of the year, Dad would get a load of fertilizer with the horses for the orchard. He would give all of us a certain sized can and we would go around to each tree and spread one can around the outer branches of the tree. They always grew a big garden, so we always had lots of fresh vegetables. My mother always canned a lot so we had canned fruit and vegetables for the winter. My father didn't hunt or fish because he couldn't stand the sight of blood. My mother always killed and dressed the chicken for Sunday dinners. Dad took the cattle and hogs to neighbors to have them butchered. We cut the beef up and canned most of it. The pork was smoked and the sausage was fried, and then covered with grease in crocks to help preserve it until it was to be used. We had an ice house. My father went to Duck Lake in the wintertime and cut big blocks of ice to haul home. He then covered it with sawdust to preserve it for our icebox in the summertime.

When I was about 14 years old, my father got a Fortson steel-wheeled tractor that he started farming with that took some of the work away from the horses. He also got a milking machine to milk the cows with. I had two younger brothers that were always trying to get out of work. Dad gave them a job of keeping the hogs' trough full of water. He kept hearing the hogs squealing, so he went to check on them. The trough was full of water. He went into the pen and discovered a covered wire running to the hog trough, hooked up to the electric fence. They had water, but couldn't drink it because it would have shocked them.

When I graduated from high school, Montgomery Ward's sent me away to cashier training because I had worked there in the summertime and on Saturdays for my last two years of school. When I came home from Saginaw, my father chose to bring 100 head of Herfords cattle home from our other pasture. We started driving them up the road, like we had done many times in the past. We had a very steep hill to drive them up. As we got them all in the road and started up the hill, a car came over the top of the hill. Instead of slowing down like the cars usually did, the farther this car came, the faster it came. My dad yelled for us to get up the banks, to not mind the cattle. The car plowed into the whole herd, killing about five of them. They broke the legs and wounded a lot more. My dad

asked us if any of us had gotten the license plate number. About this time, a second car came along really slow. The driver said the other car wasn't going very far; he had pushed him over the top of the hill. The other car had no brakes of battery. They were just taking it to have it repaired. We took the cattle that could walk on home and put them in the barnyard. In a short time, some neighbors came and helped my dad load the injured cattle to slaughter. Some couldn't be used, as they were busted up too bad. My parents sure had a loss because the man that killed and wounded the cattle had no insurance, had a family, and was already in debt. These cattle were the biggest share of my parents' bread and butter.

After I had worked at Wards for a while, I met a fellow that I had gone with a few times just before he went into the Army. We dated for around six months before he asked me to marry him. We married on October 23, 1948 and had two sons and a daughter.

Depression Era Fisherman
By Viola McVey of Mackinaw City, Michigan

On the shores of Lake Huron, I was born in a little country home to my mom and dad. We had a large icehouse as my dad was a commercial fisherman and he made his own ice from the lake. He cut ice out of the lake and set gill nets. My mother and I rowed the boat out for him while he set the nets. We used to take the fish out through the country and sell them. There was no work around as it was the Depression and President Roosevelt was in the White House and had formed the W.P.A.

He also had a smokehouse and a fish house too. It was beautiful there. We had a big dock so we went swimming there off of it.

I went to the little country school called Freedom school. It was 3 miles and I walked to it every day. I went there till 4th grade when they closed the school and transferred us to Mackinaw City. We also picked blueberries and sold them. I used my bike and my dog Pal would watch my bike.

In 1941, my mother had twin girls born and my father got work on the railroad in Mackinaw City where we later moved to. I went and finished school, graduating in 1944.

We also took the fish and berries and sold them all through the country between Mackinaw City and Cheboygan. After school, I later went to Detroit and as World War I was on, I got work in a Defense factory there through the war. When I later came home and the War had ended, I met my future husband. He was home from the War and we were married.

✓The Uncooperative Canoe
By Rebecca M. Norris of Kewadin, Michigan
Born 1942

This occurred at our grandparents' cottage on Torch Lake. My sister was seven and I five. Our mother was very nervous about letting her precious little girls play in a canoe because canoes were so tippy and she didn't want us to drown. Our father was supremely talented at just about anything, including the control of canoes.

We explained to our father that canoes were dangerous, having been so informed by our mother. He was charmed and amazed by this information. In fact, he asked us to demonstrate the difficulty. It was arranged that we would perform in shallow water with Dad right there to rescue us so there would be no danger. With that proviso, Mom was agreeable to the project.

So, we set to and tried to tip over the

Tina and Becky

canoe. We were short stuff, of course, at our ages. We pushed. We pulled. We rocked. We worked up mighty sweats. But nothing we could do would convince that darned canoe to tip over!

It was much later in life that we learned useful knowledge of levers and understood that a bit more height could have helped in our demonstration. The old family canoe and the old family cottage are both gone now. But I still have a home on Torch Lake. And I have a canoe that tips over only when I want it to because of what Dad taught me about how to control it.

✓The Secret Ingredient to Blood Sausage
By Norma Buczkowski of Rogers, Michigan
Born 1932

As a child, I lived in Detroit. I would spend my summers up north. I remember Grandpa had an outhouse, a 3 holer: big, medium, and small. Us 3 girls would go out and sit down all at the same time. We always left the door open for more light. There was no toilet paper, only Spiegel and Montgomery Ward catalogs for paper. Grandpa would walk by and yell, "Don't wipe with the shiny pages!"

Baths were on Saturdays. Each person bathed in a laundry tub. We never changed the water between people, only added more hot water.

I went to the hospital to have a baby, and my husband did the washing. He used the ringer type and put the rubber pants through them. They got air in them and blew big holes in all of them.

My husband was born during the Depression. It was Easter time and there were nine kids in the family. His father took the last money in the house and bought some oranges to put in the baskets. When his mom found out, she cried, as he had taken the last money. He said, "It's Easter." They had to have something, besides some cookies she had baked.

I walked to the county schoolhouse each day, 2 ½ miles. When we got home, Mom would have the oven on and we would sit on chairs and stick our feet in to warm up.

We raised a pig for meat. When Dad killed the pig, he asked me to stir the blood in the pan so it wouldn't gel. I put my one hand over my eyes and started to cry. My mom always made blood sausage. I always loved it, but never realized she put *blood* in it. I never ate it again.

I am now 80 years old.

✓ We Won WWII by Recycling
By David R. Whetsell of Tampa, Florida
Born 1935

I was born in a small town on the east side of Michigan just before WWII. During the time of that war, I learned about recycling at a huge scale as I was growing up.

After school, some days we boys would take our wagons and go through the neighborhoods and pick up discarded metal things people had put out at the curb or sidewalk to be used towards the "war effort": aluminum pots and pans, iron fry pans, squashed tin cans, all was needed.

A tin can was opened, the contents used, then the other end of the can was removed, both ends put inside the can, then all was squashed flat to be recycled.

Cigarette packs had a thin sheet of aluminum foil used as an inner wrapping, which we would salvage and roll up into a ball, which would become a contest on who could make the largest. Then it too would go to the "scrap pile."

The scrap pile in town was staged in a section of our school playground. It wasn't fenced off so needless to say we kids did find a few "neat things" to play with.

Grease and oils created from our cooking was poured off into a separate container, saved until nearly full, then was taken to one of the grocers in town who saw that it was picked up and taken to be used for whatever in the war.

Girls and boys would go to the country and pick milkweed pods. They were put into usually old orange bags with a drawstring so they could be contained. The pods had a lot of fuzzy seeds inside, which were used for insulation in the jackets used by the Army Air Corp. The planes then weren't heated and were very cold inside.

I could go on but you see how we learned so long ago, how things could be re-used. We won a war with it.

✓ Love at a Hot Dog Stand
By Louis E. DeCaire of Alpena, Michigan
Born 1921

I was born in this small town, Alpena, in northeast Michigan, in September 1921. My parents and grandparents immigrated to Michigan from Canada, and were known as "French Canadians." Lumbering was the prime occupation in the late 1800s and early 1900s. Both of my grandfathers were in that business.

I remember the winter seasons as being quite severe. There were no snowplows in the late '20s and '30s to keep streets and sidewalks opens. In some areas, there were no sidewalks. One of my uncles had a farm a few miles north of Alpena. Once a week he would come to town with a large four-runner sled pulled by two heavy workhorses. Snow and ice would build up to three and four feet in the street and turn into solid ice. Horses and sled would just travel over it.

The school I attended, St. Anne, was seven blocks from my home. I walked it four times a day. Starting in the 7th or 8th grade, we would have class parties once a month. Each student would take a turn having it at their parents' home. Plenty of chaperones and no drugs!

I remember a wind-up record player that had a lot of static on the record and sounded like chalk on a blackboard. Also, there were wringer washing machines by Maytag that saw a great deal of service. No detergents in those days, a shaved bar of Fels Naptha soap was all there was. It was very strong and contained a lot of lye.

Depression years were difficult. My father worked at Huron Portland Cement Co., the largest cement plant in the world at the time. However, rather than laying anyone off the company had everyone work half shifts. It was better than no job at all.

There were two theaters in Alpena called the State and the Lyric. The latter would seat about 250 people. Saturday afternoons was serial time. I became a part time projectionist and we would show one chapter per week of Tarzan, Zorro, Buck Rogers, etc., each one running 10 to 12 weeks. Admission price was somewhere around 10 to 25 cents.

I recall a wooden icebox and one of my duties was to make sure that water didn't overflow from the large pan under the icebox.

I also remember the milkman and his horse-drawn wagon. He would leave several quarts of milk on the porch and after a short time, the milk and cream would separate, cream at the top and milk at the bottom! Shortly after this, a machine called a separator was invented.

At Halloween time, outhouses took a beating, as did pumpkin patches around the city.

Party line telephones were a real pain. You would always know how many busybodies were on the line by the number of phone clicks you would hear.

I met my first love at a hot dog stand in 1939. We dated for several years, then came Dec. 7, 1941. That changed everything for years to come. We were hoping to get married, but decided to wait until after the war.

I was working at GM Yellow Truck and Coach as a Draftsman when my draft number came up. Rather than being drafted into the Army and living in a foxhole, I joined the Navy and was inducted on October 22, 1942. I was stationed at Great Lakes Naval Station, north of Chicago, for 18 months as a medic. I was transferred to Galveston, Texas, in June 1944, and assigned to an LCI (Landing Craft Infantry) which was capable of transporting 250 troops. I was in the Navy's Amphibious Forces.

Our entire crew consisted of 35 men and 4 officers. The ship was only 150 feet long, bow to stern! The ship was commissioned on June 26, 1944. We left for the Pacific the next day, south through the Caribbean and west through the Panama Canal and out on to that large "pond" called the Pacific Ocean. Five plus weeks later we finally saw land.

First stop was Espiritu Santo in the New Hebrides island group. We refueled and went northwest to New Guinea to a port called Jayapura where there was an American Naval Base. It was 90% jungle with very poor dirt roads.

Next stop was the Philippines. Manila was to be our operating base. We arrived in early August 1944. We had not received any mail for about 6 weeks and when it did arrive, there was a telegram stating that my father had passed away on July 26, 1944. Since he had been ill for quite some time, his death was expected.

The war with Japan had settled down somewhat, but kamikaze pilots were still buzzing around overhead. We were assigned many different tasks, such as transporting Philippine families back to their original islands and homes, exploding mines that had been planted in the waters around the islands, and taking part in numerous convoys and assault operations. We once put ashore 250 Australian troops on the island of Borneo.

Soon it was 1945 and all was under control.

The Navy introduced a point system in October 1945 which would determine who was eligible to return home (USA) first. By early November 1945, I had enough points to return to the states. It took about 3 weeks, aboard a Liberty ship, to get a look at the Golden Gate Bridge.

I was processed at the Naval Station in San Francisco and received my honorable discharge on Nov. 20, 1945. My fiancée, Eunice Bailey, and I had been making marriage plans while I was still in service. I arrived home on Nov. 26, 1945, and we were married in December 1945.

It has been a great marriage. We had four girls and one boy, and have 12 grandchildren and 9 great-grandchildren at last count!

Like all families, there have been ups and downs. I'm presently 91 years old and my wife is 87, and still in reasonably good health.

The Great Ice Storm of 1922 and the Best Snow Fort
By James R. Frisbie of Cadillac, Michigan
Born 1913

When we were still quite young, probably about 1925, my brother Doug and I, together with two old friends, Morris Hodges and Joe Greeley, built a snow fort in Morris's backyard. Morris had a playhouse he had used as a child, no larger than 9'x9'. For whatever reason, as if kids needed a reason for doing something, we started rolling up heavy, wet snow and stacking it around the old playhouse. Nearing completion, we decided to extend the walls above the playhouse, creating a castle-like area. This required a ramp up which to carry or roll the snowballs. With still lots of energy and snow available, we voted to extend the ramp and wall in the fort, ending

407

with a 36'x36' enclosure with 9' walls.

Boy, was this work! Had our parents asked us to put this much effort to something useful our enthusiasm would have melted. This was our idea; our enthusiasm expanded along with the project.

We became so interested in the fort that nothing superseded its completion. Up early each morning, work until noon, lunch and change to dry clothes, then back to work until suppertime.

In a picture of the old fort, which I took, brother Doug is standing on the castle, Morris Hodges and Joe Greeley are manning the walls. I cannot recall the little girl's name but from her size, you can estimate that of the fort. The hole, visible in the picture's lower left corner, is the entrance. It was a tunnel carved within the wall itself, snaking around the corner, and exiting in the inner courtyard. Broom handles were inserted through the tunnel walls to signal an unauthorized entry attempt.

Finishing our fort in time for the spring thaw, we shed no tears but moved quickly to a new project, our interest being satisfied with the picture of our accomplishment.

The Great Ice Storm of 1922 was, without a doubt, the storm of the century, a major disaster, probably unequaled in the history of Cadillac. Imagine awakening, as we did, to seeing ice everywhere: buildings, trees, and power and phone lines, all thickly coated with ice. This was not just a sleet storm, as many of us have experienced, but the most damaging storm I have witnessed in my over 90 years in Cadillac. Snow banks were coated so heavily we could skate across the fields to visit friends.

Power lines were so heavily laden they sagged to the ground or broke the wires, sending them twisting and writhing on the ground, flashing and sparking as they short circuited and grounded out. Phone and power poles and trees were toppled into the streets, making travel a hazard to life and limb.

Of course, to us kids this was a feast of fun. Warned by our parents to stay well clear of downed wires, hanging poles and branches, we put on ice skates, and toured the neighborhood with our friends. Cutting across lots, up and over the ice coverage of a recent heavy snowfall, we literally had the place to ourselves. It seemed there had been a period of extreme cold and very heavy snow followed quickly by an unusually high upper air warming trend that switched the weather to a violent ice storm.

By the swing in our backyard were two apple trees, originally standing about 10 feet high. The ice stripped the branches, leaving only a stub, in the same manner as a hungry bear would strip a wild cherry tree of its fruit in the fall.

Schools and business were closed, deliveries, as were done in those days, were impossible. For a least a week, Cadillac was like a dead city while repair crews cleared fallen trees, poles, and Consumer's Power and Bell Telephone crews restored their lines.

I cannot recall how my dad's business adjusted to the storm; his was a business from which mothers with babies expected daily deliveries. His business, in turn, was dependent on milk deliveries from several outlying farms. To understand the full impact of the storm, we need to consider this was a time when no roads were plowed and most farmers still came to town by horse and buggy or sleigh.

Fun Times with My Brother Joe
By Sharell (Pierce) Balentine of Traverse City, Michigan
Born 1938

I was born and raised in Traverse City. Where the bridge is over the Boardman River on Grandview Parkway there used to be a wooden train trestle. My parents always told my brother Joe and I never to cross it when we went downtown. Of course we did. Joe hurried ahead of me, and then started yelling, "The train is coming!" I didn't know whether to run or jump. He stood there laughing. No train was in sight!

Every Saturday we each got 25 cents to go to the Tra Bay Theater: 12 cents admission and 13 cents for popcorn and candy. What a treat!

My father was foreman of the city street department and was highly allergic to poison ivy. He would be a mess; his eyes would swell shut. At the end of East Front Street, past Shadowland Bar, was a dirt two track in the woods with a pond we used to call the frog pond—our favorite hang-out. One day Joe told me I was sitting in poison ivy. I told him I couldn't get it and proceeded to eat some. Needless to say, he couldn't wait to get home to tell my father. I never got poison ivy, but I sure got a sore bottom!

When I was probably around 12, I babysat for a younger cousin. One day we sat in an open field and watched a house being put on a basement. Sometime later, the police department used it for East Side boys, who boxed in the basement. My brother Joe was one of those boys. I now live in that house!

Tra-Bay Theatre

✓ Those Days 'Out On the River'
By Laura Gettle of Prudenville, Michigan
Born 1949

Memories are a precious pleasure and I am fortunate enough to have a plethora of them to choose from. They are a temporary escape from the day to day and a harmless way to entertain your grandchildren.

Our closest village was called Eagle. My parents, my younger brother and sister, and myself lived in a log cabin that sat at the top of a lazy sloping hill. The Looking Glass River marked the edge of our property. Fields and forest surrounded us. We had a beat up

old toboggan and in the winter 'us three kids' would slide down that big hill, across the frozen river, and into the woods on the other side. We made our own skis from any pieces of wood and leather we could find.

On weekdays, we walked three quarters of a mile (one way) to the one room schoolhouse we all attended. Our teacher was Mrs. Babbit and I adored her. She taught kindergarten through eighth grade. There were four students in my class, myself and three boys. Thanks to my classmates, I became extremely proficient at tree climbing, baseball, and fishing. Dolls? Didn't have one. They were for sissys.

Summer time was the best. We wandered through the woods helping ourselves to wild berries and green apples.

Our swimming hole was a short walk along the river. Carp and suckers liked to congregate there on hot days, but quickly disappeared once we jumped in. The two Randall kids from 'down the road' were our closest friends and neighbors and frequently joined us. We fished or swam in whatever clothing we happened to be wearing. We were experts in the fine arts of 'frogging' and 'crabbing.' One day I caught the granddaddy of all green frogs, stuck it in my pocket and forgot about it. That evening, while sorting laundry to be washed the following day, my mother let out a loud screech. Uh oh. Mom found the frog.

We seldom wore shoes during the summer but when we did they were always saddle shoes; the only kind Mom would buy. I dreamed of having shinny shoes with buckles like the other girls, but alas, it was never to be. To this day, I hate, loathe, and despise saddle shoes.

Allen Randall was my best friend and first boyfriend. I loved him with all the passion a nine year old is capable of. There was a barn on the Randall property and I literally got my first kiss 'out behind the barn'. It was accomplished after much hesitation, shyness, and giggling. Allen once asked me why I laughed so much. The goofus. It was because I was happy! I was devastated when the Randalls moved away. Allen remained the king of my heart until years later when Paul McCartney of the Beatles finally replaced him.

We had a tree house in the woods. It was actually an abandoned hunting blind but once we found it, it was ours. I got stuck one day trying to climb out and none of us wanted our parents to know. The boys panicked and it took them nearly an hour to rescue me but they did it.

One day a small flat bottom boat came drifting down the river. 'Us kids' caught it and claimed it. There were no paddles so we grabbed rakes, hoes, and shovels from the shed and used them to steer our boat around. Unfortunately, we didn't put the tools back when we were done and someone took them. We were in big trouble. Capital punishment was rare in our family but always memorable. My backside throbs just thinking about it.

We lost the boat a few days after we found it. We were careless and it just drifted off.

When I was twelve we moved to the big city where every child in the whole room was in my grade. I was expected to behave like a lady. No more ball games or foot races with the guys. No more wrestling matches or marbles. Just silly tea parties and boring gossip with the girls. And I still couldn't have buckle shoes! It was the hardest adjustment I've ever had to make. I did learn to dance though and that I enjoyed.

Those days 'out on the river' remain among my happiest and most treasured memories. As long as I have them I'll never grow old.

My Dad the Milkman (and Part Time EMT)
By Doris E. Tuffts of Kalkaska, Michigan
Born 1935

Back in the 1940s, my dad Tobe Root was a milkman. He delivered milk, cream, cottage cheese, and chocolate milk to grocery stores, restaurants, and homes in Kalkaska and Mancelona, MI. When I was about 10 years old I would help him deliver house to house.

I would take the milk that the customer had ordered to their front door or porch and bring empty bottles back. Sometimes there would be an unfriendly dog, and then Daddy would take the milk in. Daddy would park the milk truck and he would take one side of the street and I would take the other.

I remember one time when I was 12 years old. I was taking milk to a customer and returned with the empty bottles. I had three of them in one hand. I had my three fingers stuck in the neck of the bottles. I stumbled getting into the truck and caught myself with those bottles. When I put my weight on the bottles the tops gave way and I cut my wrist. Daddy quickly grabbed my wrist and put pressure on it to stem the flow of blood. The County Road Bldg. was across the street. He took me there and they put a rag around my cut, put me in the County Road Car, and took me to Graying Mercy Hospital, as we didn't have one in Kalkaska at that time. The doctor said I was very lucky because I was 1/8 inch from losing my right hand, but he was able to put it back together and all I got out of it was a little crooked finger. It was quite an experience.

I continued helping Daddy for the next few years. We always had a good time together.

He worked for Kirtpatrick Dairy for about 13 years. When Kirtpatrick Dairy went out of business, he worked for Nelson's Dairy out of Traverse City. He worked for Nelson's for a short time. When the dairies quit delivering house-to-house Daddy retired from being a milkman.

Doris's parents, Arlie and Jobe Root with Doris in 1937

Fishing on the Shores of Lake Huron
By James F. Smith of Brighton, Colorado
Born 1929

I was born and raised in the small village of Rogers City, located on the shore of Lake Huron, seventy miles south of the Straits of Mackinac.

There is no train or bus service available in Rogers and the nearest commercial airport is in Alpena, Michigan, 35 miles south of Rogers City.

Born in 1929, I vaguely remember things about Prohibition or the Great Depression.

Located one mile south of the city limits, is the largest open pit limestone mining operation in the world. The company then was the Michigan Limestone and Chemical Company, locally called "Calcite," which was one type of limestone mined there. The whole area's economy revolved around the "Calcite Plant," which employed about 500 workers. My dad drove a company bus for 45 years.

During the summer, swimming in Lake Huron and fishing at nearby Trout River were favorite activities of mine. Another summertime activity was picking wild berries. The berry-picking season started with the strawberries, then raspberries, blueberries, and blackberries. We also gathered wild hazelnuts and beechnuts. We would go to the woods and pick wild flowers for our moms, i.e., Mayflowers (Trailing Arbutus) and yellow and pink Lady slippers, they being the only true orchids that grew in Michigan. The Trailing Arbutus and pink Lady slippers are now considered an endangered species and the picking thereof, is prohibited.

Joining me in all these pursuits was my cousin, Ralph, who, although 4 years older than me, was a constant companion. The first time we found a pink Lady slipper, was like finding a gold mine, and is a treasured memory. When my cousin and I would go fishing at Trout River, which was quite often, we walked an old abandoned road for about a mile to the river. Just before getting to the river, there was a marshy area, where there usually were snakes in the ruts of the road. The snakes were quite harmless, but since I had an innate fear of snakes, Ralph would take the lead and chase the snakes away. When I was six or seven, I caught my first fish, a chub about 4" long, which I proudly took home and my mother fried it for me.

Ralph and I discovered that gathering acorns could produce cash. The cemetery in Rogers had a lot of large oak trees and subsequently, a treasure trove of acorns. We would pick the acorns until we had a coffee can full and then dump them into a bushel basket. When we had a full bushel, we would sell them to a local Polish family named Pokorski for pig food. They raised pigs in a pen in their backyard. Raising pigs in the backyard was not uncommon in Rogers, in the '30s and '40s. We received 25 cents for a bushel of acorns. You can imagine how many acorns it takes to fill a bushel basket! But 25 cents was quite a lot of money back then.

Sometimes I would go to the local fish dock and fish for shiners between the cracks in the dock. During this period of time, huge catches of Menominee Whitefish and Mackinac Trout were caught in the nets of the four fish tugs operating from the fish dock. One could go to the dock and pick out and purchase these fish for 25 cents a pound. The bulk of the catch was shipped, in ice, to larger markets.

Fall brought partridge (Ruffed Grouse) and the deer hunting. Opening day of deer season was like a national holiday. Schools gave excused absences for deer hunting students. One of my most memorable events growing up was bagging a buck with a large rack of horns when I was 16.

Winter produced skiing and sledding at local hills, but my favorite winter sports were ice fishing and Snowshoe rabbit hunting. Anyone in town owning a good rabbit hunting beagle had a prized possession. Ice fishing, usually on Swan Lake, which was on "Calcite" property, was a pretty chilly proposition.

It entailed walking through a good deal of snow, for a mile or so, to the lake. On the way, we would cut down a good sized evergreen and drag it onto the lake, for a windbreak. Then we would build a big bonfire on the lee side of the tree, for warmth. What made it tough was carrying all of our gear, including a bucket of live minnows for bait, a spud for opening holes in the 1-1/2 feet of ice, and everything else we needed. However, our efforts were rewarded with a nice catch of Northern Pike.

Spring heralded the onset of Red Horse Sucker and Smelt fishing. Smelt were so plentiful that on a night when the spawning run was on, one could easily fill a two gallon bucket using a net. Included in the package of Smelt fishing, was quite often wet feet from leaking boots, in 30 degree temperatures. The Red Horse Sucker run would darken the bottom of Trout River and other local streams. Spearing and snagging were permitted, and most folks could get all of the suckers they wanted. Suckers might not sound like a particularly palatable dish, but these suckers, fresh out of icy Lake Huron, were quite tasty, especially smoked. Suckers are a very bony fish and I think a majority of kids in Rogers had sucker bones pulled out of their throat with pliers at one time or another.

Our town had other major attractions, to wit: ice cream parlors with 5 cent double dip ice cream cones and a theater, which cost 10 cents for admission. We would usually go to the movies on a Saturday afternoon, to see a "Hop Along Cassidy" or "Gene Autry" movie, including a serial such as Flash Gordon or Zorro.

Winter usually produced a blizzard or two, which closed roads and schools. I vividly remember skiing down the middle of Main Street after one of those storms.

Our toys, for the most part, were home-made: kites, bows and arrows, rubber band guns, and slingshots. A slingshot with a nice rounded stone, from the lake shore, was a formidable weapon, though used primarily for shooting at bottles and other targets.

At the age of 16, during the second World War, I began sailing on the lake freighters. This was a common occupation for young men in Rogers. The ships I sailed on hauled limestone from "Calcite," to Buffalo, N.Y., Gary, Indiana, and other ports on the Great Lakes. The return trip would usually consist of a load of coal loaded at Toledo, Ohio, to ports in Canada, Lake Michigan, or Lake Huron. These freighters had a capacity of 60,000 to 70,000 tons of limestone. Characteristic of many small towns of that era, living was pretty laid back. People didn't lock their doors and many folks even left the keys in cars.

Today, as in many small towns like I grew up in, things have changed.

Folks now lock their homes and cars. Hunting cabins get pillaged. Drug use has raised its ugly head. The work force has dropped to about 120 employees at "Calcite." Unemployment is over 10%.

Most egregious of all, retirees, mostly from down state, have built large homes in the outlying areas of the city and eliminated my favorite blackberry patch!

In spite of changing times, Rogers City is still a clean, neat little town, with no air pollution, a very low crime rate, and a good place to raise kids.

I moved from Michigan to Colorado in 1951, but still have friends in Rogers City and visit Rogers two or three times annually. My cousin Ralph, whom I have referred to frequently in my story, is Ralph Smith, who currently resides on Freidrick St. in Rogers City.

✓ The Good Old School Days
By Marian J. Martin of Barton City,
Michigan
Born 1919

I distinctly remember the old "one room school" days. The teacher had all 8 grades, so by the time you reached the 8th grade you had a lot of "overlearning"!

The school was built on a hill, so there were lots of "home runs," where we played ball at recess time, and in the winter, we enjoyed sliding downhill.

A big furnace heated the school. It was kept going overnight by using coal for fuel. We climbed over the coal pile in the woodshed to get the biggest chunks.

The boys wore knickers most of the time, and sometimes the girls wore dresses with bloomers. In the cold winter months, both boys and girls wore long johns and big galoshes.

The most outstanding teacher was Mary Carter. She always enforced all the rules. First, you would line up for inspection. You had to hold out your hands and show your teeth to be sure you were neat and clean. There were strict rules for passing to class: turn, rise, pass.

Everyone drank from the same dipper, from a big pail of water pumped from an outside pump.

In order to remember the important events and dates in history, we had to memorize rhymes like "In 1492 Columbus sailed the ocean blue." Also:

"In 1861 the Civil War begun,
"In 1862 'twas half way through,

Marian's family

"In 1863 the slaves were free
"In 1864 they fought no more!"
Of course, we had to memorize all of the multiplication tables. Once in a while, we had arithmetic contests. The problem was written on the board, and we would write the answer on our paper as fast as possible, then rush up and put it on the front desk. The first one there with the right answer won.

Sometimes we played indoor games like "Eraser Tag." We had to run with the eraser on our head and get back to our seat before we were tagged or the eraser fell off our head!

The Christmas program was a wonderful community event. All of the village turned out! We practiced for several weeks before the program. We had plays, poems, songs, and drills, ending with a visit by Santa Claus with his jingle bells.

All in all, learning, memorizing, entertaining, and playing, we enjoyed the "country school." Those were the Good Old Days!

✓ Tales Orin J. Hadcock Told of Central Lake
By Margaret Hadcock Gallagher of Livonia, Michigan
Born 1914

It is an honor to remember some of the memories that my father, Orin J. Hadcock, who was born and raised in Central Lake, Michigan, used to share with us as we drove around every corner of the town. Since the roads are very curvy and hilly around Central Lake, Dad would tell us about going tobogganing down this one particular hill and how they would all yell "LEAN" as they went around the curve and then they would have to climb the huge hill, carrying the toboggan.

Another memory that he would talk about was how they would attend the Boy Scout Camp on Torch Lake and look for the narrowest spot and swim across. Even the narrowest spot seemed like a long way to me!

He would also talk about how they would pick potatoes for a very small sum of money, even for those days!

He told us of a story when he was a young boy, 8 or 9, that he and his two older brothers were swimming near the Moermann Bridge in Central Lake. His one brother asked his other brother, "Where's Orin?" He had gone underwater. They pulled him from the water and revived him just in time.

My grandmother Jane Hadcock used to work at the telegram office and Dad would deliver the telegrams after school. When he got enough money, he ordered a bike from the Sears catalog. He was so excited when the day came when it arrived by train in Central Lake. He always cherished that bike and the memories it gave him. When telling this story, his eyes would still light up, remembering how special that time was.

In 1929, when Dad was home from college, due to a lack of funds and to help care for my grandmother, he convinced the local lumberman to donate lumber and another businessman to donate gravel in order to dig out the basement of the Central Lake Methodist Church. Dad and his friends, Harold and Bob Aenis, Merrill Hadcock (dad's older brother), Kenneth McKay, and others took on the

Orin J. Hadcock with Rev. Richard Matson in 1999

project of digging a basement. The building was already built, but without a basement. The walls were supported with lumber and the dirt was dug out by hand and hauled by horse and cart down to Intermediate Lake. After dumping the dirt, they would bring rocks from the lake back to shore up the walls. The basement is still used for the famous Swiss steak dinners each Saturday evening during the summer.

Since we spent a great deal of time at the old Torch Tip Cabins in Eastport, we would go into Torch Lake, cold as ever, walking over the huge rocks in order to get out into the clear lake. Once this was achieved and our bodies had turned the next thing to being blue because of the cold water, we would swim and get to the raft that was in the lake. I remember standing on it and my dad would rock it back and forth saying, "Come on, you've got better sea legs than that!"

Another great memory, simple as it is, was going to the old Kruse's Store, which had housed the post office. The special treat was always looking to see if they had an orange sherbet push up to eat in the hot weather. Great memories of those times.

The Many Uses of Grandpa's Well
By Barbara Kane of Traverse City, Michigan
Born 1940

One of the most vital necessities on a farm was a good well. My grandpa's stood about fifty feet from the back door of the house and down a little incline, and produced the clearest, best tasting water of all the farms around his. The well pit itself was about five feet square and six feet deep. Boards were nailed in place to cover the top, and mounted on the boards was an iron pump.

It was a simple device consisting of the iron shaft, the spout, and the handle. It took only three or four "pumps" to prime it before the water came gushing from the spout. This was the source of all drinking water; water used for cooking and canning, for the dogs, pigs, chickens, and Saturday night baths, and even water in the large wooden tub where the horses drank before they went out to the fields. My grandpa usually filled it immediately afterwards, so that water would be available when the horses returned.

The wooden tub was refilled at noon, and again late in the afternoon after the day's work was finished. After an extremely hot day, the horses might be led again to the well so they could drink their fill in the evening. Each stop necessitated a lot of pumping on my grandpa's part.

Sometimes during a long hot summer with very little rainfall, the well near the house would dry up. Then my grandpa would hitch up one of the horses and put two big empty rain barrels on a wooden skid and drive down through the lane to a nearby creek to get water there.

There was always water in that creek although it might be low. And the water might taste a little funny, but it was better than no water at all. My grandma would use the water sparingly, but the animals at the farm came first: pigs, dogs, chickens, and other livestock that couldn't make it to the creek such as the cows and horses.

Even the laundry might be delayed for a week; and Saturday night baths were done using a couple of basins of water rather than washing in the big galvanized tub that hung outside. Usually it was brought into the house and set down in a corner of the kitchen.

Besides the few times during an extremely dry summer when water had to be carried from the creek, an extreme cold spell in the winter might also prove to be a problem. Water deep in the shaft would freeze and no amount of hand power on the pump would release it. My grandma always kept a kettle with hot water on the cook stove overnight so water could be poured down the shaft in the morning to break up the ice and allow the water to flow out again.

Whether the water was used cold as it came from the pump or was heated on the cook stove for whatever use, every drop had to be pumped by hand and carried by the pail full. Consequently, after all those numerous trips all day long, back and forth between the well and the house, one learned to conserve water and use it wisely. And so often, the water pail seemed to run low when my grandma was in the midst of cooking a meal! So when the grandchildren came to visit, it was always a big help having them pump water, even if they were able to bring back only a half pail at a time.

I was used to sinks and faucets and running water at my home in Grand Rapids where I lived, and thought that all that pumping at the well was a novel thing. In fact, one time I remembered elbowing my sister out of the way so I could operate the pump handle.

Acting quite important at the time, I remembered saying, "Grandma is waiting for this water, you know. She doesn't have a speck of it in the house."

Despite these two infrequent cases of malfunction, the well was a great gathering place. Water was always free for the taking. When company came, my grandma didn't have to offer a cup of coffee right away because the visitor had usually stopped at the well for a refreshing drink.

No country well was ever without a tin cup hanging from a wire loop near the pump handle. No one thought about germs in those days and the same cup was passed around from person to person. Enjoying a cold drink was the uppermost thought in everyone's mind.

My grandpa would always take a drink coming in from the fields before he washed up outside the house before dinner or supper. He wouldn't have ever thought about going in the house and then reaching for the dipper in the pail. Likewise, when company was ready to leave, everybody seemed to stop at the well for one last drink for the road. "Goodbyes" might last for a half-hour before everyone had had his or her fill before they departed.

The pump was just the right place to wash off the mud and sand after running around barefoot, or getting rid of the bloodsuckers after swimming in the creek during a hot summer afternoon. The water in the creek was fine; one picked up the bloodsuckers sometimes from wading near the muddy bank when one got out.

My sisters and I were always admonished never to wash in the tub that contained the water for the horses. The horses not only would not drink from it, but our grandpa would have had to clean out the tub and refill the whole thing with fresh water.

Another time that the well was an absolute necessity was for pumping water for Monday morning washdays. Preparation actually began on Sunday night when my grandpa would pump copious pails of water to fill the wash boiler that was heated overnight on the wood stove, plus several more pails of water for the rinse tub.

After the hot water was transferred in the morning to the washing machine, my grandma would shave off thin pieces of soap from a Fels Naptha bar and swish it around a few times with a clean stick used just for that purpose. Her "do it yourself" machine was actually a wooden tub standing on four legs with a couple of paddles attached to the underside of the cover.

She moved the handles back and forth in a 180-degree arc, for a while first with her right hand, then with her left. Of course, clothes that were extra soiled were scrubbed first on a washboard using the bar of soap.

White clothes were always done first, such as sheets, pillowcases, white shirts, bath towels and kitchen towels, and the heavy cloths used to strain the milk in the separator. Underwear, handkerchiefs, and colored clothes such as housedresses, aprons, and play clothes came next. And there might be two or more loads of each of these depending on the season of the year. And, of course, the same wash water was used for each succeeding load. Lastly were the dark work shirts, stockings, and the overalls which my grandpa wore doing chores and farm work.

After each load was washed, every piece was wrung out by hand and placed in the rinse tub. A few drops of bluing were added to the rinse water; this helped to keep white clothes white, although there was nothing like the hot sun for bleaching out stains. After dunking the clothes up and down in the rinse water, each piece was fed through the hand wringer and placed in a laundry basket for transfer to the clotheslines.

The winger was a contraption fastened to the rim of the rinse tub, consisting mainly of two rollers about ten inches long and operated by a hand crank. As the clothes were fed between the rollers, the water was squeezed out and allowed to flow back into the rinse tub. This was one procedure that my grandma wouldn't allow me to do until I was at least nine years old. She was afraid I might catch my little fingers between the rollers. Besides it being almost impossible to "feed and crank" at the same time, there was always the chance that something might drop on the ground and would have to be washed all over again.

After the clothes were hung on the lines

or spread over bushes to dry, the dirty wash water was emptied out on the ground behind the wood shanty, and the rinse water was carried by the pail full to the flowerbeds that grew near the house. I had always thought that my grandma's roses and peony bushes grew so well from the "bluing" that had been added. Oh, how nice the clothes smelled after having been dried outdoors all day! I was always sure that it was the water from my grandpa's well that did it.

✓ Growing Up at Woodside Dairy
By Thomas Groesser of Traverse City,
Michigan
Born 1935

My grandfather Edward Groesser started his dairy back in the 1900s in Suttons Bay, Michigan. The cows were all milked by hand until he purchased a 2-cow milking machine. Ed was married to Jenny (Bahle) Groesser and they had two sons, Milton (my father) and Gordon, and one daughter, Nellie (Groesser) Budd. The two boys helped their father on the farm for many years. They delivered milk in glass bottles door to door with a horse and the milk wagon. When my grandfather left the farm to work on the car ferry out of Ludington, his boys took over the dairy. It was called "Woodside Dairy."

My memory goes back to the time I was 8 years old. My family (Milton's) lived on

Woodside Dairy

one side of M-633 farming 80 acres but the dairy was located on the opposite side of the road where the barn and home of Gordon was located and was on 120 acres. We milked approximately 20 Guernsey cows morning and evening. We had the 2-cow milking machine but Dad would milk by hand as well. We raised most of our own grain (hay, oats, and corn), all of which we fed our livestock. It was loose hay, no hay balers back then, and no tractor, just horses. After milking the cows, the milk would go into the icehouse to be cooled. The icehouse was back of the milk house but the milk had to be carried down the steps in 5-gallon milk cans into the cooler, which was under the icehouse. In the winter, the men would take the horse and sleigh to the lake and saw off blocks of ice, bring them home, and place them in the icehouse and cover them with sawdust. It would last through the summer. After that, we would have to buy our ice.

All the glass bottles had to be washed and sterilized before filling. We had a boiler in the milk house fired by coal to heat the water. Dad would carry up the 5 gal milk cans and dump the milk into the clean tank so now we could fill the bottles, 2 bottles at a time. My job was to place the filled bottle under the capper and pull the lever down to cap the milk. The caps came in a long tube. Both the caps and the bottles had our name "Woodside Dairy" stamped on them. The bottles, which were put into a 12-compartment case, were then carried back down into the cooler until it was time to deliver the milk.

One quart of milk cost 18 cents and

Milton and son, Tom

416

whipping cream cost 20 cents for half a pint. We delivered milk/cream door to door in the village of Suttons Bay and to the school and stores, on Monday, Wednesday, Friday, and Saturday. I would ride along with Dad in his panel truck and when we stopped at a customer's house, run up to their door with the fresh milk, pick up the empty bottles left outside by the door and run back to the truck. One customer (Nellie Johnson, sister of Jenny) would sometimes give me a candy bar. She also offered to take me fishing. She started my lifelong hobby of fishing in the area.

It was a great time to be a kid but the work was never done. It instilled in me a strong sense of work ethic, which I have never regretted. Woodside Dairy would become the first dairy in Leelanau County to own a "pasteurizer" machine.

Grandpa Groesser

✓On the Farm between Bear Lake, Kaleva, and Chief
By Carol J. (Widgren) Urbanus of Bear Lake, Michigan
Born 1939

Seventy-three years ago, I was born in a suburb of Detroit, far from the roots of both my parents. Mom's parent's homesteaded in Bear Lake Township, in Manistee County, Michigan in the 1860s. Dad's parents bought a farm not too many miles from there in the

1890s. My father, Eli Widgren eventually worked as a hired hand for my mother's father, and he ended up marrying the farmer's daughter, my mother, Hilda Cushing in 1914.

Income was never plentiful in the Depression years, plus a growing family, necessitated a move to southeast Michigan to seek employment. In December of 1939, exactly 25 years to the day of their marriage, I was born in the Detroit suburb of Hazel Park. I was the fifth and last child in our family. Three years later, we left Hazel Park and moved back to my paternal grandparents' farm after the death of my father's mother. My step-grandfather still resided on the farm. At that time, only my brother and I still lived at home. Two sisters and one brother remained in Detroit.

The farmhouse was two stories with a Michigan basement. It did have electricity and Dad fixed it so water could be pumped into the house from the outside pump house to a big barrel in the dining room. (No room in the kitchen). A two-hole outhouse served as the toilet facility. It was about 60 feet from the main residence. An overnight toilet need was served by a chamber pot under the bed.

I remember the time a frisky rooster frequently attempted to ambush an unsuspecting person on the way to the outdoor facility. Mom gave it an attitude adjustment with her broom one day. Worked wonderfully!

Etched into my memory are the times I accidentally stepped in crusted cow patties in the barnyard or pasture. The contents would squish up between my toes, as I was usually barefooted in the warmer weather. Any experienced farm kid knew to pull several weeds between the toes to remove most of the odoriferous material. The rest eventually wore off until clean-up time.

A farm kid also learned to respect electric fences after seeing the reaction of a farm animal that unknowingly touched one. Actually, I learned a harder way when my brother tricked me into touching one.

Once a Blue Racer snake chased me when I stumbled onto its nest of younguns'.

Another time Dad captured a Milk snake in the barn. We sold it to a guy for $1.50. He collected snakes for some purpose and he told me that if I caught a Michigan rattler he'd pay me $5.00. That was a lot of money back then, but I could never collect on that prize.

Carol's mother, Hilda Cushing (Widgren)

There was the time we observed a Hog-nosed snake (Puff Adder) for the first time. We were fascinated by the way it rolled over on its back, writhed around, and played dead with its tongue hanging out when it felt threatened. When we'd flip it right side up it would flip back over on its back again, tongue still hanging out. Pretty good accomplishment for a "dead" snake. Very amusing.

At the age of four I started school at Kaleva, a Finnish town. My brother was seven years older than I. We walked about half a mile to the bus pick-up point. During bad winters when the snow on our dirt country road was too deep for me to walk and a plow hadn't passed through yet, I missed school. Those were unhappy events for me, as I loved school.

My favorite afterschool activity was to make a sandwich with butter, sugar, and cinnamon, accompanied with a glass of milk from our cows. Then I'd perch next to our big old radio that was up on a kitchen shelf to listen to my favorite afternoon programs: "Sky King," "B-Bar-B Ranch," and "The Shadow Knows" plus a few others I can't remember. At other times the family enjoyed "Amos and Andy", "Fibber McGee and Molly," and the "Jack Benny Show." We had no television or other electronic devices, just one radio.

With two working parents, no close neighbor kids to play with, and no siblings close to my age, any entertainment was left up to myself. When a little older I wandered the 80 acre farm in good weather. I put my imagination to good use. Eventually I discovered the joy of reading as I entered the world of Hans Brinker and the Silver Skates, Heidi, Black Beauty, and Bambi.

Since I was a late-in-life child of my parents, in the summer I played with the kids of my two much older sisters and brother when they came up for a visit from the city. This brings to mind the time when the older of my two sisters was visiting for a couple of weeks with her three boys. The oldest of these three nephews of mine was a year older than I. One day he decided he could run across the crusted-over manure pile in the barnyard. He didn't make it. There he was, down to his waist in cow poo. With the aid of a rope, my sister and mother hauled him out. They poured pails of water from the animal drinking water tank over Jimmy, and to say that the three of them were unhappy is an understatement. The other two nephews and I thought it was quite entertaining.

I'm not sure how old I was when I almost was injured, maybe five? I was playing down by the barn and pigpen when I heard our big sow squealing. When I looked up, I saw her charging toward me and I froze. That pig was about as tall as I was! My brother's little Sheltie dog Mickey was close by. She raced at the sow, caught her by her back leg, and clamped on tightly. The sow stopped her charge at me, and spun around as she tried to grab Mickey, who was being flung around in the air as she hung on. By this time Dad, who was working in the barnyard, heard the commotion, grabbed his pitchfork, ran over, and drove the sow back into her pen. Dad fixed where she had broken out. We figured that because she had a litter of piglets she felt they were threatened. Needless to say our Mickey was a hero!

Other entertainment in the summertime was attending free shows in neighboring towns. While I watched the free outdoor movie in an open field with friends, Dad would entertain himself in the local tavern. Dad often made trips to Chief, a very small town with about three businesses and just a few residences. Back then a railroad ran through the town.

Chief was just a few miles from our home. I'd go along with Dad, as it was a sure thing I'd get a double-dip ice cream cone for just five cents a dip at Coe Brother's store.

Mom eventually worked at a newspaper publishing office in Bear Lake. Dad worked for the Manistee County Road Commission. The Michigan winters made it difficult at times for them to get to work, made especially difficult because of the rural setting of the homestead on a back road.

The dining room was heated by an oil space heater. The living room received heat from a coal stove. During cold weather we froze upstairs. The old farmhouse had very little insulation—perhaps some newspapers stuffed between studs. Dad had cut small registers in the ceilings to allow some heat upstairs. I can remember standing over a register to allow the rising heat from downstairs to bellow up into my nightgown. Then I'd sprint for the bed to keep the trapped heat with me as long as possible. Hot water bottles also helped to warm the feet.

I shudder now to think of the firetrap that old house was, with its narrow stairway to the second floor, positioned between the dining room and living room with the stoves close by. No such thing back then as a smoke detector, fire extinguisher, or a phone to call for help.

Now back to everyday living. One day, out of boredom and perhaps from the wish to have a riding horse of my own, an idea entered my head. I proceeded down to the barnyard where Teddy, a big plow horse, was relaxing. Teddy belonged to my uncle and was on loan to help Dad till the fields. I was about ten years old and only my step-grandfather was at home. Using a method I'd seen Dad use, I slipped the bridle bit into Teddy's mouth as I gave him an ear of corn to munch. As I was short, I used the top rail of the wooden barnyard fence

Carol's father, Eli Widgren in the center

to enable me to position the bridle and then to hoist myself upon his very broad back.

Proudly I rode out to the rural road, but soon wanted more speed out of Teddy as he plodded along. So, I broke off a small branch from a tree we were passing, and switched Teddy's rump. He began to trot and because my short legs couldn't grasp his broad sides, I began to bounce up and down, and right off his back! I slammed onto the hard clay road, landing on my back. I thought I was dying, as the wind had been knocked out of me and I couldn't catch my breath. Teddy trotted back home to the barnyard area. Slowly I got back up, walked the distance to the barnyard, let Teddy into the barnyard, took off the bridle, and NEVER told Mom or Dad about my escapade. Fortunately my step-grandfather was unaware of what I had done.

The eighty-acre farm was my playground. I had a secret glen down at the edge of the swampy woods. My mother and I would hunt for mushrooms in special spots. As I grew older, I explored farther into the woods where a small creek meandered through our property. Dad would occasionally take me fishing in James Lake, a small pothole lake not too far from our farm. Dad made his own scow boats and we spent hours fishing with bamboo poles for bluegill, sunfish, bass, and perch. It was my job to help him dig for worms and to catch grasshoppers or crickets. The red-winged grasshoppers were the best ones, he said.

Eventually Mom tired of the conditions on the farm and the difficulties it presented. On her own, she purchased an old house in the village of Bear Lake and the family helped her to fix it up to make it livable. When I was eleven, Mom and I moved to our new home. Dad split his time between the farm and Bear Lake. I was happy as could be, as now I had village friends to play with on a regular basis. In warm weather I could walk to the lake to swim. No longer did I have a long bus ride to school at Kaleva, as I could walk to the Bear Lake School just two blocks away. We had an indoor bathroom with a real bathtub and heat furnished by a central oil floor furnace. There was an open stairwell to let heat upstairs. I could walk to the Cub Theater to see a movie.

Life, indeed, was good! I had both a more comfortable living situation in Bear Lake and also my memories of living on an eighty-acre farm between Bear Lake, Kaleva, and

Chief in Manistee County. I enrolled at Bear Lake School while entering sixth grade, and graduated from it in 1957. After four years of college, teaching at the local school, mother of a daughter and son, and widowed after many years of a great marriage, I still reside in the village of Bear Lake.

√ Poor, But Had All the Good Food We Could Eat
By Raymond Edward Purvis of Traverse City, Michigan
Born 1928

My name is Raymond Purvis. I've lived my entire life in the Traverse City, Michigan area. I was raised on my family farm on Potter Road in East Bay Township. The farm was approximately 120 acres in size, a quarter of which was woods. Growing up we had no running water or electricity in our home. We used kerosene lanterns to help light the house.

Living on the farm, I learned to use the land to help sustain our life. We chopped down trees that would heat our wood range. The wood range had a reservoir on the side of the stone for water, which provided us with hot water.

The water supply was from a windmill. The windmill would catch the air and then start to run water into an underground cistern. After enough water had collected, we would hand pump the water for usage in the house and barn. During the winter months, we would cut ice from Chandler Lake. These blocks were cut 24" x 24" by 16"-18" thick. After the ice was cut, it would be brought back by horse drawn sleighs. The ice was then stored

Raymond's father, Edward purvis with Raymond in 1942

Raymond riding his pony Dollar with his cousin, Frank in 1938

in a large icehouse packed with sawdust so it could last all summer.

The family farm had an abundance of crop varieties, as well as barnyard animals. We grew apples, hay, oats, wheat, green beans, potatoes, and many other types of vegetables. The small apple orchard provided all the applesauce and apples you would want to eat. Each crop had a lot of work that needed to be done to ensure its harvest. The hay was all loose. The hay would be cut, raked into rows, and piled into small stacks. The stacks would be pitched into a horse drawn wagon and hauled to the barn.

When the oats and wheat harvest was due, the Eikey brothers would bring down their thrashing machine. This helped harvesting the wheat and oats. On these days, we always knew Mom would make a good meal.

The farm had other crops like green beans, potatoes, and field corn. When it was time to pick the green beans Dad would hire high school boys. After they were harvested, we would sell them to wholesalers. Potatoes were a very unique harvest. Each year school would be shut down for a week to allow for their harvest. The potatoes were all dug by hand using 6 tine forks and stored in our large basement to sell at the best time for potato prices. The field corn would be harvested, stacked in piles, husked, and then placed in a silo for animal feed. After harvest, my mother would be busy canning and storing all our finished goods.

We were poor but we always had all the good food we could eat. Handmade ice cream, fresh chicken dinners, eggs, pork, beef, and all the vegetables and fruits all grown and cultivated on our family farm. The ice cream was made by a hand crank ice cream maker. You would add ice and side walk salt, and that makes the ice cream colder. You would crank it till the ice cream gets hard.

My education was unique. I attended a 1-room country school by the name of Potter School. This is where I went from kindergarten through 8th grade. Every class was taught by the same teacher. Each day our class would be called in front of the teacher. There was a long bench so that we would sit and face the teacher's desk. Then he would discuss the previous day's assignment and give us our next assignments. There were only 3 people in my grade, myself and 2 other girls. Since it was a small 1-room school, my younger sisters were in the same classroom as me. I always tried to do my best because I had 2 younger sisters who would tell on me when I arrived home.

There was no running water or electricity in the school. The older boys would have to transport well water from their homes to help the school with their water supply. We would use roughly 5 gallons a day. The school was heated using a wood furnace. There was no school bus for students. Everyone walked to school; no one to my knowledge walked more than 4 miles. School rarely ever shut down for snow days.

When I moved on to my senior high school, I had a job as a milkman before school. I delivered using a horse drawn carriage. I was allowed to miss the first class of school each day to work.

I remember the sounds of the farm, being sung to sleep by the sounds of frogs singing, exploring our land and the country on my beautiful Welsh pony named Dollar, and quenching my thirst from a spring on the side of a hill in the woods.

Colorful Characters of the '40s and '50s in Traverse City
By Arthur "Bud" Homan of Traverse City, Michigan
Born 1929

I was born in Traverse City in 1929 and have lived in the area all my life. I went to a one room school when I was in the first grade,

Bud is behind the cute little girl
1936

which had kindergarten through seventh grade with a total of eight students (I have a picture). I walked two and one half miles to get there… that was when Michigan winters were winters.

A couple of events that happened when I was very young include the time my mother was burning leaves and the fire got away from her. We ran to a creek about a block away to get water, her with a pail and me with a teakettle. I guess it was faster than pumping water by hand. We somehow got it out. Then there was the time I was with my dad going down Bunker Hill in an old Model T Ford when a rear wheel came off and rolled right past us.

Some of the things we as kids did when we lived in the small of Grawn (1937-1939): all the boys had an old car tire that we rolled wherever we went. Sometimes the smaller boys would squeeze in the center of the tire and be rolled around by the bigger boys. When we moved to Traverse City, the games changed. We had a hoop and wheel. The hoop was usually made with an old plaster lathe cut about three feet long with another eight or ten inch piece fastened across the bottom end, which you pushed and steered a wheel in front of you. The wheel was usually from an old baby buggy, as they were about the right size and had a hard rubber tire that made them easy to steer. We also played "Anti-Ay-Over" a lot. It was played by having an equal number of players on opposite sides of a low building, usually a garage or small house. You would yell "anti-ay-over" and throw a ball over, and if someone caught it, they would run around and try to touch the one that threw it. How you knew who threw it I don't remember.

Another pastime was to stomp on empty evaporated milk cans until they would curl up and clamp to the heel of our shoes, making make believe horseshoes. The 'Tra-Bay"

Theater in downtown Traverse City had a Saturday matinee every week. In the alley behind the theater would be a line of smashed milk cans waiting for us to put on and gallop off into the sunset as Gene Autry, Roy Rogers, Cisco Kid, or whoever we had seen on the screen that day.

There are many things that I remember about Traverse City, but the times that come back to me mostly when I think back are the 1940s and 1950s. I often think about the colorful characters of that era that could be seen around the area. There was Police Chief "Charlie Woodrow" who very often was standing at the corner of Front and Cass Street, by the "Dalquist 5 & 10 Cent" store, greeting people as they passed by. That was back when the police were respected, maybe a little fearful, especially by the kids. Then there was "Smokey Joe" who was a crippled street person who did odd jobs for the downtown businesses and others. He would get a kick out of scaring the kids, but he really was a nice guy who would help anyone out. He spent a few weeks one summer in a hole in the ground at the "O-Ak-A-Beach" dance pavilion as "The Man Buried Alive." You could pay ten cents or a quarter and talk to him down a chute. There was a larger area down there that the public couldn't see that he used as a living area. O-Ak-A-Beach dance pavilion was on US-31 at 4 Mile Rd. It was a large open air dance hot spot in the summer.

There were two fellows with the nickname of "Shorty." One "Shorty Burden" who sold the RecordEagle in downtown TC. He would be in a half run, moving around and in between cars near Front St. and Union St., selling the paper to people waiting for the light to change, all the time hollering "TC Record Eagle." The other one was "Shorty Bracket" who could be seen rushing from business to business to do odd jobs, waving to everyone that yelled "Hi Shorty." He also worked at the local roller rink. He was the one that blew the whistle at you if you skated too fast. There was also "Cecil Dill," son of the original owners of "Dill's Restaurant" on Union St. He would roam about downtown playing simple tunes, such as "The Old Grey Mare" by clasping his hands together and then squeeze the air out to make the different notes. And you could actually recognize the tune.

We had a bag lady named "Emma"

Bud in the mid-1940s

who also could be seen almost anywhere in town, with her burlap potato sack picking up anything that she could use or sell. She looked almost like the ones you see in movies about "The Bowery" in New York.

Some of the popular places that have been gone for a long time were "The Coliseum" roller rink. It had a big skating area, snack bar, and a railed-in spectator area. It was known as the meeting place of the town. It was very popular place for the sailors during WWII, when there was a Navy base here. You could rent clamp-on skates. I was a "skate boy" who would put the skates on people's feet for tips and the sailors were good tippers.

There were several dance places, such as "The Brook" on Maple St. that was built over "Asylum Creek" (now Kid's Creek). One spring the creek overflowed and came up over the dance floor. We had our share of bands, like The Joe Dolen Trio, Freddie Gleason Orchestra, and Satler's Nite Hawk, which played Saturday nights at a dance hall south of town. It was there that many of the younger generation got their "parking lot education" of life: cigarettes, beer, wine, and back seat love.

I guess reliving life of '40s and '50s must be a hobby for me. A few years ago, my wife gave me some '40-'50s style clothing for Christmas, saying, "If you are going to live back in those time, you might as well dress like it!"

The Big Blizzard of LeRoy Michigan
By Patricia Johnson of Nashville, Tennessee
Born 1924

The years were 1936 and 1937. It was a very severe winter in our village of LeRoy, Michigan then and still is a small village 77 years later. The snow was piled deep. School was never cancelled in those days. There was a blizzard, and the temperature was 20 degrees below zero when it was time to go home from school. My dad came and met us and led us home. We had to stay by the fencerow so we wouldn't get lost or frozen in the storm. Our faces were covered with knitted scarves so that we could see some but had protection from the snow.

It is and will always be "home" in our hearts.

The Snowstorm Birth
By Judy Smith of Flint, Michigan
Born 1947

As long as I can remember, whenever the subject of giving birth or snowstorms came up, my mother always told this story. The year was 1947. The small town of Posen, Michigan, located toward the tip of the eastside of the Lower Peninsula (also known as the mitten of Michigan), was hit with another major snowstorm. It was the end of March. Our town of Posen was getting slammed for the second time in three months with a major blizzard. Posen had already experienced a terrific snowstorm in January 1947.

My mother was about the give birth to her first child. Her due date was March 27th. My parents, Dominic and Kay Lewandowski, lived in the small farming community of Posen with my Grandma Rose. This is my dad's mom. Rogers City, located on the shores of Lake Huron, was the nearest town. Dr. Edward Arscott's office was located in Rogers City. Dr. Arscott was my mom's doctor. There was no hospital in Rogers City, just a maternity home where women went to have their babies. Alpena was the nearest town with a hospital, but it was miles away, so they decided to use the maternity home in Rogers City. That was the plan, that is, until the snowstorm hit Posen.

Since my mom's due date was near and the storm started, my parents decided to go stay at my Uncle Benny and Aunt Martha's house on South Lake Street in Rogers City until it was time for my birth. My aunt and uncle talked my parents into having their baby (that would be me) at their house. Also, Dr. Edward Arscott was able to be at the house for my birth.

Finally, the big day arrived. Wednesday, April 2nd at 5:30 P.M, I was born. They named me Judith Ann Lewandowski. The blizzard was so bad that it took the Presque Isle County Road Commission weeks to clear all the roads. We stayed in Rogers City for two weeks. We could not get home by car yet, so I was brought home by a sleigh and horses. At this time, the main road (US 23) was cleared, but the other roads to my Grandma Rose's house were still impassable. After two weeks, my mom's dad—Grandpa John Pokorski, met them at the junction of US 23 and M 65. He was safely able to get the new family back home to Grandma Rose's house.

Four siblings were soon to follow. Their births were not as exciting as mine was; they were born in the hospital in Alpena.

Days in Lewiston
By Howard Bacheller of Lewiston, Michigan
Born 1932

I grew up in Oakland County, Michigan, just north of Detroit. My parents bought a log cabin on East Twin Lake, just south of Lewiston, Michigan. My parents were teachers in Ferndale, so when school was over, we headed for Lewiston for the summer. We started each spring checking for paint peeling. If it was, we repainted it. Within a few years, Perma-log became the savior of wood cabins. It was a system of wire mesh with brown mortar to make it look like wood. The spaces were painted white to make it look like caulking. My brothers and I would take our glider airplanes up to the fire tower. It was up the hill across the road from the Lewiston Lodge. One of us would take the gliders up to the fire tower and sail them while the other two would try to find them. Needless to say, we lost a lot of gliders. We feel that it is an ideal place to spend our retirement years.

Creepy Radio Programs and Odd Findings
By Shirley J. Wares of Traverse City, Michigan
Born 1933

My four sisters and our brother were born on my grandparents' 80-acre farm, which was near the schoolhouse we all attended. We listened to scary radio programs like The Shadow before our Saturday night baths. My sister Jackie would listen to every adventure and was frightened beyond words. My mother had to heat the bath water because we had only cold water for running water in the 1930s. The kitchen stove was a black cast-iron wood burner, so it took some time to heat. The tub was an old fashioned claw leg type. We made our brother bath last because he peed in the water.

On Saturday afternoons, we sometimes were allowed to go to the matinee. They were usually western, like Hop-along Cassidy, The Lone Ranger. In those days, everyone pitched in to help with the chores. I was assigned to take care of the many chickens. There were four to six dozen of them. We gathered eggs, kept pens clean, and protected chickens from predators. There were many predators such as foxes, hawks, and thieves. Some escaped and were hit by cars. I was about nine years old and continued this chore until I left home to marry.

When I was about 20 years old, my grandmother told me of an event that she witnessed. She was coming home from shopping for material to make our clothes when she noticed a car parked in an odd location. She decided to check it out and found two young adults—a girl and her twin brother. They had connected a hose from the exhaust pipe and committed suicide because her brother had made her pregnant. They were separated at birth and raised in different orphanages.

The Tornado
By Theresa Maher Nichols of Lincoln, Kansas
Born 1933

During my childhood, I lived with my parents, sister, and two brothers on the family farm four and a half miles southwest of Lincoln, Kansas. One spring day, the sky became dark and gloomy. We were accustomed to watching the sky for storms, especially tornadoes. As conditions became progressively worse, we were alerted by my mother to be ready to go to our storm cellar, which was dug into the side of the hill. We stored smoked meat and home canned goods there. We went there for protection from the storms. We were concerned about my dad making it to the cellar, as he was in the outdoor toilet. I didn't understand it then, but I expect he was worried that he might be about to lose everything and developed an upset stomach. He made it. We prayed together for our safety, our wheat crop, our home, and our baby chickens. My mother bought brooders of baby chickens earlier in the year and raised them to become fryer-sized by harvest season. My youngest brother and I were especially concerned about the chickens, which were almost fryer-sized. The sky got very dark; the air was very still. The roar of the wind, rain, and debris sounded like a locomotive train coming our way. All hell broke loose. As fast as it came, it left. My dad and oldest brother went out first. We all followed. Our home was still standing, none of the doors ever completely closed again. The large barn was twisted off of its foundation. Several outbuildings, chicken houses, and small sheds were gone. Several pieces of farm machinery were gone. Parts of the farm machinery were found 10 to 15 miles away. The baby chickens were all gone! Not even a trace was left! We were thankful we were okay and lived to tell the tale.

Bad Storms and Blackberry Muffins
By Milo G. Houghton of South Boardman, Michigan
Born 1945

I was born in 1945, but I don't have any memories of times before I was five, so that is when my "good old days" started. There were seven girls and boys in our family. We went to Fife Lake School. Back then, we had three buses. I remember that we used to get a lot of snow back then and we had very few snow days. Today, the school has 20 buses, give or take a few. They have more snow days, also. I must say that no matter how good the school year went, I was glad to get out in the summer for a short vacation.

Milo's dad, Earl Houghton in 1972

My dad was a farmer. He milked cows and grew potatoes and cucumbers. Many of the school kids helped with the harvest of those crops. We used to get time off of school for harvest days. There was a period of time when tornadoes ripped across our farm. In 1953, it tore the silo down and some other things as well. In 1956, it took some big maple trees down by the road. In 1959, the storm went across our neighbors but didn't do any damage until it got to our farm. It took about a third of the roof off of the barn.

One of the fondest memories from back in those days was when my youngest sister Pat and I were home a lot in the summer. She would say, "I'll make some muffins if you pick

Milo at age 6

the blackberries." I would ride my bike down the road to the woods and would pick enough berries to make about twelve muffins. I would get back home, clean the berries, and then it was her turn. She did a good job. Sometimes, she would help pick the berries. It is nice to remember some of the good old days, especially when you can think of what you want to.

✓Deer Camp Coffee
By Kathryn M. Gall of Hillman, Michigan
Born 1940

Outdoor sports were a big deal in our family. Archery, in particular, was a very big deal. Our parents were among the first persons to be granted a bow and arrow deer hunting license by the State of Michigan. Archery would remain a main focus in their lives for most of the next 60 years.

October was the month of archery deer season, and a huge amount of time and effort was spent in preparing for it. Great care was taken to search out the best place to set up camp. It had to be somewhere on state land. It had to be not too far from a source of safe drinking water. Most importantly, it had to have plentiful evidence of deer activity. Many hours were spent arrow sharpening and target practicing on cardboard deer silhouettes.

October in Northern Michigan is a beautiful time to be outside in the crisp autumn air in woods aglow with crimson leaves under a clear blue sky. In the frosty evenings, we sang songs around the campfire to the tune of Dad's accordion. We were always joined by a loyal group of family friends who often drove several hundred miles on a Friday night to join us at deer camp for the weekend.

Camping in the 1940s and '50s was really primitive by today's standards. We slept in bed rolls on the cold hard floor of a canvas tent. We cooked and ate outdoors in all kinds of weather. The evening meal was typically a big pot of chili or stew. We also had coffee that was brewed in a big enamel ware pot over the open fire. In the morning, a few fresh grounds and some more water would be added to the large enamel coffee pot. We would stand around the fire in the pre-dawn frosty air warming our hands around a cup of steaming coffee before stuffing our pockets with some munchies and slipping quietly off to our various hunting stands or blinds. By mid-afternoon, most of us would be back in camp to report on our luck or lack thereof, and to catch a nap before the evening's hunt.

One particular morning, there were complaints that the coffee tasted a bit odd. We heard remarks such as, "What kind of unusual coffee is this? I've never tasted anything like it," and," What in the world did you put in this coffee to make it taste so different?" It couldn't have been too bad because the hunters drained their tin cups and filled their thermoses with more to take along with them.

In the afternoon before starting the evening meal, our mother decided she needed to clean out that coffee pot. She did, and didn't find much—just a little old dead deer mouse!

✓ Working the Farm
By Betty DeKam of Falmouth, Michigan
Born 1927

I was born on September 7, 1927. Although I am 85 ½ years old right now, I still have a very good memory. I remember that when I was little, I walked to school a mile and a quarter. The school was next to a church in a small town of Vogel Center. There also was a grocery store, Ben Bower's store. They had everything in that store—groceries, boots, shoes, material, thread, needles, underwear, towels, peanut butter in large containers. We bought it by the pound. We'd have it on our homemade bread for supper on Sunday nights. That would be a real treat! Mom would make a grocery list, and Dad would take it to the store. Also, he'd take a square crate of eggs to the store to pay for the groceries. Mom knew how much she'd get for the eggs, and sometimes she'd say, "I'd better not get those three pounds of molasses cookies for 25 cents! That's too much!" After he got done at the store, Dad would go to hardware store. The men would always sit by the stove and talk about whatever had happened that week. Tom owned the store. His brother Martin did the electrical wiring the area. We didn't get electricity until I was 16 after World War II.

Yes, we had outhouses and chamber pots. We had a party line telephone as well. Our number was 21—two long rings and one short.

If we knew somebody had an accident or was sick, we'd listen in. News traveled fast. We also had a wind-up record player. Dad came home from a farm sale one time and had a wind-up record player. We did not know what it was! He would wind it up, put a record in it, and music would come from it! One record was of two men talking. When we got electricity, we listened to the radio a lot at night. We'd get the war news. A lot of the guys were overseas in the war. We'd listen to the Grand Ole Opry. We'd all sit around the kitchen table playing games, and then we'd make popcorn or get a bowl of apples out of the basement. One in a while, Dad would come in from chores with a gleam in his eyes. He would then whisper to me "I think we should have some fudge tonight; don't you?" One time, he read a little orphan Annie book to us. He would read a chapter a night. That was something since he only went halfway through the fourth grade because his dad needed him to work on the farm. He was good at math as well.

My dad's dad had a sad life. His wife died during childbirth with the seventh child. She was only 38. The baby lived, but he needed someone to nurse him. My uncle Pete Winkel's wife was nursing a six month old baby girl, so she took him and raised him until he was a couple of years old. Everybody did what they could to help. After a few years, Grandpa Dick was engaged to be married again. Unfortunately, he had a ruptured appendix and died at the age of 51. Uncle Bert was only eleven years old. Well, they had a farm sale. My mom was there. She started running a fever, so Dad took her home to Falmouth, which was five or six miles away. They rode in a horse and buggy. Well, she got awful sick with spinal meningitis and nearly died. That was when it was an epidemic. Lots of people died of it. She was so weak that it took two people to help her walk. She and Dad were going to be married in the spring, but she had to get stronger. She sat in the sun and they fed her eggnog. She hated it. Well, they got married on September 13th. She promptly got pregnant with Dick. After two days of labor, the doctor came to the house. The last day, he didn't think she'd make it. However, the lord spared her life. Mom was never real strong. I always had to help a lot. She had five children in all. I was born after Dick, then Harvey, Joanne, and Gordon.

There were three farms on the corner where we lived. One was Uncle Bill and Aunt Jenny's. They had four children. A little north of us was Mark and Maggie's farm. They had ten kids and the grandpa lived with them, too. That is where we kids all played at night. There was always a ball game. Ray was a cripple boy and couldn't run, so he was the umpire. We could hear him all the way up to our house, "Strike!" Maggie was a good lady. Her last babies were twins—a boy and a girl, Merle and Marie. Marie was my sister Joanne's age. If we got hurt, we went to Maggie. She had salve; we only had iodine. She would bake a cake and it would be gone in one coffee time. Whoever was there got a piece.

Mark and Maggie had a 13 year old boy named Elke. He was responsible for taking the cows to the pasture past our house. Dad would always take our cows to that pasture, too. Every morning, he would try to beat my dad and tease him. One day, the weather was really funny. The sun would shine, and then it would start thundering and lightning. Dad and Elke were trying to separate a couple of Mark's young cattle from our cows and there was a huge crack of thunder and a bolt of lightning. The lightning killed Elke and knocked my dad down. Dad had on rubber boots; most likely, that is what saved him. Dad had been driving the car that day, and brought Elke home in the car. When they got to Mark's house, Mark could tell that there was something wrong. He said, "Is it the boy?" Later, they had another boy that they named after their late son. On a happier note, we all had a great time growing up on that corner with 19 kids. Good and bad things happened, but it always seemed to bring us closer together.

One winter, we were snowed in for six weeks. Our road wasn't plowed, so we walked to church. I think that was the winter that Harve got strep throat. I got it from him. He got over it, but I didn't there was three days that I just don't remember. Dad was in the chicken coop crying. They called the road commissioner and got them to plow the road east of us that wasn't as bad as ours. Dr. Masselink from McBain came and concluded that I had strep throat. He had a new tiny pill for me to take, but I couldn't swallow it. Mom put it in applesauce and I finally got it down. The doctor and the nurse (his wife) sat on each side of my bed. After an hour, I started sweating and I had to change my nightie. The doctor said that I would be alright after that happened. The fever broke. When I started getting better, I had to have one person on each side of me to lean on to even walk. Needless to say, that was a bad winter!

I remember our first wringer washer. It was gasoline powered. There was a hose that you had to put outside so that fumes would go outside. If it froze over, you would get lightheaded. When that happened, we had to get a kettle of hot water to pour over the frozen hose to thaw it out. To start it, we had to pull the choke three times and then step on the starter. It had a wringer, too. The first one we had was round and had a stick that you pushed back and forth to move the agitator back and forth. The newer one was much better because we didn't have to do that.

When I got married and got pregnant, I didn't feel so well. I worked four months and finally came home right before thanksgiving. However, right afterward, my cousin needed a person to help her with her new baby. I told her that I would help for two weeks. She got a blood clot in her leg, so I had to stay with her another two weeks. I got home just before Christmas. Then, I had only three months to sew 48 diapers, 12 little flannel nighties, and basket sheets. I also had to embroider them. The girls that I worked with threw me a baby shower and gave me enough money to buy some baby essentials—a baby basket, changing table, and a nice crib. I still have the crib. Well, the baby obviously couldn't wait to get here; she was born two weeks early on April 2nd. She was a tiny little girl—only six pounds and two ounces. We named her Carol Beth after us—Carl and Betty. She grew well.

One June 27th, Grandma DeKam said that Carl was coming home from the war before the fourth of July. I told her that Carl had not written that to me, but I had better get a home perm just in case so that I would look good for him when he arrived. I didn't give Carol a bath or dress her up that day so that I could do my hair. As I was cutting my hair, I heard a car drive up in the driveway. In stepped a soldier—my hubby! I asked him why he didn't tell me that he was coming. He said that he wanted to surprise me! He certainly did!

I got my perm that afternoon and went to his folk's house. They lived a couple of miles north of Falmouth on a farm. At about four o'clock that afternoon, it started getting really quiet and dark outside. The sky got green, and then it just started to pour. Carl's sister and brother went from window to window looking outside. "There goes the barn door," they would say, or, "There goes an apple tree." We should have gone down into the basement. One farmer's barn blew down and two other's barns were damaged. There were trees in the creek, and flats blew down. The storm gave us quite a celebration for Carl's return! However, he only had a month to stay, and then was sent to Camp Aterbury to train new recruits.

We moved to Falmouth, Michigan in northern Michigan in 1985. Our son, Dave bought the farm. Carl worked the farm every day. He loved the farm. He was born and raised there. He worked six months in Grand Rapids, and then came home. When April came around, he had to work on the farm. He was in the army for almost two years during the Korean War. When he came back, we lived in a little house on the farm for a couple years. Then, we bought the farm. We had seven children. His folks moved in the little house.

to the barn. That's the time that I stuck my tongue to the pump handle. That is a day that I have never forgotten. We were snowed in for two weeks. Dad and Rinny Wirgau had to take Rinny's Ford car down through our yard about a mile to 451 Road with our team of horses. They had to shovel the way there so that they could get to work at Calcite in town. They used skis to get to the car.

If we did all of our chores, Ma (Isabel) would take us and a couple of neighbor kids to town on Saturday nights to go to a movie. We watched movies like Roy Rogers, Gene Autrey, Whip Wilson, and Woody Woodpecker.

I started school at Klee School and then went to Saint Michaels Lutheran School from the third to the eighth grade. There were 60 kids in that one-room school with kids in the first to eighth grades. I think my teacher's name was Mr. Seabolt. Back then, we had two workhorses, seven milk cows, pigs, chickens, and rabbits. Ma used to take eggs and cream to Hoeft's Pinewood Grocery and buy groceries with the money that she received from them. We kids would take turns cranking the cream separator until the bell quit ringing.

✓ Wringer Washers and Cream Separators
By Philip C. Kreft of Rockford, Michigan
Born 1938

I was born and raised in Rogers City, Michigan. I was born on August 19, 1938 the oldest of 11 children. I had three brothers and seven sisters. I remember listening to Gene Autrey on the radio singing "Back in the Saddle Again." I turned to radio off and ran to the barn where Ma was milking cows. I said, "Ma, you got to hear Gene Autrey Sing!" She just laughed. When we got back to the house, I believe either the Green Hornet or the Dark Shadow was on. She then explained to me that the radio doesn't stop there when you turn it off.

One day, Ma was washing clothes and I was putting them through the wringer, when I ran my arm up to my elbow. I was screaming. She then hit the release button. I had a sore arm for a while. It was a Maytag washer with a little gas motor.

I remember the big blizzard. I think it was 1948. We had to shovel out the pump to get water and carry it to water cows, horses, pigs, and chickens. It was about 100 yards

Philip's mom, Isabel with Alice and Philip in 1940

428

Playing with Bees and the Rooster Hero
By Richard Derry of Interlochen, Michigan
Born 1938

We had a hand pump outside for water. In the summer, we washed clothes outside by the pump. We had a wringer washer and two rinse tubs. We hung them on a rope clothesline to dry. In the winter, we washed in the kitchen, but still hung them outside. My brother and I would follow the big yellow bumblebees until we found their nest, a ball of dried grass on the ground. Then, we would put fuel on it and burn it. We would stand back to back over the nest with wooden paddles made from fruit box slats. When the bees came back, we tried to bat them out of the air before we got stung. We didn't get stung very often. In the summer when the June Bugs came out, we would take our bee paddles out under the yard light and bat them out of the air.

Back then, every bar had a shuffleboard table. Mike and I made one with boards from a chicken coop, but it wasn't real smooth. We made pucks from zinc canning jar covers filled with clay and colored with melted crayons. It was crude, but we spent many hours playing on it. An old man lived down the road from us and I mowed his lawn with a push mower. He had a small front yard, but his backyard was huge. I got $2.00. The thing I remember most is that I was paid $1.00 for cutting Alfalfa hay. I cannot remember what a bag of oats cost, but corn screenings were very cheap.

One winter day when I was in the seventh grade, I was hunting rabbits when I saw a skunk go into a hollow log. I remembered my grandpa telling me that if you picked a skunk up by the tail, he could not squirt. I plugged the log with branches and headed home to get my axe, gunnysack, and my brother. When we got back, I chopped a hole behind the skunk and my brother prodded it with a stick until the tail came into my hole. I grabbed the tail and pulled it out. He really could not squirt. I told Mike to hold the bag open so I could put it in. When I tried, it grabbed the sack, humped his back, twisted, and sprayed me from my cheek down to my shoulder. Mike threw the sack and I fell to the ground, as I could not breathe. My mother smelled me while I was still in the backroom. I washed my face several times with soap and vinegar. My jacket was thrown away.

One summer, I remember counting my animals. I had 123 rabbits, 14 ducks, 37 Bantum chickens, 40-50 pigeons, 1 pig, and 1 dog. Back then, there was a barn at almost every farm. At night, I would climb up inside the barns and catch pigeons. The barn where we lived had been a horse barn, and I screened two of the stalls for a place for the pigeons. One fall, I took the screen off so they could go free, but most of them came back every night and still had babies there. My dad had 200 white chickens that he raised for meat. One day I heard the white chickens making a lot of noise. I ran out there and saw that one of the nesting Bantum hens had flown in their yard for food and water. The white ones had ganged up on her. I started to go in the yard to save her when I heard a Bantum rooster flying into the yard. Within two minutes, all 200 were in the coop. He walked back and forth in the doorway until the hen finished eating and went back to her nest.

The War Years
By Marcella M. McNabb of Traverse City, Michigan
Born 1934

It was 1942. My twin sister and I were eight years old. The war had started and many of the boys and men were leaving to serve in the Armed Forces. Money was scarce and every family had ration books. (I still have mine.) Some of the men and women in our small town of Lake Leelanau were leaving for the big city to work at Willow Run to help the war effort. Our dad was one of them. My Aunt Rosie was a riveter. Dad left in the summer and went to Detroit. My mom was left with seven children under nine, a milking cow, some chickens, and a mean rooster. That was a hard winter in many ways. The snow was so deep and it was hard to get to the barn to take care of the animals.

My Dad had put his name in for housing for us. After a year of being without him, we moved to a place called Norwayne into a three bedroom duplex. It was brand new. I will never forget how thrilled we were to have running water and an inside bathroom. We were surrounded by families from all over the United States. For the first time, my parents had extra money, and we got to see some movies. We missed our friends and families back home, but some of them were there also living near us. My brother had a paper route, and when the war ended, we all helped him deliver the news, yelling "Extra! Extra! Read all about it! The war has ended!" We were there for two years and had a new baby brother, John, while we were there. We were so happy to go back to our house in our little town. My Dad had earned enough money to get a bathroom and running water in our house. I am sure many more families could tell a similar story about the war years. It was a time of sacrifice and daily prayers for peace. We mourned for the loved ones from our community who lost their lives in that terrible war.

✓ The Shack and the Hermit
By Marguerite Karabin of Bellaire, Michigan

This story has some historical value even though our history in Bellaire, Michigan technically began in 1994. We had been weekend visitors and property owners since 1975, but this story began in 1999. After a few years of residence my husband Ray and I decided to do something, we had never done before. We decided to open a small business in the Village of Bellaire and we became baristas in a coffee shop known as Apron Strings. This introduced us to many residents of Bellaire and also many visitors to this beautiful area.

After spending time getting acquainted with this small town, we found a piece of property on the junction of Cedar River and Intermediate River which was for sale. We purchased this property with the idea that someday we might build a home and move to the village. Our home at that time was at Schuss Mountain. This property had promise, but it was a jungle of trees and vines, which we knew needed to be cleared. However, there happened to be a small shack hidden in the overgrowth.

This shack had obviously been abandoned for a long time. We found an old wood stove, which must have been used for heat, a rickety chair, a table, and what was left of a door and window. We agreed that there was no value to anything we found so we planned to have it demolished and removed along with the trees and brush.

Before we got around to that, we had a surprise visit from the Smith Family (not from this area) inquiring about the shack. By now,

we had heard stories about a Hermit who lived in the shack and was known for feeding the wildlife and collecting bits of coal from the existing train tracks, which he must have used for heat. The Smith Family was interested in the shack because Albert Park (the hermit) was a relative of their family. They wanted to rescue the shack and move it to their family property. This was great news to us since we were interested in clearing the property anyway.

Then we really began to hear more about Albert's life on the river. He fed the ducks, geese, and swans. He also took in muskrats and other wildlife during the winter—even sharing his cot with them. People brought him stray cats, too.

Well, the conclusion of this tale came about when the Smith Family arrived with a flatbed trailer. We watched while the family members reverently took the shack apart board by board and carefully piled it on the trailer to transport this shack to the family home in the Mesick area. We now live on this property and enjoy telling this story to our friends. Albert Park lives on.

Ray and Marguerite in 1999

✓ Remembering Christmas of 1924
By Tillie Smith of Petoskey, Michigan
Born 1918

It was Christmas morning. We opened what few gifts were under the tree. Mother made many of the gifts by knitting, sewing, and other handwork. She was so talented and a very hard worker. Oranges was a very special treat, and we each got one or two of them along with some candy. Our other gifts were small and not many. The reason this Christmas has lingered in my mind is because it was a big surprise when my brother, Ronald, who was only two years older than I, convinced me that there was no such thing as a Santa Clause. I was five at the time and he was seven. After much discussion, he convinced me that the footprints in the snow from the road to the house entrance were not made by Santa as we were told, but that of our father. He said that he had compared the footprints with Dad's boots and they matched. I did not want to believe him, but I remember that I always could not quite understand why our friends and relatives children always got such expensive and many more gifts than we did. Seems like we just accepted it and were not really too unhappy about it. It was made obvious that our parents gave the gifts, and it was all made understandable that we just did not have as much money as some other people did. Our holidays were always happy ones. Mother always had a wonderful dinner for the eight of us. It was sort of a tradition to have roast, stuffed duck, her famous homemade noodle soup, and lots of desserts, pies, cookies, cake, and coffeecake.

On Christmas day, we always attended church and got there by a horse drawn sled. That evening, Mother would play her treadle organ while Dad lit the candles on the tree. During that time, we all sang Christmas hymns and carols while Dad stood by the tree for safety. It must have been a very pleasant time since that picture has never left my mind.

My father was a poor farmer who worked very hard to support his family of six children at this time. Another brother came five years later in 1929. We always had lots of food to eat. On a farm there is always many vegetables and fruits. All farms had a large orchard with apples of various kinds, pears, cherries, plums, and grapes. We had dairy cows, pigs, chickens, and ducks. Dad never butchered any beef; it may have been without electricity, beef was harder to keep than pork. Dad and Mother would take the pork and make wonderful sausages. Chops were fried and packed in crock-pots with the fat and stored in the basements. Of course, salt added helped to preserve it for a certain length of time. Many fruits and vegetables were canned. Sweet corn and apples could be dried. Another stable food was beans. In the fall, cabbage was cut fine, packed in crock-pots with salt, and left to ferment and become sauerkraut, which kept

well all winter. Dad also buried watermelons in the grain bin that kept them eatable for a short length of time. Applesauce was made and jams and jellies. The cows supplied the milk, cream, and butter. Cottage cheese was the better than what is on the market today. I was always fascinated when butter was churned. The sweet cream was put into a container like a ten-gallon barrel with a tightly secured cover. It set on a rack with a handle so the barrel would be turned over and over until the cream turned into butter. I felt honored when I could help do the cranking. The butter formed into balls the size of a baseball. There was a hole at the bottom of the barrel that was opened to drain the buttermilk, which was what was left that did not become butter. The butter was packed into small two-quart crocks and stored in the cool basement. Cellars under the houses were walled with fieldstone and the floor was dirt. Nothing froze in the winter and everything was kept cool in the summer.

Some cellars also had a cistern. That was a very large tank, which held rainwater that was directed in from outside the house. Above that on the first floor was a small room we called a washroom. It had a small sink and a small cistern pump. This was very convenient water supply for many uses except drinking. Well water from an outside well was carried in with a pail. That job was usually assigned to one of us kids, mostly the boys. The wood-fired kitchen range had a tank on one side that served as a reservoir. It was filled with well water and warmed by the fire in the stove. That was a great necessity.

Much of my playtime was spent doing something artistic or just creating something out of nothing. I do not remember ever being bored. I can only remember having one doll. Magazines always had paper dolls that we cut out, and they included clothes and accessories. I also enjoyed playing ball with my two older brothers. Playing ball and fishing was one of my brother's favorite pastimes. They also had some chores to do to help our dad. One of the chores that they helped Dad do was splitting cedar logs for kindling. This kindling was used to start fires in the stoves.

My younger sister and I played a lot of school, taking turns in being the teacher. In the winter, we played in the snow a lot. We girls did not have jackets—only coats. We had no leggings like we have today. We had to wear cotton hose that came above the knees. They were held in place by the elastic in our underwear, called bloomers. These bloomers were a far cry from the teeny-weeny panties worn now. Besides that, women and girls wore petticoats under our dresses. Females never wore pants. My sister and I were probably two of a very few girls that did. We used the ones my brothers outgrew. We were only allowed to wear them to play in.

Most of the playtime that I recall when I was wearing the blue jeans was when we played in the creek. There was a beautiful creek that flowed close to the buildings and house. I will never forget the first time I had a small bloodsucker attach itself between my toes. I was so frightened; of course, one's thoughts were to pull it off. That was a bad idea, as it took a tiny piece of flesh with it. At that point, you can imagine that we would head back to the house for help because it was bleeding. We learned then that pulling it off is the wrong thing to do. We were told to put salt on the bloodsucker and they will let loose. The pocket in the blue jeans was a great place to carry salt. I am sure a child or person would say, "Did you not wear a bathing suit?" The easy answer to this is that we could not afford one.

I do not recall if that stream of water had a name. It came from the east and flowed west into the Flint River at the west end of our farm. This waterway supplied many hours of entertainment for us. It was convenient of the animals, horses, cattle, and ducks. Sometimes we kids had to go almost to the Flint River to head the ducks back home. These tame ducks were raised so that we could have roast duck dinners and down for our pillows.

My brothers loved to fish, but we did not eat the fish. However, the barn cats loved them. In the winter, the ice was fun to play on. My brothers had ice skates that clamped onto their boots. Boots back then were called galoshes. They fit over our shoes and had buckles to close them close to our legs. It was fun just sliding on the ice. Speaking of barn cats, farmers kept cats in the barn to help with controlling the mice population. The mice were very destructive and needed to be controlled. My youngest sister Mary loved kittens and cats more than I did. We had to play with them outside because Mother did not want them in the house. They jumped on the cupboards, tables, and any place where they could smell food.

I remember when I was around nine or ten I made myself a dollhouse from a large cardboard box. I put a floor in to have bedrooms upstairs. I also put walls up to separate the rooms. I made the furniture from heavy paper like poster board. Mother had plenty of scraps of wallpaper and various materials that she let me use for curtains, bed covers, and tablecloths. The family members who lived in the house were models from the Sears and Montgomery Ward Catalogs.

Those catalogs that were printed for winter and spring had many uses besides keeping us up on the latest styles and making it very easy for us to shop. When they were outdated, some of the paper was used to start the stove fires and some went out to the outhouse to use for toilet paper. Not everyone could afford toilet tissue. Besides, looking at them kept us entertained while we were relaxing. Speaking of outhouses (or privies, as some called them), a lady friend told me when she was little and visited her grandparents on their farm. She went out to use the outhouse and did not shut the door. Soon there was a big rooster standing in front of the door, looking very mean. She was so frightened and did not know what to do. She screamed at the top of her voice and that frightened the rooster away.

Having fun with creating things artistically is still my passion. At about the age of 40, I started art lessons in oils. As years went by and after countless lessons, I started painting with watercolors and acrylics. I also do stone sculpturing and some stained glasswork. I have been juried into several art galleries and have paintings hanging in homes in 21 states and three countries. At age 94, I am still dabbling in the arts, which seems to be the spice of my long life.

Thanksgiving in Harrisville
By Mary Jo LePage of Harrison Township, Michigan
Born 1944

In today's world when life sometimes becomes very hectic and stressful, I find myself thinking about the "good old days" and wishing, at times, that I could go back there when life was simpler and not so fast-paced. I grew up in the fifties and sixties, which was before microwave popcorn, HDTVs,

Fishing on the lake

smart phones, and Kindles. Life was good!

Some of my fondest memories are when we would all gather for Thanksgiving, Christmas, and during the summer for a vacation at Grandpa and Grandma Miller's (also known as Joe and Loraine Miller) house in Harrisville. They lived in a huge two-story home that had five bedrooms upstairs. It was a good thing they had a large home because when the Miller Clan all came, there were eight adults and fifteen grandchildren! All of my relatives on the Miller side lived in the Detroit area, so they always arrived before we did because we lived outside of Chicago. It took us a lot longer to get to Harrisville since there was no I-75 at that time. Mom and Dad thought it was easier to travel with five kids at night, so hopefully we would sleep at least part of the way. Beds were made on the floor in the back, on the seat, and on the window ledge of the rear window. That was before seat belts. Yes, we survived!

By the time we arrived up north, it was around 3:00 A.M., everyone was sound asleep. Mom and Dad had a bedroom upstairs, and there were rollaway beds set up in the garage for the late arrival kids. The beds had down comforters, so it was nice and cozy.

I always have wonderful memories of Thanksgiving. I still remember the aroma of the turkey baking in the oven along with all the other goodies to complete the meal. Of course, there were always plenty of homemade pies, cakes, and cookies for dessert. It always seemed like there was enough food to feed an army.

The highlight of the day was the Jack Horner pie. For those of you who don't' know what a Jack Horner pie is, let me explain.

Grandpa would get a bushel basket and fill it with sawdust. Then, he would cut string into two-foot lengths and attach a prize to one end. The prizes could be candy, a small toy, gum, coins, or a dollar bill. The prizes were then buried in the sawdust and the edge of the string was left hanging over the basket. After everyone had eaten, all of the grandkids took turns performing. It could be singing a song, telling a story or joke, doing a dance, or perhaps playing a tune on a tissue paper-covered comb (an early version of a kazoo). After they performed, they could pull on a string of the Jack Horner pie for their prize. Even the shy ones performed, hoping the string they pulled had the dollar bill at the other end. Oh yes, even some of the aunts and uncles performed!

Grandma and Grandpa have been gone for a while, but their home still stands on the corner of Main and Huron. For a while, the home was the Lakeview Maternity Home while Grandma and Grandpa lived in the Detroit area for a few years. They moved back to Harrisville and spent the rest of their lives there. The house was sold to Jim and Mary Hamather and was the Red Geranium Bed and Breakfast for several years. When Jim became the harbormaster, the home became the harbormaster's house. Jim passed away July 3, 2012, but his wife still lives there.

Time passes and things change. However, there is one thing that will not change over time—that is all the precious memories that I have in my heart that were made at the big house on the corner of Main and Lake Streets in Harrisville.

Christmas Cheer and Huckleberry Picking
By Shirley Helwig of Alpena, Michigan
Born 1952

When I was looking for my first job, I had to list relative's phone numbers, as we did not have a phone. I recall one of my relatives was not very happy to have to make the trip to our house to let me know that I was supposed to get in touch with a place that I had placed an application.

We grew up without a TV. To this day, I am always hearing people talk about shows/cartoons they think I should know about. I don't know about them because we didn't get a TV until I got a job and bought one. I remember my parents thinking it was very inappropriate to see a woman in a nightdress on TV. They liked old westerns and Lawrence Welk. I remember getting my first brand new dress when I was 16. We didn't have running hot water when I grew up. We had to heat water on the wood stove and then carry it to the bathtub. When we were small, we had a tub in the kitchen.

My mother hand churned butter. We had a machine that we used for separating the milk and the cream. I remember putting milk in cans and then a truck would come to pick them up. My mother always saved gift-wrapping paper. We always had to be careful when we were unwrapping gifts to save the paper. However, we didn't know she also saved laundry soap. When she passed away, we found 50 gallons of laundry soap and bleach in her basement.

I remember my dad listening to the Detroit Tigers baseball games on the radio outside while he worked when they were in the World Series. I remember listening to "Aunt Bea" on the radio on Sundays. "Tell me a story; tell me a story; tell me a story Aunt Bea, Aunt Bea." I also remember a Christmas program that we listened to on the radio every year. I can't' remember what it was called.

Christmas was special. On the day before Christmas, we had to clean house. While we cleaned the house, Dad went and got the tree. He cut it from our own farm. Then that night, Dad would put the lights on it. We had some really old lights that were actually candles. We put those on, but I don't think we actually lit them. We only used the electrical ones. We all decorated the tree. The next morning when we got up was the first time we really saw the whole tree all lit and decorated with gifts under it. It was always very impressive. We couldn't open gifts until the cows were milked and fed and the dishes all done—including the milk pails.

I remember going to the drive-in movie with my parents. I remember a cow being found stuck in the creek. My dad got the tractor to help pull her out. I also remember the smell of apple blossoms in the spring, hearing the frogs, going for walks in the woods, and picking flowers. We also played in our playhouse. It was the best and more the size of a shed. We ice skated on a small pond and sleighed on hills. We worked hard to weed the garden, milk cows, haul hay, and do housework.

We spent our Sunday or Saturday nights visiting relatives and neighbors. We didn't have a phone, so we went visiting. We also had a cabin. We used to spend nice summer days there picking huckleberries, having picnics, and walking through the woods. I earned my money in the summers by picking strawberries, raspberries, and beans.

I started driving a tractor on our small farm before I could reach the clutch or brake. I remember my parents loading the hay on a wagon while I drove the tractor around the field. My dad would jump off the wagon to stop the tractor.

I remember playing with catalogs when I was young. We used to cut out the people, furniture, and clothes and then play with them.

Fishing with Dad and Chicken Butchering
By Patricia Houghton Jacobs of Lansing, Michigan
Born 1943

As I look back on my years as a child growing up in Northern Michigan, I can only wonder of the greatness of God. It truly is the most beautiful place to live. I was born during World War II, so I don't remember anything about it. However, I do remember that our neighbors and school friends were all about in the same position as us. Our families struggled to get back to normal. Our family consisted of four girls and three boys plus Mom and Dad. I was born in the middle of the boys and yet I was the only one in all of us that liked and played sports. I remember learning a lot from my dad. He taught me to make pancakes when I could barely see over the top of the stove. They had to have lots of bubbles on them before I could turn them over. That was the beginning of many pancakes I made for him. He also took us fishing a lot and I learned how to handle a cane pole pretty good. I caught my share of fish. If I wanted to fish, I was made to bait my own hook and also help clean them. My dad also taught me how to fry fish; he was a master at it. It seems we always had things happening on the back porch. Often there was cottage cheese hanging in cheesecloth so that the liquid would drain out. Sometimes sauerkraut was in a crock or there would be headcheese out there. Now, that's something that I never learned to like. My mom was an invalid and couldn't walk

Fishing on Spider Lake

without the help of us kids, but I learned the love of the piano from her. She would sit in her chair and listen to the radio for hours. Liberace was one of her favorites. She also liked country and western music. I remember that she had a small book that had all their pictures and an article written about each one of them. That was about the time that we got our first television. It was in black and white, of course. I would sit in her chair a lot with her and just be still. She would tell me little stories and sing to me. She was also the one that that taught me the importance of going to church. We were able to ride the church bus to Sunday school and church every Sunday. Back then, we were always busy with chores. The eggs needed to be gathered, cows needed to be milked, the butter needed to be churned, and the garden needed to be hoed. We cleaned chickens almost every Saturday so we could have them for dinner on Sunday. Dad would cut off their heads and we would just sit and watch them flop all over. Their blood would splatter everywhere, and then we would dip them in hot water so we could pull their feathers off. That was a pretty smelly job.

I remember my parents coming home one day with almost a trunk full of bananas. We were able to eat as many as we wanted. Well, I certainly did. I got so sick with a stomachache and was bloated so awfully. I just had to wait for it to digest to feel any better.

The neighbor girls and I could hardly wait for green apples, as we would fill our skirts with them and get a piece of salt off the cows' salt block. We would then go up in the barn and rub the salt onto the apples and eat lots of them. I don't ever remember getting a stomachache from them.

In the winter, we would make our pie in the snow and play duck-duck-goose. We had a big hill on the neighbor's property, so we went sledding a lot and also tried to ski on our so-called skis. It truly was a good time to grow up. I wouldn't trade places with kids today for anything.

Grandma and Grandpa's Home
By Aaron Coleman of Kewadin, Michigan
Born 1937

I was born in Central Lake, Michigan I was born in my grandma and grandpa's house down by the river. My grandma and grandpa were Frank and Florence Zimmerman. It was on the same street that Dr. Duffy lived on. My grandpa had a rowboat on the river. He used to take me fishing on Intermediate Lake. I was about three or four years old. He used to take me up to the school to watch my Aunt Geraldine play basketball. She was also salutatorian of her 1942 graduating class. There were also the free shows that we went to every Wednesday night in the summertime. There was an outside screen. There were benches to sit on. I remember my mother, my grandpa, and Geraldine used to take me there. We could watch old Gene Autry shows like Northwest Mounties.

I also remember watching the trains down at the depot switching boxcars. One day, the engineer got off the train and came down. He got me, picked me up, and put me on the train. The firemen were shoveling coal in the boiler. I remember it was like a big stove, I rode up there while they switched boxcars. When they said that it was time to get off, he carried me down and set me down in the bank right where I started from. I went home and told my mother. She told me not to do that again.

From Central Lake, we moved to Frankfort. My dad worked on the car ferries for the Ann Arbor railroad. We didn't live in Frankfort for long, maybe six months. In May of 1943, we moved to the farm in Kewadin. That is where I started school at Cresswell. It was a one-room country school. My dad went there, as well as all of my aunts and uncles. I had to walk 2 miles to school. We had no electricity, running water, or indoor plumbing. I attended school there in the first grade up until about two months into the fourth grade. Then, we all went to Elk Rapids.

During World War II, Traverse City had a naval base. I remember sometimes at night you could hear the planes doing their practice runs out in the bay out by the peninsula and out at Lake Michigan. I remember watching the glider planes being pulled by the other planes. Sometimes they were so low you could see the pilot and the planes. I think they were practicing bombings out in the bay and Lake Michigan one time. One of their drones hit the bank in Traverse City. I remember we used to go out and pick milkweed pods. I think we took them to the post office, and they paid us so much a pound. There isn't much that the pods are used for, but back then, they were used to make life preservers.

My mother used to wash her clothes on a scrub board. She had a wringer that she turned by hand to wring the clothes out. I still have that today. She used the washtub to wash the clothes in the same tub we took our Saturday night baths. We didn't have milking machines, so we milked the cows by hand. Sometimes when I got home at night, I would have to milk 20 cows by hand. At first, we separated the milk with a cream separator. We sold the cream to the Argo Mill in Central Lake. We fed the skim milk to the calves. We made cottage cheese out of it, too. Later we sold milk to the Mancelona Cheese Factory. We had an icebox where we kept the milk cold in the summertime. Back then, we use to get our ice from Bert Bratchi and Charlie Hanes.

Our radio was battery-operated. It ran off a car battery. Once a week when we went in to town, we went to get a quick charge in the battery. That would last until about Thursday. When I got home from school, I'd take the battery out and put it in the tractor. I would then crank up the tractor to put a charge in the battery. We could listen to our radio programs again! After that, I would go do my chores. My mother use to listen to soap operas in the daytime. At night, we'd listen to: *the Lone Ranger, Gene Autry, Big picture, Gang Busters, Bobby Benson and the Bar 8, Sky King, Straight Arrow,* and *Sergeant Preston of the Yukon.* On Saturday nights, the *Grand Ole Opry* came on. In the morning, there was WTCM with Ken Heaven and the Breakfast Club. In the summertime, we'd listen the to

the Detroit Tigers baseball games. Harry Heilmann was the announcer. Harry was a great Tiger player. I think after Harry it was Ty Tyson. Then, I think it was Van Patrick. Gobel 22 was the sponsor. It was a beer company out of Detroit. Don't forget the Gobel rooster!

I graduated from Elk Rapids High School where I played football and baseball. I coached high school baseball team with Elk Rapids High School for 22 years. I also coached Little League for a number of years. I coached a baseball with players from around the area, too. Roger Mason played on one of those teams. I helped get him signed with the Detroit Tigers in 1980. In 1954, our six-man football team was rated number three in the nation in six-man football. Back then, the smaller schools played six-man football. Now I believe that they are playing eight-man football. Bellaire I think plays eight man now. I know they did very well.

My Cousin Ron Coleman and I use to walk to the bay and go swimming in the summertime when we got our chores done. Then sometimes we'd go down to the big creek (which was by Bob White's woods) to go swimming. We used to catch Brook trout in there. We'd get to go swimming when we were not hauling or cutting hay or doing other chores on the farm. In the summertime we didn't need bathtubs; we would go to the bay to wash up. We'd pick cherries, also.

When we were going to school, we use to get two weeks off for potato digging vacation. We also grew pickles in the summertime, too. In the winter, we had lots of snow. We lived three quarters of a mile off of US 31 on Coleman Road. Plows didn't come down very often, and when they did, it would take two trucks sometimes. When we would go into town to get groceries or to get feed ground for the cows, sometimes we'd have to walk. My uncle Charlie Coleman would come over to my grandpa Coleman's over here on the farm. He would hook up the horses and the sleigh, and then he and my dad would go empty what was in the car. My mother and my aunts used to make dresses and blouses for the girls out of the feed sacks we use to get. Most of the bags had flower patterns on them. I still live on that same farm that my great-grandfather homesteaded 150 years ago.

Cereal Box Shoe Soles and Daddy in a Dress
By Ruth Hill (Wice) Witkowski of Hale, Michigan
Born 1929

I was born in 1929 in Tawas City, Michigan of Iosco County. Times during the Depression were rough. Dad was a well driller and didn't always have a job, so we had to make every cent count. I remember him getting a cow so that we kids could have milk. The cow would come up to the kitchen window in the summertime and we would feed it leftover pancakes when Mom wasn't looking. It loved them. We caught rainwater in a big wooden barrel that sat under the eaves in the corner of the house. The water was used for our Saturday night baths or to wash our clothes in.

When I was about nine years old, we moved about a mile out of town where my grandpa lived. He took our house in town. It was on the corner of Wilbur Road and M-55. He had once had a gas station on the corner until he retired. The farm consisted of 40 acres, and it didn't take us long to cover every inch of it. We found a lot of Indian spearheads. Birds laid eggs in the tops of rotted fence posts and the killdeer had nests on the ground.

The ground for a garden was worked up with an old horse and a walking plow. When the seeds were planted and came up, we crawled on our hands and knees to thin them out. We were paid about a nickel a row. Mom canned everything. We raised cows, chickens, and pigs. Every fall a pig was butchered. We always had eggs. We had a well house with a flowing well, but no pump or water in the house. It was all carried in and heated in a double boiler on top of a wood-heated cook stove. White clothes were boiled to get them clean and then put on a scrub board with Fels Naptha soap to get them real clean. They were then hung on the clothesline outside so the sun could bleach them even more. In the winter, we waded through the snow to do the same thing. The clothes froze almost as soon as they were pinned to the line. The long johns, pants, and towels looked like they would break in two it you touched them. If they weren't all the way dry, we had to hang them on foldout wooden racks near the potbellied stove to finish drying.

The first year after we moved, we walked a mile to school in Tawas. After that, we had to walk to East Tawas School, which was two miles to get to. I started in the fifth grade that year. Miss Whipple was my teacher. She kept me in the coatroom several times after school. That meant that I wasn't able to walk home with my brother and sister. The road had no houses for about a mile and a half. It was all gravel. We wore holes into the bottoms of our shoes, but we had no money to buy more. A good many times, I would take an empty cereal box, draw around my feet a couple of times, cut them out, and put them into my shoes so the stones didn't hurt my feet. In the wintertime, we would get up early to a heavy frost or snow up to our knees. Mom kept my youngest sister at that time home because it was too cold for her to walk the two miles to and from school. After a few years, we got a bus to come pick us up. Our family grew over the years to ten children—seven girls and three boys. Everyone would ask my dad how he could afford to feed all of us. My dad, the joker he was, would say, "Do you see that sawmill across the road? They eat that every day for breakfast." Eventually, we got tired of him telling everyone that, so on April Fool's Day, I got up real early and got some sawdust in a bowl and put it at the end of the table where he always sat. I put salt in the sugar bowl and sewed his silverware to the tablecloth. When he saw what I had done, he thought it was hilarious.

My mom and dad and us kids would play baseball in the backyard. Dad had to go somewhere one day, and he knew we were going to play ball. He said, "Don't break the windows in the well machine!" Well, when Mom got up to bat, she hit the ball straight through the window of the truck. We thought it was funny because she was going to be in trouble and not us!

There was another time we were all playing ball and Mom was doing laundry in between. My dad was six feet three inches tall, and my mom was only five feet and two inches. Well, Dad got the clothes that he was wearing dirty, so he took them off for her to wash them. Then, he came back out with one of her dresses on because he said he couldn't find any of his clothes. As he stood there, a car started up our driveway. We started laughing. Dad hid behind the barn and said to tell whoever it was that he wasn't home. He never did that again! There was never a dull moment.

The house is gone now and there is a doctor's office and a bank in its place. Across the road, a Methodist church takes the place of the old sawmill. On the other two corners are a carpet business and a car sales business. Of course, the road is paved now. Back then, we didn't have much, but we had a lot of fun!

✓ Nasty Cigars and Crooked Nylons
By Velma Parker of Corunna, Michigan
Born 1933

I was so glad that I grew up in the era that I did. There were no cell phones, Playstations, and computers to take up my time. Living on the farm near Kingsley, Michigan, our family had lots of work to do. There was seven of us kids, and I was the oldest. My mom got multiple sclerosis when I was around 15 years old. That left a lot of work for us older kids to do.

We had several cows to milk, plus pigs, chickens and horses. Dad planted oats, wheat, corn, and potatoes. At harvest time, Mr. Huffman came with his threshing machine. Many of the neighbor guys would all get together to help each other as the machines made their way to the farms in the area. The farm ladies would help each other to fix a dinner for the hardworking fellows. We would put a washtub full of water out by the

Velma's dad, Earl Houghton in the 1940s

back porch for them to wash their hands. We had to set potato crates around the big table to make enough seats for everyone to sit on. Then, silo-filling time came, and we went through the same routine again.

One year, Dad went to Fife Lake and bought home some citified girls to help with the potato harvest. He would scatter the potato crates along the rows of potatoes and assign each of us a section to pick up the potatoes and empty them into the crates. One day I found a nest of field mice and took them down the row to scare the city girls. They screamed and ran, of course. They told Dad, so I got in a heap of trouble.

Once in a while in the summer, Dad would tie the long cane fishing poles on top of the car and take us to the lake to fish. Usually we went to Long Lake on Ingersoll Road. When we cast our worms out into the water, I was usually the one to catch the first fish. My brothers, Bill and Milo, would whine and cry because "Velma always caught the first one;" not the biggest or the most, but always the first, even if it wasn't a keeper. We kept on fishing. It was always a special time to go to the lake for a few hours.

With our mom being sick, we older girls had to help Dad with the chores. We were responsible for fixing breakfast and getting

Velma's mom, Norva Houghton in 1948

438

the smaller kids ready for school before the bus came. When we got home from school, we had to do chores, fix supper, do dishes, and then homework. The kids in the neighborhood would come down and play softball, hide-and-seek, or tree tag in our big yard. As it started to get dark, they would all go home. That was our entertainment.

My Uncle Frank and Aunt Dorothy lived one mile straight behind our farm. Betty and I went over there one day to play with our cousins. Rosie got into a box of German cigars that someone had brought home from the service for Uncle Frank. Us three girls got some matches and took the cigars across the road from their house into a swampy area and tried smoking them. It was a wonder that we didn't set the swamp and field on fire. How awful those cigars were! Even though I tried smoking, I'm glad that it wasn't one of my habits!

As I was upstairs sitting near the bedroom window one day, I saw my little sister Patsy running across the yard. Not far behind her was a big snake. I yelled for her to get up on the front porch. Not long after, Dad drove in the driveway on his John Deere. I told him about the snake. He lifted up the cellar door, and there it was! He killed it with a pitchfork. It was a dark colored snake with diamond shapes on its back—a Michigan Rattler, maybe.

My sister Betty was close in age to me. When I was in the eleventh grade and she in the tenth, we were in study hall at the same time. She began laughing out loud and getting attention of some of the students near her—and also the study hall teacher, Mr. Farhat. When he asked what was going on, she said, "Velma's nylon stockings are on crooked." Back then, most of the nylons had seams up the back, so who had to sit up front near the teacher's desk? You guessed it, me. It should have been her, but I didn't mind. He was one of my favorite teachers, and I was his "so-called" teacher's pet.

Great-granddad Weaver used to sit in his old wooden rocker and listen to the Detroit Tigers baseball games on his radio. Great-grandma always had sugar cookies in the kitchen. They were nearly as big as a saucer. Great-grandma Bowers lived across the road from the Weavers. She had several canaries. Those birds would chirp and tweet until it made me crazy. I don't like canaries

to this day, but I do love the wild birds.

Before our mom got sick, she would can fruits, vegetables, juices, pickles, jams, and jellies. There would be hundreds of quarts of these items stored in the cellar with potatoes and squash. She didn't have the modern conveniences that we have today. She cooked on a wood stove and used a wringer washer. Her dishwasher was her two hands and she hung clothes on the line outside even in the winter.

Our Saturday night baths were in the washtub. It would hold two of the smaller kids. Our restroom was the outhouse, stocked with Sears and Roebuck and Montgomery Ward catalogs or the Daily Grand Rapids Press.

Grit Papers and Cow Births
By Elizabeth Ballou Koski of
Thompsonville, Michigan
Born 1937

I was born in 1937 on a farm about eight miles northwest of Harbor springs, Michigan. I was the last child born into the Ballou family. My sister, who was 20 years my senior, had already had a child. Yes, that means that I was an aunt from birth! We lived on Five Mile Creek Road, which was about a mile or so from the farm. I hold many memories from that farm. I cannot call them "fond" memories because they involved a lot of hard work!

That creek was our only source of water my brother and I had to go to the creek with three barrels and two pails on the back of the trucks. He dipped and I poured until the barrels were full. This water was used for drinking, bathing, cooking, and for the farm animals to drink. The use of the water also carries lasting memories. The water for drinking was put into a large crock. It had a dipper hanging on the wall above it. Everyone used that one dipper. I don't remember it getting washed very often, either!

My brother had a near accident concerning the water crock. Mom made her own lye soap. Sometimes the soap would not harden, and she also put it into a crock and dipped the soap out whenever she needed it. One of my brothers walked in his sleep and Mom caught him just in time, as he was just about to dip into the wrong crock!

The lye soap was mostly used for washing

clothes, which took a lot of water. She used a double tub wringer bench. I turned the handle to wring the clothes from the washtub after she had scrubbed them with the lye board on the washboard. Then, I helped again as we wrung out the water in the rinse tub. The clothes would freeze dry on the clothesline in the winter. Afterward, they would be hung around inside the house. Bathing took a lot of water, too. The washtub did not get emptied after each of us took one. It was nice when it was my turn to take a bath first! In the summer, the water did get changed more often, as we would usually get it really dirty. Wash tub baths only happened once in a while. Other days were just a quick sponge bath.

The reservoir on the wood stove had to be kept full of water, too. Hot water was always ready for anything that we needed it for, especially washing dishes. That was part of my work as well. Mom let us play a game while we were doing the dishes. That made the work fun even if we had to warm the water over and over again.

Of course, the animals drank a lot of water. We dipped less water in the winter, but sure carried more wood, as there were two wood stoves going then. The kitchen was hot all summer, especially on bread-baking day. Back then, we didn't even know what store-bought bread was. I remember the range always had a flat iron on the back section along with a kettle of soup. Of course, the kitchen range was let go out at night.

Winter nights had lots of fun memories. Hard work was the last thing on our minds. The kitchen was closed off, and the range fire was let go out. We all gathered around the dining room table. The pot-bellied stove in the corner was stoked and the fun would begin. Our favorite game was Mahjong. It was given to the family by a lady that mom had helped. Another enjoyment was Mom reading the continuous story in the weekly "grit" paper. The story I remember was called Oh, Skudd Hey! It was about a pair of mules. Dad came home one day and said that we were all going to a movie on Saturday afternoon. This was a real treat, as we didn't get to go very often. When we asked what movie was showing, he said, "Just wait and see." It was our favorite grit paper story! What a treat!

I was raised with my nieces and nephews as playmates because of the age difference. My mom and sister made identical dresses for my niece and I because we were only 11 months apart. They were made from flowered printed feed sacks. After we started wearing the same patterned dress, people started thinking that we were twins. We didn't have many toys that were bought at the store, but we had fun making our own. I remember making doll furniture form the big burrs on the burdock bushes. We fed the dolls chess weed plants. They were little, tiny, button-like seeds. The dolls loved them so much that they shared with us!

Life certainly wasn't all play. We worked hard pulling weeds. We got a penny a row if we did a good job. The rows were very long. Mom grew strawberries to sell. We were paid five cents a quart to pick them but only for the ones she sold. The little ones were used for canning, jams, or on shortcake. Yum! We really didn't complain about not getting paid for the small ones!

My mom told me a tale about myself that I don't really remember. One day when she came out to call us in for lunch, she said she saw me at the top of the barn roof. I don't know how old I was. She knew I must have watched my brothers do the same. I guess I would have been considered a tom-boy. There were three brothers between my sister and I she said she didn't want to startle me, as I might fall, so she called and told me that she cooked my favorite for lunch. I just turned, crawled back down, and slipped over onto the corn crib and jumped down.

Another thing that I heard of but don't remember was an incident at the beach. We only lived a couple miles from Lake Michigan. We were there for one Fourth of July picnic and I came up missing. Everyone looked and called, but couldn't find me until my oldest brother saw me floating on my back out in the lake. He swam out and brought me in. This was strange because I did not learn how to swim until after I was married. Apparently I was good at floating!

I worked with Dad also. During haying time I drove the horses to pull the "fork-full" of hay up into the mow. One time I had a book with me (I loved to read). I read while I was waiting for them to get ready. He had to tell me one too many times to go. That was the only spanking that I ever remembered getting from my dad. I sure didn't want to get another one! My mom took us into the house to spank us because the dog growled and wouldn't let her. I don't know where the dog was that day!

My dad gave us a cow of our own. Of course, the boys had to milk more than one. I learned about "life" from a cow one day. For some reason, Mom and I were home alone when it came time for her to deliver her calf. She was having a hard time and making mournful sounds. Mom said, "Her calf won't come; I think it is sideways." I watched in amazement as mom reached inside the cow and turned the calf. I was glued to the sight as it emerged, got up on its wobbly legs, and staggered around. As the mother got up and licked it clean, I knew she loved her baby no matter how much it had hurt her. I learned a lesson in love that day. My mother had gone through birth eight times!

Dad taught us a lesson in life, too. We had to work and care for the cow that he gave us. When it gave birth, if the cow was a heifer (female), it became part of the herd, giving milk and cream. If it was a male, it was sold for veal, and the money was ours. Actually, we never saw the money, but the amount was kept in an account. When we needed anything (like shoes in the fall), it was bought, and the amount was subtracted from our balance. When we wanted something, he showed us how much money we had and would ask, "Are you sure?" It made us think if it was really worth it. The decision was ours. He wanted us to make our own decision, and he went with it.

"I love you" were not words I remember hearing from my parents growing up, but I carried with me into adulthood many lessons that I learned from actions of love.

Great Memories at Camp
By Judith M. Lentz of Petoskey, Michigan

It was my first time on a train. Around ten o'clock on a June night in 1953. School had only been over for a few days. My mother had my sister and I all packed. She had bought each of us a new steamer trunk that was big enough to hold everything we would need for the two and a half months we would be gone. We would be going to a private camp for girls on Walloon Lake near Boyne City and Petoskey, Michigan called Huntington. Our trunks held mostly what was required: blue shorts, white tops, a jacket, sweatshirts, tennis shoes, jeans,

bathing suit, beach towels, and underwear. Later, I would plead for a skirt, an off-the-shoulder blouse, and a pair of Capezio shoes for the Saturday night dances with the boys from the camp next door called Sherwood. Strangely enough, we never saw the boys during the week and they were right next door, they must have got the word that there would be no fraternization during the week.

Back on the train, we were to sleep in a berth and wake up in the morning in Boyne City where a bus would then take us to Huntington. By that time, there were 10-15 girls between the ages of eight to 16. Then, my sister, mom, and dad arrived at the Detroit Central Train Station. It was huge, and even at eleven o'clock P.M, there were all kinds of people coming and going. I was so excited and couldn't wait to board, but my sister, who was seventeen months younger, probably had some reservations, yet she never mentioned them. Something that stays in my memory on that first train ride, (we ended up going to Huntington three years in a row), was that first time after we had boarded and gotten into our berths around 11:30 P.M, the nicest man, a Pullman porter, came by and asked if we were all okay. Most of the girls were asleep by then. In fact, all of them were except my sister and I. We told him we were hungry, he said that the kitchen was closed, but that he could make us a sandwich. Then that sweet man made each of us a fried egg sandwich with a coke. I still can remember just how good it tasted. They are still my favorites to this day. We thanked him and then let the sound of the rails lull us to sleep.

Camp Huntington was not our first camping experience. We first went to a church camp on Pine Lake downstate. There wasn't much to do there. I remember playing tetherball and swimming. It is where I first began to learn to dive off the dock. One time at the beginning of my lessons, I dove in headfirst and hit my head hard on the rocky bottom. That was the end of my diving. From then on, I just jumped in. There were two big houses for the girls. One was called Bird's Nest, the other Holiday House. By that time, we had another sister, Linda, who had joined us. She was only about six years old at the time. She was put in Bird's Nest by herself. Nancy and I went to Holiday House. You need to know this was Linda's first time away from home, and let's just say she wasn't a happy camper. So, by the second day, there she was sitting on her hastily packed suitcase on the side of the driveway crying her little eyes out. Mom and Dad came and got her within a couple hours and took her home. Nancy and I only stayed two weeks at the church camp.

What stays with me the most was sitting on the large wrap-around screened-in porch in the evening before vespers and listening to one of the counselors play classical piano in the background. It was so relaxing and peaceful. When things get too stressful for me now, I try to return to that porch on those soft summer nights.

The next summer, it was Girl Scout Camp for Nancy and me. Linda was through with camp forever. There is a true story that goes with our time as G.S.C. We slept four to a tent that had wood floors and canvas that could be pulled down on the sides in case of rain. There was one counselor for two tents. When at night, if one of us had to use the facilities, we had to get a "buddy" to go along. For some reason, my sister and I decided to go with our tent mate. Down the gravel path we went, three flashlights shining, to the outhouse (no inside bathrooms there). As we waited outside for her to come out, we heard a scream. When we got inside, there she was staring down the opening saying that she had dropped her flashlight. She said, "I just have to get it." I replied that it wasn't a big deal, that she could just buy another one at the camp store tomorrow. She insisted that she had to get that one. My sister and I each held a leg and lowered her down until she picked up the beloved light. We then pulled her back up and went back to bed. In the morning when the counselor had found out what had happened, she whisked her to the infirmary and went over her from head to toe. We were told never to do that again. "What if you had dropped her?" we were asked. That was something that had never entered our minds at the time. Every once in a while it enters my mind now. It is hard to believe, but it is a true story.

Huntington was the last and best camp that we attended. It was situated on beautiful Walloon Lake. There were cabins that held ten girls, five on each side, with a room in the middle for two counselors. There was also an inside bathroom. There was a phone in the foyer for incoming and outgoing calls. The sleeping rooms had built-in drawers and a dressing table. My sister Nancy and I were never again in the same cabin. The first and second year we were both in separate cabins. By the third year, she was in a building called "The Hall." It had a large stage in front for concerts, shows, and plays. It also had an arts and crafts room to the left and an area in the back for 10-15 girls to sleep. One thing that Huntington had that no other camp I ever knew of was very nice ladies who came once a week and cleaned the cabins. I never saw them because I was never in my cabin during the day. I was going to classes, swimming, sailing, or canoeing. Nancy and some of her friends would hide in their closets and watch the cleaning women. They would not come out until they left. Then, they would go back to lying on their beds reading comic books.

The third year I was able to be in the "Nest." It was called this because it was right on the lake over the area where the dances were held on Saturday nights. It was a really big deal to be able to stay in the Nest. We slept dormitory style, around 12 of us. One wall was screened and lovely breezes came in. it turned out to be my last summer at Huntington. What wonderful memories! I had some exciting times that stick in my mind. If you could be on time before lunch or dinner and you got to the ad building before too many other girls did, 10-20 of us would pile onto Mrs. Green's open-air jeep and get an extremely fast and bumpy ride to the dining hall. It was so much fun! Mrs. Green was the director of Huntington. She had an apartment in the ad building. Eventually, she married the owner and director of the boy's camp, Sherwood. There were also canoe trips and overnight campouts. We also took rides on the Nova Scotia, an open airboat that would take us from camp to the foot. It seemed like it went 200 miles per hour!

The event that I loved the most was the council fires that were held every Sunday night. We would all walk up a hill where the counselors would have built a huge fire, at least six to seven feet tall. It was a solemn affair—no talking. The lighting of the fire was special. We sang and danced around the fire. Awards were given. The scent of the pine trees, the fire, and the closeness of everyone is still with me. The last night at camp, a dinner was held where the counselors had decorated the dining room. It always had a theme. They worked so hard and it was always beautiful. We all cried because we didn't want to leave. I am not sure if I ever expressed enough gratitude to my parents for sending me to Huntington, but I remain forever grateful.

✓ Graduation for Some of Us
By Mildred Dickson of Midland, Michigan
Born 1930

Before it was National City, it was Emery Junction, a major hub of the Detroit and Mackinaw Railway. During World War II, we would stand by the tracks and wave to the trainloads of service men passing through. When we moved there in 1932, the National Gypsum Company had been in operation a few years, mining the gypsum rock and manufacturing Gold Bond Wall Board, it is still in operation.

Mrs. Johnson started the first school, in her home. I wasn't old enough to attend school, but was invited to some parties there. I do remember one valentine's party. When I started school at four and a half years old, it was held in one side of a two family home across the railroad tracks. Finally, a square brick school building was erected. It has been a Mennonite Church for some years now.

Besides the first and last days of school, the highlight of the year was the Christmas program. Many hours were spent rehearsing. One year we did "The Christmas Carol." Everyone had new clothes for the Christmas program whether homemade or bought. We all got gifts from the teacher. I remember getting pencils one year and combs another, with our names on them. One elderly man always brought the school a bag of oranges, a rare treat in our rural community. We also

National City School in the late 1930s

borrowed his phonograph for our Christmas music. It was very old, but played well.

The end of the school year brought 8th grade graduation to some of us and then we were on to Whittemore for high school. The end of the year also brought a picnic where parents and siblings were invited. In my young days summer lasted forever and by September, I was ready to don my new first day of school dress and start the school in a new grade.

✓ Famous People
By Debbie Keene of Grayling, Michigan
Born 1963

The story began during World War II about my sister, Valda. She was married for many years. She and her husband had nine kids. Many years passed and the kids were grown, she still had some youngins at home. Her husband was living in a mobile home alone for many years for they couldn't see eye-to-eye after all those years. He passed away a few years after the marriage ended. The trailer was parked in Pontiac, Michigan. She brought the trailer to Traverse City, Michigan. The vent wasn't working so when they took it apart in one of the vents, they discovered paper was stuff inside of the vent. After they pulled it out, they discovered it was money rolled in old newspaper. It totaled $3,000. While her husband lived there, he never trusted banks. He never put his money in them, so he would stash it in the vent for safekeeping.

My parents would take me to the airport in Saginaw, Michigan. I was the youngest of our family, so I would get so excited for these family trips. John F. Kenned showed up in Cadillac, Michigan. I remember him sitting there in the back of the car. I seen his face so clearly, as if it was yesterday. I was only 15 feet away from him. I remember his young face, blonde hair, and he was waving to the crowd.

When I was in Lagoon Beach, on the Kaw Kaw River in Bay City, Michigan, we would go out and down to the river. There were boatyards there. They would build the large, racing boats for famous people. This was a big deal in Detroit, Michigan. One day when I was out in my yard, Guy Lombardo was on his boat going by and actually stood up and waved to me. It made my day that a famous person would wave to me.

In 1949 in a small town called Grayling, Michigan, we lived at Wakeley Bridge. My folks, sister, brother, and I were very young at the time. I was only three years old. Our house had a working phone in the area. So our neighbors would always come over and use the phone. We had a small group of Native Americans who lived just down the road from us and close to the river. They would come up and wanted to use the phone to call a taxi to come and get them so they can go into town. We told them to knock on our front door, but they never did. They would come out from the woods at night so we didn't see them or hear them and they would come right up to our picture window press their faces up to the window and stare in and scare us half to death.

✓ Feel It Ooze Between Your Toes
By Christine Teal of West Branch, Michigan
Born 1951

When I was a kid, we played outside in all kinds of weather. If it was snowing, we made snowmen, snow forts, snow angels, igloos, and tunnels. Everyone in the neighborhood would get together and have a snowball fight or go sledding on a small hill or big hill. Sometimes we would slide on the ice, some kids had ice skates, and some didn't. The kids with skates would share with kids that didn't have them. This was also the way it was with sleds; people would share. Who shares things now?

I remember in Rogers City, Michigan there was an ice company. Men would go out on Lake Huron to cut ice for the iceboxes. We would spend hours watching them; using ice hooks to lift the ice that they had cut out. The ice was delivered to your house or you could pick it up at the icehouse. We played in the rain, wearing raincoats and rubber boots. It was fun to splash in the mud puddles and try to catch the rain on your tongue.

During the summer we would go barefoot, it was great to feel the sand or mud on your feet or let it ooze between our toes. We would see who could pick up things with our toes. We made wooden sailboats with wood, sticks, and paper to sail across the large puddles. Climbing trees was one of my favorite things

to do. I would climb as high as I could and when the top started to bend, I would lean and grab the tree nearby and jump over like the squirrels did. I was quite a daredevil.

Tree houses were always great fun to build. We would go out and find things that people were throwing away to use for building and putting in the tree house. Whatever you could find to use in the tree house made each one unique. Some had ladders, rope swings, a slide, and special escapes. You could use a bed sheet to make the slide. There were windows, but no glass, curtains usually hung on a rope. Tin can phones attached to a long string from one tree house to another.

We played hide and seek, crack the whips, hopscotch, red rover, and board games inside when it was really bad outside. All of these things were social activities where you had to learn to play and interact with each other.

When I was young and pregnant, we had a party line that was shared with 10 people. One day while my husband was at work I started having labor pains. I picked up the phone to call the doctor. Two ladies were talking, so I hung up the phone and waited 15 minutes. When I picked up the phone, again, they were still talking and another lady had joined in on the conversation. I hung up again and waited for another 15 minutes. The pains were getting worse. Again, I picked up the phone, they were still talking, this time I said, "Excuse me, I need to use the phone, how much longer will you be on the line?" One lady said, "Why do you need to use the phone?" I replied, "I think I am in labor." All of the women got excited and offered to come to help me and take me to the doctor. Sometimes people would listen in or two people would try to make a call at the same time. It wasn't very private. Sometimes it was inconvenient. It was great for finding out all the gossip.

✓ Corky, the Snake Killing Dog
By Mary Bishop of Onaway, Michigan
Born 1943

Before indoor plumbing in my early years of growing up that was all we had, an outhouse. When we stayed overnight with our grandparents they had a chamber pot so we didn't have to go out to the outhouse at night, especially in the wintertime. With no television in those days, we use to have our favorite radio shows we listened to, especially on Saturday nights. We also had to listen to the Grand Ole Opry. I can't remember all of the stories we use to listen to. We also played a lot of card games too. My grandparents also had a windup phonograph.

Saturday we always hoped for a good day because that was laundry day. It took a while to do the laundry because we did have a wringer washer and no dryer, so the clothes were hung on the line to dry, and if the weather wasn't good then the clothes had to be dried in the house. You then had to iron the shirts because the clothes weren't' permanent pressed, no dryer to dry them in, take them out and hang them up like today. I learned how to iron my dad and three brother's shirts. I was the only girl and yes my mother use to make my dresses because there just wasn't money to go shopping for clothes the way we do now. I wore a lot of flour sack dresses growing up and I thought they were beautiful because that was what I had to wear.

My favorite teacher was my 4th and 5th grade teacher, Mrs. Graves. She was a very special person. There was a young man who lived in our area that was older than us. She got permission from his parents for him to come to school and she took the extra time he needed for her to teach him how to read and she also taught him how to write his name.

One of my favorite pets growing up was our dog Corky. One of the reasons I really liked him was because he was a snake killer because I hated snakes. He would pick them up by the tail and give them a snap and break their necks. We would walk up in the plains to pick wild huckleberries and tell him to stay home. He stayed home at first, but all of a sudden when we were picking berries, we would hear something and it would be Corky. He would stay with us then and walk back home with us.

We had chores to do. When we got home from school, we had to change our clothes and carry firewood in. We had a wood cook stove and to keep us warm in the winter all we had was a wood stove. We also had to pump water into a water tank for our cattle to drink. We had an icebox to keep our stuff cool until we got a refrigerator after we finally had electricity. My maternal grandfather use to have an icehouse for people to come and get ice to put in their iceboxes. He had a team of horses and a sleigh and he would go down to the water after the ice formed and cut the ice in blocks, bring it home, and put it in his icehouse for people to get for their iceboxes. When he stacked the ice in his icehouse he use to put saw dust between the blocks to keep them separate. My grandparents also sold eggs and made homemade butter and that's how people made a living. They also raised their own beef, pork, veggies, and everything. We had our own milk so we didn't have a milkman.

As far as toys go, we had a few but not like kids do today. Mostly we created our own fun. If a bunch of cousins got together we would draw a grid for hopscotch in the driveway, get a flat stone and that's how we played hopscotch. We also played hide and seek. A lot of times, we just enjoyed spending time together as cousins. Also in the summertime on Sunday afternoons, our neighbors and our family got together and we would play a good game of baseball. A lot of fun was had by all!

The One That Got Away
By Jerry Stein of Evart, Michigan
Born 1934

Orchard Hill Farm, near Evart, Michigan, is my place of birth. This was also the birthplace of my father and his eight siblings. The farm was purchased by my great-grandparents in 1883 and is a registered Centennial Farm. Ours has been a general farm operation with dairy, beef, swine, sheep, and poultry. We had nine stanchions in the barn and separated cream, which we sold. At the age of two, I broke my leg while trying to turn the large driver wheel of a corn sheller. Evidently, I was not tall enough to complete the turn and pulled the machine onto myself. I remember my father hurrying into the barn basement in response to my cries.

While riding on the grain binder in the summer of my 10th year, I started having chills and wearing my lined jacket. I was diagnosed with spinal meningitis. I remember the preparation for the spinal tap, but thankfully, I had no adverse results from the disease. During the World War II conflicts, even the students at our country Cherry Grove School

445

were "mobilized" to help. We were supplied with mesh onion bags for the collection of milkweed pods. These were used as a buoyant material for life preservers. Our neighbor boy and I took the horse and cart to various pastures and un-harvested areas to collect the pods. We were also encouraged to collect scrap iron, which was brought together at the schoolyard and transferred for defense hardware. Scrap paper was another item of collection from the neighborhood. We deposited it in our barn until combining it for shipment. I would find a place of solitude and read the comic books we had accumulated.

During the war, and for some time thereafter, bicycles were available on a priority basis. I really desired a bike. We went to a hardware store in Cadillac and they had a smaller sized girl's bike, which did not require the priority papers. I had to make a decision of whether to wait for a larger boy's bicycle or endure the stigma of riding a girl's style. I finally decided for the here and now and was glad to get

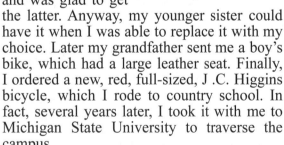

Jerry's cousin pulling market timber in 1930

the latter. Anyway, my younger sister could have it when I was able to replace it with my choice. Later my grandfather sent me a boy's bike, which had a large leather seat. Finally, I ordered a new, red, full-sized, J .C. Higgins bicycle, which I rode to country school. In fact, several years later, I took it with me to Michigan State University to traverse the campus.

At the end of WWII, former pastor friends had been assigned to the Free Methodist Church at Sault St. Marie. My parents had saved up gasoline rationing coupons to make the trip and visit this family. While we were in the tourist store at Castle Rock the news came over the radio that gas rationing had been lifted. That was welcome news! Soon thereafter, I saw a cartoon of a man getting gasoline at a station and upon hearing the news; he turned the spout and let it flow on himself in jubilation.

As a youngster, I enjoyed being part of the

farm operation even though I was too young to be of much help. On one such occasion, I was walking behind the hay loader as Dad and the hired man were loading hay with the horses. The loader had a rotating drum with tines to pick the hay up from the windrow on the ground and deposit it on ropes and slats, which carried it to the top and then dumped it on the wagon. While following too closely, the tines captured my clothing and started me up the loader. I guess that my screams stopped the loading process. The progress of equipment, techniques, and footwear is amazing. While cutting firewood and logs in our woodlot, my father taught me how to operate the opposite end of a two-man crosscut saw; now I use a much faster chain saw. As we cut the branches and poles, we loaded them on a large wood sleigh with steel runners to transport to the barn area to build into a large pile called a "buzz pile." While working, I was wearing rubber boots with buckles and flannel-like lining and my feet became extremely cold. When we completed the load, I walked in the sleigh runner track to warm up my feet as we returned to the barn. I later had the opportunity to skid logs and haul firewood with the tractor, which I enjoyed.

In the spring, after the snow and ice were melted from the "buzz pile," neighbors would come together to "buzz" the wood into blocks and stove-length firewood. This involved several men lugging the poles to the saw, which was a belt-driven circular blade with many notches. The arbor was pushed forward to cut the blocks. The dangerous job was working beside the blade and throwing the blocks into a pile. Then my sister and I would arrange the blocks into "house" outlines for our play area.

Another activity of neighborhood co-operation was threshing of the grain. Binders cut the grain and the bundles were placed in clusters called "shocks" to permit further drying. The threshing machine was brought

446

Joe's parents with their children

invented yet. The windows would frost up with ice in the winter from the condensation formed between the cold outside and warmth inside and then it would freeze. A small and low ceiling, unfinished attic became my room once I got old enough to move from my parent's bedroom. The only heat source was through the floor from the heat below plus there was a floor register in the next room allowing some heat from downstairs to come upstairs and then through my door. It would get hot during the summer, cool down some at night, and then get quite chilly in winter. Three sisters next in age to me shared a small finished room upstairs until they eventually left home and my oldest brother had a finished room next to mine where the stairway came up to, plus a younger brother had a single bed next to his. My mom and dad had their own small bedroom on the main level. The stairway to upstairs was steep and each step partially overlapped the other so if you were in a hurry you were going to catch one of your feet on a step above and trip. You had to be careful.

The house had a Michigan basement, which was used for the storage of potatoes and our canned goods, and wine that my dad made. But we managed well because it was home where love abounded amongst us and the love of God was paramount. My mom was always praying and she taught us how to pray. Dad was an "honest Abe." His word was as good as gold and I learned just how important it is to keep ones word. They were both such hard workers. Everything they did was in support of the family neighbors. Everyone was trusted. No need to be locking doors.

We had a hand pump for water in the kitchen and had to heat it on the stove for hot water to clean the dishes, keep clean, take a bath, or wash clothes. Clothes were washed using a non-electric hand-cranked wringer washer with a scrub board. We had an icebox type cooler where a block of ice was placed in a top compartment and the food on the bottom in a lower compartment to keep it cool and from spoiling. We'd get a block of ice delivered about once a week from Gauthier's Meat Market where they had ice storage. It kept frozen because it was stored in sawdust that acted as insulation. The Oscar Runge family had a farm down the road where they raised some dairy cows and sold and bottled milk in glass bottles in a small attached building with a breezeway on the back of their house. As I got older, I'd walk down there to buy milk and would often just go to their house and knock on their back door or front door if they didn't answer. Milk wasn't homogenized yet so the cream would come to the top. My dad made a little round metal scoop with a handle for removing the cream to be used for making whipping cream or adding to coffee.

Of course, we had no phone, but we did have a crank up and an electric record player that played the old 33 speed RCA records. Once my dad borrowed a recorder from where he worked and recorded each of us playing the violin with my mother at the piano. I was 14 then. We had an outhouse for our bathroom where we had an old Sears, Montgomery Wards and/or JC Penney's catalog to either look through or to use for you know what. The temperature outside was the same temperature inside so if it was hot outside it was hot inside. Same for when it was cold or freezing. However, the scent inside always remained the same. We did have three pot type containers with covers that we would use in the house that had to be emptied once a day, which was my job as I grew up. Also, I was the one to dig a new hole and move the outhouse on a regular basis with the help of one of my

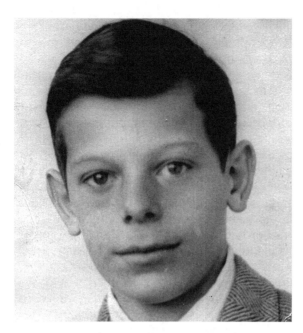

Joe in 1946

neighbor friends. We would jack it up and put several nice long round and straight logs underneath and use them as rollers to move it to the new destination. We thought that was such a big deal to do that.

Mom cooked and baked on the four-leg kerosene stove with an oven on the side where she did all her baking. She was always baking bread or making pies or fixing meals for the family. Her favorite pie to make for our annual chicken dinner at our St Mary's parish in the summer was lemon pie. I can still see her making those. They were so good. We were 100% French. Every Thanksgiving and Christmas she would bake this French pie called "Toutiere". It was definitely a holiday specialty for our family. It consisted of ground pork - as lean as possible, ground potatoes, onions, sage, and some other mixed seasonings with a piecrust on top and bottom. Then it was baked in the oven. When one of our cousins would butcher he would bring us some blood to make blood sausage. My mom would season it and maybe add something else, but she'd cook it in a frying pan like scrambled eggs. She also made head cheese into some form of gravy. It must have come from the pig's head.

The house was heated with two potbelly coal stoves and my dad had coal delivered once a year in the fall. He had built a coal bin and attached it to the backside of the house. It became my job to chop kindling for making

the fires and store some so we always had some on hand. One summer I worked hard to chop enough to fill the whole crawl space under the large attached shed we had only to find out my dad replaced the two coal stoves for one bigger oil heating stove that heated the house more evenly because it had a built-in fan plus he could regulate the heat. I wasn't happy about that because l had done such a good job. My routine chore after school was to empty the stove ashes, bring in coal and kindling for the next morning, empty the pots we used for our inside bathrooms, and sweep the shed where we were always coming in from the backyard.

Our home seemed to be about like the norm in the neighborhood where everyone was quite poor and had to work hard to make a living. There were some farms to our north that either raised cattle or had fruit orchards, which was mostly cherries or potatoes. Cherries and potatoes were big business then and cherries still are. At school, the kids got two weeks off in mid-October for (Potato Vacation) so they could earn some money picking potatoes as there were no automatic pickers in those days or they would either work at home or work out at other farms like we did and make five-cents a bushel. I could pick around 75 a day. My sisters, some neighbors, and I usually picked at the Bill Popp farm. We would get a ride early in the morning by Lavern Flees who was driving an old flatbed truck with sides and often the truck didn't have enough power to make the one steep hill on Popp Road. As soon as it would start slowing down enough we would all would jump off the back and us guys would push on it and help it make it to the top, and then we would all hurry and jump back in. We would get a big laugh out of that.

Mrs. Popp would make the best hot vegetable beef or chicken soup ever for the pickers and by mid chilly day we were all starving. When I was in 10th grade the automatic potato pickers were used so I helped on the back of the picker. I made sure the sorted potatoes would land in the crates and then the tractor would stop so we could load the full crates on a truck to be hauled to a storage area on the farm. In July the cherries would be ready to harvest so local people that weren't working out plus migrant workers would do all of the cherry picking. My mother always picked cherries until we were

450

16 and then we would get a job in the cherry processing plants.

Classes at the Courthouse
By Virginia Seguin of Alpena, Michigan
Born 1923

I was born January 14, 1923 either at home or in a hospital. Mother's version, throwing a roll of toilet paper the third time her doctor left the card game to inquire how she was doing. Dad's version, when we were out for a Sunday afternoon drive we passed McCrae Hospital. I looked in awe at the huge slide fire escape. "That's where your mother and I stood in line. When it was our turn, the nurse shoved you out. Lucky for you, I was a good catcher!"

My parents purchased a hotel on 9th across from the park. The workers who built the courthouse roomed and boarded at Park View. When a band shell was added, the park became a hubbub of activity. Concerts were held bimonthly. Mothers came pushing baby carriages, kids roller-skated on the diagonal sidewalks, and "Toots" Mac Arthur rolled his popcorn stand to the corner of 9th and Chisholm. Directly across was the Market Square city jail, housed about four cells, the sheriff, and his large family. Prisoners could look through their barred windows and watch tournament hopefuls practicing tennis on the north corner; beyond was a baseball diamond that was magically transformed overnight into a live theater via a huge tent, hastily constructed stage, and enough bleachers to seat the entire community. A loud speaker acquainted residents about the paths of unrequited love.

Bright and early Saturday mornings an old truck would transport 15-20 kids to the berry fields. The patch boss would assign us each a row to be picked "clean." We grabbed a wooden carrier lined with cardboard cartons, anxious to make our fortunes at three cents per carton. Tommy was an expert picker. He noticed the cute girl in the row next to him was not as good. With a shy smile, he backtracked with a full quart and topped four of hers. Love does not come cheap–at least six cents a week, possibly nine cents by season's end.

Cousin Marie, three years my senior and I looped our skates around our necks and hoofed it three miles to Mich-e-ki-wis. The cement block shelter had a potbellied stove, perfect for frost bitten fingers. With weak knees was wobbling to the music. Tommy raced up, grabbed my hand, and removed my mitten intent in making hand-to-hand intimacy. He said, "No girl of mine is going to wear this stuff," and began to peel off my nail polish. Forgetting I was wearing skates, I kicked him. He yelped, clutching his bleeding hand to his chest, and raced for the shelter. Two of his friends returned, told me he might lose his hand. He didn't of course, but there end my first romance.

Girls at St. Anne's wore uniforms with white collar and cuffs, a red tie, and Kleenex on their heads before entering the church. Freshman initiation day I was a lowly slave forced to sharpen pencils, carry books, and bring lunch treats to seniors.

Marie offered to let me go first. The ad read, "Painless extractions $5.00." En-route home from the dentist, we were amazed to learn we had the exact same dream. Riding the merry-go-round the horse turned down side up and stomped us.

In my junior year, the third floor of school burned down. It was decided to resume classes at the courthouse. I took my final Latin test sitting in the witness chair. Our principal, Sister Borgia, sat in the judges' chair. Momentarily I wished dad hadn't been a good catcher.

After graduation, I was employed as a cashier at J.C. Penny's, $12.50 per week plus 20% off clothes. There were no cash registers. Each department clerk deposited the cash in the money cup, clipped the sales slip on the bottom, jerked the chain, and watched hopefully as it made its way precariously up to me in the balcony. I reversed the process making correct change. Occasionally the cup would get stuck halfway. The assistant manager would grab a long pole and send it to its proper destination.

At night, I attended Alpena Business School, where I astonished even myself by testing 80 words per minute on a manual typewriter. This took twice the agility of a concert pianist playing "The Flight of the Bumble Bee."

I was engaged to Bill, but we agreed it wasn't feasible to marry until we were both 23. I had known Bill since the 2nd grade. The

D & M Railroad employed his father as a fireman. Christmas Eve, while attempting to board a slow moving train to pick up his check, he slipped and fell under the wheels, losing an arm and a leg. His co-workers commandeered a wagon and ran nine blocks with him to McCrae Hospital, where he was refused admittance unable to pay, and no insurance. His buddies threatened to bust up the place and they relented.

April 1943 Bill wrote me he was at a Port of Embarkation in San Francisco. The wire I sent him, "Made arrangements. Arriving soon with wedding ring" took seven days to reach him, since he had an APO number and was sent overseas first. Then he stood in line a block long to use the telephone. On arrival, I learned there would be a three-day delay, as California would not accept the Michigan blood test. We both were afraid his orders for overseas duty would come before we could be married. To top it off, there were no rooms to be had. Two buses and $10 of my fast depleting dollars later, I slipped the ring on my finger, and we settled for a basement room. Bill had to return to camp early the next morning. I put my hair in pin curls, wore a babushka, took a bus downtown in search of wedding finery, a black pillbox hat. I was married in my best dress–black and aqua two-piece with three large buttons featuring a Michigan wearing a sombrero riding a donkey. Mother's write up for the Alpena news, "The bride wore a white suit and carried…"

Dad Was Proud of His Family and Farm
By Hazel Yerks of Rogers City, Michigan
Born 1938

I'm very proud to have had a farmer for a dad. He had a kind and trusting heart. He was a friend to everyone; if you needed help, he was there. He shared with all; whatever he had, he would give to you. I had two brothers and one sister, all who are older than I. My sister is my soul mate now. We children were told that we would always be warm and never go hungry. Dad was true to his word.

Winter was a time for making firewood. The logs were hauled in on a dray to be cut up and burned in a potbelly stove for heat. We had a Kalamazoo kitchen stove that had a reservoir for hot water. Yummy things came

Hazel's parents, Herman and Rosena Neumann

from this stove. We had cows to milk and pigs and chickens to take care of and a dog named Carlo. Pearl and Flora, our team of horses, were great helpers before Dad had a John Deere tractor. Board games and playing cards were enjoyed during the cold winters. We also sorted kidney or navy beans for customers in town. There was always time for a visit from a neighbor, and then a cup of coffee and a piece of cake was the norm. In the cold winter weather repairing machines and running the sawmill kept dad busy. He did custom sawing. If a customer didn't have enough money to pay, dad would keep the slabs or he told the man to pay when he could.

Spring meant getting the pails and cooking pan ready for the maple syrup season. Boy, did it smell good out in the maple grove! Cooking the sap down was done in the woods in the cooking pan. It was work but it was fun. Oh, yes, spring was planting time. Grains, potatoes, peas, beans, and a big garden were planted. We cultivated this garden with a horse. I was to ride that horse and keep him from stepping on the vegetables. What a job! Dad would take his horses and work at Northern Orchards, where he had helped plant the trees in the early 1920s. He was paid a dollar a day for bringing his team of horses and working at the orchards.

Summer was time for picking strawberries and raspberries. Were they good! Then it was time for making hay; it involved mowing, raking, and hauling loose hay, no bales. Picnics were a must on weekends, maybe a little time for fishing, too. We lived on Black River. I would sit by the river with my dad and

452

enjoy talking and fishing with him. We never worked on Sunday. Dad said if you can't do it in six days it would be there later. Church was a must. God gave us the seventh day for rest and family. Visiting after church was always done. Grandpa and Grandma, here we come.

Fall meant picking potatoes and harvesting the crops. Threshing grains was a big job. We had the threshing machine and went from farm to farm. I was the one who drove the thresher with the John Deere tractor from place to place. Dad followed in the old truck. After school on fall days, dad and I would clean the peas and beans, putting them through a fan mill to remove all the chaff. This was done by hand. I must tell you before I go on that my dad had that deadly cancer, so I was his right hand "man." This one Christmas I opened a gift from dad. My eyes, I'm sure they were as big as saucers, for here was a doll! She had eyes that opened and shut rubber arms and legs and she cried when I laid her down. I called her my Dolly. Happy, happy was I! I

Hazel with her dad, Herman in 1940

still have her today.

My dad's life was cut short because of the cancer. In high school, I was talking about band and dad said he would buy me an instrument. I bought a clarinet. But sad to say, he never was able to see me perform. But I do think he was a proud dad and clapped in heaven for me. Delivering little piglets and baby calves was challenging for a teenager. You quickly understood life much better. Dad was proud of his family and farm that had a windmill to pump water. He had a big red barn with his name on it. This all happened between 1938 and 1955. I am grateful for such a kind, thoughtful, and giving dad.

We Got Plenty of Exercise
By Alice Rohl of Reed City, Michigan
Born 1935

I was born 6-½ miles north of Mio, Michigan on a farm. I was one of five children with my baby brother dying when I was three years old. I had an older brother and two sisters and mother and father. My mother made all of our clothes until we got in high school out of chicken feed packs, which back then were flowered. I was never ashamed of my clothes, as my mother was a beautiful seamstress. We had an outhouse where the old rooster would corner us in a lot of time and then we would stay out there yelling till mom would come and rescue us. It was a good healthy life as all of our food came from our garden and berries from the nearby woods. We had quite a few apple trees, our own beef, pork, chickens, and venison. All of us helped in the gardens and with picking berries and canning. I remember coming home from school and my mother would be churning butter or baking bread with a big pot of bean soup on the stove. Oh the aromas! Huge homemade cookies, pies, and cakes. The first cake I made was from scratch, by hand, baked in a wood stove oven with the door propped shut. It came out beautiful.

I remember when we got electricity. Dad had the house wired and all the switches turned on, plus a floodlight in the front yard, and when the power came on we thought the house had blown up. Before that, we had one kerosene lamp lit at night and it was in the kitchen at meal times and homework time and then it would go in the living room. We had a pitcher pump in the living room and dad got running water and an inside bathroom put in after I left home at 17, after graduation. The first television I saw was when I went to business school in Bay City, Michigan. My landlady had one and I would sit on the stairs and watch it.

My mother washed the clothes on a washboard or a wringer washer and hung them out on the line. In the winter, they would freeze before they would dry. I raised six children after I was married and even though my husband worked at Chevrolet, I washed clothes on the washboard a lot or a wringer washer and then hung them outside. I didn't have an automatic until after I had my last one and I was working in Buick, where I retired from after 24 years.

When we were young, we all helped shovel snow, which we always had a lot of. My dad was six feet and he put a tire on top of the snow bank one time and mom took his picture. It was way above his head. I came home from school pay practice, my 11th and 12th year of school, and they dropped me off by our gate. The snow was up to the top of the fence posts. I had a dress on and bare legs. I tried to walk on top of the snow, but every once in a while I would break through. By the time I got to the house my legs were all scratched up. I am now 77 and I still shovel my own snow. Habits are hard to break.

Our bathtub was a washtub, which in the summer was put out behind our house and in the winter was by our wood stove in the living room. Freeze on one side and roast on the other. The washtub was also used to cool pop, which we got one day a year on the 4th of July. Dad would put it under the big Elm Tree in our yard with a chunk of ice he would buy in Mio at the icehouse and cold water and fill it with glass bottles of pop. We could have so many as we wanted and we never wasted any. We also had potato salad, baked beans, and cold cuts and deviled eggs and we ate outside in the yard. We got to play all day after the chores were done and until chores at night. We also got cap guns and rolls of caps, which we would take with us when we went to find our cows in the morning to bring them home to be milked. We had to walk two or three miles to find them. We also got our exercise by walking to the mailbox six days a week, which was a mile and a half. If mom wanted to mail a letter or wanted stamps we would go down early and wait for the mailman.

Another day out of the year I remember so well, we would go down to the Au Sable River. There was a place where it was a big flat open space and mom would take a blanket and picnic lunch and we could play in the river all day. Mom had an old woolen bathing suit. She would dig out of the trunk and wear until one year she went to get it and it was full of holes so she threw it away. It was from the moths. We would also take a picnic lunch when we went huckleberry picking down by Mio. We would go where a fire had gone through some years before and there were a lot of berries. Mom took milk pails, lard cans, and everything had to be full when we went home. When we went strawberry, raspberry, and blackberry picking, we walked about a mile and came home with a couple of milk pails full plus three or four lard cans full and all of us singing "cool clear water." When we got home we would pump a pail of water then the water was ice cold. So good!

We didn't go to town much except to ride the school bus to school and back. At Christmas time I remember dad giving us each a quarter and we would go into the nickel and dime store and got everyone something. Then one year he gave us each a dollar and we were so tickled. We said, "Now, we can get a lot." Christmas was a big time for us, though we never had much money. Mom and dad would send for our presents Sears and Montgomery Wards and pay for them all year. I remember one year she made me a doll and made the clothes and shoes and the next year I got the same doll, but with new clothes. I loved it. We thought Santa decorated the tree and brought the presents because our folks didn't have any money. Dad would go cut the tree and put it up and we would pop popcorn and string it and leave it for Santa. When we got up, the tree was decorated and presents under it. Very pretty. My dad took a deer's foot one year and put a print out in the snow and another one some distance from it. He called us outside and said that was from Santa's reindeer. We really believed it.

Easter was another big day. My dad loved holidays. Mom decorated the eggs and made our baskets and lined them up on the bench.

They said the Easter bunny brought them and we believed them. I carried a lot over to our family. My husband and I would decorate the tree and wrap the presents, but they thought it was Santa and the same with the Easter eggs and baskets. When I found out there wasn't a Santa or Easter bunny, it wasn't the same anymore.

During World War II, we had a milkweed pod drive at school. Whoever brought the most pods to school gets an award or prize. We would go back on our farm and gather pods in gunnysacks and take them on the bus to school. They used the silk inside then for parachutes we were told. We also had a contest every year for poppy posters. We hand drew the poster and I always entered. I usually got 1st, 2nd, or 3rd. It was fun. My brother and two sisters walked a mile and a half to school for about four years. By the time I started, dad was able to help get the Mio School consolidated and busses running so I only had to walk a quarter or half a mile for one or two years then the bus came by our house. I went to a one-room Seventh Day Adventist School in my 7th and 8th grade, so I got a taste of what that was like with eight grades in one room. I had a real good teacher and I liked it. I went back to Mio High in my 9th and graduated Valedictorian. We didn't have much growing up, but I feel it made me a better and stronger person. We got one pair of shoes a year and we took care of them. When we got home from school we changed clothes and kept our school clothes good. We had a battery-operated radio that mom listened to her soaps on and Saturday night was the Grand Ole Opry.

When I was 15 my mother and older sister and I worked in a restaurant in Mio for the summer. My mother cooked, my sister washed dishes, and I waited tables. That's where I met my husband. Him and a friend had just got home from Korea and he was talking with my boss. I thought his friend was cute so I found out his name and wrote him and asked for his friend's name. He said his friend was married, but he wasn't so I kept writing him. He thought I was my sister so when we exchanged pictures, I think he was disappointed. But we went together for four years and got married and almost made 56 years. He passed away June 26, 2011 and our 56th anniversary was July 16. He got a Bronze Star and Purple Heart while in Korea and had frozen feet. He hired in Chevrolet Metal Fab a few months before we were married and retired after 30 years. He was my first and only love. I now do respite sitting and have for about five years. I do it five days a week, seven and eight hours a day plus my own shoveling and mowing and everything.

✓ The Only Time I Saw a Chicken Swim
By Kathryn Hartlep of Boyne City, Michigan
Born 1920

Kegomic, now referred to as East Bayview, was located on Little Traverse Bay. All the homes were painted dark green with red trim. All the homes in the small community were owned and rented by The Michigan Tanning and Extract Company. My father, along with most of the other men, worked at the tannery. We lived in one of those houses across the road from the Bay View Country Club. We children sat on our front porch and watched the construction of Route 31 through Kegomic. I remember how sad I was when they cut down a large tree and I saw a nest of newly hatched birds fall to the ground.

We made our own fun. I had a metal hoop and stick that I rolled down the cinder pathways every day. We also used empty canned milk cans to make mock horseshoes that made a distinctive sound like real horseshoes. We also played games like hide and seek, fox and geese, and three legged races. We also had chores. The older children carried water from the communal pump for drinking, cooking, bathing, and laundry. The water was heated on the cook stove. We also went out to our grandparent's farm to plant seeds, and later to weed. My father had a big vegetable garden. We ate fresh vegetables until frost time. Mom canned a lot of food for our winter meals. My father re-soled our shoes and Mom made most of our clothes. I remember wearing high button shoes in the winter. The five of us children had to share one buttonhook and fought about its use every morning. When we started to wear buckled arctic boots that put an end to disputes over the buttonhook. We went barefooted all summer except when we attended church.

We were sent to the company store for things we couldn't raise or pick in the wild. We had to buy the kerosene that was used to fuel our oil lamps. We also bought bananas. An orange was a tasty and very special treat. We got many things from the wild, such as mushrooms, berries, and especially black beach cherries that mom made into jam, a yummy treat that I haven't seen in decades.

We had men who traveled around who would sharpen your knives, or repair a hole in your cookware. We could also buy a cake of ice for our icebox. Horse and wagon delivered our mail. The mailman had a little shelter on the wagon in the winter. The roads were not plowed like they are today. I used to catch a ride on a wagon that hauled logs to the mill. It was slow, but a change from walking everywhere.

We didn't have trick or treat for Halloween, it was mostly trick. Our outhouse was never pushed over because it was known that dad would always rig a trip wire that would pull the pushers into the outhouse pit. Fourth of July was special. My father bought a piece of fireworks each payday to use on the fourth. He set them off in the pasture. The children were not allowed to handle them. At Christmas time, the tree was left up only one day. The tree was decorated with balls, tinsel, and real candles. The candles were lighted just once. It was a beautiful sight, but a dangerous practice.

When I stayed at my grandparents, they put me to work milking the cows, sloping the hogs, and gathering the eggs. They had a hen who was given duck eggs to sit on. When the ducklings hatched, they immediately went to the pond. The hen was so distressed that she jumped into the water to save them. That's the only time I ever saw a chicken swim. We had the usual ailments such as chicken pox and croup. My brother also got mange from a cat he had befriended. He had to eat his meals in a separate place to keep the rest of us from getting it.

I attended classes at the Edgewater School. In addition to teaching the regular subjects, one of the teachers also introduced us to dental care. She supplied each of us with a tin cup and a toothbrush and showed us how to brush our teeth. During the Great Depression, I moved to Petoskey. I was in high school. I was the first member of my family to graduate from high school. One year, I wrote a play about an old fisherman and a boy. My play was actually performed at the school. I also had a job sitting for a pair of twins, John and Mary Batsakis. I got a small income. I remember buying my first box of Kleenex and later, nail polish and anklets.

We were treated to a free movie every Saturday at the Hollywood Theatre. The owner, Mr. Levinson, made sure that we youngsters were told which movies were suitable for us. I realize how much he cared about us since he took the time to advise us. We all loved him and tried to make him proud of us. He was a wonderful man. I personally regarded Mr. Heinike as a special friend. I wanted to get a library card, but I needed a sponsor. I didn't know whom to turn to for help, but when I left the library, I saw Mr. Heinike, and decided that I would ask him for his help. I went to his beautiful china shop across from the library. I asked if he would sponsor me. He thought about it for a moment and then said that he would require a promise from me. He said that I must promise to treat the books well. I must not mark in a book or turn down the corners of the pages. I must keep the books clean and dry. He also said that if I kept them too long I would have to pay a penalty. Needless to say, I never caused him any trouble. I still think of his loving kindness.

√ Don't Forget the Fels Naptha
By Eileen Hawkins of Manistee, Michigan

Life becomes hectic at times. When that happens, I think back to my childhood and how my Aunts Martha and Lucy kept certain routines. These routines gave them a foundation to keep their lives in order and provided peace of mind. They didn't take on more than they could handle. It seems we have gotten away from structure in our lives. Many of us feel stress and strain in trying to do too many things. Modern machinery frees us from much of the physical work we used to do. But that freedom may not exist if we fill up the free time with replacement activities instead of enjoying our leisure.

I was ironing a white cotton pillow sham one day when my thoughts reverted to a picture of white 100% cotton sheets and pillowcases swaying in a gentle breeze of summer or snapping sharply in a strong winter wind, smelling so fresh from their bath in Fels Naptha Soap. In the early 1940s, many households held to the discipline of

Eileen's family in the 1950s

Monday washday, Tuesday, ironing, etc. Fond snapshots pop into my mind's eye with the memory of washday at my aunts. Their washday routine actually began on Sunday night when the galvanized washtubs were hauled up from the basement to the kitchen floor and filled with cold water and Clorox to soak the white clothes until morning. I had observed from watching my aunts that there was comfort in their working together in this routine chore. When certain things are done, it allows one's mind to be clear.

The Fels Naptha Soap made a big impression on me. Luckily, I have never been threatened with having my mouth washed out with it, but I have heard of some children who have had that experience; I'm sure they did not forget it. The pungent odor of this soap is something I can conjure up from my memory almost at will. In fact, several years ago, I purchased a bar in its still familiar wrapper, but it was smaller and did not have nearly the strong, zesty assault to my nasal passages.

When I was visiting, which was quite often, the aunts allowed me to help. I say allowed because at that time of life I had not yet learned that this was work. I looked upon it as a great adventure into the adult world. On Monday morning, the little black boiler stove in the kitchen was filled with kindling wood and a fire was started to heat the water in the adjoining tank. The soaked laundry was wrung by hand, placed in the wicker laundry basket, and carried to the basement. After disposing of the soak water, the tubs were taken to the basement to sit on a double stand with a hand-cranked wringer between them. The tubs were then filled with the hot, hot water from the kitchen boiler tank. Pail after pail was carried through the pantry, down the narrow steps, and then poured into the electric wringer washer and the hot water rinse tub. The other rinse tub received many pails of cold water.

They wouldn't let me help carry such hot water down the precarious trail from kitchen to basement. I was given the privilege to shave slivers of Fels Naptha Soap into the washer, all the while being admonished not to cut myself. I backed off as each pail of water was added and happily shaved and watched the agitator swish-swash the slivers to a frothy white foam of shiny bubbles. I felt so grownup, so helpful! Little Boy Bluing was added to the final cold rinse to make the sheets and cases look so pristine white as they were clothes pinned to the lines in the backyard. Oh, the smell! This was not a fragrance. It was an aroma!

It was very pleasant in that small northwest Michigan basement where dust motes twinkled and danced in the light sneaking entrance through the small, high windows to the dimness of the workplace. The one hanging bulb illuminated the surrounding shadows and the shelves of home-canned fruits and vegetables.

I watched the agitator push-pull the material. Bubbles of fabric with captured air inside would dance merrily on the surface, then be pulled and turned until another series of mounds formed. All the while, I would be poking the globules with the well-worn, dried sticks that had been used for hundreds of washings over the years. I always got red and sweaty from the steam as I enjoyed my game. My braids, hanging halfway down my back, absorbed the moisture as tendrils escaped to cling to my damp, warm face. After the torture of the hot water wash and the wringing to the warm rinse, we stirred the laundry and put it through the second wringer to the shock of the cold rinse. It then traveled through the wringer once more and mooshed into the waiting basket for its journey outdoors.

The newer automatic machinery that helps us do the household chores gives us more freedom to pursue other activities. If we spend that extra free time doing something enjoyable, then we have gained from it. But if we feel we must always be busy, if we pressure ourselves that, we must be doing something each and every waking moment, and then we have gained little. Have we lost sight of the fact that being a little selfish to take the time to read, nap, or spend time with a loved one is not being selfish? Must we always feel guilty for taking time for ourselves? Each of us must recognize our own needs and limitations and heed the messages our bodies give us. I am not a high-energy person. I have had to face that reality without feeling guilty.

My aunts found time for enjoying company and leisure time because their routines kept order in their lives. One worked, managing a small dress shop and kept the books for their household. The other was a highly regarded Sunday school teacher as well as keeping house. They had many friends who enjoyed the hospitality of their dinner table. I savor the memories of my Aunts Martha and Lucy and appreciate their patience with a young girl who liked to play grownup. I'll never forget the times they sent me off to the corner grocery with a wave as they called out through their cupped hands, "Don't forget the Fels Naptha!"

✓ The Raspberry Patch Debacle
By Conrad Koltys of Traverse City, Michigan
Born 1925

When I was a boy, it was a tradition for visitors, especially family, to give money to youngsters of the family they were visiting. My mother's brother, Frank Lustan, was the most generous of all. The purchasing power of a 25-cent piece was, as youngsters of today would say awesome. When given some money, sneaking over to Zambo's Grocery was difficult without some of the neighborhood kids following. I was taught to share; however if the kids did not know of my sudden wealth, sharing became a non-issue. My Uncle Frank's car parked in front of our house alerted all the free loaders and I had to employ tactics to out fox them. A five-cent Holloway caramel sucker brought joy to a kid for hours, depending on of course how quickly and diligently one licked. Demonstratively licking a Holloway at the approach of a potential sharer usually curtailed any request in this regard.

When I made my first Holy Communion my parents invited folks to celebrate the occasion. Most people gave congratulatory cards with folding money and while they were entertained, I slipped out of the house and spread the word of my wealth. Soon, more friends than I thought I had, joined me at Zambo's. Ice cream for all, followed by candy for all, followed by malted milkshakes and whatever else they wanted at the local ice cream parlor. For my final gesture of generosity, I took them to the show, both of them. The saying that refers to time flying when you are having a good time was certainly true in this case, for there was no realization that when darkness came parents would be looking for their children. This did however become apparent to me when I was suddenly snatched from my seat by my father who having worked at a steel plant developed forearms like the cartoon character Popeye. My feet occasionally touched the ground while I listened to my parents concerning my punishment was elevated to a degree of serious consideration of being sold to the Si-iee-nee. It is apparent to me that my Parents did their best during my youth to guide and direct my conduct. It also appears that spare the rod spoils the child concept had significant influence in my life. I am thankful for their effort.

From the time I was seven years old my family lived in the country on five acres of land growing a vegetable garden and raising farm animals was part of the lifestyle in those days. It wasn't long before the garden became larger so that the surplus could be sold along the road for cash money. The raspberry patch required many hours of hoeing and hand cultivating. My parents were engaged in daily chores and the garden more or less became my responsibility. One Sunday afternoon when my parents went to the city to play cards, I was faced with hours of hand cultivating. The advantages of a tractor or a horse crossed my mind many times in the past and as I labored, I wondered if our neighbor would loan me a cultivator. Mr. Cashier and his wife were leaving when I arrived and since I once accidentally burned his field of shocked corn, I had a difficult time in persuading him that I could handle this task. Without his help, I harnessed the horse, attached the cultivator, and walked him over to our garden. Boy what a great day this was going to be. I would get the job done in a fraction of the time and go swimming at the Brick Yard. The first row was perfect and as I cultivated, with ease I wondered why I did not think of this course of action before. As I proceeded to the second row the horse became alarmed and bolted on a right oblique across the patch ripping out raspberry bushes left and right. My effort to stop the horse only caused him more concern and as he ran from me, he caused more damage. Exhausted, the horse finally stopped. As I moved toward him slowly and in a soft voice I told him of my dilemma explaining in detail the severity of my punishment. My plea for his cooperation and some greens from the garden allowed me to take control. The horse was returned to his barn, rubbed down, and the harness and cultivator returned to their proper place. Returning to the garden and viewing the destruction once more, I was overwhelmed with the fact that I had never been the cause of anything so serious in my entire life. Running away was my immediate though, and while planning the details for my getaway I replanted all the salvageable raspberry bushes. I noted that my efforts in replanting were so thorough that the patch showed little evidence of wrong doing, so I dismissed my plan for running away. Several days later, I saw my father walking around the raspberry patch concerned, apparently trying to ascertain why so many bushing were dying in a strange pattern. I said nothing while my father researched books for the cause. Several years later while in the South Pacific, it occurred to me that the raspberry patch incident was insignificant compared to the trouble I was in at the moment. I later wrote to my parents and confessed my misdeed in the raspberry debacle.

During my youth, playing games, listening to adventures on the radio, and attending an occasional picture show was the extent of our play selections. With the advent of television and myriad activities today, it will be an effort for my granddaughters to imagine sitting in the dark as I did back then listening to a spooky story. Sitting in the dark listening to Hermits Cave was of my choosing and since my parents were away, it added to the degree of scare. The program started out with the sound of squeaky doors and a voice that would "advise to turn off the lights, you heard me, turn them off, while I tell you a story about the dog with the evil eye." The organ music at this time would get real spooky and loud with the sound of hollowing dogs in the back ground.

My hair, which was wavy and abundant was also scared for I felt as if it was standing straight up, It also felt as if bugs were running up and down my back and arms, the cars on the highway as they passed our house cast weird shadow movements up on the wall adding to my fright. Let me tell you, I was glued to my seat and going to the outhouse was out of the question. Invariably my Mother would ask why I wasn't in bed. Are you kidding I felt like saying, my bedroom is upstairs and the stairs are without lights.

The other day something stimulated my memory and I recalled the day I hit my first home run. I was six at the time and baseball dominated everyone's lives. Young and old listened to the ball game on the radio and quoting batting averages was commonplace. The day I hit my first homer, I was so excited that I over ran the runner on first base and beat him to home base disqualifying me. Nuts. Could I help it that the other kid was slow? Regardless, I ran home to tell my mother who was in bed giving birth to my Sister Diane. I recall seeing this little baby cuddled in the arms of my mother, but it was a momentary glance and it held no significance at the moment. My home run dominated. I don't recall any activity related to the new baby. I do however recall my sister later volunteering information regarding my misdeeds and perhaps the snitching saved me from unintended self-destruction. It was a time of children and some of the components of growing up. Sometime later, she became significant in my life and has remained so.

Mr. Tiddley-Winks
By Percy John Shooks of Grand Rapids, Michigan
Born 1924

I was born on June 8, 1924. I was the 10th child of Tony and Tillie Shooks on a farm between Ellsworth and Central Lake, Michigan in Antrim County. My grandfather homesteaded the farmland in the late 1800's. He had emigrated from the Netherlands in 1883 with his wife and a maiden sister, one daughter and four sons. The last son was born in the United States. My grandfather cleared the pine trees with his sons' help and sold them to the Essex sawmill near the property. A rail line served that activity running from Central Lake. My grandfather built the farmhouse where I was born. My father took over the farm in 1916. Grandfather lived with us until his death at age 88 in 1933.

The first six children of my parents were girls and after a short interlude (not long enough for my Mom), they had five sons. My father did general farming and developed a herd of registered Jersey cows. They had to be tested once a month to maintain their registry. He took them to fairs where he accumulated many ribbons, which we played with. The sire of these animals was named Tiddley-Winks. Many farmers found his services were important for their herds.

My farm memories were limited. I did start Mitchell Country School at age four and a half and walked about a long mile one-way to a one-room schoolhouse with my brothers. We took a short cut through my uncle's barnyard, but had to avoid a rooster who liked to chase little kids. When I had to deliver the weekly darning to my aunt, I purposely left it short of the house to avoid that creature. The socks were in a red bag so my aunt could see it. I did learn to milk a cow named Fern as she had a low container of milk. My brothers always had to strip her, as my undeveloped hands were not strong enough. Another event that had a bearing on my farm experience was watching a neighbor butcher a pig in our barnyard. I fainted at the sight.

A sad memory a year before we moved to Ellsworth, was watching for a hearse to bring the body of my youngest sister home from Grand Rapids, where she passed from pneumonia as a result of polio. She was 15 and my Mom grieved for her for the rest of her life. When I later learned to play the piano, she often asked me to play the hymns that were sung at the funeral.

In 1928, my father decided to sell his farm and buy a general store in Ellsworth for the main purpose of locating his sons nearer to a high school. My oldest brother was about to become a junior high student. He put all of his farm goods for sale along with those special Jersey cows in the spring of 1929. The animals particularly attracted out of state buyers. The calves sold in the $300 range and Mr. Tiddley-Winks went for several hundred dollars. Well there went the farm and off we went to the village of Ellsworth with a house with room for all. Unknowingly, we were about to face a depression.

I was placed in kindergarten instead of the 1st grade at the Mitchell one-room school. I went backwards. The walk to school was much shorter. When I was in the 2nd grade, I was asked to try the 3rd grade. I didn't want to lose my friends and I declined. I always liked school and the teachers. I did mess up in the 2nd grade when I giggled when a girl unfortunately piddled on the floor. I was severely reprimanded.

One summer, we had a pet crow named Harpo. My next older brother loved to fish and heard young crows in a nest along the lake where he was fishing. He went to the tree and climbed to the nest and extracted three young crows. He tucked them into his jacket and took them home. They couldn't fly yet, but he clipped their wings anyway. The littlest one died during the night and the next largest broke his foot on the woodpile. We used a small box on the car exhaust pipe with the crow in it for a merciful demise. The largest one liked us. We fed him, talked to him, and let him ride on our shoulder. He also liked to ride on our bike. He got back to flying, but stayed with us. A neighbor took a strong dislike to him, as he loved to pull clothesline pins and leave dirty foot markings on her clothes. He ranged far and wide but always came home. When we went to school in the fall, he was mistaken by a farmer for a real crow and was shot. That was the end of a lot of fun that summer with Harpo.

Growing up in Ellsworth was fun. I had brothers to play with and I had friends to swim with in the old swimming hole. In the winter, we sledded down hills and hitched rides on people's sleighs. It was not all play by any means. We all worked in the store. These were the depression years and it was tough for my father. He received cream from farmers and from some, eggs. He gave vouchers for the value of the traded goods. He turned cream and eggs over to dealers for about what he gave the farmer. In the summer, we candled the eggs and sold them to the resort hotels in Harbor Springs. I remember many instances when people would ask for credit. Men and women customers would frankly say, "We have no food in the house," as their canned goods would run out in the spring. My dad knew in many cases that he would not be paid.

He borrowed money from friends to stay in business. My dad rented plots of land and had beans and cucumbers planted for the receiving stations and we went out to pick them. We all started clerking when we were old enough.

When I did get to the 3rd grade, I got a book for geography class. A whole new world opened up for me. I devoured the book and dreamed of all the interesting places in the world. Little did I know that later in my life, my wife and I would have the opportunity to visit every continent and many countries. School was mostly studies. In high school, I played basketball and baseball. The old uniforms didn't fit and there wasn't much coaching. One basketball coach always said, "Boys, pass the ball around," and we did. We won some, lost more but we did win the district tournament when I was a senior over our arch rivals from Central Lake with the score of 16-14 after a half time score of 4-2. We never trailed Central Lake who was undefeated until that last game. I am sorry about that.

One dear high school teacher in my oldest brother's senior year (1936) put together a track team with no facilities. The runners trained on the gravel road in front of the school. He fashioned a pole vault place and also a shot put and broad jump pit. They trained hard and went to Cadillac for a regional track meet in his car. They ran and jumped as hard as they trained, and they won the meet in their class. That trophy should be in the archives somewhere. The next year the teacher found a different position and that was the end of the track team.

At age five, I started piano lessons at 25-cents an hour. My teacher was a student of the teacher who came from East Jordan to give lessons. For my first recital, my sister dressed me in a little Lord Fauntleroy outfit. I played "Flowers in the Garden." I don't think the flowers survived. I was the only boy in the recital. I kept up with the lessons into the 9th grade. I kept practicing and playing and eventually at age 16, I played the organ in my church. My only lesson was showing me where to turn on the organ. I figured out my own combination of stops and I managed.

I have no regrets of growing up in northern Michigan in Antrim County. Going through the depression years and seeing how people struggled and kids my age left school at age 16 to work on their parents' farms makes me very thankful for my hardworking, caring parents. By contrast, with many of my contemporaries, I was privileged as my family lived through the same hard times. All of my brothers and I went into military service and together we gave 17 years of service to our country. My oldest brother went ashore on D-Day in the second wave and survived. I went to Okinawa and the other brothers all served in Europe. We were glad to serve and are thankful to God that we all returned.

You Had to Wait an Entire Week to Bathe
By Marlene Hopkins of Tower, Michigan
Born 1954

I grew up in Afton, Michigan on a 40-acre farm out in the country. In order to get to school, the bus would pick me up at the end of a long, long driveway, which was walked down from the house on the hill. The school bus route was very long to pick up all the kids in the country. My first school experience was at Afton School. It was a two-room schoolhouse. In one classroom, Mrs. Brosseau would teach Kindergarten through 2nd grade. In the other classroom, Mrs. Brady would teach 3rd grade through 5th grade. We had the best cook in the world there, Mrs. Knight. She made the best peanut butter cake with peanut butter frosting I have ever tasted. Out in the playground, there were swings, a merry-go-round, and teeter-totters. All the bigger kids would get asked to "pump up" us little kids on the swings. We would go so high and swing back and forth it took forever to slow back down. Mrs. Brosseau was my favorite teacher in this school. She had a loud voice and a stern face, which would always let us know if we were in trouble. I remember learning penmanship in class and writing on my Big Chief tablet of paper.

On the farm, we didn't have any running water or any inside toilets. We had to use an outhouse for bathroom purposes; it was very cold sitting on that privy seat in the wintertime. The "outhouse" got quite hot in the summer time, but we always left the door open to let the heat escape. Every three or four years, my dad would always build a new hole to put the outhouse up on and we would be good to go for another period of time.

Our home had a "party line" for calling

461

out on the telephone. Back then, everyone's phone number would start with a name, plus one number, for example "Adams 8-5555 (AD8-5555)." Later on, they just dropped the words and went strictly by numbers: 238-5555. Every house had a special ring. Ours was two short rings and one long ring. Whenever you wanted to call a neighbor, you would dial the phone number, put the receiver down in the cradle, and listen for the "ring" (two long, one short; or one long, one short). Whenever the neighbor would receive a phone call, it would also ring into our house, if you really wanted to be nosey, you would pick up the receiver to "listen in" to their calls. Everyone owned a rotary dial phone back then. These were always black in color and had a face dial with numbers and letters and holes where you would put your fingers to dial the phone number. The receiver had a long, black cord that would allow you to walk around while you talked on the phone. I miss the sound the dial would make as it dialed a phone number.

Mondays were always washdays and we would haul up the water from the well house to be used in the wringer washing machine. Our model was a Speed Queen and it had to be filled with water by pails to do the washing. In order to rinse the clothes, you would need to swing the arm component on the washing machine over the rinse tub and run the clothes through the wringer rollers to push out all the soapy water. Once the clothes fell in to the rinse tub they would again be put through the wringer to squeeze out the water where they fell in the dry tub. From there, we would carry out the galvanized dry tub of clothes out to the clothesline in our yard. Any leftover rinse water would be then used to water the plants, trees, and shrubbery around the yard - nothing ever went to waste, not even the laundry water.

Trips to town were only once a week, on each Saturday morning. This would be about a 30-mile car ride to Cheboygan, where we bought our weekly groceries. Only one trip to town was allowed each week due to the distance and not having the money. We always went on a Saturday as my Dad got paid on Friday from his job. I remember shopping at the Woolworth's store (Five & Dime store). You bought anything you could think of there. I loved the toy aisle mostly. I would save up my pop bottle deposit money from all week

and it would be my allowance. I bought a lot with that 75-cents each week. Back then, we had penny candy and every kind of candy was bought on a candy counter, where you peeked through the glass and told the clerk what kind you wanted and it would be bought by the bulk. Another favorite store was the A&P grocery store. I later learned that A&P stood for Atlantic & Pacific Food Co. I remember the meat aisle and you only had to tell the butcher what kind of meat you wanted and he would wrap it up in some brown paper and tie it with a string and mark the price on the outside in a black marker pen.

Every Saturday night was our bath night. With no running water in our home, we had to use pails of water we would haul up from the well house. If you needed hot water, you hauled up the big, galvanized tub and put the teakettle on the gas stove and poured it into the galvanized wash dish, which was the washing basin for our baths. We did not own a bathtub or a shower. A simple washbasin was all the water we used for bathing, but it was only done one night a week. You had to wait a whole week until it was bath time again.

Snowstorms in the winter back in the 1960s and 1970s meant having at least a three-day blizzard, which meant you were stranded inside your house until a snowplow came by, but that could be up to a whole week away from when the snowstorm ended. Back roads would always be drifted shut and it was not uncommon to have school cancelled for at least three or four days. With winter came our favorite pastime of sledding and skiing. Living on a farm, meant we had many open fields to enjoy skiing on. On the farm, there were always fun and games. We had an old barn that was not used for farming anymore; up in the hayloft was a great place to play. In the lower level, was the cow stalls and it provided a cement floor to use a pair of roller-skates on. The barn was always a great place to play hide-and-seek, but the favorite place to play "King on the Mountain" was on the manure pile out back of the barn. Overgrown with tall grass, it was fun climbing up and rolling down the other side.

Springtime was my favorite time of year. The first sign of spring was the return of the red-winged blackbirds that came to our swamp each year. Then there was the sound of the peepers, or young frogs, which would burrow out of the mud and bring out their mating calls. You could always tell it was spring when the flow of water out of the trough in the well house forcefully gushed from the spring thaws in the fields. Water would come out of the artesian underground spring out of the field and find its way through a tile pipe that arrived in the well house. From there it carried the flow down the creek into the swamp, which then flooded each spring. Our yard was filled with large elm trees and each spring we would put up the birdhouse for the tree swallow's arrival in May. I don't recall ever having a year without the return of these swallows to the same birdhouse. It was always a good sign to hear their warbling birdcalls.

The Best Ride Mom Ever Had
By Len Schweitzer of Louisville, Kentucky
Born 1947

I was born in Thompsonville, Michigan in the winter of 1947 and lived there until I was 14 years old in 1961. My father owned 320 acres (1/2 section) of land—some woods, some open meadows, about four miles north of Thompsonville on County Road 669. He never "worked" the farm, except for a huge (about 2 acres) vegetable garden, a few fruit trees (a variety of apples, pears, plums, and quince) and several varieties of grape vines.

The family lived in a very modest, not quite completed structure with tarpaper walls; there was a living/dining room, a bedroom, and a pantry. I had three brothers at home for most of my boyhood. Two older brothers married and left home when I was quite young. The third brother was 18 months older than I and we were constantly together; we even slept in the same bed. He and I slept in an 8 foot by 12 foot log cabin outbuilding we called the shanty. My father was a laborer performing a number of jobs like a seasonal canning factory job and cutting pulpwood, pruning fruit trees and Christmas trees. My mother suffered from severe rheumatoid arthritis all the time I knew her. She was 41 when I was born and 54 when she succumbed to cancer in 1960 when I was 13. She didn't drive and we had no telephone, electricity, or plumbing. She led a lonely life at home cooking on a wood stove. We cooked and heated with wood stoves, pumped water from an outdoor pump, and used an outhouse.

Any story about life in northern Michigan must include "snow." Here are two humorous stories from my boyhood that include snow. The shanty where my brother and I slept was quite old and the chinking (a sand and clay material) between the logs had weathered and dried out. As a result, much of the chinking had fallen out leaving open cracks between the logs. When we would have a snowstorm with wind, it would not be unusual for us to wake up in the morning with 4-5 inch snow "drifts" on our bed where the snow had blown in through the cracks between the logs where the chinking had fallen out. We would shake the snow off the bed and go on as if that was something everyone dealt with. We had a small wood stove in the shanty, which we would fire up before we went to bed, but within a couple of hours the fire would burn out and we slept in the cold. In the morning when mom yelled from the house for us to get up, we would get out from under the covers shaking of any accumulated snow, slip on our jeans, grab our shoes and shirts, and run barefoot through the snow to the outhouse and then to the fire in the house to finish dressing. What an awakening!

The second story involves getting mom to a Christmas program at church. My mom, my brother, and I attended a rural church about four miles away. Since my father didn't go with us and mom did not drive, we relied on the country preacher to come to pick us up each Sunday morning and for any events going on at the church. In the wintertime, mom was snowbound for several months because our house was quite far off the road and no cars could come in (my father parked the car at the road and walked in). Because mom was crippled, she could not walk to or from the road in the snow. There was to be a Christmas program at church and I had memorized a piece for the program. In the afternoon of the evening of the program mom said, "I would give anything to be able to be there to see you speak your piece." I said, "I bet we can make that happen." My brother and I began making a makeshift toboggan from a sheet of corrugated steel roofing. The sheet was rolled up on one end so it wouldn't catch the snow as it moved through it. We had a rope attached to each of the front corners of the sheet of steel so we could pull it. We found a large piece of firewood, which had not been split which we set up on the end of the toboggan for mom to sit on and hang on to.

The time came to go out to the road to be picked up. We very gingerly got mom sitting on the log seat and started out for the trip to the road. About half way to the road we went over a rough spot, mom lost her balance and tumbled off the toboggan. I was quite sure we had made a bad decision to get her to the program. I had no idea how we would get mom out of the snow and back on her throne to continue the trip. I was very upset and worried. Meanwhile Mom was lying in the snow, arms and legs flailing, laughing so hard tears were running down her cheeks. What I wouldn't give for a video of that scene! My brother and I struggled to get her back on the log on the toboggan and we continued on our mission, mom laughing all the way. We got to the road, the preacher came and picked us up, and mom heard me say my piece. We all acted as if this kind of thing was just a routine and a normal part of life. After we got back home, we refused the preacher's offer to assist us getting back to the house; Mom said that was the most fun ride she had ever had!

Every May during my boyhood, I would venture to the woods in search of the "world renowned" morel mushrooms. It was quite a challenge to see them popping up under the leaves left on the ground the previous fall, but I was little so I would gather a bag full at a time. Mom would sauté them in butter and the family would make a meal of the day's gathering. I also picked wild blackberries by the bucketfuls for a neighbor lady who would pay me a nickel for a small bucket. I always picked plenty to take home for the family. Mom would bake blackberry pies and we would often just eat them before she had a chance to bake a pie.

When I was a little older, I picked strawberries for pay in June and cherries in July. It was hard work, but I had a great time working outside. I also cut grass and shoveled snow for a neighbor to earn money. When I was 10 years old, I got my first "real" job working in a small grocery store in town. I saved my money for many months so I could order a new bike from the Ward's catalogue, I think it cost about $30. I went to the train station every day for weeks to check to see if my bike came in on that day's train. The stationmaster, Mr. Hoffman, was very patient and kind with my daily pestering. When it finally came and I got it assembled, that bike was the first love of my life.

When I was 13 years old, I decided to ride my bike to Traverse City about 40 miles away to celebrate my first nephew's first birthday. I just took off by myself, not telling anyone of my plans, and rode the better part of a day in August. It was hot! I battled dusty roads, steep hills, and angry dogs at every turn. Everyone was quite surprised when I rode up to my brother's house. The next day my brother put my bike in the trunk of his car and drove me back to Thompsonville, for which I was extremely grateful! I think the return trip would have been more than my little legs and seat could withstand. One of my favorite summer time activities was riding my bike down a trail through the woods to the Betsie River swimming hole. There was a spring fed stream that entered the Betsie at the swimming hole. What a great summertime cooling off it was at the swimming hole!

✓ I Smell Glen Lake
By Susan Roelofs-Haughn of Glen Arbor, Michigan
Born 1953

I swore to myself only at first and to others later, that I would live there someday. I hated leaving the clean, dark blue and bright green waters of Glen Lake at the end of every summer. My Great-Grandfather, Boudewjn DeKorne, bless his soul, found this Michigan paradise when a friend from his hometown, Grand Rapids, Michigan, told him about it. He brought his family north one summer and the rest is my favorite part of my history.

The DeKorne family was large and my grandmother, a DeKorne twin, married a man, David Thomasma, who came from a family of 15. Often when a new relative was introduced to Glen Lake, they bought a place. There have been between 12-15 cottages on Glen Lake, in what others referred to as "Dutch Haven" owned by my relatives at various times. In fact, my father's sister, who fell in love with the area when they visited us, also bought a place on the lake in "Dutch Haven." The DeKorne family even made land available to build a church, just a three-minute walk from our cottage, so no one had to go back to Grand Rapids on Saturday night in order to attend church on Sunday. We attended every Sunday morning and evening that we were at the cottage and sang hymns with our relatives and local people who joined the church over the years.

As soon as school got out each summer my mother, sister, brother, and I would literally jump in the car and head north of Grand Rapids to Leelanau County and our cottage on Glen Lake. Dad had to stay home and work on most weekdays, but he came up every weekend and often for extra days. What awaited us there was more than the beautiful lake. There were unimaginable sunsets, dunes to climb up and run down, cousins to play with, in and out of the water, and boats in which to fly across that water. Prior to age eight, we spent two weeks at Par 5, the large cottage my mother's father gave to his five children. After age eight, we lived with my grandfather in his cottage a short way down the beach. My grandmother died just after the cottage was built and my grandfather chose my mother, his oldest, to come care for him as she had no children younger than me and the rest had babies. When he died three years later, my parents bought out the other four siblings and the cottage was ours.

I would fall asleep on the long ride to our eagerly anticipated destiny each summer and wake up and yell out, "I smell Glen Lake!" The air was fresh and clear, so much different from Grand Rapids. My mother loved to tell how I would also wake up on our way home each fall and sit up sleepily moaning, "I smell Grand Rapids." My father had a game when he was in the car with us, we went up many weekends as a family in the fall, spring and winter where he would go down a certain road and the first person to spot our lake and call out, "I see Glen Lake!" was the winner. Only after we were adults did we discover he used a tree as a landmark to help him win each time.

We loved the stories our mom would tell of coming up as a very young child herself; Model T cars, numerous flat tires, and pushing the car up hills or out of muddy holes were scenes so unbelievable to us. We tried to imagine this as we went down the two lane paved highways that existed then, before the freeways. We always stopped in Baldwin at Jones' Homemade Ice Cream Parlor. They piled on the best ice cream ever and we tried not to drip it everywhere.

At the lake, our days were spent porpoise diving in the shallow water, pushing off the hard packed sand at the bottom of our treasured lake as we dove into the clean, cool water, which later in the summer, warmed to bath water. If we swallowed water because we were laughing and splashing each other, we never worried. Jumping off the raft in the deeper water on the far side could keep us completely entertained as our imaginations created games that included whichever friends or cousins were there that week. Tree houses can still be seen in the larger trees at the edge of the nearby woods that we added to each summer. Our fun loving and somewhat crazy uncles refereed baseball games in the acreage behind grandfather's cottage or the yard of Par 5. If we begged long enough, the uncles also took us, behind whatever boat we had available, waterskiing or on some board type apparatus designed and built by my dad or my male cousins. The uncles delighted in throwing us off by taking fast, sharp turns when they wanted to hear us scream. There was never a shortage of cousins with whom to play and ride the waves.

Whenever a friend or relative visited, we went to the Sleeping Bear Dunes to climb up the very large sand hill that is now one of the main draws of a national lakeshore. Running, jumping, cart wheeling, or falling down the hill after the exhausting climb resulted in large smiles and mouths, noses, and ears full of sand. A stop at the ice cream shop across the road was part of the tradition of each trip. If we were really lucky, those visitors were a motivation to the adults for a trip down the Crystal River in canoes where we "shot the tube" that went under the roads. The deep swimming hole in the middle of the river promised opportunities to ambush and dunk each other.

At other times, my father and I would go "crabbing" in the Crystal River to get crabs for fishing bait. I was a tomboy and his fishing buddy. He would be in waders holding a stiff metal net on the bottom of the river and I would run toward him in my bathing suit scaring the crabs into his net. We would later take out the boat, rip off the head and body of the crab, peel out the tail meat to fasten to the hook, and cast out our line in our special spot in Glen Lake. Invariably we would pull in 12-14 inch perch, which my mother would fry up almost as soon as we came in for a tasty snack or dinner. I must confess that my favorite part of fishing was when my dad cleaned the fish and he cut open the stomach to reveal its contents. He always made a good fish haul, as he knew which bait they were biting. Alternatively, my dad and I would take a net, with long poles on either end, out just in front of our cottage, he on one end and I on the other, and staying close to the bottom; we would scoop up minnows and place them in a minnow bucket. Worms were an alternative bait and I taught most of my cousins, even the older boys, how to bait the hook with those slimy, squirmy things, many of which I dug myself. When the cousins would arrive at the lake for their weeks, they would ask me to take them out to where the fish were biting and often I had to remove the fish from the hook because they were afraid. My father taught me well and I was quite adept at the whole process.

At the age of 14, I had my first job at the Glen Lake Dairy Bar where I made $0.70 an hour. I was a soda jerk (real sodas), waitress, cook, and dishwasher. The next year I made $0.80 an hour and met my first love when he came in for lunch from his job at a marina nearby. We shared our love for Glen Lake for the next three years as we completed high school and started college. When I turned 16, I opted for a "better" job cleaning rooms at the Homestead Resort on Lake Michigan. My pay doubled, but so did my responsibilities and exhaustion. Throughout my late high school and college years, I worked as a waitress at the nearby Sugar Loaf Resort where I made great tips that helped put me through college. On winter vacations from college I would wait tables in the bar and get tips and free downhill ski lift tickets in exchange.

After college and graduate school at U of M, I lived and worked in Ann Arbor for seven years. After a summer of driving up to the lake every weekend to stay with my widowed mother, I found a job in the area and on a whim, made the move north. After a year on Crystal Lake and 12 years living in Traverse City, my husband, son, and I tore down my grandfather's cottage after my mother's death, and built our current home. I made my plan a

reality and now I smell Glen Lake every day and every season.

Rarely in my childhood did we go to Lake Michigan, which was so close by, or to Traverse City, the largest city within 30 miles because we simply did not want to leave the lake. I now work in Traverse City five days a week and have discovered its many treasures. The dunes look much smaller to me now, but the trails and newfound Lake Michigan beaches, which I explore regularly, in the Sleeping Bear Dunes National Lakeshore, have opened up the experience. My husband and I are the ones who now take children to the dunes, canoeing/kayaking on the Crystal River and waterskiing or wakeboarding. I still porpoise dive in the lake and water ski almost every day of the summer. Snowshoeing in the woods or cross-country skiing on the frozen lake add to the pleasure of living on Glen Lake year around. The best part of making a childhood dream come true is having the ability to share that dream with the others in your life that come along in the future. My husband and son are now as attached to Glen Lake as I was and it is expected that our grandchildren and the many generations to come will love the smell of Glen Lake.

✓ Don't Rush a Horse
By Ellsworth Handrich of Fairview,
Michigan
Born 1921

This is the story of my life. I was born July 3, 1921 on a farm in northern Michigan. The doctor lived 25 miles away and he couldn't get to my birthing in time, so I didn't even have a doctor to take care of me. Back in those days, there was no electricity, no running water, and the outhouse out back was the only place for relief with the Sears-Roebuck catalog for toilet paper; cold in the winter and bees in the summer. We didn't know any different, so we made the best of it. We had kerosene lamps for light and carried a kerosene lantern out to the cow stable to have light. I grew up in a loving, Christian family and as I remember it, we had a very good life. I had a wonderful mother, who when I was two years old, became tangled up in a belt that was pumping water and broke her back. My Dad carried her to the car and took her 50 miles to the hospital. She came home with a hump in her back, but it

Ellsworth with his wife, Mary Alice in 1943

didn't change her loving character.

I went to a one-room school to start with, but prior to that, my Dad had a school bus route with a homemade school bus box on a set of sleighs in the winter to take the students to school. It had two benches, one on each side, with a coal oil stove for heat to keep the kids warm. He had two teams going one way with one team and when he got back, he would take the other team because it was in the winter with a lot of snow and it was a tough go. My one-room schoolteacher was Lucy Layman and she was very strict, but she was a good teacher.

One day when I was five years old, my folks sent me across the road to our neighbors for the day and Mabel Pletcher, the neighbor lady, was ironing and entertained me by telling me about the little train who thought he could, thought he could, thought he could and finally made it. When I got home that evening, I had a baby brother. I knew nothing about this happening because in those days no one talked about pregnancy. My mother was especially reticent about talking about being pregnant.

My Uncle Elmer had a Delco system for electricity. It was a series of batteries hooked up to create electricity and they had light bulbs about the size of 15-watt bulbs, but we thought they were the real things. They had a radio and I can remember that they would call on the telephone when the *Amos and Andy* show was on the radio and they would hold the receiver up to the telephone so that we could listen to it since we had no way of getting that program. The telephone was on the wall with the ringer to open it up. When it rang three short rings, which were the same as our 911 today, it meant someone's house was on fire or there was an emergency. That was the way we communicated neighbor-to-neighbor because when three rings went, everyone got on the telephone to see what was happening.

We were poor in those days and all of our neighbors were poor so we didn't know the difference. We didn't have a lot of playthings or recreation other than what we made or did ourselves. We carried water out on the hill behind the house to make a slide and would shovel off the ponds to make a place to skate. I can remember going to Alpena, about 60 miles away, where my folks let me buy a bicycle. When we got home, we discovered it didn't have a chain so I would ride it down the hill and push it back up and then ride it back down because I didn't have money to buy a chain to make it complete.

For recreation, families would get together and have ice cream parties. Each family would make a freezer full of ice cream, plus a cake, and get together. Each family had its own recipe for ice cream so we young guys had to see who could eat the most and sample all the ice cream at the party. We had some great times. I well remember the bank crash in 1929 when my Dad went into the bank to get his money and the bank told him he would probably get 10-cents back on the dollar. The Kansas and Oklahoma Dust Bowl was going on then and we could see the dust in the sky in the west and it was a time of chaos in the country because even in northern Michigan we had very dry years. The corn crops were only about 4-5 feet high with very small ears.

Ellsworth with his dog

We had to cut it and shock it and save every bit of fodder because it was needed to feed the cattle. It was a tough time. We cut the corn by hand and during the winter, we would go out and shuck the corn out of the shocks and take it into the corncrib.

Back in those days, everyone burned wood for heat. We had a big kitchen range and a heating stove in the living room, making two stoves to cut wood to burn. Our farm was only about 40 acres of cleared land, as I can remember, when I was a boy. Dad would go back and cut wood with an axe and a team of horses and a bob sleigh to haul it back to the house. I can remember going along to the woods with Dad and I would get so cold that I would probably start crying so he would take me up to the horses and put my hands under the horse collars to warm them. We would then haul the full-length poles of wood up to the barnyard and later on have a wood buzzing to cut the wood into pieces for firewood. We would clear several acres of land every year to put in more crops. The old stumps would be getting rotten and we would beat the stumps with a sledgehammer and then later plow for crops. It was very rough plowing and Dad always wanted to plant potatoes in it for the first year because it was virgin soil with few weeds and it would raise excellent potatoes. Almost every year we had a potato field and later added onto the farmland for crops. Then there were stones to pick. Always stones to pick. There were small stones and then there were large stones. My Dad would put dynamite under the big ones so we could get them out of the field. Later on, when I was farming, my own family hated picking stones just as much as I did, but we had to do it to get a good crop. Day after day, we would work to kill the grass so we could plant a crop.

During the Depression, things were tough all over, especially in Detroit where the automobile business had been flourishing. I had an uncle who lived there and worked for Chrysler. During the Depression, he and his family would come to our farm to work so his family would have food to eat. One morning I was supposed to take our horses back to a pasture way down the lane and his son, little Fred, had to go along. We were chasing the horses through the gate and Fred got too close and was trying to rush them. One of them kicked back and kicked him right in the head and laid him out. I ran all the way back to the house to get Dad to pick him up and take him to the hospital. He had a mastoid operation from that and carried the scars through his life. It was a traumatic time.

My Grandpa Hopkins was Al Hopkins, who owned some acreage on McCollum Lake about 12 miles from our farm. He had lost one hand in his youth in a thrashing machine accident. He could do more with one hand off and one stub arm than most people could do with two. After his death, the property was divided up among his five daughters and each one had a strip of land. My mother, Fay, had a cabin built on her property and the highlight of the year was going to the lake if we got the haying done by July 4th. A couple of my friends and I would go out to the property and pitch a tent to fish, skinny dip, and have a great time because hardly anyone lived out there. In those days, we would go cross-country through the woods to go to McCollum Lake. There were no restrictions and my grandpa would drive those trails and most people were afraid to ride with him because he was such a poor driver, having only one hand and the two-track trails were treacherous. About that time, ex-senator Reed from Missouri bought all of the property around the lake except several pieces of land and Grandpa's land. He tried to shut off the road so that we couldn't get to the lake. Mrs. Schnable had some acreage on the frontage and when she died, she deeded her property to the DNR so that Senator Reed couldn't obtain her property.

My high school years weren't the best. They were rather traumatic because I had to stay home from school a lot to do the farming and I missed the basics of geometry and algebra. I floundered through and graduated.

If it hadn't been for playing baseball, which I loved, I probably wouldn't have graduated. I did have a highlight in that I could pitch baseball and throw curves and strikes, holding the record for quite a time of 17 strikeouts out of 21 batters. That was almost a perfect game if it wouldn't have been for one error that the shortstop made. My son Fred broke my record when he pitched baseball in high school.

Our graduating class had plays to raise money for our senior trip. We left from Fairview in a school bus with $300, went to Detroit to see the Tigers play a baseball game, stayed overnight in a hotel there and went to Niagara Falls the next day. We spent some time there and went back up through Canada to see the Dionne quintuplets, who were two or three years old. They were quite a novelty at this time. They were behind glass and we were able to watch them play. We continued through Canada to the Upper Peninsula. We camped along the way and made our own meals at times. We returned to Fairview with enough cash left from the $300 to give the bus driver a small payment.

✓ The Big Move to Grayling
By Mary Begley of Alpena, Michigan
Born 1931

In the year of 1948, when this Bay City, Michigan girl was 16 ½ years old, I was told by my parents, Jane and William Majeska, that they were moving to Grayling, Michigan to be caretakers of a 340 acre, huge, private lodge. I was supposed to have been going in September to my senior year at St. Joseph's School with the Dominican Nuns. I was devastated! My parents understood, so they asked if I wanted to stay with my married sister Edna until I could graduate. We were a very close family, so I told them that I wanted to stay with my parents and my two sisters Maureen, who was 15 years old, and Helen, who was eight years old.

So, in July, up to Grayling we went! My dad taught me how to drive (we didn't know about school buses) and there wasn't any school driver education. The car was a Chevy Coupe with a standard stick shift. With my dad hollering orders and me stopping and starting with a clutch, I made it. Now, the sheriff was the one to approve the driver for a license.

It was so different! The sheriff took me one noon hour and I had to drive and park the car as we drove right past the high school. The students all waved and hollered, but I did pass!

Being from the city, we knew no danger of the woods, so after dinner we listened to the radio for news. Then, we'd go on our evening walk. Our eyes veered under the evergreens, and we'd walk right along. If it was light enough, we saw so many deer, rabbits, snakes, raccoons, and other animals. We usually played cards in the evenings, too.

Then came September, and we started school. Our closest neighbors, William and Margaret Jenson, lived three miles away. William would drive us three more miles where we picked up the school bus on M-72 at Waverly Bridge and drive into school. Maureen and I used to sit together because we didn't know anyone. Helen (my pig-tailed sister) went to a one-room schoolhouse that held grades one through six. After that, they rode the bus to Grayling School. Now in school, our wardrobe was dresses, skirts, and blouses. We were allowed slacks on football game days only. My mother knitted angora cuffs, which we wore over our stocking cuffs with our saddle shoes! Another hair trim was to buy a piece of velvet ribbon (maybe one inch) and sew elastic to both ends and wear it like a hair band.

In our time, we could date different boys to see who we liked. We had our own school band so on Saturday nights we could dance at school, see a movie (at the one theater), go bowling, or see the boys' sports. The only sports the girls could participate in were band or fish the AuSable River. We also had canoe rides down the river and the canoe owners would pick us up at one of the bridges as we went south down the river. The seniors would have a play in April that we would audition for. Ours was "The Island Queen and I." We made our own scenery, and I won the part of a grumpy schoolteacher from our director Norine Hanson, our lovely English literature teacher.

The girls in my class were quite annoyed with a new girl coming in as a senior. However, one girl, Donna (Carlson) Wiley, was becoming a nurse at E.W. Sparrow hospital in Lansing. Donna was wonderful to me, and I decided that I would pursue a nursing career with the help of a Red Cross Scholarship that I had received. I would become a nurse upon graduation. Martha (Jenson) Austin was a daughter of our closest neighbor, and she helped me achieve this scholarship. At 17, I was too young when I graduated, so I had to wait until the February class to enter. I went back to school as a postgraduate until I left in February. I became friends with this other girl, Joan Papendick. It was a wonderful friendship.

I will end with my Senior and Junior proms. At my Senior Prom in April 1949, I had promised my old Bay City friend Leroy Goddard that he could take me. The seniors decorated the gym for a week prior for the scenery, so we painted and nailed for our magical night. The girls wore formals but the boys wore regular suits with matching flowers. There were no dinners or limos and the evening was over at midnight. I also had another enjoyable evening, as I was going with the president of the junior prom in May, Jim Feldhauser, at that time. We led the grand march and drove his classic Model-A Ford to Grayling and home by one o'clock. What fun! We were allowed to wear our cap and gown a whole week, prior to graduating in June 1949. What wonderful friends in both St. Joseph's class and the Grayling class reunions! I attend both.

My Memories

My Memories

Index A
By Name, Year of Birth, and Hometown

Florence Erdman	1920	Bellaire	Michigan	292
Marguerite Karabin	Unknown	Bellaire	Michigan	430
Valerie Murden	1950	Bellaire	Michigan	280
Laura Weighman	Unknown	Bellaire	Michigan	73
Gloria Gardner	1945	Belleville	Michigan	384
Marilyn Olsen	1938	Benzonia	Michigan	173
Eileen Pulido	1952	Benzonia	Michigan	326
Dave Beck	1948	Berkley	Michigan	103
Cloral Beeler	1948	Beulah	Michigan	388
James R. Kilgus	1944	Beulah	Michigan	189
Shirley Bishaw	1924	Boyne City	Michigan	400
Arthella Dickerson	1933	Boyne City	Michigan	333
Kathryn Hartlep	1920	Boyne City	Michigan	455
Allen L. Lawson	1937	Boyne City	Michigan	273
Glenda (White) Reinhardt	1942	Boyne City	Michigan	363
Doyle Eckhardt	1925	Brethren	Michigan	292
James F. Smith	1929	Brighton	Colorado	411
Sandy Berry	1935	Brooklyn	Michigan	160
Lela M. Sydow	1930	Brutus	Michigan	309
Ruth Moyer	1916	Buckley	Michigan	213
Donna M. Weber	1929	Buckley	Michigan	402
Susan Erickson	1960	Burton	Michigan	35
Priscilla Bennett	1927	Cadillac	Michigan	251
Shirley Fauble	1942	Cadillac	Michigan	268
James R. Frisbie	1913	Cadillac	Michigan	407
Mayme Guthrie	1922	Cadillac	Michigan	265
Bonnie Salmon	1943	Cadillac	Michigan	252
Judie Sprague	1937	Cadillac	Michigan	225
Mary Carolyn Brown	1937	Central Lake	Michigan	281
Nelson Louis Kirby	1917	Central Lake	Michigan	365
Paula Vivyan	1952	Central Lake	Michigan	110
Kaye Balch	1941	Charlevoix	Michigan	43
Rosemary McCracken Bean	1947	Charlevoix	Michigan	274
John A. Elzinga	1932	Charlevoix	Michigan	204
David F. Juilleret	1937	Charlevoix	Michigan	133
Karen Peters	1943	Charlevoix	Michigan	196
Judy Ann (Pettier) Dempsey	1948	Cheboygan	Michigan	129
Lorraine Hansen	1924	Cheboygan	Michigan	107
Betty Wartella Last	1924	Cheboygan	Michigan	145
Joyce A. Leslie	Unknown	Cheboygan	Michigan	292
Christine McDonald	1948	Cheboygan	Michigan	373
Carolyn Mousseau	1935	Cheboygan	Michigan	146
Terry Bohlander	1949	Cincinnati	Ohio	250
Jerry Rehage	1952	Cincinnati	Ohio	194
Scott R. Jones	1950	Clay	Michigan	95
Jean Smith Riggs	1935	Commerce Turnpike	Michigan	347
Nancy Jane Starlin Sanders	1941	Copemish	Michigan	62
Velma Parker	1933	Corunna	Michigan	438
Hazel Phetteplace	1924	Curran	Michigan	326
Theresa Donajkowski	1929	Davison	Michigan	17

Mark A. Mitchell	1950	Dearborn Hts.	Michigan	230
Esther Vargo	Unknown	Dearborn Hts.	Michigan	53
Marlene Rood	1950	Dimondale	Michigan	60
Kayla Koboski Briggs	1947	Durham	N. Carolina	191
Carol S. McWain Goodenough	1948	East Jordan	Michigan	121
Susan R. Gruthsch	1946	East Jordan	Michigan	354
Claribel Mason	1925	East Jordan	Michigan	280
Patricia P. Sullivan	1945	East Tawas	Michigan	279
Nedra Wagar	1927	Elk Rapids	Michigan	351
Paul Edward Doane	1930	Evart	Michigan	130
Harold L. Mowat	1937	Evart	Michigan	190
Jerry Stein	1934	Evart	Michigan	445
Ellsworth Handrich	1921	Fairview	Michigan	466
Inez Pletcher Wagner	1918	Fairview	Michigan	271
Betty DeKam	1927	Falmouth	Michigan	426
Ron Hamlin	1936	Farwell	Michigan	248
John Gordon	1954	Fife Lake	Michigan	349
Charlotte LaFeve	1937	Fife Lake	Michigan	178
Jessie M. Battenfield Tallman	1935	Fife Lake	Michigan	237
Steven Webb	1951	Fife Lake	Michigan	334
Edna Demorest	1928	Flat Rock	N. Carolina	156
Judith A. (Lewandowski) Smith	1947	Flint	Michigan	73
Judy Smith	1947	Flint	Michigan	423
Vivian J. Peterson Secrist	1929	Flushing	Michigan	105
Janet Poirier	Unknown	Fort Myers	Florida	108
Donald Kidder	1928	Frankfort	Michigan	54
Grace J.(Emerson) Langea	1941	Garden City	Michigan	239
Elizabeth Betty Dembny	1930	Gaylord	Michigan	249
Barbara Whitaker Palin	1935	Gaylord	Michigan	127
Susan Smith	1958	Gaylord	Michigan	226
Donn K. Syrett	1943	Gaylord	Michigan	40
Susan Roelofs-Haughn	1953	Glen Arbor	Michigan	464
Berniece Baldwin	1944	Glennie	Michigan	288
Roger L. Baldwin	1941	Glennie	Michigan	285
Wilbur Garrett	1924	Glennie	Michigan	375
Geri Moody	1946	Glennie	Michigan	338
Walt Plavljanich	1940	Gould City	Michigan	22
Jan Miner-Heniser	Unknown	Grand Rapids	Michigan	303
Percy John Shooks	1924	Grand Rapids	Michigan	459
James Wyatt Cook	1932	Grawn	Michigan	271
Debbie Keene	1963	Grayling	Michigan	443
Diann Murphy	1946	Grayling	Michigan	163
Peggy Schmidt Olsen	1935	Grayling	Michigan	233
Nancy Root	1944	Grayling	Michigan	25
Ruth Hill (Wice) Witkowski	1929	Hale	Michigan	437
Rick Fowler	1952	Harbor Springs	Michigan	181
Eleanor M. Jardine	Unknown	Harbor Springs	Michigan	373
William R. Kiogima	1930	Harbor Springs	Michigan	151
Kathy Mendoza	1937	Harbor Springs	Michigan	77
Sally Kay Ragan	1937	Harrietta	Michigan	345

Don Franklin	1942	Harrisville	Michigan	253
Janet Watts	1947	Hartland	Michigan	192
Teresa Louise Kenaga	1946	Haslett	Michigan	30
Ann Hempel	1943	Hawks	Michigan	394
Ann H. Gerke	Unknown	Herron	Michigan	86
Helen Hemmingson	1935	Herron	Michigan	310
Delores Troupe	1938	Herron	Michigan	262
Robert L. Uhan	1933	Higgins Lake	Michigan	293
Susan Floer	1953	Hillman	Michigan	368
Kathryn M. Gall	1940	Hillman	Michigan	425
Claude (Harriet) Hubert	1926	Hillman	Michigan	284
Justin Moreau	1947	Hillman	Michigan	45
Jack Owen	1940	Hillman	Michigan	18
Harriet Scheller	1923	Hillman	Michigan	257
Dennis Villeneuve	1950	Hillman	Michigan	221
Anita M. Armstrong	1940	Honor	Michigan	348
Alphonse Bruski	1930	Houghton Lake	Michigan	142
Irene E. Ensing	1940	Houghton Lake	Michigan	247
Lee Schrader	1931	Houghton Lake	Michigan	264
Marian Story	1928	Houghton Lake	Michigan	56
Ruth Westphal	1934	Houghton Lake	Michigan	222
Jessica Helfmann	1983	Howard	Michigan	231
Monica Urban	1957	Howell	Michigan	229
Margaret Crowl	1934	Hubbard Lake	Michigan	154
John Renauld	1931	Hubbard Lake	Michigan	377
Donald Jones	1930	Indian River	Michigan	219
Lola J. Lawrence Sell	1935	Indian River	Michigan	318
Richard Derry	1938	Interlochen	Michigan	429
Walter Zelony	1922	Interlochen	Michigan	305
Roberta Delamarter	1932	Ionia	Michigan	27
June Crawford	1928	Kackson	Michigan	125
G. Tom Whetter	1936	Kalamazoo	Michigan	54
Flo Anderson	1922	Kaleva	Michigan	59
Foster McCool	1916	Kalkaska	Michigan	328
Doris E. Tuffs	1935	Kalkaska	Michigan	410
Betty White	1924	Kalkaska	Michigan	171
Ed Barnes	1931	Kewadin	Michigan	246
Aaron Coleman	1937	Kewadin	Michigan	435
Rebecca M. Norris	1942	Kewadin	Michigan	405
Sharon Fewless	1947	Kingsley	Michigan	216
Nan Shay	1943	Kingsley	Michigan	27
Wilma P. B. Cook-Stafford	1931	Kingsley	Michigan	217
Pat Gamage	1936	Lachine	Michigan	179
John L. Flitz	1928	Lake Ann	Michigan	323
Ken Gernaat	1936	Lake City	Michigan	74
Bonnie J. Matyanczyk	Unknown	Lake City	Michigan	67
Jack McGee	1947	Lake City	Michigan	374
Patricia Houghton Jacobs	1943	Lansing	Michigan	434
Nancy Ann Priest	1934	Leelanau	Michigan	200
Betty J. Marks	1926	LeRoy	Michigan	214

Geraldine Sturdavant	1919	LeRoy	Michigan	373
Chuck Cornell	1932	Levering	Michigan	341
Howard Bacheller	1932	Lewiston	Michigan	423
Roberta Hanna	1919	Lewiston	Michigan	152
Gail Schrader	1939	Lewiston	Michigan	49
Dee Manning	1951	Lincoln	Michigan	87
Philip Naylor	1953	Lincoln	Michigan	179
Theresa Maher Nichols	1933	Lincoln	Kansas	424
Phebie Pearce	1931	Lincoln	Michigan	392
Donna L. Groulx	1937	Linwood	Michigan	316
Margaret Hadcock Gallagher	1914	Livonia	Michigan	413
Len Schweitzer	1947	Louisville	Kentucky	463
Jerry Francis	1941	Lowell	Michigan	235
Maryann Sheppard	1936	Ludington	Michigan	27
Joe Oyster	1957	Lupton	Michigan	378
Ardis Streeter	1948	Lupton	Michigan	140
Richard A. Campbell	1930	Mackinaw City	Michigan	180
Viola McVey	Unknown	Mackinaw City	Michigan	404
Randy Buyze	1951	Mancelona	Michigan	178
Richard S. Kler	1938	Mancelona	Michigan	341
Lucile Sandeen	1926	Mancelona	Michigan	146
Joseph D. Variot	1927	Mancelona	Michigan	208
Eileen Hawkins	Unknown	Manistee	Michigan	456
Marie A. Ketz	1928	Manistee	Michigan	65
Mary Johnson Pearce	1926	Manistee	Michigan	301
Maxine Pettinger	1936	Manistee	Michigan	109
Judith Shinn	1947	Manistee	Michigan	120
W. Thomas Stege	1925	Manistee	Michigan	124
Sharon Switalski	1943	Manistee	Michigan	149
Ila Bredahl	1920	Manton	Michigan	343
John Diefenbach	1936	Manton	Michigan	391
Richard T. King	1925	Manton	Michigan	183
Carole Underwood	1943	Maple City	Michigan	153
Dorothy D. Gruschow Zboyan	1918	Maple City	Michigan	276
John P. Belasco	1936	Margate	Florida	112
Jacquelyn Beebe	1946	Marion	Michigan	242
Ines Brocht	1930	Marion	Michigan	150
Martha West	1948	Marion	Michigan	147
John J. Murphy	1931	Marysville	Michigan	345
Josephine DeYoung	1920	McBain	Michigan	199
Nina Burger Myers	1909	Merritt	Michigan	85
Carlotta Myers Palozzilo	1941	Merritt	Michigan	91
Tom Finger	1929	Mesa	Arizona	100
Linda Kelley	1947	Mesick	Michigan	386
Sharon Purkiss	Unknown	Mesick	Michigan	362
Helen Braun	1925	Midland	Michigan	166
Mildred Dickson	1930	Midland	Michigan	443
Nancy Gould	1932	Millersburg	Michigan	215
Jeanette Karsten	1936	Millersburg	Michigan	20
Marie L. Cournyer Schanck	1933	Mio	Michigan	228

Shirley Groesser Balentine	1940	Muskegon	Michigan	97
Gloria Whipple	1946	Muskegon	Michigan	25
Patricia Johnson	1924	Nashville	Tennessee	423
Elvira LePard	1951	National City	Michigan	211
Gary Versen	1946	Newaygo	Michigan	241
Phyllis Kilcherman	1933	Northport	Michigan	380
Leeland Wilson	1932	Okeechobee	Florida	260
Mary Bishop	1943	Onaway	Michigan	445
Christophe Chagnon	Unknown	Onaway	Michigan	80
Newton Chapman	1940	Onaway	Michigan	382
Jennifer Folkerts Cupples	Unknown	Onaway	Michigan	56
Leonard L. LaFave	1940	Onaway	Michigan	181
Ralph L. Moore	1945	Onaway	Michigan	31
Wendell L. Orm	1940	Onaway	Michigan	21
Rozanne Curley	1949	Oscoda	Michigan	350
Brian Davis	1950	Oscoda	Michigan	210
Harriet Ellwein	1934	Oscoda	Michigan	213
Richard Griese	1930	Oscoda	Michigan	287
Ron Heinz	1943	Oscoda	Michigan	332
Hamilton D. McNichol	1942	Oscoda	Michigan	150
Paul Mouland	Unknown	Oscoda	Michigan	17
Carole Newlon	1937	Oscoda	Michigan	398
Joel V. Smith	1945	Oscoda	Michigan	47
Jim Rasche	1956	Ossineke	Michigan	386
Dr. Hans Andrews	1938	Ottawa	Illinois	378
Dennis G. Cline	1952	Owosso	Michigan	86
Helen Woodward	1938	Pellston	Michigan	106
Harry Elliott Colestock	1923	Petoskey	Michigan	38
Marilyn Stockwell Colestock	1937	Petoskey	Michigan	321
Charles Huntington	1927	Petoskey	Michigan	145
Judith M. Lentz	Unknown	Petoskey	Michigan	441
Mary Rinke-Mogle	Unknown	Petoskey	Michigan	300
Tillie Smith	1918	Petoskey	Michigan	430
Mary Jo Sobleskey	1927	Petoskey	Michigan	295
Sharon Miller Grulke	1942	Posen	Michigan	299
Joyce (Robarge) Konwinski	1946	Posen	Michigan	358
Frank Krajnik	1935	Posen	Michigan	223
Carole Lynn Orr	1944	Posen	Michigan	75
James Orr	1944	Posen	Michigan	50
Eleanor A. (Finger) Harkey	1935	Prescott	Michigan	322
Morley Kellogg	1928	Presque Isle	Michigan	212
Paul T. O'Dell	1936	Presque Isle	Michigan	116
Laura Gettle	1949	Prudenville	Michigan	409
JoAnn Croff	1938	Punta Gorda	Florida	175
Fred Putnam	1944	Redford	Michigan	342
Carol E. Bogucki	1939	Reed City	Michigan	223
Audrey Davis	1928	Reed City	Michigan	376
Meta Johnson	1925	Reed City	Michigan	109
Alice Rohl	1935	Reed City	Michigan	453
Philip C. Kreft	1938	Rockford	Michigan	428

Name	Year	City	State	Number
Norma Buczkowski	1932	Rogers City	Michigan	405
Jeanne Crawford	1953	Rogers City	Michigan	107
Diana Green Hudak	1938	Rogers City	Michigan	274
Carol Paul	1937	Rogers City	Michigan	145
Faye Plume	1952	Rogers City	Michigan	178
Ralph Smith	1925	Rogers City	Michigan	193
Hazel Yerks	1938	Rogers City	Michigan	452
William R. Frank	1947	Roscommon	Michigan	107
Richard Slater	1930	Roscommon	Michigan	187
Mary E. Grba	1940	Roscommon	Michigan	308
Stephen M. Remenar	1936	Roscommon	Michigan	330
Katie Rittershofer	1939	Roscommon	Michigan	294
Neil Frisbie	1937	Rose City	Michigan	248
Juanita Walt	1934	Rose City	Michigan	289
Jean Hafner	1933	Rudyard	Michigan	385
Dorothy V. Jennett Teplansky	1946	San Diego	California	82
Jane W. Smith	1936	Shaftsburg	Michigan	370
Judith A. Benner	1940	Sleepy Hollow	Illinois	267
Marlin F. Schmidt	1935	South Bend	Indiana	282
Milo G. Houghton	1945	South Boardman	Michigan	424
Cindy Vezinau	1953	St. Clair Shores	Michigan	361
Betty Shirey-Thayer	1921	St. Helen	Michigan	25
Bernice (Bee Houghton) Macy	1938	St. Petersburg	Florida	294
Marylou Bugh	1942	Standish	Michigan	395
David Twining	1954	Stone Mountain	Georgia	135
Ann Reynolds	1936	Sun City West	Arizona	197
Bruce Harlton	1949	Suttons Bay	Michigan	379
David R. Whetsell	1935	Tampa	Florida	406
Frank Hurst	1928	Tawas City	Michigan	241
Judy Loy	1944	Tawas City	Michigan	147
Charles M. Noel	1942	Tawas City	Michigan	353
John J. Reilly	1925	Tawas City	Michigan	396
Joan L.Cole	1944	Taylor	Michigan	111
Marion. V. (Fabera) Neely	1937	Tebbetts	Missouri	256
Wayne Bates	1942	Terrell	Texas	389
Elizabeth Ballou Koski	1937	Thompsonville	Michigan	439
Edith Thompson	1926	Three Rivers	Michigan	191
Marlene Hopkins	1954	Tower	Michigan	461
Mary Jo LePage	1944	Township	Michigan	432
Alma Leist	1939	Traverse	Michigan	243
Cleo M. Boone	1937	Traverse	Michigan	182
Mary Jane Allgaier	1934	Traverse City	Michigan	272
Phillis (McGillis) Babel	1931	Traverse City	Michigan	242
Sharell (Pierce) Balentine	1938	Traverse City	Michigan	408
James Chereskin	1943	Traverse City	Michigan	215
Nancy L. Ferrar	1923	Traverse City	Michigan	88
Dorothy Wilhelm French	1925	Traverse City	Michigan	188
Esther Dinger Gauthier	1903	Traverse City	Michigan	36
Laura Greve	1929	Traverse City	Michigan	341
Thomas Groesser	1935	Traverse City	Michigan	416

Arthur "Bud" Holman	1929	Traverse City	Michigan	421
Barbara Kane	1940	Traverse City	Michigan	414
Louise Kane	1928	Traverse City	Michigan	327
Penny Kipley	1928	Traverse City	Michigan	70
Joanne Kline	1929	Traverse City	Michigan	160
Conrad Koltys	1925	Traverse City	Michigan	458
Joseph Lamie	1934	Traverse City	Michigan	448
Jerry L. Lardie	1938	Traverse City	Michigan	25
Marge Lipp	1925	Traverse City	Michigan	342
Mary Lyon	1933	Traverse City	Michigan	212
Robert R. Martin	1937	Traverse City	Michigan	186
Marcella M. McNabb	1934	Traverse City	Michigan	429
Robert Merchant	Unknown	Traverse City	Michigan	211
Cheryl Morgan	1944	Traverse City	Michigan	376
Mariam Navachic	1918	Traverse City	Michigan	148
Betty Plough	1943	Traverse City	Michigan	120
Martha Preston	1944	Traverse City	Michigan	138
Raymond E. Purvis	1928	Traverse City	Michigan	420
Barbara Rosso	1924	Traverse City	Michigan	341
Marilyn J. (Carder) Scheck	1933	Traverse City	Michigan	313
Irma M. Schwartz	1918	Traverse City	Michigan	346
Marian Second	1928	Traverse City	Michigan	379
Vera Sparks	1930	Traverse City	Michigan	399
Dorothy Stein	1921	Traverse City	Michigan	276
Cindi Strong	1954	Traverse City	Michigan	329
Shirley J. Wares	1933	Traverse City	Michigan	424
Richard Whiting	1934	Traverse City	Michigan	383
Mary Lou Williams	1948	Traverse City	Michigan	164
Bernard H. Yantz	1958	Traverse City	Michigan	84
Donald Akers	1938	Tustin	Michigan	344
James M. Bushaw	1927	Wellston	Michigan	311
Lindsay Paul Abraham	1950	West Branch	Michigan	336
Doris Badgley Barrett	1931	West Branch	Michigan	356
Kim (Rakestraw) Gildner	1956	West Branch	Michigan	93
Darlene Groff Meske	1939	West Branch	Michigan	293
Clarice L. Sperry	1933	West Branch	Michigan	184
Christine Teal	1951	West Branch	Michigan	444
George Erickson	1929	Whittemore	Michigan	301
Agnes Moraitis	1925	Whittemore	Michigan	327
D. Elwin Hager	1927	Williamsburg	Michigan	387
R. Michael Shaft	Unknown	Williamston	Michigan	206
Robert P. Olds	1935	Wolverine	Michigan	23
Eleanore VanZyll	1918	Wyoming	Michigan	32
Stuart MacDonald	1938	Yarmouthport	Massachusetts	57
Mary L. Duda Bucklin	1937	Zephyrhills	Florida	189
Robert Bucklin	1936	Zephyrhills	Florida	352
Carol Glogovsky	1937	Zion	Illinois	381